The Political Economy of Development and Underdevelopment

The Political Economy of Development and Underdevelopment

Edited by

Charles K. Wilber

The American University

Random House New York

First Edition
987654321
Copyright © 1973 by Random House, Inc.

Library of Congress Cataloging in Publication Data

Wilber, Charles K.   comp.
The political economy of development and
underdevelopment.

1. Economic development—Addresses, essays, lectures.
I.   Title.
HD82.W525   330.9′04   73-7944
ISBN 0-394-31756-4

Manufactured in the United States of America
Composition by Cherry Hill Composition, Pennsauken, N.J.
Printed and bound by the Kingsport Press, Kingsport,
Tenn.

Typography by Juli Hopfl

Cover design by Lawrence Daniels & Friends, Inc.

For my parents, who helped me to see
and to understand . . .
For my wife, who hasn't let me forget . . .
For my children, who in turn, I hope,
will see and understand. . . .

Justicia Luego Paz

I have a dream that one day every valley shall be exalted, every hill and mountain shall be made low, the rough places will be made plain, and the crooked places will be made straight, and the glory of the Lord shall be revealed, and all flesh shall see it together.

Martin Luther King, Jr.
The March on Washington
August 1963

preface

Economists assume that the problem of a more human society is solved by expertise, by know-how. Since they assume that the question of the nature of a good society is already answered, the issue becomes one of solving certain practical problems. The good society is simply assumed to be an idealized version of the United States economy, that is, a consumer society. The key to a consumer society is growth of per capita income. Thus the vast bulk of the development literature has focused on growth rates as the *deus ex machina* to solve all problems. Even much of the socialist writing on development argues that the superiority of socialism over capitalism lies in faster growth rates.

There is much to be said for this approach because some minimum level of food, clothing, shelter, recreation, etc., is necessary before a person can be free to be human. However, the emphasis on consumption and growth of per capita income has not led to a decrease of poverty in the underdeveloped world. If anything it has increased. A thin layer has prospered while the vast majority of the population sinks ever deeper into the backwater of underdevelopment. Therefore, during the past several years a new look has been taken at the meaning of development. Dudley Seers, Mahbub ul Haq, Ivan Illich, and others have questioned the emphasis on chasing the consumption standards of the developed countries via economic growth. Instead they argue for a direct attack on poverty through employment and income redistribution policies. Denis Goulet and Paulo Freire argue that development must include "liberation" from oppression, cultural as well as political and economic.

Both of these positions have merit, and they are not necessarily mutually exclusive. That is, the study of political economy should lead one to ask whether stressing the importance of rapid economic growth has to mean that the growth will consist of movies, bikinis, deodorants, key clubs, and pollution. An analysis of political economic systems should lead one to see why growth has meant luxuries being produced for some while others go hungry.

This book is about economic development and underdevelopment, and is designed to be used with a standard textbook in advanced undergraduate and beginning graduate courses. The readings emphasize the *political economy* rather than the narrowly *economic* approach and issues.

Many of the readings are excellent examples of radical political economy. Political economy recognizes that man is a social being whose arrangements for the production and distribution of economic goods must be, if society is to be liveable, consistent with congruent institutions of family, political, and cultural life. As a result, a political economy analysis must incorporate such noneconomic influences as social structures, political systems, and cultural values as well as such factors as technological change and the distribution of income and wealth. The readings are radical in the sense that they are willing to question and evaluate the most basic institutions and values of society.

While I hope that the work presented here is objective, there is no artificial stance of neutrality. I am committed to certain values that undoubtedly influence the choice of questions asked and the range of variables considered for selection. In general, my system of values posits material progress (at least up to some minimum level), equality, cooperation, democratic control of economic as well as political institutions, and individual freedom as positive goods. It should be noted that there may be contradictions among these criteria, and thus society is faced with choices. With these values in mind the reader can judge the degree of objectivity attained.

It is a pleasure to acknowledge my indebtedness to those who have helped me shape my ideas on economic development and underdevelopment. First of all I want to thank Professors W. Michael Bailey, James H. Weaver, Celso Furtado, Branko Horvat, E. J. Mishan, Ronald Müller, Brady Tyson, Albert Waterston, and Irving Louis Horowitz—critics, colleagues, and friends. Some of my greatest debts are to those whom I know only through their writings—Karl Polanyi and R. H. Tawney. Their example of scholarship and social commitment has been a guide and inspiration. I want to thank Sandy Kelly for her invaluable help in editing and typing, and Bob Devlin for his assistance in research and editing. Barbara Conover and Nancy Perry, editors at Random House, have been invaluable in seeing the book through to publication.

My greatest debt, however, in this as in all my endeavors, is to my wife, Mary Ellen, and our children: Kenneth, Teresa, Matthew, Alice, Mary, Angela, and Louie. I owe all to their love and encouragement.

Charles K. Wilber
Washington, D.C.
September   1973

contents

ix

part one

Methodological Problems of Economic Development

economists have traditionally measured the level of "economic development" by the level of per capita Gross National Product (GNP). In the past few years serious doubt has been cast upon the validity of this measuring rod. Many countries —Brazil, Pakistan, and even Mexico—have had rapid growth rates of per capita GNP while at the same time unemployment, inequality, and the level of poverty of the mass of the population have remained unchanged or even increased. In the first reading, Dudley Seers argues that we have "misconceived the nature of the main challenge of the second half of the twentieth century." It is not to achieve high growth rates of per capita GNP but to directly reduce poverty, unemployment, and inequality. Seers analyzes the implications of this shift in emphasis for development programs and development theory.

While the first article in this part focuses on the implications of confusing development with growth of GNP, the next two articles confront, though from different angles, the problem of using traditional economic theory as the main tool for analyzing the process of development. A distinction should be made between economic growth, analyzed in terms of changes in the value of economic parameters in given institutional conditions, and economic development, when changes in the value of economic parameters are accompanied or even preceded by institutional changes. Traditional economic theory is a more efficient instrument for analysis of economic growth since long-run factors of a socio-political nature may be held constant. Economic development, however, is a process which affects not only purely economic relations but the entire social, political, and cultural fabric of society. In the dynamic world of economic development, the data usually impounded in *ceteris paribus* are in constant motion as factors making for change.

Keith Griffin points out that most of the theorizing on economic development has been done by economists who live and were trained in the developed countries of the West. Most have suffered from two serious handicaps—"lack of knowledge about the broad historical forces associated with underdevelopment and ignorance of the institutions, behavior responses and ways of life of the largest sector within the underdeveloped countries, the rural areas." Griffin maintains that this ignorance coupled with traditional economic theory has produced theories of development that are inappropriate to the reality of underdevelopment. His article focuses on theories of the dual economy developed by W. Arthur Lewis, Ranis and Fei, and others, and questions the reality of their assumptions and the empirical validity of their conclusions.

Warren Ilchman and Ravindra Bhargava argue that the major development strategies—"Big Push" balanced growth, unbalanced growth, and capital formation through unlimited supplies of labor—derived from traditional economic theory by Ragnar Nurkse, Albert Hirschman, and W. Arthur Lewis are relevant operationally only in highly specific situations. These situations are defined by crucial political, sociological, and administrative factors as well as economic ones. They analyze these development strategies in terms of the major social problems that might arise from undertaking them and the type of political regime and administrative systems they presuppose.

The last article in this part critiques W. W. Rostow's "Stages of Economic Growth" model of the development process. Rostow presented his theory as an alternative both to traditional economic theory and to Marxism. Paul Baran and E. J. Hobsbawm argue that Rostow's model fails to illuminate either the reality of underdevelopment or the process of development. They find the model to be a set of empty tautologies without predictive value whose real deficiencies are seen when juxtaposed to Marx's theory of social development. The second half of their article presents clearly and lucidly the classic Marxian approach to historical change.

Many of the readings in this book utilize the concept of the economic or social surplus introduced in Baran and Hobsbawm's article. The concept of the social surplus was widely used by the classical writers. Adam Smith labeled it the "surplus part of the produce" and David Ricardo as the "net produce." John Stuart Mill defined it as the "surplus of the produce of labour . . . the fund from which the enjoyments, as distinguished from the necessities, of the producers are provided . . . from which all are subsisted, who are not themselves engaged in production; and from which all additions are made to capital."* In view of the value connotation associated with Karl Marx's use of the concept "surplus value" and the attendant concept of "rate of exploitation," later economists discarded it completely. The social product was viewed in terms of "cost of factors," savings being no longer conceived as the result of an existing social surplus but as the result of an act of "abstinence" or "waiting." But as the contemporary developmental economist Celso Furtado points out, "from the point of view of the theory of development, in which the accumulation process acquires great importance, there is some convenience in coming back to the classic concept of the surplus, leaving aside . . . any intimation of moral values.**

The social surplus may be viewed as a residual factor—that which remains from total output after necessary consumption has been subtracted. In every organization of society, past or present, the total annual production of goods and services may be divided into two separate parts—the necessary subsistence of the population and a surplus which may be either consumed or saved in the form of additions to the country's stock of capital. Of course, the level of necessary consumption may be expected to vary from country to country and from time to time. However, for the purpose of studying the process of development this should cause no serious difficulties.

To make it more useful it is essential to differentiate three variants of the concept of social surplus.† The first is the *actual social surplus*—the difference between a country's *actual* current production and its *actual* current consumption. The second is the *potential social surplus*—difference between the output that *could* be produced in a given natural and technological environment and what might be regarded as *necessary* consumption. The third is the *planned social surplus*—the difference between a country's "optimum" production attainable in a given natural and technological environment under conditions of planned "optimum" utilization of all available productive factors and some chosen "optimum" volume of consumption.

In the context of economic development the realization of the potential social surplus would presuppose a more or less drastic reorganization of the production and distribution of output and probably imply extensive changes in the social structure of a country. The difference between the potential and the actual social surplus exists in three distinct forms. The first is that part of the potential surplus used to support the excess consumption of the upper income groups in society. The second is the development conducive output lost to society due to the existence of large numbers of unproductive workers (such as soldiers, servants, etc.). The third form is the output lost because of the irrationality and wastefulness of the prevailing economic and social organization.

The planned social surplus is, by definition, applicable only to a planned economy. It may be smaller than the potential economic surplus because of conscious decisions such as a reduced work week.

It should be obvious that the main factors of economic development have to do with the size and distribution of the social surplus. Thus it is that a development strategy must be examined in terms of its impact on the size and utilization of the surplus. In each of the succeeding parts of this book the concept of the social surplus will be utilized by various authors as a key analytical tool (in combination with other concepts of course) in their analyses of underdevelopment and development.

---

* ADAM SMITH, *The Wealth of Nations* (New York: The Modern Library, 1937), p. 17; David Ricardo, *The Works and Correspondence of David Ricardo*, Vol. I, *On the Principles of Political Economy and Taxation*, Piero Sraffa, ed. (10 vols.; Cambridge University Press, 1951), p. 391; John Stuart Mill, *Principles of Political Economy*, Sir W. J. Ashley, ed. (London: Longmans, Green and Co., 1929), pp. 163–164.

** CELSO FURTADO, *Development and Underdevelopment* (Berkeley: University of California Press, 1964), p. 79.

† PAUL A. BARAN, "Economic Progress and Economic Surplus," *Science and Society*, Vol. 17, No. 4 (Fall, 1953), pp. 289–317. See also his *The Political Economy of Growth* (New York: Monthly Review Press, 1957), pp. 22–43.

1

The Meaning of Development

Dudley Seers

The challenges of any period depend on the tasks that face those living in it. I believe we have misconceived the nature of the main challenge of the second half of the twentieth century. This has been seen as achieving an increase in the national incomes of the "developing" countries, formalized in the target of 5 percent growth rates set for the first development decade.

Why do we concentrate on the national income in this way? It is of course convenient. Politicians find a single comprehensive measure useful, especially one that is at least a year out-of-date. Economists are provided with a variable which can be quantified and movements which can be analyzed into changes in sectoral output, factor shares or categories of expenditures, making model-building feasible. While it is very slipshod for us to confuse development with economic development and economic development with economic growth, it is nevertheless very understandable. We can after all fall back on the supposition that increases in national income, if they are faster than the population growth, sooner or later lead to the solution of social and political problems.

But the experience of the past decade makes this belief look rather naive. Social problems and political upheavals have emerged in countries at all stages of development. Moreover, we can see that these afflict countries with rapidly rising per capita incomes as well as those with stagnant economies. In fact, it looks as if economic growth may not merely fail to solve social and political difficulties; certain types of growth can actually cause them.

Now that the complexity of development problems is becoming increasingly obvious, this continued addiction to the use of a single aggregative yardstick in the face of the evidence takes on a rather different appearance. It begins to look like a preference for avoiding the real problems of development.

The starting point in discussing the challenges we now face is to brush aside the web of fantasy we have woven around "development" and decide more precisely what we mean by it. "Development" is inevitably a normative term and we must ask ourselves what are the necessary conditions for a universally acceptable aim—the realization of the potential of human personality.

Reprinted from *International Development Review*, Vol. XI, No. 4 (December 1969), pp. 2-6, by permission of the publisher. Copyright 1969 © by the Society for International Development.

If we ask what is an *absolute* necessity for this, one answer is obvious— enough food. Below certain levels of nutrition, a man lacks not merely bodily energy and good health but even interest in much besides food. He cannot rise significantly above an animal existence. Recent studies show that under- nourishment of children leads to permanent impairment of both their physi- cal and their mental capacities.

Since to be able to buy food is a matter of income, the criterion can be expressed in terms of income levels. This enables it to take account also of certain other minimum requirements. People will never spend all their money and energy on food, however poor they are. To be enough to feed a man, his income has also to cover basic needs of clothing, footwear and shelter, but the utility of money clearly declines sharply as these needs are satisfied.

Another basic necessity, in the sense of something without which per- sonality cannot develop, is a job. This does not just mean employment; it can include studying, working on a family farm or keeping house. But to play none of these accepted roles—i.e., to be chronically unemployed, dependent on another person's productive capacity, even for food—is incompatible with self-respect, especially for somebody who has been spending years at school, perhaps at university, preparing for an active role.

It is true of course that both poverty and unemployment are associated in various ways with per capita income. If per capita incomes are falling, absolute poverty can hardly be reduced much, nor can unemployment (except in the very short run and exceptional circumstances). But certainly increases in per capita are far from enough, as the experience of petroleum economies shows, to achieve either of these objectives. In fact, a rise in per capita income, as we very well know, can be accompanied by, can even cause, growing unemployment.[1]

The direct link between per capita income and the numbers living in poverty is income distribution. It is a truism that poverty will be eliminated much more rapidly if any given rate of economic growth is accompanied by a declining concentration of incomes. Equality should however be considered an objective in its own right, the third element in development. Inequalities to be found now in the world, especially (but not only) outside the industrial countries, are objectionable by any religious or ethical standards. The social barriers and inhibitions of an unequal society distort the personalities of those with high incomes no less than of those who are poor. Trivial differ- ences of accent, language, dress, customs, etc., acquire an absurd importance and contempt is engendered for those who lack social graces, especially country dwellers. Perhaps even more important, since race is usually highly correlated with income, economic inequality lies at the heart of racial ten- sions.

The questions to ask about a country's development are therefore: What has been happening to poverty? What has been happening to unem- ployment? What has been happening to inequality? If all three of these have declined from high levels, then beyond doubt this has been a period of development for the country concerned. If one or two of these central prob- lems have been growing worse, especially if all three have, it would be strange to call the result "development," even if per capita income doubled.[2]

PROBLEMS OF MEASUREMENT

The challenges for the remainder of this century arise out of the analysis above. The first is how to find measures of development to replace the national income, or, more precisely, to enable the national income to be given its true, somewhat limited, significance, as a measure of development potential. (A big increase in the national income at least makes it easier in the future to achieve a reduction in poverty, if appropriate policies are adopted.)

There are two points to make here. The first is that the national income figures published for most "developing" countries have very little meaning. This is partly because of lack of data, especially on farm output, but also because, when income distributions are so unequal, prices have very little meaning as weights in "real" income comparisons.

Secondly, the lack of data on poverty, unemployment and inequality reflects the priorities of statistical offices rather than the difficulties of data collection.

The conceptual problems of these measures do not seem to be more formidable than those of the national income. We have just grown accustomed to ignoring the latter. But there are also practical problems. All the measures require information about supplementary incomes, age-and-sex composition of receiving units, etc., additional to that obtained from statistics which are prepared as a by-product of administration, at least in countries where only a small proportion of income receivers pay direct taxes.[3] It is also hard to measure even overt unemployment where unemployment registration does not exist or covers only part of the labor force. But again we must not be diverted by such technical problems from attempting the reassessment which really matters.[4]

THE INTERNAL CONSISTENCY OF THE DEVELOPMENT PROCESS

The second set of challenges to the social scientists, politicians and administrators in the decades ahead is to find paths of development which enable progress to be made on all these criteria. Since development is far from being achieved at present, the need is not, as is generally imagined, to accelerate economic growth—which could even be dangerous—but to change the nature of the development process.

A major question is whether the criteria are mutually consistent. The answer is that in many respects development on one of the criteria implies, or helps bring about, or is even a necessary condition for, development on one or more of the others.

To reduce unemployment is to remove one of the main causes of poverty and inequality. Moreover, a reduction in inequality will of course reduce poverty, *ceteris paribus*.

These propositions beg many questions, however. The reduction of unemployment means in part finding techniques which are labor-intensive, with the least damage to the expansion of production. This is of course a discussion to which many have contributed, notably A. K. Sen.

There is a well-known, indeed classical, argument that inequality is necessary to generate savings and incentives and thus to promote economic growth—which, as we have seen, can be taken as an indicator of some types of development potential. I find the argument that the need for savings justifies inequality unconvincing in the Third World today. Savings propensities are after all very low precisely in countries with highly unequal distributions; the industrial countries with less concentration of income have, by contrast, much higher savings propensities. Savings are of course also affected by the absolute level of incomes, but the explanation must also lie in the high consumption levels of the rich, designed to maintain the standards so important in an unequal society.

Moreover, the rich in most countries tend to have extremely high propensities, not merely to spend, but to spend on goods and services with a high foreign exchange content, and, for countries suffering from an acute foreign exchange bottleneck, this is a major obstacle to development. It is true that import demand can be held in check (as in India) by administrative controls, but this leads to the elaboration of a bureaucratic apparatus which is expensive, especially in terms of valuable organizing ability, and which in some countries becomes riddled with corruption. In any case, in a highly unequal society, personal savings often flow abroad or go into luxury housing and other investment projects of low or zero priority for development.

The argument that only inequality can provide the incentives that are necessary is also obviously of limited validity in a country where there are barriers of race or class to advancement. Still, we cannot dismiss it out of hand. The needs for private entrepreneurial talent vary according to the circumstances of different economies, but there are very few where this need is small. Countries relying on growing exports of manufactures, as many are, depend heavily on the emergence of businessmen with the drive to penetrate foreign markets. All countries depend in some degree on the appearance of progressive farmers. Will these emerge without financial rewards on a scale that will make nonsense of an egalitarian policy? Are rising profits of companies, especially foreign companies, an inevitable feature of growth in many countries? Or are we exaggerating the importance of financial incentives? Can other, non-financial rewards partially take their place? Can social incentives be developed to a point where people will take on such tasks with little or no individual reward (as the governments of China and Cuba are trying to prove)? This is one of the great issues to be decided, and the 1970's will throw a good deal of light on the answer.

The compatibility of equality and rising output and employment has recently become doubtful for an additional set of reasons. Can the people who are professionally necessary be kept in the country if they can earn only a small fraction of what they could earn elsewhere? Yet what are the costs in terms of human welfare and even efficiency if they are prevented from leaving?

On the other hand, there are equally serious reasons for questioning the compatibility of *in*equality and economic growth. Can a structure of local industry be created to correspond to the structure of demand that arises in a highly inequitable society (leaving aside the question of whether it *should* be created)? Will production rise rapidly if the proportion of the labor force too badly nourished for full manual and mental work is only sinking slowly? Can the government obtain the co-operation of the population in wage restraint, and in many other ways that are necessary for development, if there is visible evidence of great wealth which is being transmitted from generation to generation, so that the wage earner sees his children and his children's children doomed indefinitely to subordinate positions? Can it mobilize the energies of the total population and break down social customs which obstruct development, especially in rural areas?

I do not pretend to know the answers to this complex of questions, which point to a set of "internal contradictions" in the development process far more severe than those to which Marx drew attention. What is more, the economic and political objectives are linked closely together. An economic system with large numbers of undernourished and unemployed at the bottom end of a long social ladder, especially if they are racially distinguishable, can never provide a firm basis for political rights or for civic order. Those with high incomes from profits or salaries are not merely slow to tackle the great social problems of poverty and unemployment; they will inevitably try to find ways of maintaining privilege, resorting (as dozens of historical examples show) to political violence rather than give it up. Conversely, those without jobs or adequate incomes will sooner or later try to obtain them through a regime which would not allow organized opposition. Judging from present trends in the climate of opinion, especially among the young, it is very doubtful whether inequalities on anything like the present scale could co-exist with political liberties in the 1970's or 1980's. Yet it is hard to envisage how inequality can be reduced without setting in motion, from one direction or another, forces that reduce political liberty.

There are administrative limits to the main weapon against inequality, direct taxation, apart altogether from any conflict with incentives. Inequality cannot really be reduced so long as property ownership is heavily concentrated. So conversion of incomes from large holdings of property into life pensions (as in Cuba) or bond interest (as in Chile) or their reduction through death duties (as in Britain) are likely to be more effective than taxation, though they may be beyond the bounds of the politically feasible in many countries.

But a great deal can be done even without attacking property ownership. Practically every decision taken by government officials has implications for the degree of equality—to lend to big farmers or small, to set prices of public corporations at levels that tax or subsidize rich consumers, to build roads for private motor cars or for goods vehicles, to put the best equipment in rural or urban schools. It would not be a bad thing to put up in every civil service office a sign: "Will it reduce inequality?" Secondly, if the administrative and political organization is motivated and trained to report tax evasion, corruption, etc., all sorts of egalitarian policies, including capital taxation, become more feasible. (Where such a spirit is weak, one can hardly expect rapid development in the sense I have used the word here.)

Lastly, a reduction in inequality is very hard, if not impossible, so long as a country is dependent on a major power and shows the influence of its consumption tastes and salary levels. So is a reduction in unemployment, because one of the marks of dependence is reliance on the technology of the countries which play a dominant role in the national life, and this may well be inappropriate to local problems. On the other hand, a country that leaves its social problems unsolved is unlikely to be strong enough to achieve or maintain genuine independence; it may not even survive as a political unit.

ENDS AND MEANS

When political liberty is considered as an end, its importance, though high, is secondary so long as a substantial fraction of the people are under-nourished and unemployed. But it appears in quite a different light as a *means*. Societies lacking open opposition have shown themselves extremely inflexible in meeting the challenge of changing circumstances, whether one considers the continuation by Germany of a war for months after it was already lost, or the stubbornness of Communist regimes in clinging to unsuccessful agricultural policies. Moreover, as Soviet experience shows, there is no guarantee that political liberties will reappear as economic problems are eased.

Higher educational levels are ends in themselves, but education is also a *means*. Economists have, somewhat belatedly, come to see it as a source of development; but they treat it narrowly as a factor in the growth of national income, relating stocks of manpower with certain qualifications (e.g., university degrees) to national income levels.

But if development is not just or even mainly an increase in the national income, education takes on an entirely different aspect. We need to go a long way beyond the Harbison approach, valuable though this has been. What are important are not the "man years" at school but the methods of selec-tion and the *content* of education. Inequality can be reduced (and also eco-nomic efficiency increased) if secondary and higher education are made *genuinely* available to those with the lowest incomes (belonging to minority races), which means of course that special methods of selection must be found. Secondly, by easing shortages of high-level manpower, education can reduce the need for high salaries for those with scarce professional skills. In that case, however, the whole structure of education needs reconsidera-tion; education will hardly fulfill this function if it produces on the one hand a few distinguished academic scholars who, as in Britain, think of them-selves as superior to the rest of the population and on the other a mass of people with the wrong qualifications.

The third function of education, and this applies also to adult education and the content of radio and TV programs, is to prepare professional classes conscious of the realities of development, both the internal realities and the realities of the world scene, with such an understanding of their historical origins that they see what needs to be done and voluntarily accept the sacri-fices implied. Many of the obstacles to policies which would reduce poverty and unemployment have their origin in attitudes to manual work, especially in the countryside, to imported consumer goods, to foreign technologies, etc.

Since each generation is in some degree a copy of the preceding one, through parental influences, such attitudes can hardly be changed except by a conscious educational policy, broadly defined.

Finally, one policy area which looks different if one discards the aggregative approach is population. Conventionally, population growth is seen simply as a subtraction from the increase in the national income; the closer the growth rates of population and income, the slower the rise in *per capita* income. This line of argument is fundamentally somewhat suspect because it assumes that population and income are independent of each other. But the real case for an active population policy is simply that, so long as the labor force is growing fast, it is almost impossible to relieve unemployment and poverty, since a plentiful supply of labor keeps the wages of the unskilled, apart perhaps from a privileged modern sector, near levels of barest subsistence. Moreover, the growing pressure of population on the budget makes it very difficult to expand educational and other social services. An additional argument, on the above criteria, is that this growing pressure increases the need for foreign aid and thus postpones the attainment of genuine independence.

INTERNATIONAL POLICY

It is misleading to talk about "development" when we consider the world scene, on the criteria suggested above. One cannot really say that there has been development for the world as a whole, when the benefits of technical progress have accrued to minorities which were already relatively rich, whether we are speaking of rich minorities within nations or the minority of nations which are rich. To me, this word is particularly misleading for the period since the war, especially the "development decade" when the growth of economic inequality and unemployment must have actually accelerated. (I am alarmed at the phrase, a "second development decade." Another "development decade" like the 1960's, with unemployment rates and inequality rising by further large steps, would be politically and economically disastrous, whatever the pace of economic growth!)

Certainly in some respects, as I have said, a basis has been laid in many countries for possible development in the future. But there has not been any basic improvement in international institutions. It is true that there are now opportunities for poor countries at least to talk to the rich, but one cannot speak of international order; the international institutions lack the power to impose solutions. There is not much to show for the tremendous efforts which went into the New Delhi UNCTAD. Virtually no safeguards have been set up against a world recession—the creation of SDR's is by no means adequate in itself. Nor has much been done to open the markets of industrial countries to imports of manufactures, the only real possibility of export expansion for the Third World as a whole.

There is no fiscal system for the world. This may perhaps be foreshadowed by 1 percent aid targets, but these targets are in fact ignored and aid programs remain at very low levels. As Gunnar Myrdal warned us many years ago, the establishment of the national welfare state has turned the attention of the public in the rich countries inwards, making them less interested in the welfare of the world as a whole. The aid that does exist often plays an important economic role, but, like immigration and trade policies, it is very largely motivated by the self-interest of donors, sometimes by very short-term commercial and political interests. This often in effect leads them to support, or even help install, governments which oppose the redistribution of income and in other ways block development.

Many countries have in fact slipped further under the influence of one or another of the big powers. This itself hinders development. Independence is not merely one of the aims of development; it is also one of the means. It is a force for mobilizing popular support and the force is blunted if a government is obviously far from independent.

Yet clearly there is a basic inconsistency. Can a world system be created which will accommodate nationalism while providing a truly international and much more equitable economic and political order? And can this be done just by cerebration and logical clarity, or does it require the poorer countries of the world to organize themselves, perhaps by continent, to use what cards they possess to bring it about? How can nationalism be reconciled on the other hand with the strong tribal and regional forces which are emerging? What form of decentralization do these imply?

Such are the challenges we now face. The role of the practitioner, the politician or the civil servant is the extremely difficult one of finding a politically and administratively feasible path of development in a grossly unequal world. They can be helped by the theorist if he refrains from trying to adapt uncritically models and measures designed in and for industrial countries, where priorities are very different, but helps instead to develop policies, national and international, to mitigate the great social problems of the Third World.

By so doing, indeed, he may incidentally provide the social scientists in the rich countries with food for thought. After all, poverty and unemployment are not so starkly obvious in the North Atlantic area, compared to the conditions before the last war (and this helps explain the reduced interest of their social scientists in these problems until quite recently). Although economic inequality diminished too up to about 1950, it now seems to be growing again and to be accompanied by increasingly severe inequality between races in multi-racial societies. But above all, the aim must be to change international attitudes so that it becomes impossible for the political leaders and social scientists of Europe and North America to continue overlooking, and aggravating, often inadvertently, the obscene inequalities that disfigure the world.

NOTES

1. Thus in Trinidad the growth in per capita income averaged more than 5% a year during the whole period 1953 to 1968, while overt unemployment showed a steady increase to more than 10% of the labor force.
2. Of course, the fulfilment of human potential requires much that cannot be specified in purely economic terms. I cannot spell out all the other re-

quirements, but it would be very unbalanced if I did not mention them at all. They include adequate educational levels, freedom of speech, and citizenship of a nation that is truly independent, both economically and politically, in the sense that the views of other governments do not largely predetermine his own government's decisions.

3. Technical problems of measuring distribution are discussed in an unpublished paper, "On the Possibility of Measuring Personal Distribution of Income," by Professor Dich of Aarhaus.

4. I cannot explore here the measurement of the educational and political elements in development. In as far as the former is covered by the formal educational system, a technique for showing the changing profile over time has been developed by Richard Jolly. (See A. R. Jolly, "Planning Education for African Development," East African Publishing House, Nairobi, 1969.) Measurement of the extent to which the political aims have been achieved is of course much more difficult; possible clues include the number of prisoners held for political or quasi-political reasons; the social and racial composition of parliaments, business boards, senior public administrative grades, etc., and also of those enjoying secondary and university education; the incidence of petty theft; rates of suicide and alcoholism.

Clues on the degree of national independence include the extent to which the country votes in the same way as a great power at the United Nations, the existence of foreign military bases and overflying rights, the ratio of aid from the largest donor to total foreign exchange receipts, etc. Indirect indicators are the proportion of assets, especially subsoil assets, owned by foreigners, the extent to which one trading partner dominates the pattern of trade, and the proportion of the supply of capital (or intermediate goods) which is imported.

2

Underdevelopment in Theory

Keith Griffin

Most of the theorizing on economic development has been done by economists who live and were trained in the industrial West. Some economists, in fact, have written about the underdeveloped countries before they have seen them,[1] and others—although they may have visited an underdeveloped country—write as if they have seen only the capital and perhaps a few of the other major cities. Almost all of these economists, moreover, are ignorant of much of the economic history of the countries about which they are theorizing. Thus many writers on the poverty of nations have suffered from two serious handicaps: lack of knowledge about the broad historical forces associated with underdevelopment and ignorance of the institutions, behaviour responses and ways of life of the largest sector within the underdeveloped countries, the rural areas. Research now available or in progress is gradually reducing our ignorance of the causes of underdevelopment and the conditions under which most of mankind lives. It is almost certain that once additional evidence is accumulated many of the theories of development proposed in the last two decades will have to be abandoned.

THEORIES OF DUALISM

Perhaps the most pervasive theory is that of the dual economy. There are numerous models of economic dualism, but their common feature is the division of the economy into two broad—largely independent—sectors.[2] The names given to these two sectors vary. In some cases the division is between a "capitalist" and a "non-capitalist" sector (Lewis); in other cases it is a division between an "enclave" and the "hinterland," between a "modern" and a "traditional" sector of society[3] or, more generally, between "industry" and "agriculture" (Jorgenson).

The two sectors are separate and radically different. The "modern," "capitalist," "industrial" sector is receptive to change, is market oriented

Reprinted from the author's *Underdevelopment in Spanish America* (London: George Allen & Unwin, 1969), pp. 19-31, by permission of the author and the publishers. U.S. edition published by the M.I.T. Press, Cambridge, Massachusetts.

and follows profit maximizing behaviour. The "traditional," "feudal," "agricultural" sector is stagnant; production is for subsistence; little output passes through a market; the leisure preferences of producers are high and they do not follow maximizing behaviour. Unemployment, although "disguised," is assumed to be widespread throughout the agricultural sector and, indeed, the marginal product of labour is zero if not negative.[4] Income is at a subsistence level, which is variously interpreted as either a physiological[5] or a culturally determined minimum.[6]

The methods of production are very different in the two sectors. "The output of the traditional sector is a function of land and labour alone; there is no accumulation of capital . . . ."[7] In the manufacturing sector "output is a function of capital and labour alone."[8] The only link between the two sectors is a flow of unemployed labour (of homogeneous quality) from agriculture to industry. No flows of capital or savings are permitted—since production in the agricultural sector is done without the use of capital, and entrepreneurs are not allowed to engage in activities in both sectors—since motivations and behaviour in the two sectors differ. The economy is essentially closed and growth occurs through a transfer of labour from agriculture to industry in response to demand generated by capitalist businessmen reinvesting their profits. This process continues until all the disguised unemployed are eliminated, labour becomes scarce and the traditional sector is forced to modernize.

Dualistic models of growth, sometimes explicitly but more often implicitly, have constituted the basis on which broad development strategies have been created. The general neglect of agriculture and the bias in favour of industry, which until recently have been such a notable feature of development policy, stem directly from these models. Moreover, within agriculture, the concentration on large commercial farmers (who may be considered to belong to the modern sector) reflects the opinion that small peasants will not respond to ordinary economic incentives. Similarly, within industry, the concentration on manufactured consumer goods which use imported inputs and the failure to take advantage of opportunities to process locally available raw materials reflect the belief that the "traditional" sector is incapable of supplying the "modern" sector with the inputs it requires.

The assumptions on which dualistic models are constructed are highly suspect. First, there is very little evidence of widespread unemployment throughout the year. There may indeed be pronounced seasonal unemployment in some countries,[9] although even this has been denied in at least one densely populated underdeveloped country.[10] The usual pattern, at least in countries where imports of cheap manufactured goods have not destroyed the handicraft industries, is for seasonally available rural manpower to be fully engaged in non-agricultural activities—leather work, food processing, textile spinning and weaving, etc.[11] There is little surplus labour. Secondly, the assumption that rural incomes or wages exceed the marginal product of labour (even if the latter is not zero) could be correct only if there are no commercial farming activities whatever (e.g. share cropping, fixed rental farming), no employment opportunities outside the (extended) family farm and if all farm labour is provided by members of the family.[12] Our knowledge of tenure conditions (e.g. the interdependence of latifundia and mini-fundia in Latin America), the role of migrant labour (e.g. in Africa) and the practice of small farmers of hiring labour during the peak of the harvest season (e.g. in Asia) contradicts the assumption of the dual economy model. In other words, there is no reason to suppose that rural labour receives more than its marginal product. If there is a discrepancy between opportunity costs and incomes this is more likely to be due to the presence of monopolistic market power than to non-maximizing behaviour or a work-and-income-sharing ethic.

The presumption that members of the "traditional" sector of a dual economy are not maximizers is used to explain the alleged fact that labour supply curves are backward sloping and that peasants will not increase output when profit opportunities arise. In other words, dualistic models tend to suppose that if wages or farm prices increase the response will be to reduce the supply of labour or agricultural output. This view is clearly presented by a Dutch economist, J. H. Boeke:

> When the price of coconut is high, the chances are that less of the commodities will be offered for sale; when wages are raised the manager of the estate risks that less work will be done; . . . when rubber prices fall the owner of a grove may decide to tap more intensively, whereas high prices may mean that he leaves a larger or smaller portion of his tappable trees untapped.[13]

The extraordinary thing is that there is absolutely no empirical evidence to support the view that labour will work less if paid more. Indeed there is much evidence to the contrary. It is probable that the backward bending supply curve is a myth left over from the colonial era when the colonized peoples frequently were forced to offer their services to Europeans in order to earn sufficient cash income to pay their taxes. Obviously, in such a situation, if wages are raised, taxes can be paid more easily and the volume of labour services offered to the colonialists will correspondingly decline. Thus this third assumption of dualistic models—the perverse response of workers to wage incentives—must be dismissed.

Fourth, a large number of detailed econometric studies have demonstrated beyond a doubt that the assumption that farmers in underdeveloped countries do not respond to price signals is untenable.[14] We now know that Punjabi peasants, whether Hindus in India or Muslims in Pakistan, respond actively to agricultural policies.[15] Thai farmers, under appropriate conditions, will introduce new crops and new technologies.[16] African farmers can be induced by pricing policies to improve the quality of the output of their tree crops.[17] If in many countries the rate of growth of agriculture is too low the explanation should be sought not in the motives, values and behaviour of the inhabitants of rural areas, but in land tenure conditions, in the distribution of economic power and in government policy.

Finally, the assumption that peasants cannot save because they are too poor must be questioned, even if sufficient information is not yet available to reject it completely. Nurkse presumes that savers are found "mostly among the urban commercial classes"[18] and that "peasants are not likely to save . . . voluntarily since they live so close to subsistence level."[19] Lewis argues that only capitalists save and the reason savings are low in the underdeveloped countries is because the capitalist sector (and hence the proportion of income received in the form of profits) is small.[20]

Unfortunately, data to test these hypotheses are very scarce. One study of rural and urban incomes and savings habits in East and West Pakistan is worth mentioning, however, despite the fact that the quality of the statistical information is rather poor.

The two wings of Pakistan are separated by a thousand miles of Indian territory. East Pakistan is the poorer of the two wings.

. . . Personal incomes in West Pakistan were about 28 per cent higher than in East Pakistan. What is noteworthy is that personal savings (expressed as a percentage of gross personal income before taxes) in the rural areas of Pakistan were higher than in the urban areas and that rural savings in East Pakistan were higher than in West Pakistan. When private corporate saving is added to personal saving, so as to obtain a measure of private saving, it turns out that urban areas save more than rural but that East Pakistan still saves more than West Pakistan. In general, "rural areas . . . appear to have contributed at least three-fourths of the total private savings in the country."[21]

. . .

Clearly one cannot reject the hypothesis that the "traditional" sector does not save on the basis of a single study of one country in one year, but enough information has been provided to create a certain amount of doubt as to the validity of theories which are dependent upon this assumption. Indeed it now seems most unlikely that the assumptions of the model of economic dualism—and particularly the assumptions about the extent of rural unemployment, the relationship of wages to the marginal product of labour, the willingness of peasants to save and the response of workers and farmers to economic incentives—can withstand empirical scrutiny.

One can always maintain that the assumptions of a theory are less important than its predictions and that it is more important to foresee the development path of an economy than to describe accurately its structure and behaviour patterns. Let us, therefore, briefly examine the trends and tendencies the dual economy models would lead one to expect.

The most obvious feature of these models is the tendency for real income in the agricultural sector to remain constant. It cannot rise because there is surplus labour and it cannot fall because incomes already are at a subsistence level. Given that the marginal product of labour is zero, it must follow that all available amounts of land are fully utilized, otherwise it is very difficult to understand why the surplus labour does not combine with uncultivated land. If labour is redundant and land is fully utilized any increase in population will lead to falling *per capita incomes*—unless the increase in population is exactly offset by technical progress. The technical progress may not be of the embodied type, however, because capital accumulation in the "traditional" sector is assumed not to occur; thus the increase in technical knowledge must be entirely disembodied, i.e. it must fall like manna from heaven at precisely the rate of population increase.

These, in fact, are the assumptions many development theorists make. Jorgenson, for example, assumes that his production function "will shift over time so that a given bundle of factors will generate a higher level of output at one date than at an earlier date."[22] He also assumes "that so long as there is disguised unemployment population expands at the same rate as the growth of agricultural output."[23] Thus *per capita* income in the agricultural sector cannot fall by assumption, and since the modern, industrial sector is assumed to be increasing its relative importance in the economy the *per capita* income of the nation as a whole must rise.

Dualistic theories thus make three specific predictions about the development path of an underdeveloped country: first, aggregate *per capita* income will rise; second, agricultural output will increase at the same rate as the population; and, third, *per capita* income in rural areas will remain constant. What evidence is there that these predictions are generally correct?

In the first place, there are several areas in which *per capita* income has declined. In Africa north of the Sahara, for example, gross domestic product *per capita* declined by 0.3 per cent a year between 1960 and 1967. Looking at individual countries over the period 1960–66, GNP *per capita* grew at an annual rate of −0.1 per cent in Ghana, −0.5 per cent in Morocco, −2.6 per cent in Rhodesia, −0.4 per cent in the Dominican Republic and −1.4 per cent in Uruguay.[24] Evidently, a few countries are engaged in a process of underdevelopment which dual economy models are incapable of explaining. It is quite likely, as we shall see below, that if the economic history of today's poverty-stricken nations were examined it would become apparent that many of them descended into underdevelopment from a level of material prosperity and social wellbeing that was once considerably greater than that observed at present.

Next, there is abundant evidence that in many countries agricultural output, and particularly production of food for domestic consumption, has failed to keep pace with the rate of population increase. Comparing 1966 with the average of the period 1957–59 it appears that *per capita* agricultural production had declined in the following countries: Algeria, Burundi, Congo (Kinshasa), Liberia, Malagasy Republic, Morocco, Rwanda, Tunisia, Uganda, Iran, Iraq, Egypt, India, Burma, Cambodia, Indonesia, South Vietnam, Argentina, Bolivia, Brazil, Chile, Colombia, Costa Rica, Dominican Republic, Ecuador, Haiti, Paraguay, Peru, Trinidad and Tobago.[25] Clearly the theories of dualism have failed this simple test on a massive scale.

Finally, there is the question of whether *per capita* incomes in rural areas have remained constant. There is some evidence that rural incomes have been falling in several Spanish American countries. It is possible, of course, that our data on Spanish America are wrong or that for some reason this area constitutes a special case. Hence it is worth considering briefly what is happening in another country in a rather different part of the world.

In 1965 it was suggested, on the basis of the then existing statistical information on the *per capita* availability of foodgrains and average rural incomes, that despite the rapid growth in GNP and *per capita* income that Pakistan has enjoyed, particularly during the Second Five Year Plan, "the vast majority of the Pakistani population probably have a lower standard of living today than when the country achieved its independence in 1947."[26] Two years later additional evidence became available which showed that *per capita* agricultural output in East Pakistan declined from Rs.197 in

1949–50, to Rs.184 in 1954–55, and finally to Rs.174 in 1959–60; it then increased to Rs.188 in 1964–65 but was still lower than the level achieved in the earliest recorded period. Exactly the same pattern was followed in West Pakistan except that by 1964–65 *per capita* agricultural output had fully regained the previous peak.[27] Clearly a strong presumption exists that the standard of living in rural areas, particularly in East Pakistan, has declined in the last two decades.

The author of a more recent study has investigated in great detail the trends in rural incomes in East Pakistan since 1949.[28] According to the evidence collected by Mr. Bose agricultural value added per head of rural population declined from Rs.200.5 in 1949/50–1950/51 to Rs.182 in 1962/63–1963/64; in the same period agricultural value added per head of agricultural population declined from Rs.229 to Rs.202.5 and *per capita* rural income declined from Rs.272.5 to Rs.268.5.[29] Because of increased population density in rural areas the number of landless male workers seeking wage employment rose from 14.1 per cent of the male agricultural labour force in 1951 to 19.4 per cent in 1961.[30] The real wages of these landless agricultural labourers declined from an index of 100 in 1949 to 82.3 in 1966.[31]

In view of this evidence it seems rather pointless to construct a model of an underdeveloped economy in which the central feature is the constancy of real incomes in the largest sector. Ironically, it was during the period of falling rural incomes in Pakistan that two visiting economists published the first version of their model of a dual economy based on the assumption of a fixed "institutional or subsistence level of real wages in the agricultural sector."[32] The Fei and Ranis model subsequently became famous, particularly in the United States,[33] but in its country of origin it remains pathetically irrelevant.

It is conceivable, however, that some theorists would claim that models of economic dualism are not really concerned with the agricultural sector but are concerned with describing the pattern of growth of the modern industrial sector. In other words, it might be claimed that the dual economy models put a spotlight on one—often very small[34]—sector and leave the rest of the economy in relative obscurity.[35] If this is the correct interpretation, the validity of the theory should be tested by comparing its predictions with the performance of the "modern" sector, and the "traditional" sector should be ignored.

A prominent characteristic of the dual economy cum surplus labour theory is the lack of employment opportunities in agriculture and the growth of employment opportunities in the "modern" sector. This is a fundamental asymmetry in the model, and it is this difference in the treatment of the growth and employment potential of the two sectors which determines the development path of the economy. Given the structure of the model it is obvious that development can occur only through a process of capital accumulation in the "modern" sector and the absorption of labour in industry. In other words, the proportion of the labour force occupied in industry should increase, and in the classical version of the model "the rate of growth of manufacturing employment is, of course, equal to the rate of growth of manufacturing output."[36]

These hypotheses are contradicted by a great deal of empirical evidence. Nowhere, I believe, has industrial output and employment increased at the same rate; there has always been some increase in the productivity of labour in industry. More important, there are many countries in which the proportion of the labour force employed in industry has increased much less than the theory would lead one to expect (e.g. Turkey and Malaysia), others in which the relative size of the industrial labour force has remained constant (e.g. Egypt), and still others in which the proportion has even declined (e.g. Cyprus). . . . In a few Spanish American nations there was a smaller proportion of the labour force employed in manufacturing in 1960 than in 1925.

. . .

In a few countries, especially in Africa, there has been a decline not only in the *proportion* of the work force employed in industry and the "modern" sector, but in the *absolute level* of employment in non-agricultural activities as well. Output of the "modern" sector has increased while employment has fallen. For instance, between 1955 and 1964 the trend rate of increase of non-agricultural employment was −1.0 in the Cameroons, −0.5 in Kenya, −0.7 in Malawi, −0.4 in Tanzania, −0.1 in Uganda and −0.9 in Zambia.[37] The dual economy model is incapable of explaining these trends.

The theories we are examining make predictions not only about the level of employment in industry, but also about the aggregate rate of savings and investment in the economy. Arthur Lewis asserts that an understanding of how the savings and investment ratios rise from 4–5 per cent to 12–15 per cent of national income is the "central problem in the theory of economic development."[38] His explanation of the rise is in terms of a redistribution of income from the "subsistence" to the "capitalist" sector. Similarly, Professor Jorgenson's model implies that "if the proportion of manufacturing output to agricultural output increases, the share of saving in total income also increases."[39]

Once again, there is statistical evidence that suggests that there is no simple association between a growing modern, capitalist, industrial sector and rising savings and investment. For instance, in Colombia between 1953 and 1965 industrial output rose from 15.5 per cent of GDP to 19.0 per cent, while the gross investment ratio *declined* from 16.5 to 16.0 per cent. Similarly, in Guatemala between 1950–51 and 1962–63 the share of industry in GDP rose from 12.0 to 14.0 per cent, while private savings as a per cent of net national product *declined* from 2.6 to 2.3. The same phenomenon has occurred in Brazil: during the period 1946–48 to 1958–60 industrial production increased from 21 to 34 per cent of GDP and the ratio of gross domestic savings to GNP declined from 16.4 to 16.0 per cent. Indeed it appears that the savings ratio in Brazil has remained roughly constant since at least the late 1930s.[40] The lack of a strong positive correlation between the degree of industrialisation and the domestic savings ratio is not, of course, peculiar to Latin America; a similar lack of association can be found elsewhere. For example, in Turkey between 1954 and 1965 industrial output rose from 13.0 to 15.0 per cent of GDP, while the gross investment ratio—despite the availability of considerable amounts of foreign aid—fell from 14.5 per cent to 13.0 per cent of GDP. Thus once more the predictions of the theory are refuted by the facts.

In summary, dualistic models of development make an unhelpful division of the economy into a "traditional" and a "modern" sector. The assumptions of the theory regarding the characteristics of the "traditional" agricultural sector are not credible and, indeed, can be shown to be erroneous by even the most casual empiricism. The predictions of the theory are likewise incorrect. It has been demonstrated that in not a few countries the growth of national income *per capita*, the level of rural wages, the expansion of agricultural output, the evolution of employment in industry and the behaviour of the aggregate savings and investment ratios have differed markedly from what the theory would lead one to expect. In almost every conceivable way the theory fails to conform to the reality of a great many underdeveloped countries.

In many respects this theory of growth and development is curiously static and a-historical. Models of the dual economy assume a given and constant subsistence wage rate, a given pool of disguised unemployment and unchanged, i.e. "traditional," agrarian institutions. The real problem arises, however, when population growth rates exceed the capacity of the economy to adjust its institutions (e.g. land tenure), attitudes (e.g. toward birth control) and composition of output (e.g. the degree of industrialisation) so that real wages *fall*, seasonal unemployment in agriculture *increases* and the proportion of the labour force employed in large-scale industry *declines* or at best remains roughly constant. One cannot even begin to analyse these problems if the conceptual framework being used is one of static, unchanged, constant "subsistence" incomes and "traditional" institutions, values and modes of behaviour.

. . .

CONCLUSIONS

Underdevelopment as it is encountered today in Spanish America and elsewhere is a product of history. It is not the primeval condition of man, nor is it merely a way of describing the economic status of a "traditional" society. Underdevelopment is part of a process; indeed, it is part of the same process which produced development. Thus an interpretation of underdevelopment must begin with a study of the past. It is only from an examination of the forces of history—i.e. of the historical uses of power, both political and economic—that one may obtain an insight into the origin of underdevelopment.

The study of the uses of power in the past must be complemented by an analysis of the distribution of power in the present. The opportunities for development are conditioned by the functioning of the world economy in which the underdeveloped countries find themselves. There are some international economic forces which obviously tend to stimulate development, but there are many other forces which perpetuate inequalities and tend to retard development. . . . The transfer of ideas, knowledge, factors of production and commodities may all increase rather than decrease the obstacles to development.

The internal barriers to development—e.g. inappropriate institutions, attitudes and values—are as important as the external obstacles. . . . The types of barriers one finds, and their strength, frequently are related to the way economic and political power are distributed within the country. The concentration of purchasing power and the instruments of legitimate political force in a few hands, and the use to which this force is put, inevitably affect a country's aggregate economic performance and the welfare of its inhabitants.

Broadly speaking, the object of development policy is to turn historical constants into variables. Occasionally this can be achieved merely by changing the pattern of expenditure and the composition of investment. For example, the government might spend more of its revenues on rural education and less on central administration; investment in military installations might be reduced and expenditures on directly productive activities increased. In many cases, however, policy in underdeveloped countries cannot be concerned exclusively with allocating resources in the usual sense; it must also be concerned with creating new institutions and reforming existing ones. The major purpose of development planning, in fact, is to undertake the required structural transformation of a country in a conscious, explicit, orderly and rational manner.

The essence of development is institutional reform.[41] This process of institutional reform can act as an independent variable stimulating growth, e.g. an educational reform can stimulate growth by increasing the supply of relevant skills and improving the quality of the labour force. Alternatively, institutional reforms may be a prerequisite to development, e.g. large-scale investment in some minifundia zones may be virtually impossible unless fragmented land holdings are consolidated. Most important, institutional reforms may be complementary to other development policies and increase their effectiveness, e.g. a reorganization of the government's administrative machinery may be essential if development policies are to be properly formulated and implemented.

The three reforms we have mentioned—of the educational system, land tenure and public administration—are just a few of the many that are required. Furthermore, most of these reforms are linked to others. For example, the government administration cannot be improved unless the educational system is altered; education reform is contingent upon increased tax revenues; tax reform is impossible unless the political power of the wealthy is reduced and this, in turn, requires a land reform. The outcome of such a series of reforms is little short of a revolution. This is what Paul Baran meant when he said that "economic development has historically always meant a far-reaching transformation of society's economic, social, and political structure."[42]

NOTES

1. The most candid confession is by C. P. Kindleberger: "The book is written by one who has not been there." (*Economic Development*, McGraw-Hill, 1958, 1st edition, p. ix.)
2. The most frequently cited authors in this literature are W. Arthur Lewis,

"Economic Development with Unlimited Supplies of Labour," *Manchester School*, May 1954, and "Unlimited Labour: Further Notes," *Manchester School*, January 1958; J. C. H. Fei and G. Ranis, *Development of the Labour Surplus Economy: Theory and Policy*, Yale University, 1964; D. W. Jorgenson, "The Development of a Dual Economy," *Economic Journal*, June 1961 and "Surplus Agricultural Labour and the Development of a Dual Economy," *Oxford Economic Papers*, November 1967.

3. See W. W. Rostow, *The Stages of Economic Growth*, Cambridge University Press, 1960.

4. See R. Nurkse, *Problems of Capital Formation in Underdeveloped Countries*, Oxford University Press, 1957; P. N. Rosenstein-Rodan, "Problems of Industrialization of Eastern and South Eastern Europe," *Economic Journal*, 1943; K. Mandelbaum, *The Industrialization of Backward Areas*, Basil Blackwell, 1945.

5. Leibenstein defines the subsistence level as one where "equality between high fertility and high mortality rates exist. These are the maximum rates consistent with the survival of the population." (H. Leibenstein, *Economic Backwardness and Economic Growth*, John Wiley and Sons, 1960, p. 154.)

6. W. Arthur Lewis, *op. cit.*

7. D. W. Jorgenson, "Surplus Agricultural Labour and the Development of a Dual Economy," *loc. cit.*, p. 291.

8. *Ibid.*, p. 292.

9. See, for example, K. B. Griffin, "Algerian Agriculture in Transition," *Bulletin* of the Oxford University Institute of Economics and Statistics, 1965.

10. M. Paglin, "Surplus Agricultural Labour and Development," *American Economic Review*, September 1965. Paglin's study is of India.

11. See, for instance, M. Herskovits, *Economic Anthropology: A Study in Comparative Economics*, 2nd edition, Knopf, 1952; G. Dalton, ed., *Tribal and Peasant Economies: Readings in Economic Anthropology*, Natural History Press, 1967; J. Ingram, *Economic Change in Thailand Since 1850*, Stanford University Press, 1955.

12. A useful discussion of some of these issues is found in A. Berry and R. Soligo, "Rural-Urban Migration, Agricultural Output, and the Supply Price of Labour in a Labour-Surplus Economy," *Oxford Economic Papers*, July 1968.

13. J. H. Boeke, *Economics and Economic Policy of Dual Societies*, New York, 1953, p. 40. The backward bending supply curve of effort is also supported by B. Higgins, *Economic Development*, Constable, 1959, pp. 286–7, 504.

14. See, for example, W. P. Falcon, "Farmer Response to Price in a Subsistence Economy: The Case of West Pakistan," *American Economic Review*, May 1964; P. T. Bauer and B. S. Yamey, "A Case Study of Response to Price in an Underdeveloped Country," *Economic Journal*, December 1959; J. R. Behrman, *Supply Response in Underdeveloped Agriculture: A Case Study of Thailand, 1937–1963*; D. Narain, *The Impact of Price Movements on Areas Under Selected Crops in India, 1900–1939*; E. Dean, *The Supply Responses of African Farmers: Theory and Measurement in Malawi*, Amsterdam, 1966.

15. W. P. Falcon and C. H. Gotsch, "Two Approaches with the Same Results," *Asian Review*, July 1968.

16. J. R. Behrman, "The Adoption of New Products and of New Factors in Response to Market Incentives in Peasant Agriculture: An Econometric Investigation of Thai Corn and Kenaf Supply Responses in the Post-war Period," University of Pennsylvania, Department of Economics, Discussion Paper No. 45, mimeo, February 1967.

17. P. T. Bauer and B. S. Yamey, *op. cit.*

18. R. Nurkse, *op. cit.*, p. 37.

19. *Ibid.*, p. 43.

20. "Economic Development with Unlimited Supplies of Labour," *loc. cit.* Jorgenson assumes that "saving is equal to total profits in the industrial sector" (*op. cit.*).

21. A. Bergan, "Personal Income Distribution and Personal Savings in Pakistan, 1963/64," *Pakistan Development Review*, Summer 1967, p. 186.

22. "Surplus Agricultural Labour and the Development of a Dual Economy," *loc. cit.*, p. 292.

23. *Ibid.*, p. 293.

24. AID, Statistics and Reports Division, *Economic Growth Trends: Latin-America, East Asia, Near East and South Asia, Africa*, 1967/1968.

25. *Ibid.* Also see FAO, *The State of Food and Agriculture*, 1967.

26. K. B. Griffin, "Financing Development Plans in Pakistan," *Pakistan Development Review*, Winter 1965, p. 606.

27. G. F. Papanek, *Pakistan's Development*, Harvard University Press, 1967, Appendix Table 5B, p. 318.

28. S. R. Bose, "Trend of Real Incomes of the Rural Poor in East Pakistan, 1949–66—An Indirect Estimate," Pakistan Institute of Development Economics, Research Report No. 68, July 1968.

29. *Ibid.*, Table 1. The data are expressed in constant prices of 1959/60.

30. *Ibid.*, Table 3.

31. *Ibid.*, Table 4.

32. J. C. H. Fei and G. Ranis, "Unlimited Supply of Labour and the Concept of Balanced Growth," *Pakistan Development Review*, Winter 1961, p. 32.

33. See G. Ranis and J. C. H. Fei, "A Theory of Economic Development," *American Economic Review*, September 1961; J. C. H. Fei and G. Ranis, *Development of the Labour Surplus Economy: Theory and Policy*, *loc. cit.*

34. In Chad the non-agricultural labour force is 8 per cent of the total, in Kenya 12 per cent, in Thailand 18 per cent, in Nepal 8 per cent, in Yemen 11 per cent and in Haiti 17 per cent.

35. This rationalization certainly does not apply to Fei and Ranis who criticize Lewis for treating the agricultural sector "more or less as an afterthought" while claiming that their model "gives a more explicit treatment to the agricultural sector." ("Unlimited Supply of Labour and the Concept of Balanced Growth," *loc. cit.*, p. 29.)

36. D. W. Jorgenson, "Surplus Agricultural Labour and the Development of a Dual Economy," *loc. cit.*, p. 297.

37. C. R. Frank, Jr., "Urban Unemployment and Economic Growth in Africa," *Oxford Economic Papers*, July 1968, Table II, p. 254.

38. "Economic Development with Unlimited Supplies of Labour," *loc. cit.*

39. "Surplus Agricultural Labour and the Development of a Dual Economy," *loc. cit.*, p. 310.

40. See N. H. Leff, "Marginal Savings Rates in the Development Process: The Brazilian Experience," *Economic Journal*, September 1968.

41. In most of the literature on growth and development institutional reforms are ignored; in other cases reforms are treated in a purely formal way. For example, Mrs. Adelman writes her production function in the form $Y = f(K_t, \ldots, U_t)$, where K_t is the stock of capital at time t and U_t is the "socio-cultural environment." By differencing the production function one can determine the effect of institutional reform,

$$\sum_{g=1}^{w} \frac{\Delta Y}{\Delta Uj} \cdot \frac{\Delta Uj}{\Delta t}$$

This last expression, however, increases our knowledge of the role of institutional reforms by precisely zero. It tells us that if reforms lead to increased output, they lead to increased output; and if they don't, they don't. A more trivial result is hard to imagine. (See I. Adelman, *Theories of Economic Growth and Development*, Stanford University Press, 1961, Ch. 2.)

42. P. Baran, *The Political Economy of Growth*, Monthly Review Press, 1957, p. 3.

3

Balanced Thought and Economic Growth

Warren Frederick Ilchman and Ravindra C. Bhargava

In framing an ideal we may assume what we wish,
but should avoid impossibilities.

—Aristotle, *Politics*

In no field does orthodoxy seem to last less long than in development economics. Today's general strategy for economic growth becomes tomorrow's barrier. A factor considered crucial in one schema becomes a highly dependent variable in another. Often the whole strategy is premised on a tautology: to develop economically, a nation must develop economically. The attempts to discover basic psychological sources of the process, such as motivational patterns in a society, have pushed the answers back to deviant minority groups and the *leit-motif's* of children's fairy tales.[1] For the economic strategist in a low-income country, these latter studies, while important and interesting, are as useful in guiding his investment decisions as the studies by Max Weber.

But are the more exclusively economic strategies of greater value? It is the contention of this article that the major strategies so far advanced by economists are relevant operationally only in highly specific situations. These situations, furthermore, are not defined by economic factors alone. They are determined by crucial political, sociological, and administrative factors as well. A further contention of this article is that the only operational strategies for "development" are the products of a cross-disciplinary social science perspective with a strong contribution from political scientists.

To prove this contention, the authors have analyzed several major theorists concerned with three potentially operational strategies—"Big Push" balanced growth, unbalanced growth, and capital formation through unlimited supplies of labor.[2] These theories are not assessed in terms of their economic merits. Instead, they are analyzed in terms of the major social problems that might arise from undertaking them and the political regime and administrative systems they presuppose.[3] In other words, these strategies are analyzed in terms of what they assume about the rest of the

Reprinted from *Economic Development and Cultural Change*, Vol. XIV, No. 4 (July 1966), pp. 385-399, by permission of The University of Chicago Press and the authors. Copyright 1966 by The University of Chicago.

social system. Among the questions asked are: What is the character and membership of the elite? What is the degree of organization of two of the affected sectors—the urban working force and the peasantry? How responsive is the political system to group demands? What is the expected role of government in the strategy? How many civil servants will be required, and to what extent and in what way must they be trained? How much and what types of data are required? Detailed answers to these questions, of course, cannot be given in an article of this length. But, despite the necessary abstractions, a clear idea will be given of the "non-economic" criterion by which these strategies must be judged before they can be considered operational.

I

Balanced Growth

The "Big Push" balanced growth strategy for the development of underdeveloped countries may be attributed to Ragnar Nurkse and Paul Rosenstein-Rodan. In general, the strategy argues that the low per capita incomes which prevail in underdeveloped countries are a consequence of the low levels of productivity and that substantial increases in productivity require increased capital formation. However, another consequence of the low levels of income is that the demand for most manufactured goods is small, most of the income being utilized for subsistence. This limitation to the extent of the market implies that no entrepreneur can profitably, even with a monopoly, set up a modern factory, as the indivisibilities of capital result in the unit being of such a size that, at its low levels of operation, the costs of production are too high. Consequently, capital formation in manufacturing is not feasible, productivity does not increase, and poverty continues. To break this vicious circle, the balanced growth theorists suggest that in a country a whole set of complementary investments should be made, such that factories themselves, as well as the workers in them, can buy up all the produce either as intermediate goods or for final consumption. This will then render all the investments profitable. Thus, it is proposed to solve the demand problem by means of investment itself. In this way, capital formation will be made possible and vicious circles broken.

The most striking feature of the "Big Push" strategy is that, whereas investments in general are not profitable in the economy, there are combinations of investments,[4] which if implemented simultaneously, will prove profitable. To achieve these "right" bundles of investments, qualitatively and quantitatively, together with the time schedule for execution, is not easy. It involves planning substantial changes in production patterns with little assistance from the market mechanism and requires anticipating the market requirements once these changes have been made. In a scheme of balanced growth, every component must be at the right place at the right time in the right quantity. The entire effort is based on the capability of a country to organize its relevant sectors, enact the proper controls and incentives, and acquire and submit to the best technical judgments on the combinations of investments for balanced growth.

The capital required for the "Big Push" will come from two sources—domestic and foreign savings. For domestic savings, taxation, higher profits, and inflation will be the chief means. However, with the large requirements of the strategy, domestic savings, even under the best of circumstances, will not be adequate, and foreign capital inflows will have to be substantial. The inflow would be in the form of government grants and loans and direct private investment.

What are the so-called "non-economic factors" which might enable an underdeveloped country to adopt successfully this strategy? Above all, there must exist in the country some authority or institutional arrangement capable of planning and implementing the combination of investments. This presupposes a political ruling elite with considerable unanimity of purpose and agreement on measures that may be taken to achieve this goal, a political system supportive, in the short and at least medium run, of the resulting programs, and an administrative system capable of bearing the technical burden of preparing and implementing the strategy.

Two ruling elites are possible. They are distinguished by their membership, especially private sector representation, and the role they conceive for government to play. The first is a modernizing elite made up largely of intellectuals, the military, and civil servants. It would be, in varying degrees, distrustful of the private sector. For this elite, the government is the obvious agent for balanced growth. Any role for the private sector, if allowed at all, would have to be subject to extensive controls. Reliance on incentives and indirect controls to secure the massive complementarity of investment would contain too much uncertainty. Government ownership and operation would be preferable for this elite.[5]

The membership of a second possible ruling elite would be distinguished by heavy representation from the business sector. This elite would have to be particularly small and closely knit to achieve the cooperation necessary to plan and organize the establishment of a whole complex of industries in the balanced growth pattern. Active government help and encouragement to provide the necessary incentives and business conditions would also be required. Taxes on industries and the elite must be low (or subventions high); high profits and monopolies permitted; infrastructure investments and technical assistance provided; trade union activity controlled; and internal security maintained. Indeed, it is unnecessary to distinguish between government and the private sector; they are virtually the same.[6]

Both ruling elites will have to be narrow in membership. A broadly based nationalist elite, drawing from several social sectors, such as the urban working force, would be too susceptible to the demands of its members, and this would impede the success of the strategy. This narrow base presupposes either a quiescent population, no political opposition of a formal or informal sort, heavy expenditures on coercion, or all three.[7] This is, of course, another way to describe an authoritarian situation, for it must be apparent that the "Big Push" cannot be undertaken unless the ruling elite can effectively restrict access by the broad mass of the public to the substance of the strategy. Furthermore, ideally, the technical considerations in the "Big Push" even subordinate the elite's judgment to that of the engineers and the economists.

Therefore, for the length of time required to break the "vicious circle of poverty," the political system cannot be sensitive to group demands. But in the "Big Push," this is highly unlikely for several reasons. First, the strategy requires that within a short period of time a country will find itself with a large industrial sector superimposed on an economically primitive base. Industrialization, and attendant urbanization, means the influx of large numbers of people from the rural areas into an entirely different set of social conditions. These people would find their values and ways of life unsuited to the new environment and would need considerable readjustment to be absorbed into industry and to attain stability. Their problems would be aggravated by the fact that it would be unlikely that adequate arrangements for housing, sanitation, medical attention, recreation, etc., would exist, since the numbers involved would be so large and the capital available for these purposes inadequate. Because of the nature and objectives of either ruling elite, trade union activity would be restricted and any liberal labor legislation unimplemented. All claims for redistribution would be unacceptable. This would tend to produce a restless and dissatisfied mass of people, who will have little to say in the political system and will constitute a constant threat to the social system, necessitating an elaborate coercive apparatus. It is true that the problems of adjusting the rural population to the modern sector always create tensions and difficulties, but in the "Big Push" strategy, the magnitudes would be much larger. Industrialization would not be arriving gradually, but would be more in the nature of a "once-and-for-all" process.

Second, the problems of regional disparities would constantly press for redress. The "Big Push" strategy, however, permits this only insofar as the redress fulfills a role in the total combination of investments. Probably, the dictates of location economics, and the possible bias of the ruling elite, would lead to the concentration of economic activity in certain areas, to the neglect of other regions. The experience in several countries, Pakistan, India, and Nigeria among them, has shown how serious a situation may result from this.

Third, the financing of the strategy renders it vulnerable to group demands. On one hand, major reliance on foreign capital would be unacceptable to nations which have recently won, and intend to sustain, freedom from foreign controls. Any restriction on their use of foreign capital, whether borrowed or granted, is considered compromising to their independence. Prohibitions against foreign capital imports, restrictions on the use of foreign capital, the universal condemnation of "strings" on foreign aid, the demands for trade rather than aid, the popularity of nationalization through confiscation are common manifestations of this.[8] Under these conditions, the capital-exporting and aid-giving countries will hardly be encouraged to fill the capital needs. And to remove these impediments requires a regime unmenaced by an opposition able to exploit this sensitive issue. On the other hand, the burden of domestic saving from taxation and inflation would be borne by the non-profit-earning classes—the urban working force, the middle class, the service professions, and the rural sector. At the same time, particularly in a predominately private sector strategy, there will be increasing disparities of income. The public in all regimes tolerate the above condition to a certain degree. But if the destabilization produced by massive foreign capital is to be avoided, or if the required capital is not available, increased reliance will be placed on mobilizing domestic savings. For the authority of a regime (and consequently the strategy) to remain unaffected in this case presupposes the existence of a long-suffering and tranquil non-profit-earning class or the existence of a widely effective coercive apparatus, whose costs the "Big Push" strategist externalizes. In reality, the demands for redistribution would be great and fully exploitable by any opposition in low-income countries.

Thus, at a time when social harmony is an essential and assumed part of the strategy for economic development, it is that same strategy that is least likely to produce it.

Administratively, the "Big Push" necessitates, in the public and/or private sector, an extensive and highly skilled bureaucracy. This would have to be in addition to the existing civil service, for retraining a civil service for development objectives is a long-term process, and the needs of "law and order" would undoubtedly increase greatly under the pressure of the "Big Push." These personnel would be needed for both the formulation and execution of the strategy. New skills of many kinds and in great quantities would be called for—managerial and technical skills for operating the new enterprises, organizational and administrative skills for over-all coordination and the various forms of controls, including coercion. The experience with the execution of comparative modest development programs in several countries has revealed the shortcomings in these fields. Furthermore, formulating the strategy requires a large quantity of reliable data, not only of economic variables like elasticities of demand, income distribution, price changes, and technologies, but also of non-economic variables like changes in taste, motivations, and values. The data-gathering and processing machinery will, therefore, have to be widespread and able—far more than what exists at present in any underdeveloped country.[9]

Unbalanced Growth

Albert Hirschman developed his theory of unbalanced growth in response to the "Big Push" idea. The different kinds of resources required for the "Big Push," he contended, are ones which low-income countries have in short supply. Indeed, that is why they are underdeveloped. He also insists that development is a gradual process, and it is unrealistic to think in terms of superimposing a large modern sector on a traditional economy. But the greatest shortage, according to his analysis, is the ability to perceive and take investment decisions, even when opportunities exist. The strategy of unbalanced growth seeks to remedy this shortage by creating situations in which people are forced to take investment decisions. Such situations are achieved by deliberately "unbalancing" different sectors of the economy. If certain parts of the economy are made to grow, the shortages in the complementary parts will create pressures for their growth also, forcing investments to be made. The areas which lead the development should be so selected that investments in the complementary areas are really compulsive rather than permissive.

The most important field of application of this strategy is to governmental decisions regarding investments in economic and social overhead capital. The role of government is usually defined to include the function of providing this infrastructure, in order that entrepreneurs may make profitable investments of a directly productive nature. Hirschman, however, points out that investments in infrastructure are basically permissive of directly productive investments. They do not create any compelling situation for the latter to be made. Consequently, infrastructure investments are often uneconomic, insofar as they remain underutilized for long periods. A better sequence would be for the government to provide only the barest minimum of infrastructure and to encourage entrepreneurs through incentives, such as tariff protection and subsidies, to invest in directly productive activities. As more of these investments are made, the deficiencies of overhead facilities become marked and increase the cost of production. Entrepreneurs would then press for provision of these services. This pressure would be an indicator to government for the more rational allocation of infrastructure investments. Thus, by having infrastructure lag behind productive activities, development would be quicker, and better use would be made of the available resources.

Hirschman applies this technique to other matters, such as the choice of investments, selection of technology, and ensuring maintenance of capital. To ensure the continuance of productive investments being made, he suggests that the initial activity chosen should be one that maximizes the backward and forward linkages. Instead of starting industrial efforts by making finished goods, the investments should be made in activities which are near the middle of a triangularly arranged input-output matrix. In choosing the technology, an attempt should be made to adopt "machine-paced" operations that compel labor to work at a predetermined rate, despite such a technique being more capital-intensive. Hirschman recommends that underdeveloped countries should choose complicated techniques, where the consequence of a breakdown would be more serious and hence compel adequate maintenance.

Finally, Hirschman does not favor central planning, for it tends to internalize both the external economies and diseconomies.[10] He believes that the net effect would not necessarily be positive, and more rapid growth can be achieved by encouraging aggressive entrepreneurship in the 19th-century fashion. He would also favor a certain amount of inflation in the interest of forcing savings and making investments more profitable.

Although Professor Hirschman has insights into the problems facing at least some of the underdeveloped countries, his strategy ignores important political, social, and administrative factors. What sort of regime is necessary for adopting the strategy of unbalanced growth? Dominant power in the country, needless to say, would be exercised by one group—the business class. A regime totally sympathetic to private sector development and serving its interests would be required. There would be no governmental responsibility for comprehensive central planning and execution, and government would best fulfill its functions by providing the right social overheads at the right time and maintaining law and order. This latter task will be particularly difficult, as the urban working force and the middle class will be subject to inflation, low wages, and increasing disparities of income. At the same time, the government will be observed to tax the businessman inadequately and even to grant him subsidies to swell his profits. To compound this problem, the urban working force will be subject to the destabilizing effects of inadequate social overhead investments—in housing, education, and welfare programs. In addition, the adoption of machine-paced and capital-intensive operations would increase, or at least fail to reduce, unemployment. This would come at a time when trade union activity would be discouraged or completely curtailed by the state. Furthermore, the regime cannot be disturbed by any political objections to foreign business activity in the country. Nor would the demands of regional balance be permitted to affect the "unbalancing" decisions. This, of course, presupposes a high degree of national unity.

What regimes are excluded from adopting the strategy of unbalanced growth? Socialist regimes are, of course. So are those in which businessmen are held in low repute, and only a few businessmen, if any, are part of the core elite guiding decisions. Regimes are excluded in which trade union activity is strong and the political mechanisms sensitive to claims for redistribution. Finally, a regime which invested in social overhead for any reason other than on demonstrated need by directly productive activities would be considered hopelessly inefficient.

Administratively, the demands of the strategy, though less than those of the "Big Push," will nevertheless be considerable. The skill for taking profitable investment decisions is not the same as skills required to organize and operate enterprise. Government must gather data for rationally deciding between alternative infrastructure investments. Also, it will have to select the sectors and areas where activity is to be promoted on the basis of comparative advantage and the likely trends in the demand function. Determination of a suitable system of subsidies and sources of revenue will be necessary. Decisions, it might be added, on purely economic grounds would be difficult, owing to the differing degrees of political power various business interests would possess. Lastly, the administrative requirements for coercion would be considerable.

Capital Formation with Unlimited Supplies of Labor

W. Arthur Lewis believes that in several underdeveloped countries there are virtually unlimited supplies of labor which can be used for capital formation. Disguised unemployment in the agricultural sector, large numbers in domestic service, population growth at a rate faster than the rate of growth of productive employment, and women who can work if opportunities arise—these are the main sources.

The development of the economy takes place by the increase of the sector using reproducible capital—the capitalist sector. This sector has a higher level of productivity than the remaining part of the economy, which is at subsistence level. As development takes place, the capitalist sector expands, while the subsistence sector grows smaller. Lewis also assumes that the capitalist class, which owns the reproducible capital, has a propensity to save and reinvest a large proportion of its profits. Hence, for the growth of the capitalist sector, it is necessary for profits to grow. It is immaterial to the argument whether the state itself is the capitalist.

The capitalist sector has to hire labor to work the capital it owns. As the sector expands, the requirements for labor keep increasing. Since the model assumes virtually unlimited supplies of labor, the process of growth cannot stop because of lack of workers, at least until all the surplus labor has been absorbed. Moreover, as capital accumulates, it causes labor productivity to rise, while technological innovations have the effect of increasing the productivity of both labor and capital. Consequently, the volume of profits, and possibly the profit rate also would keep rising, assuming other factors remain unchanged, and the process of growth would continue. However, growth can be slowed, or even stopped, if the wages increase at such a rate that, despite increases in productivity, the volume of profits falls. This will lead to a decrease in savings and investments. Thus, for the success of this model, keeping wages in check is essential.

The wages paid by the capitalist sector are determined by the wages and the average product of workers in the subsistence sector. To attract workers away from the farms and the villages, the capitalist has to offer an adequate incentive in the form of higher wages. As workers are drawn away from the subsistence sector in quantities large enough to decrease the absolute numbers, the average product rises, and hence the capitalist wages also have to rise in order to maintain the differential. An even more important cause for wages to rise in the capitalist sector would be the relative increase in the price of foodstuffs, as compared with the price of industrial products. The process of drawing workers into the capitalist sector would raise real incomes and increase the demand for food, necessitating larger supplies of food being brought to the market by the farmers. If this does not happen, owing to output being inelastic, food prices would rise, and hence the wages of the capitalist sector workers must rise correspondingly. Further, as the real wages in the subsistence sector would also be increasing, the maintenance of the differential would mean a rise in the capitalist wages. However, if food output does continue to increase, wages would still have to keep rising to keep pace with the average product of the subsistence sector. The solution is twofold: increasing the output of food and, by drawing away the surplus in the form of a land tax, preventing the farmer from taking advantage of this increase. If this can be successfully done, capital formation would continue until all the surplus labor was absorbed and the productivity of the two sectors raised to a high and almost equal level.

Nurkse has a somewhat similar model. He also proposes to utilize the disguised unemployed to form productive capital, i.e., roads, dams, irrigation canals. To minimize the cost of this operation, he intends that these workers be fed from the existing food production by keeping unchanged the consumption of those remaining on the farms. This will be accomplished by the imposition of a land tax or by compulsory requisitioning of food. Nurkse realizes that the workers transferred from the farms need to be given some small increase in consumption. He also recognizes the necessity of making all the surplus population work to avoid the "demonstration effect" inducing people to return to the villages.

As with other strategies of development, these models also appear to require a specific set of conditions. Lewis's model can work either with complete state ownership of the means of production, or with a government dominated by a business elite. In either case, the rural population and the industrial working force will not be in a position to influence the allocation of resources or the distribution of income and wealth. The government has to follow a policy of keeping the wages of the subsistence sector and the industrial workers at the minimum possible level. The tools for this will largely be heavy doses of land taxation, control of the activities of organized labor, non-implementation of any liberal labor legislation, and coercion. If the industries are being developed by private entrepreneurs, the economy will have to be geared to maximize their profits, to encourage investments. Accordingly, monopolies will presumably be allowed and taxes on business and high incomes kept at low levels. The state would provide the infrastructure investments, credit facilities, and other institutional arrangements to enable entrepreneurs to make investments. Consequently, the state will have few resources to invest in general welfare activities. In any case, income transfers to the working class would not be in accordance with the logic of the model.

The model assumes that the rural and urban working population will either be docile enough to accept this situation or the state able to coerce a condition of stability. But growing income disparities, regressive taxation, and suppression of the right of organization are policies which are difficult to adhere for long. Nurkse's model has the added complication of labor conscription to make it operational. Finally, the social problems of adjustment, arising from industrialization and accentuated by the living conditions which the industrialists are likely to provide, would be as acute as in the balanced and unbalanced growth theories. Few underdeveloped countries today could undertake this strategy.

Administratively, the major task would be the maintenance of internal stability, coercion of the working class, and prevention of expressions of disaffection. An elaborate and reliable machinery for the collection of land tax would be required—a machinery not prone to leakages through corruption. In countries where land holdings are small, this problem would be even more difficult. Further, the success of the model demands rapid increase in food output. While imposing and collecting land taxes, the government would also have to embark upon an extensive program of agricultural extension. Experience in several countries has shown in recent years that this is not an easy matter and calls for high technical, administrative, and organizational skills. This has been true even where the farmers were generally cooperative, and the frictions of high taxes were not present.[11] Another task requiring substantial and advanced skills is the planning and implementing of a consistent program. If the state participated in the productive investments, the additional problem of making public enterprise efficient will have to be solved.

II

The three strategies analyzed claim that their implementation will probably lead to economic growth. No demands are made explicitly on the
regime undertaking them, except, by implication, that the regime follow
generally the prescribed program. From a social scientist's and a planner's
point of view, however, certain questions need to be asked of these and
other strategies.

1. What type of regime is required for undertaking the strategy? To
what extent are a regime's values or the ruling elites' composition limitations? Must there be separate strategies for economic growth for "liberal"
regimes, "radical" regimes, "tutelary democracies," pro-business regimes,
anti-business regimes, regimes in which labor and/or small landholders
are important components of the ruling elite, regimes in which taxes cannot be effectively collected, or where there is a low tolerance for bilateral
foreign assistance or foreign private investment? Is a moratorium on politics necessary for the period during which the strategy is being implemented? Can there be permitted opposition parties which might try to
exploit grievances against the regime and its new policies?

2. How does the strategy affect various social and economic sectors?
Will substantial disorganization result for many existing economic and
social institutions and functions? How long must this disorganization be
endured before "growth" provides new institutions and articulates new
functions? Is the strategy profligate of a society's integrative institutions,
values, and beliefs? What have been or might be some of the unintended
consequences of implementing the strategy? An increase in the number of
landless laborers? Greater urban unemployment because of increasing
capital intensiveness of investment and advancing requirements for skills?

3. What is implicit in the strategy for the distribution of wealth? Will
this "formula" change? If so, how and when will it change? What new
demands might be made on the political system as a consequence of implementing the strategy? Will there be greater demands for welfare expenditures and urban amenities? Does the strategy allow for them? Does the
strategy "internalize" their costs?

4. To what degree is the strategy dependent on coercion? Persuasion?
What, from the experience of other regimes, might be the short-term economic costs of coercion? Are they internalized in the strategy? What might
be the long-term economic and social costs of a policy of coercion? Are
social deviancy, anomie, and extremist movements likely "prices" to pay?

5. What does the strategy demand of the administrative system? Will
more personnel and new skills be needed? Will the needs of the strategy for
administrators in one sector starve the other sectors in their needs?[12] Will
existing machinery for supervision and coordination be adequate? Are new
data, and hence data-gathering machinery, required? Are these costs internalized in the strategy?

The authors of these strategies might insist that models are necessarily
abstract and that implementation must be moderated to meet each country's particular situation. At this point, the relevant political, social, and

administrative information is added. But this answer will not do. First, the authors of the strategies were inspired by the process of economic growth in specific countries. In each instance, this process took place in a sociopolitical context from which the process acquired effectiveness and without which it would be virtually meaningless. Professor Nurkse's balanced growth strategy found many precedents in the Soviet Union, Professor Hirschman's proposals in a composite of occurrences in Latin America, and the advocates of capital formation through unlimited supplies of labor in Japanese and, less enthusiastically, Soviet experience.[13] Answers to the questions posed previously are also part of the record. Advice, hence, could also be given on the political, social, and administrative prerequisites, requisites, and consequences. Important costs can be calculated. Whether or not the strategy is relevant, with the addition of the appropriate information, can be assessed. Only then, the strategy for economic growth really becomes a strategy for social, political, and administrative change as well. Second, the strategies are, in different ways, unsusceptible to moderation in economic terms. Balanced growth requires a massive complementarity of supply and demand. Anything short of a total package of investments would fail in the "Big Push." Although most countries have unbalanced growth all the time, a substantially moderated "unbalance" will probably fail to achieve Professor Hirschman's objectives. Also, most conscious efforts in this direction, despite moderated intensity, might still be destabilizing to civil authority. Any moderation in the capital formation through the use of unlimited supplies of labor strategy would be difficult, because of the small size of the profit-making sector and the declared rate of economic growth of most underdeveloped countries. For these countries, moderating any one of the three strategies really means abandoning it. Finally, the strategies might tend, if followed only "moderately," toward self-justification. For example, failure to achieve high rates of capital formation through the Lewis and Nurkse models would set up pressures to remove the political and social barriers to "efficiency." Judgment on the strategy's effectiveness would have to be postponed until a country's social and political system approximated the strategy's "hidden" requirements.

One major reason for the difficulties inherent in implementing the economic strategies is that they were constructed by tools developed for nations with different problems and needs. While this assertion is not novel, it has usually been argued within the terms of economic analysis. Part of the justification for the allegation here is an interpretation of the history of ideas. The key problems confronting underdeveloped countries are the survival of the centralized polity and the existing regime. Neither can claim the likelihood of permanence. The centralized polity, often the rather recent creation of a former colonial power, has institutions too new or too dubious to be accorded deference and legitimacy by various elites in the country. Even the nation's existence is menaced from many sources: threats of and attempts at secession; over-weening neighbors, allies, and would-be allies; and retreats into regional and village loyalties and consequent starving of resources and support for the central government's objectives.[14] The existing regime is always a changing coalition, resting in varying proportions on charisma, promises, and coercion. Each of these has built-in limitations—limitations insofar as many demands are exclusive of others in their fulfillment, limitations to the endurance of coercion and restraints by various groups, limitations in resources (which are much more than economic resources) to meet promises, limitations to the mystique of the nationalist movement, "the hero of Independence," the popular military figure. Much of modern economic analysis, however, was developed for an economic sub-system in a larger social system in which the political problems confronted by most underdeveloped countries had been largely solved or the pace of industrialization had not raised them as starkly. The centralized polity's existence could be assumed, and the ruling regime was expected primarily to help make the market mechanism more efficient and more authoritative.[15] This assumed virtual autonomy of the economic sphere was and is theoretically more acceptable for, say, Great Britain or the United States than it can be in the foreseeable future for underdeveloped countries. In the latter, the initial political prerequisites for a functioning national market are not yet met, and it is, furthermore, the intention of most of the regimes to rely (optimistically, of course) on the political marketplace in the first instance as the authoritative allocator of resources and power.

There are other reasons as well for the difficulty inherent in implementing these economic strategies. One is the extreme division of labor and consequent assumptions dominant in the social sciences.[16] Each discipline has staked out a process, defined perhaps too sharply the relevant variables, developed intrinsic indices, and tended to erect boundaries against trespassing from the other social sciences. When representatives of other social sciences have, nevertheless, successfully crossed the boundaries, the "host" social science incorporates a previously exogenous variable into its system. But there is seldom a cross-disciplinary attempt to penetrate the interrelationship of "each discipline's variables" in terms of the social system as a whole.[17] The three economic strategies analyzed in this article are premised on an essentially autonomous economic sphere in which government and/or private persons make decisions about directly productive activities and related social overhead. The strategies accept as evidence of success, among other economic indicators, an increase in gross national product or a decrease in the incremental capital/output ratio. But these decisions subsume other crucial decisions and judgments. The major judgment is simply that there *will be* a long run for which the short-term sacrifice in consumption is made. This judgment, which is more explicit in underdeveloped countries than can be imagined by analysts from politically well established nations, is the product of other judgments and decisions: a nation's laws will be honored; social conflict can be contained in the institutions of the state; the administrative apparatus is adequate and predictable enough to make just and rapid decisions; material productivity is a "good"; the present distribution of privilege, power, and resources is desirable and/or sufficiently supported, etc. As can easily be seen, the underlying judgments are narrowly social and political in character. The relevant data are not simply economic and cannot be viewed so restrictively.

Another reason stems from a misunderstanding of the mandate given by rulers of underdeveloped countries. The mandate is never a *carte blanche* for development in the most efficient way. In addition to the usual limitations on productive factors, economic development programs are limited by the character and intentions of the existing political regime and social system. The concept of "rising expectations" refers to different sectors (social and economic) and their differing demands, not a unanimous "general will" in this direction.[18] Phrases like "Arab Socialism," "communocracy, and "socialist pattern of society" may imply a "general will," but they must always be interpreted in terms of the elites endorsing these phrases. Furthermore, no nation has ever had or could have an exclusive, secular goal of economic development to which all others must be subordinated. The elites and mobilized publics of every nation, rich and poor, have many objectives for public policy: national survival, national grandeur, distributive-welfare goals, political stability, maximum public choice, maintaining a particular elite combination in power, and the "higher life" among them.[19] While it is true that economic development is necessary for some of these goals, it is also true that economic development is not sufficient. In other goals, it is dysfunctional.[20] In most cases, the other public goals and economic development are mutually necessary. Ignoring this, some economic strategists complain about "prestige" expenditures and concentration on "unproductive" activities. These complaints, heard often from professional economists in underdeveloped countries, place a great burden on the political system. Trained as they and their Western counterparts are in a discipline concerned with the most productive use of scarce resources, they are uncomfortable in the face of politics and the ambiguities of social structure and cultural values.[21] There is a growing feeling among these people that anything short of exclusive concentration on the goal of economic growth is treason by the politicians. A political system able to arbitrate many claims and move toward many common goals cannot long bear this alienation.

III

How would a more integrated social science be of greater relevance for the problems of underdeveloped countries? Basically, a new question must replace the "economic growth" question. Rather than "How should a nation allocate its scarce resources to achieve economic growth?" the question should be, "How should a government allocate its scarce resources to modernize?" This permits the social scientist and the policy-maker to look at a total social system and its institutions and puts economic growth where it belongs, as part of a broader process—the process of modernization. Modernization can be defined generally as a process of improving the capability of a nation's institutions and value system to meet increasing and different demands.[22] Theoretically, a modern nation is one in which the institutions and values are able to meet or adequately handle the increasing and different demands made on them. Political modernization, for example, involves improving the capability of the political system. The general modernization process is dependent on securing a centralized polity, its penetration into the various spheres of life, and obtaining for the polity free-floating resources, unattached to any ascriptive group, to pursue further modernizing goals. It is also dependent on changing certain values: acquiring a new time perspective, a different valuation of the objectives of the state, a changed allegiance from particularistic to broader, more functionally specific associations and institutions, and, finally, new assessments of human activity and achievement. Developing the capability to meet changing and increasing demands is by no means a settled achievement of the underdeveloped nations.[23]

How do "modernization" and "economic growth" differ? The latter becomes part of the former. As a process, modernization is social and political as well as economic. Indeed, to separate the activities is to suggest a divisible character of the phenomena which does not exist. Although economic growth is one way of increasing the stock of free-floating resources to meet demands, it is not exhaustive. The range of demands includes claims for prestige, status, and power; these demands may or may not require economic resources. But like economic growth, modernization must be planned and, above all, invested in as rationally as in the too narrowly conceived directly productive activities and social overhead capital.

Viewed from the perspective of modernization, the concept of social overhead becomes useful in formulating strategy. Social overhead or "infrastructure" permits thinking about essential conditions for building a modernized nation. In doing so, it makes more explicit the character of the social system and, particularly, the role of the state. Society must be seen in terms of developing within it new structures and sanctioning different values: institutions to integrate the members of society, who were forced to leave traditional institutions and values, into new, more materially productive relationships, values to justify modernization as a process. These, too, constitute infrastructure—social infrastructure. Likewise, a modernization strategy casts the state into a more realistic role. The state becomes more than a "fomentor" or the best instrument for capital formation, as it is for the economic development strategies; it becomes the authoritative allocator of society's scarce values and resources—even when the authoritative decision is in favor of the private sector. For the objectives of public policy, the state becomes the arbiter of claims—economic, social, ideological, and philosophical—made by the sectors of society. To fulfill these functions, particularly as they expand in later phases of modernization, a solid political infrastructure must be built: institutions to contain conflict; institutions to aggregate and simplify claims; value systems which accept the legitimacy of the state's authoritative allocations. Just such institutions and values preceded and became more implicit in the modernization of the West and were subsumed in the development of modern economic thought. Finally, an administrative infrastructure is needed. This the economic development strategists also recognize. But the modernization perspective does not allow the glib suggestion that administration must switch from "law-and-order values" to development values! Modernization brings in its wake intensified social problems for which increased expenditures on law-and-order institutions and values are required. At the same time, the administrative infrastructure must be expanded in new directions, with emphasis on values of expedition in non-law-and-order fields; on skills—economic, sociological, and managerial—to comprehend the wider range of relevant phenomena and activity; and on institutions designed to cope with the needs for coordination. Infrastructure, hence, is too inadequately conceived by strategists for economic development. The viable modernized state which would have as a major activity economic development requires conscious and rational investments in social, political, and administrative infrastructure as well.

Perhaps the concept of modernized values needs further explanation. How does a state encourage in its citizens the longer time perspective, the revised valuation on the objectives of the state, the shifting allegiance from particularistic to more universalistic associations and the new assessments of human activity and achievements? The answer is: in terms of rational planned investments. One difference, however, is that the concept of resources for investment, as understood by economic development strategists, must be expanded. Resources, as used here, include coercion, threats of coercion, economic resources, power to command resources, prestige, and security. These "factors" are brought together in different proportions for the major investments to obtain the needed value changes.[24]

Three major types of investments can be thought of for modernization of the state: stability investments, legitimacy investments, and solidarity investments. The contents, proportions, and amount of resources for each differ. Stability investments are allocations aimed at reducing potential and probable opposition to civil authority. Opposition, in this case, might take the form of secessionist groups, radical trade unions, or an urban mob of unemployed. In content, the "investment" would mainly include coercion, threats of coercion, and economic resources. By proportion and amount, there would be a heavy emphasis on coercion and meeting demands with economic resources. Legitimacy investments are very similar to stability investments, but go farther. They are investments aimed at inculcating acceptance of civil authority as right and correct, at discouraging in the public any feeling that they have a right to make authoritative allocations except through civil authorities. These investments, made for instance in educational programs, are comprised of coercion, threats of coercion, power to command economic resources, and economic resources. But the proportion of resources and coercion decreases. The decrease in coercion is primarily due to the fact that the state can rely on the traditional acceptance of authority by most citizens, and the threat of coercion, usually handled in terms of consequences resulting from the deprivation of authority, is adequate. Legitimacy investments can also be made by sharing the power to command economic resources—hitherto reserved by the central government—with local governments. Panchayati Raj is conferring legitimacy on the Indian state and its authoritative acts by sharing power with local governments.

But this last example could easily be used to illustrate the third investment level—solidarity investments. These investments are aimed at securing emotional commitments to the state and a willingness to sacrifice personal resources and forego demands for it. Coercion and threats of coercion are absent in these investments, except insofar as they define people outside the state. Prestige, security, power to command economic resources,—all are involved. Identifying a sector (such as private business) as patriotically useful, an important role at the United Nations, safeguarding the population against the "enemy," participation through representative bodies, and allocations of resources for "regional balance," stadia, national air lines—all conduce to integration into the structures and values of a modernized state. In all three types of investment, the size of each decreases over time, though reduced recurrent expenditures continue.

Free primary education might be useful in illustrating this concept. Some economic development strategists are increasingly finding free primary education a luxury consumption expenditure and argue for greater expenditures in higher and more technical education or more directly productive activities.[25] On the other hand, a modernization strategy might use free primary education in several ways. As a stability investment, it might be useful as a way of pacifying dissident groups, as part of a *quid pro quo* for civil obedience. Or, in the context of a rapidly modernizing society, the denial of free primary education might be destabilizing to large numbers of status-conscious parents. But free primary education is mostly relevant as an investment in legitimacy and solidarity. Not only does this means of human improvement (status and income) come from the state, but it provides an opportunity to teach "the rules of the game" to a modernizing nation's young citizens. As a solidarity investment, it provides a common experience for citizenship, avoids the extremes of education and the resulting social friction, provides an opportunity to stress the importance of the state, modernization, and all its other values. As an economic investment, the arguments for free primary education are obvious.

Most economic development strategists do not recognize these social and political investments. They make little room for them in their writings and calculations. When these investments are made, as they will be, the strategists label them "compromises," "politically motivated," "prestige items," and "unproductive." Yet, these investments provide the basis for subsequent investments in directly productive activities. Without these prior investments, "correct decisions" will not be made or maintained. These are investments in modernization values. And, if understood from a modernization perspective, they can be made with greater rationality and efficiency. Indeed, many of these investments would be acceptable as sound under the stricter criterion of economic development strategy.

If the appropriate question is "modernization" and not "economic growth," then social scientists must work on strategies jointly. For data, they have the tools and findings of survey research, the growing compilations of political and social quantitative indicators, and the record of modernizing activities of, among many others, Napoleon, Bismarck, the Bolsheviks, the Congress Party of India, Mexico's PRI, Nasser, and Mao Tse-Tung. Much needs to be known about the character of social change; greater precision must be achieved in defining problems and seeking relationships of variables within the wider social system. Indeed, it might be suggested that modernization first began in the social sciences.

NOTES

1. Everett E. Hagen, *On the Theory of Social Change* (Homewood, 1962); David C. McClelland, *The Achieving Society* (Princeton, 1961).

2. "Big Push" balance growth—P. N. Rosenstein-Rodan, "Problems of Industrialization of Eastern and South-Eastern Europe," in A. N. Agarwala and S. P. Singh, *The Economics of Underdevelopment* (New York, 1963), pp. 145–55; Ragnar Nurkse, *Problems of Capital Formation in Underdeveloped Countries* (New York, 1960), Ch. 1; Unbalanced growth—Albert O. Hirschman, *The Strategy of Economic Development* (New Haven, 1958); Capital formation through unlimited supplies of labor—W. Arthur Lewis, "Economic Development with Unlimited Supplies of Labour," in Agarwala and Singh, *op. cit.*, pp. 400–49; Nurske, *op. cit.*, Ch. 2.

3. Certain assumptions are made in this article about the social system and its response to economic change. First, the population is increasingly "mobilized," i.e., a population shifting to wages and a more complex division of labor, exposed to mass media and increasing education, and more easily susceptible to new forms of organization. See Karl W. Deutsch, "Social Mobilization and Political Development," *American Political Science Review* (September 1961), 493–514. Second, extreme inequalities of income, inflation over a long period of time without redistribution, and accelerated urbanization without adequate social overhead expenditures and provision for the maintenance of primary group relationships or acceptable alternatives are destabilizing to a social system. See, for example, Bert F. Hoselitz, "Urbanization and Economic Growth in Asia," *Economic Development and Cultural Change* (October 1957), 42–54; Neil J. Smelser, "Mechanisms of Change and Adjustment to Change," in Bert F. Hoselitz and Wilbert E. Moore, eds., *Industrialization and Society* (UNESCO, The Hague, 1963), pp. 32–54; Philip M. Hauser, "The Social, Economic, and Technological Problems of Rapid Urbanization," in *ibid.*, pp. 199–217; Richard D. Robinson, "Turkey's Agrarian Revolution and the Problem of Urbanization," *Public Opinion Quarterly*, XXII (Fall 1958), 397–405; Joseph A. Kahl, "Some Social Concomitants of Industrialization and Urbanization," *Human Organization* (Summer 1959), 53–74 (especially bibliographical section). An act is destabilizing when it threatens the legitimacy of the institutions of civil authority and their means of handling conflict and distribution. See, for example, Seymour Martin Lipset, *Political Man, The Social Bases of Politics* (Garden City, New York, 1960), Ch. 3; Ronald C. Ricker, "Discontent and Economic Growth," *Economic Development and Cultural Change*, XI (October 1962), 1–15. For the authors' general approach to the social system and its sub-systems, see Marion J. Levy, Jr., *The Structure of Society* (Princeton, 1953); S. N. Eisenstadt, *Essays on the Sociological Aspects of Political and Economic Development* (The Hague, 1961); David E. Apter, "System, Process and the Politics of Economic Development," in Hoselitz and Moore, *op. cit.*, pp. 135–58.

4. The probability of formulating alternative combinations of investments in underdeveloped countries is small. Indeed, at present, it is rare even to find alternative projects to choose from. See, for example, Government of Pakistan, Planning Commission, *Final Report of the Committee on Review of On-going Schemes* (Karachi, 1961), pp. 3–16.

5. See Zbigniew Brzezinski, "The Politics of Underdevelopment," *World Politics*, IX (October 1956), 55–75; Alexander Eckstein, "Individualism and the Role of the State in Economic Growth," *Economic Development and Cultural Change*, VI (January 1958), 81–87.

6. The "Big Push" strategy can also be formulated by differing proportions of authoritarian and oligarchical rule, but authoritarian and/or oligarchical, nonetheless.

7. A fourth possibility is a population almost unanimous in its commitment to economic development. This is relevant, in the authors' view, to no country now in existence. Even when a large proportion of the "effective" population has economic development as *one* of its top priorities—even its top priority—the interpretations of what "development" means, who is to sacrifice, what is to be foregone, and who is to prosper are legion,

and the view of the economic strategist, or the ruling elites, is never accepted as definitive.

8. See, for example, Donald Hindley, "Foreign Aid to Indonesia: Its Political Implications," *Pacific Affairs*, XXXVI (Summer 1963), 107–19; M. Bronfenbrenner, "The Appeal of Confiscation in Economic Development," *Economic Development and Cultural Change*, III (1954), 201–18.

9. See, for example, Albert Waterston, " 'Planning the Planning' Under the Alliance for Progress," in Irving Swerdlow, *Development Administration, Concepts and Problems* (Syracuse, 1963), pp. 141–62; "Progress in Planning in Latin America," *Economic Bulletin for Latin America*, VIII (October 1963), 129–46; John P. Lewis, *Quiet Crisis in India* (Garden City, New York, 1964), pp. 129–40.

10. Professor Hirschman has since modified his position. See Albert O. Hirschman, "Economics and Investment Planning: Reflections Based on Experience in Colombia," *Investment Criteria and Economic Growth* (Bombay, 1961), pp. 38–39. This modification, however, does not affect this article's analysis.

11. See, for example, Government of India, Planning Commission, *Reports of the Programme Evaluation Organization*, especially nos. 6 and 7; Kusum Nair, *Blossoms in the Dust* (London, 1961), *passim*.

12. See Joseph LaPalombara, "Bureaucracy and Political Development: Notes, Queries, and Dilemmas," in Joseph LaPalombara, ed., *Bureaucracy and Political Development* (Princeton, 1963), pp. 34–61.

13. Nurkse, *op. cit.*, pp. 15–16, 43, 76, 90–91, 143, 148–50; Hirschman, *op. cit.*, pp. 14, 112–13; see also Albert O. Hirschman, *Journeys Toward Progress* (New York, 1963), *passim.*; W. Arthur Lewis, *op. cit.*, pp. 422–23, 434. The experiences of other nations were also relevant, but this does not alter the argument.

14. See, for example, Reinhard Bendix, "Public Authority in a Developing Political Community: the Case of India, *Archives Europeennes de Sociologie*, IV (1963), 39–85; Selig S. Harrison, *India: the Most Dangerous Decades* (Princeton, 1960).

15. This point cannot be adequately developed in an article of this length. Indirectly, a similar argument can be inferred from: Joseph A. Schumpeter, *History of Economic Analysis* (New York, 1954), pp. 143–208; Bert F. Hoselitz, "The Scope and History of Theories of Economic Growth," *Revista de Economia Politica*, V (May 1953), 9–28; William Letwin, *The Origins of Scientific Economics* (London, 1963), *passim.*; Karl Polanyi, *The Great Transformation* (New York, 1944), Chs. 10 and 19.

16. See also Fred W. Riggs, *Administration in Developing Countries: The Theory of Prismatic Society* (Boston, 1964), pp. 19–31.

17. An obvious "heroic" exception is Talcott Parsons and Neil J. Smelser, *Economy and Society* (London, 1956).

18. An interesting study of a nation's sectors and their demands is Myron Weiner, *The Politics of Scarcity, Public Pressure and Political Response in India* (Bombay, 1963).

19. See, for example Rupert Emerson, "Nationalism and Political Development," *Journal of Politics*, XXII (February 1960), 3–28.

20. See, for example, Bert F. Hoselitz and Myron Weiner, "Economic Development and Political Stability in India," *Dissent*, VIII (Spring 1961), 172–84.

21. For an example of an economist handling the political preconditions of economic development in terms of an autonomous (i.e., less subject to the influence of the political sub-system) economic system and the consequent role for the state to play, see Joseph J. Spengler, "Economic Development: Political Preconditions and Political Consequences," *Journal of Politics*, XXII (August 1960), 387–416. Among other things, Professor Spengler argues, "Only a well-entrenched party, or a pair of parties strongly committed to economic development, is likely to be able to keep the ideology of development effectively alive, to impose the necessary costs of development on the population, and yet to remain in office long enough to get economic growth effectively underway. A dictatorship might find itself in a somewhat similar position, given that it sought to promote economic growth and had fairly widespread support. . . . a multiparty system is not compatible with economic growth; it is too likely to

give in to ever-present demands for 'liberal' welfare-state provisions." In other words, a moratorium must be called on politics to achieve the optimum product of a nation's scarce resources.

22. See S. N. Eisenstadt, "Modernization: Growth and Diversity," *India Quarterly*, XX (January–March 1964), 17–42; S. N. Eisenstadt, *The Political Systems of Empires* (New York, 1963), pp. 3–32.

23. See the excellent study by Lucian W. Pye, *Politics, Personality and Nations Building: Burma's Search for Identity* (New Haven, 1962), pp. 3 ff. See also Herbert Feith, *Decline of Constitutional Democracy in Indonesia* (Ithaca, 1962).

24. An increasing example of how the economist is now widening his concept of investment is in the sphere of education. The usual practice, when projecting future demand and production patterns, by means of input-output models or linear programming models, has been to treat the labor inputs as given, along with the capital inputs. However, it is obvious that labor is no homogeneous input, which is given, like any natural resource. Investments have to be made to create the skills required for different productive activities. The amounts of such investments are dependent on the level and nature of these activities. Therefore, if in a linear programming model, an attempt is being made to obtain the optimal allocation of all available resources, the activity by which human skills are created should also be included along with the other activities, and not as a primary input. Only in this way can the economically optimal allocation be approximated. If, however, the investments in creating skills are treated as exogeneous, to be determined on the basis of the optimal investment pattern, it is unlikely to obtain the "optimal results." For if the costs of creating the skills were attributed to different activities, the model would in all likelihood give a different pattern. This is a fact which economists are only realizing now. This article's contention is that there are other activities in which resources have to be invested, even if the only goal is the maximization of output.

25. See, for example, Sixto K. Roxas, "Investment in Education: The Philippine Experience," *The Philippine Economy Bulletin*, II (September–October 1963), 32–38. The authors are not including in the above statement the excellent recent work of Professors Harbison and Myers, although their "human resource development orientation" is concerned essentially with skills, not values. See Frederick Harbison and Charles A. Myers, *Education, Manpower, and Economic Growth* (New York, 1964).

4

The Stages of Economic Growth:
A Review

Paul A. Baran and E. J. Hobsbawm

On the jacket of W. W. Rostow's *The Stages of Economic Growth: A Non-Communist Manifesto*, the publisher advertises the product in these terms: "This book is a generalization from the whole span of modern history. It gives an account of economic growth based on a dynamic theory of production and interpreted in terms of actual societies. It helps to explain historical changes and to predict major political and economic trends; and it provides the significant links between economic and non-economic behavior which Karl Marx failed to discern." The author's own sales-pitch is equally strident: "The stages are not merely descriptions. They are not merely a way of generalizing certain factual observations about the sequence of development of modern societies. They have an inner logic and continuity. They have an analytical bone-structure rooted in a dynamic theory of production" (pp. 12f.). And the reasons for this enthusiasm are not only the light which the new theory is supposed to shed upon the process of economic and social evolution but also its alleged power to dispose once and for all of the Marxian dragon with which so many others have done battle but failed to slay. The reader is urged to "note the similarities between his (Marx's) analysis and the stages of growth; and the differences between the two systems of thought, stage by stage."

We propose to accept this invitation and to carry out the comparison which Professor Rostow suggests. In what follows, the first section will deal with the stages-of-growth scheme's contribution to the theory of economic development. The second section will attempt to answer the question whether Marxian thought is capable of surviving this newest assault.

I

Such attention as Professor Rostow's writing has hitherto been able to command in the literature on economic development has been based upon some of his earlier empirical studies. His theoretical contributions have

Reprinted from *Kyklos*, Vol. XIV, Fasc. 2 (1961), pp. 234-242, by permission of the publisher. Copyright by *Kyklos* Redaktion: Petersgraben 29, 4000 Basel, Switzerland.

been meager—in fact, largely confined to various types of classification. Does his latest effort significantly change this picture?

Professor Rostow advances three propositions. First, he insists that the problem of growth is a historical one which must be considered within a framework of a historical periodization. Second, he emphasizes—and this is perhaps his most notable point—that economic growth is not a continuous and smooth but a discontinuous and dialectical process which pivots on a sudden revolutionary transformation, the "take-off into self-sustained growth." Third, he stresses a particular aspect of this discontinuity of economic growth: that it proceeds not by a balanced development of all sectors of the economy, but by successive leaps forward of the economy's "leading sectors."

These are undoubtedly valuable insights, although it can hardly be said that they are new or that they originate with Professor Rostow. That theories of growth must be historical was perhaps the first discovery of political economy; it has merely been forgotten in the century or so in which economic growth was almost wholly neglected in academic economics, except for the Marxists and those who, like the Germans and Schumpeter, accepted much of the Marxist *Fragestellung* on the subject. The "take-off" is merely another name for the "industrial revolution" which was the basic analytic concept of modern economic history from the days of Engels to those of Mantoux until smothered by the gradualist criticism of Clapham, Ashton, and others between the two wars. The argument for uneven development is equally old. It was advanced by Marx, developed by Lenin, and underlies the Schumpeter-Kondratiev analysis of 19th-century economic development.[1] To be sure, the rediscovery of old truths is a most creditable accomplishment—particularly in contemporary "behavioral sciences" where apparently any nonsense goes as long as it has never been said before—though not one calling in itself for a major ovation.

But when we come to consider Professor Rostow's other achievements in the field of the theory of growth, the weaknesses are all too obvious. The first and most serious is that his theory of "stages" actually tells us nothing except that there are stages. The four other stages are implicit in the "take-off," and add nothing to it. Given a "take-off" there must obviously be a stage before it, but when the conditions for economic growth are not present, another when the pre-conditions for the "take-off" exist, and yet another following it when "an economy demonstrates that it has the technological and entrepreneurial skills to produce not everything, but anything it wants" (which is Rostow's definition of the stage of "maturity"), and yet another when it has acquired the capacity to produce everything it wants (p. 10).[2] Indeed, there is no departure ("take-off") of any kind—in the history of nature, of societies or of individuals—which cannot be thought of as being preceded and followed by a number of "stages." If one has a penchant for symmetry one only has to make sure that the total number of stages—the "take-off" included—should be uneven.

Thus once we have one corner, we have the entire Pentagon. One weakness of this procedure is, of course, that analysis must remain confined to its area. Accordingly, the Rostovian stage theory, despite its comprehensive historic and sociological claims reduces economic growth to a single pattern. Any and every country, whatever its other characteristics, is classifiable only in respect to its position on the stepladder, the middle rung of which is the "take-off." This gives the Rostovian stages an air of spurious generality—they appear to apply to any and all economies, to the U.S.S.R. as to the U.S.A., to China as to Brazil—which, as we shall see, is not without its ideological implications, though it overlooks the obvious fact that, however universal the technical problems of economic growth may be, different social types of economic organization can, or must, solve them in very different ways.

Yet even within its extremely narrow limits the Rostovian theory can neither explain nor predict without introducing considerations that are completely irrelevant to the stage schema. It simply fails to specify any mechanism of evolution which links the different stages. There is no particular reason why the "traditional" society should turn into a society breeding the "preconditions" of the "take-off." Rostow's account merely summarizes what these preconditions must be,[3] and repeats a version of that "classical answer," the inadequacy of which has long been evident: a combination of the "discovery and rediscovery of regions beyond Western Europe" and the "developing of modern scientific knowledge and attitudes" (p. 31). Here is the *deus ex machina*. Nor is there any reason within the Rostovian stages why the "preconditions" should lead to the "take-off" to maturity, as is indeed evidenced by Rostow's own difficulty in discovering, except long *ex post facto*, whether a "take-off" has taken place or not.[4] In fact the Rostovian "take-off" concept has no predictive value. Similarly, when it comes to analyzing the "inner structure" (p. 46) of the "take-off" or of any other stage, the Rostovian theory subsides into statements of the type that "things can happen in any one of a very large number of different ways," which constitute a rather limited contribution of knowledge.[5]

Such explanations and predictions as Rostow attempts are therefore little more than verbiage which has no connection with his stages theory or indeed with any theory of economic and social evolution, being generally based on what might be charitably called coffeehouse sociology and political speculation. The nearest he actually comes to an attempt at an explanation of *why* economic growth takes place is his emphasis on the importance of "reactive nationalism" and the crucial role of "an inherently competitive system of power" (pp. 109 and 151 n) in which states are historically enmeshed.[6] The explanation tends to be circular—when a country has economic growth it is evidence of reactive nationalism[7]—as well as openended: when an obviously nationalist country does *not* initiate a "take-off," it is because "nationalism can be turned in any one of several directions" (p. 29). Moreover, even this type of explanation is crippled by Rostow's refusal to admit the profit motive into his analysis, a refusal not concealed by an occasional parenthetical remark granting its existence.[8] Still, weak as it is, the explanation of economic growth by nationalism and the logic of international rivalry is the closest Rostow comes to an analysis of economic development as distinct from relabelling and classifying it.

And this is not very close. For in addition to an incapacity to answer relevant questions, Professor Rostow shows an astonishing lack of ability for even recognizing their existence or their import. Thus one of the crucial problems which faces both the theorist and would-be planner of economic development under capitalist conditions is that "the criteria for private profit-maximization do not necessarily converge with the criteria for an optimum rate and pattern of growth in various sectors" (p. 50), indeed, that under pre-industrial conditions or in underdeveloped areas it can be shown that they are more likely than not to diverge. The statesman or economic administrator of a backward country knows that a century of Western capitalism has failed to transfer any country across the gap which separates the advanced from the backward economies. He also knows that profit-oriented private investment can be relied on to build his country's tourist hotels but not its steelworks. Consequently he has increasingly taken to imitating the Soviet method of achieving economic growth, which does not suffer from this disadvantage, rather than relying on the 19th-century European or American method which does. Rostow neither explains any of these facts which determine the actual problem of economic development in underdeveloped areas, nor does he even seem aware of them beyond the casual mention already quoted. Conversely, the historian must explain why, in spite of this divergence, or lack of convergence, a limited number of countries around the North Atlantic in the 18th and 19th centuries actually managed to industrialize on a capitalist basis. Rostow appears equally oblivious of this problem.

This obtuseness is not accidental. Indeed, the nature of Professor Rostow's approach makes it impossible for him to solve such problems, and difficult even to realize their existence. For if we argue that the main motor of economic change was at no time "profit-maximization (in the sense of) economic advantage" (pp. 149 ff.), we can hardly deal with, let alone answer questions which arise from the fact that all economic development between the "traditional" society and the appearance of the U.S.S.R. was actually *capitalist* development and which calls therefore for an analysis of the specific characteristics of *capitalism*. If we abstract from everything that separates "eighteenth-century Britain and Khrushchev's Russia; Meiji Japan and Mao's China; Bismarck's Germany and Nasser's Egypt" (p. 1), we shall be unable to explain why Nasser's Egypt finds Khrushchev's Russia a more useful guide to economic development than 18th-century Britain. If we are anxious to minimize the element of economic advantage in the relation between advanced and dependent (colonial) economies (pp. 108–112, 137/38, 156), we shall be unable to say anything useful about problems which arise out of the fact that dependent economies are dependent.

Why, it may be asked, should a man adopt a theoretical approach so obviously defective and indeed self-defeating? At least one plausible answer may be suggested. Professor Rostow, is, on his own admission, primarily concerned not with arriving at a theory of economic development, but with writing a "non-communist manifesto." Unlike other and wiser—we shall not say abler—scholars with similar objectives, he has chosen to abandon not merely Marx's conclusions and his arguments, but even the basic posing of the problem of economic development as Marx saw it. It was, as we have tried to show, an unwise decision, for the Marxian questions are fundamental to any attempt at an understanding of the process of economic development. What is required is at least an *understanding* of Marx's questions. To that level Professor Rostow has yet to rise.

II

An examination of the principal tenets of Rostow's theory of economic growth—if it can be at all said that such a *theory* is advanced in his book— thus reveals nothing that can be considered an addition to our knowledge of the history of economic development or an enrichment of our understanding of the processes involved. But Rostow offers something much more ambitious than "merely" a new theory of economic growth. He also proposes "a comprehensive, realistic and soundly based alternative to Marx's theory of how societies evolve." Let us examine this latest effort to put Marx into the waste basket. Since, however, it is neither possible nor would it be rewarding to trace all the misconceptions and misrepresentations of Marxian thought which Rostow has managed to compress in a few pages, we will have to limit ourselves to two problems which Rostow himself considers to be central to his Manifesto.

The first relates to the nature of the engine which propells economic, social, and political evolution in the course of history. To this fundamental question, historical materialism provides a comprehensive and sophisticated answer. Far be it from us to seek to emulate Rostow in the claim that this answer supplies pat solutions to all problems raised by the complex events and patterns of history. What historical materialism does claim is to have discovered an indispensable *approach* to the understanding of historical constellations and to have focused attention on the nature of the principal energies responsible for their emergence, transformation, and disappearance. To put it in a nutshell: these energies are to be traced back to the always present tension between the degree of development of the forces of production on one side, and the prevailing relations of production on the other. To be sure, neither "forces of production" nor "relations of production" are simple notions. The former encompasses the existing state of rationality, science, and technology, the mode of organization of production and the degree of development of man himself, that "most important productive force of all" (Marx). The latter refers to the mode of appropriation of the products of human labor, the social condition under which production takes place, the principles of distribution, the modes of thought, the ideology, the *Weltanschauung* which constitute the "general ether" (Marx) within which society functions at any given time. The conflict between the two—sometimes dormant and sometimes active—is due to a fundamental difference in the "laws of motion" of forces and relations of production respectively. The forces of production tend to be highly dynamic. Driven by man's quest for a better life, by the growth and expansion of human knowledge and rationality, by increasing population, the forces of production tend continually to gain in strength, in depth, and in scope. The relations of production on the other hand tend to be sticky, conservative.

Prevailing systems of appropriation and social organization, and political institutions favor some classes and discriminate against, frustrate, oppress other classes. They give rise to vested interests. Modes of thought freeze and display a tenacity and longevity giving rise to what is sometimes referred to as "cultural lags." When the forward movement of the forces of production becomes stymied by the deadweight of dominant interests and the shackles of dominant thought, one or the other has to yield. And since a dominant class never willingly relinquishes its time-honored privileges (partly for reasons of self-interest and partly because its own horizon is more or less narrowly circumscribed by the prevailing ideology sanctifying those very privileges), the clash tends to become violent. This is not to say that obsolete, retrograde relations of production are *always* burst asunder and swept away by revolutions. Depending on the circumstances prevailing in each individual case, the process unfolds in a wide variety of ways. Violent upheavals "from below" and relatively peaceful transformations "from above" are as much within the range of possibilities as periods of protracted stagnation in which the political, ideological, and social power of the ruling classes is strong enough to prevent the emergence of new forms of economic and social organization, to block or to slow a country's economic development.

Marx's historical materialism insists, however, that the development of the forces of production has thus far been *the* commanding aspect of the historical process. Whatever may have been its vicissitudes, whatever may have been the setbacks and interruptions that it has suffered in the course of history, in the long run it has tended to overcome all obstacles, and to conquer all political, social and ideological structures subordinating them to its requirements. This struggle between the forces of production and the relations of production proceeds unevenly. Dramatic conquests are less frequent than long periods of siege in which victories remain elusive, imperfect, and impermanent. Different countries display different patterns which depend on their size, location, the strength and cohesion of their ruling classes, the courage, determination and leadership of the underprivileged; on the measure of foreign influence and support to which both or either are exposed; on the pervasiveness and power of the dominant ideologies (e.g. religion). Moreover, the course taken by this struggle and its outcome differ greatly from period to period. Under conditions of capitalism's competitive youth they were different from what they have become in the age of imperialism; in the presence of a powerful socialist sector of the world, they are not the same as they were or would have been in its absence. No bloodless schema of five (or three or seven) "stages" can do justice to the multitude and variety of economic, technological, political, and ideological configurations generated by this never-ceasing battle between the forces and relations of production. What Marx and Engels and Lenin taught those whose ambition it was to learn rather than to make careers by "refuting" is that these historical configurations cannot be dealt with by "a generalization from the whole span of modern history," but have to be studied *concretely*, with full account taken of the wealth of factors and forces that participate in the shaping of any particular historical case.

To forestall a possible misunderstanding: the foregoing is not intended to advocate renunciation of theory in favor of plodding empiricism. Rather it suggests the necessity of an interpenetration of theory and concrete observation, of empirical research illuminated by rational theory, of theoretical work which draws its life blood from historical study. Consider for instance any one of the many existing underdeveloped countries. Pigeonholing it in one of Rostow's "stages" does not bring us any closer to an understanding of the country's economic and social condition or give us a clue to the country's developmental possibilities and prospects. What is required for that is as accurate as possible an assessment of the social and political forces in the country pressing for change and for development (the economic condition and the stratification of the peasantry, its political traditions and its ideological make-up, the economic and social status, internal differentiation and political aspirations of the bourgeoisie, the extent of its tie-up with foreign interests and the degree of monopoly prevailing in its national business, the closeness of its connection with the landowning interests and the measure of its participation in the existing government; the living and working conditions and the level of class consciousness of labor and its political and organizational strength). Nor is this by any means the entire job. On the other side of the fence are the groups, institutions, relations, and ideologies seeking to preserve the *status quo*, obstructing efforts directed towards its overturn. There are wealthy landowners and/or rich peasants; there is a segment of the capitalist class firmly entrenched in monopolistic positions and allied with other privileged groups in society; there is a government bureaucracy interwoven with and resting upon the military establishment; there are foreign investors supported by their respective national governments and working hand in hand with their native retainers. Only a thorough historical-materialist analysis, piercing the ideological fog maintained by the dominant coalition of interests and destroying the fetishes continually produced and reproduced by those concerned with the preservation of the *status quo*, only such historical-materialist analysis can hope to disentangle the snarl of tendencies and countertendencies, forces, influences, convictions and opinions, drives and resistances which account for the pattern of economic and social development. And it is to this *Marxist* undertaking that Professor Rostow offers us his alternative: to assign the country in question to one of his "stages," and then to speculate on the "two possibilities" with which that country is confronted: it will either move on to the next "stage"—or it won't. And if it should move to the next "stage," it will again face two possibilities: it will either stay there for a while, or it will slide back again.

We may now turn briefly to Professor Rostow's other sally against Marx by which he seeks to provide "significant links between economic and non-economic behavior which Karl Marx failed to discern." This enterprise, he apparently feels, will deliver the "coup de grâce" to Marxian thought, "for," he assures us, "it is absolutely essential to Marxism that it is over property that men fight and die" (p. 151). What Karl Marx—"a lonely man, profoundly isolated from his fellows"—did not discern, but Professor Rostow does, is the following: "Man . . . seeks, not merely economic advantage, but also power, leisure, adventure, continuity of experience and security . . . in short, net human behavior is . . . not an act of maximization, but . . . an act of balancing alternative and often conflicting human objectives." "This notion of balance among alternatives," Professor Rostow observes "is, of course, more complex and difficult than a simple maximization proposition; and it does not lead to a series of rigid, inevitable stages of history." We submit that this "notion" may well be "complex and difficult" but that it is also singularly devoid of any ascertainable content. It is remarkable how Professor Rostow, after having constructed a strawman bearing no resemblance to Marxism finds it beyond his powers to vanquish even such a "hand-picked" enemy.

Indeed—to put it bluntly—the whole argument is too helpless to serve even as a starting point for a serious discussion. Even a passing acquaintance with the most important writings of Marx, Engels, and more recent Marxist writers is all that is required to realize the irrelevance of Rostow's caricature of Marxism. Far from asserting that "history is uniquely determined by economic forces," and far from ignoring the "significant links between economic and non-economic behavior," the theory of historical materialism advanced by Marx and his followers is nothing if not a powerful effort to explore the manifold and historically changing connections between the development of the forces and relations of production and the evolution of the consciousness, emotions, and ideologies of men. So much so that the Marxian theory of ideology has served as the point of departure and as a guide to an entire discipline known under the name of "sociology of knowledge," with all analytical history of religion, literature, art and science deriving its inspiration from the same source. Marx's theory of alienation, anticipating much of the subsequent development of social psychology, is in the center of modern study and criticism of culture. Marx's political theory has served as a conceptual basis for most that is valuable in modern European and American historical scholarship. And *The Eighteenth of Brumaire of Louis Bonaparte*—to name only one unsurpassed gem of historical and sociological study—still shines as a model of a comprehensive and penetrating analysis of the "significant links between economic and non-economic behavior" in one particular historical case.

But all this escapes Mr. Rostow who is not only incapable of contributing anything to the discussion of the relevant problems but even fails to comprehend the context within which they arise. For the problem of the "links between economic and non-economic behavior," or for that matter of the explanation of any human activity, economic or other, is not and never has been whether or not man "balances alternatives" or "adheres to the principle of maximization" (which terms, incidentally, if they mean anything at all, amount to exactly the same), no more than there is meaning to the question whether man does or does not have "freedom of will." No one in his right mind—Marxist, mechanical materialist, or idealist—has ever denied that men make choices, exercise their wills, balance alternatives, or, for that matter, move their legs when they walk. The problem is and always has been to discover what determines the nature of the alternatives that are available to men, what accounts for the nature of the goals which they set themselves in different periods of historical development, what makes them will what they will in various societies at various times. To this fundamental question: there have been several answers. The theologian's solution has been that all human acts and decisions are governed by the omnipotent and inscrutable will of God. The idealist who substituted the human spirit for the Deity arrives at a very similar position, unable as he is to explain what accounts for the actions and transactions of the spirit. The adherents of "psychologism" view human activity as an emanation of the human psyche, itself an aspect of an eternally constant human nature.[9] The historical materialist considers human actions and motivations to be complex results of a dialectical interaction of biotic and social processes, the latter continually propelled by the dynamism of the forces and relations of production as well as by the ideological evolutions deriving from them and influencing them in turn. Professor Rostow, however, has the simplest solution of all: he does not know what the answer is, nor does he appear to care. Anything can happen: man moves hither and thither, balancing alternatives, making choices, striving for power, engaged in maximization of who knows what. And this is the new, original unprecedented "theory" which makes good what Karl Marx failed to discern.

NOTES

1. Cf. also A. F Burns, *Production Trends in the United States since 1870*, New York 1934.
2. This stage Rostow misnames "the age of high mass consumption" for both by the logical requirements of his schema and by his own observations on the subject (pp. 73/74) what characterizes it is not fundamentally mass consumption (which is only one of the alternative uses to which resources can be put by society) but *abundance*. This error in nomenclature is by no means trivial; it is associated with Rostow's misleading treatment of the current stage of the United States' economic development, when *armaments* rather than mass consumption represent the economy's "leading sector."
3. And this not with any great perspicacity. Thus one would suppose that agricultural change creates the preconditions of industrialization not merely by supplying "expanded food, expanded markets, and an expanded supply of loanable funds to the modern sector" (p. 24) but also—and perhaps decisively—an expanded labor force for it.
4. Cf. the hesitations reflected in the footnotes to his table of "take-offs" (p. 38) and his inability to decide "whether the take-off period will, in fact, be successful in the six contemporary economies attempting take-off" (p. 44) as well as his failure to cope with the phenomenon of relapse after apparent take-offs. However critics, and especially statisticians, should resist the easy temptation Rostow thus provides to reject the entire concept of economic development by industrial revolution.
5. For example: "Perhaps the most important thing to be said about the behavior of these variables in historical cases of take-off is that they have assumed many different forms. There is no single pattern. The rate and productivity of investment can rise, and the consequences of this rise can be diffused into a self-reinforcing general growth process by many different technical and economic routes, under the aegis of many different political, social and cultural settings, driven along by a wide variety of human motivations" (p. 46). Or, we may add, they may not rise, and may not be diffused . . . .
6. "The general case is of a society modernizing itself in a nationalist reaction to intrusion or the threat of intrusion from more advanced powers abroad" (p. 34).
7. Cf. pp. 34/35 where the attempt is made, half-heartedly, to assimilate the pioneer industrialization of Britain to this pattern on no other grounds than that otherwise it would not fit the "general case." Admittedly, if a

theory of economic evolution cannot explain the case which needs explaining most, namely the very first "take-off" in history, it is little more than scrap paper, though Professor Rostow does not seem too keenly aware of this. Cf. p. 27.

8. Cf. on p. 28 "The merchant has always been present, seeking in modernization not only the removal of obstacles to enlarged markets and profits, but also the high status denied him," but especially the remarkably contorted pages on colonialism (p. 108–112).

9. For a somewhat more extensive discussion of this cf. Paul A. Baran, *Marxism and Psychoanalysis*, Monthly Review Press, New York, 1960.

part two

Economic Development and Underdevelopment in Historical Perspective

because the very essence of economic development is rapid and discontinuous change in institutions and the value of economic parameters, it is impossible to construct a rigorous and determinate model of the process. An economist must be willing to settle for less. Elegance and rigor are important attributes of economic theory, but they must take second place to relevance and applicability. The more rigorous the model, the higher its degree of technical success may be, but the greater its inability to explain economic development. Such a model necessarily omits too many of the most significant variables in economic development. It follows that an inquiry into the causal origins of economic development ought not to commence with a highly generalized, highly abstract model to frame the analysis. If a rigorous and determinate model is not utilized to study the process of economic development, a less rigorous but more richly textured model which accounts for the most important socioeconomic variables must be constructed. The use of economic history, together with theoretical logic, holds out the greatest prospect for success.

It has been said that scholars ". . . come to Economic History either as historians in search of a soul, or as economists in search of a body."* Many economic theorists are too fond of clever abstractions and too dependent on arbitrary concepts and models which are empty of empirical content and possess little, if any, relationship to the mutability of historical reality. Many historians allow their aversion to theory to prejudice their research and writing to the point where they become mere "fact grubbers" and "story tellers." The problem lies in a confusion between a "theoretical approach" and particular theories and concepts. A particular theory can be useful or useless, depending on the problem addressed. A "theoretical approach" is an essential step toward comprehension of historical reality. This theoretical framework, of course, should not be a Procrustean Bed in which historical reality is forced to fit. Neither does it necessarily have to be taken uncritically from the writings of economic theorists. As we saw in part one, most economic theory casts little light upon the reality of underdevelopment and development. Most of the readings in this part use the concept of the social surplus (outlined in the introduction to the first part) to order and analyze the historical and empirical evidence of the process of development and underdevelopment.

Probably the greatest weakness of economic theorists is their lack of historical knowledge and understanding of the process of development in the West between the seventeenth and twentieth centuries. The development of capitalism in the West was faced with the need of change in the social structure so that the change-oriented middle class could become the leaders of society. This often involved a more or less violent struggle for supremacy betwen the old social order and the emerging new one. The English Revolution of 1640, ending with the Supremacy of Parliament in 1688, replaced the feudal lords with the landed gentry and urban middle class as the dominant classes in England, thus preparing the way for later economic progress. The French Revolution of 1789 replaced the old aristocracy with the new middle class. The lack of such social change was a major factor in the economic stagnation of Spain after the seventeenth century.

This change in social structure enabled the social surplus to be productively used. As Dudley Dillard points out in the first reading in this part: "Productive use of the 'social surplus' was the special virtue that enabled capitalism to outstrip all prior economic systems." Dillard's article outlines some of the crucial elements in the historical development of capitalism in the West.

If there is lack of understanding of the history of development in the West there is almost total ignorance about the *history* of underdeveloped countries. The typical level of understanding can be seen in W. W. Rostow's stages of growth model. The uses of the stages of growth as a framework for analysis of the process of development assumes that present day underdeveloped countries correspond to the "Traditional Society" stage or at best the "Preconditions" stage, that the present day developed countries were once underdeveloped, and that all countries move through all the stages. This seems to obscure more than to illuminate historical reality. It denies that the underdeveloped countries have had any history, but it is obvious that India today, for example, is radically different than it was 300 years ago. The stages approach totally ignores that 300-year history, including British colonial control, except to praise that colonialism as the "intrusion" that broke through the crust of traditionalism and triggered the stage of Preconditions. It might be more illuminating to have two alternative second stages—one, Rostow's Preconditions stage, which is a transition from Traditional Society to the Take-Off; and two, Underdevelopment, the stage following the break up of traditionalism wherein the economy becomes distorted and frozen into the characteristics with which we identify underdeveloped countries. India and Japan were both traditional societies 300 years ago—neither was underdeveloped— and today Japan is developed and India is underdeveloped. Why did Japan pass from traditional society through the Preconditions to Take-Off and why did India get sidetracked into Underdevelopment? To answer requires us to pose questions about the role of imperialism and dependency in *creating* underdevelopment, that is, the relation between the *process of development* in Europe and America and the *process of underdevelopment* in Africa, Asia, and Latin America; about the role of classes in socio-economic change; and other similar questions. The stages of growth approach obscures these questions.

Both Keith Griffin and Andre Gunder Frank emphasize in their readings the importance not only of studying the history of the underdeveloped countries but also of seeing that history in the context of the world wide development of capitalism; where the underdevelopment of Africa, Asia, and Latin America was a part of the same process that led to development in Europe and North America. Griffin's article provides a succinct but richly textured historical account of the process of underdevelopment in Africa, Asia, and Latin America. Frank's article uses that historical experience to construct a theoretical model of the process of *development and underdevelopment* that took place as capitalism spread from Europe into a world wide system.

In the final reading, Paul Baran presents a detailed view of one aspect of historical underdevelopment. He argues that because of the particular historical experience of the underdeveloped countries, the class structure has evolved in a substantially different way than in the West. Capitalism entered most underdeveloped countries the "Prussian way"—not through the growth of small, competitive enterprise but rather through the transfer from abroad of advanced monopolistic business. Thus, capitalist development in these countries was not accompanied by the rise of a strong property owning middle class and the overthrow of landlord domination of society. Rather an accommodation was reached between the newly arrived monopolistic business and the socially and politically entrenched agrarian aristocracy.

Therefore, there was neither vigorous competition between enterprises striving for increased output and rationalized production, nor accumulation of the social surplus in the hands of entrepreneurs forced by the competitive system and the spirit of a middle class society to reinvest as much as possible in the continuous expansion and modernization of their businesses. The result was that production was well below the potential level, with agriculture still being operated on a semi-feudal basis, and with waste and irrationality in industry protected by monopoly, high tariffs, and other devices.

For these and other reasons the actual social surplus was much lower than the potential social surplus. A large share of the potential social surplus was used by aristocratic landlords on excess consumption and the maintenance of unproductive laborers. In addition, a large share of the actual social surplus was taken by businessmen for commercial operations promising large and quick profits, or for the accumulation of investments or bank accounts abroad as a hedge against domestic social and political hazards. Furthermore, in order to obtain social status and the benefits and privileges necessary for the operation of a business, they emulated the dominant aristocracy in its mode of living. The actual social surplus was further reduced by the substantial quantity of resources used to maintain elaborate and inefficient bureaucratic and military establishments.

Although other factors undoubtedly had much to do with the inadequacy of the amount and composition of investment, the waste of a large portion of the social surplus due to the prevailing social structure was probably one of the major causes of economic stagnation.

This process, described in the Griffin, Baran, and Frank readings, has been speeded up and changed somewhat since World War II. This is the main subject of the next part of the book on Trade and Imperialism.

---

* Sidney Pollard, "Economic History—A Science of Society?" *Past and Present*, No. 30 (April 1965), p. 3.

5

Capitalism

Dudley Dillard

Capitalism [is] a term used to denote the economic system that has been dominant in the western world since the breakup of feudalism. Fundamental to any system called capitalist are the relations between private owners of nonpersonal means of production (land, mines, industrial plants, etc., collectively known as capital) and free but capital-less workers, who sell their labour services to employers. Under capitalism, decisions concerning production are made by private businessmen operating for private profit. Labourers are free in the sense that they cannot legally be compelled to work for the owners of the means of production. However, since labourers do not possess the means of production required for self-employment, they must, of economic necessity, offer their services on some terms to employers who do control the means of production. The resulting wage bargains determine the proportion in which the total product of society will be shared between the class of labourers and the class of capitalist entrepreneurs.

. . .

HISTORICAL DEVELOPMENT

I. Origins of Capitalism

Although the continuous development of capitalism as a system dates only from the 16th century, antecedents of capitalist institutions existed in the ancient world, and flourishing pockets of capitalism were present during the later middle ages. One strategic external force contributing to the breakup of medieval economic institutions was the growing volume of long-distance trade between capitalist centres, carried on with capitalist techniques in a capitalist spirit. Specialized industries grew up to serve long-distance trade, and the resulting commercial and industrial towns gradually exerted pressures which weakened the internal structure of agriculture based on serfdom, the hallmark of the feudal regime. Changes in trade, industry and

Reprinted from *Encyclopaedia Britannica*, pp. 839-842, by permission of the publisher and the author. © *Encyclopaedia Britannica*, 1972.

agriculture were taking place simultaneously and interacting with one another in highly complex actual relations, but it was chiefly long-distance trade which set in motion changes that spread throughout the medieval economy and finally transformed it into a new type of economic society.

Flanders in the 13th century and Florence in the 14th century were two capitalist pockets of special interest. Their histories shed light on the conditions that were essential to the development of capitalism in England. The great enterprise of late medieval and early modern Europe was the woolen industry, and most of the business arrangements that later characterized capitalism developed in connection with long-distance trade in wool and cloth.

In Flanders revolutionary conflict raged between plebeian craftsmen and patrician merchant-manufacturers. The workers succeeded in destroying the concentration of economic and political power in the hands of cloth magnates, only to be crushed in turn by a violent counterrevolution that destroyed the woolen industry and brought ruin to both groups. A similar performance was repeated in Florence, which became one of the great industrial cities of Europe during the 14th century. Restless, revolutionary urban workers overthrew the ruling hierarchy of merchants, manufacturers and bankers, and were in turn crushed in a bloody counterrevolution. Thus both Flanders and Florence failed to perpetuate their great industries because they failed to solve the social problem arising from conflicting claims of small numbers of rich capitalists and large numbers of poor workers.

2. Early Capitalism (1500–1750)

By the end of the middle ages the English cloth industry had become the greatest in Europe. Because of the domestic availability of raw wool and the innovation of simple mechanical fulling mills, the English cloth industry had established itself in certain rural areas where it avoided the violent social strife that had destroyed the urban industries of Flanders and Florence. Although it was subject to many problems and difficulties, the English rural cloth industry continued to grow at a rapid rate during the 16th, 17th and 18th centuries. Hence, it was the woolen industry that spearheaded capitalism as a social and economic system and rooted it for the first time in English soil.

Productive use of the "social surplus" was the special virtue that enabled capitalism to outstrip all prior economic systems. Instead of building pyramids and cathedrals, those in command of the social surplus chose to invest in ships, warehouses, raw materials, finished goods and other material forms of wealth. The social surplus was thus converted into enlarged productive capacity. Among the historical events and circumstances that significantly influenced capital formation in western Europe in the early stage of capitalist development, three merit special attention: (1) religious sanction for hard work and frugality; (2) the impact of precious metals from the new world on the relative shares of income going to wages, profits and rents; and (3) the role of national states in fostering and directly providing capital formation in the form of general-purpose capital goods.

Capitalist Spirit. The economic ethics taught by medieval Catholicism presented obstacles to capitalist ideology and development. Hostility to material wealth carried forward the teachings of the Christian fathers against mammonism. Saint Jerome said, "A rich man is either a thief or the son of a thief." Saint Augustine felt that trade was bad because it turned men away from the search for God. Down through the middle ages commerce and banking were viewed, at best, as necessary evils. Moneylending was for a time confined to non-Christians because it was considered unworthy of Christians. Interest on loans was unlawful under the anti-usury laws of both church and secular authorities. Speculation and profiteering violated the central medieval economic doctrine of just price.

Expansion of commerce in the later middle ages stirred controversies and led to attempts to reconcile theological doctrines with economic realities. In Venice, Florence, Augsburg and Antwerp—all Catholic cities—capitalists violated the spirit and circumvented the letter of the prohibitions against interest. On the eve of the Protestant Reformation capitalists, who still laboured under the shadow of the sin of avarice, had by their deeds become indispensable to lay rulers and to large numbers of people who were dependent upon them for employment.

The Protestant Reformation of the 16th and 17th centuries developed alongside economic changes which resulted in the spread of capitalism in northern Europe, especially in the Netherlands and England. This chronological and geographical correlation between the new religion and economic development has led to the suggestion that Protestantism had causal significance for the rise of modern capitalism. Without in any sense being the "cause" of capitalism, which already existed on a wide and expanding horizon, the Protestant ethic proved a bracing stimulant to the new economic order. Doctrinal revision or interpretation seemed not only to exonerate capitalists from the sin of avarice but even to give divine sanction to their way of life. In the ordinary conduct of life, a new type of worldly asceticism emerged, one that meant hard work, frugality, sobriety and efficiency in one's calling in the market place similar to that of the monastery. Applied in the environment of expanding trade and industry, the Protestant creed taught that accumulated wealth should be used to produce more wealth.

Acceptance of the Protestant ethic also eased the way to systematic organization of free labour. By definition, free labourers could not be compelled by force to work in the service of others. Moreover, the use of force would have violated the freedom of one's calling. Psychological compulsion arising from religious belief was the answer to the paradox. Every occupation was said to be noble in God's eyes. For those with limited talents, Christian conscience demanded unstinting labour even at low wages in the service of God—and, incidentally, of employers. It was an easy step to justify economic inequality because it would hasten the accumulation of wealth by placing it under the guardianship of the most virtuous (who were, incidentally, the wealthiest) and remove temptation from weaker persons who could not withstand the allurements associated with wealth. After all, it did not much matter who held legal title to wealth, for it was not for enjoyment. The rich like the poor were to live frugally all the days of their lives. Thus the capitalist system found a justification that was intended to make inequality tolerable to the working classes.

The Price Revolution. Meanwhile treasure from the new world had a profound impact on European capitalism, on economic classes and on the distribution of income in Europe. Gold and silver from the mines of Mexico, Peru and Bolivia increased Europe's supply of precious metals sevenfold and raised prices two- or threefold between 1540 and 1640. The significance of the increased supply of money lay not so much in the rise in prices as in its effect on the social and economic classes of Europe. Landlords, the older ruling class, suffered because money rents failed to rise as rapidly as the cost of living. The more aggressive landlords raised rents and introduced capitalistic practices into agriculture. In England the enclosure movement, which developed with ever increasing momentum and vigour during the 17th and 18th centuries, encouraged sheep raising to supply wool to the expanding woolen industry. Among labourers, money wages failed to keep pace with the cost of living, causing real wages to fall during the price revolution. The chief beneficiaries of this century-long inflation were capitalists, including merchants, manufacturers and other employers. High prices and low wages resulted in profit inflation, which in turn contributed to larger savings and capital accumulation. Profit inflation and wage deflation created a more unequal distribution of income. Wage earners got less and capitalists got more of the total product than they would have received in the absence of inflation. Had the new increments of wealth gone to wage earners instead of to capitalists, most of it would have been consumed rather than invested, and hence the working classes of the 16th century would have eaten better, but the future would have inherited less accumulated wealth.

Mercantilism. Early capitalism (1500-1750) also witnessed in western Europe the rise of strong national states pursuing mercantilist policies. Critics have tended to identify mercantilism with amassing silver and gold by having a so-called favourable balance of exports over imports in trading relations with other nations and communities, but the positive contribution and historic significance of mercantilism lay in the creation of conditions necessary for rapid and cumulative economic change in the countries of western Europe. At the end of the middle ages western Europe stood about where many underdeveloped countries stand in the 20th century. In underdeveloped economies the difficult task of statesmanship is to get under way a cumulative process of economic development, for once a certain momentum is attained, further advances appear to follow more or less automatically. Achieving such sustained growth requires virtually a social revolution.

Power must be transferred from reactionary to progressive classes; new energies must be released, often by uprooting the old order; the prevailing religious outlook may constitute a barrier to material advancement. A new social and political framework must be created within which cumulative economic change can take place.

Among the tasks which private capitalists were either unable or unwilling to perform were the creation of a domestic market free of tolls and other barriers to trade within the nation's borders; a uniform monetary system; a legal code appropriate to capitalistic progress; a skilled and disciplined labour force; safeguards against internal violence; national defense against attack; sufficient literacy and education among business classes to use credit instruments, contracts and other documents required of a commercial civilization; basic facilities for communication and transportation and harbour installations. A strong government and an adequate supply of economic resources were required to create most of these conditions, which constitute the "social overhead capital" needed in a productive economy. Because the returns from them, however great, cannot be narrowly channeled for private gain, such investments must normally be made by the government and must be paid for out of public revenues.

Preoccupation with productive use of the social surplus led mercantilist commentators to advocate low wages and long hours for labour. Consumption in excess of bare subsistence was viewed as a tax on progress and therefore contrary to the national interest. Mercantilist society was not a welfare state; it could not afford to be. Luxury consumption was condemned as a dissipation of the social surplus. Restrictions on imports were directed especially at luxury consumption.

Opportunities for profitable private investment multiplied rapidly as mercantilist policy succeeded in providing the basic social overhead capital. Rather paradoxically, it was because the state had made such an important contribution to economic development that the ideology of *laissez-faire* could later crystallise. When that occurred, dedication to capital accumulation remained a basic principle of capitalism, but the shift from public to private initiative marked the passage from the early state of capitalism and the beginning of the next stage, the classical period.

3. Classical Capitalism (1750–1914)

In England, beginning in the 18th century, the focus of capitalist development shifted from commerce to industry. The Industrial Revolution may be defined as the period of transition from a dominance of commercial over industrial capital to a dominance of industrial over commercial capital. Preparation for this shift began long before the invention of the flying shuttle, the water frame and the steam engine, but the technological changes of the 18th century made the transition dramatically evident.

The rural and household character of the English textile industry continued only as long as the amount of fixed capital required for efficient production remained relatively small. Changes in technology and organization shifted industry again to urban centres in the course of the Industrial Revolution, although not to the old commercial urban centres. Two or three centuries of steady capital accumulation began to pay off handsomely in the 18th century. Now it became feasible to make practical use of technical knowledge which had been accumulating over the centuries. Capitalism became a powerful promoter of technological change because the accumulation of capital made possible the use of inventions which poorer societies could not have afforded. Inventors and innovators like James Watt found business partners who were able to finance their inventions through lean years of experimentation and discouragement to ultimate commercial success. Aggressive entrepreneurs like Richard Arkwright found capital to finance the factory type of organization required for the utilization of new machines. Wealthy societies had existed before capitalism, but none had managed their wealth in a manner that enabled them to take advantage of the more efficient methods of production which an increasing mastery over nature made physically possible.

Adam Smith's great *Inquiry Into the Nature and Causes of the Wealth of Nations* (1776) expressed the ideology of classical capitalism. Smith recommended dismantling the state bureaucracy and leaving economic decisions to the free play of self-regulating market forces. While Smith recognized the faults of businessmen, he contended they could do little harm in a world of freely competitive enterprise. In Smith's opinion, private profit and public welfare would become reconciled through impersonal forces of market competition. After the French Revolution and the Napoleonic wars had swept the remnants of feudalism into oblivion and rapidly undermined mercantilist fetters, Smith's policies were put into practice. *Laissez-faire* policies of 19th-century political liberalism included free trade, sound money (the gold standard), balanced budgets, minimum poor relief—in brief, the principle of leaving individuals to themselves and of trusting that their unregulated interactions would produce socially desirable results. No new conceptions of society arose immediately to challenge seriously what had become, in fact, a capitalist civilization.

This system, though well-defined and logically coherent, must be understood as a system of tendencies only. The heritage of the past and other obstructions prevented any full realization of the principles except in a few cases of which the English free trade movement, crystallised by the repeal of the Corn Laws in 1846, is the most important. Such as they were, however, both tendencies and realizations bear the unmistakable stamp of the businessman's interests and still more the businessman's type of mind. Moreover, it was not only policy but the philosophy of national and individual life, the scheme of cultural values, that bore that stamp. Its materialistic utilitarianism, its naive confidence in progress of a certain type, its actual achievements in the field of pure and applied science, the temper of its artistic creations, may all be traced to the spirit of rationalism that emanates from the businessman's office. For much of the time and in many countries the businessman did not rule politically. But even noncapitalist rulers espoused his interests and adopted his views. They were what they had not been before, his agents.

More definitely than in any other historical epoch these developments can be explained by purely economic causes. It was the success of capitalist enterprise that raised the bourgeoisie to its position of temporary ascendancy. Economic success produced political power, which in turn produced policies congenial to the capitalist process. Thus the English industrialists obtained free trade, and free trade in turn was a major factor in a period of unprecedented economic expansion.

The partition of Africa and the carving out of spheres of influence in Asia by European powers in the decades preceding World War I led critics of capitalism to develop, on a Marxist basis, a theory of economic imperialism. According to this doctrine, competition among capitalist firms tends to eliminate all but a small number of giant concerns. Because of the inadequate purchasing power of the masses, these concerns find themselves unable to use the productive capacity they have built. They are, therefore, driven to invade foreign markets and to exclude foreign products from their own markets through protective tariffs. This situation produces aggressive colonial and foreign policies and "imperialist" wars, which the proletariat, if organized, turn into civil wars for socialist revolution. Like other doctrines of such sweeping character, this theory of imperialism is probably not capable of either exact proof or disproof. Three points, however, may be recorded in its favour; first, it does attempt what no other theory has attempted, namely, to subject the whole of the economic, political and cultural patterns of the epoch that began during the long depression (1873-96) to comprehensive analysis by means of a clear-cut plan; second, on the surface at least, it seems to be confirmed by some of the outstanding manifestations of this pattern and some of the greatest events of this epoch; third, whatever may be wrong with its interpretations, its certainly starts from a fact that is beyond challenge—the capitalist tendency toward industrial combination and the emergence of giant firms. Though cartels and trusts antedate the epoch, at least so far as the United States is concerned, the role of what is popularly called "big business" has increased so much as to constitute one of the outstanding characteristics of recent capitalism.

4. The Later Phase (Since 1914)

World War I marked a turning point in the development of capitalism in general and of European capitalism in particular. The period since 1914 has witnessed a reversal of the public attitude toward capitalism and of almost all the tendencies of the liberal epoch which preceded the war. In the prewar decades, European capitalism exercised vigorous leadership in the international economic community. World markets expanded, the gold standard became almost universal, Europe served as the world's banker, Africa became a European colony, Asia was divided into spheres of influence under the domination of European powers and Europe remained the centre of a growing volume of international trade.

After World War I, however, these trends were reversed. International markets shrank, the gold standard was abandoned in favour of managed national currencies, banking hegemony passed from Europe to the United States, African and Asian peoples began successful revolts against European colonialism and trade barriers multiplied. Western Europe as an entity declined, and in eastern Europe capitalism began to disintegrate. The Russian Revolution, a result of the war, uprooted over a vast area not only the basic capitalist institution of private property in the means of production, but the class structure, the traditional forms of government, and the established religion. Moreover, the juggernaut unleashed by the Russian Revolution was destined to challenge the historic superiority of capitalist organization as a system of production within less than half a century. Meanwhile, the inner structure of west European economies was tending away from the traditional forms of capitalism. Above all, *laissez-faire,* the accepted policy of the 19th century, was discredited by the war and postwar experience.

Statesmen and businessmen in capitalist nations were slow to appreciate the turn of events precipitated by World War I and consequently they misdirected their efforts during the 1920s by seeking a "return to prewar normalcy." Among major capitalist countries, the United Kingdom failed conspicuously to achieve prosperity at any time during the interwar period. Other capitalist nations enjoyed a brief prosperity in the 1920s only to be confronted in the 1930s with the great depression, which rocked the capitalist system to its foundations. *Laissez-faire* received a crushing blow from Pres. Franklin D. Roosevelt's New Deal in the United States. The gold standard collapsed completely. Free trade was abandoned in its classic home, Great Britain. Even the classical principle of sound finance, the annually balanced governmental budget, gave way in both practice and theory to planned deficits during periods of depressed economic activity. Retreat from the free market philosophy was nearly complete in Mussolini's Italy and Hitler's Germany. When World War II opened in 1939, the future of capitalism looked bleak indeed. This trend seemed confirmed at the end of the war when the British Labour party won a decisive victory at the polls and proceeded to nationalize basic industries, including coal, transportation, communication, public utilities, and the Bank of England. Yet a judgment that capitalism had at last run its course would have been premature. Capitalist enterprise managed to survive in Great Britain, the United States, western Germany, Japan and other nations [with a] remarkable show of vitality in the postwar world.

·   ·   ·

6

Underdevelopment in History

Keith Griffin .

STAGE THEORIES

Economic history, and theories firmly based upon historical knowledge, would appear to be essential in understanding the nature of underdevelopment. Unfortunately, however, most of the theories which claim to view development in historical perspective begin by assuming that the underdeveloped countries are in a "low-level equilibrium trap."[1] This presumption, of course, largely precludes endogenous change, since the very essence of an equilibrium position is absence of movement.

A common procedure is to assume that all nations, rich and poor, were once equal, i.e. suffered from an equivalent degree of poverty and state of underdevelopment. The implications of Kuznets' findings that "the present levels of *per capita* product in the underdeveloped countries are much lower than were those in the developed countries in their pre-industrialization phase"[2] have been totally ignored. Instead economists have argued from an assumption of equality when inequality obviously exists. Professor Leibenstein could not be more explicit. In defining "the abstract problem" he says, "We begin with a set of economies (or countries), each 'enjoying' an equally *low* standard of living at the outset. . . . Over a relatively long period of time (say, a century or two) some of these countries increase their output per head considerably whereas others do not."[3] This being so, the thing to do is determine how today's wealthy countries escaped the "low-level equilibrium trap," and then apply the lessons to the backward countries which were left behind.

The most self-conscious attempt to do this is found in Rostow's book, *The Stages of Economic Growth: A Non-Communist Manifesto.* The terminology and analytical categories employed in this book, although severely criticized,[4] have permeated Western thinking on development problems.[5] The reasons for this have more to do with sociology than economics.

Rostow believes that all countries pass through five stages. The initial stage is called "the traditional society" and its features are similiar to those of the "non-capitalist" sector of dual economy models. Next comes a "pre-

Reprinted from the author's *Underdevelopment in Spanish America* (London: George Allen & Unwin, 1969), pp. 31-48, by permission of the author and publishers. U.S. edition published by The M.I.T. Press, Cambridge, Massachusetts.

conditioning" stage, followed by the "take-off," the "drive to maturity" and, finally, an "age of high mass-consumption." How a nation gets from one stage to another is unclear, since all Rostow presents, in effect, is a series of snapshots which freeze the development process in five different moments of time. What is clear, however, is that the present "traditional society" stage is the initial stage, and that development occurs essentially as a result of internal efforts which are largely unaffected by the workings of the wider international economy.

As Gunder Frank has stressed, Rostow's theory "attributes a history to the developed countries but denies all history to the underdeveloped ones."[6] Rostow neglects the past of the underdeveloped countries but confidently predicts a future for them similar to that of the wealthy nations. In this respect Rostow's views differ little from the Marxist doctrine that "the most industrially advanced country presents the less advanced country with the image of its future."

Marx and Rostow notwithstanding, it is exceedingly improbable that one can gain an adequate understanding of present obstacles and future potential for development without examining how the underdeveloped nations came to be as they are. To classify these countries as "traditional societies" begs the issue and implies either that the underdeveloped countries have no history or that it is unimportant.[7] No proof has yet been provided to substantiate either of these claims. Indeed it is clear that the underdeveloped countries do have a history and that it is important. Furthermore, evidence is gradually being accumulated that the expansion of Europe, commencing in the fifteenth century, had a profound impact on the societies and economies of the rest of the world. In other words, the history of the underdeveloped countries in the last five centuries is, in large part, the history of the consequences of European expansion. It is our tentative conclusion that the automatic functioning of the international economy which Europe dominated first created underdevelopment and then hindered efforts to escape from it. In summary, underdevelopment is a product of historical processes.

Historical research is gradually reconstructing the past of the underdeveloped countries for us. Enough is known to enable us to say with confidence that "by the end of the sixteenth century . . . the agricultural economies of the Spice Islands, the domestic industries of large parts of India, the Arab trading-economy of the Indian Ocean and of the western Pacific, the native societies of West Africa and the way of life in the Caribbean islands and in the vast areas of the two vice-royalties of Spanish America [were] all deeply affected by the impact of Europeans. . . . The results [of European expansion] on non-European societies were . . . sometimes immediate and overwhelming. . . ."[8]

The expansion of Europe throughout the world was an outcome of the competition among mercantilist-capitalist states for trading advantages. This competition was both peaceful and violent and its object was to obtain monopoly control of the most lucrative trading areas. In practice the quest for monopoly control led inevitably to the forceful acquisition of colonies, satellites, dependent territories and spheres of influence. But the initial impulse, from the time when the Portuguese first began to explore the Orient, was to dominate trade, not to gain territory; that came later. "The object of Portuguese colonization was not the possession of the Indies themselves, but of the trade of the Indies. Their approach was based on a concept of a *mare clausum*, secured to them under papal authority, which should save them from the inroads of other Christian states, and on a system of forts and garrisons which should save them from native opposition." The Portuguese had no wish to engage in production but "merely to divert to their own sea-routes a trade which was based on a competent native economy. Their purpose was to make the king of Portugal the only merchant trading between India and Portugal."[9]

Ironically, it was the combination of Europe's military superiority and her relative material poverty which shaped events in the early phase of European expansion. Western ascendancy was made possible by advanced military technology and it was made necessary by the inability of Europe to engage in trade on equal terms with the wealthy nations of the East. Asia had much that Europe wanted but Europe could offer almost nothing that was desired in Asia. As Professor Rich has said, "the spice trade was conditioned by the fact that the Spice Islands wanted very little of the produce of Europe save firearms."[10]

An historian of Indonesia notes that "when the first Dutch merchants and sailors had come to the island world of the Indies, they had been amazed by the variety of its nature and civilization, and the more observant among them had recognized that southern and eastern Asia were far ahead of western Europe in riches as well as in commercial ability and mercantile skill."[11] Similarly, an historian of the Middle East has written that "when Islam was still expanding and receptive, the Christian West had little or nothing to offer, but rather flattered Islamic pride with the spectacle of a culture that was visibly and palpably inferior."[12] Europe's subsequent ability to dominate the rest of the world depended not upon her cultural superiority or economic strength but upon two technological breakthroughs: the construction of large ocean-going sailing vessels and the development of gunpowder and naval cannons.[13] Indeed, Europe owed a great technological debt to the rest of the world, and particularly to China. Without Chinese science the industrial revolution would have been impossible.[14] It was European advances in specific military techniques rather than general progress in the peaceful arts of civilization which enabled her to establish hegemony in Latin America, Asia and Africa.

In the early period of expansion, in fact, a large volume of trade between Europe and the rest of the world would have been impossible because of the European tendency to run a substantial balance of payments deficit. If Europe was to obtain the products from the East which were desired she either had to force down the price of oriental products or increase the demand for goods which Europe could supply. In practice she did both. The Dutch, for instance, exacted an annual tribute in spices; for other crops they enforced compulsory deliveries at favourable prices. The English destroyed the Indian textile industry and then proceeded to supply India with cotton goods from Great Britain. How Britain was to finance the imports of tea from China presented great problems, for as the Chinese emperor said to George III, "our celestial empire possesses all things in prolific abundance" and, presumably, therefore, China had little need for English goods. This knotty problem was finally resolved by forcing opium on the Chinese and encouraging addiction. This created a large demand for the drug which the East India Company was able to supply from Bengal. The Chinese made many vain attempts to restrict the trade. Finally, Britain forced China to permit the trade and fought the Opium War of 1839–42—"a war that was precipitated by the Chinese government's effort to suppress a pernicious contraband trade in opium, concluded by the superior firepower of British warships, and followed by humiliating treaties that gave Westerners special privileges in China."[15]

It is still a matter of debate whether domination of the rest of the world was the vital ingredient in Europe's recipe for rapid economic growth. There is little doubt, however, that resources were transferred to the West, and especially to Great Britain, on a massive scale. British India had a large trading surplus with China and the rest of Asia. These surpluses, in turn, were siphoned off to England "through the (politically established and maintained) Indian trading deficit with Britain, through the 'Home Charges'—i.e. India's payments for the privilege of being administered by Britain—and through the increasingly large interest-payments on the Indian Public Debt. Towards the end of the [nineteenth] century these items became increasingly important. Before the First World War 'the key to Britain's whole payments pattern lay in India, financing as she probably did more than two fifths of Britain's trade deficits'."[16]

Going back still further, the East India Company, according to Keynes, had its origin in privateering. "Indeed, the booty brought back by Drake in the *Golden Hind* may fairly be considered the fountain and origin of British Foreign Investment. Elizabeth paid off out of the proceeds the whole of her foreign debt and invested a part of the balance (about £42,000) in the Levant Company; largely out of the profits of the Levant Company there was formed the East India Company, the profits of which during the seventeenth and eighteenth centuries were the main foundation of England's foreign connections; and so on."[17]

. . .

[W]e are concerned not with whether European expansion enriched the West, but with whether it impoverished the rest of the world. It is conceivable that the benefits to Europe of its hegemony were slight and accrued in the form of temporarily increased consumption (rather than greater investment and growth), while the costs of her dominance were heavy and fell primarily upon the dependent countries. It is to this final question that we now turn.

FRAGMENTS OF HISTORY

The concept of "underdevelopment" as it is used [here] is all-inclusive. It refers to a society's political organization, economic characteristics and social institutions. Poverty is neither a synonym for underdevelopment nor a cause of underdevelopment; it is only symptomatic of a more general problem. Poverty, in other words, forms part of a culture. Oscar Lewis had the following to say about this culture: "The culture of poverty is both an adaptation and a reaction of the poor to their marginal position in a class-stratified, high individuated, capitalistic society. It represents an effort to cope with feelings of hopelessness and despair. . . . Most frequently the culture of poverty develops when a stratified social and economic system is breaking down or is being replaced by another. . . . Often it results from imperial conquest in which the native social and economic structure is smashed and the natives are maintained in a servile colonial status, sometimes for many generations."[18]

As Lewis is the first to recognize, however, the culture of poverty is not identical in all settings; the slums of Puerto Rico produce a different culture from those of Mexico City;[19] the culture of poverty varies from place to place and from one era to another. The culture both shapes and is shaped by a people's history. It is for this reason that the differences between the developed and the underdeveloped countries cannot be explained exclusively in statistical terms; the two types of countries differ qualitatively as well as quantitatively. For similar reasons, it is almost certainly incorrect and misleading to assume that the circumstances of today's underdeveloped countries were always the same. Yet this is the view that at present prevails. Nurkse's notion of the "vicious circle of poverty"—the proposition that "a country is poor because it is poor," and presumably always has been—expresses the conventional doctrine perfectly.[20] As an alternative approach one might advance the hypothesis that the wellbeing of today's poor countries was not always so low and that their descent into underdevelopment did not occur independently of what was happening in the rest of the world.

It is our belief that underdeveloped countries as we observe them today are a product of historical forces, especially of those forces released by European expansion and world ascendancy. Thus they are a relatively recent phenomenon. Europe did not "discover" the underdeveloped countries; on the contrary, she created them. In many cases, in fact, the societies with which Europe came into contact were sophisticated, cultured and wealthy.

This is well illustrated by the case of Indonesia, an archipelago which today includes about half of the inhabitants of South-East Asia and the region which formerly acted as a magnet to Western traders and precipitated European expansion. At the beginning of the sixteenth century Indonesia was a prosperous region. "Local emporia were the equal of anything Europe had to offer: indeed Malacca was at that time regarded by Western visitors as the greatest port for international commerce in the world, clearing annually more shipping than any other."[21] The Dutch, operating through the Netherlands' United East India Company, aimed first to establish a monopoly of trade with the region. This aim was accomplished by 1641. They next established a monopsony over the purchases of the output of the islands. Finally, in the eighteenth century, the Dutch established a system of forced deliveries, forced cultivation and even the legal obligation to grow specific commercial crops on peasant holdings. Specialization was not dictated by the market but by the Company. As a consequence of this so-called Culture System "so little time was left to the Javanese for the cultivation of food crops that serious famines occurred in the eighteen-forties. The fertile island had been transformed into a vast Dutch plantation, or, from the point of view of the people, a forced labour camp."[22]

Agriculture was not the only sector that was adversely affected. The Dutch systematically discouraged and prevented local enterprise outside agriculture, and even brought in Chinese as ubiquitous middlemen. Java's indigenous commercial and industrial activities were utterly destroyed: ship building, iron-working, brass and copper founding all disappeared; weaving and peasant handicrafts declined; the merchant marine vanished and the merchants devoted themselves to piracy.

By the beginning of the present century the Indonesian economy was in a state of crisis and the Dutch government announced its intention in 1901 to "enquire into the diminishing welfare of the people of Java." Some indication of the extent to which the wellbeing of the people had declined is provided by Mr. Caldwell's figures:

Table 1   Average Annual Rice Consumption Per Head in Java and Madura

Period	Quantity (kilogrammes)
1856–70	114.0
1881–90	105.5
1891–1900	100.6
1936–40	89.0
1960	81.4

Source: M. Caldwell, *Indonesia*, Oxford University Press, 1968, p. 21.

Indonesia's experience was not unique. Indeed, President Roosevelt's comment to Lord Halifax in January 1944 that the French had possessed Indochina ". . . for nearly 100 years, and the people were worse off than they were at the beginning" is applicable to Asia as a whole. In some cases the destruction of the indigenous society was largely inadvertent. The decimation of the population of the South Pacific islands through the introduction of alien diseases is an example of this.[23] In other cases the destruction of the native economy and its institutions was deliberate. A second great example of this is India.

As late as the early seventeenth century India was more advanced economically than Europe. She had a fairly large manufacturing sector which produced mostly luxury goods—including gold and silver objects, plus glassware, paper, iron products and ships. Many of these items as well as cotton cloth, silk, indigo and saltpetre were exported to the West for payment in bullion.[24] The decline of India's industry was due to a combination of several factors: technical progress in Europe associated with the industrial revolution, domination of the East India Company and the imposition of the free trade doctrine under unequal conditions by the British. After 1833 the process of de-industrialization was accelerated and emphasis was placed on developing cash crop agriculture for export. Industrial decay was complete by the 1880s.

Parallel to the destruction of the manufacturing sector, agricultural institutions were profoundly altered and the economic wellbeing of rural inhabitants declined. Throughout the nineteenth century the proportion of the total population dependent upon agriculture increased, and the proportion of the rural population composed of agricultural labourers also increased. Data from the Madras Presidency of South India indicate that the real wages of agricultural labourers (measured in *seers* of common rice) declined sharply even as late as the last quarter of the last century. In only one of the seven districts for which data are available did real wages actually rise; in the others they declined from 13 to 48 per cent.

Table 2   Change in Real Wages of Agricultural Labour in Seven Districts of South India, Average 1873–75 to Average 1898–1900

	per cent
Ganjam	−43
Vizagapatam	−48
Bellary	−20
Tanjore	+29
Tinnevelly	−40
Salem	−13
Coimbatore	−39

Source: Dharma Kumar, *Land and Caste in South India*, Cambridge University Press, 1965, p. 164.

Conditions in the rest of India were roughly comparable. René Dumont summarizes the experience of Bengal as follows: "On 22 March 1793 Lord Cornwallis and the East India Company proclaimed that *zamindars* and *talukhars* (the men who had been charged with the collection of tribute) would henceforth be considered as permanent and irrevocable owners of the lands on which they had gathered taxes. This proclamation had far-reaching consequences. Of course, it is easy to see that the East India Company regarded it both as an improved way of obtaining a better return of tributes, and also as an easy means of making firm allies. But they never realized that, in depriving the peasant of his traditional and permanent right to occupy the land, they were making him, throughout the greatest part of India, a slave of new owners; and that exploitation of the peasant now took the place of exploitation of resources. Rural societies were not only compelled to pay taxes, but also rents which demographic development soon made outrageous; some peasants took to running away. A new law gave the *zamindars* the right to catch them, and this completed the dismemberment of traditional rural society. On the one hand great landowners; serfs on the other; the former with no incentive to improve the land; the latter with no means to do so."[25]

The conversion of tax collectors into landlords, the emphasis on production of cash crops for export, and the population explosion which began at the end of the nineteenth century were jointly responsible for the final disaster. The mass of the people were reduced to a subsistence income which hovered precariously above the famine level. Using 1900–01 as an index base of 100, agricultural production per capita had declined to 72 a half century later, while production of food *per capita* had plunged to the miserably low figure of 58.[26]

None of the preceding discussion should be taken to imply that all of the underdeveloped countries were once wealthy societies and advanced civilizations. Some of the peoples with whom the Europeans came into contact were, of course, relatively primitive. But nearly all of the people encountered in today's underdeveloped areas were members of viable societies which could satisfy the economic needs of the community. Yet these societies were shattered when they came into contact with an expanding Europe. The manner in which the indigenous societies were destroyed varied from one region to another and depended upon the precise form taken by European penetration and the wealth, structure and resilience of the native civilization. Although the method of destruction varied, the outcome was always the same: a decline in the welfare of the subjugated people. Writing about Africa, Professor Frankel notes that attempts at modernization under colonialism are "in greater or lesser degree accompanied by increasingly rapid disintegration of the indigenous economic and social structure. However primitive those indigenous institutions may now appear in Western eyes, they did in fact provide the individuals composing the indigenous society with that sense of psychological and economic security without which life loses its meaning."[27]

Although our knowledge of African history is rudimentary, it is perhaps correct to say that no continent has felt the impact of European expansion more thoroughly than Africa. The introduction, especially by the Portuguese, of large-scale trading in slaves during the sixteenth century completely disrupted West Africa from Guinea to Angola.[28] Slavery created chaos in vast areas of the continent. The population declined; wars among formerly peaceful tribes were incited; the native economy fell into decay; and the social organization of the community and the authority of the chief frequently were corrupted. The entire way of life in Africa was altered. "The increased demand for slaves arising from the plantation owners of North and South America in the seventeenth and eighteenth centuries was responsible for depopulating large parts of Africa, and for degrading what had once been settled agricultural peoples back to long-fallow agriculture or nomadism."[29]

The slaughter of the indigenous people and the depopulation of the land did not cease with the end of slavery, however. In 1919 the Belgian Commission for the Protection of the Native estimated that the number of inhabitants of the Congo had declined by as much as 50 per cent since the beginning of occupation forty years earlier. In South-West Africa during the German-Herero War of 1904 General von Trotha, after the campaign was over, issued his notorious Extermination Order which required every Herero man, woman and child to be killed.[30] As a result of this the tribe was reduced from 80,000 to 15,000, and today it has regained only half of its former strength.

As pervasive as slavery and indiscriminate slaughter may have been, they can hardly be considered the typical pattern of European penetration in Africa. One must also consider the more "normal" economic activities of colonization and mineral extraction. One cannot, of course, accurately describe in a few paragraphs all the forms which colonialism adopted in North, East and Southern Africa, but it is possible to reconstruct a simplified scheme of the effects of European activity upon the indigenous society.

The process began with the acquisition of all the good land, mineral deposits and water resources by the colonialists. Excluding West Africa, this was nearly a universal phenomenon, and was not confined to the acknowledged cases of white settlers in Kenya, Algeria and the Republic of South Africa, but was also prevalent in less prominent places. For instance, the Bechuana tribes of Botswana were continually forced to give up their most productive lands in the south and northwest in order to avoid becoming a colony and to maintain their status as the Bechuanaland Protectorate.[31] In Liberia the descendants of freed slaves (Americo-Liberians) have installed themselves as aristocratic absentee landlords of rubber farms, have required the indigenous people to supply one fourth of the labour supply gratis, and pay the remainder four cents an hour or less.[32] The mandate territory of South-West Africa is a classical example of Europeans monopolizing the land. "Whites, though only one in seven of the total population, enjoy the exclusive use of two-thirds of the land."[33]

Having lost the best lands, the indigenous population was then confined to the less desirable and more remote areas—the "bush," Reserves, the veld or Bantustans. The high population densities led inevitably to increased erosion, declining yields of food crops in native areas and falling consumption levels. Colonialism in Africa—like that in Latin America, as we shall soon see—led to underemployment both of land (in the European areas)

Table 3 Per Capita Output of Indigenous Agriculture in Algeria

	Cereals (kilos)	Cattle (head)	Sheep (head)
1863	1000	n.a.	4.5
1911	377	0.2	1.5
1938	231	0.1	0.8
1954	202	0.1	0.7

Source: R. Murray and T. Wengraf, "The Algerian Revolution," New Left Review, No. 22, p. 32, who cite A. Gorz, "Gaullisme et neo-colonialisme," Temps Modernes, March 1961.

and labour (in the African areas). *Per capita* food consumption, at least in some cases, has fallen over a considerable period of time. For example, food consumption in Algeria was perhaps between five and six times higher in 1863 than it was in 1954.

It was not sufficient, however, simply to dispossess the natives of their land and confine them to Reserves. The colonial economy—particularly the mines—also required cheap manpower; the Africans had to be compelled to emigrate and work for the Europeans. In some cases, e.g. in the Belgian and Portuguese colonies, the authorities relied to a great extent on forced labour. In most of the other colonies, however, a more subtle device was used—fiscal policy. A high tax, payable in money, was imposed on the natives. This forced them to enter a monopsonistic labour market and work for the white men at extremely low wages in order (i) to pay their taxes and (ii) to supplement the declining income obtainable from indigenous agriculture. Positive inducements in the form of incentive goods also were occasionally provided. Often this was unnecessary, however. A common technique, as in Basutoland, was to assign the responsibility for collecting taxes to the chief and allow him to take a rake-off. In this way the authority of the chief was used to favour the ambitions of the colonialists rather than the interests of his own people. The system of colonialism and indirect rule was designed to generate abundant supplies of cheap unskilled labour for Europeans who monopolized all other resources. The material wellbeing of the African was systematically lowered and his institutions were intentionally destroyed. It was this process of impoverishment and growing degradation which contributed to the urgent demands for independence in the late 1940s. By this time Africa and the other underdeveloped countries had gone through a lengthy period of growing misery which culminated in the collapse of primary commodity prices in the 1920s, the world depression of the 1930s, and the Second World War of the first half of the 1940s. The crisis of colonialism was not exclusively or even primarily a political crisis; its roots lay in the inability of the colonial system to generate economic progress and distribute it equitably.[34]

Even this rather superficial discussion of conditions in Africa and Asia should give us a broader perspective from which to consider the historical origins of underdevelopment in Latin America.

. . .

In general, colonialism in Latin America, as in the rest of the world, was a catastrophe for the indigenous people. In the areas of more primitive civilization the population virtually disappeared within less than thirty years. In the areas of advanced civilization the people were completely subjugated.

Spanish penetration of Latin America began in the Caribbean area. There they encountered Arawak, Carib and Cueva tribes with large populations tilling the soil in permanent clearings and on *conucos*. The native culture in the West Indies and on the Isthmus was not as advanced as some other civilizations, but the tribal societies were well organized and the economy was perhaps as productive as that of Indonesia. Yet within a generation the indigenous society and economy had been ruined and the native population had virtually disappeared.[35]

The Spaniards gained control over the natives by breaking their political structure. The chiefs were liquidated and the rest of the community were allocated to individual claimants. These allocations were originally called *repartimientos* and subsequently formed the basis of the *encomienda* system. These colonial institutions, in turn, were the origin of the latifundia system, under which individual rights to labour services were transformed to include the land as well. One of the features of the *repartimientos* was that the number of natives allocated to a Spaniard depended upon how much work he could extract from them, i.e. originally, how much gold for export he could get them to produce. In this way strong incentives to exploit labour were created.

The combination of brutality, slaughter, high tribute, slavery, forced labour for gold mining, destruction of the social framework, malnutrition,[36] disease and suicide led to the extinction of the indigenous population. "It has been reckoned that at the approach of the Spaniards, in 1492, total Carib population in Hispaniola was about 300,000. By 1508 it was reduced to about 60,000. A great decline had brought it to about 14,000 by 1514, as serious settlement began; and by 1548 it had reached a figure which indicated virtual extermination, about 500."[37] The population of the other islands declined even more rapidly. The Bahamas lost their population first. Puerto Rico was decimated in little more than a decade, and Cuba followed soon after. By 1519 Jamaica was almost uninhabited. Those who survived were a pitiable lot. "A well-structured and adjusted native society had become a formless proletariat in alien servitude. . . ."[38]

As the population declined the *conucos* on the islands were abandoned and the terrain became rangeland for cattle and pigs; in Central America the continuous savanna reverted to a tropical rain forest. The Spaniards responded to the labour shortage by introducing extensive grazing on their estates. The few natives who managed to escape fled to the jungle and adopted the slash-and-burn shifting agriculture that can still be observed today.

A similar story may someday be told, perhaps, of the sparsely settled regions of the Amazon basin. It is usually assumed that this region was inhabited by extremely primitive people: this assumption, however, may well turn out to be incorrect. The inhabitants of this area may once have had a more advanced civilization and a higher standard of living than is currently believed. A noted anthropologist who has had considerable research experience in Brazil, Claude Lévi-Strauss, is too cautious to advance a positive hypothesis, but the question he poses is worth pondering. "Is it not also possible to see them [the tribes in Brazil] as a regressive people, that is, one that descended from a higher level of material life and social organization and retained one trait or another as a vestige of former conditions?"[39]

We do not know what the answer to his question is as regards Brazil, but in the two cases of Mexico and the Inca Empire the answer is clearly "yes." Space does not permit us to recount the downfall of the Aztecs. Let us only note that the native population of Mexico was decimated. From about 13 million at the time of the Spanish Conquest, the population had declined to about 2 million by the end of the sixteenth century.

In the Inca Empire, which covered a very large portion of western South America, the impact of the Spanish was not quite so fatal, yet it is still true that one of the greatest tragedies in Latin America was the destruction of this civilization. The Spanish Conquest of Peru was accompanied by profound social, institutional and demographic changes. The wars, the epidemics and the fierce exploitation of the Indians reduced the indigenous population by one-half to two-thirds.[40] It was only towards the end of the nineteenth century that the Indian population began to increase again, and it is now estimated that this population only slightly exceeds the number of inhabitants of the Inca Empire. The catastrophic decline in population was accompanied by the utter ruination of the Andean civilization. Cities vanished; the communal customs of the Inca became an historical curiosity; terraced hillsides were abandoned; agricultural productivity declined. The survivors of the conquest became a miserable, starving, diseased and disorganized mass of humanity. In short, they became an underdeveloped people.[41]

The new civilization constructed from the debris of the earlier indigenous society was markedly different. The colonizing Spaniards and their descendants enslaved what remained of the indigenous population. Indians were sent to the mines by the thousands to extract the mineral wealth of the continent. Following the precedent established in the Caribbean, the best lands were appropriated and huge estates were distributed to the favoured few. The great mass of the underprivileged, on the other hand, were pushed on to the mountain slopes where they attempted to eke out a living on small plots. In this way the distinctive economic system of Spanish America—the latifundia-minifundia complex—was created.

The essential feature of the new economic system was the monopolization of land. This by itself was sufficiently important to shape the social and political relationships of the colonial civilization, since in a predominantly agricultural economy one's livelihood depends almost entirely upon access to land. Exploitation did not stop here, however. Water rights were tightly controlled by the large landowners; the majority of the population had very little access to credit; rural education was practically non-existent. Thus the latifundium acquired a monopoly of the major factors of production—land, capital, water and technology, and its position as virtually the only large employer gave it a strong monopsonistic position in the labour market as well. The economic power of the minifundium was nil; its role in the system was to provide an abundant supply of cheap, unskilled labour.

Low productivity and an unequal distribution of income were inevitable characteristics of the new social and economic system. The universal syndrome of the latifundia-minifundia complex was the continuous pressure upon the Indians to move to poorer lands, the consequent accelerated erosion of the mountain slopes, falling yields of food crops on the subsistence plots, and a decline in consumption standards of the mass of the population. In contrast to the intensive agriculture of the minifundium and its declining productivity, the latifundium adopted highly labour extensive techniques of production and the large landowners were able to prosper at the expense of the rest of the community. Thus it was the social and political systems imposed by the colonists, in combination with the demographic changes which followed the Conquest, which were responsible for creating underdevelopment in Spanish America. One cannot explain the poverty of the region today without referring to the region's history.

NOTES

1. The phrase is taken from R. R. Nelson, "A Theory of the Low-Level Equilibrium Trap in Underdeveloped Economies," *American Economic Review*, December 1956. Also see by the same author "Growth Models and the Escape from the Low-Level Equilibrium Trap: The Case of Japan," *Economic Development and Cultural Change*, July 1960.
2. S. Kuznets, *Economic Growth and Structure*, London, 1966, p. 177.
3. H. Leibenstein, *Economic Backwardness and Economic Growth*, John Wiley and Sons, 1960, p. 4. Italics in the original.
4. See, for example, P. A. Baran and E. J. Hobsbawm, "The Stages of Economic Growth," *Kyklos*, 1961; S. Kuznets, "Notes on the Take-Off," in W. W. Rostow, ed., *The Economics of Take-Off into Sustained Growth*, Macmillan, 1964.
5. For instance, in presenting their dualistic model Ranis and Fei claim that

Rostow's "well-known intuitive notion has been chosen as our point of departure." ("A Theory of Economic Development," *American Economic Review*, Sept. 1961, p. 533.)

6. A. G. Frank, "Sociology of Development and Under-Development of Sociology," *Catalyst*, Summer 1967, p. 37.

7. A typical view is exemplified by Trevor-Roper's arrogant assertion that "the history of the world, for the last five centuries, in so far as it has significance, has been European history." (*The Rise of Christian Europe*, 1965, p. 11.)

8. E. E. Rich, "Preface," in E. E. Rich and C. H. Wilson, eds, *The Cambridge Economic History of Europe*, Vol. IV, *The Economy of Expanding Europe in the Sixteenth and Seventeenth Centuries*, Cambridge University Press, 1967, p. xiii. The contributions of Professor Rich to this volume, and especially the "Preface," are brilliant.

9. E. E. Rich, "Colonial Settlement and its Labour Problems," *ibid.*, p. 304.

10. *Ibid.*, p. 368.

11. B. H. M. Vlekke, *The Story of the Dutch East Indies*, Harvard University Press, 1946, p. 178.

12. B. Lewis, *The Emergence of Modern Turkey*, Oxford University Press, 1961, p. 40.

13. See C. M. Cipolla, *Guns and Sails in the Early Phase of European Expansion, 1400–1700*, Collins, 1965.

14. See J. Needham and W. Ling, *Science and Civilization in China*, Vol. IV, Part II.

15. J. K. Fairbank, E. O. Reischauer and A. M. Craig, *East Asia: The Modern Transformation*, George Allen and Unwin, 1965, p. 136.

16. E. J. Hobsbawm, *Industry and Empire*, Weidenfeld and Nicolson, 1968, p. 123, citing S. B. Saul, *Studies in British Overseas Trade 1870–1914*.

17. J. M. Keynes, *A Treatise on Money*, Vol. II, *The Applied Theory of Money*, Macmillan, 1930, p. 156.

18. Oscar Lewis, *La Vida*, Secker and Warburg, London, 1967, p. xli.

19. See Oscar Lewis, *The Children of Sanchez*, Secker and Warburg, 1961.

20. R. Nurkse, *Problems of Capital Formation in Underdeveloped Countries*, Oxford University Press, p. 4.

21. M. Caldwell, *Indonesia*, Oxford University Press, 1968, p. 39.

22. *Ibid.*, p. 47.

23. See A. Moorehead, *The Fatal Impact*, Hamish Hamilton, 1966, Part I.

24. S. C. Kuchhal, *The Industrial Economy of India*, Chaitanya Publishing House, 1965, p. 64.

25. R. Dumont, *Lands Alive*, Merlin Press, 1965, p. 139.

26. See K. Mukerji, *Levels of Economic Activity and Public Expenditure in India*, Asia Publishing House, 1965.

27. S. H. Frankel, *The Economic Impact on Underdeveloped Societies*, Basil Blackwell, 1953, p. 134.

28. See J. Duffy, *Portuguese Africa*, Harvard University Press, 1959, especially Ch. VI. See also the well-known study by E. Williams, *Capitalism and Slavery*, University of North Carolina Press, 1944. J. Pope-Hennessy, *Sins of the Fathers: A Study of the Atlantic Slave Trade, 1441–1807*, 1967, is a lively popular account.

Slave raiding in Eastern and Central Africa had been introduced earlier by Arab traders operating out of Zanzibar and Khartoum. This naturally disturbed the native economy and society, but the effects were insignificant in comparison with the devastation created by European and American slaving expeditions.

29. Colin Clark, *Population Growth and Land Use*, Macmillan, 1967, p. 136.

30. See R. First, *South-West Africa*, Penguin, 1963, pp. 69–83.

31. E. S. Munger, *Bechuanaland*, Oxford University Press, 1965, Ch. II.

32. G. Dalton, "History, Politics, and Economic Development in Liberia," *Journal of Economic History*, December 1965.

33. R. First, *op. cit.*, p. 142.

34. See B. Davidson, *Which Way Africa?*, Penguin, 1964, Ch. 6.

35. See C. O. Sauer, *The Early Spanish Main*, University of California Press, 1966, especially chapters III and VII.

36. There was never a deficiency of cassava bread and sweet potatoes on the islands. Malnutrition occurred after the Spaniards suppressed native fishing and hunting and the supply of protein and fat declined.

37. E. E. Rich, "Colonial Settlement and its Labour Problems," *loc. cit.*, p. 319. The author adds that "European diseases had played their parts in this decimation of the Carib population, but the main cause was without doubt a passive revulsion from the changes which white occupation brought."

38. C. O. Sauer, *op. cit.*, p. 204.

39. Claude Lévi-Strauss, *Structural Anthropology*, Anchor Books, 1967, p. 101. Also see by the same author, *Tristes Tropiques*, 1958.

40. In Latin America as a whole Colin Clark estimates that the population declined from 40 million in 1500 to 12 million in 1650. (*Population Growth and Land Use*, p. 64.)

    In North America the indigenous population was not very large, but the Indian was destroyed nevertheless. A former U.S. Commissioner of Indian Affairs has described in detail how "a policy at first implicit and sporadic, then explicit, elaborately rationalized and complexly implemented, of the extermination of Indian societies and of every Indian trait, of the eventual liquidation of Indians, became the formalized policy, law and practice." (John Collier, *Indians of the Americas*, Mentor, 1948, p. 103.)

41. The classic study of this process is W. H. Prescott, *The Conquest of Peru*.

7

On the Political
Economy of Backwardness

Paul A. Baran

I

The capitalist mode of production and the social and political order concomitant with it provided, during the latter part of the eighteenth century,
and still more during the entire nineteenth century, a framework for a
continuous and, in spite of cyclical disturbances and setbacks, momentous
expansion of productivity and material welfare. The relevant facts are well
known and call for no elaboration. Yet this material (and cultural) progress
was not only spotty in time but most unevenly distributed in space. It was
confined to the Western world; and did not affect even all of this territorially
and demographically relatively small sector of the inhabited globe.

. . .

Tardy and skimpy as the benefits of capitalism may have been with
respect to the lower classes even in most of the leading industrial countries,
they were all but negligible in the less privileged parts of the world. There
productivity remained low, and rapid increases in population pushed living
standards from bad to worse. The dreams of the prophets of capitalist
harmony remained on paper. Capital either did not move from countries
where its marginal productivity was low to countries where it could be
expected to be high, or if it did, it moved there mainly in order to extract
profits from backward countries that frequently accounted for a lion's share
of the increments in total output caused by the original investments. Where
an increase in the aggregate national product of an underdeveloped country
took place, the existing distribution of income prevented this increment
from raising the living standards of the broad masses of the population.
Like all general statements, this one is obviously open to criticism based on
particular cases. There were, no doubt, colonies and dependencies where
the populations profited from inflow of foreign capital. These benefits, however, were few and far between, while exploitation and stagnation were the
prevailing rule.

Reprinted from *The Manchester School* (January 1952), pp. 66-84, by permission of the publisher.

But if Western capitalism failed to improve materially the lot of the peoples inhabiting most backward areas, it accomplished something that profoundly affected the social and political conditions in underdeveloped countries. It introduced there, with amazing rapidity, all the economic and social tensions inherent in the capitalist order. It effectively disrupted whatever was left of the "feudal" coherence of the backward societies. It substituted market contracts for such paternalistic relationships as still survived from century to century. It reoriented the partly or wholly self-sufficient economies of agricultural countries toward the production of marketable commodities. It linked their economic fate with the vagaries of the world market and connected it with the fever curve of international price movements.

A *complete* substitution of capitalist market rationality for the rigidities of feudal or semi-feudal servitude would have represented, in spite of all the pains of transition, an important step in the direction of progress. Yet all that happened was that the age-old exploitation of the population of underdeveloped countries by their domestic overlords, was freed of the mitigating constraints inherited from the feudal tradition. This superimposition of business *mores* over ancient oppression by landed gentries resulted in compounded exploitation, more outrageous corruption, and more glaring injustice.

Nor is this by any means the end of the story. Such export of capital and capitalism as has taken place had not only far-reaching implications of a social nature. It was accompanied by important physical and technical processes. Modern machines and products of advanced industries reached the poverty stricken backyards of the world. To be sure most, if not all, of these machines worked for their foreign owners—or at least were believed by the population to be working for no one else—and the new refined appurtenances of the good life belonged to foreign businessmen and their domestic counterparts. The bonanza that was capitalism, the fullness of things that was modern industrial civilization, were crowding the display windows—they were protected by barbed wire from the anxious grip of the starving and desperate man in the street.

But they have drastically changed his outlook. Broadening and deepening his economic horizon, they aroused aspirations, envies, and hopes. Young intellectuals filled with zeal and patriotic devotion travelled from the underdeveloped lands to Berlin and London, to Paris and New York, and returned home with the "message of the possible."

Fascinated by the advances and accomplishments observed in the centers of modern industry, they developed and propagandized the image of what could be attained in their home countries under a more rational economic and social order. The dissatisfaction with the stagnation (or at best, barely perceptible growth) that ripened gradually under the still-calm political and social surface was given an articulate expression. This dissatisfaction was not nurtured by a comparison of reality with a vision of a socialist society. It found sufficient fuel in the confrontation of what was actually happening with what could be accomplished under capitalist institutions of the Western type.

II

The establishment of such institutions was, however, beyond the reach of the tiny middle-classes of most backward areas. The inherited backwardness and poverty of their countries never gave them an opportunity to gather the economic strength, the insight, and the self-confidence needed for the assumption of a leading role in society. For centuries under feudal rule they themselves assimilated the political, moral, and cultural values of the dominating class.

While in advanced countries, such as France or Great Britain, the economically ascending middle-classes developed at an early stage a new rational world outlook, which they proudly opposed to the medieval obscurantism of the feudal age, the poor, fledgling bourgeoisie of the underdeveloped countries sought nothing but accommodation to the prevailing order. Living in societies based on privilege, they strove for a share in the existing sinecures. They made political and economic deals with their domestic feudal overlords or with powerful foreign investors, and what industry and commerce developed in backward areas in the course of the last hundred years was rapidly moulded in the straitjacket of monopoly—the plutocratic partner of the aristocratic rulers. What resulted was an economic and political amalgam combining the worst features of both worlds—feudalism and capitalism—and blocking effectively all possibilities of economic growth.

It is quite conceivable that a "conservative" exit from this impasse might have been found in the course of time. A younger generation of enterprising and enlightened businessmen and intellectuals allied with moderate leaders of workers and peasants—a "Young Turk" movement of some sort—might have succeeded in breaking the deadlock, in loosening the hide-bound social and political structure of their countries and in creating the institutional arrangements indispensable for a measure of social and economic progress.

Yet in our rapid age history accorded no time for such a gradual transition. Popular pressures for an amelioration of economic and social conditions, or at least for some perceptible movement in that direction, steadily gained in intensity. To be sure, the growing restiveness of the underprivileged was not directed against the ephemeral principles of a hardly yet existing capitalist order. Its objects were parasitic feudal overlords appropriating large slices of the national product and wasting them on extravagant living; a government machinery protecting and abetting the dominant interests; wealthy businessmen reaping immense profits and not utilizing them for productive purposes; last but not least, foreign colonizers extracting or believed to be extracting vast gains from their "developmental" operations.

This popular movement had thus essentially bourgeois, democratic, anti-feudal, anti-imperialist tenets. It found outlets in agrarian egalitarianism; it incorporated "muckraker" elements denouncing monopoly; it strove for national independence and freedom from foreign exploitation.

For the native capitalist middle-classes to assume the leadership of these popular forces and to direct them into the channels of bourgeois democracy

—as had happened in Western Europe—they had to identify themselves with the common man. They had to break away from the political, economic, and ideological leadership of the feudal crust and the monopolists allied with it; and they had to demonstrate to the nation as a whole that they had the knowledge, the courage, and the determination to undertake and to carry to victorious conclusion the struggle for economic and social improvement.

In hardly any underdeveloped country were the middle-classes capable of living up to this historical challenge. Some of the reasons for this portentous failure, reasons connected with the internal make-up of the business class itself, were briefly mentioned above. Of equal importance was, however, an "outside" factor. It was the spectacular growth of the international labor movement in Europe that offered the popular forces in backward areas ideological and political leadership that was denied to them by the native bourgeoisie. It pushed the goals and targets of the popular movements far beyond their original limited objectives.

This liaison of labor radicalism and populist revolt painted on the wall the imminent danger of a social revolution. Whether this danger was real or imaginary matters very little. What was essential is that the awareness of this threat effectively determined political and social action. It destroyed whatever chances there were of the capitalist classes joining and leading the popular anti-feudal, anti-monopolist movement. By instilling a mortal fear of expropriation and extinction in the minds of *all* property-owning groups the rise of socialist radicalism, and in particular the Bolshevik Revolution in Russia, tended to drive all more or less privileged, more or less well-to-do elements in the society into one "counterrevolutionary" coalition. Whatever differences and antagonisms existed between large and small landowners, between monopolistic and competitive business, between liberal bourgeois and reactionary feudal overlords, between domestic and foreign interests, were largely submerged on all important occasions by the over-riding *common* interest in staving off socialism.

The possibility of solving the economic and political deadlock prevailing in the underdeveloped countries on lines of a progressive capitalism all but disappeared. Entering the alliance with all other segments of the ruling class, the capitalist middle-classes yielded one strategic position after another. Afraid that a quarrel with the landed gentry might be exploited by the radical populist movement, the middle-classes abandoned all progressive attitudes in agrarian matters. Afraid that a conflict with the church and the military might weaken the political authority of the government, the middle-classes moved away from all liberal and pacifist currents. Afraid that hostility toward foreign interests might deprive them of foreign support in a case of a revolutionary emergency, the native capitalists deserted their previous anti-imperialist, nationalist platforms.

The peculiar mechanisms of political interaction characteristic of all underdeveloped (and perhaps not only underdeveloped) countries thus operated at full speed. The aboriginal failure of the middle-classes to provide inspiration and leadership to the popular masses pushed those masses into the camp of socialist radicalism. The growth of radicalism pushed the middle-classes into an alliance with the aristocratic and monopolistic reaction. This alliance, cemented by common interest and common fear, pushed the populist forces still further along the road of radicalism and revolt. The outcome was a polarization of society with very little left between the poles. By permitting this polarization to develop, by abandoning the common man and resigning the task of reorganizing society on new, progressive lines, the capitalist middle-classes threw away their historical chance of assuming effective control over the destinies of their nations, and of directing the gathering popular storm against the fortresses of feudalism and reaction. Its blazing fire turned thus against the entirety of existing economic and social institutions.

III

The economic and political order maintained by the ruling coalition of owning classes finds itself invariably at odds with all the urgent needs of the underdeveloped countries. Neither the social fabric that it embodies nor the institutions that rest upon it are conducive to progressive economic development. The only way to provide for economic growth and to prevent a continuous deterioration of living standards (apart from mass emigration unacceptable to other countries) is to assure a steady increase of total output—at least large enough to offset the rapid growth of population.

An obvious source of such an increase is the utilization of available unutilized or underutilized resources. A large part of this reservoir of dormant productive potentialities is the vast multitude of entirely unemployed or ineffectively employed manpower. There is no way of employing it usefully in agriculture, where the marginal productivity of labor tends to zero. They could be provided with opportunities for productive work only by transfer to industrial pursuits. For this to be feasible large investments in industrial plant and facilities have to be undertaken. Under prevailing conditions such investments are not forthcoming for a number of important and interrelated reasons.

With a very uneven distribution of a very small aggregate income (and wealth), large individual incomes exceeding what could be regarded as "reasonable" requirements for current consumption accrue as a rule to a relatively small group of high-income receivers. Many of them are large landowners maintaining a feudal style of life with large outlays on housing, servants, travel, and other luxuries. Their "requirements for consumption" are so high that there is only little room for savings. Only relatively insignificant amounts are left to be spent on improvements of agricultural estates.

Other members of the "upper crust" receiving incomes markedly surpassing "reasonable" levels of consumption are wealthy businessmen. For social reasons briefly mentioned above, their consumption too is very much larger than it would have been were they brought up in the puritan tradition of a bourgeois civilization. Their drive to accumulate and to expand their enterprises is continuously counteracted by the urgent desire to imitate in their living habits the socially dominant "old families," to prove by their conspicuous outlays on the amenities of rich life that they are socially (and therefore also politically) not inferior to their aristocratic partners in the ruling coalition.

But if this tendency curtails the volume of savings that could have been amassed by the urban high-income receivers, their will to re-invest their funds in productive enterprises is effectively curbed by a strong reluctance to damage their carefully erected monopolistic market positions through creation of additional productive capacity, and by absence of suitable investment opportunities—paradoxical as this may sound with reference to underdeveloped countries.

The deficiency of investment opportunities stems to a large extent from the structure and the limitations of the existing effective demand. With very low living standards the bulk of the aggregate money income of the population is spent on food and relatively primitive items of clothing and household necessities. These are available at low prices, and investment of large funds in plant and facilities that could produce this type of commodities more cheaply rarely promises attractive returns. Nor does it appear profitable to develop major enterprises the output of which would cater to the requirements of the rich. Large as their individual purchases of various luxuries may be, their aggregate spending on each of them is not sufficient to support the development of an elaborate luxury industry—in particular since the "snob" character of prevailing tastes renders only imported luxury articles true marks of social distinction.

Finally, the limited demand for investment goods precludes the building up of a machinery or equipment industry. Such mass consumption goods as are lacking, and such quantities of luxury goods as are purchased by the well-to-do, as well as the comparatively small quantities of investment goods needed by industry, are thus imported from abroad in exchange for domestic agricultural products and raw materials.

This leaves the expansion of exportable raw materials output as a major outlet for investment activities. There the possibilities are greatly influenced, however, by the technology of the production of most raw materials as well as by the nature of the markets to be served. Many raw materials, in particular oil, metals, certain industrial crops, have to be produced on a large scale if costs are to be kept low and satisfactory returns assured. Large-scale production, however, calls for large investments, so large indeed as to exceed the potentialities of the native capitalists in backward countries. Production of raw materials for a distant market entails, moreover, much larger risks than those encountered in domestic business. The difficulty of foreseeing accurately such things as receptiveness of the world markets, prices obtainable in competition with other countries, volume of output in other parts of the world, etc., sharply reduces the interest of native capitalists in these lines of business. They become to a predominant extent the domain of foreigners who, financially stronger, have at the same time much closer contacts with foreign outlets of their products.

The shortage of investible funds and the lack of investment opportunities represent two aspects of the same problem. A great number of investment projects, unprofitable under prevailing conditions, could be most promising in a general environment of economic expansion.

In backward areas a new industrial venture must frequently, if not always, break virgin ground. It has no functioning economic system to draw upon. It has to organize with its own efforts not only the productive process *within* its own confines, it must provide in addition for all the necessary *outside* arrangements essential to its operations. It does not enjoy the benefits of "external economies."

There can be no doubt that the absence of external economies, the inadequacy of the economic milieu in underdeveloped countries, constituted everywhere an important deterrent to investment in industrial projects. There is no way of rapidly bridging the gap. Large-scale investment is predicated upon large-scale investment. Roads, electric power stations, railroads, and houses have to be built *before* businessmen find it profitable to erect factories, to invest their funds in new industrial enterprises.

Yet investing in road building, financing construction of canals and power stations, organizing large housing projects, etc., transcend by far the financial and mental horizon of capitalists in underdeveloped countries. Not only are their financial resources too small for such ambitious projects, but their background and habits militate against entering commitments of this type. Brought up in the tradition of merchandizing and manufacturing consumers' goods—as is characteristic of an early phase of capitalist development—businessmen in underdeveloped countries are accustomed to rapid turnover, large but short-term risks, and correspondingly high rates of profit. Sinking funds in enterprises where profitability could manifest itself only in the course of many years is a largely unknown and unattractive departure. The difference between social and private rationality that exists in any market and profit-determined economy is thus particularly striking in underdeveloped countries.

. . .

But could not the required increase in total output be attained by better utilization of land—another unutilized or inadequately utilized productive factor?

There is usually no land that is both fit for agricultural purposes and at the same time readily accessible. Such terrain as could be cultivated but is actually not being tilled would usually require considerable investment before becoming suitable for settlement. In underdeveloped countries such outlays for agricultural purposes are just as unattractive to private interests as they are for industrial purposes.

On the other hand, more adequate employment of land that is already used in agriculture runs into considerable difficulties. Very few improvements that would be necessary in order to increase productivity can be carried out within the narrow confines of small-peasant holdings. Not only are the peasants in underdeveloped countries utterly unable to pay for such innovations, but the size of their lots offers no justification for their introduction.

Owners of large estates are in a sense in no better position. With limited savings at their disposal they do not have the funds to finance expensive improvements in their enterprises, nor do such projects appear profitable in view of the high prices of imported equipment in relation to prices of agricultural produce and wages of agricultural labor.

Approached thus *via* agriculture, an expansion of total output would also seem to be attainable only through the development of industry. Only through increase of industrial productivity could agricultural machinery, fertilizers, electric power, etc., be brought within the reach of the agricultural producer. Only through an increased demand for labor could agricultural wages be raised and a stimulus provided for a modernization of the agricultural economy. Only through the growth of industrial production could agricultural labor displaced by the machine be absorbed in productive employment.

Monopolistic market structures, shortage of savings, lack of external economies, the divergence of social and private rationalities do not exhaust, however, the list of obstacles blocking the way of privately organized industrial expansion in underdeveloped countries. Those obstacles have to be considered against the background of the general feeling of uncertainty prevailing in all backward areas. The coalition of the owning classes formed under pressure of fear, and held together by the real or imagined danger of social upheavals, provokes continuously more or less threatening rumblings under the outwardly calm political surface. The social and political tensions to which that coalition is a political response are not liquidated by the prevailing system; they are only repressed. Normal and quiet as the daily routine frequently appears, the more enlightened and understanding members of the ruling groups in underdeveloped countries sense the inherent instability of the political and social order. Occasional outbursts of popular dissatisfaction assuming the form of peasant uprisings, violent strikes or local guerrilla warfare, serve from time to time as grim reminders of the latent crisis.

In such a climate there is no will to invest on the part of monied people; in such a climate there is no enthusiasm for long-term projects; in such a climate the motto of all participants in the privileges offered by society is *carpe diem*.

IV

Could not, however, an appropriate policy on the part of the governments involved change the political climate and facilitate economic growth? In our time, when faith in the manipulative omnipotence of the State has all but displaced analysis of its social structure and understanding of its political and economic functions, the tendency is obviously to answer these questions in the affirmative.

Looking at the matter purely mechanically, it would appear indeed that much could be done by a well-advised regime in an underdeveloped country to provide for a relatively rapid increase of total output, accompanied by an improvement of the living standards of the population. There are a number of measures that the government could take in an effort to overcome backwardness. A fiscal policy could be adopted that by means of capital levies and a highly progressive tax system would syphon off all surplus purchasing power, and in this way eliminate non-essential consumption. The savings thus enforced could be channelled by the government into productive investment. Power stations, railroads, highways, irrigation systems, and soil improvements could be organized by the State with a view to creating an economic environment conducive to the growth of productivity.

Technical schools on various levels could be set up by the public authority to furnish industrial training to young people as well as to adult workers and the unemployed. A system of scholarships could be introduced rendering acquisition of skills accessible to low-income strata.

Wherever private capital refrains from undertaking certain industrial projects, or wherever monopolistic controls block the necessary expansion of plant and facilities in particular industries, the government could step in and make the requisite investments. Where developmental possibilities that are rewarding in the long-run appear unprofitable during the initial period of gestation and learning, and are therefore beyond the horizon of private businessmen, the government could undertake to shoulder the short-run losses.

In addition an entire arsenal of "preventive" devices is at the disposal of the authorities. Inflationary pressures resulting from developmental activities (private and public) could be reduced or even eliminated, if outlays on investment projects could be offset by a corresponding and simultaneous contraction of spending elsewhere in the economic system. What this would call for is a taxation policy that would effectively remove from the income stream amounts sufficient to neutralize the investment-caused expansion of aggregate money income.

In the interim, and as a supplement, speculation in scarce goods and excessive profiteering in essential commodities could be suppressed by rigorous price controls. An equitable distribution of mass consumption goods in short supply could be assured by rationing. Diversion of resources in high demand to luxury purposes could be prevented by allocation and priority schemes. Strict supervision of transactions involving foreign exchanges could render capital flight, expenditure of limited foreign funds on luxury imports, pleasure trips abroad, and the like, impossible.

What the combination of these measures would accomplish is a radical change in the structure of effective demand in the underdeveloped country, and a reallocation of productive resources to satisfy society's need for economic development. By curtailing consumption of the higher-income groups, the amounts of savings available for investment purposes could be markedly increased. The squandering of limited supplies of foreign exchange on capital flight, or on importation of redundant foreign goods and services, could be prevented, and the foreign funds thus saved could be used for the acquisition of foreign-made machinery needed for economic development. The reluctance of private interests to engage in enterprises that are socially necessary, but may not promise rich returns in the short-run, would be prevented from determining the economic life of the backward country.

The mere listing of the steps that would have to be undertaken, in order to assure an expansion of output and income in an underdeveloped country, reveals the utter implausibility of the view that they could be carried out by the governments existing in most underdeveloped countries. The reason for this inability is only to a negligible extent the nonexistence of the competent and honest civil service needed for the administration of the program. A symptom itself of the political and social marasmus prevailing in underdeveloped countries, this lack cannot be remedied without attacking the underlying causes. Nor does it touch anything near the roots of the matter to lament the lack of satisfactory tax policies in backward countries, or to deplore the absence of tax "morale" and "discipline" among the civic virtues of their populations.

The crucial fact rendering the realization of a developmental program illusory is the political and social structure of the governments in power. The alliance of property-owning classes controlling the destinies of most underdeveloped countries cannot be expected to design and to execute a set of measures running counter to each and all of their immediate vested interests. If to appease the restive public, blueprints of progressive measures such as agrarian reform, equitable tax legislation, etc., are officially announced, their enforcement is wilfully sabotaged The government, representing a political compromise between landed and business interests, cannot suppress the wasteful management of landed estates and the conspicuous consumption on the part of the aristocracy; cannot suppress monopolistic abuses, profiteering, capital flights, and extravagant living on the part of businessmen. It cannot curtail or abandon its lavish appropriations for a military and police establishment, providing attractive careers to the scions of wealthy families and a profitable outlet for armaments produced by their parents—quite apart from the fact that this establishment serves as the main protection against possible popular revolt. Set up to guard and to abet the existing property rights and privileges, it cannot become the architect of a policy calculated to destroy the privileges standing in the way of economic progress and to place the property and the incomes derived from it at the service of society as a whole.

Nor is there much to be said for the "intermediate" position which, granting the essential incompatibility of a well-conceived and vigorously executed developmental program with the political and social institutions prevailing in most underdeveloped countries, insists that at least *some* of the requisite measures could be carried out by the existing political authorities. This school of thought overlooks entirely the weakness, if not the complete absence, of social and political forces that could induce the necessary concessions on the part of the ruling coalition. By background and political upbringing, too myopic and self-interested to permit the slightest encroachments upon their inherited positions and cherished privileges, the upper-classes in underdeveloped countries resist doggedly all pressures in that direction. Every time such pressures grow in strength they succeed in cementing anew the alliance of all conservative elements, by decrying all attempts at reform as assaults on the very foundations of society.

Even if measures like progressive taxation, capital levies, and foreign exchange controls could be enforced by the corrupt officials operating in the demoralized business communities of underdeveloped countries, such enforcement would to a large extent defeat its original purpose. Where businessmen do not invest, unless in expectation of lavish profits, a taxation system succeeding in confiscating large parts of these profits is bound to kill private investment. Where doing business or operating landed estates is attractive mainly because it permits luxurious living, foreign exchange controls preventing the importation of luxury goods are bound to blight enterprise. Where the only stimulus to hard work on the part of intellectuals, technicians, and civil servants is the chance of partaking in the privileges of the ruling class, a policy aiming at the reduction of inequality of social status and income is bound to smother effort.

The injection of planning into a society living in the twilight between feudalism and capitalism cannot but result in additional corruption, larger and more artful evasions of the law, and more brazen abuses of authority.

V

There would seem to be no exit from the impasse. The ruling coalition of interests does not abdicate of its own volition, nor does it change its character in response to incantation. Although its individual members occasionally leave the sinking ship physically or financially (or in both ways), the property-owning classes as a whole are as a rule grimly determined to hold fast to their political and economic entrenchments.

If the threat of social upheaval assumes dangerous proportions, they tighten their grip on political life and move rapidly in the direction of unbridled reaction and military dictatorship. Making use of favourable international opportunities and of ideological and social affinities to ruling groups in other countries, they solicit foreign economic and sometimes military aid in their efforts to stave off the impending disaster.

Such aid is likely to be given to them by foreign governments regarding them as an evil less to be feared than the social revolution that would sweep them out of power. This attitude of their friends and protectors abroad is no less short-sighted than their own.

The adjustment of the social and political conditions in underdeveloped countries to the urgent needs of economic development can be postponed; it cannot be indefinitely avoided. In the past, it could have been delayed by decades or even centuries. In our age it is a matter of years. Bolstering the political system of power existing in backward countries by providing it with military support may temporarily block the eruption of the volcano; it cannot stop the subterranean gathering of explosive forces.

Economic help in the form of loans and grants given to the governments of backward countries, to enable them to promote a measure of economic progress, is no substitute for the domestic changes that are mandatory if economic development is to be attained.

Such help, in fact, may actually do more harm than good. Possibly permitting the importation of some foreign-made machinery and equipment for government or business sponsored investment projects, but not accompanied by any of the steps that are needed to assure healthy economic growth, foreign assistance thus supplied may set off an inflationary spiral increasing and aggravating the existing social and economic tensions in underdeveloped countries.

If, as is frequently the case, these loans or grants from abroad are tied to the fulfilment of certain conditions on the part of the receiving country regarding their use, the resulting investment may be directed in such channels as to conform more to the interests of the lending than to those of the borrowing country. Where economic advice as a form of "technical assistance" is supplied to the underdeveloped country, and its acceptance is made a prerequisite to eligibility for financial aid, this advice often pushes the governments of underdeveloped countries toward policies, ideologically or otherwise attractive to the foreign experts dispensing economic counsel, but not necessarily conducive to economic development of the "benefitted" countries. Nationalism and xenophobia are thus strengthened in backward areas—additional fuel for political restiveness.

For backward countries to enter the road of economic growth and social progress, the political framework of their existence has to be drastically revamped. The alliance between feudal landlords, industrial royalists, and the capitalist middle-classes has to be broken. The keepers of the past cannot be the builders of the future. Such progressive and enterprising elements as exist in backward societies have to obtain the possibility of leading their countries in the direction of economic and social growth.

What France, Britain, and America have accomplished through their own revolutions has to be attained in backward countries by a combined effort of popular forces, enlightened government, and unselfish foreign help. This combined effort must sweep away the holdover institutions of a defunct age, must change the political and social climate in the under-developed countries, and must imbue their nations with a new spirit of enterprise and freedom.

Should it prove too late in the historical process for the bourgeoisie to rise to its responsibilities in backward areas, should the long experience of servitude and accommodation to the feudal past have reduced the forces of progressive capitalism to impotence, the backward countries of the world will inevitably turn to economic planning and social collectivism. If the capitalist world outlook of economic and social progress, propelled by enlightened self-interest, should prove unable to triumph over the con-servatism of inherited positions and traditional privileges, if the capitalist promise of advance and reward to the efficient, the industrious, the able, should not displace the feudal assurance of security and power to the well-bred, the well-connected and the conformist—a new social ethos will become the spirit and guide of a new age. It will be the ethos of the collective effort, the creed of the predominance of the interests of society over the interests of selected few.

The transition may be abrupt and painful. The land not given to the peasants legally may be taken by them forcibly. High incomes not confis-cated through taxation may be eliminated by outright expropriation. Cor-rupt officials not retired in orderly fashion may be removed by violent action.

Which way the historical wheel will turn and in which way the crisis in the backward countries will find its final solution will depend in the main on whether the capitalist middle-classes in the backward areas, and the rulers of the advanced industrial nations of the world, overcome their fear and myopia. Or are they too spell-bound by their narrowly conceived selfish interests, too blinded by their hatred of progress, grown so senile in these latter days of the capitalist age, as to commit suicide out of fear of death?

8

The Development of Underdevelopment

Andre Gunder Frank

We cannot hope to formulate adequate development theory and policy for the majority of the world's population who suffer from underdevelopment without first learning how their past economic and social history gave rise to their present underdevelopment. Yet most historians study only the developed metropolitan countries and pay scant attention to the colonial and underdeveloped lands. For this reason most of our theoretical categories and guides to development policy have been distilled exclusively from the historical experience of the European and North American advanced capitalist nations.

Since the historical experience of the colonial and underdeveloped countries has demonstrably been quite different, available theory therefore fails to reflect the past of the underdeveloped part of the world entirely, and reflects the past of the world as a whole only in part. More important, our ignorance of the underdeveloped countries' history leads us to assume that their past and indeed their present resembles earlier stages of the history of the now developed countries. This ignorance and this assumption lead us into serious misconceptions about contemporary underdevelopment and development. Further, most studies of development and underdevelopment fail to take account of the economic and other relations between the metropolis and its economic colonies throughout the history of the world-wide expansion and development of the mercantilist and capitalist system. Consequently, most of our theory fails to explain the structure and development of the capitalist system as a whole and to acccount for its simultaneous generation of underdevelopment in some of its parts and of economic development in others.

It is generally held that economic development occurs in a succession of capitalist stages and that today's underdeveloped countries are still in a stage, sometimes depicted as an original stage of history, through which the now developed countries passed long ago. Yet even a modest acquaintance with history shows that underdevelopment is not original or traditional and that neither the past nor the present of the underdeveloped

Reprinted from *Monthly Review*, Vol. 18, No. 4 (September 1966), pp. 17-31, by permission of Monthly Review Press. Copyright © 1969 by Andre Gunder Frank. All Rights Reserved.

countries resembles in any important respect the past of the now developed countries. The now developed countries were never *under*developed, though they may have been *un*developed. It is also widely believed that the contemporary underdevelopment of a country can be understood as the product or reflection solely of its own economic, political, social, and cultural characteristics or structure. Yet historical research demonstrates that contemporary underdevelopment is in large part the historical product of past and continuing economic and other relations between the satellite underdeveloped and the now developed metropolitan countries. Furthermore, these relations are an essential part of the structure and development of the capitalist system on a world scale as a whole. A related and also largely erroneous view is that the development of these underdeveloped countries and, within them of their most underdeveloped domestic areas, must and will be generated or stimulated by diffusing capital, institutions, values, etc., to them from the international and national capitalist metropoles. Historical perspective based on the underdeveloped countries' past experience suggests that on the contrary in the underdeveloped countries economic development can now occur only independently of most of these relations of diffusion.

Evident inequalities of income and differences in culture have led many observers to see "dual" societies and economies in the underdeveloped countries. Each of the two parts is supposed to have a history of its own, a structure, and a contemporary dynamic largely independent of the other. Supposedly, only one part of the economy and society has been importantly affected by intimate economic relations with the "outside" capitalist world; and that part, it is held, became modern, capitalist, and relatively developed precisely because of this contact. The other part is widely regarded as variously isolated, subsistence-based, feudal, or precapitalist, and therefore more underdeveloped.

I believe on the contrary that the entire "dual society" thesis is false and that the policy recommendations to which it leads will, if acted upon, serve only to intensify and perpetuate the very conditions of underdevelopment they are supposedly designed to remedy.

A mounting body of evidence suggests, and I am confident that future historical research will confirm, that the expansion of the capitalist system over the past centuries effectively and entirely penetrated even the apparently most isolated sectors of the underdeveloped world. Therefore, the economic, political, social, and cultural institutions and relations we now observe there are the products of the historical development of the capitalist system no less than are the seemingly more modern or capitalist features of the national metropoles of these underdeveloped countries. Analogously to the relations between development and underdevelopment on the international level, the contemporary underdeveloped institutions of the so-called backward or feudal domestic areas of an underdeveloped country are no less the product of the single historical process of capitalist development than are the so-called capitalist institutions of the supposedly more progressive areas. In this paper I should like to sketch the kinds of evidence which support this thesis and at the same time indicate lines along which further study and research could fruitfully proceed.

II

The Secretary General of the Latin American Center for Research in the Social Sciences writes in that Center's journal: "The privileged position of the city has its origin in the colonial period. It was founded by the Conqueror to serve the same ends that it still serves today; to incorporate the indigenous population into the economy brought and developed by that Conqueror and his descendants. The regional city was an instrument of conquest and is still today an instrument of domination."[1] The Instituto Nacional Indigenista (National Indian Institute) of Mexico confirms this observation when it notes that "the mestizo population, in fact, always lives in a city, a center of an intercultural region, which acts as the metropolis of a zone of indigenous population and which maintains with the underdeveloped communities an intimate relation which links the center with the satellite communities."[2] The Institute goes on to point out that "between the mestizos who live in the nuclear city of the region and the Indians who live in the peasant hinterland there is in reality a closer economic and social interdependence than might at first glance appear" and that the provincial metropoles "by being centers of intercourse are also centers of exploitation."[3]

Thus these metropolis-satellite relations are not limited to the imperial or international level but penetrate and structure the very economic, political, and social life of the Latin American colonies and countries. Just as the colonial and national capital and its export sector become the satellite of the Iberian (and later of other) metropoles of the world economic system, this satellite immediately becomes a colonial and then a national metropolis with respect to the productive sectors and population of the interior. Furthermore, the provincial capitals, which thus are themselves satellites of the national metropolis—and through the latter of the world metropolis—are in turn provincial centers around which their own local satellites orbit. Thus, a whole chain of constellations of metropoles and satellites relates all parts of the whole system from its metropolitan center in Europe or the United States to the farthest outpost in the Latin American countryside.

When we examine this metropolis-satellite structure, we find that each of the satellites, including now-underdeveloped Spain and Portugal, serves as an instrument to suck capital or economic surplus out of its own satellites and to channel part of this surplus to the world metropolis of which all are satellites. Moreover, each national and local metropolis serves to impose and maintain the monopolistic structure and exploitative relationship of this system (as the Instituto Nacional Indigenista of Mexico calls it) as long as it serves the interests of the metropoles which take advantage of this global, national, and local structure to promote their own development and the enrichment of their ruling classes.

These are the principal and still surviving structural characteristics which were implanted in Latin America by the Conquest. Beyond examining the establishment of this colonial structure in its historical context, the proposed approach calls for study of the development—and underdevelopment—of these metropoles and satellites of Latin America throughout the following and still continuing historical process. In this way we can understand why there were and still are tendencies in the Latin American and world capitalist structure which seem to lead to the development of the metropolis and the underdevelopment of the satellite and why, particularly, the satellized national, regional, and local metropoles in Latin America find that their economic development is at best a limited or underdeveloped development.

III

That present underdevelopment of Latin America is the result of its centuries-long participation in the process of world capitalist development, I believe I have shown in my case studies of the economic and social histories of Chile and Brazil.[4] My study of Chilean history suggests that the Conquest not only incorporated this country fully into the expansion and development of the world mercantile and later industrial capitalist system but that it also introduced the monopolistic metropolis-satellite structure and development of capitalism into the Chilean domestic economy and society itself. This structure then penetrated and permeated all of Chile very quickly. Since that time and in the course of world and Chilean history during the epochs of colonialism, free trade, imperialism, and the present, Chile has become increasingly marked by the economic, social, and political structure of satellite underdevelopment. This development of underdevelopment continues today, both in Chile's still increasing satellization by the world metropolis and through the ever more acute polarization of Chile's domestic economy.

The history of Brazil is perhaps the clearest case of both national and regional development of underdevelopment. The expansion of the world economy since the beginning of the sixteenth century successively converted the Northeast, the Minas Gerais interior, the North, and the Center-South (Rio de Janeiro, São Paulo, and Paraná) into export economies and incorporated them into the structure and development of the world capitalist system. Each of these regions experienced what may have appeared as economic development during the period of its respective golden age. But it was a satellite development which was neither self-generating nor self-perpetuating. As the market or the productivity of the first three regions declined, foreign and domestic economic interest in them waned; and they were left to develop the underdevelopment they live today. In the fourth region, the coffee economy experienced a similar though not yet quite as serious fate (though the development of a synthetic coffee substitute promises to deal it a mortal blow in the not too distant future). All of this historical evidence contradicts the generally accepted theses that Latin America suffers from a dual society or from the survival of feudal institutions and that these are important obstacles to its economic development.

IV

During the First World War, however, and even more during the Great Depression and the Second World War, São Paulo began to build up an industrial establishment which is the largest in Latin America today. The question arises whether this industrial development did or can break Brazil out of the cycle of satellite development and underdevelopment which has characterized its other regions and national history within the capitalist system so far. I believe that the answer is no. Domestically the evidence so far is fairly clear. The development of industry in São Paulo has not brought greater riches to the other regions of Brazil. Instead, it converted them into internal colonial satellites, de-capitalized them further, and con-solidated or even deepened their underdevelopment. There is little evidence to suggest that this process is likely to be reversed in the foreseeable future except insofar as the provincial poor migrate and become the poor of the metropolitan cities. Externally, the evidence is that although the initial development of São Paulo's industry was relatively autonomous it is being increasingly satellized by the world capitalist metropolis and its future development possibilities are increasingly restricted.[5] This development, my studies lead me to believe, also appears destined to limited or underdevel-oped development as long as it takes place in the present economic, politi-cal, and social framework.

We must conclude, in short, that underdevelopment is not due to the survival of archaic institutions and the existence of capital shortage in regions that have remained isolated from the stream of world history. On the contrary, underdevelopment was and still is generated by the very same historical process which also generated economic development: the devel-opment of capitalism itself. This view, I am glad to say, is gaining adher-ents among students of Latin America and is proving its worth in shedding new light on the problems of the area and in affording a better perspective for the formulation of theory and policy.[6]

V

The same historical and structural approach can also lead to better devel-opment theory and policy by generating a series of hypotheses about development and underdevelopment such as those I am testing in my current research. The hypotheses are derived from the empirical observa-tion and theoretical assumption that within this world-embracing metropo-lis-satellite structure the metropoles tend to develop and the satellites to underdevelop. The first hypothesis has already been mentioned above: that in contrast to the development of the world metropolis which is no one's satellite, the development of the national and other subordinate metropoles is limited by their satellite status. It is perhaps more difficult to test this hypothesis than the following ones because part of its confirmation depends on the test of the other hypotheses. Nonetheless, this hypothesis appears to be generally confirmed by the non-autonomous and unsatisfactory eco-nomic and especially industrial development of Latin America's national metropoles, as documented in the studies already cited. The most important and at the same time most confirmatory examples are the metropolitan regions of Buenos Aires and São Paulo whose growth only began in the nineteenth century, was therefore largely untrammelled by any colonial heritage, but was and remains a satellite development largely dependent on the outside metropolis, first of Britain and then of the United States.

A second hypothesis is that the satellites experience their greatest economic development and especially their most classically capitalist industrial development if and when their ties to their metropolis are weakest. This hypothesis is almost diametrically opposed to the generally accepted thesis that development in the underdeveloped countries follows from the greatest degree of contact with and diffusion from the metropolitan developed countries. This hypothesis seems to be confirmed by two kinds of relative isolation that Latin America has experienced in the course of its history. One is the temporary isolation caused by the crises of war or depression in the world metropolis. Apart from minor ones, five periods of such major crises stand out and seem to confirm the hypothesis. These are: the European (and especially Spanish) Depression of the seventeenth century, the Napoleonic Wars, the First World War, the Depression of the 1930's, and the Second World War. It is clearly established and generally recognized that the most important recent industrial development—especially of Argentina, Brazil, and Mexico, but also of other countries such as Chile—has taken place precisely during the periods of the two World Wars and the intervening Depression. Thanks to the consequent loosening of trade and investment ties during these periods, the satellites initiated marked autonomous industrialization and growth. Historical research demonstrates that the same thing happened in Latin America during Europe's seventeenth-century depression. Manufacturing grew in the Latin American countries, and several of them such as Chile became exporters of manufactured goods. The Napoleonic Wars gave rise to independence movements in Latin America, and these should perhaps also be interpreted as confirming the development hypothesis in part.

The other kind of isolation which tends to confirm the second hypothesis is the geographic and economic isolation of regions which at one time were relatively weakly tied to and poorly integrated into the mercantilist and capitalist system. My preliminary research suggests that in Latin America it was these regions which initiated and experienced the most promising self-generating economic development of the classical industrial capitalist type. The most important regional cases probably are Tucumán and Asunción, as well as other cities such as Mendoza and Rosario, in the interior of Argentina and Paraguay during the end of the eighteenth and the beginning of the nineteenth centuries. Seventeenth- and eighteenth-century São Paulo, long before coffee was grown there, is another example. Perhaps Antioquia in Colombia and Puebla and Querétaro in Mexico are other examples. In its own way, Chile was also an example since, before the sea route around the Horn was opened, this country was relatively isolated at the end of the long voyage from Europe via Panama. All of these regions became manufacturing centers and even exporters, usually of textiles, during the periods preceding their effective incorporation as satellites into the colonial, national, and world capitalist system.

Internationally, of course, the classic case of industrialization through non-participation as a satellite in the capitalist world system is obviously that of Japan after the Meiji Restoration. Why, one may ask, was resource-poor but unsatellized Japan able to industrialize so quickly at the end of the century while resource-rich Latin American countries and Russia were not able to do so and the latter was easily beaten by Japan in the War of 1904 after the same forty years of development efforts? The second hypothesis suggests that the fundamental reason is that Japan was not satellized either during the Tokugawa or the Meiji period and therefore did not have its development structurally limited as did the countries which were so satellized.

VI

A corollary of the second hypothesis is that when the metropolis recovers from its crisis and re-establishes the trade and investment ties which fully re-incorporate the satellites into the system, or when the metropolis expands to incorporate previously isolated regions into the world-wide system, the previous development and industrialization of these regions is choked off or channelled into directions which are not self-perpetuating and promising. This happened after each of the five crises cited above. The renewed expansion of trade and the spread of economic liberalism in the eighteenth and nineteenth centuries choked off and reversed the manufacturing development which Latin America had experienced during the seventeenth century, and in some places at the beginning of the nineteenth. After the First World War, the new national industry of Brazil suffered serious consequences from American economic invasion. The increase in the growth rate of Gross National Product and particularly of industrialization throughout Latin America was again reversed and industry became increasingly satellized after the Second World War and especially after the post-Korean War recovery and expansion of the metropolis. Far from having become more developed since then, industrial sectors of Brazil and most conspicuously of Argentina have become structurally more and more underdeveloped and less and less able to generate continued industrialization and/or sustain development of the economy. This process, from which India also suffers, is reflected in a whole gamut of balance-of-payments, inflationary, and other economic and political difficulties, and promises to yield to no solution short of far-reaching structural change.

Our hypothesis suggests that fundamentally the same process occurred even more dramatically with the incorporation into the system of previously unsatellized regions. The expansion of Buenos Aires as a satellite of Great Britain and the introduction of free trade in the interest of the ruling groups of both metropoles destroyed the manufacturing and much of the remainder of the economic base of the previously relatively prosperous interior almost entirely. Manufacturing was destroyed by foreign competition, lands were taken and concentrated into latifundia by the rapaciously growing export economy, intraregional distribution of income became much more unequal, and the previously developing regions became simple satellites of Buenos Aires and through it of London. The provincial centers did not yield to satellization without a struggle. This metropolis-satellite conflict was much of the cause of the long political and armed struggle between the Unitarists in Buenos Aires and the Federalists in the provinces, and it may be said to have been the sole important cause of the War of the Triple Alliance in which Buenos Aires, Montevideo, and Rio de Janeiro, encouraged and helped by London, destroyed not only the autonomously developing economy of Paraguay but killed off nearly all of its population which was unwilling to give in. Though this is no doubt the most spectacular example which tends to confirm the hypothesis, I believe that historical research on the satellization of previously relatively independent yeoman-farming and incipient manufacturing regions such as the Caribbean islands will confirm it further.[7] These regions did not have a chance against the forces of expanding and developing capitalism, and their own development had to be sacrificed to that of others. The economy and industry of Argentina, Brazil, and other countries which have experienced the effects of metropolitan recovery since the Second World War are today suffering much the same fate, if fortunately still in lesser degree.

VII

A third major hypothesis derived from the metropolis-satellite structure is that the regions which are the most underdeveloped and feudal-seeming today are the ones which had the closest ties to the metropolis in the past. They are the regions which were the greatest exporters of primary products to and the biggest sources of capital for the world metropolis and which were abandoned by the metropolis when for one reason or another business fell off. This hypothesis also contradicts the generally held thesis that the source of a region's underdevelopment is its isolation and its precapitalist institutions.

This hypothesis seems to be amply confirmed by the former super-satellite development and present ultra-underdevelopment of the once sugar-exporting West Indies, Northeastern Brazil, the ex-mining districts of Minas Gerais in Brazil, highland Peru, and Bolivia, and the central Mexican states of Guanajuato, Zacatecas, and others whose names were made world famous centuries ago by their silver. There surely are no major regions in Latin America which are today more cursed by under-development and poverty; yet all of these regions, like Bengal in India, once provided the life blood of mercantile and industrial capitalist development —in the metropolis. These regions' participation in the development of the world capitalist system gave them, already in their golden age, the typical structure of underdevelopment of a capitalist export economy. When the market for their sugar or the wealth of their mines disappeared and the metropolis abandoned them to their own devices, the already existing economic, political, and social structure of these regions prohibited autonomous generation of economic development and left them no alternative but to turn in upon themselves and to degenerate into the ultra-underdevelopment we find there today.

VIII

These considerations suggest two further and related hypotheses. One is that the latifundium, irrespective of whether it appears as a plantation or a hacienda today, was typically born as a commercial enterprise which created for itself the institutions which permitted it to respond to increased demand in the world or national market by expanding the amount of its land, capital, and labor and to increase the supply of its products. The fifth hypothesis is that the latifundia which appear isolated, subsistence-based, and semi-feudal today saw the demand for their products or their productive capacity decline and that they are to be found principally in the above-named former agricultural and mining export regions whose economic activity declined in general. These two hypotheses run counter to the notions of most people, and even to the opinions of some historians and other students of the subject, according to whom the historical roots and socio-economic causes of Latin American latifundia and agrarian institutions are to be found in the transfer of feudal institutions from Europe and/or in economic depression.

The evidence to test these hypotheses is not open to easy general inspection and requires detailed analyses of many cases. Nonetheless, some important confirmatory evidence is available. The growth of the latifundium in nineteenth-century Argentina and Cuba is a clear case in support of the fourth hypothesis and can in no way be attributed to the transfer of feudal institutions during colonial times. The same is evidently the case of the postrevolutionary and contemporary resurgence of latifundia particularly in the North of Mexico, which produce for the American market, and of similar ones on the coast of Peru and the new coffee regions of Brazil. The conversion of previously yeoman-farming Caribbean islands, such as Barbados, into sugar-exporting economies at various times between the seventeenth and twentieth centuries and the resulting rise of the latifundia in these islands would seem to confirm the fourth hypothesis as well. In Chile, the rise of the latifundium and the creation of the institutions of servitude which later came to be called feudal occurred in the eighteenth century and have been conclusively shown to be the result of and response to the opening of a market for Chilean wheat in Lima.[8] Even the growth and consolidation of the latifundium in seventeenth-century Mexico—which most expert students have attributed to a depression of the economy caused by the decline of mining and a shortage of Indian labor and to a consequent turning in upon itself and ruralization of the economy —occurred at a time when urban population and demand were growing, food shortages became acute, food prices skyrocketed, and the profitability of other economic activities such as mining and foreign trade declined.[9] All of these and other factors rendered hacienda agriculture more profitable. Thus, even this case would seem to confirm the hypothesis that the growth of the latifundium and its feudal-seeming conditions of servitude in Latin America has always been and still is the commercial response to increased demand and that it does not represent the transfer or survival of alien institutions that have remained beyond the reach of capitalist development. The emergence of latifundia, which today really are more or less (though not entirely) isolated, might then be attributed to the causes advanced in the fifth hypothesis—i.e., the decline of previously profitable agricultural enterprises whose capital was, and whose currently produced economic surplus still is, transferred elsewhere by owners and merchants who frequently are the same persons or families. Testing this hypothesis requires still more detailed analysis, some of which I have undertaken in a study on Brazilian agriculture.[10]

IX

All of these hypotheses and studies suggest that the global extension and unity of the capitalist system, its monopoly structure and uneven development throughout its history, and the resulting persistence of commercial rather than industrial capitalism in the underdeveloped world (including its most industrially advanced countries) deserve much more attention in the study of economic development and cultural change than they have hitherto received. Though science and truth know no national boundaries, it is probably new generations of scientists from the underdeveloped countries themselves who most need to, and best can, devote the necessary attention to these problems and clarify the process of underdevelopment and development. It is their people who in the last analysis face the task of changing this no longer acceptable process and eliminating this miserable reality.

They will not be able to accomplish these goals by importing sterile stereotypes from the metropolis which do not correspond to their satellite economic reality and do not respond to their liberating political needs. To change their reality they must understand it. For this reason, I hope that better confirmation of these hypotheses and further pursuit of the proposed historical, holistic, and structural approach may help the peoples of the underdeveloped countries to understand the causes and eliminate the reality of their development of underdevelopment and their underdevelopment of development.

NOTES

1. *América Latina*, Año 6, No. 4, October–December 1963, p. 8.
2. Instituto Nacional Indigenista, *Los centros coordinadores indigenistas*, Mexico, 1962, p. 34.
3. *Ibid.*, pp. 33–34, 88.
4. "Capitalist Development and Underdevelopment in Chile" and "Capitalist Development and Underdevelopment in Brazil" in *Capitalism and Underdevelopment in Latin America*, New York, Monthly Review Press, 1967.
5. Also see, "The Growth and Decline of Import Substitution," *Economic Bulletin for Latin America*, New York, IX, No. 1, March 1964; and Celso Furtado, *Dialectica do Desenvolvimiento*, Rio de Janeiro, Fundo de Cultura, 1964.
6. Others who use a similar approach, though their ideologies do not permit them to derive the logically following conclusions, are Aníbal Pinto S.C., *Chile: Un caso de desarrollo frustrado*, Santiago, Editorial Universitaria,

1957; Celso Furtado, *A formaçao econômica do Brasil*, Rio de Janeiro, Fundo de Cultura, 1959 (recently translated into English and published under the title *The Economic Growth of Brazil* by the University of California Press); and Caio Prado Junior, *Historia Econômica do Brasil*, São Paulo, Editora Brasiliense, 7th ed., 1962.

7. See for instance Ramón Guerra y Sánchez, *Azúcar y Población en las Antillas*, Havana, 1942, 2nd ed., also published as *Sugar and Society in the Caribbean*, New Haven, Yale University Press, 1964.

8. Mario Góngora, *Origen de los "inquilinos" de Chile central*, Santiago, Editorial Universitaria, 1960; Jean Borde and Mario Góngora, *Evolución de la propiedad rural en el Valle del Puango*, Santiago, Instituto de Sociología de la Universidad de Chile; Sergio Sepúlveda, *El trigo chileno en el mercado mundial*, Santiago Editorial Universitaria, 1959.

9. Woodrow Borah makes depression the centerpiece of his explanation in "New Spain's Century of Depression," *Ibero-Americana*, Berkeley, No. 35, 1951. François Chevalier speaks of turning in upon itself in the most authoritative study of the subject, "La formación de los grandes latifundios en México," Mexico, *Problemas Agrícolas e Industriales de México*, VIII, No. 1, 1956 (translated from the French and recently published by the University of California Press). The data which provide the basis for my contrary interpretation are supplied by these authors themselves. This problem is discussed in my "Con qué modo de producción convierte la gallina maíz en huevos de oro?" *El Gallo Ilustrado*, Suplemento de *El Día*, Mexico, Nos. 175 and 179, October 31 and November 28, 1965; and it is further analyzed in a study of Mexican agriculture under preparation by the author.

10. "Capitalism and the Myth of Feudalism in Brazilian Agriculture," in *Capitalism and Underdevelopment in Latin America*, cited in note 4 above.

part three

Economic Development in a Revolutionary World: Trade and Imperialism

With the pioneering historical studies of underdevelopment by Celso Furtado, Andre Gunder Frank, and others,* a whole new approach to an understanding of the process of development and underdevelopment has been in the making in Latin America. This method builds on the historical perspective presented in the previous section. The development of capitalism and the world market is seen as a twofold process—the *underdevelopment* of Africa, Asia, and Latin America is the other side of the *development* of Europe and North America. This process creates a situation of *dependence* between the developed and underdeveloped. This new approach emphasizes the role of this dependence in shaping the internal economic, social, and political structures and external relations of underdeveloped countries that impede any real development.

In the first reading, Theotonio Dos Santos provides an overview of the issues contained in the theory of dependence. He stresses that by dependence he means a situation in which the economy of one country is conditioned by the development and expansion of another economy to which the former is subjected. Thus the concept of dependence leads us to view the internal structure of the underdeveloped countries as a dependent part of the capitalist world economy. Dos Santos argues that this perspective illuminates the reality of underdevelopment in a way no other approach does.

Celso Furtado's article complements both the historical articles in the last part and the Dos Santos article by focusing on the historical development of external dependency. He emphasizes the importance in underdeveloped countries of the upper income groups' adoption of the consumption patterns of their counterparts in the developed countries. Furtado argues that this shaped the structure of both the import and domestic manufacturing sectors of the underdeveloped countries. The luxury consumption demands of this group were catered to instead of the subsistence needs of the vast majority. In addition, because of the unequal income distribution the small size of the upper income class was unable to support a full range of industrialization. Furtado points out that in the last two decades the multinational corporation (MNC) has played the leading role in furthering dependence on this particular pattern of consumption and on the type of technology necessary to produce those consumer goods.

In the third reading in this part, Ronald Müller analyzes the specific ways in which these MNCs contribute to the development (or underdevelopment) of underdeveloped countries. Dos Santos refers to the post World War II period as "the new dependence." This new type of dependence is based on MNCs which began to invest in industries geared to the internal market of the underdeveloped countries. He considers this form of dependence to be basically technological-industrial in form. Utilizing the results of recent research, Müller analyzes the contribution of MNCs to technological, financial, and balance-of-payments requirements. His conclusions are that MNCs have had a negative impact in these three areas and that the main result has been an increased dependence of the underdeveloped countries on the MNCs.

The statement by the Tanzanian delegation to the Non-Aligned Nations Summit Conference included in the last part of this book contains an analysis in the first third of the article of how the international financial system, including the World Bank, is structured to preserve the status quo of development and underdevelopment between rich and poor countries. It would be useful to read that material at this point. The last reading in this section contains an analysis of how developed capitalist countries attempt to maintain the dependency relations with underdeveloped countries. Alfonso Inostroza, President of the Chilean Central Bank, recounts the ways in which the World Bank has attempted to pressure Chile into reversing those policies, particularly nationalization, that displeased the Bank's major donor countries, particularly the United States.

---

* See CELSO FURTADO, *The Economic Growth of Brazil* (Berkeley: University of California Press, 1957); Andre Gunder Frank, *Capitalism and Underdevelopment in Latin America* (New York: Monthly Review Press, 1967).

9

The Structure of Dependence

Theotonio Dos Santos

This paper attempts to demonstrate that the dependence of Latin American countries on other countries cannot be overcome without a qualitative change in their internal structures and external relations. We shall attempt to show that the relations of dependence to which these countries are subjected conform to a type of international and internal structure which leads them to underdevelopment or more precisely to a dependent structure that deepens and aggravates the fundamental problems of their peoples.

I. WHAT IS DEPENDENCE?

By dependence we mean a situation in which the economy of certain countries is conditioned by the development and expansion of another economy to which the former is subjected. The relation of interdependence between two or more economies, and between these and world trade, assumes the form of dependence when some countries (the dominant ones) can expand and can be self-sustaining, while other countries (the dependent ones) can do this only as a reflection of that expansion, which can have either a positive or a negative effect on their immediate development [7, p. 6].

The concept of dependence permits us to see the internal situation of these countries as part of world economy. In the Marxian tradition, the theory of imperialism has been developed as a study of the process of expansion of the imperialist centers and of their world domination. In the epoch of the revolutionary movement of the Third World, we have to develop the theory of laws of internal development in those countries that are the object of such expansion and are governed by them. This theoretical step transcends the theory of development which seeks to explain the situation of the underdeveloped countries as a product of their slowness or failure to adopt the patterns of efficiency characteristic of developed countries (or to "modernize" or "develop" themselves). Although capitalist development theory admits the existence of an "external" dependence, it is unable

Reprinted from *American Economic Review*, Vol. LX, No. 2 (May 1970), pp. 231-236, by permission of the American Economic Association and the author.

to perceive underdevelopment in the way our present theory perceives it, as a consequence and part of the process of the world expansion of capitalism—a part that is necessary to and integrally linked with it.

In analyzing the process of constituting a world economy that integrates the so-called "national economies" in a world market of commodities, capital, and even of labor power, we see that the relations produced by this market are unequal and combined—unequal because development of parts of the system occurs at the expense of other parts. Trade relations are based on monopolistic control of the market, which leads to the transfer of surplus generated in the dependent countries to the dominant countries; financial relations are, from the viewpoint of the dominant powers, based on loans and the export of capital, which permit them to receive interest and profits, thus increasing their domestic surplus and strengthening their control over the economies of the other countries. For the dependent countries these relations represent an export of profits and interest which carries off part of the surplus generated domestically and leads to a loss of control over their productive resources. In order to permit these disadvantageous relations, the dependent countries must generate large surpluses, not in such a way as to create higher levels of technology but rather superexploited manpower. The result is to limit the development of their internal market and their technical and cultural capacity, as well as the moral and physical health of their people. We call this combined development because it is the combination of these inequalities and the transfer of resources from the most backward and dependent sectors to the most advanced and dominant ones which explains the inequality, deepens it, and transforms it into a necessary and structural element of the world economy.

II. HISTORIC FORMS OF DEPENDENCE

Historic forms of dependence are conditioned by: (1) the basic forms of this world economy which has its own laws of development; (2) the type of economic relations dominant in the capitalist centers and the ways in which the latter expand outward; and (3) the types of economic relations existing inside the peripheral countries which are incorporated into the situation of dependence within the network of international economic relations generated by capitalist expansion. It is not within the purview of this paper to study these forms in detail but only to distinguish broad characteristics of development.

Drawing on an earlier study, we may distinguish: (1) Colonial dependence, trade export in nature, in which commercial and financial capital in alliance with the colonialist state dominated the economic relations of the Europeans and the colonies, by means of a trade monopoly complemented by a colonial monopoly of land, mines, and manpower (serf or slave) in the colonized countries. (2) Financial-industrial dependence which consolidated itself at the end of the nineteenth century, characterized by the domination of big capital in the hegemonic centers, and its expansion abroad through investment in the production of raw materials and agricultural products for consumption in the hegemonic centers. A productive structure grew up in the dependent countries devoted to the export of these products (which Levin labeled export economies [11]; other analysis in other regions [12] [13]), producing what ECLA has called "foreign-oriented development" (*desarrollo hacia afuera*) [4]. (3) In the postwar period a new type of dependence has been consolidated, based on multinational corporations which began to invest in industries geared to the internal market of under-developed countries. This form of dependence is basically technological-industrial dependence [6].

Each of these forms of dependence corresponds to a situation which conditioned not only the international relations of these countries but also their internal structures: the orientation of production, the forms of capital accumulation, the reproduction of the economy, and, simultaneously, their social and political structure.

III. THE EXPORT ECONOMIES

In forms (1) and (2) of dependence, production is geared to those products destined for export (gold, silver, and tropical products in the colonial epoch; raw materials and agricultural products in the epoch of industrial-financial dependence); i.e., production is determined by demand from the hegemonic centers. The internal productive structure is characterized by rigid specialization and monoculture in entire regions (the Caribbean, the Brazilian Northeast, etc.). Alongside these export sectors there grew up certain complementary economic activities (cattle-raising and some manu-facturing, for example) which were dependent, in general, on the export sector to which they sell their products. There was a third, subsistence economy which provided manpower for the export sector under favorable conditions and toward which excess population shifted during periods unfavorable to international trade.

Under these conditions, the existing internal market was restricted by four factors: (1) Most of the national income was derived from export, which was used to purchase the inputs required by export production (slaves, for example) or luxury goods consumed by the hacienda- and mine-owners, and by the more prosperous employees. (2) The available manpower was subject to very arduous forms of superexploitation, which limited its consumption. (3) Part of the consumption of these workers was provided by the subsistence economy, which served as a complement to their income and as a refuge during periods of depression. (4) A fourth factor was to be found in those countries in which land and mines were in the hands of foreigners (cases of an enclave economy): a great part of the accumulated surplus was destined to be sent abroad in the form of profits, limiting not only internal consumption but also possibilities of reinvestment [1]. In the case of enclave economies the relations of the foreign companies with the hegemonic center were even more exploitative and were comple-mented by the fact that purchases by the enclave were made directly abroad.

IV. THE NEW DEPENDENCE

The new form of dependence, (3) above, is in process of developing and is conditioned by the exigencies of the international commodity and capital markets. The possibility of generating new investments depends on the existence of financial resources in foreign currency for the purchase of machinery and processed raw materials not produced domestically. Such purchases are subject to two limitations: the limit of resources generated by the export sector (reflected in the balance of payments, which includes not only trade but also service relations); and the limitations of monopoly on patents which leads monopolistic firms to prefer to transfer their machines in the form of capital rather than as commodities for sale. It is necessary to analyze these relations of dependence if we are to understand the fundamental structural limits they place on the development of these economies.

1. Industrial development is dependent on an export sector for the foreign currency to buy the inputs utilized by the industrial sector. The first consequence of this dependence is the need to preserve the traditional export sector, which limits economically the development of the internal market by the conservation of backward relations of production and signifies, politically, the maintenance of power by traditional decadent oligarchies. In the countries where these sectors are controlled by foreign capital, it signifies the remittance abroad of high profits, and political dependence on those interests. Only in rare instances does foreign capital not control at least the marketing of these products. In response to these limitations, dependent countries in the 1930's and 1940's developed a policy of exchange restrictions and taxes on the national and foreign export sector; today they tend toward the gradual nationalization of production and toward the imposition of certain timid limitations on foreign control of the marketing of exported products. Furthermore, they seek, still somewhat timidly, to obtain better terms for the sale of their products. In recent decades, they have created mechanisms for international price agreements, and today UNCTAD and ECLA press to obtain more favorable tariff conditions for these products on the part of the hegemonic centers. It is important to point out that the industrial development of these countries is dependent on the situation of the export sector, the continued existence of which they are obliged to accept.

2. Industrial development is, then, strongly conditioned by fluctuations in the balance of payments. This leads toward deficit due to the relations of dependence themselves. The causes of the deficit are three:

a) Trade relations take place in a highly monopolized international market, which tends to lower the price of raw materials and to raise the prices of industrial products, particularly inputs. In the second place, there is a tendency in modern technology to replace various primary products with synthetic raw materials. Consequently the balance of trade in these countries tends to be less favorable (even though they show a general surplus). The overall Latin American balance of trade from 1946 to 1968 shows a surplus for each of those years. The same thing happens in almost every underdeveloped country. However, the losses due to deterioration of the terms of trade (on the basis of data from ECLA and the International Monetary Fund), excluding Cuba, were $26,383 million for the 1951–66 period, taking 1950 prices as a base. If Cuba and Venezuela are excluded, the total is $15,925 million.

b) For the reasons already given, foreign capital retains control over the most dynamic sectors of the economy and repatriates a high volume of profit; consequently, capital accounts are highly unfavorable to dependent countries. The data show that the amount of capital leaving the country is much greater than the amount entering; this produces an enslaving deficit in capital accounts. To this must be added the deficit in certain services which are virtually under total foreign control—such as freight transport, royalty payments, technical aid, etc. Consequently, an important deficit is produced in the total balance of payments; thus limiting the possibility of importation of inputs for industrialization.

c) The result is that "foreign financing" becomes necessary, in two forms: to cover the existing deficit, and to "finance" development by means of loans for the stimulation of investments and to "supply" an internal economic surplus which was decapitalized to a large extent by the remittance of part of the surplus generated domestically and sent abroad as profits.

Foreign capital and foreign "aid" thus fill up the holes that they themselves created. The real value of this aid, however, is doubtful. If overcharges resulting from the restrictive terms of the aid are subtracted from the total amount of the grants, the average net flow, according to calculations of the Inter-American Economic and Social Council, is approximately 54 percent of the gross flow [5].

If we take account of certain further facts—that a high proportion of aid is paid in local currencies, that Latin American countries make contributions to international financial institutions, and that credits are often "tied"—we find a "real component of foreign aid" of 42.2 percent on a very favorable hypothesis and of 38.3 percent on a more realistic one [5, II-33]. The gravity of the situation becomes even clearer if we consider that these credits are used in large part to finance North American investments, to subsidize foreign imports which compete with national products, to introduce technology not adapted to the needs of underdeveloped countries, and to invest in low-priority sectors of the national economies. The hard truth is that the underdeveloped countries have to pay for all of the "aid" they receive. This situation is generating an enormous protest movement by Latin American governments seeking at least partial relief from such negative relations.

3. Finally, industrial development is strongly conditioned by the technological monopoly exercised by imperialist centers. We have seen that the underdeveloped countries depend on the importation of machinery and raw materials for the development of their industries. However, these goods are not freely available in the international market; they are patented and usually belong to the big companies. The big companies do not sell machinery and processed raw materials as simple merchandise: they demand either the payment of royalties, etc., for their utilization or, in most cases, they convert

these goods into capital and introduce them in the form of their own invest-ments. This is how machinery which is replaced in the hegemonic centers by more advanced technology is sent to dependent countries as capital for the installation of affiliates. Let us pause and examine these relations, in order to understand their oppressive and exploitative character.

The dependent countries do not have sufficient foreign currency, for the the reasons given. Local businessmen have financing difficulties, and they must pay for the utilization of certain patented techniques. These factors oblige the national bourgeois governments to facilitate the entry of foreign capital in order to supply the restricted national market, which is strongly protected by high tariffs in order to promote industrialization. Thus, foreign capital enters with all the advantages: in many cases, it is given exemption from exchange controls for the importation of machinery; financing of sites for installation of industries is provided; government financing agencies facilitate industrialization; loans are available from foreign and domestic banks, which prefer such clients; foreign aid often subsidizes such invest-ments and finances complementary public investments; after installation, high profits obtained in such favorable circumstances can be reinvested freely. Thus it is not surprising that the data of the U.S. Department of Commerce reveal that the percentage of capital brought in from abroad by these companies is but a part of the total amount of invested capital. These data show that in the period from 1946 to 1967 the new entries of capital into Latin America for direct investment amounted to $5,415 million, while the sum of reinvested profits was $4,424 million. On the other hand, the transfers of profits from Latin America to the United States amounted to $14,775 million If we estimate total profits as approximately equal to trans-fers plus reinvestments we have the sum of $18,983 million. In spite of enormous transfers of profits to the United States, the book value of the United States's direct investment in Latin America went from $3,045 million in 1946 to $10,213 million in 1967. From these data it is clear that: (1) Of the new investments made by U.S. companies in Latin America for the period 1946–67, 55 percent corresponds to new entries of capital and 45 percent to reinvestment of profits; in recent years, the trend is more marked, with rein-vestments between 1960 and 1966 representing more than 60 percent of new investments. (2) Remittances remained at about 10 percent of book value throughout the period. (3) The ratio of remitted capital to new flow is around 2.7 for the period 1946–67; that is, for each dollar that enters $2.70 leaves. In the 1960's this ratio roughly doubled, and in some years was con-siderably higher.

The *Survey of Current Business* data on sources and uses of funds for direct North American investment in Latin America in the period 1957–64 show that, of the total sources of direct investment in Latin America, only 11.8 percent came from the United States. The remainder is in large part, the result of the activities of North American firms in Latin America (46.4 percent net income, 27.7 percent under the heading of depreciation), and from "sources located abroad" (14.1 percent). It is significant that the funds obtained abroad that are external to the companies are greater than the funds originating in the United States.

V. EFFECTS ON THE PRODUCTIVE STRUCTURE

It is easy to grasp, even if only superficially, the effects that this dependent structure has on the productive system itself in these countries and the role of this structure in determining a specified type of development, characterized by its dependent nature.

The productive system in the underdeveloped countries is essentially determined by these international relations. In the first place, the need to conserve the agrarian or mining export structure generates a combination between more advanced economic centers that extract surplus value from the more backward sectors, and also between internal "metropolitan" centers and internal interdependent "colonial" centers [10]. The unequal and combined character of capitalist development at the international level is reproduced internally in an acute form. In the second place the industrial and technological structure responds more closely to the interests of the multinational corporations than to internal developmental needs (conceived of not only in terms of the overall interests of the population, but also from the point of view of the interests of a national capitalist development). In the third place, the same technological and economic-financial concentration of the hegemonic economies is transferred without substantial alteration to very different economies and societies, giving rise to a highly unequal productive structure, a high concentration of incomes, underutilization of installed capacity, intensive exploitation of existing markets concentrated in large cities, etc.

The accumulation of capital in such circumstances assumes its own characteristics. In the first place, it is characterized by profound differences among domestic wage-levels, in the context of a local cheap labor market, combined with a capital-intensive technology. The result, from the point of view of relative surplus value, is a high rate of exploitation of labor power. (On measurements of forms of exploitation, see [3].)

This exploitation is further aggravated by the high prices of industrial products enforced by protectionism, exemptions and subsidies given by the national governments, and "aid" from hegemonic centers. Furthermore, since dependent accumulation is necessarily tied into the international economy, it is profoundly conditioned by the unequal and combined character of international capitalist economic relations, by the technological and financial control of the imperialist centers, by the realities of the balance of payments, by the economic policies of the state, etc. The role of the state in the growth of national and foreign capital merits a much fuller analysis than can be made here.

Using the analysis offered here as a point of departure, it is possible to understand the limits that this productive system imposes on the growth of the internal markets of these countries. The survival of traditional relations in the countryside is a serious limitation on the size of the market, since industrialization does not offer hopeful prospects. The productive structure created by dependent industrialization limits the growth of the internal market.

First, it subjects the labor force to highly exploitative relations which limit its purchasing power. Second, in adopting a technology of intensive capital use, it creates a very few jobs in comparison with population growth, and limits the generation of new sources of income. These two limitations affect the growth of the consumer goods market. Third, the remittance abroad of profits carries away part of the economic surplus generated within the country. In all these ways limits are put on the possible creation of basic national industries which could provide a market for the capital goods this surplus would make possible if it were not remitted abroad.

From this cursory analysis we see that the alleged backwardness of these economies is not due to a lack of integration with capitalism but that, on the contrary, the most powerful obstacles to their full development come from the way in which they are joined to this international system and its laws of development.

VI. SOME CONCLUSIONS: DEPENDENT REPRODUCTION

In order to understand the system of dependent reproduction and the socioeconomic institutions created by it, we must see it as part of a system of world economic relations based on monopolistic control of large-scale capital, on control of certain economic and financial centers over others, on a monopoly of a complex technology that leads to unequal and combined development at a national and international level. Attempts to analyze backwardness as a failure to assimilate more advanced models of production or to modernize are nothing more than ideology disguised as science. The same is true of the attempts to analyze this international economy in terms of relations among elements in free competition, such as the theory of comparative costs which seeks to justify the inequalities of the world economic system and to conceal the relations of exploitation on which it is based [14].

In reality we can understand what is happening in the underdeveloped countries only when we see that they develop within the framework of a process of dependent production and reproduction. This system is a dependent one because it reproduces a productive system whose development is limited by those world relations which necessarily lead to the development of only certain economic sectors, to trade under unequal conditions [9], to domestic competition with international capital under unequal conditions, to the imposition of relations of superexploitation of the domestic labor force with a view to dividing the economic surplus thus generated between internal and external forces of domination. (On economic surplus and its utilization in the dependent countries, see [1].)

In reproducing such a productive system and such international relations, the development of dependent capitalism reproduces the factors that prevent it from reaching a nationally and internationally advantageous situation; and it thus reproduces backwardness, misery, and social marginalization within its borders. The development that it produces benefits very narrow sectors, encounters unyielding domestic obstacles to its continued economic growth (with respect to both internal and foreign markets), and leads to the progressive accumulation of balance-of-payments deficits, which in turn generate more dependence and more superexploitation.

The political measures proposed by the developmentalists of ECLA, UNCTAD, BID, etc., do not appear to permit destruction of these terrible chains imposed by dependent development. We have examined the alternative forms of development presented for Latin America and the dependent countries under such conditions elsewhere [8]. Everything now indicates that what can be expected is a long process of sharp political and military confrontations and of profound social radicalization which will lead these countries to a dilemma: governments of force which open the way to facism, or popular revolutionary governments, which open the way to socialism. Intermediate solutions have proved to be, in such a contradictory reality, empty and utopian.

REFERENCES

1. PAUL BARAN, *Political Economy of Growth* (Monthly Review Press, 1967).
2. THOMAS BALOGH, *Unequal Partners* (Basil Blackwell, 1963).
3. PABLO GONZALEZ CASANOVA, *Sociologia de la explotación*, Siglo XXI (México, 1969).
4. CEPAL, *La CEPAL y el Análisis del Desarrollo Latinoamericano* (Santiago, Chile, 1968).
5. Consejo Interamericano Economico Social (CIES) O.A.S., Inter-American Economic and Social Council, External Financing for Development in L.A. *El Financiamiento Externo para el Desarrollo de América Latina* (Pan-American Union, Washington, 1969).
6. THEOTONIO DOS SANTOS, *El nuevo carácter de la dependencia*, CESO (Santiago de Chile, 1968).
7. _____, *La crisis de la teoría del desarrollo y las relaciones de dependencia en América Latina*, Boletín del CESCO, 3 (Santiago, Chile, 1968).
8. _____, *La dependencia económica y las alternativas de cambio en América Latina*, Ponencia al IX Congreso Latinoamericano de Sociología (México, Nov., 1969).
9. A. EMMANUEL, *L'Echange Inégal* (Maspero, Paris, 1969).
10. ANDRE G. FRANK, *Development and Underdevelopment in Latin America* (Monthly Review Press, 1968).
11. I. V. LEVIN, *The Export Economies* (Harvard Univ. Press, 1964).
12. GUNNAR MYRDAL, *Asian Drama* (Pantheon, 1968).
13. K. NKRUMAH, *Neocolonialismo, última etapa del imperialismo*, Siglo XXI (México, 1966).
14. CRISTIAN PALLOIX, *Problemes de la Croissance en Economie Ouverte* (Maspero, Paris, 1969).

10

The Concept of External Dependence in the Study of Underdevelopment

Celso Furtado

Underdevelopment was originally characteristic of economies in which an increase in productivity was largely the result of reallocation of resources aimed at obtaining static comparative advantages in international trade. Changes in demand, on a global level, opened the way to significant increases in productivity, through geographic specialization. This type of increase in productivity can be obtained with a minimum of change in the productive process (as in the case of tropical agriculture) or with significant change but under the form of an "enclave" controlled from outside (as in the case of mineral production). Thus, in the period when the system of international division of labor was created, certain countries (those already in the process of industrialization) specialized in activities where technical progress penetrated rapidly and others specialized either in activities where technical progress was negligible or in the exploitation of nonrenewable natural resources. The "law of comparative advantage" provided a valid explanation for the existence of trade but concealed the extremely uneven diffusion of technical progress. Thus the difference between developed and underdeveloped economies stems from the global process of resource allocation and structuring of a world economy provoked by the industrial revolution.

The relations between "central" and "peripheral" countries are, however, much more complex than would appear from conventional economic analysis. A fundamental aspect which is usually overlooked is the fact that when certain countries got to be peripheral, they were transformed into importers of new consumer goods, which were the fruits of technical progress in the central countries. Furthermore, this process of adopting new patterns of consumption was bound to be a very uneven one. The increase of economic productivity in a peripheral country benefits only a small part of the population (usually less than one tenth) depending on agrarian structure, relative abundance of land and labor, control of trade by foreigners or natives, and similar factors. Because the benefits were concentrated, the ruling classes of the peripheral countries were able to adopt the patterns of consumption created in the rich countries by the industrial revolution. Let us call *modernization* (with permission of the sociologists) this process of adoption of

Paper presented to the Union for Racial Political Economics, Washington, D.C. November 10, 1972. © Celso Furtado.

patterns of consumption, which occurs without the corresponding process of capital accumulation and assimilation of technical progress in productive methods.

The formation of a social group (whose relative importance varies, but which is always a small minority of the population) with consumption patterns similar to those of countries with higher levels of productivity became the basic factor in the transformation of the peripheral countries. The significance of this appears when one bears in mind that in the rich countries there is a close positive correlation between the degree of diversification of the basket of consumer goods on the one hand, and the level of capital accumulated per employed person and degree of assimilation of technical progress on the other. This correlation does not prevail for the peripheral country where the increase in consumption of the modernized minority stems from static comparative advantage in foreign trade. But what happens when the new basket of goods has to be produced within the country?

"Import substitution" tends to take the form of local manufacture of the same articles which were previously imported for consumption by the modernized minority. Now, the *quality* of the basket of consumer goods determines, within relatively narrow margins, the productive processes to be adopted and, ultimately, the relative intensity of capital accumulation. In other words, if we have to add ten dollars to the consumption of a rich person, we need more capital than is required to add ten dollars to the consumption of a poor person. In the latter case, abundant resources (land and labor) are bound to be more used, and scarce resources (capital, skilled labor, and foreign exchange) less used than in the former case. Furthermore, to increase consumption of rich people means to introduce new products, and this implies paying for more research and development; whereas increasing the consumption of the poor is mainly a process of diffusing the use of already known products. Thus, the peripheral country getting into the process of industrialization is bound to see the discontinuity previously formed at the cultural level (patterns of consumption based on imported goods versus traditional patterns of consumption) transferred to the structure of the productive system. The slow absorption of labor in the activities which produce primarily for the modernized minority, that is, for the highly diversified basket of goods, has a strong impact on the process of income distribution. The wage rate in the urban zones tends to remain stable, while the income of the propertied groups increases in absolute and relative terms. Since the industries which benefit most from ·economies of scale are also those which produce durable consumer goods, the decline in the relative prices of such goods (when it occurs) benefits only the high-income groups consuming such products.

Economic underdevelopment as a historical process can be summarized as follows: increased economic productivity, resulting from increased exports of raw materials, caused an increase in and a diversification of consumption of the well-off minority, which was geared to the cultural values of the central countries. In a more advanced stage, when exports of raw materials and import substitution no longer played the role of a transforming factor, growth occurred only when the market created by the modernized minority was compatible with the techniques required to locally produce the diversified basket of consumer goods. The alternative to this has been the so-called outward-oriented strategy of industrialization, usually known as the Hong Kong model. With the exception of this special case, whose generalization will require a thorough restructuring in the developed economies, growth in the underdeveloped countries has depended on the ability of such countries to concentrate income in the hands of the modernized minority.

This process of transplanting consumption patterns, provoked by the industrial revolution and operating through a system of international division of labor imposed by the industrialized countries, gave rise to peripheral capitalism, a capitalism unable to generate innovations and dependent for transformation upon decisions coming from the outside. I call external dependence the structural situation in which such a peripheral capitalism prevails in certain countries, the countries where modernization started on the basis of static comparative advantage and has operated as a framework for the process of cultural domination. It may exist in the absence of any direct foreign investment and, conceivably, even in the relations of a socialist country with capitalist countries commanding the flow of new products and processes of production. But this is only a theoretical hypothesis. Once the dependence has been created, the doors are open to the introduction of all the forms of economic exploitation which typify the relationships between underdeveloped and developed countries. To isolate such forms of exploitation from the framework of cultural domination is to miss the essentials of the problem.

The ability of certain countries to control technical progress and to impose consumption patterns became the decisive factor in the structuring of the productive apparatus of other countries, which in consequence became "dependent." From an economic point of view, this process appears as a discontinuity in demand, and industrialization, in the form of import substitution, transferred this discontinuity to the structure of the productive apparatus. For the economist looking at an underdeveloped economy as a closed system, this phenomenon appears as a "disequilibrium at the factors' level" provoked by the fixed coefficients in the production functions, that is, by the "inadequacy" of the technology being absorbed. He does not realize that the above-mentioned phenomenon stems originally from a cultural process, namely, the transplantation of consumption patterns. If the patterns of consumption of the modernized minority have to keep up with those prevailing in the rich countries, no policy aimed at "adapting" the technology can alter the situation. Taking into account that dependence has been permanently reinforced through the introduction of new products, it is not difficult to understand why underdevelopment has become self-sustaining. In the stage of full industrialization, underdevelopment corresponds to the inability of the economic system to spontaneously generate the demand profile required to assure the growth of the industrial sector linked to the modernized minority. Only those who benefit from property incomes and/or are entitled to high incomes through different forms of privilege granted by the State have access to the basket of consumer goods where new products must be introduced. Growth in this kind of economy relies heavily on the ability of the ruling class to keep income concentrated. Furthermore, the rich minority has to be large enough to justify a process of industrialization capable of operating at adequate standards of efficiency. Concentration of income is necessary, but not sufficient to attain a successful industrialization process under the conditions of dependence. The country's average per capita income and demographic dimensions are also important factors. The same can be said of the limits to which social inequality can be pushed, South Africa being an example of the elasticity of such limits.

We can now see the different ways in which the growth process functions in conditions of dependence. Within the classic system of international division of labor, certain economies succeed in increasing productivity without changing the productive processes, resulting in little accumulation of capital. Occasionally technical progress penetrates as a *consequence* of the increase in economic productivity. This penetration has been linked mainly to the creation of a physical infrastructure and to the expansion of urban life. What always accompanies the rise in economic productivity is the transplantation of new consumption patterns, namely, the modernization of the way of life of a small minority of the population. During the period of industrialization based on import substitution, the external demand for primary products no longer plays a dynamic role in transforming the dependent economies. The assimilation of technical progress feeds the process of growth for a time, but once the substitution process exhausts its main possibilities, the dynamic role has to be assumed by the new products produced domestically for the rich minority. This is possible only if the dimensions of the economy allow a full process of industrialization and if the political system is repressive enough to maintain income concentration.

The various means of growth of the above-mentioned peripheral economies all constitute processes of adaptation in the face of the structural evolution of the dominant centers. It is a well-known fact that the international economy, linked to geographic specialization and static comparative advantage, is being replaced by another in which markets are superseded by the internal transactions of multinational corporations (MNCs). The main feature of this new international economy is that technology, embodied in equipment and in the design of the final consumer goods, tends to be less and less the object of market transactions. Decentralizing their productive activities in response to the dimensions of the local markets of the dependent economies, MNCs have transferred technology into transactions internal to the new firms. On the other hand, access to technical innovation constitutes a necessary condition for growth based on the patterns of consumption created in the rich countries. Working on the basis of blueprints and minimizing the cost of research and development, MNCs can overcome some of the limitations imposed by the smallness of local markets and the lack of external economies. Thus, a precondition for keeping the process of industrialization going is the cooperation of MNCs. Other channels of transmission of technical progress, required by this type of industrialization, are more expensive and less accessible.

If we look at the same problem from a different angle we could say that the present growth of the dependent economies consists of increasing participation on the part of the MNCs in the international economy. They are able to control the diffusion of new techniques or to minimize the cost of the techniques required by the model of development prevailing in the dependent economies. Since they provide new products vital to the expansion of consumption of the modernized minorities, they play the role of an engine of growth in such countries, while tightening the links of dependence. The more the rich countries rely on the introduction of new products for growth (and this is inherent in modern capitalism, where competition on the basis of product innovation prevails more and more over competition on the basis of price reduction), the more the modernized sector of the dependent economies is bound to do the same. Consequently, capital accumulation in the sector of the economy producing for the rich is more rapid than it is in the economy as a whole, which means that the pace of income concentration is accelerated. In fact, income concentration is proceeding at a steady rate and even accelerating in the more successful industrializing dependent countries such as Pakistan, Mexico, and Brazil.

Focusing on the problem from yet another angle, we see that an increasing imbalance in the structure of the global system results from the present process of growth in the periphery as steered by the MNCs. On the one hand we have a relative reduction of real flows (decline of the traditional system of international division of labor), and on the other an increasing number of instances of multinational corporations reaping the benefits of increased productivity in dependent economies. In other words, the expansion of MNCs entails an increasing flow of invisibles from the center to the periphery, and the cost of such invisibles has to be matched with a flow of goods from the periphery to the center. The problem is how to reconcile this with the present slow growth or relative decline in the dependent countries' ability to make international payments. While import substitution is being practiced, the potential disequilibrium can be absorbed, albeit with heavy strain on the balance of payments in the dependent countries. But when the more advanced stage of dependent industrialization is reached, there is a tendency toward increasing external indebtedness. It is enough to mention this problem in order to realize that new methods have to be found if the present system structured around the MNCs is to keep its rate of growth. The way that best meets the requirements of the MNCs seems to be the opening of markets in the rich countries to products manufactured in the peripheral economies. In a way, this would be a return to the system of the international division of labor based on static comparative advantage; the underdeveloped countries will go on being deprived of access to the superior activities of creating technology, but given access to the expanding markets of the rich countries, they would find opportunities for growth. The relative price of technology, that is, the terms of trade between the countries creating new productive processes and new products and the countries manufacturing products already known under the control of the MNCs, can be used as an instrumental variable to keep the system in equilibrium.

This process does not avoid an increasing disparity in the productivity levels of the center and the periphery, and it implies a widening gap between the consumption levels of the modernized minorities and the mass of the population in the dependent countries, although it creates conditions in which the new international economy can work and expand. Indeed, if such tendencies prevail, from the point of view of the underdeveloped countries, growth will continue to thwart their efforts at overcoming dependence, improving living conditions, and reducing inequality within their societies.

11

The Multinational Corporation
and the Underdevelopment of the Third World

Ronald Müller

INTRODUCTION

In the two decades since World War II, there has been an increasing awareness that two revolutionary phenomena have occurred in the less developed
countries of the Third World. The first phenomenon is reflected in the
most recent recognitions of the plight of less developed countries (LDCs)
after some twenty years of so-called development attempts. This phenomenon, revolutionary in terms of its impact on the lives of roughly two-thirds
of the world's people which it affects, is the maintenance of underdevelopment. It is a phenomenon which is unique to the Third World and which
is mirrored in the statistical findings on increasing unemployment, the
growing inequality in income distribution, and the fact that anywhere from
40 percent to 60 percent of the populations of most LDCs have suffered not
only relative but also absolute declines in consumption compared to ten,
fifteen, twenty years ago.[1]

A second revolutionary phenomenon, which has occurred in the past
twenty years but which is not unique to the Third World, is the occurrence
of a new institution in the political economy of nations, the multinational
corporation (MNC). Although it had its historical antecedents in the late
nineteenth and early twentieth centuries, the multinational corporation in
its modern form has been the subject of concern in a recent deluge of
books, Ph.D. dissertations, and articles in newspapers, magazines, and
scientific journals. Part of this deluge has focused on definitions (is an MNC (sic)
a company which makes a certain percentage of its sales overseas or
should the criterion be a certain percentage of its profits) while at the
same time debating terminology (some choose to call the MNC a transnational corporation while others prefer the terminology of a global corporation).

 Whatever we choose to call it, a multinational corporation is a company with its parent headquarters located in one country and subsidiary
operations in a number of other countries. The central characteristic of a
multinational corporation is that it seeks to maximize the profits not of
its individual subsidiaries, but rather of the center parent company. This,

This article was written expressly for this book of readings. © Ronald Müller.

as we shall see, may even mean operating certain of its subsidiaries at an "official" loss. The best way to define an MNC is to name a few, for they are familiar to us whether we reside in a more developed or a less developed part of the world. They are companies such as Du Pont, Ford Motor, National Biscuit, ITT, Bayer, Unilever, Procter & Gamble, Dow Chemical, Volkswagen, Squibb, etc.

The objective of this present work is to explore whether these two phenomena, the maintenance of underdevelopment, a human condition, and the rise of a new worldwide institution, the modern multinational corporation, are related to each other. Specifically our exploration of this question will focus on three main aspects: (a) the empirical reality of the role played by MNCs in the economies of the Third World, with a specific focus on Latin America as an illustrative case; (b) the methods and practices utilized by MNCs in their Third World operations; and (c) the results of these operations and their impacts on the development potential of LDCs. Since many readers may not be intimately familiar with the operations of MNCs and/or the political economy of Third World nations, we have chosen a particular breakdown for the remainder of our discussion that should be sufficiently intelligible to both the expert and non-expert alike. The discussion will be broken down into the most-often-cited contributions of multinational corporations to the economic development of LDCs. For example, it is often said that the multinational corporation makes a fundamentally important *technological contribution* to the development of Third World countries. In what follows, this and other contributions will be individually examined to see whether or not they represent myth or reality.

Before proceeding, however, it is critical to an understanding of the impact of MNCs in LDCs to have a certain degree of familiarity with the institutional conditions and economic structure of these economies. This familiarity coupled with the use of some simple tools of economic analysis can aid us in analyzing the contributions of MNCs. In addition, a familiarity with the politico-economic circumstances of LDCs will shed further light on why it cannot be assumed that the contributions of, for example, a United States corporation's subsidiary in West Germany to that economy are the same as the contributions of that corporation's subsidiary in Peru to the Peruvian economy.

MNCs AND THE MEANING OF UNDERDEVELOPMENT

Underdevelopment: The Institutional Setting

In turning to the economic environment of Third World nations, let us first review the reasons why these countries are called "less developed." First, there is a lack of adequately trained civil servants to examine and investigate whether or not commercial and business laws are being complied with by MNCs or locally owned companies. Secondly, the implications of this lack of expertise indicate that the very laws themselves are usually quite old, designed for times past, when the holding of a patent, the legal institution which sets the limits on the market power of technology, had far different implications than it does today. The laws, as well as taxation practices and other governmental functions, have remained unrevised too long to take cognizance of the major changes in the origins of economic power. And lastly, whereas we normally think of the institutions of organized labor in advanced countries as a countervailing force or check upon the power of the corporation, this is not the case in most LDCs where organized labor is either weak or absent.

Thus, a basic part of the meaning of underdevelopment is a set of institutions which are either lacking or malfunctioning relative to similar institutions in industrialized societies. For those of us accustomed to life in the advanced nations, a fundamental understanding of this basic aspect of underdevelopment is essential when analyzing the impacts of MNCs on Third World economies. Whether we look at legal institutions or those of organized labor or those of financing, we shall find that the "bargaining power" of the MNC to maximize profits is far greater in the Third World than in rich countries because of the absence or weakness of institutional mechanisms to control the behavior of subsidiaries. Stated in Galbraithian terms, Third World countries are characterized by an absence of the "countervailing" power of government and organized labor for setting limits on the power of the modern corporation.

The institutional conditions characterizing underdevelopment are one aspect explaining the power of the multinational corporation in LDCs, but there is another aspect of underdevelopment which further intensifies this power, and that is the economic structure of societies in underdevelopment. In assessing the power of MNCs, there are two key characteristics of this economic structure which are important to grasp: first, the need for and the sources of *technology*; and second, the need for and the sources of investment *financing*.

Underdevelopment: The Structure of Technology

Fortunately or unfortunately, most Third World countries have already set in motion a process of industrialization highly similar to that found in the advanced capitalist nations of the West. This industrialization is not only similar in terms of the output of industry (capital goods and private consumption goods), but also in terms of the mechanical technology and human technical skills needed for its implementation. In other words, the voluntary or involuntary institutionalization of Western consumption values as the goal of economic growth has, in turn, brought about the need for a technology which can satisfy this pattern of consumption. Given this need, what are the sources of this technology? Tables 1 and 2 provide the answer.

The meaning of these statistics is clear. LDCs are virtually entirely dependent upon foreign sources, specifically the advanced nations of North America, Western Europe, and Japan, for their technology. Not even these figures reflect the absolute dependency involved, however, for if we look

Table 1 Patents Granted to Foreigners as a Percentage of Total Patents Granted Between 1957 and 1961 Inclusive

"Large" Industrial Countries		"Smaller" Industrial Countries		Developing Countries	
U.S.A.	15.72	Italy	62.85	India	89.38
Japan	34.02	Switzerland	64.08	Turkey	91.73
West Germany	37.14	Sweden	69.30	United Arab	
United Kingdom	47.00	Netherlands	69.83	Republic	93.01
France	59.36	Luxemburg	80.48	Trinidad and	
		Belgium	85.55	Tobago	94.18
				Pakistan	95.75
				Ireland	96.51

Source: Statistical information appearing in United Nations, "The Role of Patents in the Transfer of Technology to Developing Countries," New York, 1964, pp. 94-95, as cited in Constantine Vaitsos, "Patents Revisited: Their Function in Developing Countries," *The Journal of Development Studies* (1973), p. 6.

Table 2 Percentages of Patents Registered in Chile

Year	Owned by Nationals	Owned by Foreigners
1937	34.5	65.5
1947	20.0	80.0
1958	11.0	89.0
1967	5.5	94.5

Sources: Corporacion de Fomento de la Produccion (CORFO), "La Propiedad Industrial en Chile y su Impacto en el Desarrollo Industrial," preliminary unpublished document, Santiago (September 1970), p. 15; also in Vaitsos, "Patents Revisited . . .," *op. cit.*, p. 8.

at the ownership of patents actually utilized for producing goods versus patents granted but not utilized in production we find that:

> . . . if the number of patents is weighted by their economic or technological worth (i.e. volume of sales or value added) most developing countries are likely to find that the so weighted patents belonging to their own nationals amount to a fraction of 1 percent of the total patents granted by such countries.[2]

Also, the foreign versus local control of technology does not indicate the actual concentration of control in the hands of a very small number of foreign corporations. In the United States, for example, of the five hundred largest industrial corporations, the top thirty own 40.7 percent of the patents in their respective industries.[3] The mirror image of this concentration of technology control in the advanced nations is found to an even greater extent in the underdeveloped areas. In Colombia, for instance, in the pharmaceutical, synthetic fiber, and chemical industries 10 percent of all patent-holders own 60 percent of all patents, and these 10 percent are all foreign MNCs.[4]

Concentrated control of technology is one of the most effective means to establish oligopoly power over the market place, restricting the development of local competition and permitting, as we shall see, an astounding rate of profits, the greater majority of which leave the country. Once such a process is under way, it becomes cumulative and self-perpetuating (see

Table 2). The initial institutional purpose of patent rights, i.e., to stimulate *domestic* inventiveness, is self-defeating, since the wherewithal to pursue research and development (R&D) goes increasingly to foreign firms. Over time local business enterprises lose access not only to mechanical technology to compete, but perhaps more importantly to the human technical skills which can be accumulated only through experience in order to allow further development. In the end domestic firms are either absorbed by the MNCs or must resort to the "licensing" of their technology, as is the actual case today in Latin America. With such licensing comes a number of restrictions, enumerated below, on the ability of these enterprises and their nations to develop in the future.

Underdevelopment: The Structure of Finance

Such are the vicious circles which emerge in the interplay between the economic structure of underdevelopment in the LDCs and the technological power of the MNCs. A similar set of vicious circles is also at play in the financial patterns of these countries. Of first importance in assessing the investment financing aspects of the particular industrialization process described above is the expensiveness of the technology being used. It is also well-known that in almost all LDCs there is a scarcity of local savings available to be channeled into financial capital for productive investments. This scarcity of savings is due not only to the LDCs' low level of income, but also to the fact that a certain portion of savings leaves the country. That is, foreign firms repatriate a significant part of their profits, and indigenous wealth-holders also channel a part of their savings out to MNCs (the so-called phenomenon of "capital-flight"). Adding to the outflow of savings through repatriated profits and capital-flight is the increasing debt-repayments to bilateral (e.g., AID) and multilateral (e.g., World Bank) aid agencies on loans granted in the 1960s. Taken together, the magnitude of these outflows has led a number of writers to comment that in aggregate terms the poor countries of the world are now ironically helping to finance the rich countries, that is, the financial outflows from LDCs far exceed the inflows.[5]

There is thus a twofold dilemma in the financial structure of LDCs. On the one hand, there is a growing gap between the supply of *available* local savings and the demand for investment funds to alleviate the growing poverty *and* the growing awareness of it by the people of these countries, via increased literacy, improved communications, and the ensuing demonstration effects. On the other hand, the particular technology which the industrialization process necessitates not only is expensive, but must be paid for in foreign, not local, exchange. The relative reduction in LDCs' exports which has reduced their ability to generate foreign exchange,[6] plus the relative increase in foreign exchange outflows versus inflows, has brought about the well-known problem of the "foreign exchange bottleneck." Even when there are sufficient savings to finance needed investment projects, the investment may not take place because savings in local currency cannot be translated into foreign exchange for the purchase of the imported technology required by the project.

The upshot of this twofold dilemma (inadequate amounts of local savings and foreign exchange), from the viewpoint of domestic enterprises, is a rather perverse form of non-competitive financing patterns in most LDCs. Contrary to accepted notions about multinational companies in poor countries, these firms do not bring their own finance capital from abroad, but rather the overwhelming majority of their financing is derived from local (host country) sources. This fact will be given statistical clarity below, but what is important for the present discussion is the impact on domestic enterprises. Namely, the subsidiaries of MNCs in LDCs borrow from local financial institutions with the credit rating and financial resources backup of the entire global network of the parent MNC of which they are a part. This is in contrast to the credit rating and financial resources backup of the infinitely smaller, typical local business enterprise when it attempts to obtain finance capital. The vicious circle begins to close. The local financial institution, faced with limited loan capital relative to its demand and, like any other business, interested in risk-minimization and profit-maximization, will inevitably show a lending pattern biased toward the subsidiaries of MNCs.

This conclusion is even more obvious when the local financial institution is, in fact, a branch or subsidiary of a so-called private multinational bank, such as Bank of America, First National City Bank of New York, etc. These banks are playing a powerful role in the financial structures of the Third World where in many instances they control close to 50 percent of the private deposits of a country.[7] The LDC operation of a multinational bank will prefer lending to the subsidiaries of MNCs for the same reasons that locally controlled financial institutions do. In addition, in such a lending operation there is more at stake than just the particular profitability of one or a series of loans in a single country.

It is a well-established fact that the worldwide parent networks of banks and corporations are not two distinct entities, separated "at arm's length" by a competitive market in which one is a seller and the other a buyer. Instead there are interlocking interests of common ownership, management, and technical personnel in the groups that control banks and corporations.[8] Furthermore, whatever the consequences of these interlocking interests may be, there is a second well-established fact of a near perfect correlation between the worldwide expansion of MNCs and the commensurate expansion by multinational banks.[9] Whether the banks or the corporations led in this expansion is not of key importance; rather, what is important is that a mutual process of interdependent expansion characterized by common familiarity, experience, and objectives has developed. The commonalities lock together in a theme of expansion, where the expansion is based on the facilitation of an industrialization model most particularly suited to the competitive advantages of the MNC and, therefore, to the multinational banks. Thus, even if domestic businesses in LDCs could offer the branch offices of multinational banks better borrowing terms than MNCs, it is highly unlikely that these banks would forego their long-range global interests for the short-range local interests of a branch office.

The vicious circles emanating from the financial structures of under-development are now closed. The results for the development of national enterprises are similar to those in the case of our analysis of the technology structures: the bargaining power of MNCs to obtain finance capital is far greater than for local competitors, the degree of this financial bargaining power being greater the more dynamic a particular industry is.[10] This relatively greater bargaining power in finance has, over time, the same consequences as it does in technology. It becomes the equivalent, as noted above, of what the economist calls oligopoly power, meaning the power to erect "barriers to entry" against potential new competition or, on the other side of the same coin, the power to eliminate existing competition usually through the absorption of or buying into local firms.

Structural Impact of MNCs: Concentration and Power

Our analysis of the economic structure of LDCs, with reference to technology and finance, has shown why MNCs have a relatively high and ever-growing degree of oligopoly power in contrast to national firms in LDCs. Just how great this power is can be determined from the empirical reality of societies in underdevelopment. A focus on pre-1970 Chile will reflect this reality for almost all LDCs in which MNCs operate. In the industrial sector between 1967 and 1969, foreign participation (in terms of assets owned) increased from 16.6 to 20.3 percent, while domestic participation diminished from 76.1 to 63.0 percent, the difference between the two being made up of state owned firms. Of the 100 largest industrial firms (on the basis of asset size) in the country, 49 were effectively controlled by MNCs; when the sample was expanded to the largest 160 firms, over 51 percent were under the control of MNCs. Even these figures do not accurately convey the degree of concentration involved. When we look at control by industry, we see that in 7 of the more important industries of Chile, 1 to 3 foreign firms controlled not less than 51 percent of production in each industry. In a behavioral analysis of 22 of the largest MNC operations in the country, 5 of the MNC subsidiaries were monopolists in their respective industrial markets, 6 were duopolists, and 8 were oligopolists with each of these 8 being the largest supplier in its market. For 18 of these subsidiaries for which rate of growth in sales data were available, 16 showed a growth rate much higher than the average for the industrial sector as a whole. These figures reflect not only the reality of Chile prior to 1970, but are representative of most LDCs where MNCs are currently operating. Taken together, these concentration indicators demonstrate the degree of oligopoly power of MNCs in the Third World as well as their ability to increase that power over time.[11]

Thus far this work has attempted to convey to the reader a basic understanding of the meaning of underdevelopment as it relates to the power of MNCs. This understanding of the economic environment of Third World countries should facilitate the analysis of the impacts of MNCs on these nations, which follows in the next section. We have shown that the bargaining power, or its equivalent, the oligopoly power of the multinational corporations, is a function of the institutional conditions and the economic structure of LDCs. As the term underdevelopment implies, the institutions of poor countries are either weak and outdated or largely non-existent. Thus, compared to the more developed countries, there is little countervailing power or "checks and balances" via government and organized labor to set limits on the power of the modern international corporation. The institutional conditions described refer basically to non-business institutions which, because of their malfunctioning and/or absence, make the MNC in a Third World country a different institutional force than need necessarily be the case when it operates in an advanced industrial society.

If the non-business institutions of government and organized labor cannot act as a sufficient check on the power of the MNC in a Third World country, there still remains the check of other business institutions, namely, domestic competition. But the nature of the economic structure of under-development, exemplified in the technological and financial spheres, makes it highly unlikely that domestic business institutions will be able to perform this function, because most LDCs have embarked upon an industrialization process, highly similar to those of advanced industrialized nations, as the chief means of bringing about economic growth. Given this industrialization process and the nature of the technological and financial needs to implement it, the result is a diminution in the power of domestic enterprises to compete and a further augmentation in the oligopoly power of MNCs. Having presented the rationale and evidence for the manner in which MNCs achieve their relatively powerful positions in the economies of LDCs, we turn now to an analysis of how that power reflects itself in their day-to-day operations and of the resulting impact upon the people of these countries.

MYTH OR REALITY:
THE CONTRIBUTIONS OF MULTINATIONAL CORPORATIONS

The description and evaluation of the behavior of MNCs in the Third World will be divided into three specific sections. The choice of this breakdown for our analysis is based on what many believe to be the three most potentially important areas in which MNCs can contribute to the development of LDCs: in technology, in financial inflows, and in the alleviation of balance of payments problems. Within each of these sections, we shall proceed from a description of operational behavior to an evaluation of its impact. It is important here to mention briefly the overall criterion which serves as the basis of our evaluation.

The criterion is a simple one, although one which until recently has been relatively ignored by students of development, particularly by economists who have been trained in the orthodoxy of neo-classical analysis. We shall employ the analytical tools of the latter, but our definition of development, i.e., our evaluation criterion, shall be different than that most frequently used. It will not be assumed that an increase in average per capita income constitutes "development." Instead, a MNC activity and its impact will be judged a contribution to development only if it results in an increase in the consumption potential of the poorest 60 percent of a LDC's population. For we believe that unless economic growth brings some alleviation to those suffering most, such growth is a contribution not to development but rather to the continued underdevelopment of Third World nations.

The Technology Contribution:
Employment, Income Distribution, Costs

The United Nations estimated that in 1960 approximately 27 percent of the population of Third World countries were unemployed. By 1970, the estimate of the percentage of the active population unemployed had gone beyond 30 percent.[12] Even these global macro figures for LDCs as a whole, however, underestimate the dramatic dimension of the unemployment problems in Latin America, ironically called the "more developed" region of the Third World relative to Asia and Africa. A 1968 study estimated that by 1971, 36 percent of Colombia's labor force would be unemployed, and later studies from Colombia have confirmed that the estimate is more than being fulfilled.[13] A 1965 analysis of manpower in Peru showed that of the available Peruvian labor force, "43 percent are not needed in the production of that nation's national product."[14] In 1960 (the last year for which comparative country estimates are available), the unemployment equivalent ranged from 22 percent in Argentina, Brazil, and Mexico to 42 percent in the poorer countries of Central America and the Caribbean, and as noted, unemployment has been progressively increasing since then.[15]

Employment: Causes and Impact. Is there any hope for at least a partial diminution of the problem in the near future? If the past is any indication, the answer is no. All projections indicate that the problem will worsen, not diminish. The Prebisch report concluded that with population growing at approximately 3 percent in many countries of the region, total output would have to grow by 8 percent per annum between 1970 and 1980 in order to absorb current unemployment as well as the new additions to the labor force. To maintain the 1960 unemployment levels, total output would have to grow at a yearly rate of 6 percent for 1970 to 1980, a rate never before achieved in the region.[16]

An underlying cause of the unemployment crisis rests in the particular industrialization process being utilized to bring about economic growth. One important impact of this process was emphasized earlier, namely, that almost all of the technology in LDCs comes from, and is controlled by, foreign sources, that is, the MNCs. There is yet another and equally important impact of this industrialization process and the technology it necessitates; the technology transferred to the Third World by the MNCs has been designed for the resource conditions of the advanced industrialized nations where there is a relative abundance of capital and a relative scarcity of labor. In other words, this technology is incapable of absorbing labor because it has been designed to do just the opposite, i.e., to be "labor saving and capital using." Thus the MNC drug companies use a technology in which only 3.4 percent of total costs are due to labor.[17] There is, of course, an obvious contradiction to have such technology entrenched in the indus-

trialization processes of Third World countries where the resource conditions are an abundance of labor and an acute scarcity of capital. An example
of the change in the employment capacity of the industries where MNCs
have their most intensive expansion will show the dimensions of the
contradiction in which the MNCs are pivotally involved.

A recent study in Colombia has derived an estimated index of the
capital to labor requirements for the five modern manufacturing industries
in which MNCs have concentrated most of their investments between 1960
and 1967.[18] In all five industries similar results were found. In the chemical
products industry in 1960, it took 1.63 units of capital investment to employ
1 unit of labor; by 1967 it took 4.45 units of capital for 1 unit of labor
employment. Thus, within the eight-year period, the investment requirements to employ a unit of labor almost tripled. This study also revealed
that the increase in fixed investment to employ a unit of labor was smaller
for the industrial manufacturing sector as a whole compared to the five
specific industries where MNCs were concentrating their new investments.
The International Labor Organization, in its independent analysis of
Colombian unemployment, came to almost identical conclusions. It found
that in the period 1957–1961 it took an average fixed investment of 45,000
pesos to employ one person in a modern manufacturing industry in which
MNC technology was most used; in contrast, during the 1962–1966 period the
figure had risen to 100,000 pesos (the figures are in constant 1958 pesos,
corrected for inflation).[19] Finally, in a still more recent study of 257 manufacturing firms throughout Latin America, it was found that MNCs use
almost one-half the number of employees per $10,000 of sales as do local
firms.[20]

It is this process of ever more intensive substitution of capital for labor
in the technology transferred by the MNCs which is one of the prime causes
of the startling degree of unemployment in the Third World, a situation
which Africa and Asia only recently have begun to face but which has been
gnawing at Latin America since the 1920s. Between 1925 and 1960 the manufacturing sector was able to absorb only 5 million of the 23 million people
who migrated into urban centers from the countryside,[21] and while the total
output of modern manufacturing industries expanded relative to other
activities so that it increased its share of national product from 11 percent
in 1925 to 25 percent in 1970, the percent of the Latin American work force
which it employed actually decreased from 14.4 to 13.8 over the same time
period.[22] This, then, is the employment contribution of the technology of
the multinational corporation to Third World countries: MNCs are eliminating many more jobs than they are creating.

Unemployment is only one dimension of poverty; the other is income
distribution. It is clear that when a person becomes unemployed, without
the assistance of social security and/or unemployment insurance, which is
the case in LDCs, he will become economically impoverished. What many,
particularly those unfamiliar with economics or LDCs, forget, however, is
that poverty can also be the reflection of a highly unequal distribution of a
country's income. Technology is a key variable in explaining unequal income
distribution in countries undergoing increasing industrialization based to a
large degree on private ownership of the required technology and in which

there are no governmental programs for redistribution, again the case in LDCs.[23]

Income Distribution: Causes and Impact. In focusing on the relationship between MNCs' technology and income distribution in LDCs, we find that capital is replacing labor at a growing rate. Who receives the income generated by capital resources? Most LDC economies are based on the legal institutions of capitalism, meaning that the owners of capital resources receive the income generated by those resources. Where there are only a very small number of owners (and thus a very large number of non-owners) of capital, and where the technology used generates a larger proportion of income from capital than labor resources, then, by definition, income distribution will be highly unequal. In addition, where there is a relatively rapid change in technology biased toward labor saving techniques, and where capitalist legal institutions are not modified via, for example, more progressive tax rates to keep pace with this change, then, again by definition, income distribution will become even more unequal over time. This then is the second dimension of the growing poverty in LDCs, namely, the impact of the modern technology of the MNCs on the income distribution of these nations. Just how unequal is the distribution of national income in LDCs and how has it changed over time?

Irma Adelman and Cynthia Taft Morris, in a worldwide study of income distribution, noted a profound change in income distribution from a subsistence level to an average per capita income level of $800 during the industrialization period in Third World countries undergoing the type of industrialization described above. During this "take-off," the richest 5 percent of LDC populations experienced a "striking" increase in incomes both relatively and absolutely compared to the poorest 40 percent of the population.[24] Latin American countries in the midst of this industrialization provide a dramatic verification of this finding. In the 1960s, for example, Chile's average per capita income was approximately $600, but the richest 10 percent were receiving 40 percent of the national income or an actual per capita income of some $2,400, giving a family income higher than the majority of families in Western Europe.[25] In Mexico and Brazil, the situation is worse, and it is notable that these two countries have been by far the most favored investment targets of the MNCs in Latin America.

In Mexico in the early 1950s the ratio of individual income of the richest 20 percent to individual income of the poorest 20 percent was 10 to 1. By the middle 1960s, the ratio had increased to 17 to 1.[26] Yet even these aggregate figures becloud the actuality of what is taking place in the urban industrial zones where MNC investment is concentrated. For example, in the Mexico City area, the richest 20 percent received 62.5 percent of the area's income, while the poorest 20 percent attempted survival on 1.3 percent of the income.[27] In Brazil, where unprecedented increases in industrial output are being achieved, almost all of the benefits of that increase are going to the richest 5 percent. In the short span of ten years, their share of national income went from 27.8 percent (a U.S. Government estimate) or, depending on the source, 44 percent (a U.N. estimate) to a 1970 figure of 36.8 percent (U.S.) or 50 percent (U.N.).[28] And the income share of the poorest 40 percent, some 40 million of the Brazilian people, using the U.S.

Government figures as the conservative estimate, dropped from 10.6 to 8.1 percent during the ten years between 1960 and 1970.

This then is the second aspect of the contribution of the modern technology being transferred to the Third World by the MNCs. It is a contribution to the richest 5, 10, or 20 percent of these populations, but an absolute disservice to the human condition of the greater majority of the populations of LDCs.

The Dollar Cost of MNC Technology. We have one final note on the technology contribution, and this refers to the dollar value that MNCs place on their technology when it is transferred as part of their overall investment in their subsidiaries in LDCs. The sum of the investment value in establishing a subsidiary operation of an MNC is made up largely of the costs of plant and equipment. Of this sum, anywhere from 50 to 65 percent represents the cost of the subsidiary's technology, as valued by and received from the parent MNC. The dollar value placed on this technology is crucial to the overall investment figure claimed to have been made by the MNC and is important for both economic and political reasons. In many LDCs, for example, the tax rate on profits and/or excess profits is based on the dollar sum of profits calculated as a percentage of the value of fixed investment. This is the "rate of return"; it will be lower, and so too will be the tax liability of the subsidiary, the higher the value of fixed investment claimed. In addition, many LDCs place limitations on the amount of profits that can be repatriated by an MNC subsidiary in any given period, based on the value of the fixed investment; thus, the higher the fixed investment, the greater will be the dollar amount of profits that can be transferred out of the LDC.[29]

The declared fixed investment via the declared rate of return also has political significance to the managers of the MNCs. To maintain political stability in hospitable host countries is always a sensible business objective of MNC management. A key operational criterion then is to avoid charges of "exploitation" or, in the parlance of Western economists, charges of "excess profits." Since the empirical basis of such charges relies on the rate of return in the first instance, it is wise to keep that rate as "normal" as possible. MNCs thus wish to keep their declared values of transferred technology, and therefore fixed investment, as high as possible.

We can now look at some of the findings on the actual values of MNCs' transferred technology. From Mexico there have been numerous reported cases of secondhand technology being transferred to subsidiaries declared as either new equipment or valuated at prices much higher than could have been obtained on independent markets.[30] In Colombia, where detailed investigations have been undertaken, excessive overvaluation of the technology was found in *all* cases. For example, a parent MNC was selling machinery to its own subsidiary at prices 30 percent higher than those it was charging an independent Colombian firm for the identical items.[31] In another case, investigation revealed that the valuation of machinery declared at $1.8 million was in fact overstated by 50 percent, the true figure being $1.2 million. In the paper industry, an MNC subsidiary applied for an import permit for *used* machinery which it claimed had a value in excess of $1 million. The government agency then asked for competitive bids internationally on *new* models of the same machinery. The MNC's declared value for the used machinery was found to be 50 percent higher than bids received on the new machinery. Finally, in research being conducted by the author for a forthcoming book, interviews were held with managers of subsidiaries in LDCs. In a number of cases, after a lengthy discussion of the impact of their operations on the host countries, these managers admitted that overvaluing their technology was a common practice.[32]

It is not difficult to understand how MNCs are able to commit these practices when we recall the introductory remarks on the meaning of underdevelopment in the sense of inadequate alternative sources of technology intensified by relative ignorance of international markets on the part of LDC buyers relative to their contemporaries in advanced industrialized nations.

The Financial Contribution and Absorption of Domestic Firms

A traditional argument in favor of MNC expansion in the Third World has been that they bring much needed finance capital. This argument holds that LDCs cannot generate sufficient savings in the form of foreign exchange holdings to purchase the foreign technology needed to implement investment projects. Another variant of this argument contends that even in the cases where there is no foreign exchange shortage, there is still a general shortage of domestic savings relative to the investment needs of these countries. Thus, the MNC is envisaged as contributing foreign savings, i.e., finance capital, to alleviate the general dearth of domestic savings and/or foreign exchange. The key assumption here is, of course, that the MNCs in fact do utilize foreign savings to finance their LDC operations. This assumption, incidentally, is also made by Marxist scholars who have held that MNCs expand from their capitalist home countries because of an excess of surplus finance capital relative to inadequate domestic investment opportunities.

The Origins of MNCs' Finance Capital. Upon investigation of the empirical facts, however, the assumption proves to be incorrect. Table 3 shows the argument to be more myth than reality.

Only 17 percent of the total finance capital used by MNCs in their gross investments came from non-local savings. It should be noted that in the last three years of the overall 1957–1965 period the figure dropped to 9 percent. Of more importance is the use of local savings in manufacturing, the most rapidly expanding of the three sectors. Here the figure of 78 percent of total local financing has been constant since 1960. Individual country studies covering 1965–1970 have also shown no change in this constancy.[33]

Of the finance capital being used by MNC subsidiaries in manufacturing, 38 percent comes from local "internal" sources, largely reinvested earnings, and 40 percent from local capital markets. While in an official accounting sense reinvested earnings are classified as funds from the home country, such a classification misses the real economic meaning of these reinvested earnings. That is, they were generated by the use of largely local resources to start with, both local financial and other resources. These reinvested

Table 3   Percentage of U.S. MNC Gross Investments in Latin America
Financed from Local versus Foreign Savings

			Origin of Finance Capital 1957–1965	
	(A)	(B) Reinvested Earnings and	(C) Local, Host	(D) Total Local
Area and Sector	USA	Depreciation	Country*	(B+C)
Latin America, total	17	59	24	83
Mining and Smelting	8	78	14	92
Petroleum	13	79	8	87
Manufacturing	22	38	40	78

* The original source labels "Local, Host Country" as "Local and Third Countries." Since the participation of third countries is such a small part, we have omitted the designation to avoid misleading labels.

Source: Fernando Fajnzylber, *Estrategia Industrial y Empresas Internacionales: Posicion Relativa de America y Brasil* (Rio de Janeiro: Naciones Unidas, CEPAL, November 1971).

earnings are local savings in the same sense that they are for a 100 percent domestically owned and controlled corporation, with one big exception. Whereas the future net profits (after taxes) from earnings reinvested today constitute, in the case of local firms, a net gain to the income of the LDC that most likely will stay *internalized* to the country, this is not the case for an MNC subsidiary. For the MNC's profit, although it represents a net gain in income for itself, will be largely *externalized* from the LDC and, therefore, will not be for the consumption or investment benefit of the local citizenry. This is borne out by the fact that over the period 1960–1968 MNCs repatriated on the average some 79 percent of their net profits, not to mention the additional remissions of royalties, interest, and other fees.[34] In manufacturing, repatriated profits were somewhat lower but increasing, going from 42 percent of net profits in 1960–1964 to 52 percent in 1965–1968.[35] For each dollar of net profit earned by an MNC subsidiary, 52 cents will leave the country *even though* 78 percent of the investment funds used to generate that dollar of profit came from local sources. If we look at all sectors in which MNCs operate in Latin America, the inflow-outflow accounting gets even worse. Each dollar of net profit is based on an investment that was 83 percent financed from local savings; yet only 21 percent of the profit remains in the local economy.[36]

MNCs not only use local savings to finance their equity investments, but also draw more heavily than domestic firms on local credit markets for short-term working capital loans. In fact, studies show that the MNCs operate on roughly one and one-half to two and one-half times the level of indebtedness of their domestic competition for any given level of total assets.[37] Again the use of largely local savings, in this case working capital, makes possible a productive activity, the profits of which largely benefit recipients external to the local economy.

Do the MNCs make a financial contribution to LDCs, that is, do they make a net addition to the supply of available local savings over time? The answer is no. Although we cannot make an exact quantitative estimate of this loss, from the magnitudes of the above indicators it is clear that there is a net decrease in the amount of local savings that are being utilized for the benefit of either indigent consumers or investors in the local economies of LDCs.

The Buying Out of Domestic Firms. The preceding paragraphs have attempted to correct the first of the two most prevalent misconceived notions about the financial contributions of MNCs to the economies of Third World nations. We turn now to the second of these two notions, namely, the specific use to which MNCs put their finance capital. It is commonly held that when a MNC invests in a LDC, even if it uses largely local savings, it at least channels that investment into the creation of *new* production facilities, facilities which otherwise would have been absent from the local economy. In turn, it is concluded that these new facilities represent a net addition to the productive assets of the LDC.

Again reference to the facts shows this notion to be more myth than reality and its implications therefore largely erroneous. The error can be seen when we refer to the information available on the "method of entry" by the MNCs into LDC economies. By method of entry is meant the use of the MNCs' investment capital, i.e., creation of a new production facility, expansion of a branch office into a subsidiary operation, or the buying out of a local, domestically controlled business. We have argued earlier that the vicious circles of the technology and financial structures of LDCs generate a process whereby the multinational corporations slowly and then increasingly absorb local business enterprises. This, in fact, is actually happening in Latin America.

Data now available on the 187 largest United States MNCs, which account for some 70 percent of all United States foreign investment in the region,[38] show that between 1958 and 1967 these firms established 1,309 subsidiaries. Of the 1,136 subsidiaries for which information on method of entry was available, the breakdown is as follows: 477 or more than 36 percent of these subsidiaries were formed by buying out local enterprises; of the 642 new subsidiaries, 503 or 45 percent of the total 1,309 actually were for new production, with the other 139 established as sales subsidiaries only; the remaining 17 of the total represented the expansion of branch into subsidiary operations. The figures become even more convincing when we examine the method of entry of new subsidiaries in the manufacturing sector in which the majority of the total were established and in which the MNCs are expanding fastest. For the 717 known new manufacturing subsidiaries, 331 or 46 percent did not establish new production but rather purchased existing domestic firms. Compared to the percentage of finance capital devoted to such acquisitions since 1929, the rate of increase is notable throughout. In addition, it was observed that in industries where the percentage of foreign investment going to acquisitions had decreased, the decline was "probably attributable in part to the scarcity of local firms (remaining) in these industries."[39]

The implications of this analysis for the Third World are clear in regard to the so-called financial contributions of MNCs. In the manufacturing sector, currently the most important to the future of development of Latin America, 78 percent of MNCs' foreign investments are financed from local savings. Of this finance capital, 46 percent is used to buy out existing locally controlled firms, whose profits would otherwise be retained domestically and thus contribute to local consumption and/or savings. But from the date of the acquisition and henceforth, some 52 percent of those profits leave the country, resulting in a net decrease in the LDCs' savings which would have been available *and* a net increase in their already acute shortage of foreign exchange. Given these results, it is impossible to see how the MNCs' financial impact on Third World countries could possibly assist in the alleviation of their underdevelopment.

Balance of Payment Contributions:
Restrictions, Pricing, Actual Profits

We have already alluded to the acute foreign exchange shortages, termed "the balance of payments problem," which most Third World countries experience. It is well known that Latin America is experiencing the severest of difficulties in maintaining its ability to pay off foreign debts. There is an increasing negative gap between exports and imports, and the region's foreign debts are growing at a rapid rate in terms of repayments of past public and private loans. Concomitantly, outflows continue to mount on payments of profits, royalties, and interests for past MNC direct investment. While in the period 1951–1955 these latter items accounted for some 13 percent of the annual export earnings of the Latin American countries, by the 1966–1969 time period, they took 21 percent of those earnings.[40]

Thus it is not surprising that experts in both the offices of Wall Street and the government buildings of the Third World are taking an intense interest in the balance of payments impacts of the multinational corporations. And it is perhaps also not surprising that experts come to different conclusions on the matter.[41]

Our prior discussion of the sources and uses of MNCs' finance capital indicated that the impact on foreign exchange is largely negative. In this section, we shall go beyond an analysis of the sources and uses of finance capital to explore a second dimension of the balance of payments impacts of MNCs, the export and import behavior of these global corporations and their remittances of royalties and service fees. The latter item is the so-called managerial fee paid to the parent MNC for technical assistance rendered to its own subsidiaries and joint ventures, as well as to licensees of technology. These royalty and fee payments have reached significant proportions, accounting for some 25 percent of the total returns from all United States MNCs' foreign investments in 1970.[42] As for the significance of MNCs' export and import operations, in 1968 United States MNCs were responsible for 40 percent of Latin America's manufactured exports and in 1966, some 33 percent of its total exports, while accounting for more than a third of the region's imports from the United States in 1964.[43] It should be emphasized here that these percentages refer only to so-called *intra-company transactions*, exports and imports between subsidiaries of the same parent network. From the United States side, these intra-company transactions were very important, reflected by the fact that United States MNCs shipped some 33 percent of *total* United States exports directly to their subsidiaries overseas.[44] Thus the internal, intra-company transactions of exports and imports and the payments of royalties and fees between subsidiaries of the same parent are both a significant part of the MNCs' total revenues and an important component of the foreign exchange outflows and inflows of the countries in which they are located.

It has been claimed that the MNCs can make a significant contribution to raising the foreign exchange earnings of Third World countries through their ability to export, particularly manufactured goods. On the surface this argument would appear correct, given the competitive advantages of the technology and worldwide marketing systems of the MNCs compared to local firms. There are a number of considerations, however, which this argument overlooks. First, if MNCs have subsidiaries manufacturing similar products in many countries, which most of them do, would the subsidiaries of the same parent want to compete with each other through exports? Second, even where the parents have complementary production between subsidiaries so that intersubsidiary exports and imports are desirable, what are the prices on such exports and imports since they are internal transactions and not subject to the competitive pressures of the open market? Third, what are the tax and other financial criteria at work which would make these prices different from those received or paid by local firms dealing with independent buyers and sellers on the international market? Fourth, what does the available empirical evidence tell us concerning the initial argument and the considerations we have introduced? Finally, besides the exporting by MNC subsidiaries, what impact does the licensing of their technology to local firms have on the latter's ability to export?

The MNCs and Exports: Restrictions. We shall start with the last question first. One study, investigating the licensing agreements between local firms in LDCs and the MNCs, has shown that in most cases there are total prohibitions on using this technology in the production of exports. The study was based on 409 "transfer of technology" contracts in the five countries of the Andean Group, i.e., Bolivia, Colombia, Chile, Ecuador, and Peru. The results showed that 92 percent of the nationally owned firms and 79 percent of the wholly owned MNC subsidiaries were totally prohibited from exporting by the MNC parent from whom they had licensed their technology.[45]

As telling as these figures are, they are, nevertheless, biased downward. In many of the contracts which permitted some exporting, the effect was really total prohibition, since either they limited the firms to a small neighboring market in which the MNCs had no interest or they limited exports to distant countries which local firms could not hope to penetrate. And these practices are not unique to the Andean countries. Similar results have been revealed by government and U.N. studies in India, Pakistan, the Philippines, Mexico, Iran, etc.[46] There is a profound impact of these "restrictive business practices," to use the formal language of the U.N., on the export capacity of domestic firms and their LDC economies. At a time when the political leaders[47] of the more developed countries are encouraging Third World countries to export more, their own MNCs are making it virtually impossible for them to enter the one export market which in the long run is viable, namely, manufactured exports.

We turn now to the question of the export performance of the MNC subsidiaries themselves. As the above study illustrates, it does not necessarily follow that the MNCs will export from LDC locations even though they may have the technological and marketing prerequisites. For in the Andean Group 79 percent of the MNC subsidiaries were prohibited by their parents from engaging in exporting, and these findings are again not unique to these countries. In fact, studies have found that in Latin America, manufacturing MNCs on the average export less than 10 percent of their total sales; while in Europe, United States firms average about 25 percent.[48] There are exceptions, however. Some MNC subsidiaries do export significant *volumes*, depending on the country and industry in which they are located.

MNCs and Exports: Performance and Pricing. American MNCs account for some 40 percent of Latin America's manufactured exports, and they have achieved this level of export participation within the span of the past twenty years. Yet the figure is a deceptive one if it is intended to imply that MNCs are therefore making a significant positive impact on the balance of payments of Third World countries in general. Manufactured exports constitute only 16.6 percent of the region's total exports, and well over half of these exports are from only three of the twenty-one countries, Argentina, Brazil, and Mexico.[49] Further, a detailed econometric analysis has determined that, relative to local firms, MNC subsidiaries performed significantly better only in these three countries and only in terms of export sales to other Latin American countries.[50] In contrast, for exports to the rest of the world, where one would expect the technological and marketing superiority of the MNCs to be most crucial, their export performance was not significantly different from domestic enterprises. For the remaining countries of the region, the MNCs were outperformed on exports to the rest of the world by firms which had substantial domestic participation, while on exports to other Latin American countries the MNCs performed no differently than their domestic counterparts.[51]

Finally, in terms of the potential export contribution of MNCs, we turn to the question of the prices they received for exports relative to domestic companies trading with independent buyers. Let us first note, however, some of the reasons why the export price received by an MNC subsidiary will be different from the international market price received by a local firm exporting a similar item.

The price put on an export or import between MNC subsidiaries of the same parent is termed in the business literature an intra-company transfer price, or "transfer price." The business literature is also replete with reasons and documentation on why and how transfer prices frequently deviate sharply from the market price of these goods.[52] For example, if a subsidiary exporting in country X is faced with higher corporate tax rates than the importing subsidiary of the same parent in country M, then the parent will pay less *total* taxes for both subsidiaries and earn more *total* net profits by directing the exporting subsidiary to undervalue its exports. Another and even more profitable variant of this pricing technique is to direct the underpriced exports first to a tax-free port (so-called tax-havens) and then re-export the goods at their normal market value (or perhaps now overvalued) to the subsidiary of final destination. Either way total profits are higher than they would be had the MNC followed the "spirit of the law." Of more importance here, however, is the obvious impact on the local economy of the LDC in which such exports originate. LDC governments severely short of needed tax revenues to service the masses of illiterate, undernourished, and unemployed people in their countries are now deprived of that much more tax revenue so that a MNC can "maximize," as economists are prone to say, their global profits. All this through a simple but modern accounting technique called transfer pricing.

But we are getting ahead of our facts at this point. Let us first look at the information on export pricing and then import pricing by MNCs in Latin America. A look at the export pricing of a large number of MNCs in manufacturing industries in Mexico, Brazil, Argentina, and Venezuela shows that 75 percent of these firms sold exports only to other subsidiaries of the same parents. In turn, these 75 percent on the average *underpriced their exports by some 40 percent* relative to the prices being received by local firms.[53] The bulk of the exports of these countries and these MNCs were going to Latin American destinations, and it was for these destinations that the underpricing took place. Moreover *an average level of underpricing of 50 percent* was found in six other Latin American countries where MNCs were engaged in exporting to subsidiaries in rest of the world destinations.[54]

MNCs and Imports: Tie-in Clauses. The transfer price placed on the imports of an MNC subsidiary will be *higher* than the normal market price in the event that the parent desires to transfer funds extra-legally from that subsidiary to some other part of its network. In other words, the overpricing of imports accomplishes the same objectives and is done for similar reasons as the underpricing of exports. As a professor of business administration has recently observed:

> . . . there is the problem of transfer pricing: in a cluster of corporations (subsidiaries) controlled by the same top management, earnings may be changed at will by changing the charges for goods and services within the cluster. Presumably, rational management will use the mechanism of transfer prices in a way that will minimize the total tax burden on the (parent) company, showing higher earnings in countries where the rate of taxation is lowest.[55]

Before examining the empirical facts of overpricing of imports, we should first mention an additional "restrictive clause" in the transfer of technology contracts negotiated between MNC parents and their subsidiaries and licensees. This is the so-called "tie-in clause" which requires the subsidiary or the licensee (depending on who is acquiring the technology) to purchase intermediate parts and capital goods from the same parent MNC which supplies the basic technology. This practice is quite common and part of the day-to-day operational behavior of MNCs in the Third World. For example, in the Andean Group study, 67 percent of the investigated contracts had tie-in clauses.[56] The results were no different in other countries like India, Pakistan, etc.[57]

It is ironical that although this type of clause is in basic violation of the antitrust laws of the MNC's home countries, it continues to be put into practice in LDCs.[58] The fact that the legal institutions of LDCs cannot yet

cope with these problems strongly underlines the differences in the oligopoly power of MNCs in advanced industrialized versus Third World
countries.

MNCs and Imports: Pricing. Having noted this oligopoly power of the
parent MNCs with reference to the imports of both subsidiaries and
domestic companies, we can now examine the empirical evidence on import
overpricing. Since the information is relatively unknown to economists and
non-economists alike, particularly outside of Latin America, we shall
devote some detail to it in Table 4.

The Colombian data on overpricing are not unique to that country.
Similar results have been discovered in other parts of Latin America and in
other regions, such as the Philippines and Pakistan. In Chile, overpricing
ranges from 30 to more than 700 percent, in Peru from 50 to 300 percent,
and in Ecuador from 75 to 200 percent. Apparently the techniques for
extra-legally transferring funds out of LDCs does not stop short of overpricing actual imports. During a two-day interview with the head of a
European MNC subsidiary in a South American country, the author was
shown shipping crates which had just cleared local customs. In this isolated
case, the shipping crates contained less than 30 percent of their declared
contents although the payment to an offshore subsidiary of the parent was
for 100 percent of the declared contents at an overpricing of 2500 percent.[59]
One can only speculate as to what extent this case represents the day-to-day
behavior of MNCs in the Third World.

But even these *average* figures on overpricing, as high as they are, do
not portray the actuality of what was happening in the case of specific
products. Thus, tetracycline, a modern antibiotic increasingly replacing
penicillin, was overpriced by 948 to 987 percent. And in the case of librium
and valium, drugs used in the treatment of mental illness, the overpricing
reached figures of 6500 and 8200 percent, respectively; while in electronics
transistors were overvalued by 1100 percent and electric motors by 404 percent.[60] Who paid for the overpricing of such items as tetracycline? The
Colombian consumer paid, in a country where the average per capita income
is around $300. The total value of the overpricing for the *actually sampled*
items in the four industries was more than $4 million. If the average over-
pricing is extended and assumed to hold for the rest of the products and
MNCs in the drug industry, and there is no reason to assume otherwise,
then the total loss to the 1968 Colombian balance of payments was on the
order of $20 million with a loss in governmental tax revenues of some $10
million, and this from one industry alone![61]

The Triangular Trade: Pricing and Royalties. In the Colombian investigation, it was found that a large proportion of the overpriced imports involved
a "triangular trade." That is, they were shipped from a United States or
European based parent or subsidiary of the parent to a holding company in
Panama. In Panama, a tax-haven, the prices of these articles were raised
to their stated overpriced levels and then re-exported to Colombia.[62] Thus,
the MNCs involved avoided tax payments on their true profits *both* in the
country of export origin and in Colombia.

Panama also serves another function. The holding companies of many
United States and European MNCs in Panama are the companies for which

Table 4 Overpricing of Imported Intermediate Parts by Foreign Ownership Structure: Colombia 1968

Ownership Structure	Pharmaceutical Industry			Rubber Industry			Chemical Industry			Electronics Industry		
	a	b	c*	a	b	c	a	b	c	a	b	c
Foreign Owned	50%	25%	155%	33%	60%	40%	30%	12%	25.5%	40%	90%	16%–60%
Joint Ventures	n.a.	n.a.	n.a.	n.a.	n.a.	n.a.	45%	37%	20.2%	50%	90%	6%–50%

Code: a: approximate percentage of sales of sample firms relative to total sales of firms with a similar ownership structure
b: total volume of imports sampled and evaluated as a percentage of the firm's total imports
c: weighted average of overpricing of evaluated imports
n.a.: not available

* Individual firm data are as follows (in percent): #1: 253.6; #2: 133.7; #3: 132.8; #4: 306.2; #5: 483; #6: 39.5; #7: 179.4; #8: 79.1; #9: 58.3; #10: 73.8; #11: 475.4; #12: 374.7; #13: 177.5; #14: 164.8; #15: 60.4; #16: 476.9; #17: 34.4.

Source: Constantine Vaitsos, "Interaffiliate Charges by Transnational Corporations and Intercountry Income Distribution," submitted in partial fulfillment of the requirements for the degree of Doctor of Philosophy at Harvard University, June 1972, p. 48.

many of their foreign investments in Latin America are registered. In Peru, for instance, Panama is the second largest foreign country in which foreign investments are registered.[63] This procedure permits the channeling of royalty and fee payments to Panama, thereby giving the MNCs a substantial flexibility as to where they ultimately report their income. The income generated from royalties and fees alone is large and, in fact, most often considerably greater than reported profits received from subsidiaries. In the Andean Group, for MNC subsidiaries, royalties paid to the parent are fixed at anywhere from 10 to 15 percent of gross or net sales, depending on the particular company.[64] Since a considerable part of the final sale price is based on imported parts which are overvalued, the MNCs multiply their unearned profits, first via the import overpricing and second through that component of royalties derived from an inflated sales price due to the overpricing. The earnings thus generated are impressive relative both to the MNCs' reported profits and to the foreign exchange shortages of these countries. Thus in Chile the outflow of royalties is three times greater than profit remittances, and in Colombia the payments for royalties alone use up approximately 10 percent of non-coffee export earnings.[65]

Reported vs. Actual Rates of Return. The above figures speak well enough for themselves. We can now add these figures to the "reported profits" and the payments of royalties and fees from MNC subsidiaries. Taken together, overpricing of imports plus reported profits, royalties, and fees give the total dollar value of profits generated by a subsidiary in a given year. This total dollar value of "effective profits" can then be divided into the subsidiary's declared net worth of its investment (including reinvested earnings). The resulting answer is called the "annual rate of return on investment." Vaitsos and his group have performed this exercise for 100 percent parent owned MNC drug subsidiaries in Colombia. The results are shown in Table 5.

Table 5   On Investment: Annual Rate of Return:
Wholly Owned MNC Drug Subsidiaries: Colombia, 1968

MNC Subsidiary	Rate of Return	MNC Subsidiary	Rate of Return	MNC Subsidiary	Rate of Return
#1	197.3%	#6	38.1%	#11	88.8%
#2	94.4%	#7	402.3%	#12	256.8%
#3	247.0%	#8	126.1%	#13	56.5%
#4	708.3%	#9	44.2%	#14	378.9%
#5	962.1%	#10	138.0%	#15	352.8%

Average of Declared Returns to Colombian Tax Authorities	6.7%
Average of Effective Returns	136.3%

Source: Vaitsos, "Interaffiliate Charges . . .," *op. cit.*, pp. 69-73.

As astoundingly high as these rates of return are, they undoubtedly *understate* the actual sums earned by these MNCs. First, the above calculations do not include the probability of export underpricing, which as previously shown is quite high. Second, these returns are based on the net worth of investment as declared by the subsidiaries. As pointed out earlier, all evidence to date indicates there is substantial overvaluation of declared investment of approximately 30 to 50 percent. Thus, the correction for this overvaluation would significantly raise the above figures. One Colombian economist has commented on the fact that between 1960 and 1968 the average *reported* rate of return for MNCs in all manufacturing sectors of the country was 6.4 percent. He found it "difficult to accept" that these MNCs would continue to enter Colombia at this rate of reported profitability while national firms were showing higher returns and the interest rate in financial markets was running between 16 and 20 percent.[66] Hopefully, the foregoing analysis helps to explain why the MNCs continue to expand in Third World countries like Colombia.

SUMMARY AND CONCLUSIONS

There can be little doubt as to our overall conclusions concerning the impact of MNCs on Third World nations. We have found more myth than reality in the claims made about the three most important contributions of MNCs. Our analysis of the contribution in technology revealed a basic cause of further unemployment and a further concentration of already extremely unequal income distribution, while noting the excessive prices being charged by the MNCs in transferring this technology. Upon examination, the financial contribution turns out to be a financial drain, decreasing both current consumption and available local savings and, thus, future consumption for the vast majority of LDC inhabitants. The third area of analysis, the balance of payments contribution, led to similar conclusions. In contrast to a contribution, the empirical information showed no superior export performance by MNCs relative to local firms unless it was accompanied by export underpricing. Concomitantly, exports were further limited via restrictions placed on their technology by the MNCs. While potential inflows were minimized, the balance of payments outflows were accentuated through import overpricing and inflated royalty payments.

There can be little doubt that such an impact can only contribute to the further inpoverishment of the poorest 60 to 80 percent of Third World populations. Summing up the specific consequences discussed in this paper, however, leads to an overall consequence which should be briefly mentioned. In the Third World, the MNCs are involved in a structural process which cannot be ignored. We have already referred to the fact that this process permits an ever greater control over the technology and finances of the majority of LDCs, resulting in what Celso Furtado, among others, has shown to be an ever-growing external dependency of the poor nations on the few rich nations of the world. Besides the transfer-in of inappropriate technology and the transfer-out of financial resources, this process includes one further destabilizing force, the transfer, via advertising and mass-media programming, of a consumption ideology, the goals of which only 30 percent at best and, more realistically, 20 percent of LDC populations can hope to achieve in the foreseeable future. These consumption goals do not go unheeded by the greater majority of these countries; rather, they are observed, absorbed, and become part of the poor, the not-so-poor, and the rich. Thus, just as the MNCs are involved in the restructuring of the production sector, so too are they a major force in restructuring the consumption "sector." Yet there is a rather blatant contradiction at work here, for the new structure of consumption is in serious imbalance with the inadequate consumption capacity generated by the very production structure which the MNCs have so pivotally helped to create; and, therefore, the MNCs themselves have negated any possibility for attaining the new consumption goals by all except a small minority. It is perhaps here that we can discover a major cause for the profound and growing frustration that is often found in underdeveloped countries. When many share the same basic and intense frustration, the problem goes beyond the realm of economics and becomes truly a social and political one.

Latin America, the region which has nurtured this frustration relatively longer than any other Third World area, has already witnessed three patterns of political response to this problem. The political decision of Brazil and Mexico has been to continue the present reliance on the MNCs via the expedient of growing political oppression. Cuba and Chile are attempting to detach themselves from industrialization via the MNCs by establishing socialist institutions. And the Peruvian military appears to be in the midst of deciding to what extent it desires, let alone is able, to minimize and/or modify the role of MNCs in order to pursue a new form of national development. What the long-run viability of any of these three responses will be cannot be dealt with here. There is, however, a clear message. The continued and unaltered expansion of the MNCs into the Third World will increase the instability of these societies and bring about significant political change.

To the extent that such political change will reduce the bargaining power of the MNCs in these countries and thereby diminish the transfer of income to MDCs, the result will be a negative impact in the general level of affluence in advanced nations. Such an interpretation could, in fact, be given to the creation of the Organization of Petroleum Exporting Countries (OPEC) and the growing "Energy Crisis" being faced in the United States and other MDCs. OPEC has succeeded in significantly reducing the flow of income from poor to rich nations. This means that by the late 1970's the rising price of energy, the backbone of modern industrial society, will have negatively affected the consumption levels of the greater majority of people residing in MDCs. If new mechanisms for increasing Third World bargaining power over MNCs in the manufacturing sector are found, then there will be even more profound implications for maintaining present consumption styles in the rich nations. Whether or not the United States, Japan, and Western Europe will permit such mechanisms to become reality can only be speculated upon and such speculation lies within the domain not of economics but of an analysis of power and the use of power by the major actors in the world political economy.[67]

NOTES

1. On unemployment, see Dudley Seers, "Poverty in the Third World," lecture for The American University's Social Science Seminar, Washington,

D.C., December 16, 1972; also International Labor Organization (ILO), *Hacia el Pleno Empleo*, Un Programa para Colombia, Preparado por una Mision Internacional Organizada por la Oficina Internacional del Trabajo, Ginebra 1970. On income distribution, see Cynthia Taft Morris and Irma Adleman, "An Anatomy of Income Distribution Patterns in Developing Nations: A Summary of Findings," Economic Staff Paper No. 116, IBRD (September 1971). On income distribution in Brazil, see H. P. Miller, unpublished study (Washington, D.C.: U.S. Bureau of the Census, 1971). On income distribution in Latin America, see United Nations Economic Commission for Latin America (ECLA), *The Distribution of Income in Latin America* (E/CN-12/868) (New York: UN, 1970); UN-ECLA, *Economic Survey for Latin America, 1971* (E/EN-12/935) (New York: UN, June, 1972); UN-ECLA, *Economic Survey for Latin America* (New York: UN, 1969); UN-ECLA, *The Process of Industrial Development in Latin America* (New York: UN, 1966).

2. Constantine Vaitsos, "Patents Revisited: Their Function in Developing Countries," *The Journal of Development Studies* (1973).

3. John M. Blair, *Economic Concentration: Structure, Behavior and Public Policy* (New York: Harcourt Brace Jovanovich, Inc., 1972), p. 205.

4. Vaitsos, "Patents . . . ," *op. cit.*, p. 12.

5. See R. Prebisch, *Change and Development: Latin America's Great Task*, report submitted to the Inter-American Development Bank, Washington, D.C., July 1970; UN-ECLA, *Economic Survey for Latin America, 1971, op. cit.*

6. From 1950 to 1970 LDCs' exports decreased from 33 percent of world exports to 19 percent. Peter Peterson, Presidential Task Force on International Development, *U.S. Foreign Assistance in the 1970's: A New Approach* (Washington, D.C.: Government Printing Office, 1970), p. 8.

7. Miguel Wionczek, "La Banca Extranjera en America Latina," report prepared for Novena Reunion de Technicos de los Bancos Centrales del Continente Americano, Lima, 17-22 de Noviembre, 1969; Aldo Ferrer, "El Capital Extranjero en la Economia Argentina," *Trimestre Economico*, No. 150 (Abril-Junio, 1971); Aldo Ferrer, "Empresa Extranjera: Observaciones sobre la Experiencia Argentina," seminar on *Politica de Inversiones Extranjeras y Transferencia de Technologia en America Latina*, organized by ILDIS/Flasco, Santiago, 1971.

8. See John M. Blair, *op. cit.*, pp. 75 ff.

9. Miguel Wionczek, *op. cit.*

10. Celso Furtado, "The Concept of External Dependence in the Study of Underdevelopment," in C. K. Wilber (ed.), *The Political Economy of Development and Underdevelopment* (New York: Random House, 1974).

11. The figures for Chile are taken from Luis Pacheco, "La Inversion Extranjera y las Corporaciones Internacionales en el Desarrollo Industrial Chileno," in *Proceso a la Industrializacion Chilena* (Santiago: Ediciones Nueva Universidad, Universidad Catolica de Chile, 1972); Corporacion de Fomento de la Produccion (CORFO), *Las Inversiones Extranjeras en la Industria Chilena Periodo 1960–1969*, Publicacion No. 57-A/71 (Febrero, 1971). For an analysis of Mexico, see Ricardo Cinta, "Burguesia Nacional y Desarrollo," in *El Perfil de Mexico en 1980*, III (1972), pp. 165-209. Mexico: Siglo Veintiuno. For an analysis of Argentina, see Aldo Ferrer, "El Capital Extranjero . . . ," *op. cit.*

12. The estimate of the "equivalent of the population" is based on the percentage of unemployment plus the percentage (weighted) of underemployment (i.e., less than substantial full employment throughout one work year) of the labor force. United Nations Economic and Social Council, *Development Digest*, No. 4, (1969).

13. *Survey of the Alliance for Progress, Colombia—A Case History of U.S. AID*, a study prepared at the request of the Subcommittee on American Republic Affairs by the staff of the Committee on Foreign Relations, U.S. Senate, together with a report of the Comptroller General, February 1, 1969 (Washington, D. C.: Government Printing Office, 1969). For more recent works, see William C. Thiesenhusen, "Latin America's Employment Problem," *Science*, CLXXI (March 5, 1971), pp. 868–874; ILO, *op. cit.*; Erik Thorbecke, "Desempleo y Subempleo en la America Latina," IBD/UN Seminar on Marginality in Latin America, Santiago, November 23–27, 1970.

14. Erik Thorbecke, *Employment and Output: A Methodology Applied to Peru and Guatemala* (Paris: Development Center, OECD, 1970), p. 4.

15. *Ibid.*

16. Prebisch, *op. cit.*

17. Pedroleon Diaz, *Analisis Comparativo de los Contratos de Licencia en el Grupo Andino* (Lima: Andean Group Document, Octubre 1971).

18. Dario Abad, "Las inversiones extranjeras—divergencia de interesse y posibilidades de una reconciliacion de intereses," in Albrecht von Gleich (ed.), *Las inversiones extranjeras privadas en Latin America* (Hamburg: Instituto de estudios Iberoamericanos, 1971).

19. ILO, *op. cit.*, p. 121.

20. Ronald Müller and Richard Morgenstern, "The Impact of Multinational Corporations on the Balance of Payments of LDCs: An Econometric Analysis of Pricing in Export Sales," paper presented to the Econometrics Society Program of the American Economics Association Annual Meetings, Toronto, December 28, 1972.

21. UN-ECLA, *The Process of Industrial Development, op. cit.*

22. Inter-American Development Bank (IDB), *Socio Economic Progress in Latin America* (Washington, D.C., 1971); Thorbecke, *Employment and Output, op. cit.*, p. 10.

23. As an aside, let us briefly mention another institutional aspect of the term underdevelopment, i.e., the inability of LDC governments to enforce redistribution institutions such as social security, medical and educational assistance, progressive income taxation, etc.

24. Morris and Adelman, *op. cit.*

25. Osvaldo Sunkel, "Subdesarrollo, Dependencia y Marginacion: Proposiciones para un Enfoque Integrador," IDB/UN Seminar on Marginality in Latin America, Santiago, November 23–27, 1970.

26. James P. Grant, "Multinational Corporations and the Developing Countries: The Emerging Job Crisis and its Implications" (Washington, D.C.: Overseas Development Council, January 1972).

27. UN-ECLA, *Economic Survey for Latin America, op. cit.*

28. The United States estimate is from Miller, *op. cit.* The Latin American UN estimate is from UN-ECLA, *The Distribution of Income, op. cit.*

29. For further elaboration of these reasons, see James A. Shulman, "Transfer Pricing in Multinational Business," unpublished Ph.D. dissertation, Harvard Graduate School of Business Administration, 1966; also Michael Z. Brooke and H. Lee Remmers, *The Strategy of Multinational Enterprise: Organization and Finance* (New York: American Elsevier Publishing Company, Inc., 1970).

30. See citations in Leopaldo Solis, "Mexican Economic Policy in the Post-War Period: The Views of Mexican Economists," *American Economic Review*, XVI, No. 3, Part 2, Supplement (June 1971); also Miguel Wionczek, "Nacionalismo Mexicano e Inversion Extranjera," *Comercio Exterior* (December 7, 1967), pp. 980–985.

31. This and the other cases in Colombia are presented in Constantine Vaitsos, "Interaffiliate Charges by Transnational Corporations and Intercountry Income Distribution," submitted in partial fulfillment of the requirements for the degree of Doctor of Philosophy at Harvard University, June 1972, pp. 55–56.

32. Richard Barnet and Ronald Müller, *The Earth Managers . . . Their Global Corporations* (New York: Simon and Schuster, forthcoming).

33. Abad, *op. cit.*; Ferrer, "El Capital Extranjero . . . ," *op. cit.*; Ferrer, "Empresa Extranjera . . . , op. cit.*; Corporacion de Fomento de la Produccion (CORFO), *Analisis de la Inversiones Extranjeras en Chile . . . Periodo 1954–1970*, No. 20 (Enero 1972); CORFO, *Comportamiento de las Principales Empresas Industriales Extranjeras Acegidas AL D. F. L. 258*, Publicacion No. 9-A/70, (Santiago: Division de Planeficacion Industrial, Departmento de Diagnostico y Politica, 1970); CORFO, *Las Inversiones Extranjeras, op. cit.*; CORFO, *La Propiedad Industrial en Chile y Su Impacto en el Desarrollo Industrial*, Santiago (Septiembre de 1970) (documento preliminar); ODELPLAN, *El Capital Privado Extranjero en Chile en el Perido 1964–1968 a Nivel Global y Sectorial*, #R/PL/70-007, Santiago (Agosto de 1970).

34. Fernando Fajnzylber, *Estrategia Industrial y Empresas Internacionales: Posicion Relativa de America y Brasil* (Rio de Janeiro: Naciones Unidas, CEPAL, November 1970), p. 59. On royalties and fees, see pp. 143–145 in this article.

35. Fajnzylber, *loc. cit.*

36. Tax revenues, which for LDCs constitute internalized local savings from MNCs, are so low that they do not change the basic conclusion of this paragraph. In addition, to be shown later, the amount of tax revenue lost due to unreported and extra-legally repatriated profits more than compensates for the omission of collected tax revenues in the present argument.

37. See sources in note 33 above, particularly Dario Abad.

38. The data and its breakdown are from J. W. Vaupel and J. P. Curhan, *The Making of Multinational Enterprise* (Boston: Harvard Business School, 1969), pp. 254–265.

39. *Business Latin America* (January 15, 1970). Parentheses are mine.

40. Felipe Pazos, "El Financiamiento Externo de la America Latina: Aumento Progresivo o Disminucion Gradual?" *Trimestre Economico*, No. 150 (Abril–Junio 1971).

41. For a pro-MNC analysis of impacts, see: Herbert K. May, *The Effects of United States and Other Foreign Investment in Latin America* (Council for Latin America, January 1970); also Herbert K. May and J. A. Fernandez, *Impact of Foreign Investment in Mexico* (Washington, D.C.: National Chamber Foundation, undated, ca. 1971).

42. Susan B. Foster, "Impact of Direct Investment Abroad by United States Multinational Companies on the Balance of Payments," *Monthly Review of the Federal Reserve Bank of New York* (July 1972), p. 172.

43. United Nations Conference on Trade and Development (UNCTAD), *Restrictive Business Practices*, TD/122/Supp. 1, Santiago de Chile, January 7, 1972, p. 32; May, *op. cit.*, 1970; Samuel Pizer and Frederik Cutler, "U.S. Exports to Foreign Affiliates of U.S. Firms," *Survey of Current Business*, XLV, no. 12 (Washington, D.C.: U.S. Department of Commerce, 1965).

44. Foster., *op. cit.*, p. 174.

45. Constantine Vaitsos, "The Process of Commercialization of Technology in the Andean Pact: A Synthesis," Andean Group Document, Lima, October 1971, pp. 20–26; Diaz, *op. cit.*, pp. 10–14.

46. UNCTAD, *Restrictive Business Practices, op. cit.*, pp. 9–11.

47. See Peterson, *op. cit.*

48. Andean group statistics are from Vaitsos, "The Process of Commercialization . . . ," *op. cit.* For micro-derived Latin American figures, see Müller and Morgenstern, *op. cit.* For aggregates in Latin America and Europe, see David R. Belli, "Sales of Foreign Affiliates of U.S. Firms," *Survey of Current Business*, L, No. 10 (Washington, D.C.: U.S. Department of Commerce, October 1970), p. 20.

49. IDB, *op. cit.*; UN-ECLA, *Economic Survey for Latin America, 1971, op. cit.*

50. Müller and Morgenstern, *op. cit.*

51. *Ibid.*

52. See Shulman, *op. cit.*; Brooke and Remmers, *op. cit.*, Part II; Charles Levinson, *Capital, Inflation, and the Multinationals* (London: George Allen and Unwin Ltd., 1971), pp. 99 ff.

53. Müller and Morgenstern, *op. cit.*

54. *Ibid.*

55. Yair Aharoni, "On the Definition of a Multinational Corporation," in A. Kapoor and P. D. Grubs (eds.), *The Multinational Enterprise in Transition* (Princeton: Darwin Press, 1972), p. 11. Parentheses are mine, added for explanation.

56. United Nations Conference on Trade and Development (UNCTAD), *Transfer of Technology Policies Relating to Technology of the Countries of the Andean Pact: Their Foundations; A Study by the Junta del Acuerdo de Cartagena.* TD/107, December 29, 1971, pp. 14–15.

57. UNCTAD, *Restrictive Business Practices, op. cit.*, pp. 44-45. These technology contracts also include many other restrictions, e.g., the MNC can

determine final selling prices and volume, select key personnel in the licensee's business, etc.

58. Diaz, *op. cit.*, pp. 19–23; Vaitsos, "Interaffiliate Charges . . . ," *op. cit.*, p. 52.
59. Further details on this and other interviews will be given in Barnet and Müller, *op. cit.*
60. *El Espectador* (daily newspaper) citing the official Colombian Court transcripts, "Overpricing by Foreign Drug Companies," Bogota, Colombia, February 6, 1970, pp. 1A, ff; Vaitsos, "Interaffiliate Charges . . . ," *op. cit.*, Appendix 3.
61. *Ibid.*, pp. 49–50.
62. *Ibid.*, p. 49.
63. Diaz, *op. cit.*, pp. 24–25.
64. *Ibid.*
65. CORFO, *La Propiedad Industrial en Chile, op. cit.*, pp. 26–27. Diaz, *op. cit.*, pp. 18–19; UN-ECLA, *Economic Survey for Latin America, 1971, op. cit.*
66. Abad, *op. cit.*, p. 43.
67. A detailed analysis of the changing nature of bargaining power between MNCs and LDCs and its implications for advanced nations can be found in Barnet and Müller, *op. cit.* For an analysis of the variables affecting bargaining power and policy tools for increasing bargaining power over MNCs by LDC governments, see Ronald Müller, "The Political Economy of Direct Foreign Investment: An Appraisal for Latin American Policy Making," prepared Summer 1969 for the Prebisch Group (Washington, D.C.: Inter-American Development Bank, Special Studies Division, 1970), Chapters 1–3 and Appendix 1.

12

The World Bank and Imperialism

Alfonso Inostroza

Chile views with concern the discrepancy that appears to exist between the policy actually adopted by the Bank's management toward our country in the recent past and many of Mr. McNamara's words and comments at last Monday's meeting.

One of the subjects which the Bank's President particularly stressed in his address was the dilemma or conflict that apparently exists between rapid global growth in a country's economy and the improvement in similar terms of the income levels of its poorest sectors. On this point, he emphasized that it was the ineluctable responsibility of every government to adopt the reforms needed to prevent this unjust paradox.

The present Government of Chile has made a very great effort to overcome this problem. In 1971, after several years of economic stagnation, the overall rate of growth in our economy rose to over 8 per cent. The unemployment rate, which had been more than 8 per cent, dropped to under 4 per cent, a figure that compares favorably not only with the usual indices for developing countries but also with those for many highly industrialized nations. There has been a very notable improvement in the distribution of income, in favor, precisely, of the large low-income sectors of the population to which Mr. McNamara referred. Chile has implemented extraordinarily important and far-reaching measures to modify the distribution of wealth and economic power, measures which it was necessary to impose in view of the economic and financial situation of our country. The agrarian reform process has been expanded and accelerated. Productive sectors of a monopolistic type that were operating at a low level of their installed capacity have been brought under social ownership. Credit has been rationalized and made democratic, with the banking system being incorporated in the area of social ownership. The production of basic resources has been nationalized. Such production constitutes over 80 per cent of the value of our country's exports but, until now, accounted for a very considerable flight of foreign exchange owing to the excessive profits obtained by foreign enterprises which in certain years, as in the case of some U.S. copper producers, made profits of over 200 per cent in relation to book value.

This statement was read for Chile at the Joint Annual Discussion of the Board of Governors, IMF and IBRD, 1972 Annual Meetings, Washington, D.C., September 28, 1972.

The Government of Chile has carried out all these changes at a time when the price of copper, its principal export product, has shown a considerable decline. This resulted last year in a drop of approximately $200 million in Chile's foreign exchange receipts. In addition, there has been a large increase in world prices for fundamental import items and an increased demand for certain consumer goods that results from the improvement in the income of the poorest sectors, which has naturally had an effect on our balance of payments situation. This situation has been aggravated by the decision of various foreign sources, which have traditionally granted financial assistance to Chile, to close their operations with our country.

At this time I want to refer only to the attitude adopted by the management of the World Bank, because this institution traditionally has constituted one of our country's most important bases of external financial support, and also because the World Bank is an institution whose multilateral character we believe it necessary to preserve, as we consider that the present attitude of the Bank's management not only affects Chile but foreshadows a dangerous negative trend that, to a greater or lesser extent, may affect a large number of developing countries.

In the 22 months of the present Administration, our country has received not one new loan from the World Bank, in spite of having submitted elaborate projects for its consideration. Examples of these are a project to develop fruit growing, of great importance to Chile and with substantial effects on its balance of payments, which has been under consideration since July 1970; a project for the second stage of a program of cattle breeding development, which was initiated with the Bank's cooperation and analyzed on the spot by a mission which visited Chile in January 1971; a power program under the responsibility of our National Electricity Enterprise (ENDESA), a sector in which the Bank has been active in Chile since 1948, i.e., for over 20 years, and for which the Chilean Government has had to resolve to seek other sources of financing so as no longer to suffer the prejudicial effects of the Bank's dilatoriness. These projects have the features of feasibility, financial return, and other technical conditions that fully comply with the requirements laid down in the Bank's Articles of Agreement and in its general operating policies. The projects are entirely in accordance with the purposes of development, which is stated by the Bank to be the primary objective, and in some cases their technical analysis has been completed in full by the management. And yet their presentation to the Bank's Board of Executive Directors has been held up.

The origin of this behavior is the situation resulting from the decision of the Government of Chile to nationalize five private U.S. enterprises which were exploiting our principal copper deposits, as senior representatives of the Bank have informed the authorities of my country, including myself. This nationalization was the result of a reform of the Constitution which received the unanimous favorable vote of the members of the Chilean Congress, a reform establishing procedures that are entirely in concord with the principles of international law embodied in United Nations Resolution 1803. In accordance with the Chilean Constitution, it has been agreed that these enterprises shall receive compensation based on their book value. In some cases, also in accordance with the Constitution, deductions have been applied on account of excess profits, taking as a reasonable level of profit a percentage which in practice amounts to 12 per cent a year. This process of determining the amount of compensation appropriate in each case has not yet been formally completed. However, it is possible to indicate that, following decisions recently adopted by the Special Copper Court established by our Constitution for the formulation of claims in these matters, only some of the five large copper companies nationalized will not have a balance in their favor when the deductions for excess profits are applied. It should be added that one of the nationalized U.S. enterprises was not affected by this type of deduction as it had not obtained profits of this kind. Furthermore, there are no significant differences of opinion between that enterprise and the Government of Chile as to the amount of the compensation, and the amounts presently under discussion before the competent Chilean court are really minimal within the overall context of these proceedings.

What is really unusual is that the management of the World Bank more than a year ago—even before the companies actually concerned took the matter before the Special Copper Court—decided to suspend new loans to Chile and indicated to the Chilean representatives that it was Bank policy not to grant credits to countries that were in conflict with other member countries on account of nationalization of foreign investments. Even if the words of the Bank spokesmen were a trifle ambiguous, in one way or another they alluded to the existence of a Bank policy along these lines. Neither the Articles of Agreement of the Bank nor the resolutions of its Board of Governors or Board of Executive Directors have ever laid down a general policy of this nature. It is true that the Bank, unfortunately, has on various occasions applied restrictive measures vis-à-vis certain countries which have carried out sovereign acts of nationalization of their natural resources. However, this casuistic application of restrictions or difficulties in approval of financing for certain countries obviously does not amount to proof of the existence of a general Bank policy regarding nationalization, which would not, in any case, be appropriate as it is not a function of the World Bank to be the universal judge for interpreting or pronouncing upon situations that are governed by the domestic legislation of each country and by the principles of international law contained in the resolutions of the United Nations.

In the case of Chile, the Bank's management acted in a manifestly precipitate and prejudiced manner, long before the Chilean copper nationalization process was the subject of a final decision in regard to compensation. We do not understand on what grounds or in virtue of what powers the management of the World Bank takes decisions which definitely amount to pressure to affect the outcome of a legal case still *sub judice* and regarding which it is not really entitled to do any more than carry out certain analyses if the nationalization measures were to directly affect the feasibility of projects submitted to it for financing. In acting as it did, the World Bank acted not as an independent multinational body at the service of the economic development of all its members, but in fact as a spokesman or instrument of private interests of one of its member countries. In any case, it is obvious for us that if the nationalization of natural resources undertaken by Chile involved any conflict with the Bank's general development policies, the management of the Bank is not the proper authority to suspend financing for Chile, which should in fact be done, if occasion were to arise, by the Board of Executive Directors or the Board of Governors.

Among the immediate action items which Mr. McNamara mentioned in his opening address, and which we consider highly apposite, he failed, however, to mention one that is of fundamental importance, namely, the position of economic dependence of the developing countries occasioned to a considerable degree by the obtaining of excessive profits by big foreign consortia, which is just what the Chilean Government has sought to correct. Neither did Mr. McNamara refer to the clear necessity that the Bank's management should act with independent and objective criteria and, moreover, that matters of general policy for the Bank should be discussed and decided upon by the full Board of Executive Directors.

We are perfectly well aware that to maintain and expand its operations the Bank must necessarily resort both to the capital markets and to allocation of public resources by the developed countries, and that the possibility of it obtaining more funds depends on the attitude and disposition of the Governors for such countries. It is public knowledge that the government of one of the chief contributor countries to the Bank has differences of opinion with Chile regarding the nationalization of our copper. This is commonly known. However, the Bank is not expected to take sides in any differences of opinion between its member countries, and it should not be forgotten that one of its basic purposes is to foster the development of the most needy nations, that Chile is a member country which was one of the initial group of signatories to the Bretton Woods Agreements, that our country has always performed all its obligations to the Bank and that, obviously, Chile cannot be arbitrarily deprived of its rights as a Bank member country.

This dilemma with which the Bank appears to be confronted, between the desirability of not creating problems with any of its sources of funds versus its obligation, on the other hand, to pursue its fundamental purposes of cooperating in the efforts of the developing nations to achieve social change and economic growth, just has to be solved. It is not possible to make declarations of multilateral convictions if, at the same time, what is actually done in practice appears to indicate that international financial instruments are being used for the foreign policy ends of a particular country. The World Bank cannot be an instrument of bilateral policy of any of its member countries. If those responsible for its management do not deploy all their efforts, clearly and resolutely, in defense of this principle they will be committing a serious historical error and will, furthermore, be contributing by their passivity or indifference to a rapid deterioration of one of the most important instruments of international cooperation established through the collective efforts of a large number of countries.

If certain governments are not able to recognize this truth at the present moment, it is essential that the Bank should make a serious review of the arrangements for obtaining its resources, which originated from the ideas prevailing at Bretton Woods. If the views of Bretton Woods as regards the international monetary system are now subject to a searching review and certain to be changed, we do not see why the World Bank could not also initiate a comparable review of the machinery by which it obtains its resources, with a view to preserving its multilateral character. On more than one occasion reference has been made to the possibility of seeking mechanisms by which the funds of the Bank could be derived from fixed allocations from its member countries, in accordance with their economic capacity, and similar schemes.

As noted by President Allende at the UNCTAD meetings held in Santiago in April and May of this year, "the ideas of Bretton Woods which brought forth the World Bank and the International Monetary Fund were characterized by monetary systems, trade, and development financing based on the interests of a few countries—ideas which, in practice, have proved incapable of raising the living standards of more than half of mankind and are not even capable of maintaining the economic and monetary stability of their creators."

The Government of Chile, faced with a balance of payments situation governed by the factors already referred to, decided at the end of 1971 to renegotiate its external debt, the service of which was taking up over 30 per cent of the value of its exports. In this, as in other matters, our country received the timely assistance of the International Monetary Fund, which I wish here to stress and recognize once again. Nothing of the sort has happened as far as the World Bank is concerned. The management of the Bank has declared on various occasions that while, in general, the Bank prefers not to take part in debt refinancing arrangements, it is prepared to speed up disbursements of loans already approved and to grant additional loans, which amounts in practice to supporting the balance of payments of the country concerned and a contribution similar to that made by the creditor countries taking part in the refinancing arrangements. The World Bank has not followed this policy with Chile, since it has not granted us one single loan, while Chile has continued punctually to meet its debt service obligations to the Bank. In actual fact, the disbursements now being received in respect of loans approved by the Bank before President Allende's Government took office are approximately equal to the payments we are making to the Bank. If no fresh credits are granted to us, the time will soon come when Chile's debt service payments to the Bank exceed the sums which it receives from it. The paradox would then come to pass of Chile becoming a net exporter of capital to the World Bank, instead of the Bank assisting Chile. This would, of course, constitute a most flagrant and unacceptable negation of the necessity referred to by Mr. McNamara to increase the flow of financial resources to the developing countries.

Mr. McNamara sought to stress the efforts of the World Bank Group to achieve an improvement in the geographic distribution of its lending and investments. We are convinced, however, that these efforts will not meet with true success while the World Bank persists in interposing factors which are unrelated to the technical and financial circumstances of the projects when decisions are made regarding the financing involved. Of the slightly more than $3 billion which the World Bank Group loaned or invested in the past fiscal year, the Bank and IDA placed approximately $1 billion in the Western Hemisphere, excluding—of course—the United States and Canada. Of this total, 82 per cent went to three countries and not one single investment loan appears to have been made to Argentina, Peru or Chile. Can this be termed an equitable geographic distribution of the resources of the Bank and its affiliates? We recognize that a large number of factors, of varying natures, enter into these matters, but we wish to stress that there is no proper geographic distribution of resources at present and that this situation is in many cases determined by factors unconnected with those which should be uppermost in the Bank's decision-making.

The Chilean Delegation has sought to state with all frankness and in the most constructive spirit the observations and objections that we have concerning certain policies followed by the management of the Bank. We believe that it is advisable to speak in this way, since only insofar as we do so will it be possible to refine and perfect the valuable instrument of cooperation and development that the World Bank ought to be. If we are forthright in saying what we think regarding matters we consider should be reviewed, we are equally so in recognizing the progress achieved by the Bank in various fields of its operations, such as the greater emphasis placed recently on its activities designed to assist the education sector and agricultural development.

part four

Agricultural Institutions and Strategy

professors Johnston and Mellor have listed five important ways in which agriculture contributes to economic development. First, economic development expands the demand for food which, if unfulfilled, would impede further development. Secondly, exports of agricultural products increase badly needed foreign exchange earnings. Thirdly, agriculture must supply a significant part of the expanding labor needs of the industrial sector. Fourthly, agriculture, as the dominant sector in a peasant economy, must provide capital for industry and social overhead investment; and fifthly, rising cash incomes in agriculture can be an important source of demand.*

In addition, if we adopt Dudley Seers' meaning of development (the first reading in the book), an increase in the income of the poorer rural classes *is development* by definition since poverty is being reduced. The first reading in this section is taken from a World Bank Working Paper on agricultural development. The reading focuses on the problem of alleviating poverty, increasing incomes, and reducing unemployment in the small farm sector of agriculture. The emphasis is on alleviating the poverty of peasants within the constraints of existing institutions. No attempt is made to deal with such structural problems as land tenure systems.

There is little disagreement that in the long run the agrarian structure in most underdeveloped countries must be radically transformed if agriculture is going to make its contributions and development is not to be seriously impeded. But, as Oscar Delgado points out in the second reading, this transformation is not easy to carry out for it involves fundamental social and economic change.

With the transition from feudalism to capitalism and the destruction of the feudal system in the West, two different agrarian structures emerged. One was the structure of small peasant holdings that was typified by those that arose out of the destruction of the feudal estates in the French Revolution of 1789. The other was the relatively large-scale capitalist family farm that developed out of the enclosure movement from the sixteenth to eighteenth centuries in England.

Most land reforms involving "parcellation" (i.e., the creation of small peasant holdings) have been of such limited scope and of such recent date that no valid generalizations about their efficacy can be made. Mexico has the longest standing land reform of this type. While Mexican agricultural production has increased greatly since 1940, small-scale peasant farming has not been responsible. The private sector produces the vast bulk of the agricultural output, and within the private sector it is the holdings of over 100 hectares that account for the bulk of the output.

161

Corn, the most important subsistence crop, occupies nearly one-half the total harvested area and makes up the vast bulk of the produce of all small holdings. Most of the corn is grown by traditional methods, and it yields less per acre in Mexico than anywhere else in Latin America, a region of low corn yields compared with the rest of the world. Professor Rene Dumont sums up his study of the Mexican agrarian reform by saying:

> Mexican agriculture doubled its production between 1945 and 1955, and is progressing very much faster than that of any other Latin American country: so the agrarian reform after all can be called progress. But, instead of being due to the peasants who have "inherited," the success comes from the irrigation works, and from the efforts of the so-called "victims" of the reform; the agents of success are the dynamic expropriated *hacienderos* cultivating smaller estates, and doing their best to recoup by higher yields what they have lost in extensive area.**

He goes on to say, however, that without the agrarian reform and the revolution of 1910–1921, agriculture might have remained stagnant. The revolution and reform acted as catalysts in transforming the basis of Mexican agriculture from a semi-feudal one to a modern capitalist one. The foregoing is not an attempt to demonstrate that "parcellation" is incapable of providing the basis for development, only that in Mexico it is the large capitalist farm that has done so. If anything, the small holding has been a drag on Mexican economic development. It is true, however, that "parcellation" may lead to the growth of large-scale capitalist farming through the more successful buying up the less successful.

A second type of agrarian structure is large-scale capitalist "family" farms. There is no question that capitalist farming in the West has been the most efficient and productive agricultural system ever known. This is particularly true in the United States. The major problem is how to establish and nurture this type of agricultural structure in a present day underdeveloped country. There seem to be four basic ways of doing so. The first, applicable in countries where the bulk of land is held in landed estates, would be the creation of incentives to turn feudal minded landlords into capitalist farmers. To some degree this is what occurred in German agriculture in the nineteenth century. The major problem is that this would involve radical revision of the existing tenure system, since the majority of these large estates are actually cultivated in small plots by tenant farmers.

The second approach would involve the settlement of relatively virgin land where ownership rights have not already been established, such as occurred in the United States, Canada, Australia, and New Zealand (the ownership rights and tenure system of the local inhabitants in each case were easily eradicated). A number of Latin American countries are presently attempting to utilize this approach. Its virtue, of course, is that it does not infringe upon existing property rights. The major drawback is that there is not enough virgin land available in most countries for this approach to be of much importance.

A third way would be to follow the example of England and Germany and inaugurate an enclosure movement to remove the peasants from the land and consolidate the holdings into capitalist farms. However, this process takes time and a docile peasant class (or the power to suppress peasant discontent). It appears unlikely that social and political conditions in most underdeveloped countries today make this approach very feasible. Of course some "enclosure" will occur simply by the "pull" exerted by an industrializing urban center.

The final approach to establishing a capitalist agricultural structure appears to be the most feasible and likely. This would involve an agrarian reform that gave free title to the land to individual peasants. Then, with free sale, the more successful would buy out the less successful. Many peasants would be "pushed" and "pulled" to the industrializing urban areas (presuming they exist) and eventually a capitalist agricultural structure would emerge. This seems to be what is happening in Mexico on the privately held lands. Aside from the question of political feasibility, there is the problem of how long it will take to carry out this transformation.

While in some ways the Delgado article is dated, the basic theses remain relevant. Agrarian structures remain today little changed from what they were in 1961. The three basic approaches to land reform outlined by Delgado are still current policy issues. The attitude of the United States government toward land reform certainly is not more liberal under Nixon than it was under Kennedy.

Since effective land reform does involve a radical transformation— governments can't give land to the tenants as it might give pensions to old soldiers —capitalist governments have turned to a technological solution for the agricultural problem. That technological solution is the "Green Revolution." In the third reading Harry Cleaver evaluates this "revolution" and argues that because there has been no land reform the results so far are to increase inequalities among regions and classes, to increase MNC control of the agricultural sector through control of the new inputs, and to threaten massive ecological damage.

The last two authors in this part, Charles K. Wilber on agricultural development strategy in the Soviet Union and Joan Robinson on agricultural communes in China, analyze the operation and results of socialized agrarian structures as alternatives to the capitalist agricultural institutions discussed in the first three readings. Wilber argues that collective agriculture in the Soviet Union fulfilled the contributions of agriculture listed by Johnston and Mellor. Joan Robinson argues that the commune system, in addition, directly reduced inequality and unemployment. Unfortunately, a definitive solution to the agricultural problem still eludes us. Soviet agricultural strategy succeeded in aiding industrialization but has left agriculture itself a backwater in the economy. The Chinese experiment seems quite successful so far but it is too soon to draw many firm conclusions.

---

* Bruce F. Johnston and John W. Mellor, "The Role of Agriculture in Economic Development," *American Economic Review,* Vol. 51, No. 4 (September 1961), pp. 571–572.

** Rene Dumont, *Lands Alive* (London: The Merlin Press, 1965), p. 93.

13

Agricultural Development

World Bank

A major policy issue in almost every developing country is how to raise the incomes of the rural poor—small farmers, landless laborers, the unemployed, and their families. These groups represent a large proportion of both the total and the rural population; they constitute the poorest segment of society, and they have been largely bypassed by the progress of the past decade. Policies and techniques for raising their incomes and productivity have not yet been devised for application on a massive scale. Yet development cannot have much meaning if it does not include the alleviation of rural poverty.

The size of the problem is immense. About 700–800 million—about one-third of the total population of the developing world[1]—are economically-deprived rural people. The gap between them and the rest of the population will continue to grow unless determined efforts are made to better their lot.

There is considerable potential in the small farm sector for reducing underemployment, alleviating poverty and increasing agricultural production. The marketable production of individual units is small, since most small farmers live at or near the subsistence level, but their combined output constitutes an important, and sometimes dominant, share of total agricultural production. Because productivity is low, incomes are low even though they may be supplemented by small farmers and their families undertaking off-farm work. Changes in technology and access to services would boost productivity and incomes, and serve to reduce underemployment. Even marginal increases in productivity in the small farm sector would make a substantial contribution to total output, though the total growth in output is constrained by the growth of effective demand.

There has been limited success in bringing the benefits of development to this economically-disadvantaged group. Several governments have initiated programs to combat poverty in rural areas.

.   .   .

The scope of the problem is enormous in terms of the number of families involved and the capital and institutional services required. Moreover, the rural poor have the highest illiteracy rate, the worst health condi-

Reprinted from *Agriculture: Sector Working Paper* (Washington, D.C.: World Bank, June 1972), pp. 25-36.

tions and the poorest access to markets, all of which make innovation and investment more difficult. The average investment per farm family in a selected group of recent Bank-financed projects was $1,100. This investment level cannot be sustained in a world where there are more than 100 million small farm families. The total investment in agriculture in developing countries is estimated at $7,000–10,000 million per year, which would be equivalent to less than $100 per small farm family if all the investment was for them.

The analogy of the housing problem in developing countries may be instructive. In that area, too, the capital cost of even minimum housing units far exceeds the available resources. The emerging solution is a "sites and services" approach, whereby governments provide the infrastructure but the urban poor have to construct their own dwellings. A comparable approach—substituting idle labor for capital—is indicated for the rural poor.

However, even the provision of extension, credit and other services to enable small farmers to increase their productivity requires massive resources. The total supply of trained personnel is grossly inadequate; moreover, only a small proportion of the staff available at present provides services for the rural poor. In addition, the rural poor are less well supplied with other public services, such as education, health, electricity and water.

Since growth in agricultural production is unlikely to exceed 4–5 percent per annum, and the rural population is expected to increase at about 1½ percent per annum for some decades, production per head in agriculture cannot be expected to increase by more than about 3–3½ percent per year. The increases in net income will be less since more purchased inputs will be required to boost production. But these are average figures. Unless new measures are devised, the increases will be concentrated among the larger farm units and the real incomes of the rural poor will change very little.

There are no ready-made, generally-applicable solutions to the problem. If maximum impact is to be achieved, programs will have to be devised which encourage initiative and self-help among small farmers and increase their productivity. However, increases in primary production alone cannot provide sufficient opportunities for increasing the incomes of small farmers and others among the rural poor.

It is proposed to outline here some of the difficulties and opportunities in the development of the small farm sector. While the problem is clear, the framing and implementation of programs to assist small farmers remain a major challenge to the ingenuity of those engaged in agricultural development.

Economies and Diseconomies of Scale

Many agricultural operations can be performed quite efficiently on a very small scale. For example, from the standpoint of crop biology there is no reason for yields to change according to size of field or of farm. However, some inputs require a certain minimum scale of operations if they are to be used efficiently. This is true of machinery of various types and of certain fixed investments, such as tubewells. Similarly, a certain minimum size of herd or flock is needed for efficient livestock breeding.

It is often possible for small farmers to share the services of these inputs by the creation of machinery pools, by contract hire, by setting up public or cooperative tubewell systems serving several farms, and by group ranching. However, such arrangements create organizational and managerial problems, and there have been many failures. Miniaturization of machinery is also possible, but usually at the cost of some loss of efficiency. In general, then, small farmers are at some disadvantage because of technological economies of scale, but usually the disadvantage is slight.

On the other hand, financial economies of scale in agriculture are often quite significant. For example, the small farmer suffers, sometimes considerably, from being able to purchase only small quantities of inputs, and to sell only small quantities of produce at a time. He also finds it hard to obtain credit on reasonable terms: he usually has little security to offer against loans and finds it difficult to make an initial down payment in cash. Banking institutions tend to find it too expensive to administer loans to small farmers because the amount of each loan is small. Since it is difficult to get credit on reasonable terms for storing their output, small farmers usually are forced to sell their produce at harvest time when prices are normally low.

The ratio of labor to land and capital on small farms tends to be high. Off-farm employment opportunities are often lacking, limited or inconvenient to exploit, so that family labor tends to be used on the farm, even if its marginal productivity is low. This tendency is reinforced by the willingness of small farmers to work hard, under the spur of poverty. The result is that labor-intensive production techniques tend to be used, and labor productivity is low. However, the productivity of land in small farms is frequently as high as, or even higher than, in large farms. Provided that he is not too handicapped by other disadvantages—in particular, as discussed below, by restricted access to modern technology—the small farmer can, through hard work and careful management, use land efficiently.

Adoption of Innovations

Small farmers tend to be slower to adopt innovations than large farmers. Such behavior does not imply that the profit motive is lacking; rather, it arises from the objective circumstances of the situation. Most innovations involve risks, and a small farmer can ill-afford to take additional risks when the annual crop is all that stands between his family and starvation. The tactic of adopting the innovation on a small experimental scale, to see if it works, is hardly available to him when the scale of his whole operation is so small: it is far more rational for him to wait and see how others fare. New technologies also usually require increased expenditure on cash inputs, such as improved seeds, fertilizers and weedicides. The small farmer cannot always afford such expenditures, and his access to credit is limited. If he does secure credit it is likely to be from a moneylender and to carry a high interest charge, so that he will want to be reasonably sure of a high pay-off before he borrows.

For these reasons, large and medium-sized farmers are at an advantage in a period of rapid technological change. Some evidence from India illustrates the point. Before the "green revolution," small farms commonly showed higher yields per hectare, but subsequently the reverse relationship has been observed, owing to the larger farmer's greater propensity to adopt the new yield-increasing methods. The large farmer will have a permanent advantage if there is a continuing flow of potential innovations from research and development activity—even though the new technology itself is neutral to scale.

Extension services, credit agencies and similar institutions find it easier to deal with a few large farms than with many small ones. Apart from the fact that administrative costs are lower, large farmers tend to be more receptive to advice and more creditworthy; they are also less likely to be isolated by social barriers or by illiteracy. While large farmers can play an important role in demonstrating the effectiveness of new techniques, deliberate efforts are required if governments are to reach small farmers through extension services and credit agencies.

Policies which neglect the small farm sector tend to widen income disparities, sharpen social tensions in rural areas, and do little to assist the bulk of the rural population. In a situation of population pressure and widespread unemployment, small farms have the not inconsiderable social virtue of providing more employment per unit area than large farms. They are also capable of farming their land intensively. If they are offered the knowledge and the means to use new techniques, the social advantages of small-scale farming can be gained without harming production.

However, a substantial effort is required to plan and implement schemes for developing the small farm sector. It is seldom useful to offer only credit without also providing complementary facilities such as extension services and marketing infrastructure (including roads and physical facilities as well as marketing institutions). Such integrated schemes are thus apt to draw heavily on the financial and manpower resources of governments; and it is easy to succumb to the temptation to provide less than the minimum necessary for success (sometimes, on the other hand, such schemes are provided with an excessive share of scarce resources in order to push them through).

LAND POLICY

The pattern of land ownership and the contractual and customary relationships between landlords and tenants can have a considerable influence on production, employment and income distribution in agriculture. In developing countries, land represents a much higher proportion of total wealth than in developed countries, and inegalitarian patterns of land ownership are a major source of income inequality. Furthermore, the owners of land usually possess political and economic power which can be exercised in ways that harm the interests of the bulk of the rural people. Land reforms aimed at securing a more equal distribution of land have been prosecuted successfully in a number of countries, though in some cases at the cost of an initial drop in agricultural production. Some land reform measures have been little more than political gestures and have been ineffective, or even counterproductive.

Whether measures designed to break up large holdings—such as land distribution, progressive land taxes, or the imposition of ceilings on the size of individual holdings—will be undertaken depends on what society considers equitable, and on the balance of political forces. However, the need for productive efficiency and employment creation also has to be considered. Although a landholding is not necessarily the same thing as a farm operating unit, the pattern of land ownership does affect the way in which land is used, and does so in two main ways.

First, because the amalgamation or sub-division of owned parcels of land to form operating units involves transaction and coordination costs,[2] there is a tendency for landholdings and farm operating units to coincide. If the economies or diseconomies of scale are strong, operating units will tend to become of optimum size, despite the transaction and coordination costs. But the economies of scale generally are not very strong. It is the pattern of land ownership, therefore, that largely determines the size of operating units. Size, in turn, influences the character of farm operations. With small holdings, the agriculture is likely to be more labor-intensive, with lower output per man but probably no less output per acre. It will also require more publicly-provided credit and extension services but probably use fewer purchased inputs.

Second, the incentive to improve the land and use it efficiently depends in part on whether the person who cultivates the land also owns it; and, if not, on the contractual arrangements between the owner and the operator.[3] Ownership and operation will tend to be divorced if the size of the owned parcel of land is very different from the optimum-sized operating unit. (Absentee ownership also implies the separation of operation from ownership.) Under tenancy arrangements there is frequently little security of tenure, nor are there guarantees that the tenant will be compensated for the improvements he may make on the farm. His incentive to invest in farm improvements is thus blunted. Similarly, the tenant's or manager's incentive to farm efficiently is reduced if he does not share fully in the rewards of efficient operation.

These deficiencies in contractual relationships are usually not simply the result of landlords and tenants being thoughtless, but reflect the fact that there are difficulties and costs involved in devising tenancy contracts that preserve all the incentives. Tenancy reforms which give the tenant greater scope for exercising entrepreneurship usually reduce the landlord's entrepreneurial role correspondingly, so that the gain in efficiency is not clear-cut; there may, in fact, be a loss. Tenancy is a device whereby landlord and tenant combine their resources in a common enterprise: there are bound to be conflicts of interest and some blunting of incentives.

Owner-operated farming is often favored because it avoids the need to reconcile the interests of owners and operators through rental and other contractual arrangements. It is also favored because, with the rent component of farm income accruing to the operator, a more egalitarian pattern of income distribution is generally promoted. The inclination to provide land to the largest possible number of small farmers means that the size of the operating unit tends to become as small as is compatible with reasonably efficient operation and the provision of a socially-acceptable minimum standard of living for the operators.

More recently, as the implications of demographic changes have become clearer, the principal virtue seen in small-scale family farming is that it can provide employment and, to a lesser extent, can economize on purchased inputs. If small holdings tend to be more socially-productive than large holdings—in that they produce as great an output per unit area using more of the abundant and less of the scarce resources—the conflict which many have perceived between an equitable distribution of land and efficiency in farming may be largely illusory.

Belief in the existence of this supposed conflict was often bolstered by an exaggerated idea of the economies of scale that could be realized in agriculture. Some governments therefore favored the establishment of large-scale cooperative or collectively-owned farm enterprises. However, the management of such enterprises has often been weak. Current approaches favor retaining owner-operated production units but assisting them through cooperative, collective or state-owned organizations that can realize economies of scale and exercise bargaining advantages in the provision of off-farm and some specialized on-farm services.

Whatever size of farm it is desired to promote, it is not merely a matter of breaking up large holdings; some farms are so small that they could never support a family, even if modern techniques are used to increase production. Such units can be viable if suitable opportunities exist for off-farm employment but, where they do not, land reform measures are required to bring farm sizes up to some minimum level.

This can sometimes be accomplished by combining small farms with land that is being redistributed: in Tunisia, for example, land taken over from *colons* was available for redistribution. But since it is politically difficult to enlarge holdings by dispossessing some smallholders (unless they can be induced to leave to take up other jobs), often the best that governments can do is to try to prevent the situation from getting worse. Inheritance laws which prohibit the subdivision of land below a certain size of holding can help in this respect.

Small farmers suffer from a number of disadvantages, of which perhaps the most serious are meager financial resources, restricted access to credit, and the consequent reluctance to adopt new techniques. Land redistribution therefore needs to be accompanied by the extension of credit, marketing and technical advisory services to small farmers. Often these services or functions were previously performed by landlords. If they are not provided, the impact of land reform on production, and possibly also on the welfare of the new smallholders, is likely to be adverse.

The Impact of New Technology

New agricultural technology which increases output per unit area is essentially land-substituting in character, since it enables a given output to be produced from fewer hectares of land. Its widespread adoption will tend ultimately to diminish the relative importance of agricultural land and the share of agricultural revenue attributable to land. On a global basis this tendency does exist. But in regions that have been favored by the new technology, land values have risen. For example, the introduction of the new high-yielding varieties has increased the value of wheat land in many parts of Asia.

However, in areas where the new technology has not been applied, the value of wheat land will tend to fall—since the overall increase in wheat production will tend to depress wheat prices. The danger therefore is that in regions where the new technology is being adopted, income inequalities may worsen—the tendency being reinforced by the fact that the larger farmers are usually the first to adopt the new techniques. Far from reducing social tensions in rural areas, the spread of the new technology is likely to sharpen them, and lead to greater demand for the implementation of measures, such as land reform, for the redistribution of income and wealth.

Use of the new technology may often be accommodated only with difficulty by existing tenancy arrangements. Although the latter are not without their deficiencies, they are often reasonably well adapted to the conditions of traditional agriculture. But they may need extensive revision if the new technology is to be adopted and its benefits equitably shared. For example, under crop-share tenancy—which, as compared with cash tenancy, or the use of hired labor, serves the purpose of dividing risks between the landlord and the tenant—each party has an incentive to supply too little of the inputs for which he is responsible. In practice, it appears that this tendency is often held in check so that each tends to adhere to customary norms of performance: at any rate, there is little evidence that share-rented farms are operated much less efficiently.

However, new technology, particularly since it involves increased use of purchased inputs, will require a new set of commitments from landlord and tenant, and perhaps also changes in the customary shares into which produce is divided. Until the revisions are made, the incentives to adopt new techniques that depend on the use of purchased inputs may be seriously impaired.

Furthermore, it appears that rather than entering into revised tenancy agreements, landlords in areas favored by the new technology have been tempted to let their tenancy agreements lapse and to farm the land themselves, using hired labor and machinery. Several considerations probably explain this behavior: it may be easier for landowners to introduce new techniques by directly supervising hired workers; being uncertain about the yield increases that can be attained, they may have found it difficult to negotiate revised tenancy agreements; and legal protection of tenants—or the threat of it—may have prevented the negotiation of contracts acceptable to the landlord. Another possible explanation is simply that modern agriculture is intellectually more engaging and financially more rewarding than traditional farming.

There is a good deal of fragmentation of landholdings in some countries, especially in South Asia. Under traditional agriculture and with underemployment of labor, fragmentation probably does little to constrain production, and reduces risks to some extent. The effects of fragmentation are more serious under modern agricultural conditions since it increases the costs of distributing inputs, of appraising credit requests and of arranging for custom services. It becomes highly inconvenient when labor is in short supply, as now happens in some areas at harvest time.

The inconvenience of fragmentation is greatest in irrigated areas, since it raises the costs of distributing water (both directly and through the loss of cultivable land to additional canals). Also, labor shortages at harvest time are more likely to occur in areas served by irrigation. Consolidation of land is difficult to arrange in practice; farmers are usually reluctant to participate voluntarily because they fear that the land they receive may be less valuable than the land they give up.[4]

Implementation of Land Reforms

The historical record shows a tendency for land reforms to be enacted in law but not successfully—or only partially or slowly—implemented in practice. Where the program has been vigorously prosecuted, the results have sometimes been adverse, in that agricultural output has fallen and the condition of those whom it was intended to benefit has not been improved, or has even deteriorated. The record is, in a sense, unfair to land reform in that it has often been implemented in times of great social tension, and against strong opposition, by radical governments. But even in a favorable environment, successful implementation requires a good deal of political courage and administrative finesse.

Land reform is expensive, both in terms of the fiscal cost of compensating the former owners, and of the human and material resources required to administer it properly and to provide services to the newly-created smallholders or cooperative enterprises. It also suffers from perverse announcement effects: owners faced with the threat of losing their land—usually compensation is incomplete, so that a degree of expropriation is involved—cease to improve it and allow existing facilities to deteriorate; and laws which promise tenants security of tenure lead landlords to dismiss their tenants and replace them by hired laborers and/or machinery. Thus a difficult dilemma arises if the adverse announcement effects are to be minimized: the redistribution of land should be done rapidly, but a piecemeal approach is more in keeping with the limited fiscal and administrative resources of governments.

Attempts to bring about land reforms have sometimes been frustrated by vested interests, and governments may feel they have to proceed cautiously because production might be disrupted in the initial stages. In some cases governments, bowing to the pressure for land reform, but lacking the will to take effective action, have enacted token legislation. However, such political expediency usually worsens the existing situation, as landlords take evasive or defensive actions to the detriment of both production and the employment opportunities of tenants and rural workers.[5]

It is clear that agricultural development cannot do all it might to improve rural life if the distribution of land ownership is highly skewed. Despite the political and administrative difficulties involved, governments should pursue land policies which help disperse the benefits of agricultural progress widely rather than allowing them to go to only a small segment of the population. Steps should at least be taken to tax the higher rental incomes arising from public investments, and to reinvest the proceeds in infrastructure so as to increase the income-earning opportunities of wider strata of the population. If this is not done, rising land values will make it increasingly difficult to redistribute the land later.

NOTES

1. Excluding Mainland China.

2. Voluntary participation may be more readily encouraged if consolidation is accompanied by land improvement works, such as irrigation or land levelling within existing irrigation schemes. Since all participants are likely to benefit, each may be less concerned—so the argument runs—as to whether he receives precisely the same share of improved land as he had of the original unimproved land.

3. These include the cost of negotiating contractual arrangements, each party's uncertainty regarding the competence and good faith of the other, and, in general, all the monetary, psychic and time costs involved in the association of two or more persons in a single enterprise. These costs are the basic source of the disincentives to efficiency which inhere in many rental arrangements and which are discussed in the next paragraph.

4. Communal ownership of land is not discussed in this paragraph. However, it should be noted that in some cases it provides sufficient incentives to cultivators.

5. A study of the impact of land reform legislation on two Indian villages showed that although laws were framed to improve the position of tenants (by limiting the amount of rent payable, and by giving them greater security of tenure and the right to purchase land) the results left them worse off. Owners were able to evade the legislation by various means, including the replacement of tenants by hired laborers. It is interesting to note that a new tenurial relationship—a form of quasi-tenancy (but not legally classifiable as tenancy)—was devised to meet the situation.

14

Revolution, Reform, Conservatism:
Three Types of Agrarian Structure

Oscar Delgado

Latin America had a population of 199 million in 1960, according to a United Nations estimate. Of this total, 108 million or 54 per cent live in rural areas, and of these 28.5 million are economically active.

All rural dwellers who are economically active have family and social responsibilities, but almost all of them are underemployed and many are victims of seasonal unemployment. Their income is extremely low, and considerable numbers of them live only on the margin of money economy. Generally speaking, they work the soil in a primitive or almost primitive fashion. The average percentage of rural Latin America is around 80; but vast areas have no schools at all and an illiteracy rate of 100 per cent.

Indians form some 15 per cent of Latin America's rural population. The majority of them speak only an Indian language, though some of them are bilingual. The Indian policy of Latin American governments generally aims to keep them isolated from the white peasantry of their countries. Moreover, Indian communities benefit very little from government aid or not at all, and it is an open secret that such programs have been a complete failure because of inadequate funds and lack of any real interest on the part of the governments concerned.

In spite of these obstacles, some Indians have established contact with the white peasants. These have adopted the cultural patterns of that peasantry. Wherever such cultural contacts take place, the Indians suffer from exploitation not only by the white bourgeoisie but also by the white and *ladino* (mestizo) peasants.

These 28.5 million have to produce food not only for themselves but also directly for their 70.5 million dependents and, more indirectly, for the 91 million urban dwellers. Moreover, in terms of national economy, they have to produce a surplus for economic development. And yet, 63 per cent of them—18 million adult farmers—have no land at all. Some 5.5 million have an insufficient amount of land; 1.9 million have enough land, and 100,000—mostly absentee landlords—have too much land.

One out of every 185,000 Latin Americans—or one out of every 100,000 rural Latin Americans—owns over 1,000 hectares.* For 107,955 landlords,

Reprinted from *Dissent*, Vol. IX, No. 4 (Autumn 1962), pp. 350-364, by permission of the publisher. Translated by I. A. Langnas.

or 1.5 per cent of all landholders, own 471 hectares, or 65 per cent of all land in private hands.[1] Each of them owns an average of 4,300 hectares; but many have more than 10,000, and some have hundreds of thousands— even millions.

So much for individuals. But properties belonging to several members of a family can be registered under the name of its head. There are Latin American families who own more land than is occupied by a number of sovereign nations. In fact, there are families or groups of interrelated families in the Argentine, Brazil, Chile, and Venezuela, of which each has more land than several countries put together. This is a situation with no parallel elsewhere. Statistically speaking, Latin America has the highest index of concentrated accumulation of rural property in the world.

Latin America is now beginning to develop, however, slowly. Its indices of urbanization[2] and industrialization are progressively rising. However, this progress is generally unnoticeable because the population rapidly increases at one of the highest rates of growth in the world. Internal migration to the cities is constant and growing, but it does not absorb the rural population explosion caused by the rising birth rate and the falling death rate. This migration, a product of urbanization and industrialization, makes the rural population decrease relatively, in proportion to urban population; but it does not decrease it absolutely.

It is estimated that the percentage of rural population will fall from 54 to 46 in 1970. However, the rural population as a whole and hence also the number of actual and potential agricultural workers, will actually rise by that date from 108 million to 133 million. . . . There can be no question that the rural—and agricultural—population of Latin America is increasing today in a geometrical progression. Every year, every month, and every day there are new mouths to feed and new hands to be provided with work, land, tools, and money. Given an annual rate of increase of 3 per cent, this means about 6 million new mouths and new pairs of hands every year in all Latin America, and 3.8 million in the rural sector.

"PARCELLATION" AND COLONIZATION

How can this problem be solved? The answer is simple and can be reduced to four words: economic and social development.

We can deal here only with one aspect of this urgent problem: the different agrarian policies which can become stimulants or obstacles to the improvement of agricultural production and productivity, and to the white, mestizo, and indigenous rural population which participates—or is unable to participate—in growing crops and raising cattle.

In three countries of Latin America, a political revolution produced an agrarian policy of redistributing the property and tenancy of land: Mexico (1915), Bolivia (1953), and Cuba (1959). In these countries, new ruling groups[3] and new ideologies replaced the old and changed the traditional values. The old ruling groups had governed with the support of traditional

* A hectare = approx. 2½ acres.

ideas, and their rule was tolerated by the masses who lived in utmost ignorance, submission, and political apathy.

In two other countries, conservative governments, representing a bourgeois-landlord-military-clerical coalition, have introduced a land reform: Venezuela (1959) and Colombia (1961). This reform has meant a "parcellation" of cultivated land or a "colonization" of virgin soil.

"Parcellation," as used in this article, means:

a. The acquisition by a government agency of land used for crops or cattle by purchase from its private owners paid in cash and at once and

b. the subdivision of this land for resale as private property to landless or landpoor peasants by payment of an amount of money equal or similar to that laid out by the government agency on the installment system, with a fixed term and a low interest rate.

Similarly, "colonization" means here the opening or preparation of new agricultural, cattle-raising, or forest land owned by the government or of no definite ownership, and the settlement in it of rural population.

In all the remaining countries of Latin America, there has been no serious program of redistribution or parcellation. The countries which tried colonization in the course of the present century were successful only as regards a few fortunate individuals; for the rest, colonization completely failed to solve their agrarian problem.[4]

Parcellation, as a method of land reform, leaves the large estates practically intact. The concentration of land in a few hands is not affected by it, and it leaves the problems of the rural population unsolved. This is why it is the favorite method of land reform in "rural conservative" countries.

This phrase also requires some explanation. At first sight it seems strange to apply the label of "rural conservative" to seventeen countries which differ so much economically, socially, and politically. They include two countries at the very extremes of economic and social development: Argentina and Haiti. This is also true of political development. They include, on the one hand, the Central American republics dominated by "strong executives" and custodians of foreign interests and, on the other, a country like Uruguay, with its markedly developed democracy. Nor is it easy to include in the same group countries which never had any significant colonization or foreign immigration with others which have intermittently tried out colonization ever since the beginning of the 19th century, though on a small scale in relation to their open spaces and settled population.

Still, it is convenient to group together the countries of recent parcellation (Venezuela and Colombia), those of colonization (Argentina, Brazil, Chile, and Uruguay), and those dominated by large estates (the rest of the seventeen). They have something in common—rural conservatism—which distinguishes them from the countries of revolutionary land reform, which we may call countries of "agricultural transformation."

A closer look at the three countries where a revolution occurred with a broad popular participation will reveal certain distinctions which will require separate categories.

In Cuba, the large estates and ranches were not divided by the Castro Revolution; they continue in operation by either a government agency or a peasant cooperative. Both in Mexico and in Bolivia, land reform marked a notable social progress, though it was limited to only a part of the rural population. The national economy of these two countries benefited somewhat from the land reform,[5] but the benefits were limited by an excessive fragmentation of the estates which were distributed. Also, neither country made a sufficient effort to foster government, collective, or cooperative operation of agriculture and cattle-breeding.[6]

We can now classify the Latin American countries as follows:

I. *Agricultural Transformation:*
   1. Agrarian revolution (Cuba)
   2. Land reform (Mexico and Bolivia)
II. *Rural Conservatism:*
   1. Parcellation (Venezuela and Colombia)
   2. Colonization (Argentina, Brazil, Chile, and Uruguay)
   3. Rural conservatism, in the narrower meaning of that phrase (the remaining countries)

The countries of agricultural transformation have a dynamic agrarian situation. Their agricultural population—or at least a large part of it—has a genuine opportunity to raise its standard of living. The countries of rural conservatism have a static agrarian situation; such an opportunity is limited or non-existent in them. . . .

The reason Cuba falls into a different category from Mexico and Bolivia is that the transformation happened there with surprising efficiency and speed. This is no longer land reform; it must be called an "agrarian revolution." In Mexico and Bolivia, the rhythm of change has been much slower than in Cuba, for all the positive achievements of their land policies. But it has been very fast by comparison with Venezuela and Colombia.

LAND REFORM LAWS

In Mexico today, forty-seven years after the Land Reform Law was signed, 106 million hectares remain in private hands, and 71 million (76 per cent) belong to private individuals who own more than 1,000 hectares each. In Bolivia, land reform has moved at a faster pace than in Mexico; but even here, nine years after the law was passed, 28.5 million hectares—87 per cent of all utilized land—are still in the hands of landlords who own more than 1,000 hectares each.[7]

The land reform laws of Cuba, Mexico, and Bolivia stipulate that the former owners of expropriated land be indemnified with long-term bonds. But, in actual practice, none of these countries has paid the compensation required by the law. The small payment was made in money, not in bonds. How else would it have been possible to redistribute 61 million hectares (52 in Mexico, 5 in Cuba, 4 in Bolivia)?

The laws of Venezuela and Colombia, on the other hand, authorize the expropriation of land, with payment partly in cash and partly in medium-term bonds. Both, however, have actually preferred parcellation.

The Venezuelan government has bought about half a million hectares, at market prices, from landlords who sold their land voluntarily. They actually received payment, almost full and immediate. This land has not been given to the peasants, as happened in Cuba, Mexico, and Bolivia. It was sold to them at cost price, which included the value of improvements and the wages of the officials in charge of the transactions. The peasants pay in annual installments for a medium-term period.

In Cuba, the large estates and ranches were taken from individual owners and national and foreign companies. They were not subdivided, but continue to be operated as wholes by the government or by peasant cooperatives.

In Mexico and Bolivia, on the contrary, they were subdivided into very small farms—an average of 4 hectares of unirrigated lands—and handed over to the peasants. But the beneficiaries of the land reform were, in both countries, abandoned to their fate. Because of financial stringency or for other reasons,[8] they have received hardly any credit, technical assistance, and other services needed for efficient farming.

Among the different types of rural conservatism, parcellation deserves special treatment. In most of the literature on the subject, "land reform" actually means parcellation. This is because, for many people, parcellation means an "agrarian transformation," and so they associate what is happening in Venezuela and Colombia with what happened in Mexico, Bolivia, and Cuba.

Several Latin American countries are planning to start a parcellation program in 1963. Only they are careful to call it "land reform." (This is also true of Venezuela and Colombia with their "land reform" laws.) The Congresses of two "colonization" countries (Brazil and Chile) and of two "rural conservative" countries (Peru and Ecuador) are now studying several "land reform" projects. If they are approved in the form they were presented,[9] they will certainly not provide the legal basis for an agrarian transformation, but only for parcellation. And their practical efficiency will depend on the amount of public funds assigned to buy land from private owners.

We stated earlier that parcellation permits preservation of the traditional structure, based on large estates. The case of Venezuela will prove this. That country is now engaged in the most expensive "land reform" ever made in the world, even more expensive than those of Italy and Japan, with their special difficulties.

Venezuela has financial resources unmatched by any Latin American country. Its annual per capita income is, through the revenue derived from petroleum, the highest in Latin America—$500, as against $92 in Bolivia, and a general average of $292. Also, Venezuela has an unusually small number of agriculturally active population—only 705,000, as against 10,300,000 in Brazil and 28,500,000 in all of Latin America. No other Latin American country could afford to invest the equivalent of $750 million in a program devoted exclusively to parcellation and its auxiliary agricultural services.[10]

The sum seems disproportionately high when compared with the cost of land reform in Japan and Italy. Japan spent $390 million to distribute 2 million hectares among 4 million beneficiaries. Italy spent only $120 million to give to over half a million beneficiaries 750,000 hectares of redistributed land and 28.5 million hectares of improved and colonized land.[11]

The Venezuelan four-year program proposes to settle 200,000 peasants on the parcelled land; but in its first three years (1960–1962) only 50,000—a quarter of the number planned—have been actually settled.[12] This means 7 per cent of the active agricultural population, as opposed to 41 per cent in Mexico and 32 per cent in Cuba. The Venezuelan beneficiaries occupy 1.5 million hectares of land: one third taken from public lands (colonization); one third bought by the government from private owners (parcellation); and one third confiscated from the friends of the deposed dictator Perez Jimenez who had obtained it illegally when in power.

Venezuela has 29.6 million hectares of land used to raise crops and breed cattle. Before parcellation was started, 22 million hectares were occupied by large estates, over 1,000 hectares.[13] Three years later, when the four-year plan is coming to its close, this figure has fallen to only 21.5 million.

Another difference between parcellation and agrarian transformation is that the latter limits the amount of land a person may legally own, and the former doesn't. Thus, in Cuba the limit, for a private person or a corporation, is 403 hectares; in Mexico, 100 hectares of irrigated and 200 of unirrigated land; in Bolivia, the limit varies according to the geographical zone.[14] No other country has such restrictions.

The amount of money Venezuela spent on its "land reform" would seem fabulous if we didn't compare it with the cost of agrarian transformation, truly insignificant by comparison: $133,000 in Bolivia for 4 million hectares;[15] $14.5 million in Mexico for 52 million hectares;[16] and $8.9 million in Cuba for 5 million hectares.[17] (In all three cases, the land was expropriated.)

In Colombia, the government assigns annually, from 1962, $12 million for "land reform," some 3 per cent of the national budget. (Venezuela makes an annual assignment of $187.5 million; the Peruvian draft law foresees one of $11.5 million or about 3 per cent of the budget.) In the year since the Colombian law was passed (November 1961), the Colombian Institute of Land Reform has so far parcelled out only 15,000 hectares, which were handed over to 750 persons. The two-year plan of the Colombian Ministry of Agriculture for 1962–1963 proposes an expenditure of $18 million for the purchase of land to be distributed to tenant farmers and sharecroppers.

Colombia and Peru have an active agricultural population of 2,023,000 and 1,546,000 respectively, i.e. roughly three times and twice that of Venezuela. Colombia has 27.7 million hectares of agricultural land. Of this, 7.4 million are owned by landlords with over 1,000 hectares each.[18]

POLITICAL AND JUDICIAL RESTRAINTS

Some "colonization" and "rural conservative" countries are preparing a parcellation for 1963. In Brazil and Chile there is a hope, still vague and distant, that parcellation may be transcended and a genuine land reform achieved. This hope is based on changes in the composition of their Congresses (Brazil will have elections in October 1962) and on the election of a new president of Chile.

As things are now, Brazil and Chile cannot be expected to go beyond a modest parcellation. Any serious land reform there is blocked by juridical considerations—always the most conservative and change-resisting in Latin America. The constitutions of these two countries bar any expropriations without a cash payment in advance for the property to be expropriated, and at market prices. Large parts of Brazilian and Chilean public opinion believe that such constitutional provisions make land reform impossible and they are pushing for constitutional amendments which would permit a deferred payment of the indemnification. In the present pre-election campaigns they are concentrating upon obtaining more representative Congresses so as to neutralize—to say the least—parliamentary domination by big landowners and their allies.

It is worth recalling that, in the last ten years, 208 projects of land reform laws or relevant legislation have been presented to the Brazilian Congress.[19] Not one of them was able to pursue its normal course through the commissions appointed to "study" them. None of these laws were actually rejected; they were simply buried in the commissions.

Much the same thing happened in Peru and Ecuador. And yet a conference of agricultural economists agreed that "the majority of the tenancy contracts now prevalent in Latin America are archaic, unequal, rigid and unsuitable for the full utilization of human and natural resources."[20]

Generally speaking, in the countries of agrarian conservatism, the big landowners have exercised a powerful political and economic influence ever since Independence. Conditions vary from country to country;[21] but, except in one or two cases, the landed interests have been completely successful in blocking any structural change.[22]

Their resistance is certainly not without a logic of its own. An agrarian transformation may well make the landlords feel "lost." Their lands would be confiscated outright or they would receive an indemnity which they consider too small for investment in business. Moreover, they would not receive it in cash but in long-term bonds. They would lose their political power and their social status, which they derive from the ownership of land. Not only would they lose their prestige, but they would fall into the depths of unpopularity and be blamed by society as a whole for having prolonged a fundamentally unjust situation. From the point of view of defending their interests, the resistance of landlords to the land reform is perfectly logical, even if it is irrational in the present historical situation.

But whether they resist or not, the landlords are doomed to lose the fight for the retention of their long-held privileges.[23] Since society asked them to give up their lands, they have won many skirmishes and even some technical battles. But they are losing strategically and the fortress of their privileges—inherited rather than acquired—is beginning to succumb.

The more intelligent among the landlords will adapt themselves to the new situation. They will try to forget a lost world which had seemed ideal to them but which was too unjust to resist the passage of time. That ideal world, in which they had been the center of attention and power, is now colliding with industrial civilization.

The landlords will find a refuge in the big cities (or will remain in them if they are absentee owners). They will be shareholders in industrial, commercial, and service enterprises. Some of them will stick to their old values, and would rather become the victims of the hurricane of social transformation than give up an inch of their land. This type of landlord will die with his boots on and with his gun cocked.

UNITED STATES POLICY

Meanwhile, the United States government insists that the Latin American countries carry out a land reform. But it has not, so far, clearly stated what kind of land reform it wants. Its pronouncements are marked by vagueness, diversity, and even contradiction.

President Kennedy himself has said in a speech that there exists in the rural areas of Latin America "an immediate necessity of a better distribution of wealth and income and of a broader participation in the process of development"—and that "the unequal distribution of land is one of the gravest social problems in many Latin American countries. . . . It is evident that, when the ownership of land is so concentrated, the efforts to increase agricultural productivity will benefit only a very small percentage of the population." To help solve these difficulties, the President added, the Bank for International Development (BID) has allotted $309 million for *colonization* and improved *utilization* of the soil.[24] (Emphasis ours.)

The nations of Latin America, gathered under the leadership of the United States and with the promise of its aid, have signed two documents which refer to the land question.

The Bogota Act of September 12, 1960, mentions "the improvement of rural life and use of the soil" and "the revision of legal systems with regard to the holding of land with the view of insuring a broader and juster distribution." The Charter of Punta del Este of August 17, 1961, outlines a program for the decade of 1961–1970. One of its aims is "to prompt, within the particular conditions of each country, programs of integral land reform oriented towards the effective transformation of structures and of unjust systems of tenancy and exploitation of land wherever it is required and with a view of replacing the regime of *latifundia* and *minifundia* by a just system of property."

The Subcommittee on Inter-American Economic Relationships of the United States Congress, headed by Senator Sparkman, has recently published an extensive volume, *Economic Policies and Programs in South America, 1962*, which formulates its basic criteria of land reform. A careful reading of it will justify our reservations on the efficacy of the Alliance for Progress as an instrument of agrarian transformation. The key passages are:

> *The concept of agrarian reforms.* It seems to us that an official clarification of the meaning and objectives of "agrarian reform" in the context of the Alliance for Progress, especially the role of U.S. government as a participant is not only in order but imperative. . . . Land reform is not exclusively a tenure problem but a problem of improved farming practices

generally (rural education, research, extension services, credit institutions).
. . . Land reform would include real estate tax reform. . . . The objective of
land tenure change is not to be punitively directed against large landholdings or absentee landowners as such; on the contrary, existing property
rights under law are to be respected. The programming and administration
of agrarian reform is, and must remain, an internal matter for each of the
several nations. Certainly the United States is not pressing for any pre-
conceived patterns of land tenure or agrarian reform; least of all can it
undertake unilaterally to assure individual croppers of its support of ultimate
landownership, no matter how seemingly meritorious cases may be. . . . As a
first step in land reform and possible redistribution, the respective participating countries should first look to public lands and lands not presently
under appropriation. To this end (1) an accurate survey of acreage and use-
ability of the public domain, (2) an appropriate adaptation of the U.S. provisions for land grants in aid of schools and colleges dating back to 1859, and
(3) the so-called homestead acts dating from back to 1861 are recommended
for consideration.[25] [And:]

[The Charter of Punta del Este] recognizes that conditions and needs
will vary from country to country. Largely as the result of events in Castro
Cuba, the specter of wide-spread and uncompensated expropriation has unfortunately been read into the Alliance program and one of the conditions
of U.S. aid. . . . To what extent are we committing ourselves in such internal
matters as land tenure reform? In view of the sorry history of international
commodity stabilization agreements, to offer another example, we had best
be quite wary that the United States is not put in position of going along at
the risk of being charged with their possible if not probable failure.[26]

These documents need no comment; they speak for themselves. It is
enough to say that if the Alliance for Progress is to be guided by such concepts, its failure is practically certain. It will be even more certain unless
the Alliance quickly acquires what it presently lacks—a program of
specific measures to deal with controversial issues, to be formulated, in the
first place, by the American government. The only such measure formulated
so far is the fixing of restrictive limits by the various governments with
regard to land reform. This being so, it is not difficult to view the Alliance,
paradoxically, as a subtle form of resistance to social and cultural change—
including a true land reform.

The Charter of Punta del Este refers to the "effective transformation
of structures and of unjust systems of tenancy and exploitation of land."
It seems to do it on the naive assumption that the neo-traditional oligarchies
might be moved by an instinct which Durkheim called "altruist suicide."

ALTERNATIVE POLICIES

Some of these oligarchies seem to have found a magic formula which would
permit them to maintain the existing agricultural structure while proclaim-
ing that they had transformed it. The formula is "parcellation," i.e., the
subdivision of large properties and the fostering of homesteads. . . . What
this formula means in practice, however, is the stimulation of the *mini-
fundia* in a disguised and uneconomic form, within the framework of a
subsistence rather than market-oriented agriculture. The rural population

will remain poor, and the backward tenancy systems and the exploitation of agricultural labor will continue. The levels of rural income and buying power will not stimulate savings and consumption, so that they will not benefit industrialization. There will be, in fact, no social or political change.

As the president of the University of California, Clark Kerr, puts it: "the successful perpetuation of the family homestead . . . serves to maintain contact with the old society."[27] In other words, the old elites will continue in power at the expense of representative democracy and the participation of the mass of the population in national life. Other investigators also point out this danger.[28]

There exist alternative policies to parcellation, namely cooperative and/or communal exploitation of land. A number of Latin American experts favor cooperatism on a large scale[29] while the American experts are divided.[30] But the official U.S. policy, as embodied in the Alliance for Progress, does not take these alternatives into consideration.

Of the Latin American countries themselves, the laws of Venezuela and Colombia indulge in some rhetoric in favor of cooperatives, but the actual policies of these countries have restrained rather than favored the growth of different types of cooperatives. In Mexico and Bolivia, official support of cooperatives has considerably fallen off as their governments gradually veered away from revolutionary agrarianism.[31]

To sum up: The Alliance for Progress will make only an insignificant contribution to Latin American industrialization and land reform so long as it lacks effective means of coercion and a clear formulation of the means required to realize its objectives. It offers Latin American countries money —in amounts insufficient for the needs of their development—but does nothing to resolve the grave problem of the "terms of trade" which is an essential precondition of any increase in the rates of capital formation.

Politically speaking, the Alliance stimulates an irrational and unconditional adherence of Latin American governments to the foreign policy of the United States without any serious discussion on an international level. It gives the United States nineteen unconditionally favorable votes at the United Nations. It favors the Western bloc in the Cold War and prevents Latin American countries from becoming neutralist.

All this is, however, achieved upon a tacit condition, namely that of United States support for the established political and economic oligarchies of the various Latin American countries. Their power would be seriously jeopardized if that support were to be withdrawn. This means a limitation on the supposed American pressure in favor of replacing these oligarchies by political, agrarian, industrial, and financial democracy.

NOTES

1. Oscar Delgado, *Estructura y Reforma Agraria en Latino-america*, Bogota, Sociedad Economica de Amigos del Pais, 1960; Thomas F. Carroll, *The Land Reform Issue in Latin America*, pp. 161–201 in Albert O. Hirschman, ed. *Latin American Issues*, New York, The Twentieth Century Fund, 1961; T. Pompeu Accioly Borges, *A Reforma Agraria na America Latina*, in Desenvolvimento e Conjuntura. Rio. V. 12:51–68; VI, I:55–83, 1962; Rene Dumont, *Terres Vivantes*, Paris, Plon, 1961, pp. 1–123.

2. Philip N. Hauser, ed., *Urbanization in Latin America*, Paris, UNESCO, 1961; Pedro C. M. Teichert, *Economic Policy, Revolution and Industrialization in Latin America*, University of Mississippi, 1959; Howard S. Ellis, with Henry C. Wallich, eds., *El Desarrollo Economico y America Latina*, Mexico, Fondo de Cultura Economica, 1960.

3. Gino Germani believes that the dissolution of the old-style army of the *ancien regime*, generally a bulwark of rural conservatism, is a necessary condition of agrarian transformation: "It may be a coincidence but it is certainly very significant that no military regime ever seriously modified the concentration of landed property and that the only countries which managed to achieve a true land reform dissolved their army and either substituted for it a workers' militia (Cuba and Bolivia) or a new army (Mexico)." Germani, *La Democratie Representative et les Classes Populaires en Amerique Latine*, in Sociologie du Travail, Paris, October–December, 1961.

4. "It is disillusioning, says the FAO, that the effective progress has been so scanty and inadequate so as to create the impression that the distribution and colonization of land, even if carried out with efficiency, benefit only a very limited number of people and affect only a small fraction of the idle land and underdeveloped resources of these countries. . . . Considering that in most of them the population increases at a rate of 2.5 to 3 per cent and that, generally speaking, a large part of the families own no land, it is obvious the programs now in operation are far from providing a solution." Thomas F. Carroll, ed., *La Creacion de Nuevas Unidades Agricolas*, Report of the Second Latin American Seminar on Problems of the Land, Santiago, FAO, 1961, pp. 15–16 and 19.

5. Edmundo Flores, *Tratado de Economia Agricola*, Mexico, Fondo de Cultura Economica, 1961; Giuseppe Barbero, *Realizaciones y Problemas de la Reforma Agraria en Boliva*, in El Trimestre Economico, Mexico, 112; 612–650, 1961.

6. "It is necessary to create a firmer foundation for collective organization— here lies, one might say without exaggeration, the salvation of the *ejido*." R. Fernandez y Fernandez and Ricardo Acosta, *Politica Agricola*: *Ensayo sobre Normas para Mexico*, Fondo de Cultura Economica, 1961. A FAO document says: "Mexico, which carried out its land reform years ago, faces today's new problems which require new kinds of action." Carroll, ed., *op. cit.*, p. 16. The Mexican economist Jesus Silva Herzog asks for "a reform of the Mexican land reform," i.e., the abrogation during the Aleman administration, which has acted as a brake. *El Agrarismo Mexicano y la Reforma Agraria*, Mexico, Fondo de Cultura Economica, 1959. Hernandez y Hernandez writes: "The numerical predominance of small peasant property, possession and usufruct will maintain the foundation of the present agrarian regime, with its exploitation of poor and medium peasants by the local merchants and bosses. The system of small-scale production for the market will not free the peasant masses from misery and oppression. . . . The preconditions of total collectivization are: integration of the trading set-up which now favors the big operators; taking over of basic industries by the government; growth of agricultural cooperation; creation of big state farms; the struggle to hand all the land to the *peasants*." Jesus Silva Herzog, *El Movimiento Campesino*, in *Mexico: Cincuenta Anos de Revolucion*, Vol. II, Mexico, Fondo de Cultura Economica, 1961, pp. 235, 238–239.

  On the other hand, the XI International Conference of Agricultural Economists held at Cuehavaca in 1961 criticized the land reform in Bolivia "because insufficient attention has been paid to the transformation of Indian communities into market-oriented cooperative societies." *Report on Tenant Farming*, p. 4. Giuseppe Barbero says that Bolivia today "is characterized by the absence of the large estate but is dominated by a primitive type of agriculture though she has large unexploited natural resources." *Op. cit.*, p. 650.

7. Pan-American Union, *La Estructura Agropecuaria de las Naciones Americanas*, Washington, 1960, and *America en Cifras: 1960*, nr. 2, 1961; *Bolivia*, in FAO, *Documentacion del II Seminario de la FAO sobre Problemas de la Tierra*, Montevideo, 1959, Doc. IP-2; CEPAL, *Actividad Reciente en Materia de Reforma Agraria en America Latina*, pp. 123–157, in *Estudio Economico de America Latina 1959*, Santiago, CEPAL E/CN. 12/541, 1960.

8. "The lack of sufficient and timely credit and the bad faith of the officials in charge made the *ejidatarios* fall once more into the hands of unscrupulous operators and moneylenders. . . . Another reason is the small operating capital of the Banco Nacional de Credito Ejidal—only 72 million dollars per annum, while the actual credit needs are estimated at 400 million." Victor Manzanilla Schaffer, *La Reforma Agraria*, in *Mexico: Cincuenta Anos de Revolucion*, Vol. III, pp. 254–255. See also the study by Charles Erasmus of the important cotton area of the Yaqui Valley, with its ample documentation of corruption in official agencies in charge of agricultural credit. *Then Land Reform (in Northeastern Mexico)* in *Man Takes Control*, Minneapolis, University of Minnesota Press, 1961, pp. 209–237.

9. Jorge Alessandri, *Proyecto de Ley sobre Expropiaciones Agricolas* and *Mensaje Presidencial*, in *Boletin de la Camara de Disputados*, Santiago, nr. 165, 1962. In accordance with this project, all expropriations have to be paid for in cash and in advance except "abandoned or notoriously ill-worked estates" when the compensation can be paid on installments and according to the market value, as follows: down payment of no less than 20% . . . and the rest in equal six-monthly installments, in cash, for a maximum total of 10 years and with adequate interest." According to a cable just received from Santiago, the Chilean Congress has passed this draft, which is now a law. Chile thus joins Venezuela and Colombia as another country which accepts "parcellation." Here, too, this false kind of land reform is bound to fail.

On Ecuador, see R. Fernandez y Fernandez, *Reforma Agraria en el Ecuador*, in El Trimestre Economico, Mexico, 112, 569–594, and Ecuador, Junta Nacional de Planificacion y Coordinacion Economica, *Anteproyecto de una Ley Agraria*.

On Peru, *La Reforma Agraria en el Peru, Exposicion de Motivos y Proyecto de Ley*, Lima, Comision para la Reforma Agraria y la Vivienda, 1960.

10. Romulo Betancourt, *Discurso de Carabobo*, in *Reforma Agraria Integral en Venezuela*, Mexico, no date. Also, *Reforma Agraria*, 6 vols., Caracas, Ministerio de Agricultura y Cria, 1959.

11. On Japan, Pan-American Union, *Report on the Agrarian Reform Program of Certain Countries*, Washington, 1960, p. 5.

On Italy, Giuseppe Barbero, *La Reforma Agraria Italiana*, in Boletin de Estudios Especiales, Mexico, XVII, 202; 486–490, 1960.

12. The Instituto Agrario Nacional, in a Statement to the Associated Press, July 1, 1962.

The reports of governments which speed up the re-distribution of land are often distorted by exaggerating the area of the land and the number of beneficiaries. This happened in Cuba as well as in Venezuela. For the sake of curiosity we collected and examined the reports of various officials and commissions in charge of these programs. We found serious contradictions between them. . . . President Betancourt, in his last Message to Congress, said that in three years—December, 1958 to December, 1961—1.3 million hectares were granted to 42,000 beneficiaries. However, the National Peasant Confederation corrected these figures to 15,000 beneficiaries who received official title to the land and 10,000 peasants settled on land without official title in the period under review. It seems advisable not to trust official data too much.

Similarly, in Bolivia, one official report says that 4.2 million hectares were given to 47,585 beneficiaries in 1955-1960. But another such report gives 1.5 million hectares and 63,414 beneficiaries, and a third, 1,065,000 hectares and 32,608 beneficiaries. All three reports are official and refer to the same period.

13. Carroll, *op. cit.*, p. 187.

14. Bolivia, Decreto-Ley de Agosto 2, 1953; Cuba, Decreto-Ley de Mayo 17, 1959; Mexico, Codigo Agrario, Diciembre 31, 1942, art. 104.

15. The budget for 1959; expenditure for assignment of 270,000 hectares, in Joao Gonsalves de Souza and Manuel Diegues Junior, *Resumen de las Respuestas al Cuestionario Enviado a los Paises Latinoamericanos*, Washington, Pan-American Union, p. 90. However, the government bonds to be used for compensation have not been issued to date, in spite of demands and reminders. Cf. Barbero, *op. cit.*, p. 648.

16. Edmundo Flores, *op. cit.*, pp. 335–344. From 1915 to 1962, the Mexican government has paid only $14.5 million in indemnification. Two million dollars were paid to 170 Mexican ex-owners in bonds which were later cashed by the government at a depressed market value of 5 to 16 per cent of the nominal. From 1938 to 1955, $12.5 million were paid to American ex-owners for lands expropriated in 1927–1940.

17. Cuba, Instituto Nacional de la Reforma Agraria, Report of the Director, Antonio Nunez Jimenez, in *Bohemia*, La Havana, May 28, 1961.

18. Carlos Lleras Restrepo and others, *Tierra*, Bogota, Ediciones Tercer Mundo, 1962; Alberto Aguilera Camacho, *Derecho Agrario Colombiano*, Bogota, Ediciones Tercer Mundo, 1962; Hernan Toro Agudelo, Minister of Agriculture, *Plan Bienal para la Reforma Agraria*, in *El Tempo*, June 3, 1962.

    For Peru, see note 9.

19. T. Pompeu Accioly Borges, in a private communication. References to forty-one projects in Universidade do Brasil, Instituto de Ciencias Sociais, *Bibliografia sobre Reforma Agraria*, Rio, 1962, pp. 4–7.

20. XIth International Conference of Agricultural Economists, *op. cit.*, p. 2.

21. On the political power of landlords see Merle Kling, *Toward a Theory of Power and Political Instability in Latin America* and John H. Kautsky, *An Essay on the Politics of Development*, both in John H. Kautsky, ed., *Political Change in Underdeveloped Countries: Nationalism and Communism*, New York, John Wiley, 1962; C. Wright Mills, *Listen, Yankee!* and *The Marxists*, New York, Dell, 1962. An ECOSOC report issued in November 1961 says on p. 24: "The necessity of a land reform in Latin America and the Middle East has been accepted on the international plane, but little has been achieved on the national scale. In actual practice, the national development programs have tended to concentrate on the non-agricultural sectors of the economy, where it is easier to achieve visible progress and where the resistance of interests opposed to progress and reform is less entrenched."

22. "The land reform progressed little against a decided resistance by the landlords. A partial success was registered only by a violent social cataclysm, as in Mexico and Bolivia. . . . The forms in which the *ancien regime* accommodated itself to the new order have varied greatly. The strongest resistance came from the big landlords. Though their political control had disappeared, their economic power had been destroyed and their social monopoly broken, they successfully resisted land reform everywhere except in Mexico and Bolivia." Edwin Lieuwen, *Armas y Politica en America Latina*, Buenos Aires, Sur, 1960, pp. 73 and 79.

23. Cf. A. J. Toynbee, *The Present Revolution in Latin America*, lecture given at the University of Puerto Rico in February 1962: "There exists in Latin America an oligarchy of landlords, a dominant minority surely doomed to disappearance, but dying with difficulty and refusing to die before it puts its mark on the 'new rich' of industry and commerce. . . . The oligarchs are now fighting from their last bastions a battle which they are losing." (Retranslated from Spanish text.)

24. John F. Kennedy, Message to the Congress of the United States on Latin America, March 14, 1961.

25. Congress of the United States, *Economic Policies in South America* (Joint Economic Committee, Subcommittee on Inter-American Economic Relationship), Washington, Government Printing Office, 1962, pp. 24–25.

26. *Ibid.*, p. 79.

27. Clark Kerr, *Changing Social Structures*, pp. 348–359 in W. E. Moore and A. S. Feldman, ed., *Labor Commitment and Social Change in Developing Areas*, New York, Social Science Research Council, 1960, p. 354.

28. The economist John F. Timmins writes: "The Homestead Acts gave millions of acres to the settlers; but, only a few years later, almost a third part of that land had fallen into the hands of speculators and absentee landowners who rented it to the farmers. Our error lay in not taking complementary measures to assure to the farmers the permanent ownership of their land." *Tenencia y uso de la Tierra en America Latina*, in Selected Studies of the Latin American Seminar on Land Problems, Campinas, Brasil, 1953, published in Problemas Agricolas e Industriales de Mexico, Vol. VI, No. 1, January–March, 1954, p. 254.

29. For example, the Mexican economist Victor L. Urquidi: "It is very prob-able that, unless a new effort, combined with cooperative or collective forms of agricultural production, is made, economic development will not receive from agriculture all the contribution it requires." *Viabilidad Economica de America Latina*, Mexico, Fondo de Cultura Economica, 1962, p. 87.

30. Among the American officials and Congressmen who favor cooperatives are Chester Bowles, Hubert Humphrey, and Wayne Morse.

31. Cf. Giuseppe Barbero, *op. cit.*; Fernando Chaves, *Las Cooperativas, Ele-mento de Cambio Social*, in Americas, Washington, 13, 9:7–11; Rosendo Rojas Coria, *Introduccion al estudio del cooperativismo*, Mexico, Talleres Graficos de la Nacion, 1961.

15

The Contradictions
of the Green Revolution

Harry M. Cleaver, Jr.

Radical intellectuals have been noticeably absent from recent discussion of the Green Revolution. This neglect is surprising given the importance being openly attached to this new agricultural strategy by the same foreign policy institutions which are often targets of radical research. The Ford and Rockefeller Foundations, the Development Advisory Service, the World Bank, and USAID have all provided either financing or managers for the Green Revolution. The neglect is also strange in a generation of radical economists who have been more impressed by the peasant revolutions of China and Vietnam than by Marx's vision of revolution by an industrial proletariat. Even a cursory review of the easily available literature shows an omnipresent fear on the part of capitalist policy makers that in parts of Asia the Green Revolution may have a sizable negative impact on social stability and increase the possibility of peasant insurgency. This paper attempts to bring the Green Revolution to the attention of radical economists and to open a discussion about the importance of the phenomena to U.S. imperialism and revolutionary strategy at home and abroad.

I. THE GREEN REVOLUTION AND IMPERIALISM

Narrowly defined, the Green Revolution is the rapid growth in Third World grain output associated with the introduction of a new package of tropical agricultural inputs. The package consists essentially of a combination of improved grain varieties, mainly rice and wheat, heavy fertilizer usage and carefully controlled irrigation. Without fertilizer or without controlled irrigation the new varieties usually yield no more and sometimes less than traditional strains. With them they give substantially higher yields per acre.

The development of this new technology is very much a part of the efforts of the American elite to direct the course of social and economic development in the Third World. With a foreign policy devoted to facilitating the expansion of U.S. multinational business, the elite is always

Reprinted from *American Economic Review*, Vol. LXII, No. 2 (May 1972), pp. 177-186, by permission of the American Economic Association and the author.

concerned with creating new investment and sales markets. But it also tries to plan for the longer-run problem of economic or political upheaval which might upset the stability of those markets. Although overt military and covert CIA type intervention is used whenever necessary to put down threats, the more lucid members of the elite have tried to develop ways of warding off instability before it irrupts.

The Growth of a Strategy

The Rockefellers sent plant pathologist J. George Harrar to Mexico in 1943 to develop an agricultural research program. The resulting research effort can be seen as a friendly gesture to soften rising nationalism and to hang on to wartime friends, but the Green Revolution it produced has clearly developed into one aspect of a Third World strategy to open profitable new markets and to avoid both rural and urban turmoil caused by growing hunger and poverty. The focus on agriculture is designed to increase the availability of basic foodstuffs in potentially unstable areas and to create outlets for agribusiness products. Population control is another part of the strategy and is aimed at slowing the growth of an unemployable, unproductive labor force. Publicly the diagnosis of Third World nationalism and revolts against U.S. imperialism has been population versus food supplies.

By 1963 the Mexican research project had grown from a small team to a large organization: the International Center for the Improvement of Corn and Wheat (CIMMYT). CIMMYT became the nucleus for research and the training of native technicians. The Foundations and AID have also carried on this work. But technicians are not enough to manage an empire and a new organization. The Agricultural Development Council (ADC) was set up to provide a special focus and analysis capability for the training of a higher level elite. The goal was the formation of agricultural economists and managers who could take over agricultural policy formulation in their home countries and, with help from their teachers, mold it into forms compatible with stability and profit.

The ADC was founded by J. D. Rockefeller III in 1953. At that time the capitalist world, still reeling from the loss of China, was fighting in Korea; and much of Asia was wracked by rural guerrilla war. That same year Rockefeller made a survey trip to the Far East. Soon after, ADC advisors were dispatched to Asia to set up new programs in the universities and to ferret out promising young students for stateside training. While small in terms of the number of personnel and students it supports, the ADC, together with the U.S. universities, has helped coordinate much of the research and thinking on agricultural development policy and foreign student training.

As this new effort was getting underway to save Southeast Asia, the earlier Mexican research was beginning to pay off. Rust resistant wheat strains had been widely distributed by 1951 and a new wheat package was developed that gave high yields in the newly opened irrigation lands of Mexico's northwestern deserts. A rapid increase in yields coupled with expansion of acreage caused dramatic increases in total wheat production throughout the 1960's. Mexico, which had been a sizable net importer of wheat at the time of the Rockefeller team's arrival, was able to achieve "self-sufficiency" by the early 1960's and is today exporting a portion of her crop.

Encouraged by these successful results the Rockefeller Foundation joined with the Ford Foundation to expand research operations into Asia. In 1962 they founded the International Rice Research Institute (IRRI) in the Philippines to develop new rice varieties comparable to the Mexican wheats. The Philippine project gave results even quicker than the effort in Mexico. Within barely four years "miracle" rices were boosting yields in the Philippines. Like the Mexican wheats the new rice varieties were dwarfs and their similar requirements for a lot of inputs seemed to open new vistas for agribusiness salesmen.

The new Institute began to train agricultural technicians for Asia to complement the economists and managers being trained under Foundation, AID, and ADC auspices. These trainees and their mentors came to form an international team of agricultural experts ready and willing to spread the seeds of the Green Revolution. Their big push began in 1965, the same year as the beginning of a major turnaround in U.S. aid policy toward the capitalist Third World.

That turnaround was of great importance in opening the way for the Green Revolution and the expansion of rural markets. Since the war the U.S. government had been stopgapping socially disruptive food shortages in the Third World by the provision of grain supplies from U.S. surpluses, first on an *ad hoc* basis and then from 1954 on under P.L. 480. This program, which began as a subsidy to U.S. agribusiness, bought time for the new agricultural strategy to be put together. But in 1965 Johnson announced the reversal of this policy. No longer would U.S. surpluses be handed out freely. Future deliveries were made dependent on the satisfaction of a number of conditions by the receiving countries—primarily a shift of emphasis from industrialization to agricultural development, expansion of population control, and an open door to U.S. investors.

The crunch came with the application of this "short-tether" policy to India during the 1965–66 famine. Successive droughts had brought about major food shortages and U.S. capital was knocking at the door with plans for new fertilizer plants and demands for control over prices and distribution. Faced with upheaval at home and Johnson's intransigence, the Indian government opened her doors to some U.S. capital and most of the Green Revolution.

Since 1965 the international team handling the spread of the new technology has had mixed success. In the capitalist Third World only about 17 percent of its wheat acreage and 8 percent of its rice acreage have been planted with the new seeds. In some particular countries on the other hand, the new varieties have been diffused with considerable success. There can be little question that a Green Revolution has come to India, West Pakistan, and the Philippines. In India and Pakistan the growth rates of wheat production have increased dramatically while in the Philippines the growth rate of rice production has risen moderately.

Spreading Capitalism

The integration of the agricultural sector into the capitalist market is achieved through the adoption of the new technological package which itself makes the peasant producer more dependent on the market. He must now buy the manufactured inputs and sell part of his crop for cash in order to be able to buy next year's inputs. The international team has also been making an effort to teach personal gain and consumerism where it feels peasants lack sufficient motivation. In his handbook, ADC president Arthur T. Mosher harps repeatedly on the theme of teaching peasants to want more for themselves, to abandon collective habits, and to get on with the "business" of farming. Mosher goes so far as to advocate extension educational programs for women and youth clubs to create more demand for store-bought goods. The "affection of husbands and fathers for their families" will make them responsive to these desires and drive them to work harder. These tactics of the ADC are more than efforts to bring development to rural areas. They are attempts to spread capitalism with all its business-based social relations and the markets such relations support.

Profits from Progress?

Many Green Revolutionists have had an eye to international corporate profits all along. Lester Brown has hailed the multinational corporation as "an amazingly efficient way of institutionalizing the transfer of technical knowledge in agriculture." He sees international agribusiness as a major source of new investment in both inputs and international marketing.

In Jalisco, Mexico, an experiment financed by AID is underway to involve foreign private capital investment in a new kind of corporation which would provide inputs to "independent" peasants and then market their combined output (in this case corn). Such a corporation is designed to earn an annual income of 50 percent on equity after the third year. Its involvement in "fighting hunger" is expected to provide a good public relations cover to the foreign capital involved.

But for all the best laid plans of apologetic economists and corporate planners, exploitation is not always an easy business and market creation can be costly. Bilateral and multilateral financing for complementary irrigation systems, fertilizer and tractor imports, and joint production ventures have provided large profits to international agribusiness. Local government grain support prices, overvalued currencies, and special tariff structures have cheapened the costs of importing inputs and have helped increase sales. But ESSO recently sold its oft cited fertilizer distribution network in the Philippines because of low profits. And after all the arm twisting in India the actual amount of foreign investment in fertilizer was limited. The increase in input sales to countries adopting the new technology seems to be far less than expected and the marketing of food-grain output almost nil. It seems unlikely for now that international agribusiness will be able to move into Third World grain marketing in a big way. If projects like that at Jalisco work out, they may eventually make headway, but such a development is not around the corner.

The most profitable international investments in agriculture are outside the area of food grains and in traditional export crops like meat, oil palm, fruit, and vegetables. If the aid lobby succeeds in increasing economic aid appropriations for agricultural development, input sales and profits will probably increase, though it is likely that they will continue to be financed more through foreign aid than through direct commercial contracts. This will add to the growing debt burden of aid recipients and bring them even more closely under imperial control.

In sum, the new agricultural strategy is giving mixed results in terms of its planners' aims. Corporate investment and profit opportunities have not been as great as hoped. On the other hand, there have been sizable increases in food output in some of the biggest and most important Third World countries. How much this increased output will insure stability in those countries remains in doubt. In the process of trying to resolve one contradiction of neocolonialism—that between a rapidly growing, poverty stricken population and the inability of satellite capitalism to provide food —the Green Revolutionists appear to be creating or accentuating a whole series of other contradictions which not only threaten national social stability but the ecological balance of wide areas.

II. THE EFFECTS OF THE GREEN REVOLUTION ON THE CONTRADICTIONS OF CAPITALIST DEVELOPMENT

The simultaneous existence of poverty and wealth is a fundamental characteristic of capitalism. That unevenness, which results from investing where the private rate of return is greatest, is what John Gurley has called "building on the best." The Green Revolution is now intensifying this pattern in the Third World.

Contradictions between Regions

By breeding new grain varieties that give maximum results only on carefully irrigated land, the Rockefeller scientists insured that only limited areas of Third World agriculture would benefit. This was partly due to their concentrating on the best potential lands. It was also because within capitalist systems there is little hope of reversing the dictates of "efficiency" by transferring wealth from rich regions to poor ones. Irrigated land represents only a small proportion of the total cultivated land in most countries and well-controlled irrigation is even rarer. The resulting regional bias of the new technology has been obvious from the beginning. In Mexico the new wheats were planted overwhelmingly in the new, irrigated districts of the Northwest, and it has been this area alone which is responsible for the rapid growth in wheat output. The rest of the country, where most of the people live, has remained virtually untouched by the new varieties. India has only some 20 percent of her cultivated land under irrigation and only about half of that has assured water supplies. The adoption has thus been primarily in the north and northwestern states like the Punjab where irrigation facilities are concentrated. In Turkey wheat adoption has been limited to the coastal lowlands. In Thailand, their new rice varieties have been confined largely to the Central Lowlands.

The most striking case of uneven regional development being exacerbated by the Green Revolution is that of Pakistan. In West Pakistan, where nearly all the cropland is under controlled irrigation, the spread of the new wheats was very successful. There has been hardly any success in flood-irrigated Eastern Pakistan. The result has been to transform the West into a food surplus area while leaving the East heavily dependent on food imports and its people in greater relative poverty than before.

In all of these countries the Green Revolution is benefiting those regions which are already the most developed and neglecting the poorest and least developed areas. Moreover, the prospects for future extension into these latter areas are not very promising. There has been some work but very little success with the development of new varieties adaptable to dry or flood areas. It is also unlikely that the bulk of current drylands and flooded areas will be able to develop adequate irrigation facilities.

Contradictions between Classes

Just as the Green Revolution appears to be accentuating regional contradictions in capitalist development, there is also evidence that it is intensifying inequalities within the regions it has affected directly. Foundation and government officials often turned first to established, commercial farmers for initial field trials. The results of numerous studies on both rice and wheat have been far from unanimous, but if there is a trend it is that "them what has gets." This usually has meant larger, commercial farmers but it also has meant small peasants close to extension and market centers, and sometimes tenants where landowners supplied financing. At least two of the studies show that in some areas where the initial adoption rate was higher for larger farmers, there was a rapid catching up by others. The problem with most of these studies is that they concentrate on the diffusion of the new seeds alone, whereas the real question is that of the package. There is some indication that while more wealthy farmers may not use a higher percentage of seeds they do use more of the complementary inputs.

How representative these studies are is hard to judge, but they do indicate that, while the new combination of inputs is largely neutral with respect to technical economies of scale, there are other costs like financing and education which are not.

For those wealthier farmers who can adopt the new grains and afford all the complementary inputs, the change can be a very profitable one. A study by AID shows impressive differentials in average cash profits between traditional and new methods. Viewed together with the higher adoption rate for the entire package by large farmers, the implied greater profit differential suggests that the Green Revolution is resulting in a serious increase in income inequality between different classes of farmers in those areas where it is being adopted.

Wolf Ladejinsky claims that in the Indian Punjab such high profits have resulted in an increased demand for land which has driven its price up as much as 500 percent. He says there is a growing effort by landlords to acquire more land and to convert their tenants into hired laborers in order to reduce their costs. Under some situations this does seem to be an optimal strategy for a landlord trying to optimize his own profits. Such a change could have significant implications for the class structure of the countryside. A shift from a quasi-feudal structure of tenancy and share-cropping to a concentration of land in large operational units dependent on wage labor suggests a trend toward some variation of the classical capitalist two-class dichotomy.

With the growth of a rural proletariat, already sizable in India, is also coming the "reserve army" of the unemployed. Encouraged by increasing profits and new land acquisitions, capitalist farmers are accumulating more and more of their capital in the form of mechanical equipment. Investment in such capital is also being encouraged by the structure of input prices. Overvalued currencies and government subsidies have sharply reduced the relative cost of equipment to farmers. "Labor shortages" in some Green Revolution areas are also accentuating this trend by raising cash wage rates. Mechanical pumps, tractors, threshers, reapers, and combines all contribute to raising yields and output. There is considerable evidence that their net effect is to be labor displacing. These labor-displacing effects are tending to offset the much heralded positive impact on labor utilization caused by the new seed-fertilizer package. In the absence of mechanical equipment the new technology not only requires more labor for planting and cultivation but also, by increasing output and, in some cases, permitting double cropping, there is a considerable increase in harvest labor require-ments. The impact of reapers, threshers, and combines during harvest periods will be dramatic because the absolute number of men displaced will be higher during harvest, the one period of relatively sure employment for the seasonally unemployed rural laborers.

The overall outlook indicated by the various available studies points in the direction of considerable increase in rural unemployment in those areas where mechanization proceeds rapidly. This effect, especially if combined with the eviction of an appreciable number of tenants, will generate a growth in both size and insecurity of the rural landless labor force.

Growing numbers of the unemployed undoubtedly will leave the coun-tryside and join the migration to the cities—swelling the urban slums. This movement, coupled with the inability of neocolonial capitalism to create urban jobs through industrial growth, is affecting the class structure of the cities. The rising tide of urban unemployment threatens to transform an already large urban "reserve army" into a vast and permanently unemploy-able lumpen proletariat which will swamp even the new rush by multi-national corporations to capitalize on cheap foreign labor.

To date there has been little government action either to increase capital costs or to bring about land reform. Pakistan recently abandoned its 50 percent subsidy of fertilizer—a non-labor-displacing input. Another land reform law, which appears no more effective than those which came before it, has been passed by the Philippines. The United States and the puppet regime in Saigon have introduced land reform as part of their war effort. There has been no substantial recent land reform at all in the other major countries affected by the Green Revolution. Indeed, in some countries the discussion of land reform without action may have hastened the process of tenant eviction.

Contradictions in Price and Trade Relations

The Green Revolution countries are now experiencing one of the fundamental contradictions of capitalist agriculture: to achieve higher output of rice and wheat, their prices must be raised to make the necessary investment profitable to farmers. This has and is being done. But maintaining high support prices keeps consumer prices up and encourages surplus accumulation. High consumer prices are a cost of living increase that hits all who must buy food for cash. It does not hit all classes equally. In India, for example, lower income groups often pay more than the rich for the cereal foods that make up so much of their diet.

Any fall in support prices will result in decreased incentives to capitalist producers and perhaps a reduced output. Such a fall will hit the poorer peasants with narrower profit margins more than the big commercial adopters of the whole new package. A sufficient decline might push many of these small producers back into subsistence or off the land. Rising production must be either sold domestically or exported to avoid downward pressure on prices and surpluses. The chances of substantially raising the incomes of the millions of rural and urban poor through employment or welfare programs in order to increase domestic demand sufficiently to absorb the rising production is out of the question. Unemployment is getting worse, not better, and the size of the welfare program needed would bankrupt the United States, not to mention the countries of the Third World.

It is increasingly being said that continued success of the new agricultural strategy will depend on the readiness of the developed countries to import the increased grain production of the Third World. As Third World imports are being replaced with surpluses only the rich countries appear to have the potential effective demand to absorb the excess. There is little reason to believe that these countries are about to open their doors to food grains from others when they themselves are major exporters. It is the entry of Japan's highly subsidized rice exports and substantial increases in U.S. subsidized rice exports which are major factors in the growing glut of the international rice market. "Rice prices have declined to the lowest levels of the past decade and a half and export earnings from rice of the developing countries have been drastically reduced." The share of the underdeveloped countries in world rice exports has dropped from 66 percent in 1959–63 to only 45 percent in 1969, while that of the imperialist countries has risen from 19 percent to 40 percent in the same period. The current glut on the world wheat market is due to an unnoticed "Green Revolution" which has been taking place in the imperialist countries. Yields have been rising for both traditional importers and traditional exporters.

England has drastically reduced her imports. Production has been rising in Canada, the United States, and Australia, all traditional exporters. Rather than the Third World countries turning to the developed world for markets the opposite is taking place.

If the Third World governments are forced to strangle the Green Revolution by lowering prices radically to avoid surpluses and budget deficits, we have an idea of what could happen—marginal producers for the market may be pushed back into subsistence and further spread of the new technology would be limited. The widespread hopes stimulated by the new programs would be demolished either slowly or all at once.

Ecological Contradictions

The most difficult to foresee but the most potentially devastating of all the contradictions of the Green Revolution are those involving the ecosystem. The extension of capitalist agriculture to the tropics brings with it all of the serious ecological contradictions that we have been discovering in the United States. These contradictions are more than just technical problems because the technology itself is a product of the capitalist economic system. Pesticides, which are widely required in heavy doses for the new varieties, are primarily developed in the laboratories of private business. Their efforts to minimize research costs and to reach as wide a market as possible are dictated by capitalist competition. The resultant products are both undertested and designed to kill a broad spectrum of pests. The lack of kill specificity is bad enough in the United States. When transferred to the much more complex tropics, the results can be catastrophic. It is one thing to kill a few bald eagles. It is quite another to poison fish ponds and their protein supply while spraying rice fields. The runoffs from the heavy inorganic fertilizer applications called for by the new technology will also add to the process of protein destruction as it results in massive eutrophication of lakes, streams, and rivers.

The rapid distribution of a few plant varieties has created the danger of oversimplified ecosystems. The recent southern corn leaf blight in the United States is an example of what may be in store for Green Revolution areas. There were over 50 percent losses in many areas of the Gulf states and a one billion dollar loss to the country as a whole. The vulnerability of the crop was apparently due to the efforts of commercial hybrid breeders to reduce labor costs involved in detasseling corn plants. They used a particular kind of sterility gene which eliminated detasseling, but also conferred susceptibility to the leaf blight. Serious problems of this kind have already impeded wheat production in Turkey in 1968 and 1969. The Philippine rice boom was set so far back in 1971 by a virus disease that rice will have to be imported. The United States can afford a limited number of such "mistakes"; the Third World cannot. When such crises arise a team of breeders may patch things up. But patchwork won't solve the basic problem of having food production tied to a profit-maximizing system where the input manufacturers profit but don't have to bear the cost of error.

If the Third World is to avoid widespread ecological crises, then it must be freed from a system that insists on selling them its most deadly technology. Whether the Third World accomplishes this before the ecological contradictions of the Green Revolution negate all of its successes remains to be seen.

III. THE IMPACT OF THE NEW STRATEGY ON REVOLUTION

The most important effects of the Green Revolution on political tensions might be grouped into four categories: intensified regional conflict, changes in the form of rural class struggle, the growth of an urban lumpen, and the speedup of change.

There can be little doubt that while the Green Revolution didn't cause the victory of the Awami League in East Pakistan it certainly added to the regional bitterness which did. The differential regional success of the new technology came on top of a history of exploitation of the East by the West. This exploitation has been accomplished through capitalist institutions in a kind of internal imperialism.

How important is the factor of regional exploitation and neglect for revolution? Eric Wolf has commented on the important rule of "frontier areas" in his studies of revolution in Mexico, Vietnam, Algeria, and Cuba. Today we can see this tendency to revolt by neglected or exploited regions within many of the Green Revolution countries: Bangladesh in Pakistan, Assam and West Bengal in India, the North and Northeast in Thailand, the North in Malaya, West Irian in Indonesia, Guerrero in Mexico, as well as in countries untouched by the Green Revolution, such as Eritrea in Ethiopia, the South in the Sudan, and the North in Chad.

The impact of the Green Revolution on class structure will also have an influence on the form of revolutionary activity. A major restructuring of rural society would destroy the stability of both quasi-feudal and village relationships and lay a broader basis for a struggle for land and higher wages. The example most often cited was a clash between organizing laborers and scabs which occurred in the Green Revolution area of Tanjore, India, in 1968. Forty-three peasants were burned to death in a fight over wages. India has also seen the rise of the Naxalites, a coalition of Maoist intellectuals and landless peasants. This guerrilla group has carried on an increasing campaign of assassination and land seizure. In some areas the Naxalites developed before the new technology was introduced. How much and what kind of influence it is having on their activities, support, and tactics I don't know.

In the Philippines a guerrilla force is reported to be growing both in the Green Revolution areas of the Central Luzon rice bowl and in the outer islands. Most of its recent activities have been centered on struggle against landlords and in defense of small farmers.

Perhaps the most important effect of the Green Revolution is on the rate of urbanization. Shifts in rural class structure call for a rethinking of optimal strategy in the countryside but do not call into question the basic Maoist or Cuban "models" of revolution based on peasant support. An increased rate of urbanization, caused by unemployment and impoverished peasants pouring into the cities, however, raises serious questions about the continued applicability of these models in some countries. In the Third World the rate of change in the distribution of the population between countryside and city has been great. This has led some revolutionary groups to abandon the rural areas and to try and develop new forms of urban guerrilla war such as the Tupamaros in Uruguay.

A final and very important question raised by the Green Revolution is one of time. How fast are these effects taking place in relation to the development of revolutionary groups capable of leading revolt toward socialist goals? In Pakistan the independence of Bangladesh has come before such a political group, based on popular support, could develop. Finally, lurking ominously behind the social turmoil is the ultimate question: can capitalism be replaced in these countries before its profit-born technology destroys all hope for survival by poisoning the environment?

For radicals in the developed countries there is at least one lesson. The Green Revolution provides a striking illustration of how imperialist intervention, no matter how well-intentioned, can have far-reaching negative effects on the Third World. The problem of hunger in the capitalist world has rarely been one of absolute food deficits, particularly when the productive capacity of the developed countries is taken into account. It is one of uneven distribution caused by a system that feeds those with money and, unless forced to do otherwise, lets the rest fend for themselves.

16

The Role of Agriculture
in Soviet Economic Development

Charles K. Wilber

INTRODUCTION

Contrary to popular belief, agriculture has contributed successfully to the economic development of the Soviet Union in both labor and capital. It has provided the two forms of capital (food and raw materials) that are necessary for an expanding industrial sector, the exports required to pay for imports of scarce capital goods, and a large share of the industrial labor force. This article attempts to outline and evaluate the role of Soviet agricultural strategy in relation to the requirements of economic development.

AGRICULTURE'S CONTRIBUTION

Professors Johnston and Mellor have listed five important ways in which agriculture contributes to economic development. First, economic development expands the demand for food which, if unfulfilled, would impede further development. Second, exports of agricultural products increase badly needed foreign exchange earnings. Third, agriculture must supply a significant part of the expanding labor needs of the industrial sector. Fourth, agriculture must provide capital for industry and social overhead investment. Fifth, rising cash incomes in agriculture can be an important source of demand.[1]

In the Soviet case, however, the first requirement loses some of its urgency because of the large number of controls available in a socialist economy. The fifth requirement is, of course, relatively unimportant in a planned economy since the plan determines the size and composition of demand. Thus, there remain essentially two major roles for the agricultural sector: the provision of capital in the form of food and raw materials for industry and for export; and the freeing of large numbers of rural workers to join the urban labor force. The key to these requirements is twofold: a growing marketed surplus of agricultural products and a freeing and utili-

Reprinted from *Land Economics*, Vol. XLV, No. 1 (February 1969), pp. 87-96, by permission of the University of Wisconsin Press.

zation of surplus labor through structural reorganization and increasing agricultural productivity per man. The collective farm system in the Soviet Union was designed to provide these solutions.

There were several characteristics of the collective farm system that made it fit into the Soviet strategy of economic development. The goal set for the collective farms was maximization of the marketed agricultural output to be achieved by emphasizing increased output per man instead of increased yields per acre. The distribution of the collective farm output was regulated by a set of general priorities established by the collective farm charter.[2] In descending order of priority these were (1) deliveries of the share of output purchased by the state, (2) payment of direct taxes in kind to the state, (3) reimbursement for cost of seed and outside production costs such as services of the machine tractor stations, and (4) distribution of the residual (the wage fund) among collective farm members in accordance with their contribution of labor to production.

Collection of the Agriculture Surplus

The most crucial question was how to obtain sufficiently large marketings of agricultural products to meet the needs of the rapidly growing industrial sector and the vital export sector. After four years' debate, collectivization was chosen eventually as the solution for the agricultural question. This decision was based partly on the successful performance of the few existing state and collective farms which had been established in the 1917–24 period. These farms were achieving yields per acre only slightly better than the peasant average but these output levels were achieved with substantial savings in manpower. The net result, due to the lower wage bill, was a favorable showing with respect to the share of output available for marketing. In providing a marketed surplus, agriculture was a source of savings and, in the Soviet economy where saving and investment decisions coincided, it was a source of capital accumulation. This put the Soviet agricultural problem back in the world of classical economics where capital accumulation was limited by the wages fund (conceived as a stock of food).

The collection of the marketable agricultural surplus was facilitated by the collective farm system in two ways. First, it was possible for Soviet planners to override the market determined "terms-of-trade" between the industrial and agricultural sectors because the collective farms had to accept both the amount and the prices of the marketed output set by the state. Thus the planners decreased the prices of agricultural products relative to manufactured goods. This shift in the rural-urban "terms-of-trade" forced the agricultural sector to save. Second, the collective farm organization enabled the marketed share of output to be determined independently of the size of total agricultural output. Any short-fall in total production was absorbed by a reduction in the residual received by peasant households. Thus, 25 million tons of grain were delivered to the state in 1937 and 24 million tons were delivered in 1939 out of a harvest 20 million tons smaller.[3] There were, of course, constraints in the form of minimum peasant health and morale.

The collective farm system was successful in capturing the marketable agricultural surplus as can be seen from the following figures. The percentage of total agricultural output marketed was 20.3 per cent in 1913 and during the crucial period of industrialization it was 28.8 per cent in 1937 and 36.2 per cent in 1939.[4] The marketed output of grain averaged 18.2 million tons per year over the period 1928–32, 27.5 million tons over the 1933–37 period, 32.1 million tons over 1939–40, and 43.5 million tons over the period 1954–58.[5] Marketings of all agricultural products were 65 per cent greater in 1940 than in 1913.[6]

Limiting the size of the collective farm's wage fund facilitated economic growth in another way. The resulting low incomes of the peasants, coupled with the high prices of manufactured consumer goods, repressed the effective demand for these goods. Thus, the Soviets were able to restrict investment in consumer goods industries and concentrate most of the investment in capital goods industries, which increased the growth rate of the strategic sectors of industry. It can be concluded, therefore, that ". . . the socialization drive in agriculture achieved to a large extent its major economic purpose of serving as a basis for the industrialization drive."[7]

Agricultural marketing provided a source of capital, not only by feeding the rapidly expanding industrial labor force, but also by providing exportable products. The large imports of capital equipment in the 1930's were paid for with foreign exchange earned by food and raw material exports. The effectiveness of agricultural exports, however, was severely restricted by the decline of primary product prices on the world market in the 1930's. In addition, agriculture played an important role in a policy of import substitution. Industrial crops such as cotton and sugar beets were rapidly expanded to replace imports of these goods and thus free foreign exchange for the importation of capital goods.

The Release and Utilization of Agricultural Labor

In the Soviet Union potentially "surplus" labor existed mainly as seasonal unemployment or underemployment of self-employed farmers, tenants, and hired agricultural workers. Year-round disguised unemployment was less important because, given the existing technique (the essence of which was individual, small-scale cultivation), a significant proportion of agricultural labor could not be transferred without causing a fall in total farm output. There was little possibility of freeing labor for year-long, off-the-farm work or for seasonal work on capital formation projects in Soviet agriculture without structural reorganization and mechanization.

In the off seasons, farm operations were handled by just part of the farmers, each continuing to work full time, instead of all the farmers working a few hours each. The labor of the released farmers was then utilized in capital formation. The average number of days worked per year was greatly increased by this method. Thus, in the Soviet Union the work-year per person at work in agriculture was lengthened from around 120 days to approximately 185 to 190 days.[8]

The Soviet collective farm system served as a convenient organizational framework for the mobilization of seasonal unemployment for capital formation. The Fergana irrigation canal was dug by 165 thousand collective farm members from Uzbekistan and Tadjikstan. The Uralo-Kushumshii canal in Kazakhstan and the Samur-Divichinskii canal in Azerbaijan were each constructed by tens of thousands of collective farmers. In addition, the collective farms supervised the implementation of the statutory obligation of peasants to work six days a year on road construction. All together the collective farms contributed labor equal to an annual average of about one million yearly workers.[9]

Off-season employment of agricultural labor in construction, transportation, forestry, and even in mining and manufacturing existed under the traditional agrarian structures of Tsarist Russia and the Soviet New Economic Policy of the 1920's. The collective farm system, however, did more. It enabled the Soviets to organize and control the flow of temporary off-the-farm labor. The Soviet Union established *Organizovannvi Nabor* (organized recruitment) among the collective farms which in turn assigned certain members to work off the farms for various time periods. The total number recruited between 1931 and 1940 was 28.7 million workers. While the number working off-the-farm declined over the period, the average time worked off-the-farm per person increased from five to six months during 1933–35 to eight to nine months in 1940.[10] The demand for this type of seasonal labor declined over the period for several reasons. There was a decrease in demand for unskilled labor in general, an increase in labor recruitment through vocational schools, and an increasing demand for permanent rather than seasonal labor in nonagricultural work.

While the organized use of seasonal farm labor on agricultural capital formation projects and temporary urban work was important, even more important was the release of agricultural labor for permanent relocation in the urban areas. Mechanization, by increasing labor productivity, released labor for permanent nonagricultural work. The increase in nonagricultural employment in the Soviet Union increased very rapidly after 1928. The number of workers employed outside of agriculture increased from 9.0 million in 1928 to 19.6 million in 1932, 28.2 million in 1940, and 61.8 million in 1963.[11] The same trend is evident when data reflecting the transfer of the rural population to urban areas are examined. Between 1926 and 1939, 18.7 million people moved from rural to urban areas and between 1939 and 1959 another 24.6 million moved, for a total of 43.3 million as compared to a net increase in the urban population of 73 million between 1926 and 1959.[12]

PERFORMANCE AND PROBLEMS OF AGRICULTURE IN THE SOVIET MODEL

Soviet agriculture succeeded in fulfilling its two major functions of providing a growing marketed surplus of agricultural products and of freeing and utilizing surplus agricultural labor. The collective organization of agriculture was the key to this success. Increases in output per man and in man days worked were effected through land reorganization and mechanization. These increases enlarged the potential marketable surplus (which was then taken by the state for investment in industry) and freed the labor necessary for the expanding industrial sector. Most Western scholars argue that Soviet agriculture was a handicap, not an aid, to development. This judgment is usually based, however, on an inappropriate comparison. Present-day Soviet yields are compared with those in the United States. This ignores geographic and cultural differences, relative capital endowments, the element of time, and differential development strategies.

Better evidence on the relative success or failure of Soviet agriculture can be obtained from a comparison of Soviet agricultural *growth* with other countries. Table 1 compares the growth of total agricultural production in

Table 1   Average Annual Growth Rates of Agricultural Production in
Selected Countries

Countries	Total	Per Capita
U.S.S.R.:		
1928–1964/65	2.3	1.1
1928–1940 and 1948–1964/65	3.0	1.5
(Effective years)[1]		
U.S.A.:		
1870–1900	3.3	1.2
1910–1940	1.0	−0.2
1928–1959	1.6	0.3
Great Britain:		
1760–1790	0.6	−0.3
1801/11–1831/41	1.2	−0.5
Germany:		
1882–1909/13	1.8	0.6
France:		
1830/4–1860/4	1.6	0.8
1860/4–1895/9	0.4	0.2
Sweden:		
1861/65–1891/95	1.7	1.0
1896/1900–1926/30	1.0	0.4
Japan:		
1878/82–1913/17	2.0	0.8
Mexico:		
1940–1960	5.1	2.2

[1]The eight-year period of war and reconstruction, 1941–1948, is excluded.

Sources: Agricultural output statistics were obtained from the following sources. Arcadius Kahan, "The Collective Farm System in Russia: Some Aspects of Its Contribution to Soviet Economic Development," *Agriculture in Economic Development*, Carl Eicher and Laurence Witt, editors (New York, New York: McGraw-Hill Book Co., 1964), p. 268. United States Department of Agriculture, *The U.S.S.R. and Eastern Europe Situation* (Washington, D.C.: Government Printing Office, 1966), p. 2. United States Bureau of the Census, *Historical Statistics of the United States: Colonial Times to 1957* (Washington, D.C.: Government Printing Office, 1960), pp. 7, 288. United States Bureau of the Census, *Historical Statistics of the United States: Continuation to 1962 and Revisions* (Washington, D.C.: Government Printing Office, 1965), pp. 1, 44. B. R. Mitchel and Phyllis Deane, *Abstract of British Historical Statistics* (Cambridge, England: Cambridge University Press, 1962), pp. 3, 8. Phyllis Deane and W. A. Cole, *British Economic Growth: 1688–1959* (Cambridge, England: Cambridge University Press, 1964), pp. 78, 170. Colin Clark, *The Conditions of Economic Progress*, 3rd edition (London, England: Macmillan & Co., Ltd., 1957), pp. 262–3, 268. D. V. Glass and E. Grebenik, "World Population, 1800–1950," *The Cambridge Economic History of Europe*, M. M. Postan and J. J. Habakkuk, editors, Vol. VI (Cambridge, England: Cambridge University Press, 1965), pp. 61–2. W. W. Lockwood, *The Economic Development of Japan: Growth and Structural Change, 1868–1938* (Princeton, New Jersey: Princeton University Press, 1954), p. 86. Kazushi Ohkawa and Henry Rosovsky, "The Role of Agriculture in Modern Japanese Economic Development," *Agriculture in Economic Development*, Eicher and Witt, eds., *op. cit.*, p. 47. Howard F. Cline, *Mexico: Revolution to Evolution, 1940–1960* (New York: Oxford University Press, 1963), p. 336. Robert L. Bennett, *The Financial Sector and Economic Development: The Mexican Case* (Baltimore, Maryland: The Johns Hopkins Press, 1965), p. 187. New estimates of Japanese agricultural growth by Professor Nakamura reduce the average annual growth rate from 2.0 per cent to 1.0 per cent. See James I. Nakamura, *Agricultural Production and the Economic Development of Japan, 1873–1922* (Princeton, New Jersey: Princeton University Press, 1966), pp. 114–23.

the Soviet Union with selected other countries. Since the concern of this paper is with the role of agriculture during the industrialization period, corresponding time periods have been chosen, wherever possible, for the respective countries. Because of the inadequacy and unreliability of official Soviet statistics most of the data used in this paper are taken from computations made by Western scholars. In comparison with other countries the growth of total and per capita agricultural output in the Soviet Union has been high. Only Mexico and the United States had higher average annual growth rates. In the Mexican case the result is somewhat distorted by the exclusion of the first thirty-year period following the revolution of 1910. In the case of the United States the growth of *total*, but not per capita, agricultural output is biased upwards by the large influx of immigrants.

Another measure of the success or failure of Soviet agriculture is the increase in output per man over time. Table 2 summarizes data on changes in labor productivity for a number of selected countries. Here again the Soviet Union has a respectable performance; only the United States exceeds it in the period 1928 to 1959.

Table 2   Average Annual Growth Rates of Agricultural Output Per Man in Selected Countries

Countries	Growth Rate
U.S.S.R.:	
1928–1959	3.1%
1928–1940 and 1948–1959	
(Effective Years)	4.1
U.S.A.:	
1910–1940	1.7
1928–1959	3.4
Great Britain:	
1801/11–1831/41	0.2
Germany:	
1882–1909/13	0.6
France:	
1830/4–1860/4	2.1
1860/4–1895/9	0.9
Sweden:	
1861/5–1891/5	1.6
1896/1900–1926/30	0.8
Japan:	
1878/82–1913/17	2.1

Sources: Table I. United States, *Historical Statistics, op. cit.,* pp. 42, 280. Mitchell and Dean, *Abstract of British Historical Statistics, op. cit.,* p. 143. For Germany, France, and Sweden the only agricultural labor force statistics available are for male workers. The growth of output per man was obtained by dividing the index of agricultural output by the index of agricultural work force.

Another indicator of performance is the increase in agricultural output per unit of land. Table 3 summarizes the available data for the Soviet Union, the United States, and Japan. Land area used is not available for the remaining countries listed in Table 1. The Soviet Union did less well on this indicator than on increases in total output or output per man. This result is to be expected, of course, given the Soviet strategy of emphasizing output per man.

The data used in constructing Tables 1, 2, and 3 are estimates in most

Table 3 Average Annual Growth Rate of Agricultural Output Per Unit of Land in Use in Selected Countries

Countries	Growth Rate
U.S.S.R.:	
1928–1964/65	0.5%
1928–1940 and 1948–1964/65	
(Effective Years)	0.7
Grains, potatoes, vegetables, and industrial crops:	
1929–1959	0.9
1928–1940 and 1948–1959	
(Effective Years)	1.2
U.S.A.:	
1910–1940	0.7
1928–1959	1.1
Japan:	
1878/82–1913/17	1.2

Sources: Table I. United States, *Historical Statistics, op. cit.,* p. 281. United States, *Historical Statistics Continuation to 1962, op. cit.,* p. 42. D. Gale Johnson, "Agricultural Production," *Economic Trends in the Soviet Union,* Abram Bergson and Simon Kuznets, eds. (Cambridge: Harvard University Press, 1963), pp. 220, 227. TSSU, *Narkhoz, 1964, op. cit.,* p. 267. The index for grains, potatoes, vegetables, and industrial crops was constructed by Johnson, *op. cit.,* p. 227. For the United States the figures are for crop production per harvested acre. Thus, the United States figures are closer in concept to the Johnson index.

cases, and the degree of accuracy varies widely. However, the sum total of the data does reveal, a pattern that is probably reasonably accurate. The picture that emerges does not support the contention that Soviet agriculture has been a "failure." Rather, in the context of its role as a development aid, it has been reasonably successful. Growth was purchased by "successfully" deferring some agricultural problems to the future. These are now coming home to roost. Fortunately for the Soviet Union they are easier to solve at this stage of development.

The respectable performance of Soviet agriculture since 1928 does not, of course, imply that it is highly productive. The usual comparison of current yields in the Soviet Union and the United States proves how relatively backward Soviet agriculture is. Soviet agriculture makes such a poor showing in this type of comparison in spite of its relatively rapid growth since 1928 because of (a) the headstart possessed by other countries, (b) soil and climate conditions, (c) excesses of the collectivization drive, (d) incentives, and (e) differential development strategies.

The Headstart of Other Countries

The growth of Soviet agriculture has been as rapid as that of most developed countries whether the measure is total output, output per man, or output per unit of land. However, countries such as the United States, Great Britain, and Japan have been developing for a much longer period. Great Britain began industrializing in the eighteenth century, the United States around 1820–40, and Japan after 1868. The Soviet Union, while there were some abortive spurts under the Tsars, began a systematic effort only after 1928. As a result these countries have had more time to accumulate capital in agriculture, to diffuse technical knowledge, and to implement modern techniques.

Soil and Climatic Conditions

While mechanical equipment and fertilizer can do wonders for agriculture, geography is still the single most important determinant of relative productivity between countries. The richest Soviet land, the Ukraine, lies along the same parallel that divides Montana and North Dakota from the Prairie Provinces of Canada. Because of the importance of grain in both countries, it is pertinent to compare yields in the Soviet Union with these geographically similar areas in the United States. North Dakota, South Dakota, Nebraska, Montana, and Wyoming in the United States and the Prairie Provinces of Canada are the most climatically comparable areas.[13] Three of these states (North Dakota, South Dakota, and Nebraska) compare climatically quite closely with about half of the total Soviet grain area. The major difference is that in the eastern parts of Nebraska and South Dakota corn can be grown reasonably well, and corn land makes up about 30 per cent of the area sown to grain.

Professor Johnson prepared a detailed study of comparative agricultural yields in the 1950's between the Soviet Union and similar areas of the United States and Canada. He found that grain yields in the Soviet Union were 86.6 per cent of the yield obtained from wheat, oats, and barley grown in the Prairie Provinces of Canada and North Dakota, South Dakota, Nebraska, and Montana in the United States. But Soviet grain yields were 99.0 per cent of the yield obtained in North Dakota, South Dakota, and Nebraska. Professor Johnson concludes from this comparison ". . . that grain yields in that country (Soviet Union) are at reasonable levels."[14] Given these geographic and climatic limitations, Soviet agriculture seems to have performed reasonably well.

Excesses of the Collectivization Drive

Collectivization did have one major negative effect on Soviet agriculture. The attempt to go too far too fast led to resistance by the Russian peasant, particularly by the livestock owning kulaks, and resulted in a massive slaughter of livestock (as well as people). Between 1928 and 1933 the number of horses fell from 33.4 to 14.9 million, of cattle from 70.4 to 33.7 million, and of sheep and goats from 145.9 to 41.8 million.[15] Collectivization was carried out by urban activists who were ignorant of rural life and unsympathetic to the peasants. The process was a crude improvisation. Even the organizational pattern of a collective farm was unclear. The decision to collectivize all livestock, soon reversed, was a costly mistake—a mistake that adversely affected agriculture in the Soviet Union. The slaughter of livestock meant that much of the mechanization of the 1930's merely went to replace work animals. As a result *net* investment in agriculture was sharply lowered compared to gross investment. In addition, the loss of livestock led to a large reduction of fertilizer available for crops.

The experience of Chinese collectivization in the early 1950's indicates that there is nothing inherent in collectivization that requires the repetition of such disastrous results as the massive slaughter of livestock that occurred in the Soviet Union. A country that looks to Soviet agricultural strategy as a model need not repeat all of the mistakes made by the Soviet Union.

Incentives

As long as wage differentials (in collective farming, different numbers of workdays earned for different tasks) exist, then monetary incentives exist. Monetary incentives for industrial workers do not seem to have been any less efficient in the Soviet countries than in capitalist ones.

In agriculture, however, prices paid by the state for the required deliveries of the collective farms were far below equilibrium prices and often were below the cost of production. The crops were then sold in state retail stores at much higher prices. The price differential was one of the major sources of capital accumulation in the Soviet Union. This price structure had a disincentive effect on the collective farm workers, particularly since they could sell the produce (or at least a part of it) from their private plots at free market prices. Thus, there was an incentive to minimize effort on the collective farm lands and to maximize effort on the private plots. Higher prices for the required deliveries would have reduced this disincentive effect. While this would have reduced the original capital contribution of agriculture to development, a larger annual agricultural production might have been obtained over a longer period.

It is sometimes argued that because the individual plots are privately owned collective farm workers expended more effort on them. There is no evidence to sustain this view while there is evidence to support the importance of price differentials between sales to the state and in the collective farm market. This is the view implied by Professor Arcadius Kahan when he states that "the collective farm system by itself is mostly 'neutral' with regard to incentive policies."[16]

The problem with analyzing the importance of private property is the impossibility of separating out other factors. Comparisons between capitalist and socialist countries are possible if conditions are the same. Usually they are not. Thus differences in capital endowments, fertility of soil, cultural receptiveness to change, and the general level of development makes it almost impossible to measure the efficiency of private property relative to the collective farm system.

There are, however, enough bits and pieces of evidence to cast reasonable doubt upon the importance of private property. Why, for instance, was the average wheat yield per acre between 1955 and 1959, 22.3 bushels in the United States, 58.8 bushels in Denmark, 43.3 bushels in East Germany, 30.0 bushels in Czechoslovakia, and 16.2 bushels in Rumania?[17] Differences in climate, soils, capital equipment, and technology were probably the major causes. There seems to be no compelling evidence that the collective farm system itself has disincentive effects. Rather, particular policies, such as low delivery prices, are probably the major causes of existing disincentives.

Differential Development Strategies

The Soviet strategy of using agriculture primarily to aid industrial development meant that agricultural development *per se* was given low priority. This is a major reason for Soviet agriculture's relative backwardness. The relative backwardness of Soviet agriculture in comparison with that of the United States can be summed up by the statement of Professor Alec Nove:

> Soviet soil, is, on average, less naturally fertile; the climate is very much less favorable, the risk of drought and frost damage much greater; there is a much greater density of rural population in relation to the area of cultivatable land, and it was scarcely possible to shift peasants into non-agricultural employment faster than was in fact done.[18]

In addition to the natural limitations of Soviet agriculture, Naum Jasny points out a strong sociological limitation:

> Serfdom in Russia ceased to exist in 1861, two years before the emancipation of the slaves was proclaimed in the United States. . . . Where would the agriculture of the United States be now, had it depended entirely for its advancement on the South? . . . The situation in Russia was more unfavorable.[19]

CONCLUSION

Soviet agricultural strategy succeeded in fulfilling its role in the development process and made possible the construction of a modern industrial economy. Collectivization increased output per man, thus releasing labor for industry and rural capital formation projects. Collectivization also made possible the collection of the agricultural surplus and its allocation to the industrial and export sectors. In this way Soviet agriculture has been a success when evaluated in terms of its assigned development goals. Of course, as the Soviet economy approached maturity in the 1950's this agricultural strategy became less and less appropriate.

A number of obvious questions remain to be answered. Is the collective farm solution possible in a non-socialist economy? Can an agricultural strategy based on Soviet experience be implemented without the dogmatism and totalitarianism of Communism? How does the success of the Soviet agricultural strategy compare with the success of the "Japanese strategy" or the "Mexican strategy"? Given the importance of agricultural strategy in the development plans of underdeveloped countries, and the efficacy of Soviet strategy demonstrated in this paper, these questions should provide worthwhile research for economists interested in economic development.

NOTES

1. Bruce F. Johnston and John W. Mellor, "The Role of Agriculture in Economic Development," *American Economic Review*, September 1961, pp. 571–2.

2. See Arcadius Kahan, "The Collective Farm System in Russia: Some Aspects of Its Contribution to Soviet Economic Development," *Agriculture in Economic Development*, Carl Eicher and Laurence Witt, editors (New York, New York: McGraw-Hill Book Co., 1964), pp. 252–5.

3. *Ibid.*, p. 259.

4. *Idem.*

5. Tsentralnoye Statisticheskoye Upravleniye pri Sovete Ministrov SSSR, *Narodnoye Khozyaystvo SSSR v 1961 Godu: Statisticheskiy Yezhegodnik* (Moscow, U.S.S.R.: Gostatizdat, 1962), p. 341 (hereafter TsSU, *Narkhoz*).

6. *Ibid.*, p. 296.

7. Naum Jasny, *The Socialized Agriculture of the U.S.S.R.: Plans and Performance*, Grain Economic Series No. 5 (Stanford, California: Stanford University Press, 1949), p. 33.

8. See United States Congress, Joint Economic Committee, *Comparisons of the United States and Soviet Economies*, 86th Congress, 1st Session, 1960, p. 213. It is worth noting that, in their new study, Moorsteen and Powell find that the "dominant source of Soviet growth has been the increase in the quantity of productive resources employed." See Richard Moorsteen and Raymond P. Powell, *The Soviet Capital Stock, 1928–1962* (Homewood, Illinois: Richard D. Irwin, Inc., 1966), p. 292.

9. Kahan, *op. cit.*, p. 268.

10. *Ibid.*, p. 255. An interesting question concerning the use of surplus agricultural labor was the transportation cost incurred in getting labor to the job site. The Soviets minimized this cost by full utilization of existing transportation facilities. Railroad passenger cars designed to hold 100 riders were loaded with maybe double that number. The real cost was absorbed, therefore, by the reduced comfort of the riders.

11. United States Congress, Joint Economic Committee, *Current Economic Indicators for the U.S.S.R.*, 89th Congress, 1st Session, 1965, p. 71.

12. Kahan, *op. cit.*, p. 256.

13. D. Gale Johnson, "Agricultural Production," *Economic Trends in the Soviet Union*, Simon Kuznets and Abram Bergson, eds. (Cambridge: Harvard University Press, 1963), pp. 255–7. Also, D. Gale Johnson, *Climatic and Crop Analogies for the Soviet Union: A Study of the Possibilities of Increasing Grain Yields*, Research Paper No. 5716: University of Chicago, Office of Agricultural Economics, December 16, 1957. In one respect these areas are not comparable with the Soviet Union. Since these low yielding areas are not the only source of grain supply for Canada and the United States a large portion of the land can be left fallow in any one year. This cannot be done in the Soviet Union. This, in itself, will favor higher yields in these United States and Canadian areas.

14. Johnson, "Agricultural Production," *op. cit.*, p. 226.

15. Jasny, *op. cit.*, p. 324.

16. Kahan, *op. cit.*, p. 254.

17. United States Department of Agriculture, *Agriculture Statistics: 1964* (Washington, D.C.: Government Printing Office, 1964), pp. 5–6.

18. Alec Nove, *The Soviet Economy* (New York, New York: Frederick A. Praeger, Inc., 1961), p. 297.

19. Jasny, *op. cit.*, p. 133.

17

Chinese Agricultural Communes

Joan Robinson

The basic problem of the under-developed economies is to increase efficiency in agriculture, starting from a low level of productivity and, in most cases, a high labour/land ratio, a low capital/labour ratio and methods of cultivation which fail to take advantage of modern discoveries.

As a basis for improvements, the choice of the scale of organisation is an important matter and by no means a simple one.

For the deployment of labour, a rather small scale is required. Workers are spread out over space so that discipline is hard to enforce; an incentive wage system is not easy to arrange or to administer; there has to be a great diffusion of managerial responsibility; every field is different, every day is different and quick decisions have to be taken. For getting work out of the workers a peasant family is hard to beat. Discipline and responsibility are imposed by the pressing incentive to secure the family livelihood. But for the deployment of land the family unit is much too small. Transport and marketing are costly: specialised production is worthwhile only for valuable cash crops. The bulk of consumption is provided for on the spot. The various products required must be raised on whatever land the family happens to command. There are obvious advantages in a number of families pooling their land and allocating each crop to the area best suited to it.

The deployment of knowledge requires still larger units. A team of experts can service a wide area, but generalised science has to be digested and adapted to local conditions and its results demonstrated convincingly. The peasant cannot afford to risk his daily bread in experiments. Investments in water control and land reclamation require a larger scale again.

The land reform in China created a mass of very small-scale freeholders. It could not make the basis for a drive to increased efficiency. A slow start was made towards collectivisation. Mutual-aid teams for cultivation were encouraged and "lower-form co-operatives" began to be set up, in which proceeds were shared as to 30 per cent in respect to land and stock put into the pool and as to 70 per cent according to work contributed. There were a few "higher-form co-operatives" in which property was merged and only work counted for income. In 1956 this type swept the board.

Reprinted from *Co-Existence* (May 1964), pp. 1-7, by permission of the author.

These co-operatives proved to be too large from one point of view and too small from another. When a thousand or more workers are sharing their joint proceeds, the relationship between individual effort and individual earnings is too much diluted to make a strong incentive for conscientious work. The personal and technical problems of control and accounting were a strain on available managerial capacity, especially where the co-operative comprised a number of separate villages. On the other hand, an area of a few hundred acres was often insufficient for the best deployment of land, while both the labour force and the area were much too small to exploit the possibilities of improvements through irrigation, drainage, afforestation and so forth. The communes, which were inaugurated in a burst of enthusiasm in 1958 and hammered into shape in the three bad years that followed, have evolved into an ingenious system for reconciling the requirements of large and small scale.

The organisation is in three tiers. The team is a smaller unit than the co-operative of 1956. In some cases it corresponds to the preceding "lower-form co-operative." Where villages are large, there are several teams in one village. The brigade, usually between five and ten teams, covering a single village in plains where the villages are large, is often a continuation of a "higher-form co-operative" formed in 1956. A commune may comprise five brigades or thirty, covering as much as fifty thousand acres, or, for intense cultivation, as little as one thousand acres. Broadly speaking, the team is the unit for labour management; the brigade for the crop programme; the commune for the external relations of the group, for investment projects and for industrial enterprises ancillary to agriculture.

THE TEAM

In the standard case (with many variations) the team is the basic accounting unit for production and distribution. It consists of the labour force of some thirty families; it controls a particular block of land, with working animals and implements (tools are individually owned). Sometimes its fields are the very same that these families formerly owned or received at the land reform twelve years ago; sometimes they have been regrouped for convenience in cultivation. The team, provided with the appropriate seed, fertilisers, etc., accepts responsibility for a particular plan of production over the crop year; and for a particular quota of sales, at fixed prices, to the Government procurement agency. It may also contract with neighbouring city co-operatives for sales of vegetables, meat and so forth.

From the annual income of the team, in kind and cash, is deducted:
1. The agricultural tax. The tax was assessed on the national productivity of each piece of land and is guaranteed not to be changed for at least the next three years. The nominal rate is 11 to 13 per cent of gross produce. Since productivity has generally been increasing, the actual rate is less: 4 or 5 per cent is common. I came upon one case, where land had been turned over to highly profitable market gardening since the assessment was made, in which the tax was less than 1 per cent. On the other hand a team which fails to achieve the assessed productivity is penalised by a higher burden of

tax. An effective rate of 14 per cent or more may occur, but is said to be rare. When failure is due to "natural disasters"—drought, flood, typhoon, unseasonable frost—the tax is forgiven. The tax is collected simply as part of the deliveries to the state procurement agency.

2. Costs of production. Fodder, seed, etc., are replaced in kind. Fertilisers, fees for tractor ploughing, electric power, etc., are paid for out of cash income.

3. Contribution to accumulation. This varies according to the margin above the needs of subsistence and according to the keenness of the team on socialist construction.

4. Contribution to the welfare fund. This is generally 1 or 2 per cent of gross income. It is used to secure for member families who are in difficulties the *five guarantees*—food, clothing, shelter, medical care and funeral expenses. Poor teams provide them at a pretty meagre level. Prosperous teams support schools, and provide free medical care and other amenities to all member families.

5. A management fee. A management fee, usually 1 per cent of team income, is paid to the commune.

The remainder, usually about 60 per cent of the team's gross income, is distributed to the members. There is an elaborate system of job evaluation, acceptable to public opinion among the workers, in terms of work points. Points given for organisational work, attending meetings and so forth must not exceed 2 per cent of the team's total points earned in the field. Forward estimates of the value of a work point are made and members of the team are partially paid in advance (out of the proceeds of last year's harvests) in three or four instalments. Then, after the autumn harvest, there is a grand reckoning and the balances are paid out.

The leader, deputy and accountant are elected by the team members, and a meeting is called from time to time to discuss any personal or technical problems that may arise.

A team may choose to sell more than its quota of grain to the state (thus having so much the more cash to distribute); it may have some side activities such as pig breeding for the market or for the benefit of members who, for instance, will take a piglet to rear (they, in turn, can sell or consume the product as they please); it may operate small enterprises such as a brick kiln, but this is more common at the brigade level.

THE BRIGADE

The teams forming a brigade elect a management committee and appoint a leader, deputy and accountant. The brigade, in consultation with its teams on the one side and the commune management on the other, controls the allocation of land to special uses, such as planting orchards, and works out the annual crop programme. It may operate enterprises employing wage workers and provide conveniences such as grinding flour and making noodles for member households. It breeds draft animals, and may own a truck. Profits from its activities may provide an independent accumulation fund or it may take a levy from the accumulation funds of its member teams to finance investment, for instance, in electrification of pumps, chaff-cutters, etc. A family depends upon the team that it belongs to for daily bread, but something like regimental morale attaches to the brigade; rivalry stimulates production.

THE COMMUNE

The director of the commune, with his staff of ten or twenty "cadres," is from one point of view the representative of the co-operative, from another of the administration. The commune has absorbed the lowest level of local government (the *hsiang*) and in that capacity is responsible for registration of births, deaths and marriages, taxation, controlling the militia (police and law-courts are at county level) and gearing the commune's contribution to education and health services into the county's.

It is the point of contact between the co-operative and the administration for purposes of framing the annual plan and looking after its implementation, for receiving loans, for receiving assistance in time of trouble, for organising procurement in the broad (actual contracts are made with the respective accounting units) and for digesting and disseminating technical progress.

It may operate enterprises such as manufacture and repair of tools (some of the famous miniature blast furnaces have found a useful function here). In some cases it owns a park of tractors. (Elsewhere a county tractor station or a state farm will plough for neighbouring communes on contract.)

The original nucleus of the commune system was the pooling of resources by a number of co-operatives to organise schemes, too large to be undertaken individually, of land reclamation, irrigation, drainage and communications—investments which in effect create land. This remains a continuing function of the communes and the work goes on from year to year. Where the terrain requires a plan covering an area larger than a single commune, it is easy for two or three to organise to work together and to arrange how the benefit is to be shared, which would have been impossible for dozens of co-operatives, let alone thousands of peasant households.

As well as such positive functions, the communes have the no less vital task of coping with the effects of natural disasters. They can claim credit for preventing the breakdown of the economy in the "bitter years" 1959–61, and they are still called upon, in the smaller misfortunes that every season brings in one district or another, to mobilise labour, distribute relief and organise reconstruction as may be required.

THE HOUSEHOLD

The average size of households ranges, between one commune and another, from three to five souls, which indicates that families of eight or ten members must be quite common. Normally three generations live together in a house that they have always had, or received at the land reform, or have newly built. Standards vary. In one province, a miserable dark hovel, shared with the chickens, is typical; in another, a little mud-walled homestead, with a vegetable garden, a pigsty in the corner, the courtyard shaded by grape vines, and clean, airy, well-roofed rooms.

The system of rations distributed irrespective of work points earned, which was introduced in the first, Utopian, phase of the commune system, had to be abandoned in the bad years. Family income now depends primarily on the earnings of its members in the team. Besides this, the household has the use of a private plot. The team (which retains property in the land) allocates not more than 7 per cent of its cultivable area to plots, so much per head. The plots are very small: a family of six has one tenth or one fifth of an acre. Vegetables, pigs and chickens around the house and handicraft production for use or sale further supplement the family income. Subsidiary production is important to the family but it is reckoned to contribute less than 10 per cent to marketed supplies for the nation.

Where the household is too small an economic unit for its own activities, spontaneous co-operation develops. For instance, individually owned goats and sheep are herded in common. Team dining rooms have gone out of fashion, but some groups of unmarried workers organise a common kitchen for themselves.

VARIATIONS

The general scheme of organisation is adjusted to local conditions with great flexibility. Different treatment is required for a poor grain-growing district, where 90 per cent of produce is consumed on the farm, for a cash-crop area where income in money accrues from sales to the state procurement agency and grain for food has to be brought in, and for suburban market gardens supplying city distributors on contract. History also creates local differences; the old liberated areas have proud traditions and even in the last six years experience has moulded policy in many ways. There are considerable variations upon the standard pattern of relations between team, brigade and commune. Among a casual sample of a dozen communes in four provinces which I was able to visit in the summer of 1963, there were three where one of the brigades was different from the rest. In each case it was the continuation of a higher-form co-operative that had taken root and chose to continue as a basic accounting unit. Control of land and equipment then inheres in the brigade, and teams are merely convenient sub-divisions of the labour force. The peasants have formed and tested their own leaders and a strong collective spirit makes them less dependent upon individual incentive. This promotes efficiency in a number of ways and is rewarded by material success. In these brigades average earnings are markedly above (in one case double) those of the other teams in the commune.

Quite a different pattern was found in a commune where the teams were old lower-form co-operatives which seem to have been very little affected by the subsequent stages of collectivisation.

In some of the prosperous, sophisticated market gardens near Peking, the brigades are accounting units; it is said that in a few cases the whole commune is the accounting unit.

There are considerable variations in methods of forming the annual plan, in details of the distribution system, in the management of subsidiary enterprises and so forth.

There are differences also in the level of morale. In some revolutionary *élan* has been maintained through the difficult years. In some slackness and even corruption crept in. The general mass, between the brilliant and the bad, are more or less satisfactory and steadily improving.

SOCIAL SERVICES

There are great variations also in the organisation of medical and educational services. There is no cut-and-dried system of rights and obligations— the communes do what they can and the county fills in the gaps. One way or another there is a complete network of schools, hospitals and clinics covering the rural areas. Generally brigades (sometimes teams) are responsible for primary schools and communes for secondary schools. The buildings—often an old landlord's house or a temple—are usually provided; teachers' salaries (not much above a labourer's wage) are sometimes paid partly or wholly from the welfare fund. Parents sometimes have to pay for books and sometimes not. In the poorest communes the county authorities carry all the costs.

Similarly a hospital is usually provided by the commune and clinics by brigades. Sometimes everything is provided free, including drugs; at the other extreme a doctor is merely invited to come in and collect what he can for fees. Fees for indigent patients must be paid from the welfare fund, according to the *five guarantees*.

Public entertainment is provided by loudspeakers for those who have not a wireless of their own, and a film projection unit which gives a show in each village about once a month. There are occasional visits from theatrical companies, dance troupes, etc. The schools provide adult literacy classes.

MARKETING

Like production, sales are organised in three tiers. At the lowest level there are periodic fairs at which households can sell eggs, fruit and so forth in small quantities. A team may send in a cart-load of vegetables. Prices are freely formed under the pressures of supply and demand.

At the next level, individual teams and brigades can sell products such as noodles, sauce and wine to the Supply and Marketing Co-operative, to be retailed in the village or supplied to town, and such products as hog bristles to be passed on to industry. Here prices are fixed in what is considered to be a reasonable relation to costs.

The main outlet for agricultural produce is through the state procurement agency, which has the sole right to handle the main crops. Deliveries are agreed in advance in the annual plan and prices have been held substantially unchanged since the currency stabilisation of 1950. Retail prices are also fixed. In some cases the margin is not sufficient to cover transport and handling charges, so that the urban population is partly getting its food below cost. Where a team is allotted some specialised work and has to buy its grain, purchases must be made through the state organisation, though the grain may come physically from next door.

The vegetable market for the cities is highly organised. Plans are framed in the broad between the city authority and the commune. Within that framework, state retailers contract directly with teams and receive daily deliveries straight from the field. In the summer flush, procurement prices are lowered so as to keep earnings fairly stable, while selling prices are pushed down to clear the market. The consequent loss to the city authorities is made good out of the profits on early spring crops. Winter prices are reckoned to cover hothouse and storage costs.

Fruit and vegetable production is far and away more profitable than grain (though it involves more continuous work). Chinese economists are discussing the problem of "socialist rent" and the means to syphon it off for the benefit of the nation without upsetting the system of incentives in agriculture. For the time being it lies where it falls.

The procurement system for cash crops, surplus grain, and market-garden products, which guarantees to the producer a stable market for fixed quantities of output at fixed prices, is the basis of the whole system, and makes all the rest possible.

part five

Industrial Institutions and Strategy

Industrialization has always been considered the very basis of economic development. And rapid growth has been seen as the means to that industrialization. In the first reading, the historical experience of rapid growth in the Soviet Union is used to analyze questions of industrial development strategy. The article proceeds on two fronts: it is a critique of both development *theory* and development *practice.* After a review of traditional economic theory, the article analyzes the policy issues of the role of central planning, the choice of an investment rate, balanced vs. unbalanced allocation of investment, and the choice of production techniques.

Another crucial issue in industrial development is the question of the efficiency of managerial decision-making. It is often argued that capitalism is superior to socialist or cooperative alternatives because it provides an incentive system for managers and entrepreneurs that is the most efficient known. In the second reading, Seymour Melman asks what the options are with respect to the organization of production and the decision-making process. The development of industrialism has been accompanied by managerial-hierarchical control over industrial work. Does the introduction of industrial production require the use of this managerial-hierarchical mode of decision-making? Melman does an empirical study of managerial and cooperative decision-making by comparing capitalist versus kibbutz operated industrial firms in Israel. The high efficiency rating achieved by the kibbutz operated firms enables Melman to conclude that industrial enterprises of a modern technical sort can be operated under various modes of decision-making. The work of Barry Richman on industrial management in China somewhat reluctantly comes to the same conclusion.*

Industrialization strategy in the underdeveloped world must face environmental problems similar to those the developed world is now experiencing. Some commentators have argued in fact that industrialization of the underdeveloped countries would destroy the world environment. Since the developed countries are the overwhelming cause of environmental destruction, it might be more appropriate to argue for deindustrialization of those countries. Putting the question of responsibility to one side, the problem remains.

It is not industrialization alone that is the cause of environmental destruction. The amount of pollution per unit of output is excessively high in the developed countries because of the structure of their economic systems. There are at least three reasons for this. First, profit maximizing firms in the developed capitalist countries and output maximizing firms in the developed socialist countries attempt to minimize their internal costs of production by avoiding pollution abatement costs, thus letting the public bear the cost by suffering with the pollution. Second, large private firms resort to planned physical obsolescence of products and frequent model and styling changes in order to maintain their profits in competition with each other. This causes a greater use of resources than is necessary. Third, emphasis on individual, rather than collective, consumption means that many more durable consumer goods are produced than is necessary. A washing machine, sewing machine, and lawn mower in every house that sits idle most of the time again means using up more resources than is necessary. Underdeveloped countries need to bear in mind these points in developing their own industrialization strategy.

In the third reading, Leo Orleans and Richard Suttmeier analyze the environmental effects of the Maoist approach to development. The Chinese minimize environmental destruction through stress on agricultural development as opposed to industrialization, employment of labor-intensive production methods, use of local resources, and extensive conservation policies. Thus, they find that there is reason to hope that development is possible while at the same time minimizing environmental destruction.

In the last reading in this part, Mahbub ul Haq argues against the policy of concentrating on the growth of per capita GNP as the primary objective of development strategy. He contends that employment should become the primary goal of planning because if development means reduction in poverty, employment is the most important variable. In agreement with Dudley Seers, ul Haq thinks that our concentration on growth of GNP at the expense of employment and income distribution policies has spelled defeat in the war against poverty. The reader might refer to the earlier article on industrial strategy in the Soviet Union and consider the employment effects of a dual technology (combining labor intensive techniques with modern processes of production). That is, it is not clear that the pursuit of a high growth rate and the use of advanced technology are incompatible with a policy of maximizing employment. In the Soviet Union, for example, they combined the policy of a dual technology with on-the-job training and overstaffing (compared to Western standards) that substantially reduced unemployment.** These policies would be difficult to transfer to an underdeveloped country with a capitalist economy because they would be inefficient from the point of view of the firms (but not of the economy as a whole) and, therefore, unprofitable.

---

* See Barry Richman, "Capitalists and Managers in Communist China," *Harvard Business Review* (January-February, 1967), pp. 57–78; and his *A Firsthand Study of Industrial Management in Communist China* (Los Angeles: University of California, Graduate School of Business, Division of Research, 1967).

**Charles K. Wilber, *The Soviet Model and Underdeveloped Countries* (Chapel Hill: University of North Carolina Press, 1969), pp. 101–103.

18

Economic Development, Central Planning and Allocative Efficiency

Charles K. Wilber

INTRODUCTION

This paper is concerned with the question of central planning and allocative efficiency in the context of a backward economy trying to achieve the one overriding goal of economic development. No pretense is made of constructing a complete theory of a centrally planned economy. Rather, the aim is much more limited. This study is concerned only with the development process and within this process only with the problem of resource allocation.

This paper will first critique the usefulness of static equilibrium analysis in evaluating allocative efficiency under conditions of rapid economic development. Second, the paper will construct a model of dynamic allocative efficiency derived mainly from the historical development experience of the Soviet Union, modified where appropriate by the later experience of the other Socialist countries.

CRITIQUE OF STATIC EQUILIBRIUM ANALYSIS

A persistent criticism levied against Soviet-type central planning by Western economists is that it leads to a misallocation of resources. It is argued that since there is no market for intermediate goods, no interest charge on capital, and subsidies and taxes are used to arrive at final prices, prices do not reflect relative scarcities and thus distort resource allocation.

It is true that there are many examples of miscalculation and misallocation in centrally planned economies. However, similar examples of misallocation can be found in every economy including market economies. No economy does a perfect job of allocating resources. Rather, the important question is in what type of economy do the fewest misallocations occur. While this writer feels an advanced market economy (not, however, an underdeveloped one) probably allocates resources better than a centrally planned economy, there is insufficient empirical evidence to give a conclusive answer.

Reprinted from *Jahrbuch der Wirtschaft Osteuropas*, Band 2, 1970, pp. 221-243, by permission of Günter Olzog Verlag.

Since empirical proof is not available, Western economists have turned to static equilibrium analysis to prove the inefficiency of Soviet-type central planning. With the recent advances in linear programming, input-output-analysis, and similar mathematical tools, equilibrium analysis has become an invaluable method for solving the problem of constrained maximization of an objective function for sub-units within an economy. Despite the problem of quantifying costs and benefits, General Motors and the U.S. Defense Department can use equilibrium analysis to increase the efficiency of resource allocation within their respective units.

However, recent advances in welfare economics and particularly the theory of second best show that static equilibrium analysis breaks down when it comes to evaluating the efficiency of resource allocation for an economy as a whole and particularly for an economy in the process of rapid economic development. Static equilibrium analysis indicates that maximum efficiency is attained when available resources are allocated in such a way as to maximize the particular output mix determined by consumers' preferences (in a market economy) or planners' preferences (in a centrally planned economy). To achieve this allocation the first-order welfare conditions, which for simplicity can be summarized as price equals marginal costs, must be fulfilled in all markets. These first-order or marginal conditions are derived from the rules of the calculus regarding maximization of functions. They constitute a set of necessary conditions for the attainment of maximum efficiency, but are not sufficient conditions. They do not guarantee that it is maximum efficiency being attained; it might be minimum efficiency.

In addition, it is necessary to have second-order, convexity conditions of all cost and utility functions. Even with this, however, one cannot be sure a *maximum maximorum* has been reached. There is nothing in the first-order and second-order conditions to differentiate the top of a molehill from that of a mountain.

For efficiency to be at a maximum, the "total conditions," as J. R. Hicks calls them, must also be satisfied. They state that if efficiency is to be maximized, it must also be impossible to increase efficiency by introducing a new product or by withdrawing an old product.

If the marginal, second-order, and total conditions are all satisfied, static efficiency will be a maximum. However, it is not a unique maximum; it is merely one of an infinite number of Pareto optima because it presupposes a given distribution of income that is not itself determined by the conditions of maximum efficiency. Changes in the distribution of income will cause variations in the most efficient outputs of the various products and allocations of the various inputs.

A Pareto optimum as a position of maximum efficiency loses its validity when external effects (i.e., external economies and diseconomies, interdependence of preference functions) in consumption and production and public goods are taken into account.

Since there are institutional or technical obstacles that preclude the satisfaction of at least some of the conditions of maximum efficiency in all economies, static equilibrium analysis breaks down as an evaluative tool. There is no logical way of determining whether an economy with only one sector failing to attain the price equals marginal cost condition is more efficient in resource allocation than an economy with no sector fulfilling the first-order conditions. That is, if any one price does not reflect relative scarcities (i.e., price equals marginal cost) there is no way of theoretically saying that one set of prices is more rational than another. The conclusion from this is that probably ". . . it is impossible to demonstrate the irrationality—or rationality—of centrally planned economies on the basis of standard welfare economies."[1]

CENTRAL PLANNING AND DYNAMIC EFFICIENCY

All of the above is concerned with a static welfare analysis of resource allocation. If the problem of resource allocation is placed in the context of economic development then an entirely different approach to evaluation is required. In a developmental setting, the questions of external economies and changing resource scarcities become of prime importance.

The Soviet Union's approach to the specific resource allocation problems of investment rate (choice between present and future), investment allocation and choice of production techniques (including factor proportions) will be analyzed in the next section. For now it is enough to say that their approach centered on the capture of external economies and economizing the obviously scarce factors—capital and skilled labor.

In addition, recognition of constantly changing resource scarcities led to the use of a pricing system that deviated markedly from current resource scarcities. It is worthwhile to analyze the Soviet price system in some detail at this time.

The Pricing System

To repeat, almost every Western specialist on centrally planned economies has argued that the Soviet pricing system is irrational, that is, it does not reflect the relative scarcities of resources derived from the structure of planners' preferences. Two important points are made. First, it is argued that Soviet prices do not include an interest rate on capital. While an appropriate interest rate is theoretically determinable, practically it is very difficult. The Soviet use of the "coefficient of relative effectiveness" has been a rough, if inadequate, substitute.[2] Second, it is argued that Soviet subsidization of some capital goods and taxation of consumer goods distorts present relative scarcities, and, more importantly, the low price of capital relative to the price of labor does so also. However, as seen above, these arguments cannot be logically derived from static equilibrium theory. Furthermore, in the context of economic development this pricing system might even be rational.

A centrally planned economy attempts to secure a coordinated set of investment decisions *ex ante*, that is, in advance of any commitment of resources. In a market economy the allocation of investment is the result of the estimates and expectations of independent entrepreneurs, revised in the long-run by *ex post* movements of market prices. The differences between the planned and market approach are important. Current investment changes both productive capacity and employment and thus exercises an important influence upon market prices by changing relative scarcities. Accordingly, the present structure of market prices cannot be used as a sure measure of the future structure of prices, or, therefore, of what will be the return on any particular investment project. Professor Kenneth Boulding argues that "there is not the slightest reason . . . to suppose that the equilibrium price set, in the sense of classical or neoclassical equilibrium theory, is the price set which will go with the maximum rate of economic development."[3]

The appropriate price structure will depend on a number of considerations. Where there is a divergence between the private and social returns on investment in a particular area due to external economies:

> . . . there is a strong argument for distorting the price structure away from what would be a market equilibrium by deliberately lowering the relative prices and hence discouraging investment in those industries where the external economies or the nonfinancial returns are small, and raising prices and encouraging investment in those industries where the external economies or the nonfinancial returns are large.
> . . . (or) the general principle of the taxation of vice and the subsidization of virtue can be extended to include the taxation of those commodities the production of which we wish to discourage from the point of view of economic development and the subsidization of those the production of which we wish to encourage.[4]

The Soviets accomplished this end by subsidizing strategic material and industries such as steel, engineering, chemicals, and electrical equipment; and taxing low priority products such as textiles and most consumer goods.[5]

In the context of economic development, "personal consumption should have a low claim on resources, and the static welfare criterion of equating price to marginal cost must recede in the background."[6] This the Soviets have done by imposing high turnover taxes on most consumer goods. Some consumer goods which have significance for development, such as paper which plays an imporatnt role in the spread of literacy are favored. Soviet pricing policies, thus, have a rationale in a development context.

Central Planning

The process of industrialization and economic development was facilitated in the Soviet Union by the centralized disposal of economic resources. All of the country's resources were concentrated on certain objectives and their dissipation on other objectives which were not conducive to rapid industrialization was avoided. The lack and weakness of industrial cadres made it desirable to concentrate the available talent on high priority objectives. Thus in the Soviet Union planning in the early stages of development was characterized by administrative management and administrative allocation of resources on the basis of priorities centrally established. The Soviet model in the early stages of the development process can be best described as a *"sui generis* war economy."[7]

A major advantage of public ownership and central planning is its ability to overcome Nurkse's famous "vicious circle of poverty."

> On the supply side, there is the small capacity to save, resulting from the low level of real income. The low level of real income is a reflection of low productivity, which in its turn is due largely to the lack of capital. The lack of capital is a result of the small capacity to save, and so the circle is complete.
>
> On the demand side, the inducement to invest may be low because of the small buying power of the people, which is due to their small real income, which again is due to low productivity. The low level of productivity, however, is a result of the small amount of capital used in production, which in its turn may be caused, at least partly, by the small inducement to invest.[8]

The Soviet Union was able to break the circle on the supply side (i.e., raise the savings rate) because of its ability to collect the economic surplus from the agricultural sector and its control over the division between consumption and investment in the industrial sector.[9] Public ownership allowed the former luxury consumption from property income to be converted into savings for investment purposes. The ability of central planning to concentrate on the one goal of development permitted the Soviet Union to channel savings and thus resources into the most productive purposes and to reduce the proportion of savings going into (from the point of view of rapid growth) unproductive investment.

The demand side of the problem did not exist in the Soviet Union. Long-range development, not short-run profits, was the goal. The problem of finding buyers for what was produced did not exist. The state, through central planning, created the necessary demand by its decision to produce.[10] In making decisions about the allocation of resources between the production of capital goods and consumer goods, the state made *ipso facto* a savings decision. In real terms both investment and savings must refer to the difference between total production and consumer goods production. Thus, there is an identity of savings decisions and investment decisions.[11]

A closely related problem is that of external economies.[12] If an economy is far from equilibrium, current market prices and profit maximization are poor signals for investment decisions. In neo-classical terms, equilibrium occurs when firms (and the industry) are at the bottom of their long-run cost curves, that is, where there are constant or decreasing returns to scale. In addition, *ex ante* coordination of investment decisions is excluded. However, in underdeveloped countries such as the Soviet Union in the 1930's firms (and industries) are likely to be on an increasing return section of the cost curve. And since they are far from the technological frontier, the cost curves will shift downward over time. The presence of potential external economies makes pre-planned coordination among development projects highly desirable. Moreover, in many development schemes there exists a high degree of physical interdependence among different projects such that the productivity of anyone cannot be maximized in isolation. Multipurpose river basin planning, hydroelectricity generaton, organization of an iron and steel industry, and the development of chemicals are examples of this nature. The individual project within such a scheme can seldom be examined by itself and in estimating its operational efficiency it has to be jointly considered with its related units.

In underdeveloped countries, private marginal productivity of capital frequently falls short of its social marginal productivity. In developed economies, external economies of various industries support each other and thus help to bridge the gap between private and social productivity. However, lack of basic industrial structures and of social overhead capital does not permit the capture of potential external economies and complementarities in underdeveloped countries. The net productivity of capital, therefore, does not attain a sufficiently high level to stimulate productive private investment. Thus, since a modern industrial structure is highly interdependent, any particular investment project, by itself, frequently appears uneconomic, unless viewed in the perspective of interrelated growth of other firms and industries. Since "the lifetime of equipment is long . . . the investor's foresight is likely to be more imperfect than that of the buyer and seller or of the producer. The individual investor's risk may be higher than that confronting an overall investment program."[13] The volume and cost of production have to be computed on the basis of the anticipated future, and since each project has to be so viewed, the plans for any one project cannot be finished until the plans for all the others are known. The price system fails in these computations because the external economies of individual projects get interrelated and the supply prices depend upon the levels of outputs, which in turn are related to the overall input requirements of the entire development scheme. It is important to remember that when the economy is far from equilibrium, present prices are poor indicators of future prices, and there is no guarantee that the *sequence* of investment dictated by the market will maximize the rate of growth toward equilibrium. To promote coordinated industrial expansion, therefore, the perspective of growth must be known well in advance. This is what the state, through central planning, provided in the Soviet Union.

The most important question is where are most of the external economies and complementarities to be found. In the present context, they can be classified into two types—horizontal external economies and complementarities of demand and vertical externalities and complementarities of forward and backward linkage. These two types lie at the heart of both the debate over balanced growth versus unbalanced growth and the question of investment criteria. As such they will be considered in detail in the next section of this paper when the strategy of resource allocation in the Soviet Union is discussed. For now it is enough to say that because of interdependence of demand and of industries, a system of central planning more easily maximizes the potential external economies.[14] Individual investors will be less motivated to do so because the benefits of external economies accrue to society as a whole, or at least to some members of it, without bringing a direct return to the investor that can be anticipated by using profit maximization and current prices as criteria.

DEVELOPMENT STRATEGY AND RESOURCE ALLOCATION

In discussing resource allocation within the context of economic development, three major problems arise. First is the problem of allocation between the present and future, that is, the choice of an optimum rate of investment. Second is the allocation of investment among sectors and projects. The third problem is the choice of production technique.

The Rate of Investment

What is the optimum rate of investment for a poor country beginning a development program? There is no uniquely determinate economic solution to this question. Increasing the rate of investment today means lowering the share of consumption in gross national product (though not necessarily the absolute amount) in the present in exchange for a larger income and consumption in the future. A lower rate of investment will yield greater consumption in the present, but lower amounts in the future, than would higher rates of investment. The key to the solution, therefore, is the trade-off between present and future consumption.

In an ideal market economy individuals' time preferences would determine the relative values of present and future consumption. A market rate of interest or discount of future income streams would emerge from the particular configuration of time preferences. The market determined rate of investment would be the rate at which the marginal productivity of investment equals the market rate of discount that emerges from the interplay of unilateral decisions of savers and investors. Economists are fairly well agreed that this market determined rate is not necessarily an optimum rate from either a welfare or a growth viewpoint.

> . . . we reject the twin notions (1) that the rate of interest determined in an atomistic competitive market need have any normative significance in the planning of collective investment, and (2) that the market-determined rate of investment, and hence the market-determined rate of economic growth, need be optimal in any welfare sense.[15]

The market rate of interest as a device for discounting the worth of future income streams, however it may be justified for an individual, is inappropriate for the community as a whole, at least within the context of economic development. By determining the rate of saving and investment, time preferences of individuals would decide not only their own future income and consumption but that of future generations as well. There seems to be an inevitable short-sightedness in the individual's choice, owing to the limited perspective in time from which the individual, *qua* isolated individual, necessarily views the range of available alternatives. This limitation in regard to time has often been referred to as the deficiency of the "telescopic faculty" of the individual with regard to the future, and the fact that it gives rise to a "psychological discount" of his future income does not appear to be relevant to planning economic development.[16] In fact, even ". . . the accuracy of its basic assumption that an anticipated satisfaction is always less attractive the more distant the future date to which the actual satisfaction is assigned appears to be questionable, as anticipation can also be enjoyable."[17] This last point is valid both for an individual at different points during his lifetime and even, beyond his lifetime, in the case where satisfaction is received from passing on wealth to heirs.

Professor Holzman points out several other problems[18] of time preference. The present evaluation of the present versus the future will differ from the future evaluation of the present versus the future. The hindsight of the future will overcome the "weakness of imagination" and "defective telescopic faculty" of the present. Thus, he argues, the rate of investment undertaken in the present would be higher if it could be chosen by the population from the vantage point of the future instead of the present. In addition there is a particular time preference configuration for every possible income distribution. If the income distribution changes between the present and the future, then *ceteris paribus*, the investment rate will also change. He argues that the optimum rate is indeterminate between a lower limit set by the present evaluation and an upper limit set by the future evaluation.

Professor Sen introduces the concept of the "isolation paradox"[19] in arguing the limitations of time preference in choosing an investment rate. An individual may be unwilling to give up one unit of consumption today so that a future generation's consumption can be increased by three units. However, if someone else agrees to give up one unit of consumption now if he does likewise then he might very well change his decision. To the first individual, the loss of one unit today will be compensated by a gain of six units for the future. Therefore, while he is not prepared to make the sacrifice alone, he is ready to do so if others join in.

A central planning board cannot simply imitate the rate of investment that would emerge from individual time preferences. The social perspective of the future and the time horizon of a community differ significantly from those of an individual. The community cannot and does not discount its future in the same manner and at the same rate as an individual.[20] What rate of investment does the planning board choose? As noted above, Professor Holzman says it is indeterminate between the lower limit set by the present evaluation of the future and the upper limit set by the future evaluation of the future. Professor Sen argues that the rate is indeterminate between a lower limit set by the rate necessary to utilize existing productive capacity and to maintain a constant consumption level for a growing population and an upper limit set by the rate of investment which maintains the present level of consumption and does not yield negative marginal returns.[21] The indeterminancy in practice is not so great as these limits might imply. The rate of investment is not determined in isolation. The past allocation between consumption and investment production will physically limit the present alternatives. The rate of investment chosen in the present will, in turn, limit the alternatives in the future.[22] More importantly, the choice of investment rate cannot be determined independently of the choice of investment projects and technique.

Once the specificity of productive capacity is recognized to have an important bearing on the question, the problem of the allocation of investment between different sectors becomes the present-day equivalent of choosing future rates of saving. If, for example, we assume that investment goods are of two types, viz., those that make consumer goods and those that produce investment goods, the present-day allocation of productive *capital* between these two sectors comes to very much the same thing as the determination of the future division of national output between consumption and investment. The allocation of *investment* between the two becomes the means of influencing the rates of investment in the future.

If one assumes further specificity, so that investment goods to make investment goods to make consumer goods are different from investment goods to make investment goods to make investment goods, the decision has to be taken one further step backwards, and so on.[23]

Thus, the decision on investment rate is dependent on the *allocation* of investment and vice-versa. In a centrally planned economy particularly, the decision on allocation greatly affects the final determination of the rate of savings and investment. This problem of allocation between sectors and projects is the next aspect of resource allocation to be considered.

The Allocation of Investment

Exponents of "imbalanced growth," such as Hirschman, have stressed that if a country decides to industrialize, the correct development strategy is not to seek an optimal allocation of resources at any given time nor to dissipate scarce resources by attempting to advance on all fronts simultaneously, but rather to concentrate on a few major objectives most conducive to transforming the economy to a higher stage. Efficiency is attained in the dynamic sense of finding the most effective sequences for converting a stagnant, backward economy into one which is dynamic and modern. In other words, to be breathlessly climbing a peak in a mountain range is considered more important than standing poised on the crest of a ridge in the foothills.

There is not an infinite number of alternative investment allocation patterns. Because of complementaries and indivisibilities each individual investment project cannot be evaluated in isolation. The construction of a steel industry requires increased coal mining and investment in steel using industries. The capture of external economies requires that the entire range of investment projects be evaluated as a whole.

. . . problems of economic planning seem to acquire a resemblance to the problems of military strategy, where in practice the choice lies between a relatively small number of plans, which have in the main to be treated and chosen between as organic wholes, and which for a variety of reasons do not easily permit of intermediate combinations. The situation will demand a concentration of forces round a few main objectives, and not a dispersion of resources over a very wide range.[24]

Investment allocation in the Soviet Union gives us an historical example of this strategy. They pursued a "shock" strategy of bottlenecks successively created and resolved. Thus, Soviet planning concentrated on certain key branches in each plan to overcome particular bottlenecks. Scarce capital and managerial talent were then concentrated on these key targets. This gave Soviet planning its peculiar nature of planning by "campaigning." During the first Five Year Plan the main target was heavy industry with particular emphasis on machine building. During the second and third Five Year Plans the target was again heavy industry with metallurgy, machine building, fuel, energetics, and chemicals singled out for emphasis. This emphasis on key branches yielded high growth rates. The average annual rates of growth in Soviet heavy industry between 1928/29 and 1937 were 18.9 percent for machinery, 18.5 percent for iron and steel, 14.6 percent for coal, 11.7 percent for petroleum products, 22.8 percent for electric power, and 17.8 percent for all heavy industry.[25] Sectors which did not contribute directly to further growth (consumption) were neglected while sectors which enhanced growth (capital goods) were emphasized. Growth tempos such as these caused acute shortages and strains. The bottlenecks which appeared then became the new targets.

Much of the balanced growth versus imbalanced growth debate boils down to the question of where external economies are the greatest. One of the key questions in choosing investment criteria, in turn, hinges on how best to take advantage of external economies and avoid external diseconomies. Economic theorists usually argue that investment should be allocated in such a way that its social marginal product (SMP) is equal in all uses. While this is true as a formal statement it has little meaning unless the "empty box" entitled SMP can be filled with some content. To date no one has done so. One advantage of the imbalanced growth strategy is that it provides a practical signal for reallocating investment. When bottlenecks appear the planner can be sure that the SMP of investment is not equal in all uses. The industries that are the bottlenecks will have a high SMP and thus should receive large investment allocations in the next period. In this sense the SMP will be equated in all uses through time, that is, in a dynamic sense. Thus the campaign method of imbalanced growth, though crude, does have a logic. It also, of course, entails a large risk of waste. If the bottlenecks are not quickly opened they can seriously retard economic growth.

The logic of the campaign method does not ensure that any particular campaign is the right one. The search is for industries which are particularly potent in starting a chain reaction through the capture of external economies. An indication of which industries these are may be found, according to Hirschman, by calculating the backward and forward linkage effects of the industry.[26] Backward linkage represents the degree of input requirements or derived demand which every nonprimary economic activity generates. Forward linkage represents the degree to which output is utilized as an input for activities other than final demand. Thus, the establishment of a new industry with a high backward linkage will provide a new and expanding market for its inputs whether supplied domestically or from abroad. Similarly, the domestic production of a product will tend to stimulate the development of industries using this product. Of course, the domestic availability of a product will not "compel" the construction of industries using the product, but it will create conditions favorable to their development. Hirschman admits that backward linkages are much more clear cut in their stimulating effects than foward linkages. While backward linkage creates demand, forward linkage is dependent upon the existence or anticipation of demand. Therefore, forward linkage cannot be regarded as an independent inducement mechanism. It acts, however, according to Hirschman, as an important and powerful reinforcement to backward linkage. Industries with a high combined backward and forward linkage should, therefore, play a powerful role in inducing industrial development through "creating the demand" or "paving the way" for other supplier or user industries. Indeed, examination of the process of development of a number of mature economies such as Great Britain, Germany, and the United States reveals the crucial role in development played by leading sectors with high-linkage effects.

The identification of high-linkage industries should enable us to put our finger on the crucial sectors or sub-sectors whose growth has maximum impact on an economy's development. Data prepared by Professors Chenery and Watanabe based on input-output tables for the United States, Italy, and Japan indicate that industries with the highest combined linkage effect include (in order of rank) iron and steel (144 of a possible combined 200); nonferrous metals (142); paper and paper products (135); petroleum products (135); grain mill products (134); coal products (130); chemicals (129); textiles (124); metal mining (114); petroleum and natural gas (112); and coal mining (110). Two other industries, transportation equipment (80) and machinery (79), would certainly have scored substantially higher and been among the above group of industries had the sales of these industries not been construed in input-output tables as final demand under capital formation.[27]

The list of industries, derived without reference to Soviet experience, is very similar to a list of the "leading sectors" given priority in Soviet development. The Soviet Union did not give high priority to paper and paper products, and textiles. In the case of grain mill products the high linkage effect, in this case largely backward, is explained by the industry being a satellite of agriculture. It is an outgrowth rather than a cause of agricultural development and for this reason could properly be excluded from the original list. Of the industries given high priority by the Soviet Union only electric power production is omitted from the list. The relatively low combined linkage effect (86) would not apply in the Soviet Union, however, where a much smaller share of electric power output is used by households or for municipal lighting.[28] When these qualifications are taken into account, the lists very nearly overlap and the similarity of the two lists is surely not coincidental.

While linkage is not the same thing as external economies, it is probably a good indicator of where they lie. Hirschman, however, stresses the incentive effect of linkage. The creation of bottlenecks forces entrepreneurs to invest in the bottleneck industries. Presumably an overall plan would account for linkage effects and thus the incentives of linkage would be minimized. However, economic planning of the type used by the Soviet Union during the industrialization period and by extension in less developed countries today, is a relatively crude affair, "Campaigns," with their ensuing bottlenecks, substitute for the profit motive in keeping the planning bureaucracy on its toes.

> . . . the entire *rationale* of the Soviet "campaign" approach to economic planning rests upon . . . the need to stimulate not only the executants but also the controllers. . . . Campaigns are, among other things, a means of goading the goaders, of mobilizing the controllers, of providing success indicators for officials at all levels. . . .
> . . . Hence the vital role of campaigns as controller mobilizers. Hence the value of bottlenecks as stimulators to effort.[29]

The Soviet campaign method of planning thus has logic when viewed in the light of Hirschman's imbalanced growth theory and concept of linkage. When the SMP of investment is viewed as containing the return on external economies, allocation of investment to bottleneck industries through time appears to be not only good practice but good theory as well. This does not imply, of course, that the Soviets deliberately created bottlenecks or that they understood the meaning of imbalanced growth. Rather, the bottlenecks and imbalanced growth were necessary by-products of the high growth tempos that the planners adopted. It is also true that the Soviets have pushed imbalanced growth so far at times that waste occurred with a consequent reduction in the potential growth rate. However, during periods of rapid growth and structural change misallocation errors are of relatively minor importance.

> . . . Soviet development technique is more effective: choose a few "leading branches" and concentrate on them. The details and the secondary industries can catch up later. The fact that such a programme is unbalanced and violates "scarcity" rules matters less than its superior speed. . . . A certain increase in growth is worth any amount of minor allocation errors. . . . There are two main reasons for this. . . . The mere fact of growth floats off even a *permanent* misallocation of resources. . . . Secondly, the misallocation need not be permanent. . . . Scarcity need not be violated always in the same direction. . . . We have here again the dichotomy: good resource allocation versus rapid growth.[30]

Professor Wiles is referring, of course, to static resource allocation. Because of external economies, imbalanced growth can lead to a proper resource allocation through time, that is, in a dynamic sense. But even when imbalanced growth is pushed too far the resulting allocation errors may be a small price to pay, if concentration on leading sectors yields a faster tempo of growth.

As an economy becomes more sophisticated, "campaign" planning becomes less appropriate. The number of products multiply and "balance" becomes more important. Since there is little structural change, and firms and industries are operating closer to equilibrium, marginal calculations become more feasible. This seems to be the present situation of the economy of the Soviet Union. Failure to pull up lagging sectors, particularly agriculture, and to develop more sophisticated planning methods is causing the Soviets many problems and slowing their growth tempo.

Finally, it must be remembered that investment allocation is not independent of the investment rate and the investment rate is not independent of the growth rate of national income. The decision on the pace of economic growth determines both the share of national income that is to be devoted to investment and also the physical nature of the required investment. To attain a certain growth rate a certain investment rate must be maintained. To maintain this investment rate over time the physical output of the growing capital goods industries must match this rate. Thus, a high growth rate means a high investment rate, which in turn means a large allocation of investment to capital goods industries. Therefore, given the indivisibilities and complementarities of production, the range of choice in allocating investment becomes small. This makes the rather crude Soviet strategy of investment allocation more feasible.

The Choice of Production Technique

The final question which arises in regard to resource allocation in the context of centrally planned economic development is the choice of technique in production.

This problem usually resolves into a question of whether capital should be devoted to large-scale units using advanced and expensive technology or to smaller-scale enterprises using simple tools and employing relatively more workers. It is often argued that since, practically by definition, there is a shortage of capital and a surplus of labor in underdeveloped countries, labor-intensive techniques should be used wherever possible so as to conserve on capital and provide as much employment as possible.[31] But, to a large degree, this is a false issue. The decision on the type of technology to use cannot be divorced from the decision regarding the allocation of investment. Once the allocation of investment to sectors and industries has been decided, the choice of technologies is severely limited. The range of processes available for the production of steel, electric power, tractors, and machine tools is not a continuous function where capital and labor are substitutable at the margin in infinitesimal increments. More realistically, the production function in these key industries is sharply discontinuous with probably only two or three alternative processes which make any sense from the purely engineering point of view. Further, many of the most modern technologies tend to be both labor *and capital* saving, as witnessed by the declining capital/output ratios of the advanced countries during their industrialization.[32]

Since Great Britain each succeeding country to industrialize has capitalized on its ability to borrow the most advanced technology from the more developed countries. Professor Gerschenkron points out that "borrowed technology . . . was one of the primary factors assuring a high speed of development in a backward country entering the stage of development."[33] Professor Patel also argues that the explanation "of the progressively higher rates of growth of industrial output for each new entrant to the process of industrialization lies in the opportunity of benefiting from accumulated technological advance."[34] Since many of these modern technologies are both labor- *and capital*-saving the choice can be made on purely engineering grounds rather than economic.

Wholesale borrowing of the most advanced technologies that are labor-saving *but not capital-saving* would be desirable, however, only if the factor proportions in the underdeveloped country were somewhere near those in the developed country. This is seldom the case. Where it is not, redesigning and adapting the most advanced technology to its own factor proportions will yield a larger output.[35]

Soviet development policy has been aware of this conflict between requirements of progress and factor endowment and has dealt with it by adopting the strategy of a "dual technology." On the one hand, in the key industries, they utilized to the maximum the advantage of borrowing the most advanced technologies developed in economies with very different factor endowments. On the other hand, they allowed for these differences by utilizing manual labor in auxiliary operations and by aiming at high performance rates per unit of capital instead of per man.[36]

In many Soviet plants it is common to find the most advanced capital equipment in the basic processes and, at the same time, the most primitive labor intensive methods in maintenance, intra-plant transport, and materials handling. In such enterprises as the Gorky Automotive Plant, which was a direct copy of the Ford River-Rouge plant, they allowed for their lower level of skills by redesigning job descriptions so that each worker performed fewer and simpler tasks.[37] Thus, the Soviets obtained the advantages of advanced technology, conserved scarce capital in auxiliary operations that did not affect output, and utilized their relatively abundant labor.

In addition, the Soviets aimed at high performance rates per unit of capital instead of per man in further adapting advanced technology to their factor endowments. Typical are their records in output of pig-iron per cubic meter of blast furnace. In 1958 they obtained 1.25 tons of pig-iron per cubic meter of blast furnace capacity per day compared with about 0.92 tons per cubic meter in the United States. Without this utilization differential they would have needed an additional 39 blast furnaces to produce the same output.[38] Thus, again, they economized on the scarce factor.

Both use of labor-intensive techniques in auxiliary operations and the intensive utilization of capital tend to lower the capital/output ratio or at least keep it from rising. Thus, the benefits of modern technology are reaped while at the same time minimizing the demand for capital, which is the scarce factor. Undoubtedly the Soviets did not perfectly accommodate modern technology. There are many examples where they did not adapt borrowed technology but instead imitated it exactly.[39]

As indicated above, the key to adoption of this dualistic technology was the desire of Soviet planners to conserve scarce capital. In certain cases, such as the choice between hydroelectric and steam-generated electric power, a means for more accurately measuring the relative scarcity of capital is crucial. The Soviets have used the crude "period of recoupment," or its inverse, the "coefficient of relative effectiveness" as a substitute for an interest rate. While this leaves much to be desired it must be remembered, as was pointed out above, that no one has yet been able to measure the SMP of capital when it is being allocated through time. The capture of external economies and changes in relative scarcities make use of the interest rate derived from static equilibrium analysis inappropriate.

A final factor in the choice of technique, and another reason the determination of an appropriate interest rate is so difficult, is the external economies created by the stimulus of advanced technology to the creation of a disciplined industrial work force.

> New technologies do much to educate industrial labour to become a reliable and disciplined social stratum, psychologically adjusted to the requirements of the modern factory. In order to operate with modern machinery some attitude of responsibility and some habits of punctuality are necessary. The education of such a stratum is a protracted process and involves no less difficulties than the creation of the necessary savings.[40]

CONCLUSION

As already seen above, static equilibrium theory has little to say about the efficiency of resource allocation where marginal cost equals price conditions do not prevail in all markets. One of the major weaknesses of equilibrium analysis is the assumption of resource mobility. In reality, mobility of resources, at least in the short run, is not from one sector of employment to another, but, rather, from a state of unemployment or underemployment to a sector of employment. Further, it may be that the major cause of resource immobility in an economy and, therefore, of inefficient allocation is the full-employment of resources. As an economy approaches full-employment, the pool of skilled labor, for instance, dries up and all kinds of shortages and bottlenecks begin to appear.

The fact that centrally planned economies have typically aimed at full-employment of capital and skilled labor may explain what seems to be their poor record of resource allocation. Constantly operating at full-employment has left little slack to cover the inevitable shortages and rigidities. They have reduced the consequences of this tautness by diverting resources from low priority sectors (primarily the consumer goods sector) to cover the shortages in high priority sectors.

In market economies the normal slack in the use of capital goods' capacity and employment has provided greater flexibility. The normal pool of unemployed resources has been used to cover allocation errors. Whenever a market economy approaches sustained full-employment, rigidites and shortages similar to those in centrally planned economies begin to appear.

Unemployed resources can be likened to an Army commander's troop reserves that are used to plug a gap that develops in the battle line. The conclusion seems to be that increased inefficiency in resource allocation may be an unavoidable concomitant of full-employment. This makes centrally planned economies' efforts at reform more difficult. The system of central planning and resource allocation derived from Soviet experience was developed for use in a backward economy trying to achieve the one overriding goal of economic development. The methods are basically those of a war economy. As such, when the economy has reached some level of sophistication, the required economic strategy then changes from one of maximum concentration of available resources on a few main goals towards successively greater dispersion. Since a number of the centrally planned economies seem to have reached this stage, either the planning system will have to become much more effective or pools of unemployed resources will have to be allowed to develop since low priority sectors, particularly consumer goods, can no longer be drawn on to provide the necessary flexibility to cover allocation errors.

SUMMARY

This paper analyzes the question of allocative efficiency within the context of a backward economy using a system of central planning to achieve rapid economic development. The paper first critiques static equilibrium analysis and finds that its usefulness is limited in a developmental context. Second, the paper constructs a model of dynamic allocative efficiency derived mainly from the historical development experience of the Soviet Union, modified where appropriate by the later experience of the other socialist countries.

When the problem of resource allocation is placed in the dynamic context of economic development, the questions of external economies, complementarities, and *changing* resource scarcities become of prime importance. The resource allocation problems of investment rate (choice between present and future), investment allocation among sectors and projects, and choice of production techniques (including factor proportions) are analyzed in the light of the above questions. Central planning is analyzed in terms of its role in solving these resource allocation problems.

The model of central planning and resource allocation set forth in this paper is based on a backward economy trying to achieve the one overriding goal of economic development. The strategy is basically that of a war economy. As such, when the economy has reached some level of sophistication, the required economic strategy then changes from one of maximum concentration of available resources on a few main goals toward successively greater dispersion.

NOTES

1. Alastair N. D. McAuley, "Rationality and Central Planning," *Soviet Studies*, Vol. 18, No. 3 (January, 1967), p. 353. There may not be a satisfactory second-best solution at all or a third-best, fourth-best, or nth-best, and if there is, the rules for achieving it may be almost impossible to implement. For a thorough treatment of resource allocation see E. J. Mishan's, "A Survey of Welfare Economics, 1939–1959," and "A Reappraisal of the Principles of Resource Allocation," both in E. J. Mishan, *Welfare Economics* (New York: Random House, 1964), pp. 3–97, 155–183.
2. The "coefficient of relative effectiveness" (CRE) is given by the formula $e = \dfrac{V^1 - V^2}{K^2 - K^1}$ where V^1 and V^2 represent the annual operating costs (including depreciation) of two alternative projects producing the same output,

and K^1 and K^2 represent the corresponding capital outlays. Since capital outlays usually vary inversely with operating expenses, e represents the savings in operating expense realized per ruble of additional capital outlay. The choice between two projects depends on whether $e \overset{>}{\underset{<}{=}} E$, where E is some CRE taken as a standard. Thus K^1V^1 is chosen if $e < E$; K^2V^2 if $e > E$: and the two projects are equally desirable if $e = E$.

3. Kenneth E. Boulding and Pritam Singh, "The Role of the Price Structure in Economic Development," *American Economic Review*, Vol. LII, No. 2 (May, 1962), pp. 29, 30.

4. *Ibid.*, pp. 29, 33.

5. Subsidizing an industry has the same effect as increasing the price of its output, and, conversely, taxation has the same effect as decreasing price. Also, the effect of subsidization can be achieved by simply taxing some goods less than others. The effect is that some goods are priced below and others above what their relative equilibrium prices would be in a free market.

6. Boulding and Singh, p. 35.

7. Oskar Lange, "Role of Planning in Socialist Economy," *Problems of Political Economy of Socialism*, ed. Oskar Lange (New Delhi: Peoples Publishing House, 1962), p. 18. During the first World War and even more so the Second World War, capitalist countries used war economy methods. Resources were concentrated towards the one basic objective of producing war materials. Resources were centrally allocated to prevent leakages to production not connected with the prosecution of the war. Essential consumer goods were rationed. The production of consumer durables such as automobiles and refrigerators was prohibited. The average work week was lengthened. Patriotic appeals were used to maintain labor productivity and discipline. The share of consumption in gross national product in the United States declined from 75.4 percent in 1940 to 53.9 percent in 1944. These same features characterized the Soviet economy during its war on economic underdevelopment. It is somewhat strange that Western economists who applauded war economy methods in the Second World War do not understand their analogous use in the Soviet Union's industrialization and by extension in underdeveloped countries today.

8. Ragnar Nurkse, *Problems of Capital Formation in Underdeveloped Countries* (Oxford: Basil Blackwell, 1958), pp. 4–5.

9. A planned economy is, of course, still limited in raising the savings rate by the minimum standard of living necessary to maintain the efficiency and morale of the agricultural and industrial work force, and, more importantly, by the absorptive capacity of the economy.

10. It is in a planned economy that Say's Law can be said to hold (at least for capital goods). Supply does create its own demand, or rather, more correctly, demand creates its own supply (within the limits of available resources of course).

11. There are certain problems with the mechanism necessary to ensure this result. The amount of real investment is susceptible to market influence if enterprise managers have discretion as to the size of inventories they hold, and even under the most centralized planning they are bound to have considerable *de facto* discretion. See Maurice Dobb, *Soviet Economic Development Since 1917* (London: Routledge & Kegan Paul Ltd., 1960), pp. 356, 382. R. W. Davies, *The Development of the Soviet Budgetary System* (Cambridge: Cambridge University Press, 1958), pp. 158, 231.

12. At this point, external economies can be considered the divergence between private profit and public benefit. See Tibor Scitovsky, "Two Concepts of External Economies," *The Economics of Underdevelopment*, ed. A. N. Agarwala and S. P. Singh (Oxford: Oxford University Press, 1958), pp. 295–308. P. N. Rosenstein-Rodan, "Problems of Industrialization of Eastern and South-Eastern Europe," *The Economics of Underdevelopment*, pp. 245–256. Maurice Dobb, *An Essay on Economic Growth and Planning* (London: Routledge & Kegan Paul Ltd., 1960), pp. 5–13. Hla Myint, *The Economics of the Developing Countries* (New York: Frederick A. Praeger, Publishers, 1964), pp. 118–125.

13. P. N. Rosenstein-Rodan, "The Flaw in the Mechanism of Market Forces,"

Leading Issues in Development Economics, ed. Gerald M. Meier (New York: Oxford University Press, 1964), p. 417.

14. ". . . complete integration of all industries would be necessary to eliminate all divergence between private profit and public benefit." Scitovsky, p. 305. And, it is necessary that the ". . . whole of the industry to be created is to be treated and planned like one huge firm or trust." Rosenstein-Rodan, "Problems of Industrialization of Eastern and South-Eastern Europe," p. 248.

15. Stephen A. Marglin, "The Social Rate of Discount and the Optimal Rate of Investment," *Quarterly Journal of Economics*, Vol. LXXVII, No. 1 (February, 1963), p. 111. Also see Franklyn D. Holzman, "Consumer Sovereignty and the Rate of Economic Development," *Economia Internazionale*, Vol. IX, No. 2 (1958), pp. 3–17. Maurice Dobb, *An Essay on Economic Growth and Planning*, pp. 15–28. A. K. Sen, "On Optimising the Rate of Saving," *The Economic Journal*, Vol. LXXI, No. 283 (September, 1961), pp. 479–496.

16. Roy Harrod refers to pure time preference as ". . . a polite expression for rapacity and the conquest of reason by passion." Roy Harrod, *Towards a Dynamic Economics* (London: Macmillan & Co., Ltd., 1948), p. 40. Also see S. S. Wagle, *Technique of Planning* (Bombay: Vora & Co., 1961), pp. 165–169.

17. G. L. S. Shackel, *Time in Economics* (Amsterdam: North-Holland Publishing Co., 1958), p. 37.

18. Holzman, pp. 8–10.

19. Sen, pp. 487–489.

20. "It should be noted that the problem of inadequate foresight on the part of individuals, where collective needs are under consideration, is not restricted to the rate of economic development undertaken by the state. A similar situation exists in the cases of both trade unions and large corporations. Union leaders may call a strike which they know will reduce the total income of their members over the subsequent five-year period but which, in their opinion, will strengthen the position of the union (and the labor movement) and the earnings of its members over the longer-run period. The conflict between rank and file stockholders and management of large corporations on dividend and reinvestment policy is too well-known to need repeating." Holzman, p. 11.

21. Professor Horvat argues that this upper limit is the optimum rate of saving and investment. His argument, in effect, ignores completely *any* discount of the future. See Branko Horvat, "The Optimum Rate of Investment," *The Economic Journal*, Vol. LXVIII, No. 272 (December, 1958), pp. 747–767.

22. If the allocation between consumption and investment is changed too abruptly, excess capacity will appear in the sector receiving the reduced allocation.

23. Sen, pp. 493–494. Also see H. B. Chenery, "Comparative Advantage and Development Policy," *American Economic Review*, Vol. LI, No. 1 (March, 1961), p. 41. Maurice Dobb, *Some Aspects of Economic Development* (Occasional Paper No. 3; Delhi: Delhi School of Economics, 1951), pp. 52–53.

24. Dobb, *Soviet Economic Development Since 1917*, p. 6.

25. Alexander Gerschenkron, "Soviet Heavy Industry: A Dollar Index of Output, 1927–1937," *Economic Backwardness in Historical Perspective* (New York: Frederick A. Praeger, Publishers, 1962), p. 247.

26. This approach is feasible only for a country with population and resources capable of maintaining a full industrial structure. Those too small to do so must modify the strategy by a much greater reliance on international trade.

27. Hollis B. Chenery and Tseunehiko Watanabe, "International Comparisons of the Structure of Production," *Econometrica*, October, 1958, p. 493, quoted in Albert O. Hirschman, *The Strategy of Economic Development* (New Haven: Yale University Press, 1958), pp. 106–107.

28. The United States uses about half its electric power for industrial purposes while the Soviet Union uses perhaps 80 percent, W. W. Rostow,

"Summary and Policy Implications," *Comparisons of the United States and Soviet Economies,* Part III (Washington: Joint Economic Committee, GPO, 1959), p. 291.

29. Alec Nove, *The Soviet Economy* (New York: Frederick A. Praeger, Publishers, 1969), p. 292. Also see Gregory Grossman, "Soviet Growth: Routine, Inertia and Pressure," *American Economic Review,* Vol. L, No. 2 (May, 1960), pp. 62–72.

30. P. J. D. Wiles, "Growth vs. Choice," *The Economic Journal,* Vol. LXVI (June, 1956), pp. 244–255. Reprinted in Jesse W. Markham (ed.), *Capitalism, Market Socialism, and Central Planning* (New York: Houghton Mifflin Co., 1963), pp. 296–297, 299. Also see Tibor Scitovsky, *Welfare and Competition* (Homewood: Richard Irwin, Inc., 1951), pp. 8–11.

31. See Nurkse, *Problems of Capital Formation in Underdeveloped Countries,* p. 45.

32. In the United States the capital/output ratio first rose, then fell. This was in part technological and in part reflected an initial build up of capital ahead of demand; e.g. the railroads. See Simon Kuznets, "A Comparative Analysis," *Economic Trends in the Soviet Union,* ed. Abram Bergson and Simon Kuznets (Cambridge, Mass.: Harvard University Press, 1963), pp. 353–358.

33. Gerschenkron, *Economic Backwardness in Historical Perspective,* p. 8.

34. Surendra J. Patel, "Rates of Industrial Growth in the Last Century, 1860–1958," *The Experience of Economic Growth,* ed. Barry E. Supple (New York: Random House, 1963), p. 69.

35. For fuller theoretical treatments of this, see Joseph Berliner, "The Economics of Overtaking and Surpassing," *Industrialization in Two Systems,* ed. Henry Rosovsky (New York: John Wiley & Sons, 1966), pp. 170–174. R. S. Eckhaus, "Factor Proportions in Underdeveloped Areas," *American Economic Review,* Vol. XLV, No. 4 (September, 1955), pp. 539–565. Hirschman, pp. 150–152.

36. See Alfred Zauberman, "Soviet and Chinese Strategy for Economic Growth," *International Affairs,* Vol. XXXVIII, No. 3 (July, 1962), pp. 347–349. Berliner, pp. 172–174. Gregory Grossman, "Scarce Capital and Soviet Doctrine," *Quarterly Journal of Economics,* Vol. LXVII (August, 1953), pp. 311–343. Professor Granick's studies cite evidence for these Soviet policies but his evaluation is much more negative. See David Granick, *Soviet Metal-Fabricating and Economic Development* (Madison: The University of Wisconsin Press, 1967).

37. Berliner, p. 172.

38. Robert W. Campbell, *Soviet Economic Power* (Boston: Houghton Mifflin Co., 1960), p. 61.

39. See Berliner, p. 173. M. Gardner Clark, *The Economics of Soviet Steel* (Cambridge, Mass.: Harvard University Press, 1956), pp. 65–66, 84.

40. S. Swianiewicz, *Forced Labour and Economic Development: An Inquiry into the Experience of Soviet Industrialization* (London: Oxford University Press, 1965), p. 263.

19

Industrial Efficiency Under Managerial vs. Cooperative Decision-Making: A Comparative Study of Manufacturing Enterprises in Israel

Seymour Melman

The development of industrialism has been accompanied by managerial-hierarchical control over industrial work. Indeed, it has been generally assumed that industrialism and managerialism are necessarily linked, that each is in some way necessary for the other. It is not only of historical interest to know whether this association merely reflects parallel development or involves a necessary interrelation. In contemporary social thought, a mystique of technological determinism is often seized upon to explain or criticize social phenomena. Thereby, responsibility for the character of the industrial corporation and its consequences is assigned to technology (e.g., the computer). Man, individually and in groups, is viewed as the servant of the machine, the latter being endowed with initiative and direction of its own. The machine Golem dominates the scene, shapes society, and leaves to each man only the task of adapting himself to the social forms that are machine-dictated. Since the managerial mode of industrial organization is seen as a prime example of technology-determined social form, the intelligent man's problem is, essentially, how to adapt to managerial organization. One aim of this paper is to challenge the mystique of technology-determined social form in the organization of production.

Engineers and administrators in modern industry have a different perspective from that of the mystique of technology. They have a well-developed tradition for selecting among alternatives in production methods and hence know that men shape technology by the criteria that are applied in designing technology. With respect to modes of decision-making, however, the concept of major alternatives is underdeveloped. The textbooks and handbooks on the organization of production give no instruction on other than managerial styles of administration. Little attention is paid to the possibility that alternatives to managerial control may compare favorably in economic efficiency and/or be desirable on other grounds. Yet, in American industry the number of administrators has risen steadily, per 100 production workers, from 10 administrative employees in 1899 to 38 by 1963. Moreover, this growing cost of decision-making has not been necessarily correlated with growth in productivity.[1] Hence, it is reasonable to

Reprinted from *Studies in Comparative International Development*, Vol. VI, No. 7 (1970-1971), pp. 47-58, by permission of Transaction, Inc.

expect that as the rising cost of managerial decision-making becomes onerous, someone will be interested in developing less costly ways of making production decisions.

Also, managerial control has included qualities of competitiveness and expansionism that are disliked by many people as ways of interpersonal relations. But if these qualities are integral to managerialism which, in turn, is viewed as essential to modern industry, then there would seem to be little choice—except to discard industrialism itself.

A related issue occurs in the developing countries where there are options with respect to the selection of types of industry and industrial processes. What are the options, if any, with respect to the organization of production, with respect to decision process? Or, are there substantially none? Does the introduction of industrial production require the use of the managerial-hierarchical mode of decision-making? This paper is intended as a contribution toward broadening perspectives on options for organization of production.

MANAGERIAL VS. COOPERATIVE DECISION-MAKING

Apart from relatively primitive societies, the managerial mode of organization is clearly the dominant one, worldwide, in private as well as publicly owned enterprise. The managerial mode of decision-making may be identified by three primary features. First, there tends to be an occupational separation between decision-making and producing. Especially in firms beyond the workshop size, those who mainly do decision-making have distinctive occupational roles from those who primarily do production work. This differentiation is reinforced and formalized by unionization, for then the "bargaining unit" differentiates those who do the production work from those who do decision-making. A second feature of management is the hierarchical organization of decision-making. At the peak of successive layers of fewer and more powerful decision-makers, there is the final decision-maker, the person whose decision cannot be vetoed by anyone else. A third feature of managerial organization is the built-in criterion of enlarging the scope and intensity of decision-making as the priority objective for the enterprise. In this perspective, money making in the form of profit is a necessary, but not a primary objective in its own right.

What sort of alternative is conceivable—as against the managerial mode of decision-making so defined? First, decision-making could be done by those who also do production work. This is feasible especially as decision process is differentiated between particularized decisions concerning details of work, and condition-setting decisions which define major goals, criteria for design, or limits (like product class) within which an enterprise is to operate. Thus, decisions about the choice of class of products, or decisions about major capital expansions are made infrequently. All persons in an enterprise have a stake in such choices and can conceivably participate in making them. Once defined, such condition-setting decisions become the boundaries within which detailed operating decisions can be made by administrators and technicians. In a non-hierarchical organization, work assignments, including the administrative and technical posts, can be subject to final decision, including removal and replacement, by the general body of persons engaged in an enterprise. Finally, it is conceivable to operate industrial facilities according to primary criteria like providing useful work and regulating volume of output to serve specified social priorities—instead of profit maximization or extension of managerial control.

These analytically abstracted contrasts in types of decision process define key elements of a cooperative as against the conventional managerial mode of production organization.

A COMPARATIVE STUDY IN ISRAEL

Such variation in mode of decision process is found within Israel where, in addition to a considerable population of industrial firms under managerial control, there is also a population of 170 industrial enterprises that are operated under a cooperative decision process. The latter group of enterprises is located in the cooperative communities called Kibbutzim. There are 230 such communities in Israel* of which 170 operate industrial enterprises with 20 to 250 persons working in each unit. These cooperative enterprises use modern machine technology and techniques and are engaged in a broad array of manufacturing industries: metalworking, chemicals, various types of machinery production, tools, home appliances, woodworking, food processing, instruments, electrical goods, plastics, and others.[2]

In view of the wider theoretical interest in the problem of alternatives for decision-making on production, I decided to inquire into the comparative industrial efficiency of enterprises operating under managerial as opposed to cooperative control. How efficient can an industrial enterprise be under cooperative control? In terms of accepted criteria of labor and capital productivity, and profitability, can there be an efficient alternative to managerial control over industry?

In Israel, such an analysis could be performed within one country. Two sets of industrial enterprises could be examined, differing markedly in organization, but operating under similar conditions of language, government, currency, markets, prices, types of population engaged in the enterprises, and the like. Accordingly, after 1963 I did the necessary field work in Israel with the cooperation of the Israel Institute of Productivity and the Kibbutz Industries Association.

It is well-appreciated that there is some degree of variation among nations in "styles" of industrial administration. However, average national industrial efficiency, as in productivity of labor and capital, is determined decisively by relative costs of labor and machinery to industry, which, in turn, regulate the cost-minimizing intensity of mechanization. It is signifi-

---

* Total Kibbutz population: 1949–63, 500; 1964–80, 900. *Annual Statistical Abstract of Israel*, Central Bureau of Statistics, Government of Israel, Jerusalem, 1949, 1965.

cant that Israeli industry is permeated with personnel trained in the United States and Western Europe, and that the Israeli schools of business and technology emulate the same models as do industrial associations and others who have continuing access to the literature of modern industrial management. From this standpoint, therefore, Israeli industry shares in the knowledge and practices of western industrialism.

The criterion for the selection of enterprises for this study was that each should represent a technically modern industrial operation, including substantial capital investment and producing standard products for sale in an open market. Of course, it was essential that the enterprise administrators in each case should make available the required data for analysis. In the case of the Kibbutz enterprises a special criterion was applied: Kibbutz enterprises that involved more than about 10 percent of hired employees were not to be included in the sample. During the last years, numbers of Kibbutzim, endeavoring to enlarge their industrial output, sought to employ persons on a temporary basis. This arrangement sometimes continued. Since this introduced an employment relationship in what was formerly a cooperatively operated enterprise, industrial units that had this characteristic were excluded from the sample.

PROCEDURE

About 25 industrial enterprises were contacted, and it was possible to develop a paired sample of 12 enterprises, 6 of them under managerial control and 6 under cooperative control. These enterprises were matched with respect to industry and product. It seemed important to include in each group enterprises that produced similar products, hence using similar raw materials, similar manufacturing technologies and processes, and selling their products in similar markets.

The list of industries represented by these two groups of enterprises and the capital investment in each enterprise are shown in Table 1. The plants manufacturing tools mainly made metalworking tools. The manu-

Table 1   Capital Investment of Each Matched Enterprise in This Study

Industry	(£I 000's) Managerial Decision-Making	Cooperative Decision-Making
Tools	942	647
Instruments	753	8,393
Diecasting	20,953	461
Plastics	330	2,656
Machine Shop	335	1,077
Canning	6,746	4,148
Median	£I 847	£I 1,866
Average	5,010	2,897
Ranking	3	3
No. sets where each type enterprise leads		

facturers of instruments produced equipment for commercial and home use. The diecasting shops in the sample were mainly engaged in zinc diecasting. The plastics plants produced diverse products by plastic moulding. The two machine shops in the sample were mainly operating batteries of automatic screw-machine lathes. The canning factories both processed comparable sorts of locally grown fruits and vegetables.

In terms of capital invested, each type of enterprise led in three industrial pairs. However, the median capital investment was £I, 847 for the managerial firms and £I, 1,866 for the Kibbutz factories. (The large size of the managerially controlled diecasting plant produced a substantially larger mean value for capital investment in the managerially controlled enterprises as a group.)

The enterprises under study were selected by a purposive, stratified sampling method. It was necessary to "pair" the enterprises by industry (product class) thereby requiring a selective dropping of "unpaired" firms. The resulting sample represented a variety of industries, industrially important product classes, and diverse technologies and skills. This sample was selected solely on the basis of industrial type and without any *a priori* knowledge of operating characteristics of individual enterprises. Each enterprise is an independent entity. The data from each enterprise came from the ordinary records of operations which were checked for comparability of definition of data categories. Moreover, the data came from unpublished records, which were examined after the sample was selected. Prior to the analyses for this paper, there were no data on the comparative input-output behavior of the sampled firms.

In each of the sampled firms it was possible to obtain parallel sets of data from the financial and production records.* These data were all for the same year, between 1963 and 1967. The actual year is not disclosed in order to shield the identity of the enterprises.

There are special features of accounting data for the cooperatively administered enterprises. The cost of labor in the managerially controlled enterprise is measured by wages paid. In the cooperatively administered enterprise no wages or salaries are paid, there being no internal money exchange within the framework of the cooperative community. (Money is used in the economic relations of the cooperative community to the rest of society and for recording inputs and outputs in the component enterprises of the cooperative community.) The cost of labor, as part of the cost of production in the Kibbutz enterprise, was measured by using an accounting category which the Kibbutzim calculate regularly and carefully: the

---

* For each of the sampled enterprises I secured the following data from their balance sheets and profit-and-loss statements: capital invested, value of fixed assets, sales and profits. These data categories are the ordinary sorts of financial records that are kept by industrial firms. In each instance, the financial statements were private, unpublished data. The following employment data were also obtained: administrative personnel, production manhours per year. The accountants or bookkeepers made the data available, being directed to do so by the responsible administrators of each enterprise. In each instance I checked for consistency of definition of the data categories, and in several enterprises I found it necessary to reclassify the data in order to assure consistency. The data, arrayed for all the enterprises, were altered by an unstated factor—thereby shielding the identities of the cooperating firms while retaining proportional relationships.

"cost of a day of labor." This means the average cost of maintaining a person in the cooperative community per day of labor worked. This statistic reflects the sum of all expenditures for consumer goods and services during a year divided by the total number of man-days worked in the various production sections of the cooperative village economy. The resulting figure is the best available estimate of the cost of using labor by a Kibbutz enterprise and was accordingly used for accounting purposes in these calculations. (The Kibbutz "cost of a day of labor" has tended to equal or exceed industrial wages in managerial enterprise.)

In the cooperative enterprises, "capital investment" and "fixed assets" do not include the cost of land. The land used is rented, not purchased. Therefore, the rent appears as a current expense in the annual costs of operations. This feature has no determining effect on the main results of this investigation.

The cost of capital is a significant factor in all industrial enterprises and has special importance as it affects capital investments, degree of mechanization, and availability of working capital. The cooperative and the managerially controlled enterprises must obtain capital from essentially the same sources. The Israeli government facilitates low interest rate loans to certain new enterprises, especially to preferred industries locating in development areas. Foreign investor, managerial enterprises have been the main beneficiaries. For the rest, however, both the managerially controlled and the cooperative enterprises obtain capital from the ordinary private capital market. A check on the structure of loans in a number of firms showed that the sampled firms were paying ordinary capital market interest rates. In this respect, however, the cooperative enterprises may gain an advantage insofar as they are a part of a larger cooperative community. Thus, the industrial enterprise that is part of the Kibbutz has the automatic standing of being backed by the population and assets of the entire cooperative community. This gives the cooperative enterprise an advantage in credit ratings, apart from other considerations that a banker uses to decide on lending his money. This is akin to the credit advantage of a borrower enterprise that is part of a large firm with diverse assets.

Industrial efficiency is measured here in terms of: productivity of labor, productivity of capital, profit generated per production worker, and the cost of administration. Labor and capital productivity reflect on the efficiency with which key industrial inputs are utilized. The general competence of enterprise administration in optimizing outputs in relation to inputs is reflected in the profit that is generated per production worker. Lastly, the manpower used for administration measures the outlays made for the productionally necessary function of decision-making: Who can do it at lesser cost?

RESULTS

The comparative productivity of labor in managerial and cooperative enterprises was measured by contrasting output (net sales) to inputs (production worker manhours). These data (Table 2) were calculated for the

Table 2   Productivity of Labor (Sales Per Production Manhour)

Industry	Managerial Decision-Making		Cooperative Decision-Making	
Tools	£I	7.88	£I	6.31
Instruments		13.64		12.67
Diecasting		15.48		14.71
Plastics		5.40		14.26
Machine Shop		5.66		13.26
Canning		14.08		13.97
Median	£I	10.76	£I	13.61
Average		10.36		12.53
Ranking		1		2
No. sets where each type enterprise leads		3 — almost equal		

sampled enterprises on an equal weighting basis. This procedure is signifi-cant for the purpose of the investigation. If the total sales in each set of enterprises were divided by total production worker manhours, the result would assign substantial weight to the enterprises in each group that were larger than the others. The present objective, however, is to contrast types of enterprises. Therefore, the enterprise is necessarily the unit of observa-tion, and the productivity of labor and other measures of efficiency were calculated separately for each enterprise, then grouped with median and average values shown for the managerial and cooperative groups.

The results appearing in Table 2 show that the cooperative decision-making enterprises had median sales per production worker manhour of £I 13.61, 26 percent higher than the £I 10.76 for the managerially controlled enterprises. It is important that the sales statistics do not simply reflect undifferentiated money-valued sales. They represent quantities of similar products sold in similar markets, and therefore at similar prices, for each set of enterprises.

A second measure of productivity was that of productivity of capital (Table 3). This was measured in two forms, output (profit) as percent of input (capital invested), and output (sales) as a percent of input (fixed assets). For the cooperative enterprises median profit was 12.9 percent of capital invested as against 7.7 percent for the managerially controlled enter-prises. Sales (median) were 3.6 times fixed assets for the cooperative enterprises and 2.7 for the managerially controlled enterprises. These meas-ures of capital productivity reflect the overall effectiveness of the use of fixed assets for generating output for sale. In this respect the cooperative enterprises outperformed the managerially controlled firms—by 67 percent greater profit/investment, and by 33 percent greater sales/fixed assets.

In order to gain another view of the overall effectiveness of the admin-istration of these enterprises, I measured net profit per production worker (Table 4). In these terms, the cooperative enterprises showed a median profit per production worker of £I 1,912, 115 percent greater than the £I 899 for the enterprises under managerial control.

A further contrast for these two sets of enterprises is given in Table 5, showing the comparative cost of administration. This is measured in terms of the number of administrative employees required per 100 production

Table 3 Productivity of Capital
      (a) Profit as Percent of Capital Invested
      (b) Sales as Percent of Fixed Assets

Industry	Managerial Decision-Making		Cooperative Decision-Making	
Tools	a)	.659	a)	.021
	b)	2.9	b)	3.7
Instruments	a)	.300	a)	.0195
	b)	2.5	b)	4.7
Diecasting	a)	.038	a)	1.125
	b)	1.1	b)	3.6
Plastics	a)	.024	a)	.095
	b)	3.4	b)	4.3
Machine Shop	a)	.117	a)	.200
	b)	2.5	b)	2.6
Canning	a)	.026	a)	.164
	b)	2.96	b)	2.6
Median	a)	.077	a)	.129
	b)	2.7	b)	3.6
Average	a)	.194	a)	.271
	b)	2.6	b)	3.6
Ranking	2		7	
No. sets where each type enterprise leads			3 — almost equal	

Table 4 Efficiency of Management (Net Profit Per Production Worker)

Industry	Managerial Decision-Making		Cooperative Decision-Making	
Tools	£I	3,190	£I	118
Instruments		2,880		556
Diecasting		1,335		4,350
Plastics		74		2,771
Machine Shop		463		2,287
Canning		461		1,537
Median	£I	899	£I	1,912
Average		1,401		1,937
Ranking	2		4	
No. sets where each type enterprise leads				

Table 5 Cost of Enterprise Administration
      (Administrative Staff Per 100 Production Workers)

Industry	Managerial Decision-Making	Cooperative Decision-Making
Tools	12.1	19.2
Instruments	24.0	15.4
Diecasting	21.5	21.1
Plastics	26.5	24.1
Machine Shop	11.1	13.3
Canning	18.3	14.2
Median	19.9	17.3
Average	18.9	17.8
Ranking	2	2
No. sets where each type enterprise has lower value		2 — almost equal

workers. In the cooperative enterprises, the median value was 17.3; the same relationship for the managerially controlled enterprises was 19.9.

In sum: the cooperative enterprises showed higher productivity of labor (26 percent), higher productivity of capital (67 and 33 percent), larger net profit per production worker (115 percent) and lower administrative cost (13 percent).

The relative performance of the two types of enterprises may also be viewed by ranking the position of each of the firms in the study with respect to each criterion. In Table 6, there is an entry M (managerial) in the

Table 6 Summary Ranking of Managerial (M) vs. Cooperative (C) Enterprises By Criteria of Efficiency

Industry	Labor Productivity	Capital Productivity	Profit per Production Worker	Cost of Administration
Tools	M	M C–M	M	M
Instruments	M–C	M C	M	C
Diecasting	M–C	C C	C	C–M
Plastics	C	C C	C	C–M
Machine Shop	C	C C–M	C	M
Canning	M–C	C M–C	C	C

Note: The M,C designations in this table may be used as rank values in the sign test of significance of difference, single-tailed. Were the cooperative enterprises, as a group, significantly more efficient than the managerial enterprise, with 15 of the former and 7 of the latter emerging first in the various measures of industrial efficiency? Chance factors alone would produce the cooperative lead at probability .067. This gives confidence in the inference that the sampled cooperative enterprises, as a group, were significantly more efficient than the others. See S. Siegel, *Nonparametric Statistics for the Behavioral Sciences*, McGraw-Hill, New York, 1956, pp. 68 ff.

Tools industry row under the *Labor Productivity* column. This means that for the labor productivity criterion in the tools industry, the managerial enterprise was the better performer. Again, under *Labor Productivity* for the *Instruments* industry, the managerial and cooperative firms were almost equal, with the managerial unit being somewhat better than the cooperative, hence the designation in the table as M–C. Similarly for the rest of the table.

Discounting the 8 almost-equal performances (M–C or C–M), in 15 enterprise-criteria cases the cooperative units were better performers, compared with 7 where the managerial units led. By industry type, only in the *Tools* case was there a clear first for the managerial type in more than two criteria. In ranking under efficiency criteria, the cooperative units led in capital productivity and profit per production manhour, were ahead in labor productivity and broke even in cost of administration.

ANALYSIS OF RESULTS

The data assembled here bear upon three widespread assumptions: first, that there is no workable alternative to the managerial form of control for operating modern industry; second, that even if there were an alternative, the managerial mode of organization is inherently most efficient; and finally, that technology itself sets the requirement for managerialism. Whatever constraints may be assigned to the data of this paper, it is evident that they do not support these familiar themes. Evidently, there is a cooperative mode of organization that is a workable alternative to managerialism for industrial operations, and the use of machine technology does not itself exclude the use of cooperative decision-making.

However, some reservation is in order for interpreting the data of this study for the second proposition. It is not warranted, given the characteristics of the data, to infer any general statement as to the degree or predictability of relative efficiency of cooperative versus managerial decision-making in industrial operations. Thus, while the enterprises examined here tend to show greater efficiency for the cooperative units as a group, the limitations on the data (number of units, single time and single locale of observations) point to the following as the relevant inference: cooperatively administered industrial enterprises can be as efficient as, or more efficient than, managerially controlled units. This, albeit qualified, inference suggests that the cooperative organization of industry can be a workable option for some societies. What characteristics of cooperative organization account for its apparent effectiveness in industry?

The main differentiating features of cooperative organization of production include the following. (1) Authority for major decisions is vested in all the participants; there is no occupationally-codified separation between those who decide and those who do the work. (2) The mode of internal decision-making is based upon mutuality and is essentially democratic, as against the hierarchical organization of managerial control. (3) In the cooperative organization there is formal, institutionalized equality and anti-inequality in decision-making and in consumption through the pervasive system of sharing final authority in decision-making and in consumption. This contrasts with the managerial pattern of differential, competitive gain (i.e., one man's gain, to be a competitive gain, must include another's relative loss). (4) Finally, the cooperative enterprise is oriented toward enlarging its output and affording participation in useful work for members of the cooperative community, rather than profit maximization or expansion of managerial control.

The above-mentioned characteristics of the cooperative organization have not been ordinarily linked to industrial efficiency. Indeed, some of these features are often presumed to lead to industrial inefficiency. It seems appropriate at this point to examine each of the above features of the cooperative system in light of its possible consequences for industrial efficiency.

Participation and Democracy in Control

In the cooperative industrial enterprise, final authority over basic decisions —products, capital investment, number of workers—is vested in the general body of workers in the enterprise and in the cooperative community as a whole. Responsibility for organizing implementation of basic decisions is the task of democratically elected enterprise administrators who are required to report regularly to the general body and to justify their decisions and proposals.

As a consequence of cooperative control, the workers in these enterprises tend to have interest and concern about technical conditions of work which is rare in the managerially controlled enterprise. Thus, instead of the suggestion box and individual money rewards for particular technical suggestions, the cooperative industrial enterprise operates with a fairly sustained free flow of communication among all members of the enterprise, both in production and administration.

The cooperative enterprises deal with mechanization and automation of production in ways that contrast with the managerial firm. Thus, the elimination of a manual work task by mechanization benefits all concerned in the Kibbutz-managed enterprise since the gains are shared by all. Also, the Kibbutz industrial enterprises usually operate under conditions of labor shortages relative to goals for enlarging production. As a result there is little problem of having useful work available for people whose tasks have been mechanized. Furthermore, each person knows that the members of the cooperative care for each other. There is little likelihood here of producing a situation where a particular work skill, no longer required, could cause a person to be discarded, no longer needed or wanted. Such an event contradicts the essential conditions of mutuality and cooperation in the Kibbutz.

Equality in "Income"

In the cooperative enterprise, the principle of equality in major decision-making is paralleled by a code of consumption equality—more exactly, consumption without money exchange and on the basis of need, community capability, and in accordance with mores of anti-inequality and material non-ostentation. There are no problems of wage systems administration since there are no wages. The cooperative enterprise has no trade union relations problems or costs in the absence of an employment relationship. Production work-load problems are usually resolved by the working group in terms of mutual understanding of what is an acceptable day's work, taking into account the capabilities of production equipment and the requirements of the enterprise.

Instead of individual financial incentives, the people in the cooperatively controlled enterprise receive an acceptable level of living, the right and duty to participate in mutual decision-making, mutual care and esteem—especially for carrying group decision responsibilities. For example, the Kibbutz enterprise gets the benefit of wide-ranging cooperation among its members owing to the use of extra-workshift hours on behalf of the enterprise. Frequently, when some of the administrators or workers of an enterprise eat dinner together in the community dining room and discuss the problems of the work place, this is not an "overtime" task that requires special payment as would be the case in a managerially controlled enterprise where work is done by employees. Though discussions on enterprise problems in the dining hall of the cooperative can be lengthy, it is unthinkable to "charge" for this, for there is no theory, category, or procedure by which such a "charge" could be made.

It is commonly assumed that the presence of individual money incentives combined with opportunity for rising in a managerial hierarchy comprises a very powerful incentive system for efficiency in industry. In the Kibbutz there is no differential income reward for varied work. Therefore election to a post of administrative responsibility confers status only. Also, it is ordinarily assumed that the managerial decision process, because of the attraction of individual gain, uniquely produces a major incentive to minimize costs in production and to maximize net return to the enterprise. The administrator of the cooperative enterprise does strive for efficiency, and meeting enterprise goals of profit, output, and employment, for that is the requirement for his status. However, in contrast with the managerial system, success in Kibbutz industry administration does not necessarily bring accretions of decision-power, for rotation of administrative personnel is a general policy in cooperative enterprises. This produces a sophisticated administrative cadre because people with these talents are moved among administrative tasks within and among enterprises. The unwritten code of the cooperative community often requires that administrators do manual production work as one of their rotating responsibilities.

Among the administrators and technicians in the cooperative enterprise, there is considerable pressure to have good personal relations with the other men in the work place. This is owing to the fact that only by mutual agreement are major decisions made and effectively implemented.

None of this is to say that in the Kibbutz community all men are equal. Work tasks differ. Differences of ability make for inequality of responsibility, and those who bear it receive the esteem and attention of their fellows while having to devote typically more than average hours to their work. In the cooperative community a person's standing, the degree to which others take him seriously, means a lot. The use of a vehicle often goes with some administrative jobs and that gives a fringe-benefit of mobility as a result of simply doing the work. But the vehicle goes with the job not with the man. Identification of the individual with the wider community and cooperation to achieve its goals are the main operative incentives of the cooperative enterprise—in contrast with the individual competitive incentive pattern of managerially controlled production.[3] The apparent workability of the cooperative form of organization in production suggests the importance of greater understanding of the worth of non-monetary and other than direct-work-efficiency factors in influencing productiveness in industry.

Useful Work and Increased Output as Goals

Historically, manufacturing industry was introduced into the Kibbutz communities as a way of providing productive work for men and women who were no longer physically able to work in agriculture. This resulted in selection of industries of a highly capitalized and mechanized sort. In recent years, the design of work places has often been performed with a special eye to human engineering considerations so as to allow older (gradually retiring) members to put in all or part of a day's work in a factory. Among the factories visited by this writer, four of the cooperatively run plants included significant technical innovations in production processes that were developed by the people on the spot. These ranged from unusual sets of jigs and fixtures to special-purpose multi-station machine tools.

A diverse literature in industrial administration, during the last decades, has repeatedly emphasized the factor of integrated operation, especially by securing cooperation among employees, as an efficient means for inducing conditions of stability.[4] The combined effect of the main features of cooperative organization, summarized above, is to induce automatically a pervasive pattern of detailed cooperation in the performance of work. Such cooperation is the crucial element for stable, hence optimal, operation of a given production system. This is a key factor, in my judgment, for explaining the efficient performance of cooperatively controlled industrial enterprise.

Optimum input-output performance in modern industrial facilities is expected, on both theoretical and empirical grounds, when the unit functions as a stable system.[5] A stable system is one whose output varies within predictable and acceptable limits. When operations are, in this sense, "under control," there is an optimum production result from the combined inputs of machines, men, and services that constitute the principal inputs of an industrial facility.

The sort of cooperative pattern of workaday functioning that is found in the Kibbutz enterprise is rarely found, or even approximated, in the managerially controlled enterprise. This is owing to the conditions of competitive individual incentives and competitive bargaining between managers and employees within the managerially operated enterprise. Beyond a certain level of intensity these competitive incentive factors produce conditions which work against stable operation of the production system. Stated differently: competitive managerial rule over production often interferes with the optimization requirements of modern production technology.

This is not to say that stability in production is not obtainable under managerial control. However, the price is usually costly managerial control over production workers (one foreman to ten workers) or the creation of conditions which induce cooperation among production workers and between production workers and management. The latter can significantly alter the competitive incentive factors that differentiate the managerial from the cooperative mode of decision-making.[6] Having considered the efficiency effects of features that are unique to cooperative decision-making, we now turn to other factors that may bear on the findings of differences in efficiency between the two types of organizations.

Size, Environment and Ideology

In manufacturing industry it is widely appreciated that large enterprises operate with significant advantages over small enterprises. Larger firms have superior access to capital and technical talent and usually operate with higher rates of profit. Also, investigations of administrative costs[7] show that larger enterprises, on the average, have lower administrative to production ratios than smaller enterprises.

The managerially controlled enterprises of this study were all located within or near large urban centers. Therefore, the managers of these enterprises had access to a large and diverse labor pool. By contrast, the cooperatively run enterprises in this study were, in each instance, located on the premises of a particular cooperative community and could draw their labor supply only from the members of that community or from neighboring ones. The cooperative village populations vary in size within a range of 300 to 2,000. This is, at maximum, a significantly smaller labor pool than the one that is open to the management of the managerially run enterprises.

In some ways, however, the cooperative enterprises can get advantages that ordinarily accrue to enterprises of large size. For example, the cooperative enterprises have formed joint purchasing and marketing organizations for buying raw materials, machinery, and various industrial supplies that are used by many factories. Thereby they get benefits of quantity purchasing and expertise. Similarly, the Kibbutz industries have set up common marketing arrangements for diverse products.

In the present study, advantages of size for the paired enterprises are substantially balanced out since in three industries the managerial enterprises are larger (tools, diecasting, and canning) and in three the cooperatively controlled units have larger investments (instruments, plastics, and machine shop). Therefore, the average differences in enterprise efficiency that have appeared here must be explained primarily in terms of factors that are specific to, and associated with, the contrasting types of decision-making among the paired enterprises. These associated factors include conditions of environment (integration of the enterprise in a wide community), ideology, and motivation.

There are definite relations between the mode of functioning of an organization and the social structure of its wider society. The Kibbutz enterprise is sharply differentiated from the managerial unit by its total integration into the surrounding Kibbutz community. Thus the individual does not differentiate sharply between his role in the Kibbutz enterprise and his role in the community. He is not, as in a managerial enterprise, an "employee"— while being a "citizen" of a wider community. The conventional firm is a work organization, formally unconnected with the family, home, consumption activities, and the provision of various community services. In the Kibbutz, all these functions are integrated and the individual sees them as related parts of one community. As a result members identify with and have a strong commitment to the whole community of which the enterprise is a part. This is a central characteristic of Kibbutz organization, apart from variation in individual behaviors owing to all manner of reasons.

The operation of the cooperative enterprise is strongly influenced by the integration of the enterprise within the cooperative community where it is one among several "branches" of the economy. Integrated operation produces certain economies for component enterprises. For example, when manpower is needed in the industrial enterprise for a short period of time, say to make up for persons away for military training, then, depending on community priorities, manpower from other branches of the community can be temporarily assigned to the industrial enterprise.

When a Kibbutz factory needs the use of special equipment like a tractor for moving heavy machinery, then this equipment and its driver are borrowed from their normal work to do the special task. Thereby, there are no problems of renting heavy equipment, billing, paying for transportation time of the equipment to and from the industrial location, etc. Similarly, when Kibbutz vehicles go to town the drivers are able to do chores that are helpful to the industrial plant, like picking up or delivering materials or machine parts. Also, the cooperative community often includes manpower for particular tasks needed by industrial administration. For example, if a letter has to be written in a foreign language which someone in the community knows, he is easily asked to do this job and would normally do the task of letter translation and writing during an off hour. A similar task in the managerial enterprise usually requires hiring a secretarial service.

However, integration and commitment of the individual to the enterprise is by no means unique to the cooperative enterprise. The professional behavior and life style of modern corporate executives include extensive involvement of the individual with his occupational role: work is carried home at night, to the golf course, and to the dinner table. As in the Kibbutz enterprise, it is unthinkable to "charge" for this "overtime" (not counting the expense account). This sort of integration of occupation with other facets of life is ordinarily appreciated as contributing to the effectiveness of the managerially controlled enterprise.

It may appear from the above that the managerial and cooperative organizations are more alike than different with respect to commitment of members to the enterprise. The similarity, however, lies particularly in the commitment and integration of individuals who are decision-makers. In the managerial enterprise this means the management. But in cooperative organization this includes the total work group. To the extent that involvement of the individual in responsibility for the enterprise and its purpose affect morale and work efficiency, then the cooperative organizations have an inherent advantage in this respect.

Even allowing for the built-in strengths of cooperative organization, it would be erroneous to infer its competence from the structure of decision-power alone. An important contribution to its competence is the support that comes from the explicit ideology and moral values of the community: mutual care, responsibility, and cooperation. This is different from the ideal value system that permeates the managerial organization, with its affirmation of individualism and competitiveness—values that contradict the operational efficiency requirements of modern productive systems. The conditions of involvement of the individual in the Kibbutz enterprise, and accompanying ideological factors, are important in motivating the individual.

The people working in the Kibbutz enterprise are motivated to feel needed and wanted within the context of the total community. Such feelings, among people who share in a common task, are powerful motivating forces for individuals to give their best in the performance of shared responsibility. The entire social system of the cooperative reflects voluntary participation, voluntary cooperation, and mutual control: these are democratic communities that operate internally without coercion (no courts, no police, no jails) and without money. The Kibbutz approximates—within community capabilities and priorities—the principle "from each according to his ability, to each according to his needs."

The prospect for industrial enterprises in the Kibbutz is reflected in the fact that in a number of cooperative communities the value of industrial production equals or exceeds that of agriculture. This is a turning point for the general development of the Kibbutzim, which began with agriculture as their economic base. Manufacturing industry, even along sophisticated technical lines, can become a new frontier for the further economic development of cooperative communities.

Is there a feature of cooperative decision-making that may, automatically, restrict the size of such enterprises? From the experience of managerially controlled enterprise, it is evident that the size of a unit factory is a separable issue from size of firm. A large firm can be the sum of many factories or divisions, each of "medium" size. The size of a factory, with an array of technology options and markets, can be varied according to the size of a workable decision-making sub-unit, and the capability of acceptable planning and control techniques for regulating the activities of many sub-units.

When cooperative enterprise is organized to take into account the separate function of condition-setting as against particularized (detailed-specified) decisions, then there should be, theoretically, broad limits for conceivable size of enterprise. This expectation is abetted by the known capability of modern data-handling techniques for integrating varied and even far-flung industrial operations. At this writing, I have learned that about 50 Kibbutzim are making use of modern data processing facilities for economic, including production, planning, and for control of operations. Computers, appropriately programmed to suit the criteria of integrated economic planning, can be put to work on behalf of the cooperative community, as well as (with differing programs) for the managerial enterprise. This expectation is consistent with the data of this study which are at variance with the idea that the main alternatives for society are either value-oriented or technology-determined. The assumption is that the latter means individual incentives, inequality, social stratification, and elite rule in the name of technological advance and efficiency. Value-oriented is taken to mean egalitarianism, humanism—meaning, necessarily, anti-technology.

All this, however, is based upon the erroneous idea that technology has a direction or initiative of its own. This theory does not survive close scrutiny. Technology is shaped by using knowledge about nature to satisfy social criteria: hence, change the criteria (durability versus cost, safety versus style) and the resulting technology is changed. Several lines of evidence converge on the point that technology can be fashioned to suit man's requirements for life or for war-making, for industrial production to serve private profit-making or adapted to man's sensory-motor abilities. Plainly, technology is man's servant, bearing the imprint of who decides on technology and the sort of criteria that are applied in the process of design.

Accordingly, industrial technologies under managerial control bear the imprint of managerial criteria. As cooperative control continues, then, to the extent that its criteria are used to control production, some technology is bound to be fashioned, increasingly, in its image.[8]

SUMMARY AND CONCLUSION

The data of this comparative study in Israel of six managerially controlled enterprises and six cooperative administered enterprises indicate the following:

1. Industrial enterprises of a modern technical sort can be operated under various modes of decision-making. Factory production with powered equipment and division of labor can be efficiently performed without parallel use of managerial decision-making. These findings contradict the mystique of technology-determined form in organization of production.

2. Cooperative decision-making is a workable method of production decision-making in the operation of industrial enterprise.

3. The equal or greater efficiency of operation found in the cooperative, as opposed to the managerially controlled enterprises, is not anticipated from conventional knowledge in economics and industrial management.

4. This investigation does not establish the probability by which cooperative decision-making in industrial production may be, systematically, more efficient than managerial control. It is demonstrated that cooperative decision-making in modern industry can be as efficient, or more efficient, a mode of decision-making than managerial control. This capability is linked to the pervasive motivational and operational effects of cooperation in decision-making and in production, pressing toward stability in operations, and thereby toward optimal use of industrial facilities.

The findings of this comparative study suggest that social scientists, and others engaged in research on organization, ought to explore the problems of cooperative versus managerial decision-making within various economies and cultural contexts, as well as in laboratory and field experiments. Diverse approaches to these problems, exploring the variability of performance of diverse modes of organization, should add to knowledge and have operational importance—insofar as variation in organization can produce meaningful differences in economic efficiency, or enlarge the available array of options for viable social organization. How much of the experience of cooperative decision-making is relevant to managerial organization, and vice versa, is an open and interesting question.

NOTES

1. S. Melman, "The Rise of Administrative Overhead in the Manufacturing Industries of the United States 1899–1947," *Oxford Economic Papers*, 1951; *Dynamic Factors in Industrial Productivity*, John Wiley, New York, Basil Blackwell, Oxford, 1956; *Decision-Making and Productivity*, John Wiley, New York, Basil Blackwell, Oxford, 1958.

2. *A Directory of Kibbutz Industry* is published by Kibbutz Industries Assn., 13 Tiomkin St., Tel Aviv, Israel. For background, see E. Kanovsky, *The Economy of the Israeli Kibbutz*, Harvard University Press, Cambridge, Mass., 1966. This volume includes a bibliography (pp. 155–160) that covers principal books and articles on the organization and economy of the Kibbutz.

3. Among the relatively few organizational studies that are relevant for a comparison of managerial versus cooperative decision-making, two are noteworthy: Stephen C. Jones and Victor H. Vroom, "Division of Labor and Performance Under Cooperative and Competitive Conditions," *Journal of Abnormal and Social Psychology*, 68 (March 1964), pp. 313–320; Bernard M. Bass, "Business Gaming for Organizational Research," *Management Science*, 10 (April 1964), pp. 545–556, esp. fn. 3.

4. A fairly extensive bibliography in the field of organization is found in James G. March (ed.), *Handbook of Organizations*, Rand McNally, Chicago, 1965; also, the unusual volumes by James L. Price, *Organizational Effectiveness*, Richard D. Irwin, Homewood, Ill., 1968; and Amitai Etzioni, *Complex Organizations*, Holt, Rinehart & Winston, New York, 1961.

5. S. Littauer, "Technological Stability," *Transactions of the New York Academy of Science*, December 1950; S. Littauer, "Stability of Production Rates as a Determinant of Industrial Productivity Levels," *Proceedings of the Business and Economic Statistics Section* (Washington, D.C.: American Statistical Association, 1955), pp. 241–248; S. Melman, *Decision-Making and Productivity*, *op. cit.*, pp. 165–166.

6. This is one consequence of bilateralism in production decision-making. See diagnosis of bilateralism in L. B. Cohen, "Workers and Decision-Making on Production," in L. Tripp (ed.), *Proceedings of the Eighth Annual Meeting, Industrial Relations Research Association*, 1956, pp. 298–312; also see data on impact of bilateralism on management in S. Melman, *Decision-Making and Productivity*, *op. cit.*

7. S. Melman, "Administration and Production Cost in Relation to Size of Firms," *Applied Statistics*, (*Journal of Royal Statistical Society*), 1954.

8. See S. Melman, "Who Decides Technology?" *Columbia Forum*, Winter 1968; *Dynamic Factors in Industrial Productivity*, *op. cit.*

20

The Mao Ethic
and Environmental Quality

Leo A. Orleans and Richard P. Suttmeier

It is only recently that apprehension over the rapidly intensifying problems of environmental quality in the industrialized world has reached a point where it has become obvious that solutions will require much more money, effort, and desire on the part of both government and people. It may come as something of a surprise, therefore, to find that as early as the 1st century B.C. the Chinese *Record of Rites of the Elder Tai*[1] warned against man's polluting his environment, and that Communist China, at best only a partially industrialized nation, has shown some concern regarding questions of environmental quality for almost all of the 20 years of its existence. Taking great satisfaction in their professed accomplishments in this field, the Chinese news sources have been quick to report and comment on U.S. problems of pollution, citing them as among the more serious weaknesses of the capitalist system. They even referred to President Nixon's State of the Union Message, commenting that he "helplessly wailed that [in 10 years] the so-called 'pollution' problem in the United States would 'become insoluble?'"[2] They have also pointed to reports in the *Wall Street Journal* that the production of antipollution devices has become the new "glamor industry," stating that American antipollution programs are a guise for further exploitation of the American people by "monopoly capitalists."[3]

SETTING FOR CHINESE ENVIRONMENTAL CONCERNS

The fight against environmental contamination in Communist China, which has taken various forms over the years, was recently manifested in the ideological struggles of the now waning Cultural Revolution—the struggle between the all-powerful thoughts of Mao Tse-tung and the black deeds of Liu Shao-chi, the former President of the People's Republic of China, who took the "capitalist road." Liu, as politician and development strategist, has often been identified by the Maoists with China's "bourgeois experts"—those

Reprinted from *Science*, Vol. 170 (December 11, 1970), pp. 1173-1176, by permission of the publisher and authors. Copyright 1970 by the American Association for the Advancement of Science.

managers, engineers, and scientists whose positions in the technically oriented bureaucracy implied the emergence of a technocratic elite. Thus it
was not only Liu but also the "experts" and all they represented in terms
of economic growth and social modernization that became subjects for
attack during the Cultural Revolution. According to Maoist news sources,
the approach of Liu Shao-chi and the technical experts toward industrial
wastes was to treat these as "industrial 'garbage,' . . . [maintaining that]
because they could not be reused to produce large quantities of valuable
products, it would not pay to utilize them. They [Liu followers] not only
threw away these valuable materials, but let them pollute the air and
rivers."[4] Thus "Liuism" has come to represent a position of opposing the
comprehensive utilization of resources, of relying on the opinions of experts,
and of being insensitive to environmental pollution.

   Maoism, on the other hand, is first and foremost an ethic of frugality, of
"doing more with less." It is an ethic of self-reliance, but of self-reliance
tempered with the cooperation that theoretically results from the mobilization of all sectors of the society for given tasks. Maoism is an ethic of
progress, but of progress that relies more on the transformation of the
Chinese masses than on the directions and recommendations of a scientific
and technological elite. Hence, progress and the resulting changes in the
means of production—the development of new technologies—are to remain
under human control. It is therefore an ethic that appears to make technological development dependent on social development, instead of letting
social development slip completely out of phase with technological progress.
As an environmental ethic, then, Maoism may seem very attractive indeed
to many of the citizens of the complex industrial societies of the West, who
are increasingly disturbed about the secondary and tertiary ecological
effects of their technologies.

   When the Communist Party seized power in China, the new regime
established as two of its primary goals "socialist construction" and "national
defense." In some respects both these goals entailed new relationships
between man and nature. Attitudes of the new regime toward the natural
environment, although this is rarely explicitly stated, were, on the one hand,
necessarily exploitative and, on the other hand, curative. Nature was to be
exploited for the good of society, and the fostering of modern science and
technology was considered an appropriate means to that end. Yet, the
vastness of China's population and the primitive exploitation of nature that
characterized the old society had resulted in a highly degraded environment
which manifested itself as totally inhospitable in time of famine, plague, or
flood. Therefore, in addition to exploitation, there was a need for therapeutic
action in such areas as afforestation, water conservancy, land reclamation,
and sanitation and public health.

   To increase their inadequate knowledge of the nation's resource base
and natural environment, the Chinese leaders promoted a rather extensive
series of surveys of tropical resources in south China. These activities
became known as "comprehensive expeditions" and were often conducted
in collaboration with Soviet scientists. More than ten of these highly
organized multidisciplinary expeditions were made during the 1950's. The
foci of the expeditions ranged from water and soil conservation surveys in

the middle reaches of the Yellow River to surveys of tropical resources in south China; from studies of the developmental potential of the Amur River basin to studies of the feasibility of developing water resources in west China. The composition of the expedition teams varied according to task and location, but the teams typically included geographers and geologists, hydraulic engineers, pedologists, foresters and agriculturists, and public health officials.[5]

These attempts to explore and inventory China's natural environment were institutionalized with the establishment of a high-level Committee on Comprehensive Expeditions, within the Chinese Academy of Sciences. This committee, with meteorologist Chu K'o-chen as chairman, was established in 1956, the year in which the long-range, 12-year plan for the development of science and technology was initiated. The committee had responsibility not only for promoting the expeditions themselves and for coordinating them with the Soviet Union but also for producing, on the basis of the data obtained, reports and plans for the exploitative and curative environmental management of the regions studied. Although the final disposition of these plans is unclear, presumably they formed the basis for subsequent planning and development in many regions of China.

At a different level, the responsibility for research on specific measures designed to improve the environment, and for their implementation, was distributed among numerous institutions. The Ministry of Public Health had perhaps the major share of the total responsibility, since much of the emphasis was on the health and well-being of the workers. But some of the most important research on pollution was conducted in the Ministry of Labor's Institute of Scientific Research on Labor Protection, in the Division of Research on Labor Sanitation of the Chinese Academy of Medical Sciences, and in other such institutions. There were also special research institutions in the research organizations of the ministries of Metallurgy, Coal, Chemicals, Railways, and Construction, and departments and special courses on labor protection in many universities and colleges.[6] Thus, to use one of their favorite expressions, the Chinese Communists attacked the environmental problem "on many fronts."

HUMAN POLLUTION

In the past, health conditions in China have been notoriously poor, and, for most of the people, sanitation measures virtually unknown. As a result, the death rate tended to fluctuate between high and very high, depending on the extent and intensity of famines, natural disasters, military conflicts, and epidemics of such "filth diseases" as typhus, cholera, plague, typhoid, and dysentery. Improvement of the health of the Chinese population was high on the priority list of the Chinese Communists. Since there were not enough doctors and medical facilities to provide medical care for those who were sick, emphasis was concentrated on preventive medicine and on environmental sanitation, so that the number of people requiring medical attention would be reduced. Through massive programs of vaccination, through periodic nationwide "patriotic health campaigns," and through concurrent long-range campaigns to control kala-azar, schistosomiasis, hookworm, malaria, filariasis, and other diseases, the Chinese have achieved considerable success in improving the environmental conditions and, consequently, the health of the population.

A feat that has received much publicity in the West has been the elimination of flies and mosquitoes through the mobilization of virtually every man, woman, and child in the country. It seems quite possible that the Chinese may have gone a long way toward accomplishing another feat of almost equal proportions—that of cleaning up many of the polluted streams, small rivers, and lakes which for centuries have been receiving much of the human and animal waste that was not used for fertilizing fields. Careful management of water and manure in the rural areas is one of the most important functions of medical and sanitation personnel, while medical and public health journals publish many articles on the subject and print detailed instructions on how to build and protect wells, how to manage manure, where to place latrines, and what personal hygienic measures one should take after working with manure.

Since many of the cities in China continued to have inadequate sewerage systems or none at all, the Communists concentrated much effort on the proper disposal of human waste in the more densely populated areas. In order to control contamination of urban water, which usually came from adjacent rivers or lakes, the Chinese adopted a twofold approach. First, over the years the Communists made considerable progress in expanding urban sewerage and sewerage treatment facilities; second, much of the urban waste was transported into the countryside to be used for the irrigation and fertilization of farms. The latter process undoubtedly helped the cities but apparently intensified health problems in the villages. Reports indicated some serious increases in the incidence of dermatosis and various infectious diseases. These reports were followed by increased discussion of problems and of possible solutions in the public health and sanitation publications.

Other pollution problems in the cities were handled through extensive cleanup campaigns—not unlike recent community efforts in some of the cities of the United States, but on a vastly larger scale. Masses of people were mobilized in China's cities to remove refuse that had accumulated in residential districts. To keep the streets and alleys of residential areas clean, regulations that such areas must be swept were enforced, and residents were organized to transport refuse. In this process great care is taken to salvage anything that may have some residual value. For example, pieces of metal are always collected; furnace cinders are gathered, to be used in construction materials or as fill for swampy areas; and so forth. A side effect of the "keep your city clean" campaigns, Chinese style, is one that foreigners who had been in China prior to 1950 would find almost unbelievable: apparently the people no longer expectorate or blow their noses on the street.

To judge from the periodic introduction of new cleanup campaigns, however, the authorities have not been able to rest on their laurels, since people tend to slip back into old habits. After almost three years of the Cultural Revolution, much space in the Chinese press was given this year's spring cleanup, which was described as a "spring patriotic sanitation movement." It was organized by local revolutionary committees and focused on picking up accumulated litter and garbage from residences, farms, and factories; on cleaning up local waters; on eliminating pests; on collecting reusable wastes; and on stressing public health measures.

INDUSTRIAL POLLUTION

Throughout the period of the Peking regime, industrial pollution has been fought primarily under various slogans relating to frugality; workers have been told that, if they will properly implement Mao's thoughts, "wastes" will indeed be transformed into "treasures." Of particular importance during the last few years has been the concept of "comprehensive use," introduced as a Maoist injunction to workers and peasants to recover and reuse (recycle) industrial and agricultural wastes. Although the comprehensive-use concept had its foundations in perceived conditions of scarcity and in Maoist frugality as a response to those conditions, it has nevertheless been explicitly linked to environmental quality. During the first four months of 1970 the tempo of the comprehensive-use campaign increased. The campaign became a "vigorous mass movement" aimed at full utilization of the "four wastes" —waste materials, waste water, waste gas, and waste heat. There are indications that Chinese science and technology is being asked to focus more of its attention on comprehensive utilization.[7] This presumably will lead to research by trained scientists and engineers on the recycling of resources, to supplement the innovations of peasants and workers.

It is easy to understand why China would not be greatly concerned with air pollution. First, only about 15 percent of the population is located in the urban areas and only a small proportion of the urban labor force is engaged in industrial production. Second, pollution from automotive traffic is insignificant in Chinese cities. This is not to say that air pollution does not exist in some of China's more important industrial centers, or that serious pollution problems are completely ignored. Steel centers such as An-shan and Paot'ou and large industrial centers and urban conglomerations such as Shanghai, Tientsin, Harbin, Wuhan, and Peking certainly produce their share of air pollution and cause local concern. For example, a clinical examination of school children conducted as part of research on the effects of atmospheric contamination on the health of people living near the Shih-ching-shan Steel and Iron Factory in Peking revealed definite liver enlargement that was attributed to the toxic effects of the small amount of sulfur dioxide in the atmosphere.[8]

To cope with some of these problems, many of the old cities such as Peking, Shanghai, and Wuhan have reportedly relocated those factories that seriously contaminate the atmosphere, moving them to new industrial zones. In many of the new cities factories are being built "on the opposite side of the city from which the wind usually blows."

Some of the factories report making "wealth" from waste gases.[9]

> At the Dairen Chemical Factory, in the process of manufacturing sulphuric acid, extra gas from the surplus acid was usually expelled directly into the

atmosphere. This condition endangered the health of the inhabitants. . . . Now this company is recovering sulphuric acid fumes and ammonia, and producing fertilizers with these waste products.

Much progress has apparently been made in improving the working conditions of those involved in mining and other industries where harmful dust is prevalent. For example, it was reported that the concentration of silica dusts in metal mines has been reduced to meet government standards and that similar progress has been made in controlling dust in coal mines, chalk factories, quartz factories, and enamelware factories. As a result, diseases such as silicosis have been drastically reduced.[10]

Because the consequences of water pollution are much more immediate and serious, the industrial pollution of water is naturally more disturbing to the Chinese Communists than air pollution is. With increased industrialization and urbanization, both the nature and the degree of water pollution changed for the worse. As in the case of air pollution, however, the ameliorating factor is the concentration of most Chinese industry in less than a dozen eastern and northern provinces.

An effort is made in most cities to locate new plants and factories down-river from the most densely inhabited areas. Furthermore, the more modern and the larger installations may well have some waste-water purification systems. The most serious problems undoubtedly relate to the older and the smaller industrial facilities, which continue to dump untreated industrial waste into adjacent bodies of water. It seems doubtful that even the expanded sewerage facilities now being constructed in some of the cities can keep up with the increasing industrial development and the concurrent growth of urban populations.

The impression one gets from various articles and reports appearing in the Chinese press is that, even as in Western countries, there is an inevitable gap between identifying the sources of pollution and doing something about it. Epidemiological departments of many cities and provinces report much research on the quality and cleanliness of the water in rivers and lakes. There has been considerable research, experimentation, and collection of data by various scientific and educational institutions. Given China's economic constraints, however, the admonitions of the health and sanitation departments are not likely to result in corrective action unless the waste is particularly harmful, unless the cost of corrective action would be minimal, or unless the waste can be made economically profitable.

All three of these considerations may be discerned in recently reported activities in Shanghai, China's largest and most industrialized city. In July 1968 the Shanghai Municipal Revolutionary Committee—the effective local government, made up of representatives from the army, unpurged Party cadres, and revolutionary activists—started a campaign to clean up the waters of the Huangpu and Suchow rivers. In the course of Shanghai's industrialization, these two streams had become industrial sewers, with plants for paper manufacture, printing and dyeing, chemical-fiber manufacture, electroplating, tanning, and other industrial processes located on their banks. The campaign appeared to have economic, environmental, and sociopolitical objectives. Much of the justification for the work which ensued was based on the concept of comprehensive use of resources. It was noted that most of the raw materials for Shanghai's industries came from distant sources. In the interest of economy, therefore, "workers, revolutionary cadres and revolutionary intellectuals" were urged to make thorough use of these resources. Wastes were to be recovered and recycled for further industrial use where possible, or waste waters were to be diverted for irrigation of farmlands in the vicinity of the city. Efforts were made to develop new technologies for these purposes. This was reported in the electroplating industry, for instance, and also in a gas factory which was producing waste waters that were heavily contaminated with phenol. In attacking this pollution, it is claimed, new equipment for recovering the phenol was developed and installed at a modest cost.[11]

These efforts at comprehensive use were also seen as improving the quality of the environment. It was recognized that the reduction of stream pollution not only improved the appearance of the rivers but also represented a major step forward in sanitation and public health. Efforts were made to dredge the rivers of contaminated muck. The Revolutionary Committee used the standard Chinese Communist technique of mass mobilization for this purpose. Over a three-month period, "90,000 persons were mobilized on the industrial and agricultural fronts in Shanghai to form muck-dredging and muck-transporting teams, waging a vehement people's war to dredge muck from the Suchow River. After 100 days of turbulent fighting, more than 403,600 tons of malodorous organic mire had been dug out."[12] Most of this was to be used as fertilizer.

There are two basic reasons why the Chinese Communists seem to have been concerned with environmental pollution when the more advanced and more polluted countries of the world were still largely ignoring the problem. First, the concern was an integral part of China's efforts to improve the country's health and sanitation conditions; second, it was consistent with the Chinese Communists' policies and programs of frugality and economy.

Chinese environmental problems have been characterized by the fact that a great proportion of waste in China is organic. There are no unreturnable containers, few plastic goods, no car cemeteries—none of the wastes of our affluent society. On the contrary, because of the low economic level of the population and the national emphasis on frugality, few items are disposed of unless they are approaching a natural state of disintegration. Thus, for most of China, solutions involve intensification of sanitation measures, mass cleanup campaigns, and other measures of the "do-it-yourself" variety. In the areas of industrial pollution and urban sewerage disposal, however, the problems are much more serious, and, despite considerable progress and continuing efforts, many undoubtedly persist.

Underlying present Chinese concerns about pollution are the thoughts of Mao Tse-tung. Maoism as an environmental ethic may strike many Westerners as obvious common sense. In the real life of contemporary China, however, it is still an open question whether the Maoist ethic represents common sense or courts environmental catastrophe. However admirable the attempts at comprehensive utilization and recycling of wastes may be, there are indeed occasions when such efforts make no economic sense and many make even less ecological sense.[13] The removal of labor from productive activities for purposes of diverting industrial waste waters for irrigation is a case in point. These waters may have a highly deleterious effect on the irrigated fields. Unfortunately, we lack information on whether or not this process is scientifically monitored, whether the waste waters have been chemically analyzed, and whether the wastes in them conform to the needs of the soils.

Similarly, the encouragement of inventiveness on the part of workers and peasants and maintenance of a skeptical attitude toward "academic authorities" are in many ways eminently reasonable policies in a developing nation. However, the widespread discrediting of the expert can also have unfortunate consequences, particularly in areas of ecology where expert scientific knowledge is critical.

All conclusions with regard to developments in China these days come by way of piecemeal facts and wholesale speculation, and pollution control is no exception. It seems, however, that a summation from a 1959 Chinese medical journal is just as valid today as it was 10 years ago:[14] "Since the founding of new China, great achievements have been made in the research and practical work in the field of environmental hygiene. . . . Nevertheless, our achievements are far from meeting the requirements of socialist construction in our country."

NOTES

1. M. Conway, "Asia: the unnatural rape," *Far Eastern Econ. Rev.* 1970, 21 (23 Apr. 1970).
2. *Hung-chi* [Red Flag], No. 4 (1970).
3. *New China News Agency* (Peking) (18 Apr. 1970).
4. *Ibid.* (21 Feb. 1970).
5. "Ten years of natural resources expeditions," *K'o-hsueh T'ung-pao* [Science Journal] (July 1959).
6. *Chung-kuo Hsin-wen* [China News] (2 Apr. 1966); translated in *U.S. Joint Publ. Res. Serv. Publ. No. 36,983* (15 Aug. 1966).
7. *New China News Agency* (13 Apr. 1970).
8. "China's major scientific and technical achievements in community hygiene in the past decade," *Jen-min Pao-chien* [People's Health] 1, No. 10 (1959); translated in *U.S. Joint Publ. Res. Serv. Publ. No. 2745* (10 June 1960).
9. *Ibid.*
10. "China's major achievements in industrial hygiene and in the prevention and treatment of occupational diseases during the past decade," *Jen-min Pao-chien* [People's Health] 1, No. 10 (1959); translated in *U.S. Joint Publ. Res. Serv. Publ. No. 2745* (10 June 1960).
11. *New China News Agency* (21 Oct. 1969).
12. *Ibid.*
13. See, for instance, *New China News Agency* (21 Feb. 1970). For a look at haphazard field testing and application of a new pesticide, see *ibid.* (1 March 1970).
14. *Ch'ing-chu Chien-kuo Shih-chou-nien I-hsueh K'ohsueh Ch'eng-chiu Lun-wen-chi, Yu-fane I-hsueh Pu* [A Collection of Papers on Medical Sciences in Commemoration of the Tenth Anniversary of the Founding of the People's Republic of China: vol. 1, Preventive Medicine] (Peking, 1959); translated in *U.S. Joint Publ. Res. Serv. Publ. No. 9551* (29 June 1961).

21

Employment in the 1970's:
A New Perspective

Mahbub ul Haq

Ever since you asked me to make a presentation to this distinguished forum
—on the very dubious assumption that since I was associated with Pakistan's economic planning for 13 years, I ought to know something about
employment strategy—I became conscious of a very deep responsibility.
And despite all the gaps in my knowledge, I was determined not to let you
down. So I went on a feverish search of all the literature on employment
strategy, all the theories and policy prescriptions that the economists and
the practitioners in the field had to offer. And I came up with some
distressing discoveries.

First, it appears to me that we are assembled here to discuss a problem
whose nature and dimensions we simply do not know. I looked at various
estimates of unemployment and underemployment which had been prepared
for the developing countries—even by that distinguished organization known
as the ILO—and I was distressed to find that estimates of 5 to 10% unemployment and 20 to 25% underemployment were tossed around with a
casualness which was simply frightening. There was no agreed methodology
for measuring unemployment or underemployment, no definite ideas or
projections on what had happened in this field in the 1960's or what might
happen in the 1970's, and very poor knowledge about this "vital" concern
even in some of the largest and most affected countries like India, Pakistan
and Brazil.

Second, while we knew so little about the nature and dimensions of the
unemployment problem, we suffered from no modesty when it came to
definitive policy prescriptions. The favourite prescription of the economists
—besides the doubling or tripling of growth rates—is to correct the price
system, particularly exchange rates, interest rates, terms of trade between
agriculture and industry and prices of all factors of production. But has
this faith in the price system been tested empirically? When various developing countries corrected their exchange rates or interest rates at various
times, was this followed by a great surge in their employment situation or
merely by better utilization of capital, larger output and higher labour
productivity? In any event, how large a segment of the economy does the

Reprinted from *International Development Review*, Vol. XIII, No. 4 (1971), pp. 9-13, by permission of the publisher. © 1971 Society for International Development.

price adjustment affect when there is a large subsistence sector in these countries and the modern industrial sector generally contributes less than 10% to total output? No one will dare suggest that price corrections will not move these economies in the right direction. But are they decisive? Or do they make only a marginal impression on the unemployment problem? We need far more empirical evidence before we can pass any overall judgments.

Third, there is a fashion these days to talk about intermediate technology, something which is supposed to be more labour-intensive and more suited to the needs of the developing countries than the technology presently used in the developed world. But where does it exist? I found very little evidence of it in the developed countries, which have no real incentive for fashioning special technology for the developing countries and which export a good deal of their technology under tied assistance. There are no great improvisations going on in the developing countries themselves and no major research institutes devoting their energies to the development of intermediate technology.* The only place where I found something resembling intermediate technology was in mainland China, but there has not been much transfer of it to the developing countries, as China's trade and aid are fairly limited at present.

Fourth, I found in the literature on employment abundant suggestions that the developed world should open up its markets to the labour-intensive products of the developing countries. Here, at least, the evidence is fairly clear: no one has detected any impatience on the part of any developed country to follow this prescription.

Finally, looking at the national plans of the developing countries, it was obvious that employment was often a secondary, not a primary, objective of planning. It was generally added as an afterthought to the growth target in GNP but very poorly integrated in the framework of planning. Recalling my own experience with the formulation of Pakistan's five year plans—and I ought to know—the chapter on employment strategy was always added at the end, to round off the plans and make them look complete and respectable, and was hardly an integral part of the growth strategy or policy framework. In fact, most of the developments which affected the employment situation favourably, such as the rural works programme and the green revolution, were planned primarily for higher output, and their employment-generating potential was accidental and not planned. There were endless numbers of research teams, our own and foreign, fixing up our national accounts and ensuring that they adequately registered our rate of growth; there was not a fraction of this effort devoted to employment statistics.

The employment objective, in short, has been the stepchild of planning, and it has been assumed, far too readily, that high rates of growth will ensure full employment as well. But what if they don't? A sustained 6% rate of growth in Pakistan in the 1960's led to rising unemployment, particularly

---

* I was informed after my lecture that there is a small research institute in Britain, the Intermediate Technology Group, operating on a shoe-string budget, which is devoting all its efforts to this subject. I am sorry I missed that.

in East Pakistan. And what happens if the developing countries cannot achieve the high growth rates of 10% or more that it may take to eliminate unemployment and are confined to 5 or 6% over the present decade? Should they quietly accept rising unemployment, and the social and political unrest that accompanies it, as the inevitable price for not growing any faster?

There were uncomfortable questions of this kind which led me to a re-examination of the overall theory and practice of development. And I found it to be in an even sorrier state than the literature on employment.

HAS POVERTY DECREASED?

Here we stand after two decades of development, trying to pick up the pieces, and we simply do not know whether problems associated with dire poverty have increased or decreased or what real impact the growth of GNP has made on them. We do know that the rate of growth, as measured by the increase in GNP, has been fairly respectable in the 1960's, especially by historical standards. We also know that some developing countries have achieved a fairly high rate of growth over a sustained period. But has it made a dent on the problems of mass poverty? Has it resulted in a reduction in the worst forms of poverty—malnutrition, disease, illiteracy, shelterless population, squalid housing? Has it meant more employment and greater equality of opportunities? Has the character of development conformed to what the masses really wanted? We know so little in this field. There are only a few selected indices and they are rather disquieting.

A recent study in India shows that 40 to 50% of the total population has a per capita income below the official poverty line where malnutrition begins. And what's more pertinent, the per capita income of this group has declined over the last two decades while the average per capita income went up.

In Pakistan, which experienced a healthy growth rate during the 1960's, unemployment increased, real wages in the industrial sector declined by one-third, per capita income disparity between East and West Pakistan nearly doubled, and concentrations of industrial wealth became an explosive economic and political issue. And in 1968, while the international world was still applauding Pakistan as a model of development, the system exploded—not only for political reasons but for economic unrest.

Brazil has recently achieved a growth rate close to 7% but persisting maldistribution of income continues to threaten the very fabric of its society.

These instances can be multiplied. There is in fact need for much more work in this field. The essential point, however, is that a high growth rate has been, and is, no guarantee against worsening poverty and economic explosions.

What has gone wrong? We were confidently told that if you take care of your GNP, poverty will take care of itself. We were often reminded to keep our eyes focused on a high GNP growth target, as it was the best guarantee for eliminating unemployment and of redistributing incomes later through fiscal means. Then what really happened? Where did the development process go astray?

WHERE WE WENT WRONG

My feeling is that it went astray at least in two directions. First, we conceived our task not as the eradication of the worst forms of poverty but as the pursuit of certain high levels of per capita income. We convinced ourselves that the latter is a necessary condition for the former but we did not in fact give much thought to the inter-connection. We development economists persuaded the developing countries that life begins at $1,000 and thereby we did them no service. They chased elusive per capita income levels, they fussed about high growth rates in GNP, they constantly worried about "how much was produced and how fast," they cared much less about "what was produced and how it was distributed."

This hot pursuit of GNP growth was not necessarily wrong; it only blurred our vision. It is no use pretending that it did not, for how else can we explain the worsening poverty in many developing countries? How else can we explain our own preoccupation as economists with endless refinements of statistical series concerning GNP, investment, saving, exports and imports; continuing fascination with growth models; and formulation of evaluation criteria primarily in terms of output increases? If eradication of poverty was the real objective, why did so little professional work go into determining the extent of unemployment, maldistribution of incomes, malnutrition, shelterless population or other forms of poverty? Why is it that even after two decades of development, we know so little about the extent of real poverty—even in such "well-planned" economies as India and Pakistan?

Besides the constant preoccupation with GNP growth, another direction we went wrong was in assuming that income distribution policies could be divorced from growth policies and could be added later to obtain whatever distribution we desired. Here we displayed a misguided faith in the fiscal systems of the developing countries and a fairly naive understanding of the interplay of economic and political institutions. We know now that the coverage of these fiscal systems is generally narrow and difficult to extend. We also know that once production has been so organized as to leave a fairly large number of people unemployed, it becomes almost impossible to redistribute incomes to those who are not even participating in the production stream. We have a better appreciation now of the evolution of modern capitalist institutions and their hold on political decision making and hence we are more aware that the very pattern and organization of production itself indicates a pattern of consumption and distribution which is politically very difficult to change. Once you have increased your GNP by producing more luxury houses and cars, it is not very easy to convert them into low cost housing or bus transport. A certain pattern of consumption and distribution inevitably follows.

We have a number of case studies by now which show how illusory it was to hope that the fruits of growth could be redistributed without reorganizing the pattern of production and investment first. Many fast-growing economies in Latin America illustrate this point. In my own country, Pakistan, the very institutions we created for promoting faster growth and capital accumulation later frustrated all our attempts for better distribution and greater social justice. I am afraid that the evidence is unmistakable and the conclusion inescapable: divorce between production and distribution policies is false and dangerous. The distribution policies must be built into the very pattern and organization of production.

Where does all this lead us? It leads us to a basic re-examination of the existing theories and practice of development. It is time that we stand economic theory on its head and see if we get any better results. In a way, the current situation reminds me of the state of affairs in the developed world in the early 1930's before Keynes shook us all with his General Theory. Since existing theories fitted none of the facts in the real world, they had to be discarded. Keynes provided us with a fresh way of looking at economic and political realities. His theoretical framework was not very elegant but his ideas had a powerful impact.

The developing countries today are seeking a fresh way of looking at their problems. They are disillusioned, and somewhat chastened, by the experience of the last two decades. They are not too sure what the new perspective on development should be but at least some of the elements are becoming increasingly clear.

A NEW PERSPECTIVE ON DEVELOPMENT

First, the problem of development must be defined as a selective attack on the worst forms of poverty. Development goals must be defined in terms of progressive reduction and eventual elimination of malnutrition, disease, illiteracy, squalor, unemployment and inequalities. We were taught to take care of our GNP as this will take care of poverty. Let us reverse this and take care of poverty as this will take care of the GNP. In other words, let us worry about the *content* of GNP even more than its rate of increase.

Second, and this follows from the first, the developing countries should define minimum (or threshold) consumption standards that they must reach in a manageable period of time, say a decade. Consumption planning should move to the centre of the stage; production planning should be geared to it. And consumption planning should not be in financial terms but in physical terms, in terms of a minimum bundle of goods and services that must be provided to the common man to eliminate the worst manifestations of poverty: minimum nutritional, educational, health and housing standards, for instance. There are two major implications of this strategy. One, we must get away from the tyranny of the demand concept and replace it by the concept of minimum needs, at least in the initial stages of development, since to weight basic needs by the ability to pay is outrageous in a poor society. It will only distort the patterns of production and consumption in favour of the "haves," as has happened in many societies. Two, the case of elusive present-day Western standards and per capita income levels, which cannot be reached even over the course of the next century, must be replaced by the concept of a threshold income which each society defines for itself and which can be reached in a manageable period of a decade or so.

Third, the concerns for more production and better distribution should be brought together in defining the pattern of development; both must be generated at the same time; the present divorce between the two concerns must end. If the pattern of production (and exports and imports) is geared to satisfying minimum consumption requirements and to employing the entire labour force, higher production will itself lead to better distribution.

Fourth, and this is implicit in the third, employment should become a primary objective of planning and no longer be treated as only a secondary objective. Let a society regard its entire labour force as allocable; over this force its limited capital resources must be spread. Let us reverse the present thinking that, since there is only a fixed amount of capital to be allocated at a particular time, it can employ only a certain part of the labour force, leaving the rest unemployed, to subsist on others as hangers-on or as beggars, without any personal income, often suffering from the worst forms of malnutrition and squalor. Instead let us treat the pool of labour as given; at any particular time it must be combined with the existing capital stock irrespective of how low the productivity of labour or capital may be. If physical capital is short, skill formation and organization can replace it in the short run. It is only if we proceed from the goal of full employment, with people doing something useful, even with little doses of capital and organization, that we can eradicate some of the worst forms of poverty. With this goal, even the character and pattern of production will change, as Dudley Seers points out in his Colombia Report, since better income distribution will also mean greater production of those goods which are less import- and capital-intensive and which require more labour.

THE CHINESE EXPERIENCE

These are only a few elements in the new perspective that is needed today on development. They are neither complete nor carefully integrated nor perhaps very original. I offer them only as an invitation to further thinking. And if some of this framework sounds fairly mad, let me invite you to study the development experience of the largest developing country in the world —that of mainland China. I visited it twice in the last few years and I must say that I was greatly impressed by its economic performance measured against ours in Pakistan. It was not obvious to me what the real rate of growth of China was, but it was obvious to me that they had looked at the problem of development from the point of view of eradication of poverty and not from the viewpoint of reaching a certain prescribed per capita income level. It appears that within a period of less than two decades. China has eradicated the worst forms of poverty; it has full employment, universal literacy and adequate health facilities; it suffers from no obvious malnutrition or squalor. What's more, it was my impression that China has achieved this at fairly modest rates of growth, by paying more attention to the content and distribution of GNP. In fact, China has proved that it is a fallacy that poverty can be removed and full employment achieved only at high rates of growth and only over a period of many decades.

How has it accomplished this? Of course, its political system, its isolation, its great size, its ideological mobilization, all of these have contributed to the evolution of its pattern of development. But are there any lessons to learn, even when we do not subscribe to its political system? Is there not a practical illustration here of a selective attack on the problems of poverty, pursuit of a threshold income and minimum consumption standards, merger of production and distribution policies and achievement of full employment with a meagre supply of capital? It is no use insisting that these results must have been achieved at tremendous social and political costs; people in the developing countries are often undergoing these costs without any visible economic results so that they look at the experience of China with great envy and praise. It is time, especially as China's isolation ends, that there be an objective and detailed study of its experience in place of the usual rhetoric to which we have been subjected so far.

In conclusion, let me say that the search for a new perspective on development—of which the themes of our Conference, employment and social justice, are only two facets—has already begun in the developing countries. Many of us of these countries, who are essentially products of Western liberalism and who returned to our countries to deliver development, have often ended up delivering more tensions and unrest. We have seen a progressive erosion of liberalism, both in our own countries and amongst our donor friends abroad. And we stand today disspirited and disillusioned. It is no use offering us tired old trade-offs and crooked-looking production functions whenever we talk about income distribution and employment. It is no use dusting off old theories and polishing up old ideas and asking us to go and try them again. It is time that we take a fresh look at the entire theory and practice of development.

part six

**Comparative Models
of Development**

It is only in the last twenty-five years that economic development has so captured the attention of economists and statesmen alike. There are several reasons for this recent emphasis. First is the realization that international division of labor has not brought the benefits expected by nineteenth century economic theory. Second, the pressure for economic development exerted by the newly independent countries suggests that lack of freedom from want in underdeveloped countries may well mean lack of freedom from fear in developed countries. The third and probably most important reason is the emergence of socialism in the USSR and China as alternative models of development to capitalism.

In this part of the book, the readings present models of development based upon the historical experience of particular countries. There are both positive and negative lessons to learn from these models. The term "model" does not mean a detailing of every strategy, correct and incorrect, that was used by the particular country. Rather it is an abstraction of the essentials from the historical experience of development in that country. Despite the variation of development methods and strategies within and among countries, it is possible, and indeed necessary, to abstract from the secondary attributes of the individual cases and to concentrate on their essential common characteristics. This approach has always been the primary tool of all analytical effort—whether it be Marx's "pure capitalism," Marshall's "representative firm," or Weber's "ideal type." That the resulting model does not take into account every peculiarity of the given case does not invalidate its usefulness. Its value lies in the establishment of a framework which gives interpretation and meaning to the facts and descriptions assembled by quantitative research.

The two earliest cases of late (i.e., twentieth century) economic development are Japan and the Soviet Union. In the first reading of this section, William McCord constructs the "Japanese Model" of capitalist development from their historical experience, emphasizing both the lessons to be learned and the peculiarities of that experience. He concludes that peculiarities of culture and historical circumstance severely limit the applicability of the Japanese model today.

The Soviet Union produced the world's first example of rapid economic development centrally planned and directed; and this example—that is, both Soviet strategy and planning procedure—exercises a deep influence on the underdeveloped countries today. The full model of Soviet economic development can be found in my earlier book.* Certain specific details of the Soviet experience can be obtained from my articles in the two previous sections of this book. A quick summary of this "Soviet model" might be helpful for comparison with the models presented in the readings.

The Soviet model, as historically derived from socialist development experience, can be subdivided into three aspects: the preconditions of the model, the institutions characteristic of the model, and the strategy of development in the model.

The preconditions of the Soviet model include severence of any existing colonial bond with capitalist countries, elimination of economic domination by foreign capitalists, and redistribution of political and economic power. This is carried out by expropriating private property in landed estates and industrial enterprises.

After destruction of the old political and economic institutions and mechanisms, new socialist forms are substituted. Collectivized agriculture replaces landed estates and peasant proprietorship. Public ownership and operation replace private in industry and trade. Central planning, centralized distribution of essential materials and capital goods, and a system of administrative controls and pressures on enterprises partially supplant the market mechanism and the profit motive.

The strategy of development in the Soviet model includes a number of interrelated policies. Agricultural investment is held to the minimum necessary to allow agriculture to provide industry with a growing marketed surplus of agricultural products and an expanding source of labor supply. In addition, the collective farm system is used as a convenient organizational framework for the utilization of surplus agricultural labor on social overhead projects such as roads, canals, and irrigation works.

The strategy of development in the model encompasses a high rate of capital formation, with the bulk allocated to industry as the leading sector. Industrial investment is allocated on an imbalanced growth pattern. Soviet planning concentrates on certain key branches in each plan period to overcome particular bottlenecks. Scarce resources and talent are concentrated on these key targets. In the successive campaigns, investment is allocated to those industries that yield the largest external economies.

Choice of technique in the Soviet model encompasses a number of policies designed to utilize the most advanced technology while accounting for existing factor proportions. Soviet strategy consists of developing a "dual technology." On the one hand, in key processes, the most advanced technology is used. On the other hand, differences in factor proportions (between a developed and an underdeveloped economy) are accounted for by utilizing labor-intensive technology in auxiliary operations, by aiming at high performance rates per unit of capital instead of per man, and by utilizing plants of greatly differing vintages and technological levels in the same industries and sectors.

A major aspect of Soviet development strategy is an emphasis on human capital formation. Large amounts of investment are allocated to education and health services. Besides formal education and after-work vocational training, factories are over-staffed to provide on-the-job training. Propaganda, monetary incentives, and non-monetary rewards are all used as motivation.

The international trade policy in the Soviet model is primarily one of import-substitution. Capital goods, prototypes, blueprints, and technicians are imported in exchange for traditional exports until this imported capital can be used to construct industries that will replace the imports.

In the Soviet model of development the economy is a war economy harnessed to the attainment of one overriding objective—economic development. All physical and human resources are concentrated on the one basic objective of promoting economic development. Resources are centrally allocated to prevent leakages to production that do not promote economic development. The production of consumer goods is restricted to the minimum necessary to maintain health and morale. Propaganda and nonmaterial incentives are used. Civil liberties are restricted and conscription is utilized. These are common practices in war time. If leaders of underdeveloped countries are willing to view economic development as a war against poverty, the Soviet model offers an alternative to the capitalist methods offered by the West.

In the next two readings Robert Rhodes and Celso Furtado look at Mexico and Brazil as contemporary models of capitalist development. Rhodes argues that there is a major discrepancy between the image and the reality of Mexican development: despite impressive growth rates of GNP and industrialization, poverty has been little reduced for the vast majority, income distribution is more unequal than ever before, unemployment is still high, and land reform is a failure. Rhodes argues further that Mexico has benefited from the fortuitous circumstance of a common border with the United States. This has given Mexico a competitive advantage in the exportation of agricultural commodities to the United States and, more crucially, in attracting the tourist dollar. In his paper on the "Brazilian Model," Celso Furtado uses the theoretical framework developed in his work on "External Dependency" (the second reading in part three) to analyze and evaluate the Brazilian experience. The main feature of this experience is large scale industrialization based on the demands of a small minority of the population who possess an extraordinarily large percentage of the national income. The corollary of this is a structural tendency to exclude the mass of the population from the benefits of capital accumulation and technical progress. Both Rhodes and Furtado argue that the structure of dependency created by the capitalist world market is a major factor working against the success of a capitalist model of development today as compared with the development of Japan at the turn of the twentieth century.

In the final reading, John Gurley presents a coherent analysis of China as a contemporary model of socialist development. He argues two main points. First, even in conventional terms of GNP growth rates, Chinese development has been impressive. Second, and more important, the Chinese leadership is primarily concerned with creating a "new socialist man." When these two goals conflict, the first must give way. Gurley spells out in this context the meaning of such concepts as "walking on two legs" and "building on the worst." The reader should compare this Chinese version of socialist development with the general thrust of Dudley Seers' article in part one and Mahbub ul Haq's articles in parts five and eight. Gurley's discussion of the Chinese emphasis upon creating a "new socialist man" should also be reread after reading Paulo Freire's article on the "pedagogy of the oppressed" in part eight.

---

* Charles K. Wilber, *The Soviet Model and Underdeveloped Countries* (Chapel Hill: University of North Carolina Press, 1969).

22

The Japanese Model

William McCord

By external circumstances and by the ambitious temperament of her own
people, Japan has been obliged . . . to compress into a few decades
an economic development which most other industrialized nations have
spread over at least a century.

—M. D. Kennedy

Only one non-Western society, Japan, has succeeded in making the "great
ascent." It did so while handicapped by burdens which far exceeded those
of the West or Russia. In 1868, when the pulse of growth began to beat
faster, Japan lacked an industrial base comparable to that possessed by
Europe in 1800 or Russia in 1900. She had only tiny amounts of arable land
which could be brought under cultivation. She was critically deficient in the
basic mineral resources, a supposed prerequisite for industrialization.
Because of the international situation, she could neither impose protective
tariffs (which played a significant role in aiding continental Europe's infant
industries) nor could she depend upon colonies as a source of capital,
resources, and markets. The nation could not boast of a cadre of trained
personnel such as that which carried out Lenin's and Stalin's ambitions.
Japan's per capita income rested at a much lower level than Europe's or
Russia's at the beginning of their expansion and, thus, capital did not lie
ready at hand.

Despite unpropitious circumstances (which resemble closely the situation in today's new nations), Japan underwent an economic transformation
which surpassed Europe's and rivaled Russia's in its scope and pace. From
almost nothing in 1868, Japan built 4600 industrial concerns by 1896. Between
1878 and 1887, a critical decade of expansion, the total national product
increased by 42 per cent. From the end of the nineteenth century through
World War I, the amount of food approximately doubled. Each decade until
the 1930's, national production increased by almost 50 per cent.

A poor peasant society, almost devoid of resources, actually created a
modern economy. The transition began with a deliberate decision taken by
a small elite. Until 1868, the Tokugawa clans ruled Japan as a typically
feudal regime, consciously secluded from Western contact. The West
intruded on this isolation intermittently, but most devastatingly in 1863 and

Reprinted from the author's *The Springtime of Freedom: The Evolution of Developing Societies*,
(New York: Oxford University Press, 1965), pp. 58-64, by permission of the publisher. Copyright
© 1965 by Oxford University Press, Inc.

1864 when European ships bombarded Sotsuma and Choshu. This unde-
niable demonstration of modern technology's superiority convinced a dissident group of samurai—the "outer clans" already alienated from the ruling
clique—that Japan had to abandon its traditionalist policies. Under the
Meiji rulers who succeeded to power in a relatively bloodless manner, these
nobles vigorously pursued a program of modernization.

The tasks of the Meiji were eased by the fact that, while Japan was a
rural, traditional society in 1868, it had not been utterly stagnant under
Tokugawa rule. To some degree, Japan had already experienced a commercial revolution, similar to that in the West. Money had circulated since
1690; a small merchant class receptive to modern innovations had developed; and urban concentrations had begun to grow. In consequence, a pool
of mobile labor existed, and a base had been laid for "market-oriented"
attitudes. Further, like the West and Russia, Japan enjoyed an agricultural
surplus. As Thomas Smith has made clear, Japan under the Tokugawa had
shifted from a communal to an individual system of farming.[1] When the
introduction of new fertilizers and techniques, the substitution of rice for
unirrigated crops, and the cultivation of new products for urban markets
supplemented this change, the result was an upswing in production. Under
the Meiji, total farm output increased markedly. Japan could, therefore,
easily accommodate the population expansion which accompanied her initial
economic growth. Until the 1890's, Japan actually exported food.

While fortunate in possessing a food surplus, the Meiji rulers faced
formidable obstacles in their desire to transform the economy. Stung by
humiliations at the hands of the West, they sought to create a nation which
could recoup its military glory. Certainly, Japan's military adventures
worked to her temporary advantage in providing resources and markets.
Further, the nationalism cultivated by the Meiji may well have provided a
psychological framework which eased the burdens of economic growth. On
the other hand, the leaders squandered money on the military. The army
budget alone increased from 1 million yen in 1868 to 107 million yen by
1908. For good or ill, the drive to modernization got its impetus from an
urge to make Japan into a major military power, a nationalist goal apparently shared by the people.

To assure the foundation for military power, the nobles had to construct
a modern, growing technical base. They succeeded in doing this with extraordinary rapidity by following a series of policies which differed in basic
ways from the Western model and also in certain significant features from
that of Russia. These differences deserve the closest attention, for they
represent the first response of a non-Western nation to problems fundamentally similar to those of the contemporary developing countries.

First, unlike the West even in its mercantilist era, the government
assumed paramount importance as the stimulant to growth. The state took
a hand not only in creating the "social overhead" of railroads, irrigation
canals, and roads but also as the initiator of directly productive enterprises.
Throughout the nineteenth century, some 50 per cent of all investment came
from government coffers. The policy could be termed one of "guided capitalism." The rulers established model factories, producing silk and cement,
cotton and soap. After the enterprise had demonstrated its utility, private

entrepreneurs, often drawn from the same noble class as the government bureaucracy, took over control. This pattern of economic change differed markedly from that of the West, for the propellers of change were in no sense bourgeois entrepreneurs but rather members of the ruling nobility. As Robert Bellah has argued in his stimulating analysis of Japanese values:

> Only one class was in a position to lead the nation in breaking new ground: the samurai class. From the nature of its situation, its locus of strength was the polity, not the economy. I am insistent on this point because the tendency to regard economic developments as "basic" and political developments as "superstructure" is by no means confined to Marxist circles but permeates most current thinking on such matters.[2]

The Meiji rulers accumulated their investment capital essentially by squeezing it from the peasantry.[3] Agricultural production mounted steadily under the new government, but taxation held down the farmers' consumption and skimmed off the new profits for further investment. A land tax, imposed in 1873, forced farmers to pay a fixed charge on the value of their land amounting to about 25 per cent of the yield. As production climbed, so did tax returns.* In consequence, by 1875, revenue from the land tax accounted for 85 per cent of government income. Paul Baran has underlined the immense significance of this measure: "It is . . . no exaggeration to say that the main source of primary accumulation of capital in Japan was the village which, in the course of its entire modern history, played for Japanese capitalism the role of an internal colony."[4]

The pattern and type of industrialization undertaken also contrasted with that of the West and Russia. In those regions heavy industrial complexes formed the base of economic development. Japan, in contrast, emphasized light, cottage industries, widely decentralized throughout the country. These small workshops produced handmade consumer goods or components which were later assembled in the cities. In 1878, 81 per cent of all production in the textile industry came from light or cottage units; by 1930, the proportion was still 59 per cent, and even today it remains at 35 per cent. In a nation possessing an overabundant supply of labor, this policy had much in its favor. Since human energy could replace expensive imported machines in the productive process, capital could be conserved while, simultaneously, the talents of unemployed men could be released.

Such a program allowed Japan to grow very quickly, without the investment of enormous sums of capital. During similar periods, Japan and England invested approximately the same, relatively small amounts of capital, but Japan's growth in per capita product outraced England's by more than 2 to 1. The program also meant that economic change came gradually; rather than being ripped unceremoniously from their lands and

---

* A moderate inflationary spiral of some 8 per cent a year accompanied the process of capital accumulation and economic growth. Indeed, a "controlled" inflation was also characteristic of the Russian and European patterns of growth. As some of the "tougher-minded" fiscal experts fail to realize, moderate inflation may create a set of optimistic expectations which can serve to facilitate rather than impede economic growth in developing areas.

placed in the alien environment of a factory, the Japanese integrated new productive processes into their old ways of earning a living. One might say, too, that economic growth in Japan was "family-centered"; even today 30 per cent of Japan's labor force works in their own homes with their families, as compared to only 2 per cent in America and 0.2 per cent in Britain. The Japanese policy, therefore, demonstrated for the first time in history that "labor-intensive" light industry could serve as the vehicle for economic advance.

The nature of social change also differed in Japan. Radical alterations in the fabric of social life accompanied Europe's march into industrialization and occurred largely in a spontaneous, unplanned fashion. In Russia, the Bolsheviks precipitously and often unsuccessfully tried to destroy the traditional social order. The Meiji regime also set itself the task of initiating pervasive social reforms, aimed at facilitating economic growth. Yet many reform measures were also designed to buttress tradition, rather than to dismantle it.

In the attempt to modernize their society, the Meiji rulers attacked on several fronts. They undermined feudalism by breaking up landed estates and by encouraging the growth of small, individually-owned farms. This dismemberment of feudalism took place with remarkable ease; some former Tokugawa lords even voluntarily surrendered their land, perhaps because land in Japan did not have the supreme importance as a mark of noble status which it did in Europe. Indeed, in the whole process of feudal reform, the only serious rebellion was not triggered over the land issue, but rather occurred when the Meiji demanded that some traditionally oriented samurai should surrender their ritual swords. Antagonism arose, in other words, when the new government tampered with the symbols not the substance of the feudal order—a phenomenon which contemporary modernizers might do well to remember. New symbols were also created to ensure the people's allegiance. In particular, the rulers sought to create a cult of reverence for the Meiji emperor.

The Meiji also endeavored to "westernize" significant segments (although not all sectors) of their society. The government encouraged students to travel abroad for technical education. They opened their ports to trade and to European advisers who soon flooded every ministry. They abolished certain feudal practices such as the torture of criminals, and they even ordered civil servants to wear European clothes. They poured effort into the creation of a modern educational system, particularly technical schools. The rulers spent a very high proportion of the national budget on education, especially in contrast to Europe of the time. Within an astonishingly short period, these various measures produced a core of Japanese equipped with modern skills and attitudes.

While the Meiji desired the human resources to staff their expanding industry, they did not by any means wish to disband traditional society. In fact, they deliberately tried to cement the ties which linked a person to his family, his community, his traditional values, and to the Meiji emperor. Among other undertakings, the government legally defined the individual's responsibilities to his family and local village. The law made children responsible for support of their aged relatives (thus instituting an informal system of social security). The courts proclaimed, too, that the head of a family was legally accountable for the actions of any of its members. Only after divorces had been considered by a full family council would the courts take action. Each person had to register himself as a member of his family and the village of his origin, and legally he remained a part of these groups forever.[5] In its educational program, too, the government ensured that the cultivation of modern aptitudes would not disrupt the traditional order, by ordering all schools in 1872 to inculcate reverence for family and emperor as the prime goals of education.

For those who entered the new factories, the government strove to create a social framework which would disturb traditional life in the least possible way. Workers usually remained in the same productive group permanently and were originally recruited on the basis of their previous status in the traditional order. Various social criteria determined the worker's rewards and his position in a complicated hierarchy. As a whole, the factory system exhibited a pronounced paternalistic spirit; employers regarded workers as part of a large family.[6]

These various efforts to ensure the stability of traditional life, as well as the government's emphasis on light, decentralized industry, allowed Japan to avoid the social disorganization which industrialism occasioned in the West. Urbanism proceeded at a relatively slow pace, and the number of people engaged in agriculture remained steady; the sum of those living off the land declined by only 12 per cent between 1868 and 1940. Rates of crime, alcoholism, and other symptoms of social disorder did not skyrocket as they had in nineteenth-century Europe. Observers remarked on the "discipline" of urban laborers and their acceptance of the rigors of factory life. Militant trade unions did not emerge until the 1920's, and the entrepreneurs created by "guided capitalism" did not, as in the West, demand new political rights and power. In its early stages, industrialization for Japan became little more than the frosting on a cake of custom and tradition.

In Japan, therefore, we observe the remarkable case of a nation which truly lifted itself by its bootstraps and did so, even more surprisingly, without the wholesale destruction of tradition which economic growth normally entails. Unblessed with the resources or land or capital of Europe and Russia, Japan underwent a transformation which approached the miraculous. Certainly, the samurai relied on advantages which leaders of contemporary nations can seldom claim: they had a food surplus, export markets in Asia (provided when the Western nations had to withdraw from competition during World War I), and, eventually, colonies. The Meiji could also count on the allegiance of a peasant population long accustomed to national unity and discipline, and undisturbed by the longings for equality and affluence which have appeared in the new nations. Recognition of these differences should not, however, obscure the fact that Japan offers an exciting example of how a determined national elite once reconciled growth with the preservation of traditional society.

NOTES

1. Thomas Smith, *The Agrarian Origins of Modern Japan* (Stanford, Calif.: Stanford University Press, 1959).

2. Robert Bellah, *Tokugawa Religion* (New York: Free Press of Glencoe, Inc., 1957), p. 184.

3. The entire process of capital accumulation has been closely analyzed by Henry Rosovsky in *Capital Formation in Japan* (New York: Free Press of Glencoe, Inc., 1961).

4. Paul Baran, *The Political Economy of Growth* (New York: Monthly Review Press, 1960), p. 155.

5. See Thomas O. Wilkinson, "Family Structure and Industrialization in Japan," *American Sociological Review*, Vol. 27, No. 5, Oct., 1962.

6. See James Abegglen, *The Japanese Factory* (New York: Free Press of Glencoe, Inc., 1958).

23

Mexico—A Model for
Capitalist Development in Latin America?

Robert I. Rhodes

I. THE THESIS

Even a brief survey of Latin America suggests that Mexico is unique. In an area characterized by economic stagnation, political unrest, and military dictatorship, one finds in Mexico a rapidly expanding economy, relatively little political unrest, and a nominally democratic political system. Consequently, many students of Latin America have drawn the apparent conclusion that capitalist development is possible. It is argued that the Mexican experience need not be unique. If, somehow, other countries can carry out the same kinds of institutional reforms that emerged out of the Mexican revolution, then they too will develop.[1]

It is the thesis of this essay that the contrast between Mexico and other major Latin American countries has generally been overdrawn. Three aspects of Mexican society which have often been considered progressive are examined here. In each case one finds a discrepancy between image and reality. The evidence presented suggests that agrarian reform has been more limited than is generally believed; economic expansion may not eliminate the struggle for survival among Mexico's poor; to the extent that the Mexican economy *is* expanding, such expansion does not seem to be caused by Mexico's allegedly nationalistic economic policies, but, rather, to be the result of a fortuitous circumstance.

II. THE FAILURE OF AGRARIAN REFORM

The Mexican revolution had a profound impact on the structure of agrarian Mexico. Before the revolution 1 percent of the population controlled 97 percent of the national territory, while 96 percent of the population controlled only 2 percent. Inequality in rural Mexico is less pronounced today, but, Rodolfo Stavenhagen[2] points out, the revolution and a half century of land distribution have not created a nation of prosperous family-sized farms:

> The traditional hacienda has effectively disappeared from the national agrarian scene, with the exception, perhaps, of some remote regions of Chi-

Reprinted from *Science and Society*, Vol. XXXIV, No. 1 (Spring 1970), pp. 61-77, by permission of the publisher.

huaha or Chiapas. But the great properties which monopolize lands, waters and most other resources in prejudice of the small cultivators (as often private as *ejidal*) continue being more the norm than the exception in many parts of the country.[3]

According to the 1960 agricultural census, less than one-tenth of 1 percent of agricultural units are larger than 400 hectares, but units of this size hold more than 20 percent of total holdings. Contrastingly, 50 percent of Mexico's agricultural units are 5 hectares or smaller, but units of this size hold less than 12 percent of total holdings (Table 1).

As one would expect, there are corresponding differences in income. In 1961–62, the monthly family income of 45 percent of Mexico's rural families was 300 pesos or less (Table 2). Since there are 12.5 pesos to the dollar, this amounts to a yearly family income of $278 or less. In the same period about one-half of 1 percent of Mexico's rural families had incomes in excess of 3000 pesos per month.

Not surprisingly, low incomes are associated with short life expectancies and high infant mortality rates. Especially with regard to infant mortality rates, official government figures are quite misleading. Eduardo Cordero has found that in some areas, real infant mortality rates are two to two-and-a-half times the reported rates. According to his estimates, in 1965 five states had infant mortality rates in excess of 100 per thousand, while five states had infant mortality rates of under 60 per thousand.[4] These regional differences only suggest the enormous disparities in living condi-

Table 1   The Structure of Land Tenure in Mexico, 1960

	% of Parcels	% of Area
5 Hectares or less	49.45	11.75
From 5.1 to 10 Hectares	40.09	34.04
From 10.1 to 25 Hectares	7.47	11.94
From 25.1 to 50 Hectares	1.58	6.06
From 50.1 to 100 Hectares	0.82	6.38
From 100.1 to 200 Hectares	0.39	5.66
From 200.1 to 400 Hectares	0.12	3.78
More than 400 Hectares	0.08	20.39
Total	100.00	100.00

Adapted from: Carlos Tello, *La Tenencia de la Tierra en México*, Mexico, Universidad Nacional Autónoma de México, 1968. Untitled table, p. 69.

Table 2   Percent of Families by Income Levels and Region, 1961–62

Levels of monthly family income in pesos	% Urban	% Rural	% Total
Up to 300	9.68	45.52	26.00
From 301 to 500	20.60	27.83	23.89
From 501 to 1000	34.18	18.84	27.19
From 1001 to 3000	30.14	7.42	19.79
More than 3000	5.39	.40	3.12
Total	99.99	100.01	99.99

Adapted from: Pablo González Casanova, *La Democracia en México*, Mexico, Ediciones, ERA, 1965. Appendix table "Numero y Porciento de Familias por Niveles de Ingreso y Poblacion Urbana y Rural (1961–62)," p. 277.

tions which characterize different income strata in urban as well as rural areas.

Officially the Mexican government is deeply committed to the struggle against illiteracy and it points proudly to a history of dramatic progress. Yet, here again, there is a major discrepancy between image and reality. According to official statistics, in the decades from 1910 through 1950 literacy in rural areas increased steadily from roughly 20 to 85 percent.[5] But as late as 1961–62 more than 80 percent of rural Mexicans had at most three years of schooling (Table 3). When one considers that many parts of

Table 3 Rural and Urban Population According to Years of Approved Study (1961–62)

Years of approved study	Rural	Urban
0 to 3	81.2	29.4
4 to 6	16.3	45.5
7 to 9	1.9	14.8
10 to 11	0.2	2.9
12 or more	0.4	7.4
Total	100.0	100.0

Source: Pablo González Casanova, "Enajenación y Conciencia de Clases en México," in *Ensayos Sobre las Clases Sociales en México*, Mexico, Editorial Nuestro Tiempo, 1968. Table, p. 166.

rural Mexico are so backward that there is little opportunity to practice whatever reading skills one may have learned in school, it is obvious that the official statistics are more than optimistic.

The absence of adequate credit facilities is a major problem in rural Mexico. Cultivators of small parcels cannot obtain credit from commercial banks. They must borrow money from government banks, relatives, or local moneylenders. If one is poor, it is not likely that relatives can be of much assistance, and local credit is both scarce and expensive. This means that if one is an *ejidatario*,[6] one must borrow from the appropriate government bank—the *Banco Nacional de Crédito Ejidal*. Similarly, if one is a small landowner one must borrow from the *Banco Nacional de Crédito Agricola*. According to the *Banco de México*, these two sources account for only 20 percent of the total credit lent to Mexican agriculturalists by all sources.[7] The *Banco de México* justifies this inequitable situation in the following terms:

> Banks are merely financial middlemen; other organizations should solve social problems. Agricultural banks may have to be reorganized, as well as all primary activities, but even banks must recover loans.[8]

We find here an indirect rationalization for the government's increasingly restrictive credit policies. What lies behind this policy?

Since the establishment of the *Banco Ejidal*, yearly losses have increased rapidly. Moreover, in the period from 1936 to 1960 the bank lent over $680 million and lost more than 23 percent of this sum.[9] Since 1962, loans to small holders (*ejidatario* as well as private) have declined, but until recently officials have avoided commenting officially on the economic viability of the small agricultural units created by the Mexican revolution and its aftermath. This is no longer true. In the name of economic rationality Mexico's peasantry is being abandoned, but the real situation is very different from that put forward officially.

According to the 1960 agricultural census, *ejidos* employed 43 percent of agricultural labor and produced 43 percent of Mexico's agricultural produce. Yet, according to the census, this sector received only 30 percent of agricultural capital (this is a very generous estimate). These data illustrate a point which could be documented in much greater detail—the concentration of capital in large private agricultural holdings displaces labor but does not increase production to a significant extent.[10] Given these facts, how does one explain the heavy losses of the *Banco Ejidal* and the increasing denial of government credit to small holders?

Generally speaking, government institutions have been more concerned with the creation and maintenance of new forms of dependency and exploitation than with the economic security and independence of Mexico's peasantry.[11] Though the *Banco Ejidal* may once have been concerned with "solving social problems," its concerns have always been more political than economic or social. Loans have been utilized as a means of social control and patronage; they have been used to consolidate the power of the *Partido Revolucionario Institucional* (PRI) in areas of potential agrarian unrest.[12] Even where there may be a genuine commitment to economic development, the pervasive corruption in Mexican government hurts most those who need the greatest assistance. Truly enormous sums are accumulated in a system of corruption that reaches from the lowest to the highest levels of government.[13] Though accounts of corruption are very widespread and a whole body of humor has developed around the subject of corruption and extortion (referred to as *la mordida*—the bite), it is hard to estimate its impact on official government policies. But the nature of the problem in agriculture has been ably described by Charles Erasmus:

> The major reason for popular distrust of the Ejido Bank is its reputation for graft, which is managed in innumerable ways. For example, Bank officials may get a percentage on all purchases of insecticide, fertilizer and farm machinery ordered for ejidos. This is undoubtedly one reason why some collectives were so overloaded with debts that they were never able to show a profit. Fertilizers have been used on newly cleared lands without any preliminary soil tests and ejidatarios have often been encouraged to buy unnecessary farm machinery. One ejido was induced to dig a great many wells and install expensive pumping equipment only two years before the area was to receive water by gravity from the new irrigation system. Graft was involved in the construction of the wells and in the purchase of the equipment. A popular pun sums up the Bank's reputation: *Banjidal*, a common abbreviation of Banco Ejidal used in newspaper captions or painted on Bank equipment, is often read *bandidal* or "bandit gang."
>
> Graft extends down into the ejido itself. Only too often the president, secretary, and vigilante of the ejido come to an agreement with the Bank inspector during a friendly drinking session at a bar in town. From then on they may find many ways to graft ejido funds. Part of the harvest, for example, may never be entered in the accounts. Ejido members may be credited with more days of work than they are paid for and the difference pocketed

by the officials. Expenses may be padded, especially for repairs to equipment. Several ejidatarios told me that they had learned to read, write, and calculate since becoming ejidatarios so that they could defend themselves against the *mordilones* (grafters) within the Bank and their own ejidos. But even those who are able to read and write do not always get the chance to defend themselves. Members of several of the new Yaqui collectives complained that they never were told of ejido expenses or even the size of their harvests. They had no way of estimating for themselves what profits should be, and when they asked their credit society officials for an accounting, they were rebuffed. Some of the heads of ejidos were illiterate and did not understand the accounts; others acted insulted and accused their questioners of impugning their integrity.[14]

The political character of the *Banco Ejidal* and the pervasiveness of corruption within the bank in large measure explain the heavy losses that it has sustained through the years.

In a recent review of agrarian reform in Bolivia, Venezuela, and Mexico, Charles Erasmus concluded that the removal of old forms of economic exploitation without a change in agricultural technology results in new forms of exploitation and little change in the level and quality of life.[15] Though there have been some excellent theoretical discussions of these forms of exploitation and some suggestive descriptive studies, the available literature is meager.[16] Essentially, what is described is a system of interdependency within which the countryside is exploited by the city, and within the countryside those groups and classes in strategic positions exploit those who are dependent upon them. Pablo González Casanova has called these processes internal colonialism, and constructed a list of its forms. A partial listing of these includes:

1. Monopoly of commerce and trade by the "dominant" (relations of unfavorable interchange for the native community, speculation, acquisition of premature harvests, hoarding of merchandise).
2. Monopoly of credit (usury, control of native production).
3. Decapitalization.
4. Reinforcement of the dependence (juridical, political, military and economic measures).
5. Joint exploitation of the Indian population by the different social classes of the Ladino population.
6. Exploitation of the artisan.
7. Social discrimination (humiliation and oppression).
8. Linguistic discrimination.
9. Political discrimination (colonialist attitudes of local and federal functionaries, lack of political control by the natives in their own municipalities).
10. Fiscal discrimination (taxes and excises).
11. Discrimination in public trade.
12. Discrimination in official credit.
13. Other forms of discrimination (barter, measurements, weights).
14. Process of displacement of the Indian by the Ladino (as governor, proprietor, merchant).
15. Magico-religious culture and economic manipulation (prestige economy) and political manipulation (collective vote).[17]

It would be unfair to hold the present regime responsible for the creation and development of all of these conditions. Particularly in its early years, the Mexican revolutionary government simply did not have the resources to transform the agrarian scene. However, this is no longer the case. As we have seen, the government bureaucracy participates in the exploitation of rural Mexico. The manipulation of Mexico's peasantry becomes overtly political during Mexican elections.

In many parts of Latin America the retainers of large landowners see to it that peasants support conservative interests at the polls. In Mexico this function has been taken over by the apparatus of the ruling party—the PRI. The effectiveness of this political regime can be seen by examining support for opposition parties in Mexican elections. In the 1961 and 1964 elections in five of Mexico's most backward states, the following opposition votes were cast: Chiapas 0.73 and 1.81 percent; Guerrero 7.37 and 4.55 percent; Hidalgo 1.25 and 1.14 percent; Oaxaca 5.17 and 6.41 percent; and Tlaxcala 0.27 and 6.22 percent. In the most prosperous states opposition parties received much more substantial support in these two elections: Baja California Norte 33.01 and 28.78 percent; Distrito Federal 35.32 and 34.01 percent; Morelos 26.90 and 8.02 percent; and Chihuahua 18.09 and 23.29 percent.[18] Evidently the PRI and other political organizations controlled by the present regime have become so strong that the government need no longer finance small agriculturalists.

This political analysis of agrarian Mexico could be duplicated in other sectors of Mexican society and similar conclusions drawn. A cohesive national bourgeoisie has created a remarkable political structure that maintains the existing system of power and privilege.

III. POPULATION AND WELFARE TRENDS

The spread of public health services in the last fifty years in combination with an improvement in the standard of living of most Mexicans has created a population explosion in Mexico. In the same period a heavy migration to the cities has reduced the rate of population growth in the countryside (Table 4). But land is no longer being redistributed to any significant degree and government irrigation projects have been too limited in scale and have favored capital-intensive holdings. As a result, rural Mexico is once again becoming populated by landless agricultural laborers. Between 1950 and 1960 the number of landless agricultural workers increased from 2.079 million to 3.273 million, and became a majority of Mexico's agricultural work force.

Table 4   Annual Rates of Increase in Population

Period	Population		
	% Urban	% Rural	% Total
1930–1940	2.22	1.49	1.73
1940–1950	4.77	1.50	2.73
1950–1960	3.08	4.89	1.51

Source: Rodolfo Stavenhagen, "Aspectos Sociales de la Estructura Agraria en México," in *Neolatifundismo y Explotacion*, Mexico, Editorial Nuestro Tiempo, 1968. Table, p. 27.

Some observers remain relatively optimistic about Mexico's future despite its population explosion, and there are some grounds for optimism. Mexico's economy is expanding much faster than its population, as can be seen from Table 5. In addition, all of Mexico's social indicators have shown

Table 5 Trends in National Income, Population, and Per Capital Income

Year	% Annual Increase in National Income (1950 pesos)	% Annual Population Increase	% Per Capita Income Increase
1950	3.2	3.1	2.1
1958	5.4	3.1	1.9
1959	3.0	3.1	−0.3
1960	8.0	3.1	4.9
1961	3.4	3.3	0.1
1962	5.1	3.3	1.7
1963	6.4	3.3	3.0
1964	10.0	3.3	6.5
1965	5.3	3.6	1.6
1966	7.6	3.6	3.9

Adapted from: Joseph S. La Cascia, *Capital Formation and Economic Development in Mexico,* New York, Frederick A. Praeger, 1969. Table 17 "National Income, Population, and Per Capita Income," p. 80.

Table 6 Infant Mortality Rates

Year	Reported Rate	Calculated Rate	Index	% Omissions $\frac{(2)-(1)}{2}$
1930	147.63	244.27	100	39.6
1940	124.61	207.29	85	39.9
1950	101.29	155.52	64	34.9
1960	73.87	88.22	36	16.3
1965	65.42	77.60	32	15.7

Adapted from: Eduardo Cordero, "La subestimación de la mortalidad infantil en México," *Demografia y Economia*, Vol. II, No. 1, 1968, pp. 44–62. Table 6 "México: Cálculo de las q_0, total de la República," p. 55.

steady progress through the years. But an examination of Eduardo Cordero's revised infant mortality rates suggests a disturbing trend. An examination of Table 6 shows that between 1960 and 1965 there was relatively little improvement in these figures.[19] Moreover, a graphic projection of the existing trend indicates that Mexico's infant mortality rate seems to be approaching a plateau around approximately 60 per thousand. By way of comparison, the infant mortality rate in Mississippi is probably not over 40 per thousand.[20] A preliminary examination of Cordero's regional data suggests that there is surprisingly little relationship between regional urbanization and infant mortality. Apparently migration to the city no longer assures an improvement in the standard of living of many Mexicans. Cash incomes may be higher but everything has a price in the city.

It remains to be seen whether Mexico's continued economic expansion will improve the lives of Mexico's poor, but there is no doubt that it is providing Mexico's rich with increasing quantities of luxury goods. The available statistics often do not distinguish between luxury and nonluxury goods, but the sale of automobiles does give us a crude estimate of the rate at which luxury purchases are growing. In the period from 1960 to 1966, Mexico's real national income increased 44 percent, while in the same period sales of cars increased 152 percent.[21] And, as one would expect, it is those who have comparatively large incomes who buy cars. In 1963, approximately 90 percent of Mexico's cars were owned by Mexican families in the top income decile.[22]

Liberal students of Mexican society have generally deplored the great inequalities in Mexican society, but have argued that the masses must make sacrifices if development is to take place. But, as we shall see, development and luxury goods may not be compatible.

IV. TAKE-OFF INTO UNSUSTAINED GROWTH[23]

Mexico's economic expansion has been accompanied by the rapid development of an impressive industrial base. By 1953 Mexico was producing meaningful amounts of most basic industrial materials. If we compare production of selected items in the period 1953–64 we find the following increases: Crude oil 75 percent, electricity 175 percent, steel ingots 344 percent, electrolytic copper 133 percent, sulfuric acid 328 percent, caustic soda 628 percent, fertilizers 513 percent and cement 160 percent.[24] In this period savings in the private sector have been rougly one-tenth of national income, but they have not been growing as rapidly as Mexico's national income, and more seriously, investment of private domestic funds has generally gone into light manufacturing and service industries.[25] Mexico's infrastructure and petroleum industry have been developed by the national government, which has financed its development activities through loans from the Import Export Bank of Washington, D.C., IBRD, BID, AID, and private United States banks. The dependency of the public sector on financial institutions controlled by the United States is paralleled by the dependence on direct foreign investment (overwhelmingly United States) in key Mexican industries. The national policy of "Mexicanization" of industry has placed nominal

Table 7A   Mexico: Direct Foreign Investments (Thousands of Dollars)

Year	New Investments	*Outflow of Exchange on Foreign Investment	Balance
1950	38,010	47,578	− 9,568
1955	84,926	67,132	17,794
1960	62,466	130,996	− 68,530
1961	81,826	122,889	− 41,063
1962	74,871	123,154	− 48,283
1963	76,944	149,527	− 72,583
1964	83,075	185,863	−102,788

* All remittances.

Adapted from: Nacional Financiera, *Statistics On The Mexican Economy*, Mexico, 1966. Table 103, pp. 217, 218.

Table 7B   Mexico: Direct Foreign Investments (Millions of Dollars)

Year	New Investment	Outflow of Exchange due to Interest Payment on Foreign Investments	Balance
1961	81.8	148.1	− 66.3
1962	74.9	159.3	− 84.4
1963	76.9	185.6	−108.7
1964	95.1	236.1	−141.0
1965	120.1	234.9	−114.8
1966*	109.1	203.7	− 94.6
1967*	67.9	216.5	−148.6
1968**	44.4	39.0	5.4

* Excludes reinvested earnings, as they remained in Mexico.
** Up to June.

Source: Banco de México, *Review of the Economic Situation of Mexico* (RESM), Nov. 1968. Table, p. 11.

control in the hands of nationals, but the technology and a very large proportion of capital is supplied from outside. Thus real control of Mexico's industry lies beyond its national boundaries.[26]

Mexico's reliance on direct foreign investment for industrial development has led to an increasingly serious foreign exchange imbalance. The outflow of earnings, interest, and fees derived from direct foreign investment becomes ever larger than the investment of new capital. The loss of foreign exchange associated with direct foreign investment is now well over $100 million a year (Table 7). There is no reason to expect that this trend will be halted or reversed. A similar situation in the public sector is developing slowly but steadily. Mexico's external public indebtedness increased from $0.29 to 1.88 billion in the period 1950–66.[27] In relation to exports this represents a steadily worsening situation since 1955. In 1955 external public indebtedness was 54 percent of exports; in 1966 it was 159 percent of exports (Table 8).

There has been no fundamental change in Mexico's export structure. Despite its relatively large and sophisticated industrial base, in the period 1961–67 the export of manufactured goods varied erratically from 16.4 to

Table 8   External Public Debt Compared with Gross National Product, and with Exports (Millions of Pesos)

Year	A External Public Debt	B Gross National Product	C A/B %	D Exports of Goods	E A/D %
1950	3,747	40,600	9.2	4,339	86.3
1955	5,172	87,300	5.9	9,484	54.5
1960	10,167	154,100	6.6	9,247	109.9
1961	13,543	163,800	8.2	10,044	134.8
1962	14,075	177,500	7.9	11,243	125.1
1963	16,437	192,200	7.5	11,699	140.5
1964	21,537	224,600	9.6	12,780	168.5
1965	22,675	242,700	9.3	13,883	163.3
1966	23,637	272,100	8.3	14,905	158.6

Adapted from: Banco de México, RESM, Oct. 1967. Table, p. 6.

21.0 percent of Mexico's total exports.[28] The failure to develop a dynamic industrial export sector is particularly serious because, as Mexico has developed, its import needs have also increased. In the period 1959–66 Mexico's national income increased 56 percent. At the same time, all major categories of imports rose at roughly the same rate: consumer goods 48 percent, producer goods 62 percent, raw and semi-finished materials 56 percent, capital goods 67 percent, and total imports 60 percent.[29] In the course of rapid industrialization one expects a major increase in the importation of capital goods and some industrial materials; but here an increasing demand for luxury goods and intermediate products indicates a failure to control both the importation of luxury goods and their production at home. The inevitable result of these trends is a deterioration in Mexico's balance on goods and services. This can be seen from the following balances expressed in millions of dollars: 1950 (40.2), 1958 (−268.0), 1959 (−146.6), 1960 (−311.1), 1961 (−220.5), 1962 (−156.4), 1963 (−206.0), 1964 (−406.4), 1965 (−375.7), and 1966 (−345.8); and another series, 1966 (−296.1), 1967 (−502.2), and 1968 (−595.5).[30]

At this point one must ask how Mexico has been able to develop as far as it has despite an import-export structure and a capital dependency that is so similar to that of other underdeveloped countries. Why hasn't Mexico been faced with recurrent foreign exchange problems, devaluation, deflationary measures, and the chronic stagnation associated with these events? The answer to this question has little to do with Mexico's allegedly nationalistic economic policies. It is, rather, due to a fortuitous circumstance over which Mexico has no control. Mexico's common border with the United States has given it a competitive advantage in the exportation of agricultural commodities and, more crucially, in the income from tourism. In the period 1960–66 Mexico's income from tourism increased from $155 to 328 million—an increase of 112 percent.[31] In the same period the export of goods and services as a whole increased only 57 percent while the gross national product increased 77 percent.[32]

It seems likely that if present trends are maintained, Mexico will become a victim of the same economic forces that have led to economic stagnation in less fortunate countries, but this will occur at a more advanced stage in its economic development. But will present trends necessarily be maintained? Mexico *could* institute meaningful import quotas, restrict the production of luxury goods, and institute a highly progressive tax system. These measures would allow Mexico to protect its foreign exchange position and control its own future. But they would also alienate Mexico's middle sectors and bourgeoisie. And would the United States stand by in polite neutrality? Mexico's dependence upon the United States probably makes genuine economic nationalism impossible in anything short of a revolutionary situation.

V. STRUCTURAL CONVERGENCE AND DEVELOPMENT

Liberal social scientists have a stake in Mexican development, for as long as Mexico continues to develop, the claim can be made that capitalist development is possible in Latin America. The tendency to emphasize the progressive aspects of Mexican society is also enhanced by the historians' interest in historical differences. But I believe the importance of these differences has been exaggerated. The remarkable thing about Mexico is that, despite its glorious revolution and all the institutional changes associated with it, its class structure and economic organization are all too familiar. What would happen to Mexican politics if the Mexican economy ceased to expand? The most probable result would be increasing economic and political strife, followed by greater political repression.

It is likely that within underdeveloped capitalist nations the rapid expansion of population, the ever swifter growth of urban areas, the increased demand for sophisticated consumer goods, and the ever greater dependence upon the major industrialized countries lead to increasing structural similarity. Moreover, it is doubtful that development can take place within this context. The future course of Mexican history will provide a crucial test of this thesis.

NOTES

1. The major institutional reforms usually referred to include land and agrarian reform, a reduction in the influence of the military and the church, and a nationalistic economic policy. I would argue that it is very unlikely that these reforms can be carried out without violence, and a capitalist revolution of the kind peculiar to Mexico is no longer possible. But these issues are beyond the scope of this essay.
2. Rodolfo Stavenhagen, "Aspectos Sociales de la Estructura Agraria en México," in *Neolatifundismo y Explotacion* (Mexico, 1968).
3. *Ibid.*, p. 19.
4. Eduardo Cordero, "La subestimación de la mortalidad infantil en México," *Demografia y Economia*, II, 1, 1968, Table 9, "Mexico: Calculo de las tasas de mortalidad infantil," 1965, 59.
5. Pablo González Casanova, *La Democracia en México* (Mexico, 1965), p. 77.
6. *Ejidatarios* are peasants who have been granted control of *ejido* plots. *Ejido* lands may not be sold or leased. With government approval they may be passed on to one's children, but the parcels must be passed on to only one child—they may not be subdivided.
7. Banco de México, *Review of the Economic Situation of Mexico* (RESM), Feb. 1968, Table "Total Credits To Agriculture in Mexico, 1961," p. 10. The bank rejected several more recent estimates and suggested this was the best estimate available.
8. RESM, Feb. 1968, pp. 10, 11.
9. Emilio Romero Espinosa, *La Reforma Agraria En México* (Mexico, 1963), Table, p. 111.
10. Stavenhagen, "Aspectos . . . ," pp. 24–37.
11. The following works written by Charles J. Erasmus discuss the relationship between government and peasantry in greater detail: "Upper Limits of Peasantry and Agrarian Reform: Bolivia, Venezuela, and Mexico Compared," *Ethnology*, VI, 4 (Oct. 1967), 349–380; "Community Development and the Encogido Syndrome," *Human Organization*, XXVII, 1 (Spring 1968), 65–73; and *Man Takes Control* (Indianapolis, 1961). See also Stavenhagen, "Aspectos . . . ," especially pp. 38–40.
12. Arturo Warman, "La Corrupción en el Campo: un Medio de Control Social," in *La Corrupción* (Mexico, 1969), pp. 87–107.
13. For an estimate of the magnitude of the sums accumulated by those in key positions, and a general discussion of the spoils system in Mexico

and its contribution to political stability see Frank R. Brandenburg, *The Making of Modern Mexico* (Englewood Cliffs, 1964), pp. 156–65.

14. Erasmus, *Man Takes Control*, pp. 222, 223.

15. Erasmus, "Upper Limits . . . ," p. 379.

16. Two excellent general discussions are Pablo González Casanova, "Internal Colonialism and National Development," in *Latin American Radicalism*, ed. by Irving Louis Horowitz and others (New York, 1969), pp. 118–39: Rodolfo Stavenhagen, "Classes, Colonialism, and Acculturation," in *Comparative Perspectives on Stratification: Mexico, Great Britain, Japan* (Boston, 1968), pp. 31–63. For useful surveys of the descriptive literature see Gerritt Huizer, "Community development and conflicting rural interests," *América Indigena*, XXVIII, 3, (July 1968), 619–29; and Robert Hunt, Agentes culturales mestizos: estabilidad y cambio en Oaxaca," *América Indigena*, XXVIII, 3 (July 1968), 595–609. An historical perspective can be found in David Kaplan, "City and Countryside in Mexican History," *América Indigena*, XXIV, 1 (Jan. 1964), 59–69.

17. González Casanova, "Internal Colonialism," pp. 137–39.

18. González Casanova, *La Democracia* . . . , p. 117 and Table, p. 266.

19. The most systematic attempt that has been made to construct a poverty index for Mexico is that of James W. Wilkie. He describes his index in the following way: The items cover the persons actually stating in the census that they (1) are illiterate, (2) speak only an Indian language, (3) live in a community with less than 2500 persons, (4) go barefoot, (5) wear sandals, (6) regularly eat tortillas instead of wheat bread and (7) are without sewerage disposal (p. 205). *The Mexican Revolution: Federal Expenditure and Social Change Since 1910*, Chapter 9: "An Index of Poverty" (Berkeley, 1967). In order to measure the extent of agreement between infant mortality and Wilkie's poverty index I calculated the Spearman rank order correlation of their 1960 figures (enumerated by states and the Federal District). The coefficient r_s was a very modest .37 which suggests that they measure very different phenomena. I believe the infant mortality rate is a much more meaningful measure of real deprivation than Wilkie's poverty index. (Since Wilkie's poverty index is based upon census data I was not able to compare his index to Cordero's infant mortality rates after 1960. Both show a steady improvement in conditions through 1960.)

20. The official rate is 35.5 per thousand (1967) which is almost certainly an underestimate. If we add 15 percent (Mexico's underestimate in 1965) we have a rate of around 40. In 1967 the infant mortality rate for the United States as a whole was 22.5. *Information Please Almanac 1970* (New York, 1970), p. 645.

21. RESM, Feb., 1968, p. 12.

22. Based upon a comparison of Table 2 with Table "Number of Automobiles Owned, According to Level of Income, 1963," RESM, Feb., 1968, p. 13.

23. For a more general discussion of some of the issues raised here see David Felix, "Economic Development: Take-offs Into Unsustained Growth," *Social Research*, XXXVI, 2 (Summer 1969), 267–93.

24. Nacional Financiera, *Statistics On The Mexican Economy*, Mexico, 1966, Tables 23, 25, 36, 37, 38, 44, 54.

25. See Alonso Aguilar Monteverde, "El Proceso de Acumulacion de Capital," in *Mexico: Riqueza y Miseria* (Mexico, 1967), pp. 13–90, especially pp. 20, 27, and 53.

26. Aguilar Monteverde, "El proceso . . . ," especially pp. 32, 33.

27. See Table 8.

28. RESM, Table "Mexican Exports" (1961–1967), April 1968, p. 5.

29. Joseph S. La Cascia, *Capital Formation and Economic Development in Mexico* (New York, 1969), Table 34 "Imports by Major Commodity Groups," pp. 140, 141.

30. La Cascia, *Capital Formation* . . . , Appendix Table 38 "Balance of Payments," pp. 146, 147; and RESM, Table "Mexico's Relations with other Countries" (1961–1968), p. 21. The great variation in this downward trend is not due to an erratic demand for imports which have risen steadily.

Rather, it is due to an erratic demand for a small number of major export items. This phenomenon is characteristic of underdeveloped countries.

31. RESM, Table "Income from Tourism in Mexico" (1960–1966), Sept. 1967, p. 11. Tourism increased even more rapidly in 1967 and 1968 than in earlier years. RESM Table "Mexico's Relations with other Countries," May 1969, p. 21.

32. La Cascia, *Capital Formation* . . . , Appendix Table 38 "Balance of Payments," pp. 146, 147 and Appendix Table 51 "GNP, Population, and Per Capita GNP," p. 161.

24

The Brazilian "Model" of Development

Celso Furtado

The Brazilian economy constitutes a very interesting example of how far a country can go in the process of industrialization without abandoning its main features of underdevelopment: great disparity in productivity between urban and rural areas, a large majority of the population living at a physiological subsistence level, increasing masses of underemployed people in the urban zones, etc. The idea, implicit in the growth models of the genus started by Lewis, that steering the surplus of an underdeveloped economy toward the industrial sector (the activities absorbing technical progress) would ultimately create an economic system of increasing homogeneity (where the wage rate tends to increase in all economic activities *pari passu* with the average productivity of the system), has been thoroughly disproved.

The objectives of this paper are (a) to investigate why the worldwide diffusion of technical progress and the resulting increases in productivity have not tended to liquidate underdevelopment; and (b) to demonstrate that a policy of "development," geared to satisfy the high levels of consumption of a small minority of the population, such as that carried out in Brazil, tends to aggravate social inequalities and to increase the social cost of an economic system.

A significant element in our model is the hypothesis that underdevelopment is an aspect of the way industrial capitalism has been growing and spreading from the beginning. It is important to keep in mind that the industrial revolution took place inside an expanding commercial economy, in which foreign trade certainly was the most profitable activity; furthermore, the industrial revolution in turn spurred this trade. In the particular and fundamental case of Great Britain, the share of foreign trade in the economy increased enormously, giving rise to a complex system of international division of labor. The study of underdevelopment must start with the identification of the particular types of structures created in the periphery of the capitalist economy by this system of international division of labor. Therefore, to build a model of an underdeveloped economy as a closed system is totally misleading. To isolate an underdeveloped economy

This paper originated in a talk given to the author's Seminar in Economic Development at the American University, Fall 1972. It was put into written form expressly for this book of readings. © Celso Furtado.

from the general context of the expanding capitalist system is to dismiss from the beginning the fundamental problem of the nature of the external relationships of such an economy, namely, the fact of its global dependence. The first part of this paper will deal with this general problem, presented here in a rather schematic way. Most of the assumptions require additional empirical work to be adequately established. However, if the framework presented here helps in understanding better the different types of under-development, it will also be useful in providing more relevant interpretations of the vast empirical work currently being done on the so-called developing countries.

DEVELOPMENT AND MODERNIZATION

Let us define technical progress as the introduction of new productive processes capable of increasing efficiency in the utilization of scarce resources and/or the introduction of new products capable of being added to the basket of consumers' goods and services. And let us assume that economic development implies diffusion in the use of products already known and/or the insertion of new products into the basket of consumers' goods.

Because access to new products is with rare exceptions restricted, at least during a first phase, to a minority formed by high income people, development based mainly on the introduction of new products corresponds to a process of income concentration. And because diffusion means access of more people to the use of known products, development based mainly on diffusion corresponds to a process of greater equality in the distribution of income. Furthermore, a necessary condition in any process of economic development is accumulation of capital, as important for the diffusion of known products as for the introduction of new ones. But there are reasons to believe that the insertion of new products into the basket of consumers' goods requires relatively more capital accumulation than the diffusion of known products. For example: the introduction of a new model of automobile of a certain class requires more investment (including research and development) per unit than the increase in the production of the corresponding model already being produced. A different way of focusing on this problem is as follows: the more diversified a basket of consumers' goods, the higher has to be the income of the person consuming these goods, and the larger the amount of capital required to satisfy the needs of that person. The average American citizen receives an annual income of approximately $4,000, and a certain basket of consumers' goods corresponds to that level of income. This basket of goods has been made possible by a process of capital accumulation that now adds up to something like $12,000 per person living in the country. The average Brazilian receives an annual income of something like $400 and the capital accumulated in Brazil adds up to something around $1,000. Thus, the basket of consumers' goods to which the average Brazilian has access has to be much less diversified than that available in the United States.

Increases in the income of a community may result from at least three different processes: (a) economic development, that is, accumulation of capital and adoption of more effective productive processes; (b) the depletion of non-renewable natural resources; and (c) reallocation of resources aiming at geographic specialization, through the pursuit of comparative advantages in a system of international division of labor. Increases in income entail diversification of consumption, adoption of new products, etc. These increases, therefore, can be present in a community without economic development, that is, without capital accumulation and introduction of more efficient productive processes. They may merely be the result of an increase in income due to (b) and/or (c) above. Let us call *modernization* this process of adoption of new patterns of consumption corresponding to higher levels of income in the absence of economic development.

The countries now known as underdeveloped are those where there occurred a process of modernization: new patterns of consumption (introduction of new products) were adopted as a result of an increase in income generated by the type of changes referred to in (b) and (c) above. Brazil is a country where increases in income (economic productivity) were, during a long period, basically the result of a simple reallocation of resources aiming at maximization of static comparative advantages in foreign trade. The shift from subsistence agriculture into commercial agriculture does not necessarily presuppose a shift from traditional into modern agriculture. But, when generated by foreign trade, such a shift entails a significant rise in economic productivity, and may initiate a process of modernization. How important such a process will be depends on the institutional matrix at the time of its inception. In Brazil, because of the concentration of property in land and the abundance of labor in subsistence agriculture, the increases in productivity benefited mainly a small minority. However, because of the large population, the modernized minority was sizable enough to allow a full urban development and a beginning of industrialization.

In those countries where modernization occurred without economic development, the process of industrialization presents very particular features. Thus, the market for manufactured products is formed by two completely different groups of people: the first, consumers of very low income (the bulk of the population) and the second, a rich minority. The basket of consumers' goods corresponding to the first group is only slightly diversified and tends to remain without modifications because the real wage rate is rather stable. Industries producing this basket of goods have weak linkages: they use raw materials from agriculture (food and textile industries) and produce directly for the final consumer. Furthermore, such industries benefit little from economies of scale and externalities. The basket of consumers' goods corresponding to the second group, being fully diversified, requires a complex process of industrialization to be domestically produced. The main obstacle here stems from the dimension of the local market. This is the sector of the market that is really expanding, however, and full industrialization will only be possible if geared to it. Given the different behavior of the two baskets of consumers' goods—one expanding slowly and without introduction of new goods, and the other growing quickly, mainly through the inclusion of new products—the two industrial sectors compete only to a small degree for the same markets and may keep different standards of organization and marketing. But, once the sector catering to the rich minority comes to the fore, requirements in capital and modern technology tend to increase rapidly. Consequently, creation of new jobs per unit of investment declines and the need to keep up with the flow of new products increases. Furthermore, as a spin off of the process of full industrialization, based on the second basket of consumers' goods, the industries catering to the mass of the population are bound to pass through important transformations. Economies of scale and externalities may also benefit the mass of the population, and products such as plastics and synthetic fibers be added to the popular basket of goods. As a consequence of the progressive integration of the industrial apparatus, more capital intensive processes tend to be adopted in the industries that first developed in competition with local handicraft activities. Technical progress is no longer a matter of buying a certain type of equipment, but a question of having access to the innovations pouring into the rich countries. In this phase, the branches of the multinational corporations (MNCs) will easily supersede the local firms, particularly in the industries geared to the diversified basket. More precisely, such a diversified basket of consumers' goods would never be locally produced if the flow of technical innovations had to be paid at market prices. In spite of the fact that for an MNC operating in an underdeveloped country the opportunity cost of such a flow of innovations is practically zero, the corporation would never make it available to independent local firms except for a very high price.

The industrialization of the economies that start with the process of modernization is bound to face a double difficulty: if the local industries remain producing for the first basket (industries with weak linkage) and the second basket has to be imported, the country will never reach the point required to form an industrial system; and if the local industries get into the production of the second basket, decreasing returns may show up because of the smallness of the local market. A few countries of large demographic dimensions and with a highly productive exporting sector have succeeded in overcoming these obstacles. Such has been the case with Brazil. This does not mean that industrial capitalism can operate in Brazil following the rules that prevail in a developed economy. In the latter case, expansion of production signifies parallel expansion in the cost of labor, that is, in the value added by labor during the production process. And because demand is mainly generated by payments to labor, expansion of demand is bound to follow the increase in production. In the underdeveloped economy, value added by labor is bound to decline in relative terms during the phases of expansion. Increases in productivity created by internal economies or externalities tend to benefit the owners of capital exclusively, and, given the structure of markets, nothing will press them to transfer the fruits of increased productivity to the consumers, the modernized minority. On the other hand, raising the wage rate would increase costs without enlarging the market, because the workers are linked to a different basket of goods. The fact is that the system operates spontaneously, benefiting too small a minority, the owners of capital. How should the process of income concentration, inherent to the system, be steered in order to create a link between the increase in productivity in the industries producing the second basket and the consumers who have access to that basket? In the third part of this paper we will examine the particular type of solution used in Brazil.

THE PERFORMANCE OF THE BRAZILIAN ECONOMY

In the last twenty-five years the Brazilian economy has been growing at a relatively high rate. Given "normal" levels of agricultural production, in terms of trade and public expenditures, a growth rate of about 6 percent a year could be expected. The very rich natural resources, the size of the population, and the average level of income attained in the past through maximization of static comparative advantages in foreign trade converge to produce this growth potential. Furthermore, fluctuations in the rate of growth of the gross domestic product (GDP) had little effect on the process of capital formation. The rates of saving and investment have been rather stable. Changes in the rate of growth of the GDP basically reflect modifications in the degree of utilization of the productive capacity already installed. In the elementary language of growth models, we would say that changes in the rate of growth are mainly caused by modifications in the parameter that represents the relationship between output and the stock of reproducible capital, and that the other parameter, representing the relationship between investment and income, tends to be stable.

In fact, the first parameter (output-capital ratio) doubled between 1964–67 and 1968–69, whereas the second (rate of investment) increased only slightly. No doubt, the process of accumulation has been much steadier than the performance of the economy in general. When performance is poor, the margin of unused productive capacity is increased, but in spite of that, the global capacity of production will grow as usual. We may infer from this that the rate of profit might be rather high even when the economy underutilizes its productive capacity; on the other hand, there is reason to believe that the economy has been unable to generate the kind of demand required to obtain adequate utilization of the productive capacity.

I have not referred to the level of demand but to the *kind of demand*. As a matter of fact, we are very far from the Keynesian hypothesis of insufficiency of effective demand. During the period considered, the Brazilian economy has been operating under strong pressure from excess money demand, with a high rate of inflation in the periods of rapid growth and relative stagnation as well.

My basic hypothesis is that the system has not been capable of spontaneously producing the demand profile that would assure a steady rate of growth, and that growth in the long run depends on the exogenous actions of the government. Account must also be taken of the fact that during the period being discussed, the industries catering to the modernized minority came to be increasingly controlled by multinational corporations, along the lines of the general process of expansion of capitalism referred to above.

Rapid industrial growth, in the particular conditions now prevailing in Brazil, implies an intense absorption of technical progress in the form of new products and the new processes required to produce them. For the MNCs the opportunity costs of such technical progress are at a minimum when they can reproduce what they create and amortize in the countries responsible for the financing of research and development, and are at a maximum when they have to introduce new R & D. Consequently, industrial expansion goes on through an interlocking of local industries with the dominant industrial systems from which the flow of new technology springs. On the one hand, the MNCs stick to their blueprints as the best way of maximizing growth and profits; on the other, the modernized minorities seek to keep up with *le dernier cri* in the metropolis. Hence, although the two social forces have convergent interests, these interests do not suffice to make the system generate the kind of demand required to assure growth.

The successive waves of industrial expansion in Brazil during the post-war period cannot be explained without taking into account the autonomous role of the government in either subsidizing investment or enlarging demand. The general framework was the process of import substitution, catering to the market formed during the period of expansion of the exports of raw materials. Creating new jobs, this process enlarged the market for wage goods, but given the small size of the market for durable consumers' goods, local production of such goods tended to increase their relative prices, causing a decline in demand. Such a negative effect was checked up to the middle of the fifties by actions of the government to reduce prices of imported equipment by means of differential exchange rates, and also to subsidize industrial investments (particularly in industries that produced import substitutes) largely through loans with negative rates of interest. Part of the resources used to implement such a policy came from an improvement in the terms-of-trade which took place during this period. Cutting the real cost of the fixed capital by half helped the industries producing durable consumers' goods to realize profits, even if they had to operate with a large margin of unused capacity. In the second half of the fifties, when the terms-of-trade had deteriorated, the government embarked on a policy of external indebtedness that allowed it to proceed with the subsidies. At the same time, the government engaged in a policy of huge public works: the building of Brasilia and the construction of a national network of roads, including pioneering roads like the Belem-Brasilia. More recently, as we will see, action has been taken directly in the area of income distribution in order to produce the quality of demand that better fits the plans of expansion of the MNCs and the expectations of the modernized minority.

THE NEW STRATEGY

Brazil's high rate of growth in industrial production, attained in the last five years (1968–72) after a period of seven years of relative stagnation (1961–67), has been obtained through a very successful governmental policy which aims at attracting the MNC and fostering the expansion of the branches of such corporations already installed in the country. By various means the government has been guiding the process of income distribution in order to produce the demand profile most attractive to the MNCs. Consequently, the basket of consumers' goods which attempts to reproduce the patterns of consumption of the rich countries has expanded rapidly in both absolute and relative terms.

The State also has been playing important complementary roles by investing in physical infrastructure, in human capital (in an attempt to enlarge the supply of professional cadres and personnel), and in those industries with a low capital turnover. Industries producing homogeneous products such as steel, non-ferrous metals, and other standard inputs of the industrial system do not rely on innovation of products to compete or generate market power. They rely on innovation of productive processes and, because the turnover of fixed capital is low, the flow of innovation tends to be much slower. Furthermore, a policy of low prices, followed by such industries through concealed subsidies, may be defended as essential to foster the process of industrialization. Thus, keeping this block of industries in the hands of the State, totally or partially, may be the best way for MNCs to obtain a rapid payoff, and may maximize profits and expansion.

The firms controlled by local capitalists also have a role in this system. Industries producing for the mass of the population face a sluggish demand because the real wage rate of the unskilled worker is declining or stagnating. The markets for such industries expand horizontally, however, because of the increase in population and the transfer of people from subsistence activities into the sector paying the basic wage rate guaranteed by social legislation. Because this basket of consumers' goods does not include the introduction of new products, control of technical progress is not so important as a source of market power. Consequently, the MNCs in this sector do not have the same advantages in competing with local capitalists.

Considering the industrial system as a whole, we perceive that MNCs control the activities which rely mainly on technical progress (the activities where the flow of new products is more intense), namely, production of durable consumers' goods and equipment in general. The State has an important share in industries producing intermediate products, and local capitalists are very strong in industries producing non-durable consumers' goods. Furthermore, local firms operate under contracts as an auxiliary line of production for MNCs and for the enterprises of the State, adding flexibility to the system. No doubt, MNCs are passing through a process of vertical integration in certain sectors, absorbing local firms, and are also expanding in important sectors of non-durable consumers' goods. The food industry, under the control of MNCs, is catering to the upper income groups, introducing a myriad of products that fill the supermarkets of the rich countries. Nevertheless, the basic lines of the system are those presented above, and we may say that the three sub-sectors pursue different roles and, up to a point, are complementary. It is important to stress, however, that the dynamism of the system rests upon the intensity of transmission of technical progress as visualized by MNCs. In other words, when the opportunity costs of technical progress are practically zero for the branches of multinational corporations, the rate of growth of the industrial system tends to be maximized.

Given the characteristics of the Brazilian economy, formed by a rather small highly diversified market and another relatively large market of low diversification, durable consumers' goods industries benefit much more from economies of scale than existing consumers' goods industries. Consequently, the more concentrated is the distribution of income, the greater is the positive effect on the rate of growth of GDP. Thus, the same amount of money when consumed by rich people causes a faster rate of growth of GDP than when consumed by poor people. Let us suppose that the consumers' goods whose demand is in rapid expansion are automobiles; most probably, the building of the infrastructure will not keep pace with the increase in the stock of automobiles, and efficiency in the use of the vehicles is bound to decline. This means more consumption of fuel and more repairs per mile as a consequence of traffic jams, etc. All this will also contribute to an increase in the rate of expansion of the GDP. We can push this further. Concentration of income creates the possibility of price discrimination. In fact, some touches added to certain cars (new models) allow overpricing to occur, and the producer's rent thus created will also add to the increment of the GDP. In short, squandering resources for the superfluous consumption of a rich minority contributes to the inflation of the growth rate of GDP, and may also inflate the prestige of people in government.

Another factor to be taken into account is the rate of inflow of foreign capital. If the demand profile fits with the requirements of MNCs, the possibilities of mobilizing financial resources abroad will obviously be greater. As a matter of fact, things are not so simple, because prospects for the balance of payments depend on other factors linked to the anticipated capacity to export. Other things being equal, however, if the anticipated rate of profit of MNCs is higher, then the inflow of foreign capital will be greater, adding to local savings and giving flexibility to the economy, at least in the short run.

To sum up: a certain profile of demand, corresponding to an increasing concentration in the distribution of income and to an increasing gap between the level of consumption of the rich minority and that of the mass of the population, entails a composition of investments that tends to maximize the transfer of technical progress through MNCs, and to increase the inflow of foreign resources. Thus, the policy aiming at producing that demand profile will also tend to maximize the expansion of the GDP.

Within this general framework, the Brazilian government has been pursuing four basic objectives:

1. fostering and steering the process of income concentration (a process inherent to the underdeveloped capitalist economies in general) to benefit the consumers of durable goods, that is, the minority of the population, with patterns of consumption similar to those of the rich countries;

2. obtaining a minimum transfer of people from the subsistence sectors into the sectors benefiting from the minimum guaranteed wage rate;

3. controlling the differential between the minimum guaranteed wage rate and the level of real income in the subsistence sector. In six years the government reduced the guaranteed wage rate and succeeded in reconciling

the transfer of some people from the subsistence sectors with an intense process of income concentration; and

4. subsidizing the export of manufactured goods in order to reduce the pressure on those sectors producing non-durable consumers' goods with a sluggish demand due to income concentration, and also to improve the balance of payments.

The objectives referred to under (2) and (3) are instrumental social variables required to tackle the social tensions stemming from the process of income concentration, particularly when the real wage rate is declining. Creation of new jobs is a way of reducing the burden on people already working; since the number of dependents per family is large, the number of wage earners in each family can be increased, which makes the reduction in the wage rate easier to accept. Furthermore, such a policy brings about a reduction in the cost of labor to MNCs without shrinking their markets.

The most complex part of this policy concerns the process of fostering and steering income concentration. To obtain the desired result, the Brazilian government has been using various instruments, particularly credit, income and fiscal policies.

The first spurt of demand for durable consumers' goods originated from a rapid expansion of consumers' credit, benefiting the upper middle class. The resulting inflation reduced the real income of the mass of the population, freeing resources for a policy of public investments while helping to reduce production costs of private firms. The increase in the rate of profit of the firms producing durable consumers' goods was very rapid, creating leverage for an expansion of private investments. If we take into account the fact that the firms producing durable consumers' goods had been operating with a large margin of unused productive capacity, and that these enterprises reap substantial economies of scale during expansion, then we can easily understand the boom that took place.

The extremely high level of profit and the investment boom, particularly in the industrial sector producing for the rich minority, opened the door for an income distribution policy favoring the upper brackets of the salary scale, since the supply of professional cadres was rather inelastic. This situation, coinciding with a decline in the basic wage rate, engendered an extreme concentration of income not derived from property. A similar tendency can be observed within the public sector.

It is through fiscal policy, however, that the government has been pursuing the more ambitious objective of giving permanence to the new structures. Scores of "fiscal incentives" have been implemented, aimed at creating a sizable group of rentiers within the middle class. As a matter of fact, every person having to pay income tax (approximately 5 percent of the families) has been induced to compose an investment portfolio as an alternative to the payment of part of the tax due.* The poor, with a heavy burden of indirect taxes, are excluded from such privileges. The apparent

---

* A special provision of the tax law allows taxpayers to reduce their tax liability up to one-half if they invest that amount in government bonds or new issues of corporate securities.

objective of the government in adopting this policy is to link the purchasing power of the upper middle class to the most dynamic flow of income, the flow of profits. In this particular and important aspect, Brazil is engendering a new type of capitalism, heavily dependent upon the appropriation and utilization of profits to generate a certain type of consumption expenditure. This can only be obtained through decisive action on the part of the State to force the firms to open their capital (particularly difficult in the case of MNCs) and to pursue an adequate policy of distribution of dividends. An alternative to this would be the accumulation of an increasing public debt in the hands of the upper middle class, whose flow of interest would have to be fed with the proceeds of a tax on the profits of the corporations. Nowhere has a capitalist economy been so dependent upon the State to gear demand to supply.

The most significant feature of the Brazilian "model" is its structural tendency to exclude the mass of the population from the benefits of accumulation and technical progress. Thus, the durability of the system relies heavily on the capacity of the ruling groups to suppress all forms of opposition which its anti-social character tends to arouse.

25

Maoist Economic Development:
The New Man in the New China

John W. Gurley

While capitalist and Maoist processes of economic development have several elements in common, the differences between the two approaches are nevertheless many and profound. It is certainly not evident that one approach or the other is always superior, either in means or ends. What is evident, however, is that most studies by American economists of Chinese economic development are based on the assumption of capitalist superiority, and so China has been dealt with as though it were simply an underdeveloped United States—an economy that "should" develop along capitalist lines and that "should" forget all that foolishness about Marxism, Mao's thought, great leaps, and cultural revolutions, and get on with the job of investing its savings efficiently. This unthinking acceptance by American economists of the view that there is no development like capitalist development has resulted in studies of China that lack insight.

The practice of capitalism has not, of course, met the ideal specification for it as theorized by Adam Smith. In general, the theory holds that an economy can develop most rapidly if every person, whether as entrepreneur, worker, or consumer, is able to pursue his own self-interest in competitive markets without undue interference from government. Progress is best promoted not by government, but by entrepreneurs owning the material means of production, whose activities, guided by the profit motive, reflect consumers' demands for various goods and services. Labor productivity is enhanced by material incentives and the division of labor (specialization); economic progress is made within an environment of law and order, harmony of interests, and stability. It is by these means that economic development, according to the theory, can best be attained, and its attainment can best be measured by the national output.

In practice, many markets have been more monopolistic than competitive, government has interfered in numerous and extensive ways in competitive market processes in pursuit of greater equity in income distribution, higher employment of labor, and better allocation of economic resources. Capitalism of the individualist, competitive type has to some extent given way in most parts of the industrial capitalist world to a state welfare capi-

Reprinted from The Center Magazine, Vol. III, No. 3 (May 1970), pp. 25-33, by permission of the Center for the Study of Democratic Institutions, Santa Barbara, California.

talism, in which government plays a larger role and private entrepreneurs and consumers somewhat smaller ones than envisaged by Adam Smith and his disciples. Despite these departures from the ideal model of capitalism, however, it is fair to say that the main driving force of the capitalist system remains private entrepreneurs who own the means of production, and that competition among them is still widespread and worldwide.

There is no doubt that capitalist development, whatever importance its departures from the Smithian model have had, has been highly successful in raising living standards for large numbers of people. It has been relatively efficient in using factors of production in ways best designed to provide all the goods that consumers by and large have demanded. It has also encouraged new ways of doing things—innovative activity and technological advances.

At the same time, however, there is a heavy emphasis in capitalist development—as there now is throughout most of the world—on raising the national output, on producing "things" in ever-increasing amounts. Implicit is the view that man is merely an input, a factor of production, a means to an end. Moreover, capitalist development has almost always been uneven in several crucial ways—in its alternating periods of boom and bust; in enriching some people thousands of times more than others; in developing production facilities with much more care than it has devoted to the welfare of human beings and their environment; in fostering lopsided development, both in terms of geographical location within a country and, especially in low-income countries, in terms of a narrow range of outputs, such as in one- or two-crop economies. The lopsided character of capitalist development has been evident historically in those nations that today have advanced industrial economies, but it is especially evident in the underdeveloped countries (with their mixture of feudal and capitalist features) that are tied in to the international capitalist system—those countries that, by being receptive to free enterprise and foreign capital, regardless of whether they are also receptive to freedom, are in the "free world."

This lopsidedness shows itself more markedly, of course, in the matter of trade. As satellites to the advanced capitalist countries, the underdeveloped regions supply raw materials, agricultural products, minerals, and oil, and receive in return manufactured and processed goods as well as basic food items. Much more trade takes place between the underdeveloped and the advanced capitalist countries than among the underdeveloped countries themselves. One consequence of this is the poor transportation within South America and Africa—while there are good highways or railroads running from mines, plantations, and oil fields to the seaports, it remains difficult to travel from one part of the continent to another.

The economic development of these poor capitalist countries is lopsided in many other ways, too. A few cities in each of these countries, with their airports, hotels, nightclubs, and light industries, are often built up to the point where they resemble the most modern metropolis in advanced industrial countries—but the rural areas, comprising most of the country and containing most of the people, are largely untouched by modernization. Industry, culture, entertainment, education, and wealth are highly concentrated in urban centers; a traveler to most of the poor "free world"

countries, by flying to the main cities, can land in the middle of the twentieth century, but by going thirty miles out into the country in any direction
he will find himself back in the Middle Ages. Education is usually for the
elite and stresses the superiority of the educated over the uneducated, the
superiority of urban over rural life, of mental over manual labor. The
burden of economic development, which is essentially a restraint on consumption, is shared most inequitably among the people; the differences
between rich and poor are staggering—they are nothing less than the differences between unbelievable luxury and starvation.

While some of these characteristics are not peculiar to the poor countries
tied to the internationalist capitalist system (they can be found in the Soviet
socialist bloc, too), and while some are related more to feudalism than to
capitalism, much of the lopsided development is intimately connected with
the profit motive. The key link between the two is the fact that it is almost
always most profitable, from a private-business point of view, to build on
the best. Thus a businessman locates a new factory in an urban center near
existing ones, rather than out in the hinterlands, in order to gain access to
supplies, a skilled labor force, and high-income consumers; to maximize
profits, he hires the best, most qualified workers; a banker extends loans
to those who are already successful; an educational system devotes its best
efforts to the superior students, and universities, imbued with the private-
business ethic of "efficiency," offer education to those best prepared and
most able; promoters locate cultural centers for those best able to appreciate and afford them; in the interests of efficiency and comparative advantage, businessmen are induced to specialize (in cocoa or peanuts or coffee)
—to build on what they have always done best.

This pursuit of efficiency and private profits through building on the
best has led in some areas to impressive aggregate growth rates, but almost
everywhere in the international capitalist world it has favored only a relative few at the expense of the many, and, in poor capitalist countries, it has
left most in stagnant backwaters. Capitalist development, even when most
successful, is always a trickle-down development.

The Maoists' disagreement with the capitalist view of economic development is profound. Their emphases, values, and aspirations are quite different
from those of capitalist economists. Maoist economic development occurs
within the context of central planning, public ownership of industries, and
agricultural coöperatives or communes. While decision-making is decentralized to some extent, decisions regarding investment versus consumption,
foreign trade, allocation of material inputs and the labor supply, prices of
various commodities—these and more are essentially in the hands of the
state. The profit motive is officially discouraged from assuming an important
role in the allocation of resources, and material incentives, while still prevalent, are downgraded.

Perhaps the most striking difference beween the capitalist and Maoist
views concerns goals. Maoists believe that while a principal aim of nations
should be to raise the level of material welfare of the population, this should
be done only within the context of the development of human beings,
encouraging them to realize fully their manifold creative powers. And it

should be done only on an egalitarian basis—that is, on the basis that development is not worth much unless everyone rises together; no one is to be left behind, either economically or culturally. Indeed, Maoists believe that rapid economic development is not likely to occur *unless* everyone rises together. Development as a trickle-down process is therefore rejected by Maoists, and so they reject any strong emphasis on profit motives and efficiency criteria that lead to lopsided growth.

In Maoist eyes, economic development can best be attained by giving prominence to men rather than "things."

Recently, capitalist economists have begun to stress the importance for economic growth of "investment in human capital"—that is, investment in general education, job training, and better health. It has been claimed that expenditures in these directions have had a large "payoff" in terms of output growth. Although this might seem to represent a basic change in their concept of man in the development process, actually it does not. "Investment in human capital" means that economic resources are invested for the purpose of raising the skill and the educational and health levels of labor, not as an end in itself but as a means of increasing the productivity of labor. Thus economists are concerned with the "payoff" to investment in human capital, this payoff being the profit that can be made from such an expenditure. Indeed, the very term "human capital" indicates what these economists have in mind: man is another capital good, an input in the productive engine that grinds out commodities; if one invests in man, he may become more productive and return a handsome profit to the investor—whether the investor is the state, a private capitalist, or the laborer himself. Thus the preoccupation of capitalist economists is still with man as a means and not as an end.

The Maoists' emphasis, however, is quite different. First of all, while they recognize the role played by education and health in the production process, their emphasis is heavily placed on the transformation of ideas, the making of the communist man. Ideology, of course, may be considered as part of education in the broadest sense, but it is surely not the part that capitalist economists have in mind when they evaluate education's contribution to economic growth. Moreover, ideological training does not include the acquisition of particular skills or the training of specialists—as education and job training in capitalist countries tend to do. The Maoists believe that economic development can best be promoted by breaking down specialization, by dismantling bureaucracies, and by undermining the other centralizing and divisive tendencies that give rise to experts, technicians, authorities, and bureaucrats remote from or manipulating "the masses." Finally, Maoists seem perfectly willing to pursue the goal of transforming man even though it is temporarily at the expense of some economic growth. Indeed, it is clear that Maoists will not accept economic development, however rapid, if it is based on the capitalist principles of sharp division of labor and sharp (meaning unsavory or selfish) practices.

The proletarian world-view, which Maoists believe must replace that of the bourgeoisie, stresses that only through struggle can progress be made; that selflessness and unity of purpose will release a huge reservoir of enthusiasm, energy, and creativeness; that active participation by "the masses" in decision-making will provide them with the knowledge to channel their energy most productively; and that the elimination of specialization will not only increase workers' and peasants' willingness to work hard for the various goals of society but will also increase their ability to do this by adding to their knowledge and awareness of the world around them.

It is an essential part of Maoist thinking that progress is not made by peace and quietude, by letting things drift and playing safe, or, in the words of Mao Tse-tung, by standing for "unprincipled peace, thus giving rise to a decadent, philistine attitude. . . ." Progress is made through struggle, when new talents emerge and knowledge advances in leaps. Only through continuous struggle is the level of consciousness of people raised, and in the process they gain not only understanding but happiness.

Mao sees man engaged in a fierce class struggle—the bourgeoisie against the proletariat—the outcome of which, at least in the short run, is far from certain. The proletarian world outlook can win only if it enters tremendous ideological class struggles.

Maoists believe that each person should be devoted to "the masses" rather than to his own pots and pans, and should serve the world proletariat rather than, as the *Peking Review* has put it, reaching out with "grasping hands everywhere to seek fame, material gain, power, position, and limelight." They think that if a person is selfish he will resist criticisms and suggestions and is likely to become bureaucratic and elitist. He will not work as hard for community or national goals as he will for narrow, selfish ones. In any case, a selfish person is not an admirable person. Thus Maoists deëmphasize material incentives, for they are the very manifestation of a selfish, bourgeois society. While selflessness is necessary to imbue man with energy and the willingness to work hard, Maoists believe this is not sufficent; man must also have the ability as well. And such ability comes from active participation—from seeing and doing. To gain knowledge, people must be awakened from their half slumber, encouraged to mobilize themselves and to take conscious action to elevate and liberate themselves. When they actively participate in decision-making, when they take an interest in state affairs, when they dare to do new things, when they become good at presenting facts and reasoning things out, when they criticize and test and experiment scientifically—having discarded myths and superstitions—when they are aroused, then, says the *Peking Review*, "the socialist initiative latent in the masses [will] burst out with volcanic force and a rapid change [will take] place in production."

Finally, if men become "selfless," there will be discipline and unity of will, for these "cannot be achieved if relations among comrades stem from selfish interests and personal likes and dislikes." If men become "active," then along with extensive democracy they will gain true consciousness and ultimately freedom, in the Marxian sense of intelligent action. Together, selflessness and active participation will achieve ideal combinations of opposites: "a vigorous and lively political situation . . . is taking shape throughout our country, in which there is both centralism and democracy, both discipline and freedom, both unity of will and personal ease of mind."

It is important to note the "discipline" and "unity of will." As for the basic framework of Marxism-Leninism, Maoists believe that everyone should accept it, and they are quick to "work on" those who lag behind or step out of line. But, within this framework, the Maoists energetically and sincerely promote individual initiative, "reasoning things out and not depending on authorities or myths," "thinking for oneself," and so forth. Outside of this framework, an individual stands little chance; inside the framework, an individual is involved in a dynamic process of becoming "truly free," in the sense of being fully aware of the world around him and an active decision-maker in that world. Mao's thought is meant to lead to true freedom and to unity of will based on a proletarian viewpoint. So everyone must think alike—the Maoist way—to attain true freedom.

For Marx, specialization and bureaucratization were the very antithesis of communism. Man could not be free or truly human until these manifestations of alienation were eliminated, allowing him to become an all-round communist man. Maoists, too, have been intensely concerned with this goal, specifying it in terms of eliminating the distinction between town and countryside, mental and manual labor, and workers and peasants. The realization of the universal man is not automatically achieved by altering the forces of production, by the socialist revolution. Rather, it can be achieved only after the most intense and unrelenting ideological efforts to raise the consciousness of the masses through the creative study and creative use of Mao's thought. Old ideas, customs, and habits hang on long after the material base of the economy has been radically changed, and it takes one mighty effort after another to wipe out the bourgeois superstructure and replace it with the proletarian world outlook. This transformation of the "subjective world" will then have a tremendous impact on the "objective world."

In many ways Maoist ideology rejects the capitalist principle of building on the best, even though the principle cannot help but be followed to some extent in any effort at economic development. However, the Maoist departures from the principle are the important thing. While capitalism, in their view, strives one-sidedly for efficiency in producing goods, Maoism, while also seeking some high degree of efficiency, at the same time and in numerous ways builds on "the worst": experts are pushed aside in favor of decision-making by "the masses"; new industries are established in rural areas; the educational system favors the disadvantaged; expertise (and hence work proficiency in a narrow sense) is discouraged; new products are domestically produced rather than being imported "more efficiently"; the growth of cities as centers of industrial and cultural life is discouraged; steel, for a time, is made by "everyone" instead of by only the much more efficient steel industry.

Of course, Maoists build on "the worst" not because they take great delight in lowering economic efficiency; rather, their stated aims are to involve everyone in the development process, to pursue development without leaving a single person behind, to achieve a balanced growth rather than a lopsided one. Yet if Maoism were only that, we could simply state that, while Maoist development may be much more equitable than capitalist efforts, it is surely less efficient and thus less rapid; efficiency is being sacrificed to some extent for equity. But that would miss the more important aspects of Maoist ideology, which holds that the resources devoted to bringing everyone into the socialist development process—the effort spent on building on "the worst"—will eventually pay off not only in economic ways by enormously raising labor productivity but, more important, by creating a society of truly free men who respond intelligently to the world around them, and who are happy.

The sharp contrast between the economic development views of capitalist economists and those of the Chinese communists cannot be denied; their two worlds are quite different. The difference is not mainly between being Chinese and being American, although that is surely part of it but, rather, between Maoists in a Marxist-Leninist tradition and being present-day followers of the economics first fashioned by Adam Smith and later reformed by John Maynard Keynes. Whatever the ignorance and misunderstanding on the Chinese side regarding the doctrines of capitalist economics, it is clear that many Western economic experts on China have shown little interest in, and almost no understanding of, Maoist economic development. Most of the economic researchers have approached China as though it were little more than a series of tables in a yearbook which could be analyzed by Western economic methods and judged by capitalist values. The result has been a series of unilluminating studies, largely statistical or institutional in method, and lacking analysis of the really distinctive and interesting features of Maoist development

Like seagulls following the wake of a ship, economists pursue numbers. The main concentration of numbers pertaining to the economy of Communist China is in *Ten Great Years*, which was published in September, 1959, by the State Statistical Bureau. This volume contains a wealth of data on almost all phases of economic activity, and so it has become one of the main sources for much of the empirical work on Chinese economic development. But throughout the nineteen-fifties economic data were published in hundreds of other sources—in official reports, statistical handbooks, economics books, and articles—so that altogether massive information, of varying degrees of reliability, became available on the first decade or so of China's development efforts. After 1958, however, the release of aggregate data just about came to a halt, so little research on the nineteen-sixties has been done by economists outside of China. The data of the nineteen-fifties continue to be worked over, adjusted, and refined, though there is no longer much more that can be said about them.

Much of this research has been concerned in one way or another with China's national output—its absolute size; its rates of growth; its components, like agriculture and industrial output, or consumption and investment goods; the extent to which national output has been affected by international trade and Soviet aid; and the planning methods utilized in its production.

There are, of course, scores of studies, though mostly of an empirical nature, on specialized aspects of the economic process. A few Western economists have actually visited China in recent years and have returned with much information, but mainly of a qualitative nature.

Economic research on China suffers from an ailment common to most of economics—a narrow empiricism. Thus most of the research studies of the Chinese economy deal with very small segments of the development process, and within these tiny areas the researchers busy themselves with data series—adding up the numbers, adjusting them in numerous ways, deflating them for price changes, and doing a lot of other fussy statistical work. Each economist tills intensively his small plot, gaining highly specialized knowledge in the process, finally ending up an expert in his cramped quarters. There are not many economists in the China field who try to see Chinese economic development as a whole, as "the comprehensive totality of the historical process." If the truth is the whole, as Hegel claimed, most economic experts on China must be so far from the truth that it is hardly worthwhile listening to them.

Moreover, it is often painful. Even a casual reader of the economic research on Communist China cannot help but notice that many of the researchers are not happy—to say the least—with the object of their investigation. This is immediately noticeable because it is so very unusual in economics. Ordinarily, economists are utterly fascinated and almost infatuated with their special areas of study—even with such an esoteric one as "Game Theory Applied to Non-linear Development." But not so our China experts. Indeed, it is quite apparent that many of them consider China to be, not the Beloved, but the Enemy. And in dealing with the Enemy, their research often reveals very strong, and undisguised, biases against China.

These biases show up in a variety of ways, from such trivial things as changing Peking to Peiping (à la Dean Rusk), which reveals a wish that the communists weren't there; to the frequent use of emotive words (the communists are not dedicated but "obsessed," leaders are "bosses," a decision not to release data is described as "a sullen statistical silence," the extension of the statistical system becomes "an extension of its tentacles further into the economy"); to the attribution of rather sinister motives to ordinary economic and cultural policies (education and literacy are promoted for the purpose of spreading evil Marxian doctrines, economic development is pursued for the principal purpose of gaining military strength for geographical expansion—which is the theme of W. W. Rostow's book on *The Prospects for Communist China*); to dire forecasts of imminent disaster based on little more than wishful thinking; and on up to data manipulation of the most questionable sort.

This strong propensity to treat China as the enemy has led to some grossly distorted accounts of China's economic progress. The picture that is presented by these studies as a whole is one in which China, while making some progress for a time in certain areas, is just barely holding on to economic life. It is a picture of a China always close to famine, making little headway while the rest of the world moves ahead, being involved in irrational economic policies, and offering little reason for hope that the lives of her people will be improved. Our China experts, furthermore, know what is wrong, and that, in a word, is communism. They seldom fail to pass judgment on some aspect or other of Chinese economic development, and this judgment is almost invariably capitalist-oriented. Thus national planning and government-controlled prices cannot be good because they do not meet the criteria of consumer sovereignty and competitive markets; communes violate individualism and private property; ideological campaigns upset order and harmony; the deëmphasis on material incentives violates human nature and so reduces individual initiative and economic growth; the breakdown of specialization lowers workers' productivity. This sort of thing pervades much of the economic literature on China.

Given all this—the narrow specialized studies that are sometimes useful but not often enlightening, the distortions by omission or commission, the capitalist-oriented approaches and assessments, not to mention those evaluations of Communist China that are inspired by a strong allegiance to Chiang Kai-shek—given all this, it is little wonder that a fair picture of China's economic progress seldom gets presented. Seldom, not never: Barry Richman's book on *Industrial Society in Communist China,* Carl Riskin's work—for example, in *The Cultural Revolution 1967 in Review*—and several other research efforts are refreshingly objective, relatively free of capitalist cant, and approach Maoist ideology in a serious way.

The truth is that China over the past two decades has made very remarkable economic advances (though not steadily) on almost all fronts. The basic, overriding economic fact about China is that for twenty years she has fed, clothed, and housed everyone, has kept them healthy, and has educated most. Millions have not starved; sidewalks and streets have not been covered with multitudes of sleeping, begging, hungry, and illiterate human beings; millions are not disease-ridden. To find such deplorable conditions, one does not look to China these days but, rather, to India, Pakistan, and almost anywhere else in the underdeveloped world. These facts are so basic, so fundamentally important, that they completely dominate China's economic picture, even if one grants all of the erratic and irrational policies alleged by her numerous critics.

The Chinese—all of them—now have what is in effect an insurance policy against pestilence, famine, and other disasters. In this respect, China has outperformed every underdeveloped country in the world; and, even with respect to the richest one, it would not be farfetched to claim that there has been less malnutrition due to maldistribution of food in China over the past twenty years than there has been in the United States. If this comes close to the truth, the reason lies not in China's grain output far surpassing her population growth—for it has not—but, rather, in the development of institutions to distribute food evenly among the population. It is also true, however, that China has just had six consecutive bumper grain crops (wheat and rice) that have enabled her to reduce wheat imports and greatly increase rice exports. On top of this, there have been large gains in the supplies of eggs, vegetables, fruits, poultry, fish, and meat. In fact, China today exports more food than she imports. The Chinese are in a much better position now than ever before to ward off natural disasters, as there has been significant progress in irrigation, flood control, and water conservation. The use of chemical fertilizers is increasing rapidly, the volume now over ten times that of the early nineteen-fifties; there has been substantial gains in the output of tractors, pumps, and other farm implements; and much progress has been made in the control of plant disease and in crop breeding.

In education, there has been a major breakthrough. All urban children and a great majority of rural children have attended primary schools, and enrolments in secondary schools and in higher education are large, in proportion to the population, compared with pre-communist days. If "school" is extended to include as well all part-time, part-study education, spare-time education, and the study groups organized by the communes, factories, street organizations, and the army, then there are schools everywhere in China.

China's gains in the medical and public-health fields are perhaps the most impressive of all. The gains are attested to by many fairly recent visitors to China. For example, G. Leslie Wilcox, a Canadian doctor, a few years ago visited medical colleges, hospitals, and research institutes, and reported in "Observations on Medical Practices" (*Bulletin of the Atomic Scientists*, June, 1966) that everywhere he found good equipment, high medical standards, excellent medical care—almost all comparable to Canadian standards. As William Y. Chen, a member of the U.S. Public Health Service, wrote in "Medicine in Public Health" (*Sciences in Communist China*), "the prevention and control of many infectious and parasitic diseases which have ravaged [China] for generations" was a "most startling accomplishment." He noted, too, that "the improvement of general environmental sanitation and the practice of personal hygiene, both in the cities and in the rural areas, were also phenomenal."

While all these gains were being made, the Chinese were devoting an unusually large amount of resources to industrial output. China's industrial production has risen on the average by at least eleven per cent per year since 1950, which is an exceptionally high growth rate for an underdeveloped country. Furthermore, industrial progress is not likely to be retarded in the future by any lack of natural resources, for China is richly endowed and is right now one of the four top producers in the world of coal, iron ore, mercury, tin, tungsten, magnesite, salt, and antimony. In recent years, China has made large gains in the production of coal, iron, steel, chemical fertilizers, and oil. In fact, since the huge discoveries at the Tach'ing oilfield, China is now self-sufficient in oil and has offered to export some to Japan.

From the industrial, agricultural, and other gains, I would estimate that China's real G.N.P. has risen on the average by at least six per cent per year since 1949, or by at least four per cent on a per-capita basis. This may not seem high, but it is a little better than the Soviet Union did over a comparable period (1928–40), much better than England's record during her century of industrialization (1750–1850), when her income per capita grew at one half of one per cent per year, perhaps a bit better than Japan's performance from 1878 to 1936, certainly much superior to France's one per cent record from 1800 to 1870, far better than India's 1.3 per cent growth during 1950 to 1967; more important, it is much superior to the postwar record of almost all underdeveloped countries in the world.

This is a picture of an economy richly endowed in natural resources, but whose people are still very poor, making substantial gains in industrialization, moving ahead more slowly in agriculture, raising education and health levels dramatically, turning out increasing numbers of scientists and engineers, expanding the volume of foreign trade and the variety of products traded, and making startling progress in the development of nuclear weapons. This is a truer picture, I believe, than the bleak one drawn by some of our China experts.

The failure of many economic experts on China to tell the story of her economic development accurately and fully is bad enough. Even worse has been the general failure to deal with China on her own terms, within the framework of her own goals and methods for attaining those goals, or even to recognize the possible validity of those goals. Communist China is certainly not a paradise, but it is now engaged in perhaps the most interesting economic and social experiment ever attempted, in which tremendous efforts are being made to achieve an egalitarian development, an industrial development without dehumanization, one that involves everyone and affects everyone. All these efforts seem not to have affected Western economists, who have proceeded with their income accounts and slide rules, and their free-enterprise values, to measure and judge. One of the most revealing developments in the China field is the growing belief among the economic experts that further research is hardly worthwhile in view of the small amount of economic statistics that have come out of China since 1958. Apparently, it does not matter that seven hundred and seventy-five million people are involved in a gigantic endeavor to change their environment, their economic and social institutions, their standard of living, and themselves; that never before have such potentially important economic and social experiments been carried out; that voluminous discussions of these endeavors by the Maoists are easily available. No, if G.N.P. data are not forthcoming, if numbers can't be added up and adjusted, then the economy must be hardly worth bothering about.

What can be done? Probably not very much until a substantial number of younger economists become interested in China. It is a hopeful sign that many young economists are now breaking away from the stultifying atmosphere of present-day "neo-classical" economics and are trying to refashion the discipline into political economy, as it once was, so as to take account of the actual world and not the world of highly abstract models, scholastic debates, and artificial assumptions—all designed to justify the existing state of things and to accept without question the rather narrow, materialistic goals of capitalist society. This reformulation by the young will have to take place first, but once this task is well along, China is bound to be attractive to many of these "new" economists. Only then will we begin to get a substantial amount of research on China that makes sense.

The research that would make sense is any that takes Maoism seriously as a model of economic development, in terms both of its objectives and of the means employed to attain those objectives. A thoughtful consideration of Maoism means paying proper attention to Marxism-Leninism as well as to the Chinese past of the Maoists. The Marxist-Leninist goal of the communist man within a classless society in which each person works according to his ability and consumes according to his needs—this goal of the Maoists should be taken seriously in any economic analysis of what is now going on.

There is a core of development theory that would probably be accepted by both the capitalist and Maoist sides—that economic growth can be attained by increasing the amounts of labor, capital goods, and land used in production, by improving the quality of these factors of production, by combining them in more efficient ways and inspiring labor to greater efforts, and by taking advantage of economies of scale. Now, Maoism undoubtedly affects every one of these ingredients of economic growth, and often in ways quite different from the capitalist impact. For example, it is likely that Maoist ideology discourages consumption and encourages saving and investment, and so promotes the growth of the capital stock; it does this by preventing the rise of a high-consuming "middle class," by fostering the Maoist virtues of plain and simple living and devoting one's life to helping others rather than accumulating "pots and pans."

As another example, it is possible that Maoist economic development, by deëmphasizing labor specialization and reliance on experts and technicians, reduces the quality of the labor force and so slows the rate of economic growth. On the other hand, as Adam Smith once suggested, labor specialization, while increasing productivity in some narrow sense, is often at the expense of the worker's general intelligence and understanding. It was his view that "the man whose whole life is spent in performing a few simple operations . . . generally becomes as stupid and ignorant as it is possible for a human creature to become." The difference between the most dissimilar of human beings, according to Smith, is not so much the cause of division of labor as it is the effect of it. Consequently, while an economy might gain from the division of labor in some small sense, it could lose in the larger sense by creating men who are little more than passive and unreasoning robots. A major aim of the Maoists is to transform man from this alienated state to a fully aware and participating member of society. The emphasis on "Reds" rather than experts is just one part of this transformation which, it is felt, will release "an atom bomb" of talents and energy and enable labor productivity to take great leaps.

In addition to this argument, which is based on Maoists' interpretation of their own history and experience, it is also possible that the "universal man" in an underdeveloped economy would provide more flexibility to the economy. If most people could perform many jobs moderately well, manual and intellectual, urban and rural, the economy might be more able to cope with sudden and large changes; it could with little loss in efficiency mobilize its labor force for a variety of tasks. Further, since experience in one job carries over to others, a person may be almost as productive, in the job-proficiency sense, in any one of them as he would be if he specialized—a peasant who has spent some months in a factory can more easily repair farm equipment, and so on. Finally, a Maoist economy may generate more useful information than a specialist one and so lead to greater creativity and productivity. When each person is a narrow specialist, communication among such people is not highly meaningful. When, on the other hand, each person has basic knowledge about many lines of activity, the experiences of one person enrich the potentialities of many others.

The point is that this issue—which, I should stress, includes not only labor productivity (that is, the development of material things by human beings) but also the development of human beings themselves—this issue of generalists versus specialists, communist men versus experts, the masses versus bureaucrats, or whatever, is not to be laughed away, as it has been, in effect, by some China experts. How men, in an industrial society, should relate to machines and to each other in seeking happiness and real meaning in their lives has surely been one of the most important problems of the modern age. There is also another basic issue here: whether modern industrial society, capitalist or socialist, does in fact diminish man's essential powers, his capacity for growth in many dimensions, even though it does allocate them "efficiently" and increases his skills as a specialized input. Is man Lockean in nature—reactive to outside forces, adjusting passively to disequilibrium forces from without? Or is he essentially Leibnitzian—the source of acts, active, capable of growth, and having an inner being that is self-propelled? If the latter, how are these powers released?

The Maoists claim that the powers exist and can be released. If they are right, the implications for economic development are so important that it would take blind men on this side of the Pacific to ignore them.

part seven

The Human Cost
of Development

economic development is not a smooth evolutionary process of change. Rather it is a painful process, which involves breaking up established ways of life and hurting many strongly entrenched vested interests. Development in the past, capitalist or socialist, has meant a virtually complete destruction of the old order, its values and institutions, and their replacement with a new ethic based on a belief in the efficacy of economic progress.

In the first reading, the human costs of continued underdevelopment, of capitalist development, and of socialist development are compared. The article analyzes three types of human costs: (a) living standards, (b) mortality, and (c) human values such as freedom and dignity. It concludes that rapid economic growth, while creating and intensifying a whole new set of human costs, is the fastest way to overcome the far worse human costs of continued underdevelopment. The article emphasizes E. H. Carr's observation that the cost of conservation falls just as heavily on the underprivileged as the cost of innovation on those who are deprived of their privileges.

James Weaver demonstrates that the future is not unmixed for the underdeveloped countries even if they succeed in overcoming their underdevelopment. As he says, "Modern man is lost in a lonely crowd, beset by massive bureaucracies on all sides, alienated from his work, isolated from his fellow man, and estranged from nature." He argues that it is the core institutions of modern capitalism—markets in labor and land, bureaucratic and hierarchically organized business firms—that are the cause. The one developed socialist country, the Soviet Union, has used many of the same institutions, has been dedicated to the same goal of economic growth, and has been inflicted with the same results.

Continued underdevelopment is bringing untold suffering to millions of people. Unfortunately, as the first two articles demonstrate, both capitalist and socialist development have generated new sufferings in the process of eliminating the old. Neither the United States nor the Soviet Union has created a truly human society. The United States has been so interested in money-making and the Soviet Union in catching up that human values have been relegated to a secondary position in both countries.

In the final reading of this part, Denis Goulet argues that "liberation" must supplement "development" if the poor countries are not to escape the human costs of continued underdevelopment merely to succumb to the human costs of the modern industrialized world. The hope that Goulet holds out is that the poor countries, while eliminating the sufferings of underdevelopment as rapidly as possible, will draw upon the best from capitalist and socialist experience and combine it with their own uniqueness to produce a new liberated and humanistic civilization.

323

26

The Human Costs of Economic Development: the West, the Soviet Union, and Underdeveloped Countries Today

Charles K. Wilber

INTRODUCTION

This paper considers three types of human costs: (a) living standards, (b) mortality, and (c) human values such as freedom and dignity. The first two will be measured quantitatively while the last will be limited primarily to qualitative analysis.

An analysis of the human costs of underdevelopment will be considered first. Then a comparative analysis of the Soviet Union, Great Britain, the United States, Japan, and Mexico will be developed.

The final section of the paper will consider whether the human costs incurred were an inherent part of the development process and thus must be repeated by underdeveloped countries today. In addition, the special circumstances of underdeveloped countries today will be considered in evaluating the problem of human costs in contemporary development programs.

THE COST OF UNDERDEVELOPMENT

It has sometimes been argued that, because of the tremendous social cost of economic development, industrialization should not be attempted. Rather, increased welfare through heightened agricultural efficiency should be aimed for; or industrialization, if followed, should proceed very slowly. Some would disagree that what is needed is *rapid* economic development. They ask why the hurry—why this "obsession" with economic growth?

While it is true that social change and industrialization have always entailed a high price, the price of underdevelopment is also very high. Professor E. H. Carr has remarked that "the cost of conservation falls just as heavily on the underprivileged as the cost of innovation on those who are deprived of their privileges."[1] The cost of underdevelopment is high

Reprinted from *Conference Papers of the Union for Radical Political Economics* (December 1968), pp. 125-148, by permission of the publisher. Copyright by the Union for Radical Political Economics.

indeed; chronic disease, hunger, famine, premature death, and degradation of the human spirit which lasts not for a few years, but century after century. For example, it is estimated that prior to 1949, 50 per cent of Chinese mortality was directly or indirectly caused by chronic malnutrition, and some 4 million persons died every year as a result of contamination by human excrement.[2] And the Chinese suffered 1,829 famines during the last 2,000 years—an average of almost a famine a year.[3] Famine in China extending from 1876 to 1879 is believed to have caused 9 million deaths, and a famine in China's Hunan Province in 1929 led to 2 million fatalities.[4] As another example, ten major famines in India between 1860 and 1900 resulted in 15 million deaths.[5] The 1918 influenza epidemic killed between 15 and 20 million Indians; as recently as the winter of 1942–43, the bodies of the famished littered the streets of Calcutta so profusely that their mere removal became impossible.[6] In the days of the Tsars, Russia was known throughout the world as the country of the great famines, and as late as the middle of the nineteenth century, Western Europe was still subject to frequent famines.[7] These are just a few examples of the cost of underdevelopment.

Table 1   The Human Costs of Underdevelopment

Countries grouped by national income per capita	Infant mortality rate (average 1955–58)	Life expectancy (average 1955–58)	Caloric intake per capita (1960–62)
Group I: $1,000 and more	24.9	70.6	3,153
Group II: $575 to $1,000	41.9	67.7	2,944
Group III: $350 to $575	56.8	65.4	2,920
Group IV: $200 to $350	97.2	57.4	2,510
Group V: $100 to $200	131.1	50.0	2,240
Group VI: Less than $100	180.0	41.7	2,070

Source: United Nations, *The Economic Development of Latin America in the Post-War Period* (New York: United Nations, 1964), p. 62.

Table 1 brings together three indicators of the human cost of underdevelopment. As an example, of the estimated 22 million children born each year in the Group VI countries, approximately 4 million die before they reach their first birthday. If these countries had the infant mortality rate of Group 1 countries then the mortality of infants would be approximately 0.5 million. This means that because of underdevelopment, 3.5 million infants die *each year* in the Group VI countries.

The "mathematics of suffering" may be morbid, but it does give perspective to the human costs of economic development. Professor Holzman faces the problem of human cost squarely. His consideration of the problem is worth quoting at length.

Let us turn now to the case of the nation caught in the "Malthusian trap," nations in which: (1) there has been no increase in the standard of living for centuries—perhaps there has even been a decline, (2) increases in output lead to a corresponding fall in the death rate so that no change in the standard of living occurs, i.e., those who live remain at subsistence, (3) the death rate is so high relative to the death rate in nations which have experienced secular economic progress that it is fair to say the inability to escape the "Malthusian trap" is responsible for the (premature) death of most of those born, and finally (4) escape from the "trap" requires a rate of investment so high that increases in productivity outrun increases in population. With such nations the case for a high rate of investment for a long period of time (one which enables the nation to escape the "trap") becomes much easier to justify and value judgments easier to make. The essential distinction between this case and that of the progressive economy is that loss of life can no longer be considered an "absolute," i.e., an infinite disutility. It was reasonable to consider it in this way in a progressive economy because loss of life is not comparable, by any measure, with other changes in the level of individual welfare. In the case of the "Malthusian trap" nation, however, one is put in the position of having to compare losses of life between periods. That is to say, failure to attempt to escape the "trap" may be considered equivalent to condemning to death, needlessly, members of future generations. Under these circumstances, loss of life would seem to become a legitimate and measurable datum of the system. The question facing the planner is: shall we raise the rate of investment in the present to a point high enough to escape the "trap" even though this will involve a rise in the death rate of the present generation if we know that it will increase the life expectancy and raise the standard of living of countless future generations? No matter what his decision, the planner faced with such a question is responsible for imposing the death sentence on someone. When life and death are compared on this plane, escape from the trap might well seem to be the superior alternative since by simple addition it becomes obvious that more lives would be saved than lost in the process.[8]

Most of the peoples of the world exist in conditions of poverty which are difficult for the affluent West to understand. And the effect on the dignity of the individual, the degradation of his very being, cannot be measured.[9]

THE COST OF DEVELOPMENT

The Case of the Soviet Union

Any writer begins a discussion of the human costs of Soviet industrialization with a certain amount of trepidation. In the case of Western industrialization the human costs are detailed but are usually treated as mere aberrations from a basically sound and moral system. On the other hand, the same human cost in Soviet industrialization is viewed as an essential part of the Soviet social system. Therefore one system merely needs reform while the other is essentially evil and can never be anything but evil.

· · ·

But an evaluation must be made if an honest appraisal of the human costs of industrialization is to be attempted.

> There seems to be little doubt that living standards declined during the first Five Year Plan. There is no accurate quantitative measure of the overall decline, but it is evident from the 18 per cent reduction in net agricultural output between 1928 and 1932 and the sharply increased exportation of agricultural products.[10]

Table 2   Estimates of Average Annual Increases in Per Capita Consumption in the U.S.S.R.: Various Years

	1928–37	1928–58	1928–40 and 1948–58
Consumption of private goods:			
1928 adjusted market prices	2.2%	3.4%	4.7%
1937 adjusted market prices	−0.3	2.1	2.9
1950 adjusted market prices	0.1	2.1	2.9
Composite, 1937 base	2.2	2.7	3.8
Communal services:			
1928 adjusted market prices	16.1	—	—
1937 adjusted market prices	14.6	5.6	7.7
1950 adjusted market prices	14.7	6.3[a]	9.0*
Composite, 1937 base	16.1	6.1	8.4
Total consumption:			
1928 adjusted market prices	3.8	—	—
1937 adjusted market prices	1.1	2.4	3.3
1950 adjusted market prices	1.5	2.1[a]	2.9[a]
Composite, 1937 base	3.8	3.1	4.3

* The ending year is 1955.

Sources: Abram Bergson, *The Real National Income of Soviet Russia Since 1928* (Cambridge: Harvard University Press, 1961), pp. 225, 237, 252. Janet S. Chapman, "Consumption," *Economic Trends in the Soviet Union*, ed. Abram Bergson and Simon Kuznets (Cambridge: Harvard University Press, 1963), pp. 238–239. The 1928–40 and 1948–58 period is used so as to exclude the war and reconstruction of 1940–47. The CIA estimated that per capita consumption increased at an annual rate of 2.8 per cent between 1959 and 1965. See David W. Bronson and Barbara S. Severin, "Recent Trends in Consumption and Disposable Money Income in the U.S.S.R.," *New Directions in the Soviet Economy*, U.S. Congress, Joint Economic Committee, 89th Cong., 2nd Sess., p. 521.

However, since the Second Five Year Plan, with the exception of the World War II period, per capita consumption has increased. Table 2 gives estimates of the average annual increase in per capita consumption between 1928 and 1958. Four weighting systems have been used to estimate consumption in the Soviet Union. Professor Bergson believes that "1937 adjusted market prices" and "Composite, 1937 base" are the most soundly based. In the former, adjusted market prices for 1937 are used as weights in all years. In the latter, with 1937 as the base year, the index for 1928 is weighted by adjusted market prices of 1928, the indices for 1955 and 1958 by adjusted market prices of 1950. Bergson has not been able to decide which of these is the best so he uses both. Both will be used in this chapter in comparison with other countries. The only decline recorded in Table 2 is for the period 1928–37 using 1937 adjusted market prices. And this is only for household consumption of private goods. If communal consumption is added, consumption increases of all periods seem respectable (between 1928 and 1932, however, consumption decreased). Communal consumption primarily consists of education and medical services received from the state.

Table 3 compares changes in consumption for the Soviet Union and the United States. The rate of increase in the Soviet Union appears respectable when viewed against the experience of the United States. The increase of per capita consumption in the Soviet Union over the period 1928–1958 was between 2.4 per cent and 3.1 per cent depending on the weighting system used. The increase in the United States over the period 1869–1899 was 3.0

Table 3 Average Annual Increases in Per Capita Consumption in the U.S.S.R. and the U.S.A.: Various Years

Country and Period	Annual Rate
U.S.S.R.:	
1928–1937, 1937 adjusted market prices	1.1%
1928–1937, Composite, 1937 base	3.8
1928–1958, 1937 adjusted market prices	2.4
1928–1958, Composite, 1937 base	3.1
1928–1940 and 1948–1958, 1937 adjusted market prices	3.3
1928–1940 and 1948–1958, Composite, 1937 base	4.3
U.S.A.:	
1869–1899	3.0
1869–1958	2.0
1870/79–1900/09	2.4
1880–1894	−0.1
1899–1929	2.0
1928–1937	−0.2
1928–1958	1.4

Sources: Table 2 and Chapman, "Consumption," *Economic Trends in the Soviet Union*, pp. 246–247. The consumption data for the United States are Simon Kuznets' "Flow of goods to consumers" and include final government services to consumers. These are taken from Chapman. The weights are 1954 dollars.

per cent. Dr. Janet Chapman concludes from her study of consumption in the Soviet Union that:

> In terms of the American experience the Soviet achievement looks quite respectable, particularly since the American progress was achieved in a peaceful world . . . while the 1928–58 period for the Soviet Union was characterized by the upheavals of the revolution in agriculture and the devastation of a major war fought largely on Russia's own soil.[11]

In addition, if the Soviet industrialization period is compared to the similar period of 1869–1899 in the United States, the Soviet record appears better in a number of respects. In the Soviet Union, much less child labor was used, working hours were less, working conditions were superior, social security provisions were far better, and income was more equally distributed and steadier.[12]

Changes in living standards in the Soviet Union compare favorably with the experience of other countries during their period of industrialization. For most countries good statistical data are lacking, but some rough comparisons can be made.

Per capita consumption declined in the Soviet Union between 1928 and 1932. However, similar decreases have occurred in many other countries. Table 3 shows that there was a decline in the U.S. between 1880–1894. There were several periods during the English Industrial Revolution when per capita consumption declined for a few years.[13] In Japan, too, there were years when per capita consumption declined.[14]

Table 4 compares some components of the standard of living in the Soviet Union, Mexico, and Japan. Japan began her industrialization in 1868. Mexico marked time from the revolution in 1910 until the development program really got started in 1940. The Soviet Union began industrializing in 1928. If 1960 is taken as the comparison date, and if the World War II

Table 4   Some Indicators of the Standard of Living in the U.S.S.R., Mexico, and
Japan: 1958–1962

	U.S.S.R.	Mexico	Japan
Actual caloric intake as percentage of individual country minimum standards	112	105	100
Actual protein intake as percentage of individual country minimum standards	145	113	117
Average number of persons per room in residential housing	1.5	2.9	1.4
Life expectancy at birth, in years	67.4	51–55	67.5
Infant mortality rate per 1,000 births	32.0	70.2	26.5
Number of physicians per 10,000 inhabitants	30.3	5.8	10.6
Proportion of illiterates in the population 15 years and older	2	43	2
Number of students in higher educational establishments per 100,000 population	689	111	470
Per capita consumption of fibres, kilograms	8.5	4.0	8.3
Per capita consumption of energy, kilowatt hours	2,847	1,012	1,164
Movies attended per capita	17.7	10.4	7.0
Stock of radios, per 1,000 population	202	97	107
Stock of television sets, per 1,000 population	28	25	98

Sources: U.S. Department of Agriculture, *The World Food Budget, 1970* (Washington: Government Printing Office, 1964), pp. 25–26. U.S. Bureau of the Census, *Statistical Abstract of the
United States, 1963* (Washington: Government Printing Office, 1963), pp. 932–933. United
Nations, *The Economic Development of Latin America in the Post-War Period* (New York: United
Nations, 1964), pp. 56–61. United Nations, *Statistical Yearbook, 1963* (New York: United Nations,
1964), pp. 52–53, 641, 647, 682–683. While movie attendance and stocks of radios and tele-
vision sets may not be the best indicators of consumption levels, they are the only ones
available for all three countries.

period is excluded for Japan and the Soviet Union, then the Soviet Union
has had 24 years, Mexico 20 years, and Japan 84 years to attain the consumption levels shown in Table 4. The Soviet Union ranks first on eight of
the indicators, ties for first on one, and is second on four. Given the relative time spans since industrialization began in the three countries, Soviet
performance has been quite respectable.

The next question to be raised concerns the problem of excess mortality
in the U.S.S.R. The major loss of life occurred during the collectivization
of agriculture. Possibly the majority of poor peasants would have peacefully, if not willingly, joined the collective farms except for the opposition
of the "well-to-do" peasants.[15] They actively and forcibly resisted by killing
Party cadres and burning their crops, and, through their traditional leadership positions in the villages, persuading great numbers of poorer peasants
to resist also. This brought brutal and ruthless retaliation by the Soviets.
An observer has vividly pictured the results.

> The more well-to-do peasants continued to resist the movement, and, to
> dispose of their opposition, the Soviets proceeded to liquidate them. . . . Only
> those who visited Russian villages in those stormy days can appreciate the
> human tragedy that liquidation brought in its train. *Koolacks* had their prop-
> erty unceremoniously taken from them, and were cast out of their homes on
> to some barren or swampy piece of land outside their own, or in some other
> village, to wrest a living from a niggardly soil as best they could. Or, with
> their families, they were packed into overcrowded freight cars, sometimes

with scanty food supplies, and exiled to some northern region—to start life over again on virgin lands, in a lumber camp, or in some new construction project.[16]

What did "liquidation" of the kulaks mean? Sir John Maynard says it meant that ". . . persons numbering, with their families, some five millions, were to be dispossessed of their properties, and in many cases driven from their homes."[17] This certainly caused untold suffering among these people, but it did not cause the death of all of them. After the good harvest of 1935 confirmed the victory of collectivization ". . . it became possible to 'amnesty' a large number of the liquidated kulaks."[18] That is, many kulaks were allowed to return and join the collective farms.

Many commentators estimate that the deaths among all classes of peasants due to collectivization and the attendant famine were about 5.5 million. There are, however, no reliable data to substantiate this or any other figure. The 5.5 million figure is based on a population study prepared by Professor Frank Lorimer for the League of Nations.[19] Arguing from these data, Naum Jasny states that the decline in the excess of births over deaths from 20 per 1,000 before 1928 to 10.7 per 1,000 between 1928 and 1938 cannot be talked away.[20] The major reason for this decrease is a fall in the birth rate, but it does not necessarily follow, as Jasny argues, that it fell because of starvation. It is just as possible that the decline in the birth rate was due to a lowered desire for children during a period of great upheaval and uncertainty,[21] and the use of abortion (which was legal at this time).

Jasny's use of population statistics to estimate excess mortality is open to a more damaging criticism. How accurate is a population census taken by an inexperienced government in an underdeveloped country such as Russia? Of course possible errors could work either way. The above is not written to deny that there was a great loss of human life, but only to show that the quoted 5.5 million figure is not hard fact. The best that can be said for this figure is that it serves as the upper limit on possible losses.[22]

There are normally two causes given for the deaths: the famine of 1932–34 and the liquidation of the kulaks. It has been shown conclusively that there was a famine, but the only quantitative evidence is composed of estimates by Western journalists. These estimates range from a few thousand deaths to 10 million.[23] Indirect evidence of famine conditions is the 18 per cent decline in agricultural output between 1928 and 1932.

This lends support to the position that there was a sharp reduction in food consumption in the Soviet Union. In addition, food exports were increased in the early 1930's. However, the data throw no light on the extent or severity of the food shortage. Even if there were few deaths from outright starvation, it is probable that the debilitating effects of widespread hunger caused a large number of premature deaths among children and elderly people. To this writer's knowledge there have been no attempts to measure this abnormal mortality except by the previously mentioned population statistics.

The "liquidation of kulaks *as a class*" was not designed to kill them but rather to liquidate their power as property owners. While it is true that thousands of them were shot, most of those who died did so from the hardships of transportation to and working in the Siberian regions (which, of course, doesn't make them any less dead). Also, especially in the Cossack areas, some died of starvation and related diseases due to the fact that after they destroyed their livestock and seed grain, and refused to plant, the Soviets denied them relief.[24] Here again, there is no evidence as to the extent of these practices. It can be concluded, however, that excess mortality in the Soviet Union during the 1930's was certainly high; exactly how high, however, is unknown.

The Cost of Industrialization under Capitalism

What was the human cost of industrialization in the capitalist countries? This is probably an unanswerable question. Much depends on the viewpoint adopted, since precise causal relationships cannot be established between industrialization and social costs. In what follows no attempt is made to establish cause and effect. However, the following material must at least be considered in evaluating the human cost of capitalist development relative to the human cost of Soviet development and of underdevelopment described above.

The human costs incurred in England during the Industrial Revolution were not small. The use of women and children in factories during the Industrial Revolution was notorious. Even though adult males were not treated with quite the same cruelty, their life in the factory was hard enough. They, too, suffered from too many working hours, overcrowded and unhealthy working conditions, and from tyrannical employers.

Adding to, and a partial cause of, the evils was the absolute and uncontrolled power of the factory owner. This power was acknowledged, admitted and even proclaimed with brutal candor. It was the employer's own business and this was justification enough for his conduct. He owed his employees wages, and once those were paid he had no further obligations.

The first result of the Industrial Revolution "was deplorable, for, instead of creating a happier, wiser, and more self-respecting society, this revolution led to the degradation of large masses of people and the rapid growth of a town life in which everything was sacrificed to profit."[25] The reaction of the English government in the face of the destitution and degradation of the working classes is instructive. The Poor Law Reform Act of 1834 was its answer. The Poor Law abolished outdoor relief for the able-bodied. To receive relief the worker and his family had to move to the work-house. The Act attempted to make the receipt of relief shameful. Unemployment, for instance, was considered to be due to laziness, which could, therefore, be cured by the threat of the work-house. This, of course, was a complete misunderstanding of cyclical unemployment, which was becoming important.

The working classes did not accept their situation quietly, but there was little they could do about it. There was protest, as can be seen in the massive proportions of unrest. "Luddism, the abortive march of the 'Blanketeers' in 1817, the Peterloo massacres two years later, the revolt of the agricultural workers in 1830, the meteoric rise and precipitous decline of the Grand

National Consolidated Trades Union, Owenite socialism, the Ten Hours Movement, and Chartism,"[26] all testify to the discontent of the growing industrial working class. These attempts to revolt were suppressed in two ways: explicitly by the police power of the state and implicitly through the market mechanism. The Luddite movement was crushed after Parliament made the breaking of machines a capital offense.[27] In 1819 the passage of the Six Acts restricted civil liberties by increasing the power of magistrates to punish "subversion." Workers who protested against conditions, and those convicted of petty crimes were often exiled to penal colonies such as Australia.[28]

In spite of the very poor conditions described above, there was not great loss of life among Englishmen. However, mention must be made of the human cost incurred by others. Here again, no direct cause and effect relationship is implied; only that these costs place the costs incurred in the Soviet Union and because of underdevelopment in better perspective.[29] During the Industrial Revolution, England dominated the economy of Ireland. During the famine years of the 1840's at least one and a half million Irish died and another one million were forced to emigrate.[30]

The period of the Industrial Revolution also saw great human cost in India, as Britain began to spread her power. After the battle of Plassey in 1757, British rule began to consolidate itself in Bengal, Bihar, Orissa, and eventually in all of India. British policy consisted of expropriation of Indian land and resources for English companies, high taxation of Indian manufactures and agriculture, and through political control, artificial turning of the terms-of-trade against Indian products. English products were allowed free entry, or virtual free entry, into India, but tariffs were erected against the entry of Indian industrial products into England, and direct trade between India and any other country was prevented by the operation of the Navigation Acts. These policies led to the destruction of Indian manufactures, which prior to 1757 had been competitive with British. By the early nineteenth century, India had been converted into an exporter of food and raw materials. In Nehru's opinion, this had important consequences for India.

> The liquidation of the artisan class led to unemployment on a prodigious scale. What were all these scores of millions, who had so far been engaged in industry and manufacture, to do now? . . . They could die of course. . . . They did die in tens of millions. . . . But still vast numbers of them remained. . . . They drifted to the land, for the land was still there. But the land was fully occupied and could not possibly absorb them profitably. So they became a burden on the land and the burden grew, and with it grew the poverty of the country, and the standard of living fell to incredibly low levels. . . . India became progressively ruralized. . . . This, then, is the real, the fundamental cause of the appalling poverty of the Indian people.[31]

England was not the only industrializing country to possess colonies. The Dutch had the East Indies, the French had Indo-China and parts of Africa, and Belgium had the Congo. Japan took over Taiwan and Korea as colonies, thus shifting some of the burden of capital accumulation to the people of these countries.

A large share of the human cost of capital accumulation in the Western countries was also borne by the Negroes caught in the African slave trade.[32]

By the 1790's the value of English income derived from trade with the West Indies was about four times larger than the income from trade with all the rest of the world. And the trade with the West Indies was in many respects the ideal colonial system, since it consisted in simple exchange of cheap manufactured goods for African slaves; of African slaves for West Indian food-stuffs and tobacco; and of these products for a high return in cash from Europe.

There is no need to detail the cost in suffering to the slaves in providing this capital accumulation for the developing countries. The only question is how many Africans had to pay this price. "So far as the Atlantic slave trade is concerned, it appears reasonable to suggest that in one way or another, before and after embarkation, it cost Africa at least fifty million souls. This estimate . . . is certainly on the low side."[33]

Even in the United States, where conditions were the most advantageous for development, there was a high human cost. Too often the economic historian focuses only on the social cost to the white worker. But the role of the American Indian and the Negro slave must not be completely overlooked. In the nineteenth century the American Indian stood in the way of capitalist expansion. Thus, a policy that can only be called genocide was embarked upon. "Disease, conquest, mass executions, oppression, decay and assimilation had by about 1900 reduced the number of Indians in the United States to some 250,000 or less than one-third of the estimated population in aboriginal time."[34] The same type of policy was followed in Canada, Australia, and New Zealand.

According to Professor Douglass North, the main catalyst of United States industrialization in the 1820–40 period was exports of cotton which were produced by Negro slaves.[35] What cost did the American Negro pay, both as slave and later as a freedman for American economic development?

It should be noted again that none of the above is meant to prove a cause and effect relationship between capitalist development and the detailed human costs. The purpose of including these costs is to place the human cost of development in the Soviet Union in perspective. In both the Soviet and capitalist cases there is insufficient evidence to say that the *process* of development *required* these human costs. In fact, one of the goals of development policy today should be the attempt to minimize the attendant social costs.

FREEDOM AND ECONOMIC DEVELOPMENT

The Cost in the U.S.S.R.

The greatest human cost of Soviet industrialization has been the emergence of a totalitarian regime. It is true that the Communist Party provided the coercive leadership and development ethic necessary to successfully carry out industrialization. But communism has not just been authoritarian, it has imposed a totalitarian *weltanschauung* that has generated appalling and unnecessary social costs. This totalitarian *weltanschauung*, combined with the fear of "capitalist encirclement," led in the Soviet Union to the treatment of dissent as treason and of error as sabotage. In this atmosphere a secret police, "corrective" labor camps, and purges were enabled to thrive.

It is true, of course, that this *weltanschauung* was reinforced by the historical background of Russia. The vast bulk of the Russian people lost little freedom under the Soviet regime because they had little to lose. Secret police organizations to fight revolutionary activity had long been used in Tsarist Russia. Banishment and exile were old Tsarist institutions. Forced labor in the form of serfdom also had a long history.

Since the Russian Revolution the secret police have brought suffering and fear to millions of people. It is only in their colonial possessions that we see capitalist countries maintaining a secret police and using terror to maintain order.[36] The use of forced labor was widespread in the Soviet Union.[37] Capitalist countries utilized forced labor in their colonies and through the institutions of slavery and indentured servitude.

Presumably the more pragmatic communist leadership that has emerged since Stalin's death, combined with the decline in fear of "capitalist encirclement," will reduce these totalitarian social costs in the future. However, if the social costs of the Stalin era had to be repeated when utilizing the Soviet model, then almost any alternative would be preferable.

The Cost in the Underdeveloped Countries

In discussing the impact of rapid industrialization on freedom, it must be remembered that for the bulk of the people in underdeveloped countries, there is little freedom to be lost. Moreover, too often the meaning of freedom to Western observers is entirely unlike that understood by the masses of poor in the underdeveloped areas. The Brazilian economist Celso Furtado has argued that:

> It must be recognized . . . that the masses in the underdeveloped countries have not generally put the same high valuation on individual liberty that we do. Since they have not had access to the better things of life, they obviously cannot grasp the full meaning of the supposed dilemma between liberty and quick development. Also, if we were to assert that rapid economic development of socialist countries was achieved only at the price of restricting civil liberties, we must then accept the corollary that the liberty enjoyed by the minority in our society is paid for by the delay in general economic development, hence is at the expense of the welfare of the great majority.[38]

The problem of how to obtain present sacrifices from the present generation for the benefit of the future cannot be ignored. It might very well involve a postponement of political freedom. In England the working class did not receive the right to vote until 1867, after the "big push" stage of the Industrial Revolution was over. In both Germany and France the lower classes were effectively excluded from the franchise until development was well on its way. In Japan there were no political rights for the lower classes. Even in the United States, political rights were severely restricted during the crucial 1830–60 period. The American Negro, the American Indian, and imported foreign workers such as Chinese coolies had no political rights.

In addition, property, residence, and literacy requirements effectively disenfranchised large segments of the lower classes. Still, the Soviet record in regard to political freedom has been no better and possibly poorer than the capitalist countries of the West.

HUMAN COSTS AND ECONOMIC DEVELOPMENT PROGRAMS

There is no doubt that the human cost of economic development in the past has been very high. However, the important question for the purposes of this study is whether or not these costs are an inherent part of the industrialization process. We might analyze the Soviet example in an attempt to answer this question. A good case can be made for the position that not all of these costs are inherent, but instead are due to specific historical circumstances and mistakes.[39] Still others were due to the totalitarian nature of Stalinist communism and thus need not be repeated.[40]

A portion of the social cost in the Soviet Union can be attributed to the extraordinary speed of industrialization which was necessitated by the fear (real or imagined) of foreign attack. Professor Gerschenkron has pointed out that:

> Much of what happened at the turn of the third and fourth decades of the century was the product of that specific historical moment. . . . It must not be forgotten that the smashing defeat of the country by Germany stood at the very cradle of the Soviet regime. Foreign intervention in the Civil War, however half-hearted, certainly left memories that were long in fading . . . after Hitler's advent to power . . . the threat of a military attack began to loom larger and larger each year. There is very little doubt that . . . Russian industrialization in the Soviet period was a function of the country's foreign and military policies.[41]

The adverse impact on the people of this rapid tempo of industrialization was increased by the sharp decline in the international terms-of-trade which required larger agricultural exports to obtain the same amount of capital imports. In addition, Professor Gerschenkron points out that the Soviets' willingness to push rapidly ahead in spite of the social costs incurred was conditioned by the historical acceptance of force in Russia.

. . .

The major cause of the famine in the early 1930's was the massive destruction of livestock that occurred at the beginning of the collectivization drive. This was caused by the attempt to collectivize all of the peasants' livestock. Rather than acquiesce, the peasants slaughtered and ate their livestock. The decision to collectivize livestock was probably the single most important mistake made in the Soviet Union during the 1930's. The communist countries that began collectivization later did not repeat this mistake. The eastern European countries collectivized at a much slower rate and even stopped temporarily when resistance became strong.[42] In China, "the principal domestic animal, the pig, was left in private hands . . . the Chinese were able to avoid mass slaughter of livestock and famine in carrying through full-scale collectivization."[43]

In conclusion, while the social costs incurred in the industrialization of the Soviet Union need not be repeated in the same degree by an underdeveloped country adopting the Soviet model or some part thereof, some social costs seem almost inevitable regardless of what development model is followed.

There are a number of reasons why the industrialization process is not a painless one. First, there is the need in many countries for a radical change in social structure. In many cases this can be brought about only by a more or less violent social revolution. The old order will fight to maintain its dominance and the new will defend itself against possible counterrevolution. And the period of revolution is not restricted to just the time of open civil war (if there is one) but extends until the inhibiting features of the old social structure are eradicated. The American Civil War officially ended in 1865 but the social revolution that engendered it goes on today in the battles of Little Rock, Birmingham, Watts, Detroit, and Washington, D.C. The collectivization battles of the 1930's were a continuation of the Russian Revolution of 1917.

Second, and closely allied to the first, is the need to develop new social institutions and to educate people to new habits and values. Peasants must be turned into factory workers. A new kind of discipline must be learned. People must be convinced that new ways of doing things can be good and beneficial. This is often not easy. The Luddites rose up and smashed the new machinery in the British Industrial Revolution. The Russian peasant tried to sabotage the introduction of the kolkhoz. The type of labor discipline that is required in an industrial society is alien to the habits of a pre-industrial society. It is difficult to convince people of the need for new habits and discipline exclusively by methods of persuasion. It is not so much that the need for discipline and change is not understood; but as often happens, what is understood is not yet sufficiently willed. Thus, the change-over from one set of habits and values to another is difficult, and some compulsion is often required. This compulsion took the form of the *explicit coercion* of the state police power to expedite the movement from individual to collective farms and to enforce factory discipline in the Soviet Union of the 1930's. In capitalist countries the implicit coercion of the market mechanism transferred labor from rural to urban areas and imposed discipline through the threat of starvation and unemployment.

Third is the need to increase the rate of capital accumulation. This involves widening the margin between consumption and total output. Despite the fact that consumption levels are already deplorably low in underdeveloped countries, it is most unlikely that they can be substantially raised in the early stages of development. "Often it is argued that (the) more human approach is what distinguished economic development under democratic conditions from what would take place under a Communist regime—in my opinion a rather dangerous assertion if, realistically, living standards will have to be kept low in order to allow development."[44] This need to restrain consumption in favor of capital accumulation can cause a rise in social discontent. The poorer classes will feel that after fighting for the recent revolution, and/or reforms, they are entitled to its fruits. The middle classes and the upper classes will resent the curtailment of their former privileges and "luxury" consumption. To keep this unrest from upsetting the development plans or from leading to counterrevolution a powerful, even ruthless, government policy of coercion may be needed. This, while enabling capital to be accumulated, will increase the social cost of doing so. It is wrong to envision economic development as a smooth evolutionary process of change since ". . . the happy picture of a quiet industrial revolution proceeding without undue stir and thrust has been . . . seldom reproduced in historical reality."[45] The changes necessary to initiate economic development are more likely to resemble a gigantic social and political earthquake.

. . .

CONCLUSION

From the discussion in this paper we can draw a number of conclusions. The social cost of development in the Soviet Union was high indeed—purges, Stalinist terror, forced labor, famine, and lack of freedom. The cost of capitalist development was high also—slavery, colonialism, genocide of native races, and lack of freedom. The extent of a cause and effect relationship is probably impossible to establish. It would seem, however, that particular historical circumstances, rather than the development process itself, account for the major share of the human costs. The human cost of either capitalist or communist development appears less than the cost of continued underdevelopment. Still, some social cost seems inevitable if economic development is to take place.

Given the inevitability of some social cost, how does one evaluate the acceptability of this cost relative to the potential benefits of economic development? Seeking refuge in some predetermined ideological position doesn't solve the problem because as Richard Ohmann has pointed out:

> A man who subscribes to a moral or social ideology runs the risk that someone will put it into practice and thereby burden it with a wretched freight of human error and venality. The guillotine becomes an argument against libertarianism, juvenile gang wars an argument against permissive parenthood, the carpetbaggers an argument against emancipation. When this happens, the ideologist may recant; or he may save his ideology by disowning the malpractice as irrelevant perversion. A third response is possible: to accept *la guillotine* along with *la liberte*; but in a man of good will, this requires a strong stomach and a certain obstinacy.[46]

None of these responses seems adequate to the problem. Possibly there is no adequate answer since our normal moral standards are so ambiguous. However, the problem at least can be made clearer by briefly discussing two factors that affect moral judgments.

First, there are the "objective conditions controlling the environment in which behavior takes place."[47] An example of this would be a state of war.

Restrictions of civil liberties, for example, are usually judged more acceptable in wartime than in time of peace. Economic development is also an objective condition. The prevailing objective conditions will help determine what is acceptable behavior on the part of the state and of individuals. This may be an ambiguous standard but it seems to be accepted by most people. For example, Professor Bowles has pointed out that ". . . the death of a political enemy on a battlefield is approved, the domestic execution of a political prisoner is disapproved."[48]

Second, there is the "ideology affecting the norms by which man evaluates such behavior."[49] In the example cited above, a state of war is an objective condition, while the historical tradition and system of beliefs which shape people's attitudes about civil liberties comprise the ideology or value system. Obviously the two factors interact. The objective conditions can alter the ideological commitments. For example, given the situation of ruthless guerrilla warfare in South Vietnam, many Americans become willing to view torture and napalm bombing of peasant villages as acceptable conduct. Even with roughly similar objective conditions, a value system can yield different judgments of identical actions. For example, in the aftermath of the Cuban revolution the execution of a few thousand Batista supporters was condemned by many Americans. The shooting of several hundred thousand Communists in the recent Indonesian revolution was received, if not with approval, at least with tolerance. Also, at least until recently, a government which did not allow white people to vote would be judged a dictatorship, while one that only disenfranchised colored people could be considered a democracy. In addition, of course, different value systems will judge the same actions or behavior differently. Raising the price of a good to take advantage of a temporary scarcity in its supply would have been condemned as a sin by Medieval Catholicism; in a capitalist society it would be considered good business practice.

The above discussion highlights the complexity of the problem of evaluating the social costs of economic development. Man seems to be faced with a dilemma. On the one hand, the failure to overcome underdevelopment *allows* untold human suffering to continue. On the other hand, the process of overcoming these human costs through speeding up development will most likely *generate* some new ones; and the faster the old human costs are overcome the more severe the new. Also, there is the danger that the centralized power needed to generate rapid development will be used, as with Stalin, to consolidate personal power and establish totalitarianism.

Let me close this discussion by quoting a comment received from a close colleague, Professor W. Michael Bailey, after he had read the paper.

> It seems most ironic that to be FREE (from want and privation) man must be made a SLAVE to some political and economic gyroscope that spins off goods in abundance while grinding away at moral freedom and the possibility of real human choices. In a sense your paper is the most immoral thing of all because it portrays so clearly the necessity for evil and provides the perfect motive for doing for good reasons what so many want to do for the sheer pleasure of it and for the terrible beauty of the awesome power machine that man can make. False gods beckon on every side; only a few see God within the shadows, faint like a mist but more real than man's most titanic creations, as good is.

NOTES

1. E. H. Carr, *What is History?* (New York: Alfred A. Knopf, 1962), p. 102.
2. See Josué de Castro, *The Geography of Hunger* (Boston: Little, Brown and Co., 1952), pp. 29, 151.
3. *Ibid.*, p. 29.
4. *Colliers Encyclopedia*, 1962, Vol. 9, p. 552.
5. *Ibid.*
6. Castro, p. 177. Except for American grain shipments, there would probably have been famine in India during 1966–68.
7. *Ibid.*, p. 277. *Colliers Encyclopedia*, p. 552.
8. Franklyn Holzman, "Consumer Sovereignty and the Rate of Economic Development," *Economia Internazionale*, Vol. XI, No. 2 (1956), pp. 15–16.
9. For illuminating views on the effect of poverty on the human spirit see Carolina Maria de Jesus, *Child of the Dark* (New York: E. P. Dutton & Co., 1962), and Oscar Lewis, *The Children of Sanchez* (New York: Random House, 1961).
10. D. Gale Johnson and Arcadius Kahan, "Soviet Agriculture, Structure and Growth," *Comparisons of the United States and Soviet Economies*, Joint Economic Committee, 86th Cong., 1st Sess., 1960, p. 205.
11. Janet Chapman, "Consumption," *Economic Trends in the Soviet Union*, ed. Abram Bergson and Simon Kuznets (Cambridge: Harvard University Press, 1963), p. 245.
12. *Ibid.*, pp. 245, 254, 261, 268–270.
13. A. J. Taylor, "Progress and Poverty in Britain, 1780–1850: A Reappraisal," *Essays in Economic History*, ed. E. M. Carus-Wilson (Vol. III; London: Edward Arnold Ltd., 1962), p. 391.
14. W. W. Lockwood, *The Economic Development of Japan: Growth and Structural Change, 1868–1938* (Princeton: Princeton University Press, 1954), pp. 34, 148–149.
15. Sir John Maynard writes that the great majority of peasants did or would have joined willingly because ". . . collectivization is a step up on the social ladder, and I err greatly if this has not been an element of importance in the acceptance of the change. It was otherwise, of course, with the prosperous peasant, who desired no such change; but the prosperous peasant, in his character of *kulak* was condemned beyond reprieve." Sir John Maynard, *The Russian Peasant: And Other Studies* (New York: Collier Books, 1962), p. 388. See also Maurice Hindus, *The Great Offensive* (New York: Harrison Smith and Robert Haas, 1933). For an opposing view see M. Fainsod, *Smolensk Under Soviet Rule* (Cambridge: Harvard University Press, 1958).
16. Hindus, pp. 146–147.
17. Maynard, p. 366.
18. *Ibid.*, p. 379.
19. Frank Lorimer, *The Population of the Soviet Union: History and Prospects* (Geneva: League of Nations, 1946).
20. Naum Jasny, *The Socialized Agriculture of the U.S.S.R.: Plans and Performance* (Grain Economic Series No. 5; Stanford: Stanford University Press, 1949), pp. 322–324.
21. This is what happened in the United States during the Great Depression. The birth rate fell from 21.3 in 1925 to 16.9 in 1935. U.S. Bureau of the Census, *Statistical Abstract of the United States, 1963* (Washington: Government Printing Office, 1963), p. 52.
22. The 5.5 million figure must be the upper limit unless birth rates were *higher* and/or death rates *lower* in the 1930's than the trend of the 1920's.
23. See Dana G. Dalrymple, "The Soviet Famine of 1932–1934," *Soviet Studies*, Vol. XV, No. 3 (January, 1964), pp. 250–284.
24. "Ukraine [sic] villages which failed to deliver their quotas to the collectors were punished by the confiscation of all grain, and the stoppage of relief supplies: a measure of ruthless reprisal which was doubtless the cause of some of the local mortality." Maynard, p. 377.

25. J. L. and B. Hammond, *The Town Labourer, 1760–1832* (London: Longmans, Green & Co., 1932), p v.

26. Karl de Schweinitz, "Economic Growth, Coercion, and Freedom," *World Politics*, Vol. IX, No. 2 (January, 1957), p. 176.

27. Frightened by these internal manifestations of discontent and by the revolutionary changes in America ad France, Parliament added sixty-three new capital offenses between 1760 and 1810. "Not only petty theft, but primitive forms of industrial rebellion—destroying a silk loom, throwing down fences when commons were enclosed, and firing corn ricks—were to be punished by death." E. P. Thompson, *The Making of the English Working Class* (London: Victor Gollancz Ltd., 1964), p. 60. Professor Thompson also points out that an average of fifty to sixty persons were hanged each year for these "crimes against property." *Ibid.*, p. 61.

28. Between 1786 and 1869, some 160,000 persons were transported to Australia as convicts. Margorie Barnard, *A History of Australia* (New York: Frederick A. Praeger, Publisher, 1963), p. 210.

29. As will be explained later, it is this writer's belief that the major human costs incurred in both the Soviet and capitalist development experiences are not inherent in the systems and, therefore, need not be repeated by underdeveloped countries today.

30. See Cecil Woodham-Smith, *The Great Hunger* (New York: Harper and Row, 1963). She places a large share of the blame for the high mortality on the English policy of laissez-faire and the land-tenure system imposed by the English over the preceding years.

31. Jawaharlal Nehru, *The Discovery of India* (New York: Doubleday & Co., 1956), pp. 211–212.

32. For a detailed analysis of the contribution of slave trading to European development see Eric Williams, *Capitalism and Slavery* (Chapel Hill: University of North Carolina Press, 1944); Basil Davidson, *Black Mother* (Boston: Little Brown & Co., 1961); Daniel P. Mannix, *Black Cargoes* (New York: Viking Press, 1962).

33. Davidson, p. 80.

34. William Brandon, *The American Heritage Book of Indians* (New York: Dell Publishing Co., 1961), p. 360.

35. Douglass North, *The Economic Growth of the United States: 1790–1860* (Englewood Cliffs: Prentice-Hall, Inc., 1961), p. 189. See also Kenneth M. Stampp, *The Peculiar Institution: Slavery in the Ante-Bellum South* (New York: Vintage Books, 1964).

36. See Wilbert E. Moore, *Industrialization and Labor* (New York: Cornell University Press, 1951) and J. C. Furnivall, *Colonial Policy and Practice* (New York: New York University Press, 1956).

37. Western estimates of the peak use of forced labor vary between 3 and 13 million. See S. Swianiewicz, *Forced Labour and Economic Development* (London: Oxford University Press, 1965), pp. 25–40.

38. Celso Furtado, "Brazil: What Kind of Revolution," *Foreign Affairs*, Vol. 41, No. 3 (April, 1963), p. 530.

39. Professor Swianiewicz, however, argues that the rapid tempo of development adopted in the Soviet model necessarily causes a demand for labor that can be met at reasonable cost only through forced labor. See Swianiewicz, pp. 189–207. However, this would be profitable only if the difference in consumption between free and forced labor exceeded the difference in output between the two kinds of labor.

40. For an interesting discussion of this point see Alec Nove, "Was Stalin Really Necessary?" in his *Economic Rationality and Soviet Politics* (New York: Frederick A. Praeger, Publishers, 1964), pp. 17–39.

41. Alexander Gerschenkron, *Economic Backwardness in Historical Perspective* (New York: Frederick A. Praeger, Publishers, 1965), pp. 147–148.

42. The percentage of cows in the private sector in 1964 was 90 per cent in Poland, 47 per cent in East Germany, 22 per cent in Czechoslovakia, 57 per cent in Hungary, 62 per cent in Rumania, 35 per cent in Bulgaria, and 95 per cent in Yugoslavia. U.S. Department of Agriculture, *The U.S.S.R. and Eastern Europe Agricultural Situation* (Washington: Government Printing Office, 1966), p. 60.

43. Alec Nove, "Collectivization of Agriculture in Russia and China," *Symposium on Economic and Social Problems of the Far East*, ed. E. F. Szczpanik (Hong Kong: Hong Kong University Press, 1962), p. 19.

44. Gunnar Myrdal, *An International Economy* (New York: Harper & Brothers, 1956), p. 164.

45. Gerschenkron, p. 213.

46. Richard Ohmann, "GBS on the U.S.S.R." *The Commonweal* (July 24, 1964), p. 519.

47. De Schweinitz, p. 168.

48. W. Donald Bowles, "Soviet Russia as a Model for Underdeveloped Areas," *World Politics*, Vol. XIV, No. 3 (April, 1962), p. 502.

49. De Schweinitz, p. 168.

27

Growth and Welfare

James H. Weaver

W. Arthur Lewis has presented a persuasive case for the benefits of economic growth.[1] He argues that economic growth gives man greater control
over his environment, thereby increasing his freedom; it gives man freedom
to choose greater leisure; it permits him to have more services as well as
more goods or leisure; and it permits him to indulge in the luxury of greater
humanitarianism.

The benefits of growth are all around us and are obvious. The gross
national product of the United States was estimated at more than $1,100
billion or $1.1 trillion in 1972. If we divide that by 200 million Americans, we
find that per capita GNP was more than $5,000 in 1972—or $20,000 for the
typical family of four.

Up until the last few years the notion that growth meant progress was
the predominant view among all economists whether in the developed or
underdeveloped, capitalist or socialist countries. In fact, the main argument
used in favor of socialism was that it produced more goods and services
faster than capitalism. Many persons in underdeveloped countries are still
seeking economic development for their countries according to the traditional model. In this paper, I will try to set out some of the things they have
to look forward to should they succeed.

TRADITIONAL ECONOMIC ASSUMPTIONS

Traditionally, economists assume that people are motivated by self-interest.
People are assumed to be hedonists, desiring to maximize pleasure and minimize pain. Pleasure is thought to result primarily from the consumption of
goods and services.

The fundamental welfare postulate of traditional economic theory is
that an individual is better off as he or she moves from goods bundle A to
goods bundle B, B being the preferred goods. Welfare is increased as the
individual gets more goods and services. Simply put, more is better.

TRADITIONAL ECONOMIC CRITERIA

The traditional criteria used to judge economic systems are as follows.

1. efficiency—maximum output at minimum private cost
2. stability and full employment—no great swings in economic activity, no depressions or inflations
3. economic growth—the production of goods and services should increase over time at a faster rate than population growth so that people have more goods and services per capita

POLITICAL ECONOMY DEFINITION OF WELFARE[2]

As a political economist, I would agree with the assumption of traditional economists that people act to achieve their own self-interest. People are indeed maximizers; however, society determines what they maximize. Their self-interest would be better served by institutions other than the ones we have created, in order to achieve economic growth.

Welfare derives from activities. People derive welfare from singing, dancing, working, loving, theorizing, playing, painting, sleeping, and so forth. In order to carry out these activities, three requirements must be met.

First, we need certain instruments. We need a paint brush and paints before we can paint. We need tools—goods and services—to be able to carry out our activities. This is the main point of traditional economists. They stop here.

Secondly, we need certain capacities. In order to derive welfare from making music, we must have the capacity to enjoy music. We need encouragement and training to develop all our capabilities to the fullest.

Thirdly, we need a context or environment in which to carry out our activities. In order to enjoy the beauties of nature, we have to have access to nature. In order to enjoy the activity of fishing, we need a stream or river or sea.

CRITERIA FOR JUDGING ECONOMIC SYSTEMS[3]

How can we judge the success of economic systems in achieving these goals? Here we introduce the concept of sovereignty (used also by traditional economists in a more limited sense) as the criterion to be used in judging economic systems. Sovereignty means power. If you are sovereign, you have the ability to control things. A sculptor is sovereign over a piece of wood. He can make anything he wants out of the wood, subject to the physical constraints of the piece of wood itself, i.e., he can't make it into marble or stone. The opposite of sovereignty is alienation, when processes are separated from an individual and are beyond his or her control.

In order for an economic system to be a good system, it must meet three tests of sovereignty. The first test is consumer sovereignty. Does the system produce the goods and services people want? Is the output of goods and services the result of a proper aggregation of people's preferences? Do the people have the instruments they need to carry out their preferred activities?

The second test is worker sovereignty. Do people have the jobs they really want? Are the jobs available to people the result of a proper aggregation of their preferences? Are the jobs fulfilling and personally satisfying? Do they offer people the chance to do creative and meaningful work? A good society is one in which work enhances people's capacities and in which worker sovereignty exists.

A third test is citizen sovereignty. Do people have the communities and environments they really want? Are the communities and environments a reflection of people's true preferences?

Thus, we can pose three key questions.

1. Do we have the goods and services we want in the United States?
2. Do we have the kinds of jobs we want?
3. Are our communities and our environments the way we want them to be?

I will present the answers to these three questions from the traditional and political economists' point of view.

TRADITIONAL VIEW—CONSUMER SOVEREIGNTY

Orthodox economists would argue that consumer sovereignty holds in the United States, that consumers in a capitalist economy get the goods and services they want. Each individual's tastes are independent of everyone else's, and are taken as given. What one person consumes doesn't influence anyone else.

I like Mexican food, you like Chinese food, and there's no conflict. We let everyone express their preferences and find a mechanism that produces what they want.

What is that mechanism? The market, of course. If we allow profit maximizing firms to compete in an open market for people's money, they will produce what people want most. Through the price system, people register their preferences. The price system acts as a signaling device, controlling output in the economy. Producers respond to the price changes because they want to maximize profits, and this ensures that people get what they actually want.

WORKER SOVEREIGNTY

The same approach is applied to worker sovereignty. Neo-classical economists argue that labor markets ensure worker sovereignty in a capitalist economy. Each worker sells his labor in a market and chooses among competing firms, picking the one that gives the best deal. If people wanted satisfying jobs, they would sacrifice goods and services for such jobs. Capitalists would notice that workers wanted good jobs, and wages for such jobs would be lower. Workers would be willing to work for less in a good job, and the capitalists would hire such workers at low wages and make lots of profits, responding to workers' preferences for satisfying work. Orthodox economists argue that if jobs are unsatisfying today it's because workers want goods and services and are willing to take those jobs in order to get them. If people really wanted good jobs, they would be willing to take fewer goods and services. Work and technology have developed in conformance to what people really want. Thus, according to the traditional economists, we do have worker sovereignty in a capitalist economy.

CITIZEN SOVEREIGNTY

We have the kinds of homes and communities we want; markets in land ensure that land is used for those purposes which people want most and for which they are willing to pay the most money. Orthodox economists also argue that citizen sovereignty holds in capitalist economies, but the argument is a little different here. Consumer and worker sovereignty hold as the result of the operation of markets. But one doesn't buy and sell community, or culture, or national defense, or highways. Here we run into the problem of externalities. If I spend $10,000 toward creating a decent environment— a public park, for instance—everybody benefits. There's no way I can charge people who walk by and receive the benefits from my park, and here's where the government comes in. The state is the mechanism which aggregates preferences for what are called public goods, e.g., parks, community services, environmental quality, highways, etc. So we add liberal democracy to capitalist economy and we have the ideal system.

If people want a good community and a good environment, politicians will run on a platform to create a good community and environment. Coalitions will develop. People will come together and elect candidates to public office, and those who are elected will implement their platform. This is the meaning of democratic pluralism; a proper aggregation of people's preferences will hence occur via the political process, ensuring citizen sovereignty.

Orthodox economists argue that people in the United States have the best of all *possible* worlds. Not the best world conceivable, but the best world possible of achievement. If we have polluted environments, alienated work, a lack of community, etc., it is because that's what people want. People apparently want goods and services more than they want beautiful communities, clean air, and good jobs. They get what they want, and who are we to say that what they want isn't good for them? Who knows better than the people themselves?

POLITICAL ECONOMY APPROACH

As a political economist, I would argue that we do not have the three types of sovereignty in the United States nor in any capitalist system today. In fact, the institutions which have been designed to bring about rapid economic growth in capitalist economies *destroy* the welfare-relevant aspects of society; and this is not an aberration, but is necessary if growth is to proceed. It is obviously necessary for underdeveloped countries to produce enough food, clothing, shelter, medical care, and education to meet the needs of their people. Beyond this point, it is not at all clear that increased economic growth leads to increased welfare. In fact, I am prepared to argue that the nation which chooses to increase the gross national product as its primary goal is choosing to systematically destroy those aspects of life which enhance human welfare.

CORE ECONOMIC INSTITUTIONS

In order to understand why increasing GNP leads to declining welfare, we must examine the core institutions of a capitalist economy. There are four such institutions—markets in land, labor, and capital, and bureaucratic and hierarchical firms which are dedicated to maximizing profits and in which specialization of labor is the norm.

First let us examine the market for labor. In such a system, labor becomes a commodity, to be bought and sold on the market just like sacks of flour and bales of hay. You go to work wherever you can get the best price for your labor. Karl Polanyi described this process in *The Great Transformation* and pointed out that it is a new phenomenon. Before the Industrial Revolution, people did that task to which tradition consigned them. Now labor is a commodity. It is a factor of production and a means to an end, the end being greater production of goods and services.

The Industrial Revolution transformed people into commodities. The process involved the de-capitalization of the workers; it took their capital away from them. The Enclosure Movement drove them off the land and ended their traditional rights to use the land. The competition of the factory system eliminated the skilled craftsmen and artisans. All workers were systematically de-capitalized. They were driven into the massive cities and given the choice of becoming a commodity and entering the factory or starving. This is what creating an industrial labor force means, and a growing economy requires it.

The second institution is a market for land. Land, all of nature, becomes a commodity to be bought and sold in a market and to be used for whatever is most profitable. This is a new phenomenon also. Polanyi has pointed out that prior to the Industrial Revolution, land was not considered a commodity. It was used for traditional purposes and was owned and used socially. It wasn't bought and sold.

The third institution is a market for capital, in which tools of production are bought and sold and are used for whatever purpose will be most profitable.

The fourth institution is the bureaucratic and hierarchical firm which seeks to maximize profits. Production of goods and services is done in that manner which will produce maximum profits for the owner of the firm.

The results of such institutions in today's underdeveloped countries are becoming obvious. Those poor countries which have used a capitalist model during the post-World War II period have produced an increasing gross national product. They have also produced increasing poverty, increasing inequality, and increasing unemployment. Adelman and Morris[4] have pointed out that the income going to the bottom 40 percent of the population has actually fallen; their absolute level of income has declined. The same study showed income increasingly concentrated in the hands of a tiny minority of the population. In those capitalist countries in which growth was most rapid, there was the highest degree of income concentration, e.g., Mexico, Pakistan, and Brazil. Hans Singer has recently estimated that unemployment in the underdeveloped countries is approximately 25 percent and that unemployment is growing by 8 percent each year.[5]

However, it is not from the experience of the underdeveloped countries that we should draw our lessons concerning the relationship between growth and welfare. Rather, we should look to the developed countries, and in particular to the most spectacularly successful of the developed countries, the United States of America. We must look at the United States and examine the relationship between growth and welfare. We must ask whether consumer, worker, and citizen sovereignty really exist in the United States.

When we look at the operation of our core economic institutions we find four inevitable consequences: growing inequality, loss of community, ecological destruction, and alienated labor.

GROWING INEQUALITY

One of the inevitable consequences of markets in labor and capital is the presence of great inequality. To be sure, inequality is not a new phenomenon in the world. But somehow we had believed that with the coming of capitalism and democratic governments we would see a reduction in inequality. One of the great goals of the French Revolution, after all, was equality, and it has been an ideal of Western liberal thought for the past 200 years. What has been the actual experience?

The reality is that America today is a society of widespread and growing inequality. If we look at total income we find that in 1968 those families which received less than $2,000 per year (a typical family consists of four people, which means $500 per person per year or a little more than $1.35 per day for food, clothing, medical care, housing, trips to Europe, etc.) made up 10 percent of our families and they received less than 1 percent of our income. By way of contrast, those families who received $50,000 per year made up one half of 1 percent and they received 7 percent of our income.[6]

If we look at the gap between the median income of the top and bottom quintiles, we find increasing inequality since 1949. The *real* income gap between the top and bottom quintiles was $10,565 in 1949 and had grown to

$19,071 in 1969.[7] And the income gap between the top and bottom incomes is truly staggering. We now have multi-billionaires in this country who are estimated to receive as much as $200,000,000 per year in income while there are whole families who live on less than $2,000 per year.

And one of the startling discoveries is that taxes have virtually no impact in terms of redistributing income. "In the United States, the pre- and post-tax distribution of income are not noticeably different."[8] If poverty is defined as living on less than half the median income, then the percentage of our families living in poverty has not changed during the period for which we have data available.[9]

The same depressing story is found when we look at the distribution of wealth. If wealth is good—and as an economist and a materialist I believe it is good—then it should be spread around. But we find that wealth isn't widely distributed in America. In 1962 the wealthiest 20 percent of our families owned 75 percent of all private assets;[10] Robert Lampman has estimated that about 1 percent of the families own approximately 80 percent of the corporate stock.[11]

This information is depressing and discouraging because not only do the data contradict one of the most important ideals of Western liberal thought, but they also reveal that all of our past governmental activities which have been designed to reduce inequality have failed. And these governmental activities have indeed been impressive. They include mass, public, free, and compulsory education; taxes on inheritance; progressive income taxes; the social security system; unemployment compensation; the welfare system; the war on poverty, etc. Despite all these massive governmental programs, inequality has not been reduced and is in fact increasing.

We can conclude three things. First, it seems clear that our core economic institutions perpetuate and even worsen inequality over time. Secondly, income inequality is required for the core economic institutions to function. And finally, a good deal of income immobility is also required.[12]

In order to understand these points, it is useful to divide income into that which derives from labor and that derived from ownership of capital. Labor income, including both wages and salaries, makes up about three quarters of total income and income derived from the ownership of capital makes up the other one quarter.

Capitalism requires that capital be owned unequally. If everyone owned equal shares of capital, there would be no distinction between capitalists and workers; no one would work for anyone else. Because it is a system in which some people own capital and employ labor which owns no capital, capital ownership must be unequal, and therefore income from capital ownership must also be unequal.

The system also requires that labor income be distributed unequally. If labor markets are to work, wages must be unequal. If wages were distributed even approximately equally, who would come and clean our homes and dormitories? People in this society do not work because they find the work fulfilling, they work primarily for material rewards. Thus, if wages were distributed equally, no one would undergo schooling and training to fill certain jobs.

We have established the necessity for inequality—but must it grow?

The answer is simple and affirmative. Capital is accumulated as the result of saving, and saving is much easier for the rich than for the poor. One is appalled at how little saving is done by the residents of our central city ghettoes; they simply are not thrifty. Obviously, those who have large incomes find it easier to save and accumulate more capital. It is also easier for large capital owners to save than for smaller capital owners, so there is a tendency toward concentration within the capital-owning group. It is also possible for large capital owners to make more profitable investments. Inheritance, a necessary institution in a capitalist economy, means that such inequality is passed on and increased from one generation to the next.

The same is true of labor income, deriving from skills, education, and personality characteristics which are acquired in the home, at school, or on the job. Opportunities to develop such skills and characteristics are very different for different classes in the society, and those with the greatest initial advantages tend to have these advantages reinforced. Such differential advantages can be inherited, accumulated, and transmitted between generations.

There is also a high degree of interaction between labor and capital income. Those persons with high incomes from capital or labor can afford to send their children to the best schools, etc., so that they develop their labor power fully.

Thus, the working of markets for labor and capital ensure that income will be divided unequally, that such inequality will increase, and that income immobility will persist. All three results are necessary if the system is to operate. St. Matthew was describing the operation of the system accurately when he wrote, "For unto everyone that hath shall be given, and he shall have abundance; but from him that hath not shall be taken away even that which he hath" (Matthew 25:29). Or, as they used to say in the Ozark mountains of Arkansas where I grew up, "Them as has, gits." Government has proven itself unable to reverse these forces.

LOSS OF COMMUNITY

A further consequence of the operation of the core economic institutions is a loss of community, arising when labor becomes a commodity. Because labor goes to the highest bidder, workers move to that place where they can get the highest wage. They must be able to move around in order for the economic system, as it exists, to operate. Eighteen percent of the American people move each year,[13] and this kind of transience negatively affects feelings of community.

The operation of markets in land also makes community difficult. Homes are built by speculators who are interested in the greatest possible profit. Very little consideration is given to designing homes in such a way that people will be encouraged to develop a feeling of community. Freeways and highways are built where it is most efficient to build them. Neighborhoods are cut in half and even destroyed with little regard for the feelings of the people who live there.

Once labor markets and land markets have been allowed to operate as the primary economic institutions, the political process is virtually powerless to create a good community and a good environment. Power lies with the people who own the land, and they are the ones who determine the shape of our cities. Zoning commissions and planning boards are often dominated by real estate interests and developers. And even when this is not the case, such commissions and boards must operate so that land will be used for its most profitable purpose. There is little room for maneuvering within such constraints.[14]

Citizens in the United States are realizing that the government is virtually powerless to provide us with better communities, even though we continue to pay more taxes in order to get better communities. Indeed, conditions seem to be deteriorating rather than getting better. It appears that the state is not only unable to alter inequality of income in a capitalist society, but is also unable to provide good communities.

ECOLOGICAL DESTRUCTION

Ecological destruction is a further consequence of our core institutions. We know that each firm acts to maximize private profit and has a very great incentive to convert private costs into social costs. We also know that in a capitalist economy all of nature comes to be viewed as a commodity to be used for whatever purposes produce the greatest private profit. Thus, the environment becomes a commodity to be exploited, used, and abused for the sake of maximizing profit. It is, as John Muir said, "a gobble gobble economy"—mine the land, dump garbage in the rivers, fill the air with carbon monoxide, and assault the nerves with noise. All to the end of greater profit.

George Orwell pointed out a long time ago that in a money economy good things happen only by accident. Good things come about if they happen to coincide with making money—that is, by accident. We should congratulate ourselves that such a system has left things as they are and that things have not turned out even worse. We are lucky to be living now; we have been able to fish in clear streams, to swim in unpolluted rivers, to climb an unspoiled mountain trail. Our children and our children's children will never have these opportunities.

ALIENATED LABOR

In addition to markets for land, labor, and capital, the other important institution is the firm—the profit maximizing, pyramidically hierarchical, bureaucratic firm in which work is divided and specialization of labor obtains. Most people spend half of their waking hours in massive, undemocratic, anonymous institutions. There are captains, officers, supervisors, and foremen. Orders flow in one direction, compliance flows in the other.

Such organizations are designed to ensure that owners and managers of a firm can retain overall direction of the firm's activities.[15] This structure allows the people at the top to supervise a number of subordinates who in turn supervise other employees who watch over still other employees. The firm assumes the shape of a pyramid and this pyramidal hierarchy allows a few owners to effectively control the activities of vast numbers of people, most of whom they never see.

Workers in the hierarchy are responsible for those persons under them and are accountable to those above them, and they have very little or no role in shaping the policies they carry out. This leads to a sense of powerlessness on the part of the workers; they feel they are utterly unable to control what they will do, or how and when they will do it.

In adddition to hierarchy and bureaucracy, there is specialization of labor.[16] Work is broken down into minute tasks, and each worker is expected to be an expert in only one small task. His contribution to the final product is minimal, impersonal, and standardized; and his work is meaningless to him.

A feeling of isolation exists among workers in a modern firm, for fragmented tasks preclude solidarity and cooperation. Workers compete with each other. The worst workers are fired, and the best ones are kept and given salary increases and promotions. In such circumstances it is difficult to develop true community with one's fellow workers.

And finally the worker becomes estranged from himself. Work is treated as an instrument—a means to an end—and not as an end it itself. And work is so important to a person's self-definition that he comes to view himself as an instrument, as a means to an end.

Why do we have specialization of labor and hierarchy? The traditional answer is "for the sake of efficiency." The new technology of the Industrial Revolution required it. Stephen Marglin has argued against this explanation, however, claiming that factories were not introduced because they were efficient, for factories increased inputs more than outputs increased, with the number of hours of labor rising significantly with the introduction of the factory system.[17] We also had factories before the new technology was introduced; this casts doubt on the idea that factories were introduced to take advantage of the new technology. Marglin concludes that the main reason for specialization of labor and the factory system was to separate the worker from his product and his customers, and thereby make him dependent on capitalists and thus more subject to industrial discipline. Marglin concludes that the factory system was introduced for the purpose of ensuring control over the generation of surplus so as to be able to increase it and invest it in order to bring about increased output with which to appease the workers.

Whatever the origins of specialization and hierarchy, it is certain that these institutions are not continued today in the interest of efficiency. Workers simply don't like fragmented jobs. When job enlargement is introduced and when decision-making is in the hands of the workers, productivity and satisfaction increase and absenteeism and turnover decrease.[18] Capitalists do not introduce these techniques, however, because they pose a fundamental threat to capitalist control over the surplus.

The evidence indicates that decentralized structures are far superior when tasks are difficult, complex, and unusual. Centralized structures are efficient when tasks are simple and routinized.[19] Since firms are organized in a centralized and hierarchical manner, it is in the interests of those who control the firms to make work as simple and routine as possible. But this is done in the interest of control, not in the interest of efficiency.[20]

CONCLUSION

We have accepted this whole phenomenon of economic growth and its accompanying institutions on the grounds that we will get more and more goods and services as a result. We accept inequality, unsatisfying jobs, fragmented lives, and a degraded environment in return for more and more goods. We have neither worker sovereignty nor citizen sovereignty.

We do have consumer sovereignty, however. The drive to acquire more and more goods is a perfectly rational one for the individual within the present society. When one has little opportunity to do meaningful work, little sense of community with his fellows, and little gratification from a natural environment which has been despoiled and degraded, it makes perfectly good sense to try and maximize consumption.

There is no denying that those persons with the highest income also have the best jobs. With a high income, one can also escape the horror of living in our central cities and can afford to live in a more pleasant environment. Within the constraints under which we live, maximizing one's income is a perfectly rational goal for the individual. It is not rational, however, to accept the existing constraints.

The problems which beset us today—alienated work, increasing inequality, lack of community, and environmental destruction—are inevitable consequences of economic growth in a capitalist economy. These problems may be inevitable and insoluble in *any* industrialized economy.

Modern man is lost in a lonely crowd, beset by massive bureaucracies on all sides, alienated from his work, isolated from his fellow man, and estranged from nature. We do not have the kinds of jobs nor the kinds of communities we want. We do not have the kind of natural environment we need in order to survive. And we can't obtain these things within the existing institutional framework in the United States.

Capitalism, in overcoming the deprivation and poverty of the feudal era, has brought enormous material progress. The status-bound life of the traditional villager has been irrevocably altered. More people are living longer and better than in any previous age.

Yet most of us have suspected for a long time that the system is fatally flawed. A system based primarily on greed and the amassing of goods and services is not a good society. We have known all along that avarice is a vice, not a virtue.

And, as has often been the case, it was the young who made us realize these things. From the Bible we learn that "your young men shall see visions" (Joel 2:28). Young people in both the rich and the poor nations have had a vision of a better society and have had the courage to confront the revolutionary changes which are necessary if that society is to come into being. I can only wish them Godspeed.

NOTES

1. W. Arthur Lewis, "Is Economic Growth Desirable?" Appendix to *The Theory of Economic Development* (Homewood, Ill.: Richard Irwin, 1955).
2. Based on Herbert Gintis, *Alienation and Power*. Unpublished Ph.D. dissertation, Harvard University, 1969.
3. Based on Herbert Gintis, "Consumer Behavior and the Concept of Sovereignty," *American Economic Review*, May 1972.
4. Irma Adelman and Cynthia Taft Morris, "Who Benefits from Economic Growth?" (mimeograph, 1971).
5. Hans Singer, "Dualism Revisited," *Journal of Development Studies*, 1971.
6. Roger A. Herriot and Herman P. Miller, "Changes in the Distribution of Taxes Among Income Groups: 1962 to 1968." Paper presented to the American Statistical Association, August 1971.
7. Lester C. Thurow and Robert E. B. Lucas, *The American Distribution of Income*, Joint Economic Committee, U.S. Congress (Washington: Government Printing Office, 1972), p. 1.
8. *Ibid.*, p. 5.
9. Oscar Ornati, *Poverty Amid Affluence* (New York: Twentieth Century Fund, 1966).
10. Thurow and Lucas, *op. cit.*, p. 12.
11. Robert Lampman, *Shares of Top Wealth Holders in National Wealth, 1922–1956* (Princeton: Princeton University Press, 1962).
12. The following analysis is based on a paper by Thomas Weisskopf, "Capitalism and Inequality," in Richard C. Edwards, Michael Reich, and Thomas E. Weisskopf, eds., *The Capitalist System* (Englewood Cliffs, N.J.: Prentice-Hall, Inc., 1972).
13. U.S. Department of Commerce, *Statistical Abstract of the United States, 1971* (Washington: Government Printing Office, 1971), p. 34.
14. One of my students recently did a study of Houston, Texas, where there are no zoning and planning laws and commissions. He found that Houston had not developed in a significantly different manner than other cities of comparable size.
15. See Richard C. Edwards, "Bureaucratic Organization in the Capitalist Firm," in Edwards, Reich, and Weisskopf, *op. cit.*
16. This analysis is based on Herbert Gintis, "Alienation and Power," in James Weaver, ed., *Modern Political Economy: Radical and Orthodox Approaches* (Boston: Allyn & Bacon, 1973).
17. See Stephen Marglin, "What Do Bosses Do?" (Harvard University, mimeograph).
18. Paul Blumberg, *Industrial Democracy* (New York: Schocken, 1969).
19. Victor Vroom, "Industrial Social Psychology," in Gardner Lindzey and Elliot Aransen, eds., *The Handbook of Social Psychology*, Vol. V, 2nd ed. (Reading, Mass.: Addison-Wesley, 1969).
20. For a further discussion, see Herbert Gintis, "Alienation and Power," in Weaver, *op. cit.*

28

"Development" . . . or Liberation?

Denis Goulet

Latin Americans in growing numbers now denounce the lexicon of development experts as fraudulent. To illustrate, Gustavo Gutierrez, a Peruvian theologian and social activist, concludes that "the term development conveys a pejorative connotation . . . (and) is gradually being replaced by the term liberation . . . there will be a true development for Latin America only through liberation from the domination by capitalist countries. That implies, of course, a showdown with their natural allies: our national oligarchies."[1]

Gutierrez is a major spokesman for "theology of liberation." Numerous seminars and conferences have already been held on the theme in Colombia, Mexico, Uruguay, Argentina, and elsewhere. For Gutierrez—as for Gustavo Perez, René Garcia, Rubem Alves, Juan Segundo, Camilo Moncada, Emilio Castro,[2] and others—"liberation" expresses better than "development" the real aspirations of their people for more human living conditions. Gutierrez does not attempt to review all the changes in the definition of development since the Marshall Plan was launched in 1947. This task has already been performed by others.[3] Instead he focuses his critical gaze on three perspectives with one of which most experts in "developed" countries identify.

THREE VIEWS OF DEVELOPMENT

For many economists development is synonymous with economic growth measured in aggregate terms. A country is developed, they hold, when it can sustain, by its own efforts and after having first reached a per capita GNP (Gross National Product) level of $500 (for some observers) or $1000 (for others), an annual rate of growth ranging from 5% to 7%. According to these criteria, certain countries are highly developed, while those on the lowest rungs of the ladder are either underdeveloped or undeveloped. Similar comparisons can also be established between different regions and sectors within a single economy. Although this view is generally repudiated today, it still retains some vestigial influence, thanks to the impact of works like Walt Rostow's *The Stages of Economic Growth* and to the dominant role

Reprinted from the *International Development Review*, Vol. XIII, No. 3 (September 1971), by permission of the publisher. Copyright 1971 © by the Society for International Development.

still played by economists in planning. Even when they give lip-service to other dimensions in development, many economists continue to subordinate all non-economic factors to the practical requirements of their growth models.

The second outlook, far more prevalent today, was summarized at the start of the United Nations' First Development Decade in U Thant's phrase, "development = economic growth + social change." The trouble with this formula is that it either says too much or says too little since not any kind of growth will do, nor any kind of change.

Most social scientists adopt some variant of this conception as their own working definition of development; it is broad enough to embrace a variety of change processes emphasizing either economic, social, cultural or political factors. Nearly always, however, social scientists subordinate value judgments about human goals to the achievement of economic growth, to the creation of new social divisions of labor, to the quest for modern institutions, or to the spread of attitudes deemed compatible with efficient production. The last point is well illustrated by those who affirm that "modernity" is not the presence of factories, but the presence of a certain viewpoint on factories.

Behind an array of theories and special vocabularies, however, lingers the common assumption that "developed" societies ought to serve as models for others. Some observers, eager to minimize culture bias, reject the notion that all societies *ought* to follow patterns set by others. Nevertheless, they assert that modern patterns are inevitable, given the demonstration effects and technological penetration of modern societies throughout the world.

A third stream of development thinkers stresses ethical values. This group has always constituted, in some respects, a heretical minority. Its position centers on qualitative improvement in all societies, and in all groups and individuals within societies. Although all men must surely have enough goods in order to be more human, they say, development itself is simply a means to the human ascent. This perspective, at times called "the French school," is linked to such names as economist François Perroux, social planner Louis Lebret, theorist Jacques Austruy, and practicing politicians like Robert Buron and André Phillip. According to these men and their disciples, social change should be seen in the broadest possible historical context, within which all of humanity is viewed as receiving a summons to assume its own destiny. Their ideas have influenced United Nations agencies in some measure, but they have made their greatest inroads in religious writings on development: papal encyclicals, documents issued by the World Council of Churches and the Pontifical Commission on Justice and Peace, pastoral letters drafted by bishops in several countries. The single geographical area where the French school has achieved considerable penetration is Latin America.

This is why the conclusion reached by Gutierrez is particularly significant. According to Gutierrez, the French school, because of its historicity and its insistence on norms for social goals, is the least objectionable of the three perspectives he criticizes. Nevertheless, he argues, the realities barely hinted at by the French are better expressed by the term "liberation" than by "development." By using the latter term the French school does not dramatize its discontinuities with the other perspectives sharply enough. Worse still, its spokesmen employ such notions as foreign aid, technical cooperation, development planning, and modernization in ways which remain ambiguous at best. Consequently, in the eyes of many Latin Americans "development" has a pejorative connotation: it does not get to the roots of the problem and leads to frustration. Moreover, "development" does not evoke asymmetrical power relations operative in the world or the inability of evolutionary change models to lead, in many countries, to the desired objectives. Therefore, says Gutierrez, it is better to speak of liberation, a term which directly suggests domination, vulnerability in the face of world market forces, weak bargaining positions, the need for basic social changes domestically and for freer foreign policies.

THE LANGUAGE OF LIBERATION

To substitute for "development" the term "liberation" is to engage in what Brazilian educator Paulo Freire calls "cultural action for freedom."[4] Liberation implies the suppression of elitism by a populace which assumes control over its own change processes. Development, on the other hand, although frequently used to describe various change processes, stresses the benefits said to result from them: material prosperity, higher production and expanded consumption, better housing or medical services, wider educational opportunities and employment mobility, and so on. This emphasis, however, errs on two counts. First, it uncritically supports change strategies which value efficiency above all else, even if efficiency must be gained by vesting decisions in the hands of elites—trained managers, skilled technicians, high-level "manpower." A second failing, analyzed by Harvard historian Barrington Moore in *Social Origins of Dictatorship and Democracy,* is the dismissal of violence as unconstructive and the refusal to condemn the violence attendant upon legal change patterns.

Not theologians alone, but social scientists, planners, educators, and some political leaders in Latin America prefer the terminology of liberation to that of development. They unmask the hidden value assumptions of the conventional wisdom and replace them with a deliberate stress on self-development as opposed to aid, foreign investment, and technical assistance. Since I have written a detailed critique of the Pearson, Peterson, Jackson and other development reports elsewhere,[5] there is no need to repeat here what is there said regarding the value assumptions and critical omissions of these reports. What is germane to the present discussion is the confirmation given these criticisms by Third World spokesmen in UNCTAD (United Nations Conference on Trade and Development) and GATT (General Agreement on Tariffs and Trade) meetings.[6] Not surprisingly, more and more leaders from underdeveloped areas are coming to regard "development" as the lexicon of palliatives. Their recourse to the vocabulary of liberation is a vigorous measure of self-defense, aimed at overcoming the structural vulnerability which denies them control over the economic, political, and cultural forces which impinge upon their societies. Even to speak of liberation, before achieving it, is a first conquest of cultural autonomy. Ultimately what is sought is to alter relationships between director and directed societies, between privileged elites and the populace at large within all societies. Ever more people are coming to understand that "to be underdeveloped" is to be relegated to a subordinate position in history, to be given the role of adjusting to, not of initiating, technological processes.

The language of liberation is being nurtured in societies where a new critical consciousness is being formed. For these societies, the models of genuine development are not those billed by U.S. aid agencies as success stories—South Korea, Greece, Taiwan, and Iran. Industrialization and economic growth have no doubt taken place in these lands, but no basic changes have occurred in class relationships and the distribution of wealth and power; the larger social system remains structurally exploitative. Moreover, economic gains have been won under the tutelage of repressive political regimes. Finally, as one European has observed, "U.S. aid seems to work best in countries which are lackeys of American foreign policy."

Revolutionary Latin Americans reject this kind of development. They look instead to China, Cuba, and Tanzania as examples of success. In China, mass starvation has been abolished and a feudal social system overthrown. Elitism in rulers is systematically uprooted whenever it reappears, and technological gains are subordinated to the cultural creation of a new man capable of autonomy. Cuba, notwithstanding its economic mistakes, freely admitted, has overcome its servile dependence on the United States and asserts itself increasingly in the face of the Soviet Union, upon whom it still relies heavily for financial, technical and military assistance. Moreover, Cuba has abolished illiteracy in sensational fashion, decentralized investment, and reduced the gap in living conditions between the countryside and the cities. And Tanzania is admired because it rejects mass-consumption as a model for society, practices self-reliance in its educational system (choosing to grant prestige to agricultural skills rather than to purely scientific ones geared to large-scale engineering projects), accepts foreign aid only when the overall impact of the projects financed will not create a new elite class within the nation itself, and in general subordinates economic gains to the creation of new African values founded on ancient communitarian practices.

For liberationists, therefore, success is not measured simply by the quantity of benefits gained, but above all by the way in which change processes take place. Visible benefits are no doubt sought, but the decisive test of success is that, in obtaining them, a society will have fostered greater popular autonomy in a non-elitist mode, social creativity instead of imitation, and control over forces of change instead of mere adjustment to them. The crucial question is: Will "underdeveloped" societies become mere consumers of technological civilization or agents of their own transformation? *At stake, therefore, is something more than a war over words; the battle lines are drawn between two conflicting interpretations of historical reality, two competing principles of social organization.* The first values efficiency and social control above all else, the second social justice and the creation of a new man.

Western development scholars are prone to question the validity of the new vocabulary of liberation. As trained social scientists, they doubt its analytical power, explanatory value, and predictive capacities. Yet their scepticism is misplaced inasmuch as empirical social science has itself proved unable to describe reality, let alone to help men change it in acceptable ways. Of late, however, a salutory modesty has begun to take hold of social scientists. Gunnar Myrdal (in *Asian Drama*) confesses the error of his early days as an "expert" on development, and challenges (in *Objectivity in Social Research*) the assumptions behind all value-free theories and research methods. More forcefully still, Alvin Gouldner, in *The Coming Crisis of Western Sociology*, argues the case for a new Utopian, value-centered radical sociology for the future. And economist Egbert de Vries[7] reaches the conclusion that no significant breakthroughs in development theory have been achieved in the last decade. Western development scholars, therefore, themselves lost in deep epistemological quagmire, are ill-advised to scorn the new theories.

One finds in truth great explanatory power, analytical merit, and predictive value in the writings of Latin American social scientists on development, dependence, and domination.[8] The new liberation vocabulary is valid, even empirically, because it lays bare structures of dependence and domination at all levels. Reaching behind the neutral "descriptive" words of developmental wisdom, it unmasks the intolerably high human cost to Latin Americans of economic development, social modernization, political institution-building and cultural westernization. The reality described by these writings is the pervasive impotence of vulnerable societies in the face of the impersonal stimuli which impinge upon them. Furthermore, their vocabulary enjoys high prescriptive value because it shows this powerlessness to be reversible: if domination is a human state of affairs caused and perpetuated by men, it can be overthrown by men. Finally, the highly-charged political language of liberation has great predictive value to the extent that it can mobilize collective energies around a value which is the motor of all successful social revolutions—HOPE. Liberated hope is not the cold rational calculus of probability *à la* Herman Kahn or Henry Kissinger, but a daring calculus of *possibility* which reverses the past, shatters the present, and creates a new future.

"DEVELOPMENT" AS A HINGE WORD

In spite of its absolute superiority, however, the language of liberation remains, for many people in the "developed" world, tactically unmanageable. The historical connotations of the word sometimes lead them to resist mobilization around its theme, especially if these people are not themselves oppressors, but inert beneficiaries of impersonal oppressive systems. A second category of people may also find it difficult to respond, namely those insurgent professionals who can subvert "the system" only by mastering its tools and serving as a fifth column in alliance with revolutionary groups on the outside. Understandably, these persons will need to continue using the currently available "professional" terminology. It is considerations such as these which lie behind the question: Can "development" serve a useful hinge role in mobilization? The answer is affirmative if one agrees with political scientist Harvey Wheeler that

> . . . we don't possess a *revolutionary* social science to serve the utopian needs of the revolution. And those learned enough to create it are divorced from the activists who must prepare the way for the new utopianism. . . . Somehow, the radical activists and the radical scientists—the utopians— must come together.[9]

Desired changes within "developed" societies can ensue only in the wake of concerted (and much unconcerted) action emanating from a variety of change agents. There can be no objection on principle, therefore, to granting tentative validity to "development" as a hinge word.

For the benefit of those who have not yet been weaned from the sweet milk of palliative incrementalism,[10] "development" needs to be redefined, demystified, and thrust into the arena of moral debate. If critically used as a hinge word, it may open up new perspectives and render the leap into "liberation" possible for many people. Nevertheless, only from the third perspective on development summarized above can one find a suitable platform whence to make this leap of faith. The reason is that, of the three viewpoints, only this ethical, value-laden, humanist approach is rooted in history, and not in abstract theory. Before the language of liberation can sound convincing to the categories of people I have described, it must be shown that "development," as normally understood, alienates even its beneficiaries in compulsive consumption, technological determinisms of various sorts, ecological pathology and warlike policies. Worst of all, it makes those who benefit from development the structural accomplices of the underdevelopment of others. Surely this cannot be what authentic development is. As one reflects on its goals, he discovers that development, viewed as a human project, signifies total liberation. Such liberation aims at freeing men from nature's servitudes, from economic backwardness and oppressive technological institutions, from unjust class structures and political exploiters, from cultural and psychic alienation—in short, from all of life's inhuman agencies.

A new language, able to shatter imprisoning reality, must be born from the clash between vocabularies nurtured in different soils. The first will gestate in a Third World matrix and express the emerging consciousness of those who refuse to be objects, and declare their intent to become subjects, of history. The keys to this vocabulary are the conquest of autonomy and the will to create a new future. At the opposite pole, out of "developed" societies, must arise a subversive redefinition of development itself. Its function will be to destroy the First World's uncritical faith in the universal goodness of its notions of progress, achievement, social harmony, democracy, and modernization. Confrontation between the two is required because neither "development" alone nor "liberation" alone fully transcends both cultural domination and purely negative responses to oppression. Moreover, both terms can be used by symbol manipulators to mystify reality or rationalize palliative change strategies.

Nevertheless, it is clear that competing terminologies of development and liberation are not equally subject to distortion. On the scales of human justice, the interests which they express do not balance each other out. There is indeed, as Camus writes, universal meaning in the rebel's refusal to be treated as something less than a man. And as Marx put it, the oppressed masses are the latent historical carriers of universal human values. The battle to free men is not comparable to the struggle to maintain or expand privilege. Consequently, every trace of elitism and cultural manipulation must be purged from the development vocabulary and replaced with the symbols of liberation. Even then history will not give men any respite; rather, it will propel them into asking: Liberation for what? Ancient teleological questions reappear, concerning the good life, the good society, and men's final purposes. That they should keep arising is no sign of the weakness of men's words, but merely a clue to the grandeur of their historical task. That task is to strive endlessly to outstrip not only alienating material conditions but all particular images of the ideal society as well.

Intellectuals who discuss revolution and violence often utter irresponsible words which place bullets in other people's guns. As they debate development and liberation, the danger they face is less dramatic but no less destructive in the long run. For most of them resort to persuasive political definitions, thereby pre-empting all the intellectual ground upon which descriptive and evocative definitions might find their place. Such habits render genuine liberation impossible since true cultural emancipation admits of no sloganism, no sectarianism, no simplism. Revolutionary consciousness is critical of self no less than of others; and it brooks no verbal cheating even to achieve ideological gains. In final analysis, any liberation vocabulary must do two things. The first is to unmask the alienations disguised by the development lexicon: the alienation of the many in misery, of the few in irresponsible abundance. The second is to transform itself from the rallying cry of victims alone into the victory chant of all men as they empower themselves to enter history with no nostalgia for pre-history.

Success proves difficult because men have never fully learned the lesson implied in a statement by the Indian mystic Rabinadranath Tagore that, ultimately, only those values can be truly human which can be truly universal.

NOTES

1. Gustavo Gutierrez Merino, "Notes for a Theology of Liberation," *Theological Studies*, Vol. 31, No. 2 (June 1970), 243–261.
2. The writings of these men are found largely in papers circulated by documentary services such as LADOC (Latin American Bureau, U.S. Catholic Conference), ISAL (Iglesia y Sociedad en América Latina), and the THEOLOGY OF LIBERATION SYMPOSIUM (in Spanish), Bogota.
3. Cf. the excellent work by Jacques Freyssinet, *Le Concept de Sous-Développement*, Mouton, 1966. A brief review of the different meanings attached to the word "development" can be found in Denis Goulet, "That Third World," *The Center Magazine*, Vol. I, No. 6 (September 1968), 47–55.
4. Cf. Paulo Freire, *Cultural Action for Freedom*, Harvard Educational Review and Center for the Study of Development and Social Change, Monograph No. 1, 1970. One may also consult the same author's *Pedagogy of the Oppressed*, Herder and Herder, 1970.

5. Cf. Denis Goulet and Michael Hudson, *The Myth of Aid: the Hidden Agenda of the Development Reports*, IDOC Books, 1970. This work contains two essays, one by Goulet entitled "Domesticating the Third World," and a second by Hudson on "The Political Economy of Foreign Aid."

6. On this cf., e.g., Guy F. Erb, "The Second Session of UNCTAD," *Journal of the World Trade Law*, Vol. 2, No. 3 (May/June 1968), 346–359. For a Latin American view, see the document entitled, "The Latin American Consensus of Viña del Mar," dated May 17, 1969.

7. Egbert de Vries, "A Review of Literature on Development Theory," *International Development Review*, Vol. X, No. 1 (March 1968), 43–49.

8. Cf., e.g., such works as F. Cardoso and E. Falleto, *Dependencia y Desarrollo on América Latina*, Santiago, 1967; Theotonio dos Santos, *El Nuevo caracter de la dependencia*, Santiago, 1968; Celso Furtado, *Dialéctica Do Desenvolvimento*, Rio de Janeiro, 1964; numerous essays by Alberto Guerreiro Ramos (a Brazilian now teaching at UCLA), *et al.*

9. Harvey Wheeler, "The Limits of Confrontation Politics," *The Center Magazine*, Vol. III, No. 4 (July 1970), 39.

10. The difference between palliative and creative incrementalism is explained in Denis Goulet, *Is Gradualism Dead?*, Council on Religion and International Affairs, 1970.

part eight

What Is
To Be Done?

In the most basic sense, most of the readings in this book address themselves to the question, "What is to be done?"—either by analyzing the nature of underdevelopment or the process of development. The articles in parts four, Agricultural Institutions and Strategy; five, Industrial Institutions and Strategy; and six, Comparative Models of Development, directly discuss the varied problems of promoting development.

This concluding part deals with the problem of how to initiate a development program. That is, it deals with reforms and revolution. The first reading by Mahbub ul Haq sets the stage for the subsequent material. After demonstrating the bankruptcy of present development strategies, he calls for a frontal attack on poverty by redefining development as a selective attack on the worst forms of poverty. Thus development strategy should concentrate on redistributing income and providing employment for the poorest half of the population. He then poses the key question, "Can such a strategy of development be conceived and implemented in the present political and economic structures in the developing countries?" He believes that the mixed economy has failed and sweeping political and social changes are needed. "Whether the developing countries can manage such a change without violent revolutions is a critical question of our time."

In the second reading, the Tanzanian delegation to the Non-Aligned Nations Summit Conference, after explaining how the international system is rigged against the poor countries, argues that there is room for substantial change within the present political and social structures. The poor countries must cooperate in bargaining with the rich countries over trade preferences, controls over MNCs, etc. Thus, they must concentrate on building up the knowledge and expertise of the international economic system to effectively carry on this bargaining.

It is conceivable that the ruling classes in an underdeveloped country will voluntarily give up their vested interests in the status quo in order to promote social and economic development. It is possible that a policy of reforms within existing institutions, as outlined by the Tanzanian delegation, for example, will succeed. Many observers doubt, however, whether reform will succeed in transforming the social and political structures of the underdeveloped countries. During the process of development there are gainers and losers, both relatively and absolutely, among classes as well as individuals. Many of the underdeveloped countries fear the prospects of development, for better than we, their ruling classes realize the revolutionary potential which is contained in social change. They realize that even an attempt at peaceful evolutionary development could quickly gain momentum and proceed to a situation where whole social classes are destroyed and basic institutions remolded.

To some observers, therefore, it seems more likely that change will not come about by completely peaceful, evolutionary means, but rather by a social revolution which will destroy the power of the old ruling classes. The statement from the First Latin American Encounter of Christians for Socialism argues that only a revolutionary reconstruction of society will make it possible to carry out a major development program and eliminate poverty and inequality. The fact that this statement comes out of a Christian context, traditionally the most conservative force in Latin America, is significant itself.

In the next reading, Ivan Illich argues that the underdeveloped countries must take charge of their own development. They must reject the meaning given to development by the rich countries if for no other reason than they will never have sufficient capital to pursue that type of development. He calls for a whole new program of research and policies. For example, because educational resources are so scarce underdeveloped countries can provide each citizen only between eight and thirty months of schooling. He asks: "Why not, instead, make one or two months a year obligatory for all citizens below the age of thirty?" Further, he argues that every dollar spent on doctors and not spent on purifying water costs lives of the poor. In effect, Illich is arguing that resources available for development now and over the next several generations will simply not be adequate to support a full-scale development program. Therefore, resources must be reallocated from serving the rich—private cars, organ transplant clinics, etc.—to aiding the poor—public transportation, water purification, etc.

Illich further argues that revolutionaries in the underdeveloped world have succumbed to the same delusion. They claim that a change in political regime will permit them to expand the privileges of the rich to all. Illich's own program, however, also requires a revolution, if not of iron and blood, at least of ideas and involving a radical shift in the pattern of power. It requires the kind of "liberation" that Denis Goulet briefly discussed in the previous section of the book, and which is developed at greater length by Paulo Freire in "Pedagogy of the Oppressed," the last reading in the book. He argues that development worthy of human beings in the poor countries will come about only when the mass of people recognize their oppression and consciously act to change it. That is, a revolution in ideas and values must accompany a transformation of structures.

29

The Crisis in Development Strategies

Mahbub ul Haq

. . .

I believe that economic development is in serious trouble today. And the indications are many.

After two decades of development, the achievements are quite meagre. When you rip aside the confusing figures on growth rates, you find that for about two-thirds of humanity the increase in per capita income has been less than one dollar a year for the last twenty years.

Even this increase, miserable as it may seem, has been unevenly distributed, with the poorest 40 percent of the population hopelessly squeezed in its struggle for existence and sometimes getting even less than what it received twenty years ago.

Some successful cases of development have turned into development disasters—Pakistan and Nigeria among them.

There is "development weariness" in many developing countries today, with strident voices asking for a social and economic revolution, and there is "aid weariness" in the developed countries today, with many voices asking for an end to a partnership which was never much of a partnership.

And to cap it all, many advocates of zero growth have sprung up in the very societies where growth was always regarded as a sacred goddess and who preached to the developing countries the virtues of an undiluted commitment to growth objectives, underlining how serious the reaction really is against growth for the sake of growth.

What has gone wrong? Why is there such a disillusionment about economic development? Where are the origins of the present crisis?

I believe that the developing countries have themselves to blame for much of the present sorry mess.

Two decades ago, when the developing countries set out to accelerate their pace of economic development, they seemed to have made three basic decisions.

Dazzled by the high living standards of the developed countries and convinced that real life begins at $1,000 or thereabouts, they decided to go after high growth rates in GNP in their mad chase after certain magic figures of *average* per capita incomes.

Paper presented at the International Development Conference, Washington, D.C., April 19–21, 1972; reprinted by permission of the author.

They generally adopted "mixed economy" as a style of development, convinced that they were smart enough to combine the best features of capitalism and socialism.

They turned to the developed countries for generous assistance, hoping that this would make possible the attainment of high growth rates and living standards over a manageable period of time.

All these decisions turned out to be disastrous.

The chase of the Western living standards was illusory at best. After two decades, the evidence is painfully clear. The per capita income disparity between rich and poor nations has continued to widen in the last twenty years. Today, the average per capita income of the developed world is $2,400 compared to $180 in the developing countries. The gap has widened to $2,220. It is expected to widen by another $1,100 by 1980. And all the present indications are that the gap will continue widening and the rich nations will continue becoming richer, despite all the liberalism that is generally expressed in forums like this. To underline how hopeless it is to expect the gap between rich and poor nations to narrow, let me mention just one comparison. The increase in the per capita GNP of the United States in one year equals the increase that India may be able to manage in about one hundred years. Therefore, to conceive the objectives of development in terms of Western living standards or to focus on the widening income gap between the rich and the poor nations is not meaningful at all, except to make the rich nations feel ashamed of themselves from time to time. The developing countries have no choice but to turn inward, much the same way as Communist China did twenty-three years ago, and to adopt a different style of life, seeking a consumption pattern more consistent with their own poverty—pots and pans and bicycles and simple consumption habits—without being seduced by the life styles of the rich. This requires a redefinition of economic and social objectives which is of truly staggering proportions, a liquidation of the privileged groups and vested interests which may well be impossible in many societies, a redistribution of political and economic power which may only be achieved through revolutions rather than through an evolutionary change.

This also means that the developing countries have to search for a new development strategy. The old strategy is based on the quiet assumption that poverty can be taken care of through high growth rates which will eventually filter down to the masses. In this strategy, high growth rates are always better than low growth rates and distribution can be taken care of after growth is achieved. Both these premises have proved bankrupt by now.

It is not true that high growth rates are invariably preferable to low growth rates since they enlarge society's options. It all depends on the structure of these growth rates. If a high growth rate is achieved through rising military expenditures, or through the production of luxury goods for the rich and the privileged, it is not necessarily better than a lower growth rate which is more evenly distributed. In other words, judgements about different levels of growth rates cannot be made independently of the income distribution implicit in them. It is not merely a question of how much is produced but what is produced and how it is distributed. The GNP measurements, unfortunately, do not register social satisfaction.

Here the second part of the old strategy comes in which argues that income distribution is a subsequent consideration. If there are more material goods and services in the system, they can always be redistributed in such a way as to create more social satisfaction. This is simply not true. And it is important that this line of reasoning be rejected as it has done considerable damage already.

It is not true for at least the following three reasons.

Poor societies have often very poor means of redistributing incomes. The coverage of the fiscal systems is generally very limited. Even when income distribution is extremely skewed, it is difficult to reach through direct taxation. To illustrate, even if 60 percent of the income accrues to 20 percent of the population in India, this still implies an average per capita income level of $300 for the "rich" which is below the income tax exemption limit of $400. In other words, income transfers from one sector to the other can be arranged only to a very limited extent in poor societies through the taxation machinery.

Income flows are not financial: they are in the form of physical goods and services. They are influenced by the initial distribution of income. If the society has increased its income in the form of luxury housing and motor cars, how do you really convert them into low cost housing and public buses, short of their physical takeover by the poor?

The institutions which create growth are not neutral as to its distribution. Thus if the growth institutions are characterised by wide disparities in land holdings and concentrations of industrial wealth, the process of growth will strengthen them further and they will resist and frustrate all future attempts to take away their powers and privileges through orderly reforms. This is essentially what happened in Pakistan in the 1960's.

The new development strategy, therefore, must reject the thesis that poverty can be attacked *indirectly* through the growth rates filtering down to the masses. It must be based on the premise that poverty must be attacked *directly*.

What are the elements in such a direct attack on mass poverty? It is difficult to say at this stage since the developing countries are only beginning to perceive this problem in a new perspective. But let me mention a few elements which are critical.

To start with, the focus should shift to the poorest 40 to 50 percent in society. Who are they? How numerous are they? How have their living standards behaved over time? Let us find out a little more, even at this late stage, about the problem we set out to tackle about twenty years ago.

In planning national production targets, the basic minimum needs of these poor should be taken into account, irrespective of whether they can express them in the market or not. In other words, market demand—which is so largely influenced by existing income distribution—should be rejected explicitly in favour of fixing national consumption and production targets on the basis of minimum human needs. We have been slaves of the concept of market demand for too long. But the concept of market demand mocks poverty or plainly ignores it as the poor have very little purchasing power.

It follows that the problem of development must be redefined as a selective attack on the worst forms of poverty. Development goals should be expressed in terms of progressive reduction and eventual elimination of malnutrition, disease, illiteracy, squalor, unemployment, and inequalities. Social indicators must be developed and progress of plans must be measured in terms of specific and quantitative goals in these fields and not in terms of average per capita income. We were taught to take care of our GNP as this will take care of poverty. Let us reverse this and take care of poverty first as the GNP can take care of itself since it is only a convenient summation, and not a motivation for human efforts.

It also follows that the concerns for more production and better distribution should be brought together and not treated separately. This invariably means that employment should be treated as a primary, not a secondary, objective of development since it is the most powerful means of redistributing incomes in a poor society. Capital should not be concentrated in a small modern sector, enjoying high productivity and savings, but spread thinly over a wide segment of the economy—through public works programs, if necessary, and even at the risk of lowering the average productivity of labour and lowering the future rate of growth. The poor societies have to squarely face this choice. They have a limited amount of capital. They can either raise the productivity of a small part of the labour force quite high in the modern sector while leaving a large part unemployed or settle for a lower average productivity but full employment. Again, it appears to me that Communist China made the second choice and was, therefore, able to achieve full employment and equitable income distribution at a relatively low level of per capita income.

But can such a strategy of development be conceived and implemented in the present political and economic structures in the developing countries? And here we come to the second of the disastrous decisions: the choice of the mixed economy. In most cases, such a choice has combined the worst, not the best, features of capitalism and socialism. It has often prevented the developing countries from honest-to-goodness economic incentives and free functioning of the price system to achieve efficiency in a capitalistic framework, if not equity: in reality, there have been too many inefficient administrative controls and price distortions. At the same time, it has prevented these societies from pursuing their goals in a truly socialistic framework as mixed economy institutions were often more capitalistic than not. And the end result often is that they fall between two stools: combining weak economic incentives with bureaucratic socialism. Neither the ends of growth nor equity are served by such confusion in social and political objectives within the framework of a mixed economy.

My own feeling is that the days of the mixed economy are numbered. The developing countries will have to become either more frankly capitalistic or more genuinely socialist. The capitalistic alternative is workable only in those situations where the society is willing to accept income inequalities over a long period of time without exploding or where extremely high growth rates (10 to 15 percent) can be financed with a generous inflow of resources from Western friends. Otherwise, the only alternative is a genuinely socialist system, based on a different ideology and a different pattern of society. But this does not mean bureaucratic socialism or postbox socialism; it means a major change in the political balance of power within these societies and drastic economic and social reforms. Whether the developing countries can manage such a change without violent revolutions is a critical question of our time.

And now let me turn briefly to the third disastrous decision: the dependence on foreign assistance. Let me make it quite clear that I am one of those who has always believed in economic liberalism and in a genuine partnership between the developed and the developing countries. But the sorry record of foreign assistance in the last two decades is beginning to convince me, as it has convinced many of my liberal colleagues, that the developing world would have been better off without such assistance. Unfortunately, I do not have the time to go into the early origins of foreign assistance, its changing motivations, and its present plight, but let me offer a few observations quite baldly without elaboration.

The level of foreign assistance that is required for a meaningful change in the developing countries over a short period of a decade or so through the growth rate route is at least four to five times the present level of $7 billion. The developed countries have neither the will nor the imagination to offer such assistance.

The present levels of assistance are only of a marginal significance for the developing countries and come with so many project conditions, country tying, foreign consultants and technology, and irritating debt problems that they sap up the initiative and freedom of action of the developing world.

The developing countries must regard foreign assistance as an undependable residual in their total planning effort and turn their energies to internal institutional changes that are required for creating a different economic and social order, based on egalitarianism and second-best standard of living.

In the international field, the developing countries should organise their "poor power" to wring major concessions from the rich nations and to arrange for a genuine transfer of resources. Since the rich nations are going to shrink in the next few decades to less than 10 percent of the total world population with over 70 percent of world income, the poor will be numerous enough and annoyed enough to organise such an effort.

One element in such a confrontation will be to serve notice to the developed nations that the developing countries cannot pay their present foreign debt of $60 billion and the world community must make arrangements for its orderly cancellation.

Another element will be to exploit their collective bargaining power in their negotiations with the rich. Recent oil negotiations under OPEC are expected to yield $20 billion of additional revenues to the oil producing countries by 1980. Similarly, if the developing countries can exploit the current concern about depletion of nonrenewable resources and agitate for a 10 percent tax on consumers of these minerals, they could collect as much as $30 billion over this decade for a common international development fund. Again, they can stake their claim to the commonly-held resources of mankind, like oceans and space, and start demanding that 80 percent of the proceeds from the exploitation of such resources should go to them on the basis of world population.

. . .

What I am trying to convey here is the emerging mood in the developing countries rather than my own deeply held beliefs. I am not an apostle of confrontation, nor am I prepared to forsake my own liberalism. But I think it is important that we realize that liberalism cannot survive in an illiberal world. The developing countries are passing through a very dark and ugly mood. They are questioning all the assumptions on which they based their early development strategy. I cannot predict what may come out of this re-examination. But if I have to make any guesses today, I would expect that economic development in the next few years will be increasingly based on a new strategy embodying a direct attack on mass poverty, a genuine turn toward socialism, and a far greater degree of self-reliance. This is the new manifesto that most developing countries are trying to articulate. But there is a wide gap between articulation and implementation, between dim perception and real action. The future of the developing world will turn on how far this gap can be bridged without violent political explosions.

30

Cooperation Against Poverty

Non-aligned nations aim to make their independence a reality, both politically and economically. To do this they need to develop; and to develop in such a manner that they can make their own decisions, and not have their progress determined by politicians, or business men, in the developed world. It is therefore necessary that we consider the nature of our position as poor areas of a rich world and decide how we can obtain the changes we need.

The independence of a nation must be total or it does not exist at all. Without economic independence there can be only a limited degree of political, social, cultural, or even military independence. Economic progress is not the only thing which matters, or which we care about. But without a steady growth in the resources at our command, it is impossible for us to make sustained progress towards any of our other objectives. Political, educational, technical, and social advances—as well as the fuller realization of our independence *vis-à-vis* other nations—all require the expenditure of resources which we do not at present possess. They will only become available to us through economic development, and as we achieve greater economic independence.

None of us can hope to achieve rapidly a prosperous and full degree of economic independence by means of economic isolationism. We will make much faster, and much surer, progress by participation in the exchange of goods, services, and knowledge with other economies. At least as far as the majority of the smaller non-aligned states are concerned, an attempt at economic self-sufficiency is a road to great sacrifice and very slow (if any) growth; it is doubtful whether it will lead to development, even in the long run, and therefore it is unlikely to lead to true independence.

The importance of this to the Non-Aligned Conference lies in the fact that the member states do not only share a common policy of non-alignment. They also have a common experience of poverty. Every one of our nations must achieve rapid national development if the political independence we have won is to become a reality or to have practical meaning to our citizens. At present there is a unity in our poverty, as well as in our desire to overcome it without falling under the control of external powers. Indeed,

This paper was prepared by the Tanzanian delegation to the Non-Aligned Nations Summit Conference held in Lusaka, Zambia, in September, 1971. Reprinted from *IDOC International, North American Edition*, No. 43 (March 11, 1972). Copyright 1972 by IDOC-North America, Inc.

our common poverty is shared by some other nations who, for various reasons, find themselves unable to adopt the political policy of non-alignment. There is a unity of poverty, which is so widely recognized that the world has adopted a term to cover all those involved, and speaks of the Third World as something different, almost in kind, from the rest of the earth's nations.

STRUCTURED INEQUALITY

The poverty of the Third World and the economic dependence of the nations of the Third World are, however, an integral part of the present world economic order. To a large degree, the Third World is poor and will remain poor because the rest is rich and getting richer. The functioning of the present international economic system ensures that this is so. For national wealth, development, and effective economic independence on the one hand and national poverty, underdevelopment, and extreme economic dependence on the other hand are all complementary parts of the whole world economic system as it exists at the present time.

This reality, unpalatable though it is, must be faced. Free trade and unrestricted international investment do not normally lead to increasing economic equality; as most of us know from experience, the truth is quite the reverse. Unfortunately, joint development activities between rich and poor do not overcome the problem of international class divisions either; they ameliorate intolerable conditions here and there but have no basic effect on the division of the world between rich and poor. This is not only because the resource transfers to the poorer nations are too small in quantity. More basically, it is because these transfers take place within the context of a world economic structure which leads all the time to increasing inequality between rich and poor nations. In other words, all international economic activities at present take place within the framework of an "inequality accentuating" system.

Thus the poor nations of the world need to determine their policies in the light of two facts. First is the difficulty (and probable impossibility) of achieving growth through economic isolationism—through autarchy. Second is the nature of the present world economic system, which has a built-in impulse towards increased inequality and not towards the spreading of development. To overcome their problems the poor nations have therefore to devise methods of international economic exchange and cooperation which are different in kind from those at present operating.

There are two strategies which can be adopted, and which are complementary rather than mutually exclusive. We can strengthen the economic relationships between ourselves by improving our communications links, by increased trade, and by education and technical exchanges; and we can do this on a bilateral, regional, or global basis according to what may be possible and desirable in particular cases. Secondly, we can—either as non-aligned states or all together as the Third World—take joint action to secure major alterations in those key points of the present international economic system which militate against our interests, and which prevent it from serving our needs as well as those of the rich industrial economies.

All of us poor nations are open to criticism for not having pursued either of these lines of action with enough seriousness, or for not having demonstrated enough tenacity and ingenuity. Even what we have attempted has often been of doubtful or limited value. For our joint action in support of international economic reform has usually taken the form of statements, pleas or manifestos, addressed to the rich nations—with a marginal reference to our own responsibilities being added for public relations purposes! Further, such documents rarely pay much attention to demonstrating the power which non-aligned nations can exert to achieve the changes they desire; nor do they show why many of these changes would also serve the interests of richer countries. Yet international economic relations do not consist of sharing out a fixed quantity of resources; many of the changes we need could yield net benefits to both rich and poor countries while still reducing the present world economic inequalities. Nor is the international economic system primarily a humanitarian exercise; it is a set of relationships and institutions aimed at achieving economic gain for those who use their power and influence.

MISLEADING CONCEPTS

Power and perceived self-interest are thus the determining factors in national, corporate, and institutional economic policies. This is—or should be—as true of developing economy interest groups as of the interest groups of developed economies, although the very nature of the present dependent relationships makes it doubtful whether such is in fact usually the case. Of course, this is not to deny that humanitarian and ethical considerations play some role in policy determination; but their role is a subsidiary one— it is really power and economic self-interest which are dominant in any important decision. And this means that discussion of international development activities in terms of "aid," "cooperation," or "partnership" is dangerously misleading; it leads to reform proposals which are inherently inadequate because they do not result from an analysis of the existing patterns of power and interest, or of the impact which the proposals would have on these patterns.

"Partnership," as an international development concept, can exist, although until now it has not often done so. For "partnership" is the result of a recognized mutual self-interest which leads to joint action beneficial to all participating nations or groups. It involves a recognition of the fact that the present pattern of international economic relationships is not based on one-way transfers of resources from the developed to the underdeveloped parts of the world. And it involves a rejection of the idea that national, regional, or global economic self-sufficiency is the only practical policy for Third World economies.

"Aid" too must be recognized for what it is, i.e. the commitment of resources by wealthy economies to the goals of the "donor" group, as these goals are perceived by that group. From the point of view of those "accepting" it, on the other hand, "aid" represents the receipt of resources which can be used in the pursuit of the goals they have set for themselves. The goals of the two sides to the transaction may be the same or very different. And the motivations on either side are not necessarily simple; they may involve long as well as short term considerations and political as well as economic factors. The point is that each will decide whether and on what terms to offer, or to accept, the "aid" according to what it believes to be its interests. The fact that much of the "aid" accepted until now has been defective, or counterproductive, in relation to the goals of economic development and economic independence, merely shows that the developing countries have been making mistakes. They have allowed themselves to be bemused by talk of "aid" and have failed to consider whether the particular accession of resources which is under consideration will really speed the attainment of fuller independence and the conquest of poverty, or whether it will distort their economies and hamper the progress towards their final goal.

NO MORE SYMPATHY

It is therefore necessary that we as poor nations should cease from seeking "sympathy" or "assistance" in our international economic contacts with the industrialized wealthy nations. For in the process we are minimizing our effectiveness and also ensuring that the world economic system continues to operate against our interests. Instead of demanding our rightful place at the banquet table, we are begging for more crumbs.

We should be seeking to enter into a "dialogue" with the developed nations; it is "negotiation" we should be preparing, not an application for assistance. Thus, instead of demonstrating that the absence of certain international economic reforms will mean a perpetuation of misery in Third World nations, we should be showing that their implementation would benefit certain economies or interest groups in the developed world. Similarly, our arguments should make clear that the economic power which can be exerted by the developing nations is such that acquiescence in change will be less costly to the wealthy economies than a refusal would be. In economic matters the language of power is more convincing than an appeal to morality. Our problem is thus one of recognizing, and marshalling, our power as Third World economies, either singly or—more effectively—collectively.

Unfortunately, it is more difficult to pursue a strategy of "dialogue" and "negotiation" than to make an ethical appeal for sympathy. In the first place, perceived self-interest may be very far removed from true self-interest owing to a lack of understanding, too short a vision, or some other deficiency. In that case, agreement may be given to proposals which deny all one's basic purposes. Further, the other side in any negotiations will be anxious to preserve and extend any gap between the appearance and the reality of our self-interest. A very obvious example of these facts is that much of Africa came under colonial control in the nineteenth century because of negotiated treaties which the African rulers of that time believed (mistakenly) to be in their best interests. Even now, some years after our political independence, few of us nations in the Third World have prepared ourselves to understand our true needs and interests. Few of us have collected the data or built up the capacity for involved economic analysis; we have not accumulated negotiating team expertise and experience which is at all adequate for hard bargaining. This failure arises partly because of our absolute shortage of resources in trained manpower. A more important reason, however, is that we have given relatively low priority to this field— we have apparently been willing to rely upon the impartiality and the disinterestedness of foreign "partners"! Under these circumstances, it is hardly surprising that we are constantly feeling a sense of betrayal, as we realize that a particular "aid agreement" or "partnership contract" is working to our disadvantage.

A second difficulty in pursuing a strategy of "dialogue" and "negotiation" is even more basic. It is that many groups in the Third World—including some ruling elites and members of some governments—see their own interests as being compatible with the workings of the present international economic order. As a result, we lose the clarity and singleness of purpose which is necessary to meet the richer nations effectively; we also dissipate much of the limited bargaining power which is available to us either singly, regionally, or collectively.

THE PERILS OF POWERLESSNESS

Powerlessness corrupts just as often, and to just as great an extent, as power does—even if in very different ways. In some developing countries it has led to the widespread adoption of a client, if not a servant, mentality; it has often led to the internal dominance of groups whose personal interests are linked to the interests of external economic forces and who recognize that their continued internal power is dependent upon the power exerted by these factors. They therefore accept—or even welcome—the fact that their nation's economy is controlled by the activities of the foreign firms or governments for whom they work or with whom they are in "partnership."

Unfortunately, it is also true that a belief in absolute powerlessness is self-fulfilling, even if it is objectively unsound. A man who is afraid to use his gun because he believes it will blow up in his face is likely to surrender to his opponent even if the gun is a perfectly good one. The basic differences between those developing economies which have negotiated internal and external economic arrangements compatible with national development and those which have failed to do so lies more in their approach to the problems than in their initial economic structures, institutions, or power positions. The former made a commitment to the principle of self-reliance.

believing that this is both possible and necessary. They then assessed their external bargaining power, and were able to use it to the full, because they knew its limitations and its potential.

Thus it is clear that three things are necessary for any real progress to be made towards overcoming the present disadvantages of the underdeveloped world. First is a belief that it is possible to negotiate a pattern of external relationships which will lead towards greater international interdependence—as opposed to continued domination and dependence. Second is that careful attention is given to identifying the outside limits of national economic and other power. And third is that areas of potential joint interest with any external economic groups are recognized and understood before negotiations are begun with these or rival external forces. In all this the kind of leadership our nations are given is a crucial factor.

AUTOMATIC INCREASE IN INEQUALITIES

There are two basic ways in which the present international economic system reinforces the pattern of rich industrial world economic domination over the poor and mostly primary producing Third World. The first is through those workings of international institutions and customary procedures which would produce reasonably balanced results if all participants had roughly comparable economic resources, capabilities, and power. For unfortunately, existing inequalities are increased when the world system acts as if rough equality did exist between nations while the reverse is in fact the case. And the reason for this is that courses of action open to those economies which are poorer and weaker have been limited by "agreements," "conventions," and "customary practices" which are incorporated in the system.

The second basic means by which the present system works against the interests of the Third World is by the deliberate inclusion of certain biases which are contrary to the basic logic of the system, but which favor special interest groups within the industrial and powerful economies.

It is important to distinguish between these two aspects of the inequality accentuating tendency in the present system. For reforms in the second could lead to significant amelioration of the plight of some Third World economies even within the present international structure. And it should be possible either to redress certain of the existing biases or to create counterbalancing biases in other areas which would favor the interests of developing economies.

It is for this reason that the Pearson Report may be of value. Its authors are "respectable" members of the established international order, and the Report is framed in the context of the existing system—it neither is, nor appears to be, revolutionary. Yet it argues for the removal of a number of biases which favor the wealthy economies, and also for the introduction or expansion of other arrangements which could be negotiated into becoming significantly favorable biases for developing economies.

Examples of the latter are the Report's advocacy of preferential market access, genuinely low cost multinational economic resource transfers, and the acceptance of discriminatory economic regionalism among the developing nations.

We shall need to use to the utmost these possibilities of securing reform, even while we do not lose sight of the need to secure more radical change. For the latter is not going to be easy to achieve; even working out effective proposals for basic changes in the existing system is exceedingly difficult—let alone the greater problem of negotiating them! This is because the present system is an interlocking, self-reinforcing whole, which has served the interests of the capitalist industrial world reasonably well over the period 1945–70 and which has now begun to accommodate also the international economic interests of the socialist industrial economies.

The need for radical change in the present system is therefore very far from self-evident to the majority of those who now manage and influence the system. Further, the power which can be marshalled on behalf of basic change is limited and fragmented. Under these circumstances, the status quo in respect of metropolitan dominance in the international economy is often maintainable if important industrial-world economic interest groups are seriously committed to it.

Fortunately, while dependence and exploitation are central to the system as it affects the Third World, this is not necessarily so for the industrialized nations taken as a whole. It may of course be central to certain specialized economic groups within any industrial economy. This means that negotiated change should be more possible to achieve than any simple comparison of total economic power might suggest. Reforms which are of critical importance to us will not necessarily be of high cost to the rich nations.

IMBALANCE OF INTERNATIONAL INSTITUTIONS

The imbalance of international economic institutions arises from formal, operational, and personal factors. In the first place, there is no international organization of the first rank which was created to close the "poverty gap." It is no accident that the word "Reconstruction" comes before "Development" in the full name of the World Bank; the rebuilding of Europe after the war and the avoidance of capital market conditions which might lead to another Great Depression were central to its founding. The development roles of the World Bank and the development institutions of the United Nations are very much ad hoc structures; they are also very subsidiary when compared with things like GATT and the International Monetary Fund.

On an operational level the same bias is evident. International economic institutions are sometimes self-selected "rich men's clubs"; an obvious example is the "Group of Ten" dealing with international monetary issues. Others are so organized that only nations with very large resources in terms of data collection, analysis, and high level manpower can participate effectively. The Kennedy Round negotiations in GATT are a classic example of that. In both cases Third World countries' interests are virtually excluded, with the inevitable result of further emphasis being given to the priorities and interests of industrial economies rather than those of the world as a whole. Thus it is not the result of accident that Special Drawing Rights to deal with international liquidity crises could be negotiated but that so far no agreement has been reached as regards allocating a portion of the S.D.R.s in support of development. Nor is it coincidental that 70 percent of this newly created international purchasing power has been allocated to the rich industrial nations. The vital interests of the Group of Ten have been attended to; matters which are of peripheral concern to them have been left on one side—and will remain there unless and until the Third World nations exert themselves.

And finally, on the personal level the pattern is repeated. The majority of the managers of the international institutions are people of the capitalist industrial world. They mostly attempt to be fair to all members of their organization and to operate impartially between them. But their jobs necessitate the exercise of value judgments as well as intellectual judgments, and their whole background, upbringing, and social environment has determined the framework within which these judgments will inevitably be made.

MULTINATIONAL CORPORATIONS

The growth of the multinational corporation as a factor in world production and trade is often said to constitute a basic new factor, which alters the nature of the international economic system. The extent to which, and the ways in which, this contention holds true for developing economies needs to be thoroughly scrutinized.

First, multinational corporations are, by their nature, advocates of "free trade." For "free trade" has (with reason) normally been the policy of the strong; its practical meaning is freedom for the stronger economic unit to enter the sphere of weaker units without the hindrance of restrictive measures or serious competition. And multinational corporations are, by definition, the strong element in any business competition; they have massive resources at their command in money, men, and—therefore—power. (The annual profit of many such corporations dwarfs the yearly budget of a large proportion of the members of the Non-Aligned Conference.) Further, these organizations are able to advance the cause of free trade more single-mindedly than governments ever can, because they normally have very limited concern with—or stake in—the weak or declining sectors of any economy. (Nor are they ever concerned with the social problems arising from economic poverty.) And while their past investments may make them resist particular proposals for economic regionalism for a while, they are in general the most fervent advocates of economic unity on a regional basis, both among the developed and among the developing economies. They regard such regionalism as the step towards that kind of "freedom" which allows rationalization of their corporate production and planning without regard to social problems or political boundaries.

Second, managements of multinational corporations are an extremely important part of the de facto managing elite of the international economic system; they have heavy vested interests in its smooth operation, and its collapse would be disastrous for them. On the other hand, the major problems facing these managers in the maintenance and expansion of the corporation activities are, in practice, the major problems of the system as far as the wealthy nations are concerned. Each is part of the other; just as trouble in the international economy means trouble for such enterprises, so trouble in a major corporation means trouble for the international system. That is why "rescue operations" are undertaken by governments of developed economies if a major multinational corporation gets into difficulties; it is also the reason that these corporations are willing to "cooperate" with these same governments in tackling problems arising from the workings of the international system. (Of course, this is not to say that the interests of the two are always identical; international "scandals" do reveal divergence—usually when the industrial economy government is making some attempt to control its own economy for social purposes!)

Third, multinational corporations are nonetheless likely to be interested in raising the level of economic development in selected Third World economies, provided that they can participate as investors, managers, financiers, and suppliers. For they are sophisticated businesses, which take both a broad and a long term view of their operations. What they are interested in is their profit and their power; they will exploit any possibilities of increasing this, even if it requires shifting production from their "home" wealthy economy to developing economies. Despite being a part of the industrialized world, they have no "patriotism" in the sense of loyalty to this country or that. Their loyalty is to their own progress, and if they believe that this calls for investment in a developing country, then the investment will be made. Further, their decision on this matter is unlikely to be based on ideological considerations; more than most foreign investors they place primary emphasis on the probable stability and economic rationality of the potential host governments.

Yet such investments will not normally make the economy of the Third World nation concerned any more self-reliant as long as the multinational corporation retains its control. The satellite relationship will continue to exist while questions of output, markets, technology, research and management are determined by corporations which are basically North American, West European, Japanese, and South African.

From all this it becomes obvious that Third World countries need to consider very carefully the potentialities and the dangers of multinational corporations. We need to make deliberate decisions about when, and how, it is in our interests to work with them.

RESTRICTIVE TRADE POLICIES

Despite the basically "free trade" logic of the present economic order, the policies of the industrial economies of the world are becoming increasingly restrictive to trade in the products of the Third World. This applies both to primary commodities and (to an ever greater extent) to processed goods or simple manufactures.

Thus, the production and export of a number of primary products is subsidized in the industrial economies, despite their comparatively high costs of production. The most appalling case is that of sugar, where the uneconomic production of beet sugar by wealthy nations costs the Third World something like one thousand million U.S. dollars worth of potential exports every year. Further, the European Economic Community and (to a slightly lesser degree) the U.S.A. agricultural programs do more than protect an uncompetitive agricultural sector in their domestic market. They even promote the expansion of the subsidized crops and then compete with developing economies in export markets through so-called "commodity aid."

Established primary product processing industries in the industrial economies are also protected; sometimes the effective tariff is more than 25 percent of value added. The rational use of resources is thus impeded in a manner detrimental to the economies of the poorer countries. In the UNCTAD II discussions at New Delhi, the rich nations treated both the agricultural subsidies and this kind of protective tariff as being beyond generalized challenge.

Trade in those manufactured goods of real interest to developing countries is another area where "free trade" fails to operate. It appears that many manufacturers of simple articles in the wealthy countries are unable to compete economically with the products of new industries in the developing world, but are capable of exerting effective political pressure on their own governments. If the result was some temporary arrangement to ease the transition to other production, opposition from us might be unreasonable. Unfortunately, it always appears to result in a degree and kind of protection that destroys the incentive to change, and the potential market is thus *permanently* closed to the goods of the developing nations. It is noticeable that the Kennedy Round tariff reductions created a situation of relatively free trade in almost all manufactures—except those which are labor intensive or raw material intensive. And it is these in which developing economies are interested. Even where some improvement was achieved, draconic quota restrictions have quickly been imposed—cotton textiles is an obvious example. Various administrative devices to choke off imports of manufactured goods from developing areas or to prevent their quantity increasing have also been used to considerable effect.

The principle of generalized preferences for the manufactured exports of developing economies was supported at UNCTAD II. This, however, had been done by GATT four years earlier! And it was immediately followed by warnings from the rich countries that safeguards would be necessary; what this means can be gauged from the United States' demand that all textiles, clothing, and footwear should be excluded from such preferences, and should in fact be subjected to stringent quota limits as well as full tariff barriers!

It is also worth noting another method by which exports from developing countries are prevented from establishing a market. "Infant Industry" protective tariffs are acceptable to the world economic powers; export promotion subsidies, on the other hand, are not acceptable, and their use leads to economic sanctions. This has the effect of forcing industrialization in developing countries to become unbalanced in favor of import substitution. It militates against export promotion even where the latter would be economically rational from a world as well as a domestic point of view.

Resistance to change, promoted by certain interest groups within the industrial economies, also accounts for some opposition to economic grouping by developing countries. For the primary effect of a "free trade area" or "preferential area" consisting solely of underdeveloped nations is to increase the range of viable domestic industrial production. It does not normally reduce the total imports of the nations concerned, because these are largely determined by the foreign currencies available through export earnings and capital inflows. It is the type of imports which is changed by economic regionalism, not the total; indeed, as the economies strengthen, their total imports are likely to increase. Thus opposition originates with possessors of "traditional markets"; the authorities of the rich countries concerned are—once again—endeavoring to protect the privileged position of an interest group which has political power.

Opposition to one kind of economic grouping does not, however, preclude the rich nations from actively promoting another. For the industrial countries do initiate and support the development of preferential areas which include both developed and developing countries. The reason for this difference is very simple—and already clear. While the former lead to change —however marginal—in the international relationships, the latter tend to freeze the existing pattern and to inhibit any structural change. The dominance of the industrial and developed economies is ensured by the act of embracing the weaker partner; competition by the poor nations in industries already dominated by the rich is precluded, and—in exchange for preferences on primary imports—the poor nations allow virtually free access for the goods of the metropolitan nations even within their own economy.

All these kinds of deviations from the neo-free trade logic of the present system result from the special interests and political leverage of declining and inefficient industries within the wealthy economies. They rarely serve the overall interests of the industrial world, and they are usually opposed by (or in opposition to the interests of) the multinational corporations. Leverage for obtaining the reduction and final elimination of these biases thus exists.

CONDITIONS FOR PRACTICAL ADVANCE

Unfortunately, the ease of presenting the general case for economic reform (as distinct from economic transformation) gives a rather deceptive impression about the ease of achieving concrete action. An example of this has already been mentioned. It has been agreed in principle since 1963–64 that the manufactured goods produced by developing economies should be given preferential access to the markets of the industrial economies. On balance, however, the individual changes which have occurred since that time have tended in the very opposite direction. The general case was established and accepted; its implementation is further away now than before "agreement" was reached!

There are basic problems which have to be resolved once the general case for reform is accepted. First, it is necessary to overcome the political problem which arises from the ability of industrial special interest groups to demand protection in their own economies and domination in those of the Third World. Second, governments in the Third World must achieve enough national economic control to ensure that potentially beneficial changes actually do benefit the nation as a whole and not just multinational corporations and other foreign interest groups which operate within their territories. And third, developing nations must expand their capacity for information collection and analysis, as well as their negotiating capability, until these are qualitatively and quantitatively much superior to that possessed by most of them at present.

The first problem can be approached in a number of different ways. Protection can be phased out over a definite period, so that retraining and conversion can prevent localized political and social problems within the wealthy economies. Groups which are potential beneficiaries of reform (such as the Committee for Economic Development in the United States) can be mobilized in support of specific proposals. And special interest groups which are opposed to a reform can sometimes be split and weakened by involving some members of them in the new trade pattern. One successful example of this is the division of the United States shoe protection lobby because a number of shoe manufacturers are now major importers and distributors of foreign footwear.

The second obstacle can be cleared only if each underdeveloped nation uses its power in its own interests. Three things have to be clearly established. Foreign economic interests must be made to realize that they have a choice between negotiations within a framework which is nationally determined or being excluded from the economy. The non-aligned (or poor) government which is establishing the framework for negotiations must have substantial domestic backing. And the framework must be seen to provide areas of potential joint foreign and national interest. If these conditions are fulfilled—and probably only if they are—serious negotiations between Third World economic groups (whether public or private), on the one hand, and industrial world economic groups, on the other, are likely to follow and can prove fruitful. It will be obvious that, as argued earlier, the critical question here is whether the national leadership clearly understands the possibilities and limits of pursuing a strategy of self-reliance, and is completely committed to achieving such internal economic control and international economic interdependence.

The final problem may prove to be the most intractable. Negotiating is an extremely demanding process in respect of the data needed, the amount of attention required at policy making level, and the quality of good high level manpower. Major conferences are a very minor part of any strategy which is based on negotiation. Case by case bargaining in numerous forums, with literally scores of governments, institutions, multinational corporations, and other foreign economic units, is essential to making real progress through negotiations.

Until now, detailed negotiation of this kind is not an area in which the majority of Third World economies have been very effective; even those without high level manpower problems have shown themselves deficient—probably owing to an insufficiently high priority being given to this work. And the possibilities of cooperation between non-aligned countries in this matter have not been explored, much less systematically practiced.

If this record is to be improved upon in the coming decade, it is essential that more manpower be allocated to negotiation preparation and practice, and that there should be considerable rethinking of our priorities and approach as regards external economic forces. Yet without a real breakthrough in this respect it is difficult to see how a strategy of achieving reform through negotiation and dialogue can be made to function. We cannot even identify the areas of negotiation, much less determine our basic tactics and the minimum acceptable (as opposed to the maximum desirable) results, without far more, and far better, negotiating patterns and personnel than are now typical. We all have some good people, but we make even them ineffective by giving them inadequate backing and too much to do.

CREATION OF POWER BASES

In equipping themselves for the task of remedying their present backwardness and inequality, there are four areas in which developing economies can establish a base of power: national, regional, Third World, and global. The first is basic, while the last (with special exceptions) can only be pursued seriously in conjunction with the other three.

Economic size, or even the degree of dependence on external trade and investment, is not necessarily the crucial factor determining the economic power of a developing nation. At least as important (and perhaps more) is the degree to which the domestic economic policies are nationally formulated, and the extent to which its institutions are controlled by a public sector leadership which has clear developmental goals and broad support. A very small economy with a high ratio of foreign trade to gross domestic product can exert a substantial degree of control over "resident" foreign interests; it can also maintain some freedom to maneuver in the international economy if its domestic economy is nationally controlled, if its policies are determined realistically and largely formulated and staffed by citizens, and if they are reasonably popular.

The case for economic regionalism among developing nations is—at least in broad outline—both fairly well known and widely agreed. There is, however, a lack of clear national political and economic strategies and policies. This leads to severe problems in working out any broadly based approach to coordination or unification across national boundaries—the negotiators are often working in the dark. There is often also a deficiency in the degree of commitment and priority given to the policy of regionalism, and an absence of that patience combined with flexibility and imagination which is necessary to pursue to a conclusion the inevitably numerous and tedious negotiations. Yet without these things no economic community which provides for growth and all-around benefit can be established.

A logical extension of economic regionalism is the broader Third World cooperation. This can take a number of forms. A coordination of negotiating positions, with especial reference to tax rates on overseas companies and to investment incentives, is obviously one. Another is the development of Third World institutions, for example relating to applied research, the collection and analysis of economic data, and economic consultancy services. And there is also the possibility of establishing a variety of preferential economic agreements—possibly including shipping, reinsurance, and development and merchant banking, as well as trade.

The number of national interests to be accommodated, and of positions to be coordinated, in any Third World cooperation makes this even more difficult and time consuming than regionalism. However, at least on certain issues, the effect of pooling a large proportion of the power of non-aligned nations could be considerable. Shipping is a case in point. If the national shipping lines of countries represented at this Non-Aligned Conference were all unified, or their activities coordinated, a much more equal bargaining position with shipping conferences would be possible.

Economic power for the developing countries in the international institutions will normally follow, and not precede, the establishment of economic power at national, regional, and Third World levels. If we do not use our potential domestic power, and if we remain divided in our approach to industrial economies and multinational corporations, we are unlikely to gain significant power internationally. Yet at the moment that is the position. Many of us make little effort to control our national economies in our own interests; we wait gratefully to receive the employment by-product of foreign investment and allow such investors to determine the income distribution pattern of our economies, the type of production undertaken and where, and generally to make all major economic decisions on our behalf. And in discussions with the rich nations of the world, we Third World nations make separate agreements, or give individual support to proposals, which appear marginally beneficial to our nation individually but which are seriously detrimental to the interests of the Third World as a whole. We compete with each other in a manner that is ultimately detrimental to all our interests. While this sort of situation continues, the chances of achieving any real power—as distinct from marginally greater influence— in such bodies as the World Bank, the International Monetary Fund, or GATT, is very low. And unless we do build up a real and strong "trade union" unity among ourselves there is not the slightest chance of reversing the relative importance of agencies like UNCTAD, which are virtually controlled by the Third World, and economic industrial power centers such as GATT.

And it is urgent that the Third World should examine the implications of development operations on a world scale. The recent initiatives of the World Bank towards greater involvement in national planning and bilateral aid coordination, together with the full implementation of the Pearson and Jackson Reports, could lead to a "World Bank World" so far as the development of poor and noncommunist economies is concerned. For these proposals would lead to virtually all transfers of material, personnel, information, feasibility study, and training being routed through a World Bank/ United Nations Development Program-led consortia—with the World Bank very much the senior partner.

There is little doubt but that such a change from the present bilateral and uncoordinated arrangements would increase the efficiency of resource transfers. It would also decrease the political strings which are only too frequently explicit or implicit in current arrangements. Further, the proponents and supporters of these proposals are, without question, genuine in their serious commitment to rapid economic growth in the poor and subordinate economies.

Thus it would be absurd to say that we should reject the current proposals for multinationalism in resource transfers; simply that they must incorporate certain safeguards necessary to our position. Thus, the developing nations must secure firm control over the Regional Development Banks; two of the present three appear at present to be dominated by the wealthy industrial nations. Developing countries must also secure control over the United Nations Development Program. Then—and only then— multinationalism could be a viable strategy for securing world economic transformation through genuine dialogue and negotiation. This is assuming that the Regional Development Banks become an increasingly important channel for resource transfer, and the United Nations Development Program for information, training, and personnel transfer.

Of course, it is not clear whether the developing nations can gain control over any major United Nations activity; it depends partly upon their own level of commitment to this and partly on factors outside their control. However, if we do make a serious effort, the U.N.D.P. is a more promising area for success than most others. And if the implementation of the Jackson Report were to be coupled with the creation of a full-time Board of Directors of U.N.D.P. (like the World Bank Executive Directors) with a built-in Third World majority, significant favorable results could be achieved—provided that the developing countries were able to agree on joint positions for their directors to use.

In all these matters, the evaluation of what it is possible to achieve must take account of the probable use, as well as the actual possession, of power. Neither the representatives of the rich countries nor multinational corporations will normally find it profitable to devote more than a small fraction of their economic power or negotiating capacity to the settlement of questions concerning the developing economies. This will be especially true if the changes under discussion include areas of mutual benefit as well as straight alterations in favor of the Third World nations.

Thus, realistic hopes for the success of dialogue and negotiation can be based on a combination of two factors. Firstly, the identification (by us) of reforms which benefit industrial economies and/or multinational corporations as well as the developing economies. And secondly, the probability of partial commitment by the rich nations and these corporations being met by what could be the total commitment of non-aligned nations linked together.

CONCLUSION

This analysis suggests that as non-aligned and poor nations, we need to pursue a variety of types of economic cooperation and coordination, on a number of different levels. It also indicates that major conferences and manifestos are insufficient, even though they are important both as symbols and as providing an opportunity for major decisions of principle. To be effective they must always be followed by the necessary series of working groups, exchanges of personnel and information, and specific operational agreements—with the establishment of new institutions where appropriate.

None of this is impossible. For all of us have had some successes in international economic negotiations, and information about these could be of value to all. Yet these successes are rarely if ever described in enough detail to be of practical use to others. Still less often are our failures described; we do not always learn the lessons from these ourselves! Nor do we even look at each other's experience when we propose to adopt similar policies. And the result of this kind of reticence is that the industrial nations and other rich negotiating groups accumulate experience and become even better qualified to meet any demands, while we almost always approach them as if similar issues had never been raised before.

Further, we often act as if we are afraid of the problems of cooperation or taking action which might upset one or more powerful external economic force. We do not welcome new approaches to these problems, and therefore we fail—both nationally and jointly—to give serious attention to working out the practicability of new ideas on how cooperation can be made effective, or how specific problems can be solved. Even when these new ideas originate from citizens of the industrial economies we sometimes reject them on grounds of unorthodoxy! (At other times we allow a very reasonable suspicion to prevent our giving proper attention to the proposal being made, as distinct from the national origin of the proposer!)

And it is not only in world international affairs that things are agreed in principle without action following. Among ourselves as Third World nations similar failures occur. Many of our joint ventures in trade, planning, or particular enterprises are struggling for existence—where they have not already become moribund. This is not for lack of potential; it is because the need to pool economic power in order to expand it is recognized in principle but ignored in practice when it has short term costs.

It is essential that we should face up to our weaknesses in relation to cooperation among ourselves and in relation to our approach to the rest of the world. For until we have done so, and taken steps to overcome them, we shall make no progress in securing major change. We shall continue to achieve a new factory here and a new structure there; but we shall also continue to be "the poor" of the world, whose interests can be largely disregarded.

The only countries which have a primary commitment to the development in freedom of the non-aligned nations are the non-aligned nations. The only people to whom poverty is the central issue are the poor. We have to depend upon ourselves; only on that basis can we obtain the kind of international cooperation which is really of use to us. But we are all involved, and we are the stronger the more we act together. Whether we tackle our problems and begin to fight against our economically subordinate position depends upon our commitment and upon our willingness to recognize the implications of our common involvement in the struggle for international economic change.

31

First Latin American Encounter
of Christians for Socialism

INTRODUCTION

More than four hundred Christians from all the countries of Latin America (laymen, pastors, priests, and nuns), plus observers from the United States, Quebec, and Europe, have come together here in Santiago. In the light of our common faith, and well aware of the injustice that characterizes the socio-economic structures of our continent, we wanted to reflect about what we can and must do at this historical moment in which we are living and in the concrete circumstances that surround us. We want to define ourselves quite clearly as Christians who, in the light of the process of liberation that our Latin American peoples are living and of our own commitment, real and practical, to the construction of a socialist society, are rethinking our faith and revising our attitude of love toward the oppressed. Almost all of us are in daily contact with workers, peasants, and unemployed who painfully live their lives in misery, frustration, and economic, social, cultural, and political marginalization. There is much we have to do, and do jointly with them, with great urgency.

We have met in Santiago at the same time as the Third World assembly of UNCTAD [United Nations Conference on Trade and Development], a forum dedicated to the discussion of a small problem that is daily becoming more acute: a relatively small part of humanity is progressing and becoming richer every day by virtue of the oppression of two-thirds of the world's population. What impinges on the consciousness of the exploited people more than anything else is the realization that their precarious economic condition is nothing other than the consequence of the growing wealth and well-being of the great powers. Our poverty is the other face of the enrichment of the international exploiting classes.

How can one face up to this unquestionable injustice? At least one thing is clear: the peoples dominated by imperialist capitalism must unite in order to break the stranglehold of this situation of oppression and despoilation to which they are presently subjected. But this unity, however

Persons from three continents attended the "First Latin American Encounter of Christians for Socialism," which took place in Santiago, Chile from April 23–30, 1972. This is the final statement from the encounter. It is a copyrighted translation, from the Spanish, by the IDOC Quick Translation Service in Rome. Reprinted by permission.

logical it may seem, is not an easy thing to achieve because external dependence works in favor of division—a division, moreover, that is fomented,
either openly or underhandedly, by imperialism. Therefore, we Christians
from all the countries of Latin America, meeting here on the occasion of the
UNCTAD assembly, want to launch an appeal to the exploited social classes
and the dominated countries to unite for the purpose of defending their
rights rather than to beg for help.

The economic and social structures of our Latin American countries
are rooted in oppression and injustice, the direct consequences of the situation of a capitalism that is dependent on the great power centers. Within
each of our countries there are small minorities who are accomplices and
servants of international capitalism and who use every means to maintain
a situation created for their own advantage. In actual practice this structural injustice amounts to violence, irrespective of whether it be open or
artfully masked.

Those who for centuries have exploited the weak, and who still endeavor
to exploit them today, do nothing other than subject them to violence. This
violence, even though it may sometimes be disguised by a false order or a
false legality, is nonetheless a violence or injustice. This is not human, and
for the same reason it is not Christian.

However, it is not enough to diagnose these facts. Christ by his example
taught us to live what he proclaimed. Christ preached human brotherhood
and the love that must characterize all social structures; but above all he
lived his message of liberation through to its ultimate consequence. He was
condemned to death. The powerful among his people saw in his message of
liberation, and also in the love to which he bore witness, a serious threat
to their economic, social, religious, and political interests. This spirit of the
risen Christ is today as active as it has always been, a driving force in history that is showing itself in the solidarity, in the disinterested dedication
of those who struggle for liberty, moved by a true love for their oppressed
brothers.

The structures of our society must be transformed down to their roots.
Today more than ever before it is urgent to do this because those who
benefit from the unjust order in which we are living are aggressively defending their class interests and are making use of every means—propaganda,
subtle forms of domination of public opinion, defense of a discriminatory
legal system, dictatorship if necessary, and frequent repression—to prevent
the bringing about of such a revolutionary transformation. Only by arriving
at the centers of economic and political power can the class that today is
being exploited construct a qualitatively different society, a socialist society
in which there are neither oppressors nor oppressed, a society in which all
will have the same possibilities of human realization.

The revolutionary process in Latin America is in full swing. There are
many Christians who have committed themselves to it, but there are even
more who, immobilized by mental inertia and categories of thought impreg-
nated by bourgeois ideology, see it with fear and persist in following
impossible reformist and "modernizing" roads. The Latin American process
is a single and global process. Christians neither have nor want to have a
political road of their own. The understanding of this single and global

character turns into companions and unites in a common task all those who commit themselves to the revolutionary struggle.

This revolutionary commitment has made us rediscover the meaning of the liberative work of Christ. This work gives human history its profound unity and enables us to understand the meaning of political liberation and to place it in a wider and more radical context. The liberation of Christ is necessarily realized in liberating historical facts, but it also transcends them; it points out the limits of these facts, but above all, it brings them to their full accomplishment. Those who bring about a reduction of the work of Christ are rather those who want to remove it from the heartbreak and pulse of history, from the men and social classes who struggle to free themselves from the oppression in which they are kept by other men and social classes, those who do not want to accept that the liberation of Christ is a radical liberation from every kind of exploitation, every kind of despoilation, every kind of alienation.

If we commit ourselves to the construction of socialism, we do so because socialism is objectively founded on historical experience and because after having analyzed the facts in a rigorous and scientific manner, we have reached the conclusion that it is the only effective way of fighting imperialism and putting an end to our situation of dependence.

The construction of socialism cannot be achieved by means of vague denunciations or appeals to goodwill, but rather presupposes an analysis that will highlight the mechanisms that really drive society, an analysis that will not only put into relief oppression itself but will also be capable of unmasking and calling by their own names all those who openly or stealthily oppress the working class. Above all, it presupposes a participation in the struggle that opposes the exploited class to its oppressors. True love cannot countenance the struggle that is unleashed by the exploiters of the people with a view of either defending or increasing their privileges.

If we now publish the results of our reflections, it is because we believe that they can help other Christians and men of goodwill to reflect with us and thus to arrive at the decision to look for the road that leads to a radical transformation of the structures that dominate our continent.

PART ONE

1. The Latin American Reality: a Challenge to Christians

1.1. The socio-economic, political, and cultural situation of the Latin American peoples challenges our Christian conscience. Unemployment, malnutrition, alcoholism, infant mortality, illiteracy, prostitution, an ever-increasing inequality between the rich and the poor, racial and cultural discrimination, exploitation, and so forth, are facts that define a situation of institutionalized violence in Latin America.

1.2. We declare, first of all, that this reality is not the inevitable result of an insufficiency of natural riches, and even less so of an inexorable "fate" of an implacable "God" alien to the human drama. On the contrary, it is the outcome of a process determined by the will of men.

1.3. This "will" is the will of a privileged minority who have made possible the construction and maintenance of an unjust society, the capitalist society, based on exploitation, profit, and competition.

1.4. This unjust society has its objective basis in the capitalist production system that necessarily generates a class society.

1.5. Colonialist or neo-colonialist capitalism as an economic structure shapes the reality of the Latin American countries. In its ultimate stage this capitalist structure leads to imperialism and sub-imperialism, which assert themselves through many mechanisms, including military and economic aggression, alliances of repressive governments, multinational trusts, cultural domination, the presence of the C. I. A., the [U.S.] State Department, and so forth.

1.6. In each country imperialism acts in complicity with the dominant classes or the national bourgeoisie—dominant classes that seem to be in alliance with the institutional church.

1.7. Among the last resorts of imperialism we have dictatorships and regimes, of fascist type, that make use of repression, torture, persecution, political crimes, and so forth.

1.8. Imperialism's desperate struggle leads to economic boycotts of countries that have opted for socialism, points in case being Chile and Cuba.

1.9. Imperialism tries to divide the people by opposing Christians to Marxists, the aim being that of paralyzing the revolutionary process in Latin America.

1.10. False models of economic growth brought about at the expense of the workers and peasants endeavor to distract the people from the true overall aims of the revolution (witness the publicity given to the Brazilian and Mexican development models).

1.11. The imperialist forces and the national upper class impose a dependent type of culture through all the means of communication and education. This culture justifies and hides the situation of domination and, what is more, creates a type of man who meekly accepts his alienation. Lastly, it stimulates the oppressed to become masters and exploiters of their fellow men.

1.12. The historical process of class societies and imperialist domination leads inevitably to a class struggle. Although this struggle is becoming more obvious with each passing day, it is denied by the oppressors. Nevertheless, the exploited masses become aware of it and gradually develop a new revolutionary consciousness.

1.13. The progressive sharpening of the class struggle makes it clear that in Latin America there now remain only two possibilities: dependent capitalism and underdevelopment, or socialism. Indeed, within the different countries one can clearly see the historical failure and the impossibility of positions intermediate between capitalism and socialism, this being equally true as regards every type of reformism.

1.14. Some of the leftist nationalist movements have a certain revolutionary importance, but these movements prove to be insufficient if they do not lead to socialism as part of the present process of Latin American liberation.

1.15. Consciously or unconsciously, the present position of all Latin Americans, and therefore also that of Christians, is being conditioned by the historical dynamics of the class struggle in the process of liberation.

1.16. Christians committed to the revolutionary process recognize the complete failure of a middle-of-the-road social solution and are now endeavoring to become part of the only historical way of liberating the continent.

1.17. The sharpening of the class struggle represents a new stage in the ideological and political struggle and excludes every form of presumed neutrality or desire to remain apolitical. This sharpening of the struggle confers upon the Latin American revolutionary process its true dimension of totality.

1.18. A scientific analysis and revolutionary commitment to the struggle of the exploited necessarily leads one to discover the real elements of the situation: relations based on production, capitalist appropriation of surplus value, class struggle, ideological struggle, and so forth.

1.19. In this sense, then, the Cuban Revolution and the trend toward socialism in Chile stimulate a return to the sources of Marxism and a critique of traditional Marxist dogmatism.

1.20. The people, helped by all the effective elements of analysis provided primarily by Marxism, are becoming conscious of the need to begin to move toward a real conquest of power by the working class. Only such a conquest will make possible the construction of an authentic socialism, the only means known up to now for achieving complete liberation.

2. Attempts at Liberation in Latin America

2.1. In Latin America, following in the footsteps of Bolivar, San Martin, O'Higgins, Hidalgo, Jose Marti, Sandino, Camilo Torres, Che Guevara, Nestor Paz, and others, there is now coming into being a common process of liberation. This is a second fight for independence, a struggle that is bringing together the revolutionary forces of a continent that has as its common heritage a past of colonialism and a present of exploitation and misery.

2.2. The dependent capitalism dominant in Latin America necessarily generates the working and peasant classes. These classes, by the mere virtue of their existence, constitute an objectively revolutionary social basis and at the same time set us an urgent task of politicization so that they may gradually come to acquire the power to destroy the capitalist system and to put a more just and more fraternal society in its place.

2.3. Numerous attempts at liberation are being made all over the continent, particularly since the Cuban Revolution. These attempts are assuming a similar form as regards the rupture with dependency and the anti-imperialist struggle, even though they appear in different outward forms according to the peculiar characteristics of the various nations.

2.4. The numerous attempts at liberation appearing in the different countries are tending to become unified in spite of tactical differences. One notes the desire for a new strategy of joining revolutionary forces in a common struggle for liberation.

2.5. The revolutionary process urgently calls for the overcoming of the sterile differences between the various groups of the Latin American Left, divisions that are both fomented and utilized by imperialism.

2.6. Christians, urged on by the spirit of the gospels, are joining the proletarian groups and parties without asking for any rights or duties different from those of any other revolutionary. Christians committed to socialism recognize the national and continental proletariat as the vanguard in the process of the liberation of Latin America.

2.7. The growing popular mobilization poses new requirements, including the elimination of sectarianism, bureaucracy, the process that leads to a bourgeoisie, the corruption of leaders, and so forth.

3. Christians and the Process of Liberation in Latin America

3.1. Some Christians are becoming aware that Christian reality (institution, theology, conscience) does not stand outside the context of the struggle between the exploited and the exploiters. Rather, it is already marked by colonialism and in many cases even objectively allied with dependent capitalism.

3.2. Of ever-increasing evidence is the impact that is being felt throughout the continent by the fact that groups of Christians, in complete coherence with their faith, are assuming a firm and ever-growing revolutionary commitment by the side of the people.

3.3. At the same time, one notes a growing interest among Christian and non-Christian groups in analyzing and taking into account the sociological impact that Christianity has had and still has, both negatively and positively, in shaping the social structure of the Latin American continent.

3.4. Increasingly large numbers of Christians are now discovering the historical vigor of their faith as a result of their political action in the construction of socialism and the liberation of the continent's oppressed people. The Christian faith thus displays a new liberating and critical vitality.

3.5. Concrete action by the side of the proletariat frees Christians from the ethical-affective inhibitions that prevent them from committing themselves to the class struggle. The historical weight of these inhibitions constitutes an important and particular aspect of the cultural revolution.

3.6. By virtue of a growing commitment to the poor, to the oppressed, and to the working class, priests and pastors, inspired by a new type of theological reflection, are discovering new dimensions of their specific mission. This very commitment brings them to shoulder the political responsibility needed to render effective the love for the oppressed that is called for by the gospels, and leads them back to the prophetic tradition that forms a part of the process of revelation. Occasionally grouped together in movements and organizations of their own, they are making a positive contribution to the process of Latin American liberation.

3.7. There is now a growing consciousness of the need for a strategic alliance between revolutionary Christians and Marxists in the process of liberating the continent—a strategic alliance that goes beyond the short-term tactical or opportunist alliances, a strategic alliance that will mean traveling the same road in a common political action aimed at a historical project of liberation. For Christians this historical unity in political action does not mean an abandonment of their faith, but rather gives renewed impetus to their hopes in the future of Christ.

PART TWO

1. Some Aspects of Our Revolutionary Commitment

1.1. A revolutionary commitment implies an overall historical project for the transformation of society. Neither generosity nor goodwill will alone suffice. Political action calls for a scientific analysis of reality because there is a continuous interrelation between action and analysis. This analysis has a logic of its own, a logic that is qualitatively different than that of bourgeois social science.

1.2. The social structure of our countries is based on productive relations (predominantly capitalist relations or dependent on world capitalism) and founded on the exploitation of the workers. The recognition of the class struggle as a fundamental fact enables us to arrive at a global interpretation of Latin American structures. Revolutionary practice discovers that every objective and scientific interpretation must make use of the analysis of social classes as the key of interpretation.

1.3. Socialism presents itself as the only acceptable possibility of overcoming the class struggle. In fact, the classes are the reflection of the economic basis that in capitalist society creates an antagonism between the possessors of capital and the wage earners. The latter have to work for the former and thus become the objects of exploitation. Only by replacing private property by the social ownership of the means of production can one create the objective conditions for overcoming the antagonism between the classes.

1.4. The conquest of power that leads to the construction of socialism calls for a critical theory of capitalist society. This theory, by making obvious the contradictions of Latin American society, discovers the objective revolutionary potentiality of the working classes. Even though they are exploited by the system, the latter are capable of transforming it.

1.5. In order to arrive at socialism one has to have not only a critical theory, but also a revolutionary practice of the proletariat. This implies a change of consciousness, that is to say, an overcoming of the distance that at present separates social reality and the consciousness of the workers. This change calls for the denunciation and unmasking of the ideological mystifications of the bourgeoisie. In this way the people will be able to identify the structural causes of their misery and conceive the possibility of eliminating them. However, the change of consciousness also calls for populist parties and organizations and a strategy intended to lead to the conquest of power.

1.6. The construction of socialism is a creative process that is incompatible with every form of schematic dogmatism or uncritical position. Socialism is not a collection of unhistorical dogmas, but rather a critical theory (in constant development) of the conditions of exploitation, and also a revolutionary practice intended to lead, by way of the conquest of political power by the exploited masses, to the social ownership of the means of production and finance, and to a globally and rationally planned economy.

1.7. An inadequate recognition of the inherent logic of the class struggle has led many Christians to defective political positions. Unaware of the structural mechanisms of society or the need for being backed up by scientific theory, they attempt to deduce political conclusions from a certain humanist conception ("the dignity of the human person," "liberty," and so forth) with the inevitable result of political naïveté, activism, and volunteerism.

2. Christianity and Ideological Struggle

2.1. The class struggle is not limited to the socio-economic level, but rather extends to the ideological field. The dominant class creates a series of ideological justifications that prevent people from recognizing this struggle. The ideology of the dominant classes, popularized by means of communication and education, produces a false consciousness in the dominated class and thus hampers its revolutionary action.

2.2. For this reason revolutionary action valorizes the ideological struggle as an essential element. Its object is the liberation of the consciousness of the oppressed.

2.3. The dominant ideology adopts certain Christian elements that strengthen it and help to diffuse it among vast sectors of the Latin American population. On the other hand, the dominant ideology penetrates in some way into the expression of the Christian social doctrine, theology, and the organizations of the church. One of the central tasks of the ideological struggle is therefore the identification and unmasking of those ideological justifications that are supposedly Christian.

2.4. The profundity of the faith we profess as the free gift of Christ obliges us to criticize the ideological use, often very subtle and unconscious, that is being made of this faith. The unmasking of the prejudiced and impoverishing use of the Christian faith is an evangelical duty. However, it calls for adequate scientific instrumentation and a commitment to the poor, the oppressed, and the working class. This does not mean instrumentalizing the faith for other political ends, but rather restoring to it its original evangelical dimension. This task is an urgent one in the Latin American continent, because the ideological use that is being made of the faith paralyzes its liberating evangelical force, a force that is decisive at the present moment.

2.5. The dominant culture imposes an image of man according to which he is required to accept a preconstituted system presented to him as an objective order based on human nature and expressed in natural laws and rights. Inequalities and dependence, the division of labor, the separation of people and power, all these are presented to him as natural exigencies of society. This serves to camouflage the fact that these relations are based on the capitalist system and to push out of sight the vision of global and radical change.

2.6. The dominant culture imposes an individualistic conception of man —a man whose capacities, tasks, and destiny are exclusively individual. In its various forms of liberalism, humanism, and personalism, this culture claims to be the defender of the freedom of the person, of individual liberty, of private property, of freedom of competition, of love reduced to an inter-personal level, and so forth. In this way it covers up the structural aspects of social relations and the contradictions engendered by the system.

2.7. The culture of the dominant system imposes a "spiritual" idea of man, explaining his behavior and his history as founded principally on ideas and moral attitudes, as if the evils of the world were exclusively the result of ideological and moral deviations of a purely individual kind. We believe that the dominant culture distracts attention from a scientific study of the economic and social mechanisms that fundamentally govern the march of history, obfuscates the fundamental role of the structures involved in the oppression of men and of peoples, and plays down the fundamental impact of economic interests, and especially of class relations on political, cultural, and religious life. In this way it induces people to discard the idea of trying to change things by means of a transformation of the economic system.

2.8. The dominant culture, using the gospels in a partial and deformed way, imposes a pacifistic idea of society and describes differences, dependence, the division of labor, privileges, and so forth, as forms of pluralism, a kind of complementarity required by civil order and the common good. It therefore proposes "collaboration and dialogue" between classes and people. In this way it obscures the conflictive character of the relations between classes and peoples, and also every authentic process of liberation. Similarly, it obscures the institutionalized violence of the system and uses the term *violence* exclusively to describe opposition to the dominant class and revolutionary struggle. In the last resort it thereby delays an authentic communion among men.

2.9. The class struggle itself is therefore the reason why the majority of men are averse to it. Indeed, this class struggle becomes all the more effective for the oppressors the more it can operate without the oppressed becoming aware of its influence and its mechanisms.

2.10. The alliance between Christianity and the dominant classes explains to a large extent the historical forms assumed by the Christian conscience. It is therefore essential that Christians should place themselves firmly on the side of the exploited, thereby breaking this alliance and, by the process of the verification of practice, making it possible to rediscover a renewed Christianity which, in an endeavor of evangelical fidelity, will creatively redeem the conflictive and revolutionary character of its original inspiration.

3. The Faith and Revolutionary Commitment

3.1. One of the most important discoveries of many Christians today consists of the convergence between the radical nature of their faith and the radicality of their political commitment. The radicality of Christian love and the need for making it effective drives them to recognize the logic peculiar to the political sphere and to accept with full coherence the reciprocal implications of revolutionary action and scientific analysis of historical reality.

3.2. This living of the faith in the midst of revolutionary practice gives rise to a fertile interaction. The Christian faith becomes a critical and dynamic revolutionary ferment. The faith heightens the need for the class struggle to be decisively directed towards the liberation of all men, particularly those who suffer the most acute oppression. It also accentuates the orientation toward a global transformation of society rather than a mere transformation of the economic structures. In and through committed Christians, the faith thus makes its contribution to the construction of a qualitatively different society and the birth of a new man. The specific Christian contribution must not be thought of as something anterior to revolutionary practice, something ready-made that the Christian brings to the revolution. The truth is that in the course of its revolutionary experience the faith reveals itself as the creator of new contributions that neither the Christian nor anybody else could have foreseen from outside the process.

3.3. However, the revolutionary commitment also exerts a critical and stimulating function with respect to the Christian faith—critical as regards its historical complicities, blatant or subtle as they may be, with the dominant culture, and stimulating inasmuch as it obliges the living faith to move in new and unexpected directions. In fact, Christians committed to the process of liberation come to realize, by their own experience, that the requirements of revolutionary practice, the change of mentality and the discipline that it implies, lead them to rediscover the central themes of the evangelical message, stripped at last of their ideological disguises.

3.4. The real context of the living of the faith today is represented by the history of oppression and the liberating struggle against this oppression. In order to become situated in this vital context, however, it is essential for the holders of this faith to participate effectively in the process of liberation by joining organizations and parties that are authentic instruments of the struggle of the working class.

3.5. The Christian committed to revolutionary practice discovers the liberating force of the love of God, of the death and resurrection of Christ. He discovers that his faith does not imply the acceptance of a world that is already made, or of a predetermined history, but rather that the very living of his faith involves the creation of a new and solitary world and leads to historical initiatives fertilized by Christian hopes.

3.6. In his revolutionary commitment the Christian learns to live and to think in conflictive and historical terms. He discovers that transforming love is lived in antagonism and opposition, and that ultimate values are only received and constructed in the course of history. The Christian thus begins to understand that the struggle for a different society does not admit of neutrality and that the unity of mankind tomorrow is being forged by the struggles of today. Lastly, he discovers that the unity of the church has to be achieved through the unity of mankind, and that therefore the revolutionary struggle, inasmuch as it reveals the false unity of the church today, prepares the true unity of the church tomorrow.

3.7. Reflection on the faith is no longer a speculation estranged from commitment in history. Revolutionary practice is recognized as the generating matrix of a new theological creativity. Theological thought is thus transformed into a critical reflection within and about liberating practice as part of a permanent confrontation with evangelical demands.

As an indispensable requisite for the accomplishment of its task theological reflection adopts a complex of socio-analytical instruments that enable it to perceive critically the conflictive nature of historical reality.

3.8. In a spirit of authentic faith, this leads to a new reading of the Bible and to a Christian tradition that re-proposes the basic concepts and symbols of Christianity in such a way as not to hinder the Christian in his commitment to the revolutionary process, but rather to help him to shoulder this commitment in a creative manner.

CONCLUSION

We leave this encounter to return to our tasks in a spirit of renewed commitment, adopting as our own Che Guevara's well-known words that in some way we have already put into practice in the course of this meeting:

> Christians must opt for the revolution once and for all, and this particularly in our own continent where the Christian faith is of such importance among the popular masses. In the revolutionary struggle, however, Christians must not attempt to impose their own dogmas, nor must they engage in proselytism for their churches; they must come without wanting to evangelize the Marxists and without the cowardice of concealing their faith in order to seem similar to them.
>
> Only when Christians will have the courage to give a wholehearted revolutionary testimony will the Latin American revolution become invincible, because up to the present time they have allowed their doctrine to be instrumentalized by the reactionaries.

32

Outwitting the "Developed" Countries

Ivan Illich

It is now common to demand that the rich nations convert their war machine into a program for the development of the Third World. The poorer four fifths of humanity multiply unchecked while their per capita consumption actually declines. This population expansion and decrease of consumption threaten the industrialized nations, who may still, as a result, convert their defense budgets to the economic pacification of poor nations. And this in turn could produce irreversible despair, because the plows of the rich can do as much harm as their swords. US trucks can do more lasting damage than US tanks. It is easier to create mass demand for the former than for the latter. Only a minority needs heavy weapons, while a majority can become dependent on unrealistic levels of supply for such productive machines as modern trucks. Once the Third World has become a mass market for the goods, products, and processes which are designed by the rich for themselves, the discrepancy between demand for these Western artifacts and the supply will increase indefinitely. The family car cannot drive the poor into the jet age, nor can a school system provide the poor with education, nor can the family icebox insure healthy food for them.

It is evident that only one man in a thousand in Latin America can afford a Cadillac, a heart operation, or a Ph.D. This restriction on the goals of development does not make us despair of the fate of the Third World, and the reason is simple. We have not yet come to conceive of a Cadillac as necessary for good transportation, or of a heart operation as normal health care, or of a Ph.D. as the prerequisite of an acceptable education. In fact, we recognize at once that the importation of Cadillacs should be heavily taxed in Peru, that an organ transplant clinic is a scandalous plaything to justify the concentration of more doctors in Bogotá, and that a Betatron is beyond the teaching facilities of the University of São Paolo.

Unfortunately, it is not held to be universally evident that the majority of Latin Americans—not only of our generation, but also of the next and the next again—cannot afford any kind of automobile, or any kind of hospitalization, or for that matter an elementary school education. We suppress our consciousness of this obvious reality because we hate to recognize the corner into which our imagination has been pushed. So persuasive is the power of the institutions we have created that they shape not only our preferences, but actually our sense of possibilities. We have forgotten how to speak about modern transportation that does not rely on automobiles and airplanes. Our conceptions of modern health care emphasize our ability to prolong the lives of the desperately ill. We have become unable to think of better education except in terms of more complex schools and of teachers trained for ever longer periods. Huge institutions producing costly services dominate the horizons of our inventiveness.

We have embodied our world view into our institutions and are now their prisoners. Factories, news media, hospitals, governments, and schools produce goods and services packaged to contain our view of the world. We —the rich—conceive of progress as the expansion of these establishments. We conceive of heightened mobility as luxury and safety packaged by General Motors or Boeing. We conceive of improving the general well-being as increasing the supply of doctors and hospitals, which package health along with protracted suffering. We have come to identify our need for further learning with the demand for ever longer confinement to classrooms. In other words, we have packaged education with custodial care, certification for jobs, and the right to vote, and wrapped them all together with indoctrination in the Christian, liberal, or communist virtues.

In less than a hundred years industrial society has molded patent solutions to basic human needs and converted us to the belief that man's needs were shaped by the Creator as demands for the products we have invented. This is as true for Russia and Japan as for the North Atlantic community. The consumer is trained for obsolescence, which means continuing loyalty toward the same producers who will give him the same basic packages in different quality or new wrappings.

Industrialized societies can provide such packages for personal consumption for most of their citizens, but this is no proof that these societies are sane, or economical, or that they promote life. The contrary is true. The more the citizen is trained in the consumption of packaged goods and services, the less effective he seems to become in shaping his environment. His energies and finances are consumed in procuring ever new models of his staples, and the environment becomes a by-product of his own consumption habits.

The design of the "package deals" of which I speak is the main cause of the high cost of satisfying basic needs. So long as every man "needs" his car, our cities must endure longer traffic jams and absurdly expensive remedies to relieve them. So long as health means maximum length of survival, our sick will get ever more extraordinary surgical interventions and the drugs required to deaden their consequent pain. So long as we want to use school to get children out of their parents' hair or to keep them off the street and out of the labor force, our young will be retained in endless schooling and will need ever-increasing incentives to endure the ordeal.

Rich nations now benevolently impose a straightjacket of traffic jams, hospital confinements, and classrooms on the poor nations, and by international agreement call this "development." The rich and schooled and old of the world try to share their dubious blessings by foisting their pre-packaged solution onto the Third World. Traffic jams develop in São Paolo, while almost a million northeastern Brazilians flee the drought by walking 500 miles. Latin American doctors get training at the New York Hospital for Special Surgery, which they apply to only a few, while amoebic dysentery remains endemic in slums where 90 percent of the population live. A tiny minority gets advanced education in basic science in North America—not infrequently paid for by their own governments. If they return at all to Bolivia, they become second-rate teachers of pretentious subjects at La Paz or Cochabamba. The rich export outdated versions of their standard models.

The Alliance for Progress is a good example of benevolent production for underdevelopment. Contrary to its slogans, it did succeed—as an alliance for the progress of the consuming classes, and for the domestication of the Latin American masses. The Alliance has been a major step in modernizing the consumption patterns of the middle classes in South America by inte-grating them with the dominant culture of the North American metropolis. At the same time, the Alliance has modernized the aspirations of the major-ity of citizens and fixed their demands on unavailable products.

Each car which Brazil puts on the road denies fifty people good trans-portation by bus. Each merchandised refrigerator reduces the chance of building a community freezer. Every dollar spent in Latin America on doctors and hospitals costs a hundred lives, to adopt a phrase of Jorge de Ahumada, the brilliant Chilean economist. Had each dollar been spent on providing safe drinking water, a hundred lives could have been saved. Each dollar spent on schooling means more privileges for the few at the cost of the many; at best it increases the number of those who, before dropping out, have been taught that those who stay longer have earned the right to more power, wealth, and prestige. What such schooling does is to teach the schooled the superiority of the better schooled.

All Latin American countries are frantically intent on expanding their school systems. No country now spends less than the equivalent of 18 percent of tax-derived public income on education—which means schooling —and many countries spend almost double that. But even with these huge investments, no country yet succeeds in giving five full years of education to more than one third of its population; supply and demand for schooling grow geometrically apart. And what is true about schooling is equally true about the products of most institutions in the process of modernization in the Third World.

Continued technological refinements of products which are already established on the market frequently benefit the producer far more than the consumer. The more complex production processes tend to enable only the largest producer to continually replace outmoded models, and to focus the demand of the consumer on the marginal improvement of what he buys, no matter what the concomitant side effects: higher prices, diminished life span, less general usefulness, higher cost of repairs. Think of the multiple uses for a simple can opener, whereas an electric one, if it works at all, opens only some kinds of cans, and costs one hundred times as much.

This is equally true for a piece of agricultural machinery and for an academic degree. The midwestern farmer can become convinced of his need for a four-axle vehicle which can go 70 m.p.h. on the highways, has an electric windshield wiper and upholstered seats, and can be turned in for a new one within a year or two. Most of the world's farmers don't need such speed, nor have they ever met with such comfort, nor are they interested in obsolescence. They need low-priced transport, in a world where time is not money, where manual wipers suffice, and where a piece of heavy equipment should outlast a generation. Such a mechanical donkey requires entirely different engineering and design than one produced for the US market. This vehicle is not in production.

Most of South America needs paramedical workers who can function for indefinite periods without the supervision of an M.D. Instead of establishing a process to train midwives and visiting healers who know how to use a very limited arsenal of medicines while working independently, Latin American universities establish every year a new school of specialized nursing or nursing administration to prepare professionals who can function only in a hospital, and pharmacists who know how to sell increasingly more dangerous drugs.

The world is reaching an impasse where two processes converge: ever more men have fewer basic choices. The increase in population is widely publicized and creates panic. The decrease in fundamental choice causes anguish and is consistently overlooked. The population explosion overwhelms the imagination, but the progressive atrophy of social imagination is rationalized as an increase of choice between brands. The two processes converge in a dead end: the population explosion provides more consumers for everything from food to contraceptives, while our shrinking imagination can conceive of no other ways of satisfying their demands except through the packages now on sale in the admired societies.

I will focus successively on these two factors, since, in my opinion, they form the two coordinates which together permit us to define underdevelopment.

In most Third World countries, the population grows, and so does the middle class. Income, consumption, and the well-being of the middle class are all growing while the gap between this class and the mass of people widens. Even where per capita consumption is rising, the majority of men have less food now than in 1945, less actual care in sickness, less meaningful work, less protection. This is partly a consequence of polarized consumption and partly caused by the breakdown of traditional family and culture. More people suffer from hunger, pain, and exposure in 1969 than they did at the end of World War II, not only numerically, but also as a percentage of the world population.

These concrete consequences of underdevelopment are rampant; but underdevelopment is also a state of mind, and understanding it as a state of mind, or as a form of consciousness, is the critical problem. Underdevelopment as a state of mind occurs when mass needs are converted to the demand for new brands of packaged solutions which are forever beyond the reach of the majority. Underdevelopment in this sense is rising rapidly even in countries where the supply of classrooms, calories, cars, and clinics is also rising. The ruling groups in these countries build up services which have been designed for an affluent culture; once they have monopolized demand in this way, they can never satisfy majority needs.

Underdevelopment as a form of consciousness is an extreme result of what we can call in the language of both Marx and Freud *"Verdinglichung"* or reification. By reification I mean the hardening of the perception of real needs into the demand for mass manufactured products. I mean the translation of thirst into the need for a Coke. This kind of reification occurs in the manipulation of primary human needs by vast bureaucratic organizations which have succeeded in dominating the imagination of potential consumers.

Let me return to my example taken from the field of education. The intense promotion of schooling leads to so close an identification of school attendance and education that in everyday language the two terms are interchangeable. Once the imagination of an entire population has been "schooled," or indoctrinated to believe that school has a monopoly on formal education, then the illiterate can be taxed to provide free high school and university education for the children of the rich.

Underdevelopment is the result of rising levels of aspiration achieved through the intensive marketing of "patent" products. In this sense, the dynamic underdevelopment that is now taking place is the exact opposite of what I believe education to be: namely, the awakening awareness of new levels of human potential and the use of one's creative powers to foster human life. Underdevelopment, however, implies the surrender of social consciousness to pre-packaged solutions.

The process by which the marketing of "foreign" products increases underdevelopment is frequently understood in the most superficial ways. The same man who feels indignation at the sight of a Coca-Cola plant in a Latin American slum often feels pride at the sight of a new normal school growing up alongside. He resents the evidence of a foreign "license" attached to a soft drink which he would like to see replaced by "Cola-Mex." But the same man is willing to impose schooling—at all costs—on his fellow citizens, and is unaware of the invisible license by which this institution is deeply enmeshed in the world market.

Some years ago I watched workmen putting up a sixty-foot Coca-Cola sign on a desert plain in the Mexquital. A serious drought and famine had just swept over the Mexican highland. My host, a poor Indian in Ixmiquilpan, had just offered his visitors a tiny tequila glass of the costly black sugar-water. When I recall this scene I still feel anger; but I feel much more incensed when I remember UNESCO meetings at which well-meaning and well-paid bureaucrats seriously discussed Latin American school curricula, and when I think of the speeches of enthusiastic liberals advocating the need for more schools.

The fraud perpetrated by the salesmen of schools is less obvious but much more fundamental than the self-satisfied salesmanship of the Coca-Cola or Ford representative, because the schoolman hooks his people on a much more demanding drug. Elementary school attendance is not a harmless luxury, but more like the coca chewing of the Andean Indian, which harnesses the worker to the boss.

The higher the dose of schooling an individual has received, the more depressing his experience of withdrawal. The seventh-grade dropout feels his inferiority much more acutely than the dropout from the third grade. The schools of the Third World administer their opium with much more effect than the churches of other epochs. As the mind of a society is progressively schooled, step by step its individuals lose their sense that it might be possible to live without being inferior to others. As the majority shifts from the land into the city, the hereditary inferiority of the peon is replaced by the inferiority of the school dropout who is held personally responsible for his failure. Schools rationalize the divine origin of social stratification with much more rigor than churches have ever done.

Until this day no Latin American country has declared youthful under-consumers of Coca-Cola or cars as lawbreakers, while all Latin American countries have passed laws which define the early dropout as a citizen who has not fulfilled his legal obligations. The Brazilian government recently almost doubled the number of years during which schooling is legally compulsory and free. From now on any Brazilian dropout under the age of sixteen will be faced during his lifetime with the reproach that he did not take advantage of a legally obligatory privilege. This law was passed in a country where not even the most optimistic could foresee the day when such levels of schooling would be provided for even 25 percent of the young. The adoption of international standards of schooling forever condemns most Latin Americans to marginality or exclusion from social life—in a word, underdevelopment.

The translation of social goals into levels of consumption is not limited to only a few countries. Across all frontiers of culture, ideology, and geography today, nations are moving toward the establishment of their own car factories, their own medical and normal schools—and most of these are, at best, poor imitations of foreign and largely North American models.

The Third World is in need of a profound revolution of its institutions. The revolutions of the last generation were overwhelmingly political. A new group of men with a new set of ideological justifications assumed power to administer fundamentally the same scholastic, medical, and market institutions in the interest of a new group of clients. Since the institutions have not radically changed, the new group of clients remains approximately the same size as that previously served. This appears clearly in the case of education. Per pupil costs of schooling are today comparable everywhere since the standards used to evaluate the quality of schooling tend to be internationally shared. Access to publicly financed education, considered as access to school, everywhere depends on per capita income. (Places like China and North Vietnam might be meaningful exceptions.)

Everywhere in the Third World modern institutions are grossly unproductive, with respect to the egalitarian purposes for which they are being reproduced. But so long as the social imagination of the majority has not been destroyed by its fixation on these institutions, there is more hope of planning an institutional revolution in the Third World than among the rich. Hence the urgency of the task of developing workable alternatives to "modern" solutions.

Underdevelopment is at the point of becoming chronic in many countries. The revolution of which I speak must begin to take place before this happens. Education again offers a good example: chronic educational under-development occurs when the demand for schooling becomes so widespread that the total concentration of educational resources on the school system becomes a unanimous political demand. At this point the separation of education from schooling becomes impossible.

The only feasible answer to ever-increasing underdevelopment is a response to basic needs that is planned as a long-range goal for areas which will always have a different capital structure. It is easier to speak about alternatives to existing institutions, services, and products than to define them with precision. It is not my purpose either to paint a Utopia or to engage in scripting scenarios for an alternate future. We must be satisfied with examples indicating simple directions that research should take.

Some such examples have already been given. Buses are alternatives to a multitude of private cars. Vehicles designed for slow transportation on rough terrain are alternatives to standard trucks. Safe water is an alternative to high-priced surgery. Medical workers are an alternative to doctors and nurses. Community food storage is an alternative to expensive kitchen equipment. Other alternatives could be discussed by the dozen. Why not, for example, consider walking as a long-range alternative for locomotion by machine, and explore the demands which this would impose on the city planner? And why can't the building of shelters be standardized, elements be pre-cast, and each citizen be obliged to learn in a year of public service how to construct his own sanitary housing?

It is harder to speak about alternatives in education, partly because schools have recently so completely pre-empted the available educational resources of good will, imagination, and money. But even here we can indicate the direction in which research must be conducted.

At present, schooling is conceived as graded, curricular, class attendance by children, for about 1000 hours yearly during an uninterrupted succession of years. On the average, Latin American countries can provide each citizen with between eight and thirty months of this service. Why not, instead, make one or two months a year obligatory for all citizens below the age of thirty?

Money is now spent largely on children, but an adult can be taught to read in one tenth the time and for one tenth the cost it takes to teach a child. In the case of the adult there is an immediate return on the invest-ment, whether the main importance of his learning is seen in his new insight, political awareness, and willingness to assume responsibility for his family's size and future, or whether the emphasis is placed on increased productivity. There is a double return in the case of the adult, because not only can he contribute to the education of his children, but to that of other adults as well. In spite of these advantages, basic literacy programs have little or no support in Latin America, where schools have a first call on all public resources. Worse, these programs are actually ruthlessly suppressed in Brazil and elsewhere, where military support of the feudal or industrial oligarchy has thrown off its former benevolent disguise.

Another possibility is harder to define, because there is as yet no example to point to. We must therefore imagine the use of public resources for education distributed in such a way as to give every citizen a minimum chance. Education will become a political concern of the majority of voters only when each individual has a precise sense of the educational resources that are owing to him—and some idea of how to sue for them. Something like a universal G.I. Bill of Rights could be imagined, dividing the public resources assigned to education by the number of children who are legally of school age, and making sure that a child who did not take advantage of his credit at the age of seven, eight, or nine would have the accumulated benefits at his disposal at age ten.

What could the pitiful education credit which a Latin American Republic could offer to its children provide? Almost all of the basic supply of books, pictures, blocks, games, and toys that are totally absent from the homes of the really poor, but enable a middle-class child to learn the alphabet, the colors, shapes, and other classes of objects and experiences which insure his educational progress. The choice between these things and schools is obvious. Unfortunately, the poor, for whom alone the choice is real, never get to exercise this choice.

Defining alternatives to the products and institutions which now pre-empt the field is difficult, not only, as I have been trying to show, because these products and institutions shape our conception of reality itself, but also because the construction of new possibilities requires a concentration of will and intelligence in a higher degree than ordinarily occurs by chance. This concentration of will and intelligence on the solution of particular problems regardless of their nature we have become accustomed over the last century to call research.

I must make clear, however, what kind of research I am talking about. I am not talking about basic research either in physics, engineering, genetics, medicine, or learning. The work of such men as Crick, Piaget, and Gell-Mann must continue to enlarge our horizons in other fields of science. The labs and libraries and specially trained collaborators these men need cause them to congregate in the few research capitals of the world. Their research can provide the basis for new work on practically any product.

I am not speaking here of the billions of dollars annually spent on applied research, for this money is largely spent by existing institutions on the perfection and marketing of their own products. Applied research is money spent on making planes faster and airports safer; on making medicines more specific and powerful and doctors capable of handling their deadly side-effects; on packaging more learning into classrooms; on methods to administer large bureaucracies. This is the kind of research for which some kind of counterfoil must somehow be developed if we are to have any chance to come up with basic alternatives to the automobile, the hospital, and the school, and any of the many other so-called "evidently necessary implements for modern life."

I have in mind a different, and peculiarly difficult, kind of research, which has been largely neglected up to now, for obvious reasons. I am calling for research on alternatives to the products which now dominate the market; to hospitals and the profession dedicated to keeping the sick alive;

to schools and the packaging process which refuses education to those who are not of the right age, who have not gone through the right curriculum, who have not sat in a classroom a sufficient number of successive hours, who will not pay for their learning with submission to custodial care, screening, and certification or with indoctrination in the values of the dominant elite.

This counter-research on fundamental alternatives to current pre-packaged solutions is the element most critically needed if the poor nations are to have a livable future. Such counter-research is distinct from most of the work done in the name of the "year 2000," because most of that work seeks radical changes in social patterns through adjustments in the organization of an already advanced technology. The counter-research of which I speak must take as one of its assumptions the continued lack of capital in the Third World.

The difficulties of such research are obvious. The researcher must first of all doubt what is obvious to every eye. Second, he must persuade those who have the power of decision to act against their own short-run interests or bring pressure on them to do so. And, finally, he must survive as an individual in a world he is attempting to change fundamentally so that his fellows among the privileged minority see him as a destroyer of the very ground on which all of us stand. He knows that if he should succeed in the interest of the poor, technologically advanced societies still might envy the "poor" who adopt this vision.

There is a normal course for those who make development policies, whether they live in North or South America, in Russia or Israel. It is to define development and to set its goals in ways with which they are familiar, which they are accustomed to use in order to satisfy their own needs, and which permit them to work through the institutions over which they have power or control. This formula has failed, and must fail. There is not enough money in the world for development to succeed along these lines, not even in the combined arms and space budgets of the super-powers.

An analogous course is followed by those who are trying to make political revolutions, especially in the Third World. Usually they promise to make the familiar privileges of the present elites, such as schooling, hospital care, etc., accessible to all citizens; and they base this vain promise on the belief that a change in political regime will permit them to sufficiently enlarge the institutions which produce these privileges. The promise and appeal of the revolutionary are therefore just as threatened by the counter-research I propose as is the market of the now dominant producers.

In Vietnam a people on bicycles and armed with sharpened bamboo sticks have brought to a standstill the most advanced machinery for research and production ever devised. We must seek survival in a Third World in which human ingenuity can peacefully outwit machined might. The only way to reverse the disastrous trend to increasing underdevelopment, hard as it is, is to learn to laugh at accepted solutions in order to change the demands which make them necessary. Only free men can change their minds and be surprised; and while no men are completely free, some are freer than others.

33

Pedagogy of the Oppressed

Paulo Freire

While the problem of humanization has always, from an axiological point of view, been man's central problem, it now takes on the character of an inescapable concern.[1] Concern for humanization leads at once to the recognition of dehumanization, not only as an ontological possibility but as an historical reality. And as man perceives the extent of dehumanization, he asks himself if humanization is a viable possibility. Within history, in concrete, objective contexts, both humanization and dehumanization are possibilities for man as an uncompleted being conscious of his incompletion.

But while both humanization and dehumanization are real alternatives, only the first is man's vocation. This vocation is constantly negated, yet it is affirmed by that very negation. It is thwarted by injustice, exploitation, oppression, and the violence of the oppressors; it is affirmed by the yearning of the oppressed for freedom and justice, and by their struggle to recover their lost humanity.

Dehumanization, which marks not only those whose humanity has been stolen, but also (though in a different way) those who have stolen it, is a *distortion* of the vocation of becoming more fully human. This distortion occurs within history but it is not an historical vocation. Indeed, to admit of dehumanization as an historical vocation would lead either to cynicism or to total despair. The struggle for humanization, for the emancipation of labor, for the overcoming of alienation, for the affirmation of men as persons would be meaningless. This struggle is possible only because dehumanization, although a concrete historical fact, is *not* a given destiny but the result of an unjust order that engenders violence in the oppressors, which in turn dehumanizes the oppressed.

Because it is a distortion of being more fully human, sooner or later being less human leads the oppressed to struggle against those who made them so. In order for this struggle to have meaning, the oppressed must not, in seeking to regain their humanity (which is a way to create it), become in turn oppressors of the oppressors, but rather restorers of the humanity of both.

This, then, is the great humanistic and historical task of the oppressed:

to liberate themselves and their oppressors as well. The oppressors, who oppress, exploit, and rape by virtue of their power, cannot find in this power the strength to liberate either the oppressed or themselves. Only power that springs from the weakness of the oppressed will be sufficiently strong to free both. Any attempt to "soften" the power of the oppressor in deference to the weakness of the oppressed almost always manifests itself in the form of false generosity; indeed, the attempt never goes beyond this. In order to have the continued opportunity to express their "generosity," the oppressors must perpetuate injustice as well. An unjust social order is the permanent fount of this "generosity," which is nourished by death, despair, and poverty. That is why the dispensers of false generosity become desperate at the slightest threat to its source.

True generosity consists precisely in fighting to destroy the causes which nourish false charity. False charity constrains the fearful and sub-dued, the "rejects of life," to extend their trembling hands. True generosity lies in striving so that these hands—whether of individuals or entire peo-ples—need be extended less and less in supplication, so that more and more they become human hands which work and, working, transform the world.

This lesson and this apprenticeship must come, however, from the oppressed themselves and from those who are truly solidary with them. As individuals or as peoples, by fighting for the restoration of their humanity they will be attempting the restoration of true generosity. Who are better prepared than the oppressed to understand the terrible significance of an oppressive society? Who suffer the effects of oppression more than the oppressed? Who can better understand the necessity of liberation? They will not gain this liberation by chance but through the praxis of their quest for it, through their recognition of the necessity to fight for it. And this fight, because of the purpose given it by the oppressed, will actually constitute an act of love opposing the lovelessness which lies at the heart of the oppressors' violence, lovelessness even when clothed in false generosity.

But almost always, during the initial stage of the struggle, the oppressed, instead of striving for liberation, tend themselves to become oppressors, or "sub-oppressors." The very structure of their thought has been condi-tioned by the contradictions of the concrete, existential situation by which they were shaped. Their ideal is to be men; but for them, to be men is to be oppressors. This is their model of humanity. This phenomenon derives from the fact that the oppressed, at a certain moment of their existential experience, adopt an attitude of "adhesion" to the oppressor. Under these circumstances they cannot "consider" him sufficiently clearly to objectivize him—to discover him "outside" themselves. This does not necessarily mean that the oppressed are unaware that they are downtrodden. But their per-ception of themselves as oppressed is impaired by their submersion in the reality of oppression. At this level, their perception of themselves as oppo-sites of the oppressor does not yet signify engagement in a struggle to overcome the contradiction;[2] the one pole aspires not to liberation, but to identification with its opposite pole.

In this situation the oppressed do not see the "new man" as the man to be born from the resolution of this contradiction, as oppression gives way to liberation. For them, the new man is themselves become oppressors.

Their vision of the new man is individualistic; because of their identification with the oppressor, they have no consciousness of themselves as persons or as members of an oppressed class. It is not to become free men that they want agrarian reform, but in order to acquire land and thus become landowners—or, more precisely, bosses over other workers. It is a rare peasant who, once "promoted" to overseer, does not become more of a tyrant towards his former comrades than the owner himself. This is because the context of the peasant's situation, that is, oppression, remains unchanged. In this example, the overseer, in order to make sure of his job, must be as tough as the owner—and more so. Thus is illustrated our previous assertion that during the initial stage of their struggle the oppressed find in the oppressor their model of "manhood."

Even revolution, which transforms a concrete situation of oppression by establishing the process of liberation, must confront this phenomenon. Many of the oppressed who directly or indirectly participate in revolution intend—conditioned by the myths of the old order—to make it their private revolution. The shadow of their former oppressor is still cast over them.

The "fear of freedom" which afflicts the oppressed,[3] a fear which may equally well lead them to desire the role of oppressor or bind them to the role of oppressed, should be examined. One of the basic elements of the relationship between oppressor and oppressed is *prescription*. Every prescription represents the imposition of one man's choice upon another, transforming the consciousness of the man prescribed to into one that conforms with the prescriber's consciousness. Thus, the behavior of the oppressed is a prescribed behavior, following as it does the guidelines of the oppressor.

The oppressed, having internalized the image of the oppressor and adopted his guidelines, are fearful of freedom. Freedom would require them to eject this image and replace it with autonomy and responsibility. Freedom is acquired by conquest, not by gift. It must be pursued constantly and responsibly. Freedom is not an ideal located outside of man; nor is it an idea which becomes myth. It is rather the indispensable condition for the quest for human completion.

To surmount the situation of oppression, men must first critically recognize its causes, so that through transforming action they can create a new situation, one which makes possible the pursuit of a fuller humanity. But the struggle to be more fully human has already begun in the authentic struggle to transform the situation. Although the situation of oppression is a dehumanized and dehumanizing totality affecting both the oppressors and those whom they oppress, it is the latter who must, from their stifled humanity, wage for both the struggle for a fuller humanity; the oppressor, who is himself dehumanized because he dehumanizes others, is unable to lead this struggle.

However, the oppressed, who have adapted to the structure of domination in which they are immersed, and have become resigned to it, are inhibited from waging the struggle for freedom so long as they feel incapable of running the risks it requires. Moreover, their struggle for freedom threatens not only the oppressor, but also their own oppressed comrades who are fearful of still greater repression. When they discover within themselves the yearning to be free, they perceive that this yearning can be transformed into reality only when the same yearning is aroused in their comrades. But while dominated by the fear of freedom they refuse to appeal to others, or to listen to the appeals of others, or even to the appeals of their own conscience. They prefer gregariousness to authentic comradeship; they prefer the security of conformity with their state of unfreedom to the creative communion produced by freedom and even the very pursuit of freedom.

The oppressed suffer from the duality which has established itself in their innermost being. They discover that without freedom they cannot exist authentically. Yet, although they desire authentic existence, they fear it. They are at one and the same time themselves and the oppressor whose consciousness they have internalized. The conflict lies in the choice between being wholly themselves or being divided; between ejecting the oppressor within or not ejecting him; between human solidarity or alienation; between following prescriptions or having choices; between being spectators or actors; between acting or having the illusion of acting through the action of the oppressors; between speaking out or being silent, castrated in their power to create and re-create, in their power to transform the world. This is the tragic dilemma of the oppressed which their education must take into account.

[This paper] will present some aspects of what the writer has termed the pedagogy of the oppressed, a pedagogy which must be forged *with*, not *for*, the oppressed (whether individuals or peoples) in the incessant struggle to regain their humanity. This pedagogy makes oppression and its causes objects of reflection by the oppressed, and from that reflection will come their necessary engagement in the struggle for their liberation. And in the struggle this pedagogy will be made and remade.

The central problem is this: How can the oppressed, as divided, unauthentic beings, participate in developing the pedagogy of their liberation? Only as they discover themselves to be "hosts" of the oppressor can they contribute to the midwifery of their liberating pedagogy. As long as they live in the duality in which *to be* is *to be like*, and *to be like* is *to be like the oppressor*, this contribution is impossible. The pedagogy of the oppressed is an instrument for their critical discovery that both they and their oppressors are manifestations of dehumanization.

Liberation is thus a childbirth, and a painful one. The man who emerges is a new man, viable only as the oppressor-oppressed contradiction is superseded by the humanization of all men. Or to put it another way, the solution of this contradiction is born in the labor which brings into the world this new man: no longer oppressor nor longer oppressed, but man in the process of achieving freedom.

This solution cannot be achieved in idealistic terms. In order for the oppressed to be able to wage the struggle for their liberation, they must perceive the reality of oppression not as a closed world from which there is no exit, but as a limiting situation which they can transform. This perception is a necessary but not a sufficient condition for liberation; it must become the motivating force for liberating action. Nor does the discovery by the oppressed that they exist in dialectical relationship to the oppressor, as his antithesis—that without them the oppressor could not exist[4]—in itself constitute liberation. The oppressed can overcome the contradiction in which they are caught only when this perception enlists them in the struggle to free themselves.

The same is true with respect to the individual oppressor as a person. Discovering himself to be an oppressor may cause considerable anguish, but it does not necessarily lead to solidarity with the oppressed. Rationalizing his guilt through paternalistic treatment of the oppressed, all the while holding them fast in a position of dependence, will not do. Solidarity requires that one enter into the situation of those with whom one is solidary; it is a radical posture. If what characterizes the oppressed is their subordination to the consciousness of the master, as Hegel affirms,[5] true solidarity with the oppressed means fighting at their side to transform the objective reality which has made them these "beings for another." The oppressor is solidary with the oppressed only when he stops regarding the oppressed as an abstract category and sees them as persons who have been unjustly dealt with, deprived of their voice, cheated in the sale of their labor—when he stops making pious, sentimental, and individualistic gestures and risks an act of love. True solidarity is found only in the plenitude of this act of love, in its existentiality, in its praxis. To affirm that men are persons and as persons should be free and yet to do nothing tangible to make this affirmation a reality is a farce.

Since it is in a concrete situation that the oppressor–oppressed contradiction is established, the resolution of this contradiction must be *objectively* verifiable. Hence, the radical requirement—both for the man who discovers himself to be an oppressor and for the oppressed—that the concrete situation which begets oppression must be transformed.

To present this radical demand for the objective transformation of reality, to combat subjectivist immobility which would divert the recognition of oppression into patient waiting for oppression to disappear by itself, is not to dismiss the role of subjectivity in the struggle to change structures. On the contrary, one cannot conceive of objectivity without subjectivity. Neither can exist without the other, nor can they be dichotomized. The separation of objectivity from subjectivity, the denial of the latter when analyzing reality or acting upon it, is objectivism. On the other hand, the denial of objectivity in analysis or action, resulting in a subjectivism which leads to solipsistic positions, denies action itself by denying objective reality. Neither objectivism nor subjectivism, nor yet psychologism is propounded here, but rather subjectivity and objectivity in constant dialectical relationship.

To deny the importance of subjectivity in the process of transforming the world and history is naïve and simplistic. It is to admit the impossible: a world without men. This objectivistic position is as ingenuous as that of subjectivism, which postulates men without a world. World and men do not exist apart from each other, they exist in constant interaction. Marx does not espouse such a dichotomy, nor does any other critical, realistic thinker. What Marx criticized and scientifically destroyed was not subjectivity, but subjectivism and psychologism. Just as objective social reality exists not by chance, but as the product of human action, so it is not transformed by chance. If men produce social reality (which in the "inversion of the praxis" turns back upon them and conditions them), then transforming that reality is an historical task, a task for men.

Reality which becomes oppressive results in the contradistinction of men as oppressors and oppressed. The latter, whose task it is to struggle for their liberation together with those who show true solidarity, must acquire a critical awareness of oppression through the praxis of this struggle. One of the gravest obstacles to the achievement of liberation is that oppressive reality absorbs those within it and thereby acts to submerge men's consciousness. Functionally, oppression is domesticating. To no longer be prey to its force, one must emerge from it and turn upon it. This can be done only by means of the praxis: reflection and action upon the world in order to transform it.

Making "real oppression more oppressive still by adding to it the realization of oppression" corresponds to the dialectical relation between the subjective and the objective. Only in this interdependence is an authentic praxis possible, without which it is impossible to resolve the oppressor-oppressed contradiction. To achieve this goal, the oppressed must confront reality critically, simultaneously objectifying and acting upon that reality. A mere perception of reality not followed by this critical intervention will not lead to a transformation of objective reality—precisely because it is not a true perception. This is the case of a purely subjectivist perception by someone who forsakes objective reality and creates a false substitute.

A different type of false perception occurs when a change in objective reality would threaten the individual or class interests of the perceiver. In the first instance, there is no critical intervention in reality because that reality is fictitious; there is none in the second instance because intervention would contradict the class interests of the perceiver. In the latter case the tendency of the perceiver is to behave "neurotically." The fact exists; but both the fact and what may result from it may be prejudicial to him. Thus it becomes necessary, not precisely to deny the fact, but to "see it differently." This rationalization as a defense mechanism coincides in the end with subjectivism. A fact which is not denied but whose truths are rationalized loses its objective base. It ceases to be concrete and becomes a myth created in defense of the class of the perceiver.

Herein lies one of the reasons for the prohibitions and the difficulties . . . designed to dissuade the people from critical intervention in reality. The oppressor knows full well that this intervention would not be to his interest. What *is* to his interest is for the people to continue in a state of submersion, impotent in the face of oppressive reality. . . . "To explain to the masses their own action" is to clarify and illuminate that action, both regarding its relationship of the objective facts by which it was prompted, and regarding its purposes. The more the people unveil this challenging reality which is to be the object of their transforming action, the more critically they enter that reality. In this way they are "consciously activating the subsequent development of their experiences." There would be no human action if there were no objective reality, no world to be the "not I" of man and to challenge him; just as there would be no human action if man were not a "project," if he were not able to transcend himself, to perceive his reality and understand it in order to transform it.

In dialectical thought, word and action are intimately interdependent. But action is human only when it is not merely an occupation but also a preoccupation, that is, when it is not dichotomized from reflection. Reflection, which is essential to action, is implicit in Lukács' requirement of "explaining to the masses their own action," just as it is implicit in the purpose he attributes to this explanation: that of "consciously activating the subsequent development of experience."

For us, however, the requirement is seen not in terms of explaining to, but rather dialoguing with the people about their actions. In any event, no reality transforms itself,[6] and the duty which Lukács ascribes to the revolutionary party of "explaining to the masses their own action" coincides with our affirmation of the need for the critical intervention of the people in reality through the praxis. The pedagogy of the oppressed, which is the pedagogy of men engaged in the fight for their own liberation, has its roots here. And those who recognize, or begin to recognize, themselves as oppressed must be among the developers of this pedagogy. No pedagogy which is truly liberating can remain distant from the oppressed by treating them as unfortunates and by presenting for their emulation models from among the oppressors. The oppressed must be their own example in the struggle for their redemption.

The pedagogy of the oppressed, animated by authentic, humanist (not humanitarian) generosity, presents itself as a pedagogy of man. Pedagogy which begins with the egoistic interests of the oppressors (an egoism cloaked in the false generosity of paternalism) and makes of the oppressed the objects of its humanitarianism, itself maintains and embodies oppression. It is an instrument of dehumanization. This is why, as we affirmed earlier, the pedagogy of the oppressed cannot be developed or practiced by the oppressors. It would be a contradiction in terms if the oppressors not only defended but actually implemented a liberating education.

. . .

The pedagogy of the oppressed, as a humanist and libertarian pedagogy, has two distinct stages. In the first, the oppressed unveil the world of oppression and through the praxis commit themselves to its transformation. In the second stage, in which the reality of oppression has already been transformed, this pedagogy ceases to belong to the oppressed and becomes a pedagogy of all men in the process of permanent liberation. In both stages, it is always through action in depth that the culture of domination is culturally confronted.[7] In the first stage this confrontation occurs through the change in the way the oppressed perceive the world of oppression; in the second stage, through the expulsion of the myths created and developed in the old order, which like specters haunt the new structure emerging from the revolutionary transformation.

The pedagogy of the first stage must deal with the problem of the oppressed consciousness and the oppressor consciousness, the problem of men who oppress and men who suffer oppression. It must take into account their behavior, their view of the world, and their ethics. A particular problem is the duality of the oppressed: they are contradictory, divided beings, shaped by and existing in a concrete situation of oppression and violence.

Any situation in which "A" objectively exploits "B" or hinders his pursuit of self-affirmation as a responsible person is one of oppression. Such a situation in itself constitutes violence, even when sweetened by false generosity, because it interferes with man's ontological and historical vocation to be more fully human. With the establishment of a relationship of oppression, violence has *already* begun. Never in history has violence been initiated by the oppressed. How could they be the initiators, if they themselves are the result of violence? How could they be the sponsors of something whose objective inauguration called forth their existence as oppressed? There would be no oppressed had there been no prior situation of violence to establish their subjugation.

Violence is initiated by those who oppress, who exploit, who fail to recognize others as persons—not by those who are oppressed, exploited, and unrecognized. It is not the unloved who initiate disaffection, but those who cannot love because they love only themselves. It is not the helpless, subject to terror, who initiate terror, but the violent, who with their power create the concrete situation which begets the "rejects of life." It is not the tyrannized who initiate despotism, but the tyrants. It is not the despised who initiate hatred, but those who despise. It is not those whose humanity is denied them who negate man, but those who denied that humanity (thus negating their own as well). Force is used not by those who have become weak under the preponderance of the strong, but by the strong who have emasculated them.

For the oppressors, however, it is always the oppressed (whom they obviously never call "the oppressed" but—depending on whether they are fellow countrymen or not—"those people" or "the blind and envious masses" or "savages" or "natives" or "subversives") who are disaffected, who are "violent," "barbaric," "wicked," or "ferocious" when they react to the violence of the oppressors.

Yet it is—paradoxical though it may seem—precisely in the response of the oppressed to the violence of their oppressors that a gesture of love may be found. Consciously or unconsciously, the act of rebellion by the oppressed (an act which is always, or nearly always, as violent as the initial violence of the oppressors) can initiate love. Whereas the violence of the oppressors prevents the oppressed from being fully human, the response of the latter to this violence is grounded in the desire to pursue the right to be human. As the oppressors dehumanize others and violate their rights, they themselves also become dehumanized. As the oppressed, fighting to be human, take away the oppressors' power to dominate and suppress, they restore to the oppressors the humanity they had lost in the exercise of oppression.

It is only the oppressed who, by freeing themselves, can free their oppressors. The latter, as an oppressive class, can free neither others nor themselves. It is therefore essential that the oppressed wage the struggle to resolve the contradiction in which they are caught; and the contradiction will be resolved by the appearance of the new man: neither oppressor nor oppressed, but man in the process of liberation. If the goal of the oppressed is to become fully human, they will not achieve their goal by merely reversing the terms of the contradiction, by simply changing poles.

This may seem simplistic; it is not. Resolution of the oppressor-oppressed contradiction indeed implies the disappearance of the oppressors as a dominant class. However, the restraints imposed by the former oppressed on their oppressors, so that the latter cannot reassume their former position, do not constitute *oppression*. An act is oppressive only when it prevents men from being more fully human. Accordingly, these necessary restraints do not *in themselves* signify that yesterday's oppressed have become today's oppressors. Acts which prevent the restoration of the oppressive regime cannot be compared with those which create and maintain it, cannot be compared with those by which a few men deny the majority their right to be human.

However, the moment the new regime hardens into a dominating "bureaucracy"[8] the humanist dimension of the struggle is lost and it is no longer possible to speak of liberation. Hence our insistence that the authentic solution of the oppressor-oppressed contradiction does not lie in a mere reversal of position, in moving from one pole to the other. Nor does it lie in the replacement of the former oppressors with new ones who continue to subjugate the oppressed—all in the name of their liberation.

But even when the contradiction is resolved authentically by a new situation established by the liberated laborers, the former oppressors do not feel liberated. On the contrary, they genuinely consider themselves to be oppressed. Conditioned by the experience of oppressing others, any situation other than their former seems to them like oppression. Formerly, they could eat, dress, wear shoes, be educated, travel, and hear Beethoven; while millions did not eat, had no clothes or shoes, neither studied nor traveled, much less listened to Beethoven. Any restriction on this way of life, in the name of the rights of the community, appears to the former oppressors as a profound violation of their individual rights—although they had no respect for the millions who suffered and died of hunger, pain, sorrow, and despair. For the oppressors, "human beings" refer only to themselves; other people are "things." For the oppressors, there exists only one right: their right to live in peace, over against the right, not always even recognized, but simply conceded, of the oppressed to survival. And they make this concession only because the existence of the oppressed is necessary to their own existence.

This behavior, this way of understanding the world and men (which necessarily makes the oppressors resist the installation of a new regime) is explained by their experience as a dominant class. Once a situation of violence and oppression has been established, it engenders an entire way of life and behavior for those caught up in it—oppressors and oppressed alike. Both are submerged in this situation, and both bear the marks of oppression. Analysis of existential situations of oppression reveals that their inception lay in an act of violence—initiated by those with power. This violence, as a process, is perpetuated from generation to generation of oppressors, who become its heirs and are shaped in its climate. This climate creates in the oppressor a strongly possessive consciousness—possessive of the world and of men. Apart from direct, concrete, material possession of the world and of men, the oppressor consciousness could not understand itself—could not even exist. Fromm said of this consciousness that, without such possession, "it would lose contact with the world." The oppressor consciousness tends to transform everything surrounding it into an object of its domination. The earth, property, production, the creations of men, men themselves, time—everything is reduced to the status of objects at its disposal.

In their unrestrained eagerness to possess, the oppressors develop the conviction that it is possible for them to transform everything into objects of their purchasing power; hence their strictly materialistic concept of existence. Money is the measure of all things, and profit the primary goal. For the oppressors, what is worthwhile is to have more—always more—even at the cost of the oppressed having less or having nothing. For them, *to be* is *to have* and to be the class of the "haves."

As beneficiaries of a situation of oppression, the oppressors cannot perceive that if *having* is a condition of *being*, it is a necessary condition for all men. This is why their generosity is false. Humanity is a "thing," and they possess it as an exclusive right, as inherited property. To the oppressor consciousness, the humanization of the "others," of the people, appears not as the pursuit of full humanity, but as subversion.

The oppressors do not perceive their monopoly on *having more* as a privilege which dehumanizes others and themselves. They cannot see that, in the egoistic pursuit of *having* as a possessing class, they suffocate in their own possessions and no longer *are*; they merely *have*. For them, *having more* is an inalienable right, a right they acquired through their own "effort," with their "courage to take risks." If others do not have more, it is because they are incompetent and lazy, and worst of all is their unjustifiable ingratitude towards the "generous gestures" of the dominant class. Precisely because they are "ungrateful" and "envious," the oppressed are regarded as potential enemies who must be watched.

It could not be otherwise. If the humanization of the oppressed signifies subversion, so also does their freedom; hence the necessity for constant control. And the more the oppressors control the oppressed, the more they change them into apparently inanimate "things." This tendency of the oppressor consciousness to "in-animate" everything and everyone it encounters, in its eagerness to possess, unquestionably corresponds with a tendency to sadism.

> The pleasure in complete domination over another person (or other animate creature) is the very essence of the sadistic drive. Another way of formulating the same thought is to say that the aim of sadism is to transform a man into a thing, something animate into something inanimate, since by complete and absolute control the living loses one essential quality of life—freedom.[9]

Sadistic love is a perverted love—a love of death, not of life. One of the characteristics of the oppressor consciousness and its necrophilic view of the world is thus sadism. As the oppressor consciousness, in order to dominate, tries to deter the drive to search, the restlessness, and the creative power which characterize life, it kills life. More and more, the oppressors are using science and technology as unquestionably powerful instruments for their purpose: the maintenance of the oppressive order through manipulation and repression.[10] The oppressed, as objects, as "things," have no purposes except those their oppressors prescribe for them.

Given the preceding context, another issue of indubitable importance arises: the fact that certain members of the oppressor class join the oppressed in their struggle for liberation, thus moving from one pole of the contradiction to the other. Theirs is a fundamental role, and has been so throughout the history of this struggle. It happens, however, that as they cease to be exploiters or indifferent spectators or simply the heirs of exploitation and move to the side of the exploited, they almost always bring with them the marks of their origin: their prejudices and their deformations, which include a lack of confidence in the people's ability to think, to want, and to know. Accordingly, these adherents to the people's cause constantly run the risk of falling into a type of generosity as malefic as that of the oppressors. The generosity of the oppressors is nourished by an unjust order, which must be maintained in order to justify that generosity. Our converts, on the other hand, truly desire to transform the unjust order; but because of their background they believe that they must be the executors of the transformation. They talk about the people, but they do not trust them; and trusting the people is the indispensable precondition for revolutionary change. A real humanist can be identified more by his trust in the people, which engages him in their struggle, than by a thousand actions in their favor without that trust.

Those who authentically commit themselves to the people must re-examine themselves constantly. This conversion is so radical as not to allow of ambiguous behavior. To affirm this commitment but to consider oneself the proprietor of revolutionary wisdom—which must then be given to (or imposed on) the people—is to retain the old ways. The man who proclaims devotion to the cause of liberation yet is unable to enter into *communion* with the people, whom he continues to regard as totally ignorant, is grievously self-deceived. The convert who approaches the people but feels alarm at each step they take, each doubt they express, and each suggestion they offer, and attempts to impose his "status," remains nostalgic towards his origins.

Conversion to the people requires a profound rebirth. Those who undergo it must take on a new form of existence; they can no longer remain as they were. Only through comradeship with the oppressed can the converts understand their characteristic ways of living and behaving, which in diverse moments reflect the structure of domination. One of these characteristics is the previously mentioned existential duality of the oppressed, who are at the same time themselves and the oppressor whose image they have internalized. Accordingly, until they concretely "discover" their oppressor and in turn their own consciousness, they nearly always express fatalistic attitudes towards their situation.

> The peasant begins to get courage to overcome his dependence when he realizes that he is dependent. Until then, he goes along with the boss and says "What can I do? I'm only a peasant."[11]

When superficially analyzed, this fatalism is sometimes interpreted as a docility that is a trait of national character. Fatalism in the guise of docility is the fruit of an historical and sociological situation, not an essential characteristic of a people's behavior. It almost always is related to the power of destiny or fate or fortune—inevitable forces—or to a distorted view of God. Under the sway of magic and myth, the oppressed (especially the peasants, who are almost submerged in nature)[12] see their suffering, the fruit of exploitation, as the will of God—as if God were the creator of this "organized disorder."

Submerged in reality, the oppressed cannot perceive clearly the "order" which serves the interests of the oppressors whose image they have internalized. Chafing under the restrictions of this order, they often manifest a type of horizontal violence, striking out at their own comrades for the pettiest reasons.

> The colonized man will first manifest this aggressiveness which has been deposited in his bones against his own people. This is the period when the niggers beat each other up, and the police and magistrates do not know which way to turn when faced with the astonishing waves of crime in North Africa. . . . While the settler or the policeman has the right the livelong day to strike the native, to insult him and to make him crawl to them, you will see the native reaching for his knife at the slightest hostile or aggressive glance cast on him by another native; for the last resort of the native is to defend his personality vis-à-vis his brother.[13]

It is possible that in this behavior they are once more manifesting their duality. Because the oppressor exists within their oppressed comrades, when they attack those comrades they are indirectly attacking the oppressor as well.

On the other hand, at a certain point in their existential experience the oppressed feel an irresistible attraction towards the oppressor and his way of life. Sharing this way of life becomes an overpowering aspiration. In their alienation, the oppressed want at any cost to resemble the oppressor, to imitate him, to follow him. This phenomenon is especially prevalent in the middle-class oppressed, who yearn to be equal to the "eminent" men of the upper class. Albert Memmi, in an exceptional analysis of the "colonized mentality," refers to the contempt he felt towards the colonizer, mixed with "passionate" attraction towards him.

> How could the colonizer look after his workers while periodically gunning down a crowd of colonized? How could the colonized deny himself so cruelly yet make such excessive demands? How could he hate the colonizers and yet admire them so passionately? (I too felt this admiration in spite of myself.)[14]

Self-depreciation is another characteristic of the oppressed, which derives from their internalization of the opinion the oppressors hold of them. So often do they hear that they are good for nothing, know nothing and are incapable of learning anything—that they are sick, lazy, and unproductive—that in the end they become convinced of their own unfitness.

> The peasant feels inferior to the boss because the boss seems to be the only one who knows things and is able to run things.[15]

They call themselves ignorant and say the "professor" is the one who has knowledge and to whom they should listen. The criteria of knowledge imposed upon them are the conventional ones. "Why don't you," said a peasant participating in a culture circle, "explain the pictures first? That way it'll take less time and won't give us a headache."

Almost never do they realize that they, too, "know things" they have learned in their relations with the world and with other men. Given the circumstances which have produced their duality, it is only natural that they distrust themselves.

Not infrequently, peasants in educational projects begin to discuss a generative theme in a lively manner, then stop suddenly and say to the educator: "Excuse us, we ought to keep quiet and let you talk. You are the one who knows, we don't know anything." They often insist that there is no difference between them and the animals; when they do admit a difference, it favors the animals. "They are freer than we are."

It is striking, however, to observe how this self-depreciation changes with the first changes in the situation of oppression. I heard a peasant leader say in an *asentamiento*[16] meeting, "They used to say we were unproductive because we were lazy and drunkards. All lies. Now that we are respected as men, we're going to show everyone that we were never drunkards or lazy. We were exploited!"

As long as their ambiguity persists, the oppressed are reluctant to resist, and totally lack confidence in themselves. They have a diffuse, magical belief in the invulnerability and power of the oppressor.[17] The magical force of the landowner's power holds particular sway in the rural areas. A sociologist friend of mine tells of a group of armed peasants in a Latin American country who recently took over a latifundium. For tactical reasons, they planned to hold the landowner as a hostage. But not one peasant had the courage to guard him; his very presence was terrifying. It is also possible that the act of opposing the boss provoked guilt feelings. In truth, the boss was "inside" them.

The oppressed must see examples of the vulnerability of the oppressor so that a contrary conviction can begin to grow within them. Until this occurs, they will continue disheartened, fearful, and beaten.[18] As long as the oppressed remain unaware of the causes of their condition, they fatalistically "accept" their exploitation. Further, they are apt to react in a passive and alienated manner when confronted with the necessity to struggle for their freedom and self-affirmation. Little by little, however, they tend to try out forms of rebellious action. In working towards liberation, one must neither lose sight of this passivity nor overlook the moment of awakening.

Within their unauthentic view of the world and of themselves, the oppressed feel like "things" owned by the oppressor. For the latter, *to be* is *to have*, almost always at the expense of those who have nothing. For the oppressed, at a certain point in their existential experience, *to be* is not to resemble the oppressor, but *to be under* him, to depend on him. Accordingly, the oppressed are emotionally dependent.

> The peasant is a dependent. He can't say what he wants. Before he discovers his dependence, he suffers. He lets off steam at home, where he shouts at his children, beats them, and despairs. He complains about his wife and thinks everything is dreadful. He doesn't let off steam with the boss because he thinks the boss is a superior being. Lots of times, the peasant gives vent to his sorrows by drinking.[19]

This total emotional dependence can lead the oppressed to what Fromm calls necrophilic behavior: the destruction of life—their own or that of their oppressed fellows.

It is only when the oppressed find the oppressor out and become involved in the organized struggle for their liberation that they begin to believe in themselves. This discovery cannot be purely intellectual but must involve action; nor can it be limited to mere activism, but must include serious reflection: only then will it be a praxis.

Critical and liberating dialogue, which presupposes action, must be carried on with the oppressed at whatever the stage of their struggle for liberation.[20] The content of that dialogue can and should vary in accordance with historical conditions and the level at which the oppressed perceive reality. But to substitute monologue, slogans, and communiqués for dialogue is to attempt to liberate the oppressed with the instruments of domestication. Attempting to liberate the oppressed without their reflective participation in the act of liberation is to treat them as objects which must be saved from a burning building; it is to lead them into the populist pitfall and transform them into masses which can be manipulated.

At all stages of their liberation, the oppressed must see themselves as men engaged in the ontological and historical vocation of becoming more fully human. Reflection and action become imperative when one does not erroneously attempt to dichotomize the content of humanity from its historical forms.

The insistence that the oppressed engage in reflection on their concrete situation is not a call to armchair revolution. On the contrary, reflection—true reflection—leads to action. On the other hand, when the situation calls for action, that action will constitute an authentic praxis only if its consequences become the object of critical reflection. In this sense, the praxis is the new *raison d'être* of the oppressed; and the revolution, which inaugurates the historical moment of this *raison d'être*, is not viable apart from their concomitant conscious involvement. Otherwise, action is pure activism.

To achieve this praxis, however, it is necessary to trust in the oppressed and in their ability to reason. Whoever lacks this trust will fail to initiate (or will abandon) dialogue, reflection, and communication, and will fall into using slogans, communiqués, monologues, and instructions. Superficial conversions to the cause of liberation carry this danger.

Political action on the side of the oppressed must be pedagogical action in the authentic sense of the word, and, therefore, action *with* the oppressed. Those who work for liberation must not take advantage of the emotional dependence of the oppressed—dependence that is the fruit of the concrete situation of domination which surrounds them and which engendered their unauthentic view of the world. Using their dependence to create still greater dependence is an oppressor tactic.

Libertarian action must recognize this dependence as a weak point and must attempt through reflection and action to transform it into independence. However, not even the best-intentioned leadership can bestow independence as a gift. The liberation of the oppressed is a liberation of men, not things. Accordingly, while no one liberates himself by his own efforts alone, neither is he liberated by others. Liberation, a human phenomenon, cannot be achieved by semihumans. Any attempt to treat men as semihumans only dehumanizes them. When men are already dehumanized, due to the oppression they suffer, the process of their liberation must not employ the methods of dehumanization.

The correct method for a revolutionary leadership to employ in the task of liberation is, therefore, *not* "libertarian propaganda." Nor can the leadership merely "implant" in the oppressed a belief in freedom, thus thinking to win their trust. The correct method lies in dialogue. The conviction of the oppressed that they must fight for their liberation is not a gift bestowed by the revolutionary leadership, but the result of their own *conscientização.**

The revolutionary leaders must realize that their own conviction of the necessity for struggle (an indispensable dimension of revolutionary wisdom) was not given to them by anyone else—if it is authentic. This conviction cannot be packaged and sold; it is reached, rather, by means of a totality of reflection and action. Only the leaders' own involvement in reality, within an historical situation, led them to criticize this situation and to wish to change it.

Likewise, the oppressed (who do not commit themselves to the struggle unless they are convinced, and who, if they do not make such a commitment, withhold the indispensable conditions for this struggle) must reach this conviction as Subjects, not as objects. They also must intervene critically in the situation which surrounds them and whose mark they bear; propaganda cannot achieve this. While the conviction of the necessity for struggle (without which the struggle is unfeasible) is indispensable to the revolutionary leadership (indeed, it was this conviction which constituted that leadership), it is also necessary for the oppressed. It is necessary, that is, unless one intends to carry out the transformation *for* the oppressed rather than *with* them. It is my belief that only the latter form of transformation is valid.

The object in presenting these considerations is to defend the eminently pedagogical character of the revolution. The revolutionary leaders of every epoch who have affirmed that the oppressed must accept the struggle for their liberation—an obvious point—have also thereby implicitly recognized the pedagogical aspect of this struggle. Many of these leaders, however (perhaps due to natural and understandable biases against pedagogy), have ended up using the "educational" methods employed by the oppressor. They deny pedagogical action in the liberation process, but they use propaganda to convince.

---

* The term *conscientização* refers to learning to perceive social, political, and economic contradictions, and to take action against the oppressive elements of reality.—Ed.

It is essential for the oppressed to realize that when they accept the struggle for humanization they also accept, from that moment, their total responsibility for the struggle. They must realize that they are fighting not merely for freedom from hunger, but for

> . . . freedom to create and to construct, to wonder and to venture. Such freedom requires that the individual be active and responsible, not a slave or a well-fed cog in the machine. . . . It is not enough that men are not slaves; if social conditions further the existence of automatons, the result will not be love of life, but love of death.[21]

The oppressed, who have been shaped by the death-affirming climate of oppression, must find through their struggle the way to life-affirming humanization, which does not lie *simply* in having more to eat (although it does involve having more to eat and cannot fail to include this aspect). The oppressed have been destroyed precisely because their situation has reduced them to things. In order to regain their humanity they must cease to be things and fight as men. This is a radical requirement. They cannot enter the struggle as objects in order *later* to become men.

The struggle begins with men's recognition that they have been destroyed. Propaganda, management, manipulation—all arms of domination —cannot be the instruments of their rehumanization. The only effective instrument is a humanizing pedagogy in which the revolutionary leadership establishes a permanent relationship of dialogue with the oppressed. In a humanizing pedagogy the method ceases to be an instrument by which the teachers (in this instance, the revolutionary leadership) can manipulate the students (in this instance, the oppressed), because it expresses the consciousness of the students themselves.

> The method is, in fact, the external form of consciousness manifest in acts, which takes on the fundamental property of consciousness—its intentionality. The essence of consciousness is being with the world, and this behavior is permanent and unavoidable. Accordingly, consciousness is in essence a "way towards" something apart from itself, outside itself, which surrounds it and which it apprehends by means of its ideational capacity. Consciousness is thus by definition a method, in the most general sense of the word.[22]

A revolutionary leadership must accordingly practice *co-intentional* education. Teachers and students (leadership and people), co-intent on reality, are both Subjects, not only in the task of unveiling that reality, and thereby coming to know it critically, but in the task of re-creating that knowledge. As they attain this knowledge of reality through common reflection and action, they discover themselves as its permanent re-creators. In this way, the presence of the oppressed in the struggle for their liberation will be what it should be: not pseudo-participation, but committed involvement.

NOTES

1. The current movements of rebellion, especially those of youth, while they necessarily reflect the peculiarities of their respective settings, manifest in

their essence this preoccupation with man and men as beings in the world and with the world—preoccupation with *what* and *how* they are "being." As they place consumer civilization in judgment, denounce bureaucracies of all types, demand the transformation of the universities (changing the rigid nature of the teacher–student relationship and placing that relationship within the context of reality), propose the transformation of reality itself so that universities can be renewed, attack old orders and established institutions in the attempt to affirm men as the Subjects of decision, all these movements reflect the style of our age, which is more anthropological than anthropocentric.

2. As used throughout this paper, the term "contradiction" denotes the dialectical conflict between opposing social forces.—Translator's note.

3. This fear of freedom is also to be found in the oppressors, though, obviously, in a different form. The oppressed are afraid to embrace freedom; the oppressors are afraid of losing the "freedom" to oppress.

4. See Georg Hegel, *The Phenomenology of Mind* (New York, 1967), pp. 236–237.

5. Analyzing the dialectical relationship between the consciousness of the master and the consciousness of the oppressed, Hegel states: "The one is independent, and its essential nature is to be for itself; the other is dependent, and its essence is life or existence for another. The former is the Master, or Lord, the latter the Bondsman." *Ibid.*, p. 234.

6. "The materialist doctrine that men are products of circumstances and upbringing, and that, therefore, changed men are products of other circumstances and changed upbringing, forgets that it is men that change circumstances and that the educator himself needs educating." Karl Marx and Friedrich Engels, *Selected Works* (New York, 1968), p. 28.

7. This appears to be the fundamental aspect of Mao's Cultural Revolution.

8. This rigidity should not be identified with restraints that must be imposed on the former oppressors so they cannot restore the oppressive order. Rather, it refers to the revolution which becomes stagnant and turns against the people, using the old repressive, bureaucratic State apparatus (which should have been drastically suppressed, as Marx so often emphasized).

9. Eric Fromm, *The Heart of Man* (New York, 1966), p. 32.

10. Regarding the "dominant forms of social control," see Herbert Marcuse, *One-Dimensional Man* (Boston, 1964) and *Eros and Civilization* (Boston, 1955).

11. Words of a peasant during an interview with the author.

12. See Candido Mendes, *Memento dos vivos—A Esquerda católica no Brasil* (Rio, 1966).

13. Frantz Fanon, *The Wretched of the Earth* (New York, 1968), p. 52.

14. *The Colonizer and the Colonized* (Boston, 1967), p. x.

15. Words of a peasant during an interview with the author.

16. *Asentamiento* refers to a production unit of the Chilean agrarian reform experiment.—Translator's note.

17. "The peasant has an almost instinctive fear of the boss." Interview with a peasant.

18. See Regis Debray, *Revolution in the Revolution?* (New York, 1967).

19. Interview with a peasant.

20. Not in the open, of course; that would only provoke the fury of the oppressor and lead to still greater repression.

21. Fromm, *op. cit.*, pp. 52–53.

22. Alvaro Vieira Pinto, from a work in preparation on the philosophy of science. I consider the quoted portion of great importance for the understanding of a problem-posing pedagogy and wish to thank Professor Vieira Pinto for permission to cite his work prior to publication.

bibliography

PART ONE: Methodological Problems of Economic Development

BARAN, PAUL. "Economic Progress and Economic Surplus." *Science and Society*, 17, 4 (Fall 1953), 289–317.

DALTON, GEORGE. "Economics, Economic Development, and Economic Anthropology." *Journal of Economic Issues*, June 1968.

DOWD, DOUGLAS F. "Some Issues of Economic Development and of Development Economics." *Journal of Economic Issues*, 1, 3 (September 1967), 149–160.

FEI, JOHN C.H. and G. RANIS. *Development of the Labor Surplus Economy: Theory and Policy*. Homewood: Richard Irwin, 1964.

FRANK, ANDRE GUNDER. "Sociology of Development and Underdevelopment of Sociology." In *Latin America: Underdevelopment or Revolution?* New York: Monthly Review Press, 1969, pp. 21–94.

GOULET, DENIS. *The Cruel Choice*. New York: Atheneum, 1971.

_____. "An Ethical Model for the Study of Values." *Harvard Educational Review*, 41, 2 (May 1971).

HIRSCHMAN, ALBERT O. *The Strategy of Economic Development*. New Haven: Yale University Press, 1958.

LEWIS, W. ARTHUR. "Economic Development with Unlimited Supplies of Labour." *The Manchester School of Economic and Social Studies*, 22 (May, 1954), 139–191.

MEEROPOL, MICHAEL. "Towards a Political Economy Analysis of Underdevelopment." *Review of Radical Political Economics*, 4, 1 (Spring, 1972), 77–108.

MYRDAL, GUNNAR. *Asian Drama*. New York: Pantheon, 1968.

_____. *Economic Theory and Underdeveloped Regions*. New York: Harper and Row, 1971.

NURKSE, RAGNAR. *Problems of Capital Formation in Underdeveloped Countries*. Oxford: Basil Blackwell, 1958.

SEERS, DUDLEY. "The Limitations of the Special Case." *Bulletin of Oxford Institute of Economics and Statistics*, May 1963.

STREETEN, PAUL. "Economic Models and Their Usefulness for Planning in South Asia." In *Asian Drama*, by Gunnar Myrdal. New York: Pantheon, 1968.

PART TWO: Economic Development and Underdevelopment in Historical
            Perspective

BARAN, PAUL. "On the Roots of Backwardness." In *The Political Economy of Growth*. New York: Monthly Review Press, 1957, pp. 134–162.

DALTON, GEORGE. "History, Politics and Economic Development in Liberia." *Journal of Economic History*, 25, 4 (December 1965), 569–591.

FURTADO, CELSO. *Development and Underdevelopment*. Berkeley: University of California Press, 1964.

_____. *Obstacles to Development in Latin America*. New York: Doubleday and Co., 1970.

GERSCHENKRON, ALEXANDER. *Economic Backwardness in Historical Perspective.* New York: Praeger, 1965.

GRIFFEN, K. B. *The Underdevelopment of Spanish America.* London: George Allen & Unwin, 1969.

HYMER, STEPHEN. "Robinson Crusoe and Primitive Accumulation." *Monthly Review,* 23 (September 1971), 11–36.

POLANYI, KARL. *The Great Transformation.* Boston: Beacon Press, 1957.

ROLLINS, C. E. "Mineral Development and Economic Growth." *Social Research,* 23 (October 1956), 253–280.

ROSTOW, W. W. *The Stages of Economic Growth.* New York: Cambridge University Press, 1960.

————., ed. *The Economics of Take-Off Into Sustained Growth.* Proceedings of a conference held by the International Economic Association. New York: St. Martin's Press, Inc., 1963.

SUPPLE, BARRY E. *The Experience of Economic Growth: Case Studies in Economic History.* New York: Random House, 1963.

TAWNEY, R. H. *Religion and the Rise of Capitalism.* New York: The New American Library, 1926.

PART THREE: Economic Development in a Revolutionary World

EMMANUEL, ARGHIRI. *Unequal Exchange: A Study of the Imperialism of Trade.* New York: Monthly Review Press, 1972.

FRANK, ANDRE GUNDER. *Capitalism and Underdevelopment in Latin America: Historical Studies of Chile and Brazil.* New York: Monthly Review Press, 1967.

GOULET, DENIS and MICHAEL HUDSON. *Myth of Aid.* Marino, New York: Orbis Press, 1971.

GRIFFIN, KEITH and JOHN ENOS. "Foreign Assistance: Objectives and Consequences." *Economic Development and Cultural Change,* 18, 3 (April 1970), 313–327.

HAYTER, TERESA. *Aid as Imperialism.* Middlesex: Pelican, 1971.

HEILBRONER, ROBERT L. "Counterrevolutionary America." *Commentary,* 43, 4 (April 1967), 31–38.

HYMER, STEPHEN and STEPHEN RESNICK. "International Trade and Uneven Development." In *Trade, Balance of Payments and Growth,* edited by Jagdish Bhagwati. New York: American Elsevier Publishing Co., 1971.

JALEE, PIERRE. *The Pillage of the Third World.* New York: Monthly Review Press, 1968.

MAGDOFF, HARRY. *The Age of Imperialism.* New York: Monthly Review Press, 1969.

PREBISCH, RAOUL. "The Role of Commercial Policy in Underdeveloped Countries." *American Economic Review,* 49, 2 (May 1959), 251–273.

RHODES, ROBERT I., ed. *Imperialism and Underdevelopment: A Reader.* New York: Monthly Review Press, 1970.

SINGER, H. W. "The Distribution of Gains Between Investing and Borrowing Countries." *American Economic Review,* 40, 2 (May 1950), 473–485.

WEEKS, JOHN. "Employment, Growth and Foreign Domination in Underdeveloped Countries." *Review of Radical Political Economics,* 4, 1 (Spring 1972).

WEISSKOPF, THOMAS. "Capitalism, Underdevelopment and the Future of the Poor Countries." *Review of Radical Political Economics,* 4, 1 (Spring 1972).

————. "Dependence and Imperialism in India." *Review of Radical Political Economics,* 5, 1 (Spring 1973).

PART FOUR: Agricultural Institutions and Strategy

ALEXANDER, ROBERT J. "Nature and Progress of Agrarian Reform in Latin America." *Journal of Economic History,* 23, 4 (December 1963), 559–573.

BARKIN, DAVID. "Cuban Agriculture: A Strategy of Economic Development." *Studies in Comparative International Development,* 7, 1 (Spring 1972), 19–38.

BECKFORD, GEORGE L. *Persistent Poverty: Underdevelopment in Plantation Economies of the Third World.* New York: Oxford University Press, 1972.

CLEAVER, HARRY M., JR. "The Contradictions of the Green Revolution." *Monthly Review*, 24, 2 (June 1972), 83–111.

DUMONT, RENE. *Lands Alive.* London: The Merlin Press, 1965.

————. *Types of Rural Economy: Studies in World Agriculture.* New York: Praeger, 1957.

EICHER, CARL and LAURENCE WITT, eds. *Agriculture in Economic Development.* New York: McGraw-Hill, 1964.

GALBRAITH, J. K. "Conditions For Economic Change in Underdeveloped Countries." *Journal of Farm Economics*, 33 (November 1951), 689–696.

GEORGESCU-ROEGEN, NICOLAS. "Economic Theory and Agrarian Economics." *Oxford Economic Papers*, 12 (February 1960), 1–40.

JOHNSTON, BRUCE F. and SOREN T. NEILSON. "Agricultural and Structural Transformation in a Developing Economy." *Economic Development and Cultural Change*, 14, 3 (April 1966), 279–301.

JOHNSTON, BRUCE F. and JOHN W. MELLOR. "The Role of Agriculture in Economic Development." *American Economic Review*, 51, 4 (September 1961), 566–593.

NOVE, ALEC. "Collectivization of Agriculture in Russia and China." In *Symposium on Economic and Social Problems of the Far East*, edited by E. F. Szczpanik. Hong Kong: Hong Kong University Press, 1962, pp. 16–24.

STAVENHAGEN, RODOLFO, ed. *Agrarian Problems and Peasant Movements in Latin America.* New York: Doubleday and Co., 1970.

PART FIVE: Industrial Institutions and Strategy

BOULDING, KENNETH E. and PRITAM SINGH. "The Role of the Price Structure in Economic Development." *American Economic Review*, 52, 2 (May 1962), 28–38.

CULBERTSON, JOHN M. *Economic Development: An Ecological Approach.* New York: Alfred A. Knopf, 1971.

DOBB, MAURICE. *An Essay on Economic Growth and Planning.* London: Routledge and Kegan Paul, 1960.

HIRSCHMAN, ALBERT O. "The Political Economy of Import-Substituting Industrialization in Latin America." *Quarterly Journal of Economics*, 82, 1 (February 1968), 1–32.

HORVAT, BRANKO. *Towards a Theory of Planned Economy.* Belgrade: Yugoslav Institute of Economic Research, 1964.

NOVE, ALEC. "The Problem of 'Success Indicators' in Soviet Industry." *Economics*, 15, 97 (February 1958), 1–13.

RICHMAN, BARRY. "Capitalists and Managers in Communist China." *Harvard Business Review* (January–February 1967), 57–78.

SEERS, DUDLEY. "New Approaches Suggested by the Columbia Employment Programme." *International Labor Review*, 102, 4 (October 1970), 337–389.

PART SIX: Comparative Models of Development

BELL, PETER F. and STEPHEN A. RESNICK. "The Contradictions of Post-War Development in Southeast Asia." *Review of Radical Political Economics*, 3, 1 (Spring 1972).

BOWLES, W. DONALD. "Soviet Russia As a Model for Underdeveloped Areas." *World Politics*, 14, 3 (April 1962), 483–504.

CLINE, HOWARD F. *Mexico: Revolution To Evolution, 1940–1960.* New York: Oxford University Press, 1963.

HORVAT, BRANKO. *An Essay on Yugoslav Society.* New York: International Arts and Sciences Press, 1969.

HUGHES, GLYN. "Preconditions of Socialist Development in Africa." *Monthly Review*, 22, 1 (May 1970), 11–30.

INKELES, ALEX and OLEG HOEFFDING. "The Soviet Union: Model for Asia?" *Problems of Communism* (November–December 1959), 30–46.

LOCKWOOD, W. W. *The Economic Development of Japan: Growth and Structural Change, 1868–1938.* Princeton: Princeton University Press, 1954.

MACEWAN, A. "Contradictions in Capitalist Development: The Case of Pakistan." *Review of Radical Political Economics,* Spring 1971.

MALENBAUM, WILFRED. "India and China: Contrasts in Development Performance." *American Economic Review,* 49, 3 (June 1959), 284–309.

NOVE, ALEC. "The Soviet Model and Underdeveloped Countries." *International Affairs,* 37, 1 (January 1961), 29–38.

PERKINS, DWIGHT H. "Economic Growth in China and the Cultural Revolution." *China Quarterly,* April–June, 1967.

SEERS, DUDLEY, ed. *Cuba: The Economic and Social Revolution.* Chapel Hill: The University of North Carolina Press, 1964.

SOLGANICK, ALLEN. "Chinese Economic Development Since the Revolution." *Science and Society,* 31, 3 (Fall 1967), 342–354.

SPULBER, NICOLAS. "Contrasting Economic Patterns: Chinese and Soviet Development Strategies." *Soviet Studies,* 15, 1 (July 1963), 1–16.

SWIANIEWICZ, S. *Forced Labour and Economic Development: An Enquiry Into the Experience of Soviet Industrialization.* London: Oxford University Press, 1965.

WHEELRIGHT, E. L. and BRUCE MCFARLANE, *The Chinese Road to Socialism.* New York: Monthly Review Press, 1970.

WILBER, CHARLES K. *The Soviet Model and Underdeveloped Countries.* Chapel Hill: The University of North Carolina Press, 1969.

————. "The Soviet Model of Economic Development." In *Protagonists of Change: Subcultures in the Development Process,* edited by Abdul A. Said. New York: McGraw-Hill, 1971, pp. 124–136.

PART SEVEN: The Human Cost of Development

CASTRO, JOSUE'DE. *The Geography of Hunger.* Boston: Little, Brown & Co., 1952.

DE JESUS, MARIA CAROLINA. *Child of the Dark.* New York: E. P. Dutton & Co., 1962.

"The Executive Life in Brazil." *Fortune* (December 1972), 115–119.

HOLZMAN, FRANKLYN D. "Consumer Sovereignty and the Rate of Economic Development." *Economia Internazionale,* 11, 2 (1958), 3–17.

LEWIS, W. ARTHUR. "Is Economic Growth Desirable?" In *The Theory of Economic Growth.* Homewood: Richard D. Irwin, 1955.

NAIR, KUSUM. *Blossoms in the Dust.* New York: Praeger, 1962.

SCHWEINITZ,, KARL DE, JR. "Economic Growth, Coercion, and Freedom." *World Politics,* 9, 2 (January 1957), 166–192.

PART EIGHT: What Is To Be Done?

FRANK, ANDRE GUNDER. "Capitalist Underdevelopment or Socialist Revolution?" In *Latin America: Underdevelopment or Revolution?* New York: Monthly Review Press, 1969, pp. 371–409.

FREIRE, PAULO. *Pedagogy of the Oppressed.* New York: Herder and Herder, 1972.

GUTIERREZ, GUSTAVO. *A Theology of Liberation.* Marino, New York: Orbis, 1972.

HINTON, WILLIAM. *Fanshen: A Documentary of Revolution in a Chinese Village.* New York: Monthly Review Press, 1966.

HIRSCHMAN, ALBERT O. *A Bias for Hope.* New Haven: Yale University Press, 1971.

MYRDAL, GUNNAR. *The Challenge of World Poverty.* Middlesex: Pelican Books, 1970.

RANDALL, LAURA, ed. *Economic Development: Evolution or Revolution?* Boston: D. C. Heath & Co., 1964.

SHAFFER, HARRY G. and JAN S. PRYBYLA. *From Underdevelopment to Affluence: Western, Soviet, and Chinese Views.* New York: Appleton-Century-Crofts, 1968.

WEAVER, JAMES H. and LEROY P. JONES. "An International Negative Income Tax." *Conference Papers of the Union for Radical Political Economics*, December 1968.

ZEITLIN, MAURICE and JAMES PETRAS, eds. *Latin America: Reform or Revolution?* Greenwich, Connecticut: Fawcett Publications, 1968.

_____. *Revolutionary Politics and the Cuban Working Class*. Princeton: Princeton University Press, 1970.

contributors

Paul Baran was Professor of Economics at Stanford University before his death in 1964. His published works include *The Political Economy of Growth* (1957) and, with Paul M. Sweezy, *Monopoly Capital*. A collection of his articles has been published as *The Longer View: Essays Toward a Critique of Political Economy* (1970). **E. J. Hobsbawm** is a Reader in History at Birkbeck College in the University of London. He is the author of several books, including *Primitive Rebels, Labouring Men, The Age of Revolution, 1789–1848*, and *Industry and Empire*.

Harry M. Cleaver, Jr. is Professor of Economics, University of Sherbrooke, Quebec.

Oscar Delgado is Professor of Sociology, University of Bogota in Colombia. He is also an official with the Inter-American Committee of Agricultural Development and the editor of *Reformas Agrarias en la America Latina*.

Dudley Dillard is Professor and Chairman of Economics, University of Maryland. He is the author of *The Economics of John Maynard Keynes* and *Economic Development of the North Atlantic Community*.

Theotonio Dos Santos is Professor of Economics, University of Chile. He is a Brazilian economist who is presently director of a research project on the relations of dependence in Latin America conducted at the Center for Socio-economic Studies of the Faculty of Economic Science at the University of Chile.

Andre Gunder Frank has taught economics and social science at the University of Iowa, Michigan State University, Wayne State University, and Sir George Williams University in Montreal. He has also taught at the universities of Brasilia, Chile, and the National University of Mexico. He is the author of *Capitalism and Underdevelopment in Latin America* and *Latin America: Underdevelopment or Revolution*.

Paulo Freire was Professor of the History and Philosophy of Education in the University of Recife, Brazil, until exiled after the military coup in 1964. He then spent five years in Chile, working with UNESCO and the Chilean Institute for Agrarian Reform in programs of adult education. He is presently serving as Educational Consultant to the Office of Education of the World Council of Churches in Geneva.

Celso Furtado was formerly chief of the Development Division of the

United Nations Economic Commission for Latin America, director of the Banco Nacional do Desenvolvimento Economico in Rio de Janeiro, executive head of the Agency for the Development of the Brazilian Northeast (SUDENE), and the Minister of Planning in the Brazilian Government. He was exiled after the military coup in 1964 and is now professeur associe at the Faculte de Droit et des Sciences Economiques at the University of Paris, and Visiting Professor, The American University, Washington, D.C. He is the author of *Economic Growth of Brazil, Development and Underdevelopment, Diagnosis of the Brazilian Crisis,* and *Obstacles to Development in Latin America.*

Denis Goulet is a member of the Center for the Study of Development and Change in Cambridge, Massachusetts. Trained in philosophy and political science, he has been associated with both aid and research projects in Africa and Latin America and has taught in institutions in Europe and North America. He is the author of *The Cruel Choice.*

Keith Griffin is a Fellow of Magdalen College, Oxford. He is the author of *Underdevelopment in Spanish America, Financing Development in Latin America,* and *Growth and Inequality in Pakistan.*

John W. Gurley is Professor of Economics, Stanford University. He is the author (with E. S. Shaw) of *Money in a Theory of Finance.*

Mahbub ul Haq was Chief Economist of the Pakistan Planning Commission and was closely associated with the formulation of Pakistan's five-year development plans before joining the World Bank in April 1970 where he is presently serving as Senior Adviser to the Economics Department.

W. F. Ilchman is Professor of Political Science, the University of California at Berkeley. He co-authored *The Political Economy of Change.* **R. C. BHARGAVA** is with the Planning Department, Government of Uttar Pradesh, India.

Ivan Illich is one of the founders of the Center for Intercultural Documentation in Cuernavaca, Mexico. He was formerly Vice President of the Universidad Católica de Puerto Rico and worked for five years as a parish priest in a Puerto Rican and Irish neighborhood on the West side of Manhattan. He is the author of *Celebration of Awareness* and *Deschooling Society.*

Alfonso Inostroza is President, Banco Central de Chile, and Governor of the International Monetary Fund and World Bank for Chile.

William McCord is Lena Gohlman Fox Professor of Sociology at Rice University. He has served as a consultant on the President's Commission on Civil Unrest and the National Institute for Mental Health. He is the author of *The Springtime of Freedom* and *Mississippi: The Long, Hot Summer.*

Seymour Melman is Professor of Industrial Engineering at Columbia University. He is the author of *The Peace Race* and *Our Depleted Society.*

Ronald Müller is Assistant Professor of Economics, The American University, Washington, D.C. He is the author (with Richard Barnet) of the forthcoming book *The Earth Managers . . . Their Global Corporations.*

Leo A. Orleans is China research specialist at the Library of Congress,

Washington, D.C. **Richard P. Suttmeier** is Assistant Professor of Government at Hamilton College, Clinton, New York.

Robert I. Rhodes is the editor of *Imperialism and Underdevelopment*.

Joan Robinson is Reader in Economics, Cambridge University. One of today's most distinguished economic theorists, her books include *Economics of Imperfect Competition, Essay on Marxian Economics, The Accumulation of Capital, Economic Philosophy, The Cultural Revolution in China,* and *Economic Heresies.*

Dudley Seers is Director of the Institute of Development Studies at the University of Sussex. He was formerly Director-General of the Planning Staff of the UK Ministry of Overseas Development.

James H. Weaver is Professor of Economics, The American University, Washington, D.C. He is the author of *University and Revolution* and of the recently published *Political Economy: Orthodox and Radical Views.*

Charles K. Wilber is Professor of Economics, The American University, Washington, D.C. He is the author of *The Soviet Model and Underdeveloped Countries.*